SECOND EDITION

The Norton Field Guide to Writing

with readings

Richard Bullock
WRIGHT STATE UNIVERSITY

Maureen Daly Goggin
ARIZONA STATE UNIVERSITY

W. W. NORTON & COMPANY
New York • London

W. W. Norton & Company has been independent since its founding in 1923, when William Warder Norton and Mary D. Herter Norton first published lectures delivered at the People's Institute, the adult education division of New York City's Cooper Union. The firm soon expanded its program beyond the Institute, publishing books by celebrated academics from America and abroad. By mid-century, the two major pillars of Norton's publishing program—trade books and college texts—were firmly established. In the 1950s, the Norton family transferred control of the company to its employees, and today—with a staff of four hundred and a comparable number of trade, college, and professional titles published each year—W. W. Norton & Company stands as the largest and oldest publishing house owned wholly by its employees.

Printed in the United States of America

Editor: Marilyn Moller
Associate Editor: Ana Cooke
Project Editor: Rebecca A. Homiski
Copy Editor: Katharine N. Ings
Managing Editor: Marian Johnson
Electronic Media Editor: Eileen Connell
Production Manager: Jane Searle
Manufacturing: R. R. Donnelley, Crawfordsville
Composition: Matrix Publishing Services
Text Design: Anna Palchik
Cover Design: Debra Morton Hoyt

Library of Congress Cataloging-in-Publication Data

Bullock, Richard H.
The norton field guide to writing, with readings / Richard Bullock, Maureen Daly Goggin. — 2nd ed.
p. cm.
Includes bibliographical references and index.
ISBN: 978-0-393-93381-9 (pbk.)
1. English language—Rhetoric—Handbooks, manuals, etc. 2. English language—Grammar—Handbooks, manuals, etc. 3. Report writing—Handbooks, manuals, etc. 4. College readers. I. Goggin, Maureen Daly. II. Title.
PE1408.B8838245 2009
808′.042—dc22 2009020705

W. W. Norton & Company, Inc., 500 Fifth Avenue, New York, N.Y. 10110
www.wwnorton.com

W. W. Norton & Company Ltd., Castle House, 75/76 Wells Street, London W1T 3QT

1 2 3 4 5 6 7 8 9 0

Preface

The Norton Field Guide to Writing began as an attempt to offer the kind of writing guidelines found in the best rhetorics in a format as user-friendly as the most popular handbooks, and on top of that to be as brief as could be. It was to be a handy guide to help college students with all their written work. Just as there are field guides for bird watchers and accountants, this would be one for writers. The book touched a chord with many instructors, and it quickly became the most widely used brief rhetoric. And in response to requests for more readings, we provided a version that included an anthology of readings; we are happy now to offer that version in a second edition.

The Norton Field Guide still aims to offer the guidance new teachers and first-year writers need and the flexibility many experienced teachers want. From our experiences as teachers and WPAs, we know that explicit writing guides work well for students and novice teachers. Many instructors chafe at the structure imposed by such books, however, and students complain about having to buy books that have much more detail than they need. So we've tried to provide enough structure without too much detail — to give the information college writers need to know, and to resist the temptation to tell them everything there is to know.

Most of all, we've tried to keep the book brief and easy to use. To that end, we've designed *The Norton Field Guide to Writing, with readings* as two books in one, the rhetoric in front and the anthology in back — and used color-coded links to make it easy to navigate between the two. These links are also the key to keeping the book brief: chapters are short, but the links point to pages elsewhere in the book *if* students need more detail.

Students can access much of the *Field Guide* on the Web, where they'll find a color-coded Writer's Help Window that downloads into Word, providing help when students most need it: *as they write.*

What's in the Book

The Norton Field Guide covers 15 kinds of writing often assigned to college students. Much of the book is in the form of guidelines, designed to help students consider the choices they have as writers. Most chapters are brief, in response to students' complaints about books with too much detail—but color-coded links send them to places in the book where they can find more information if they need it. The book has 7 parts:

1. **RHETORICAL SITUATIONS.** Chapters 1–5 focus on purpose, audience, genre, stance, and media and design. In addition, most chapters include tips to help students focus on their particular rhetorical situation.
2. **GENRES.** Chapters 6–20 offer guidelines for fifteen kinds of writing, from abstracts to lab reports to memoirs. Literacy narrative, textual analysis, report, and argument are treated in greater detail.
3. **PROCESSES.** Chapters 21–28 offer advice on generating ideas, drafting, revising, editing, proofreading, compiling portfolios, collaborating, and writing as inquiry.
4. **STRATEGIES.** Chapters 29–41 cover familiar ways of developing and organizing text—writing effective beginnings and endings, coming up with good titles and developing effective thesis statements, comparing, describing, using dialogue, and other essential writing strategies. Chapters 40–41 offer useful strategies for reading and essay exams.
5. **RESEARCH / DOCUMENTATION.** Chapters 42–50 offer advice on how to do academic research; work with sources; quote, paraphrase, and summarize source materials; and document sources using MLA and APA styles.
6. **MEDIA / DESIGN.** Chapters 51–53 give general guidance on designing and presenting texts for print, spoken, and electronic media.
7. **READINGS.** Chapters 54–64 provide additional readings in ten of the genres, plus one chapter of readings that mix genres. Discussion questions help students engage with the text—reading purposefully and mining the texts rhetorically—and are color-coded to refer students to relevant details elsewhere in the book.

What's Online

A free and open website provides instant access to much of *The Norton Field Guide*. Visit the site at **wwnorton.com/write/fieldguide**.

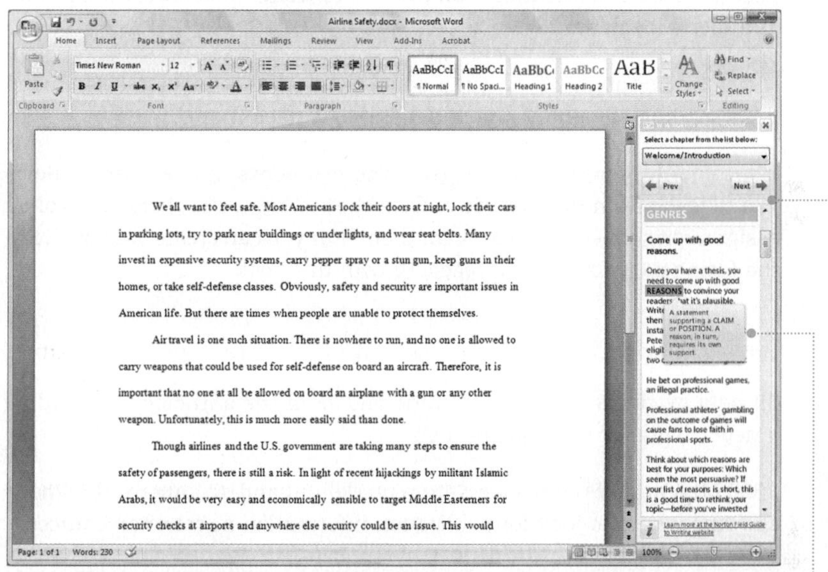

A Writer's Help Window, color-coded to match the book, downloads into Word to give writers access to a quick-reference version of the entire book—as they write.

Color-coded hyperlinks pop up more detailed information if students need it.

Model student papers demonstrate the genres taught in the book.

MLA and APA templates help students document their sources accurately.

A Handbook helps students edit what they write—with 1,000+ exercises for practicing sentence-level writing issues.

Highlights

It's easy to use. Color-coding, menus, directories, and a glossary/index make it easy for students to find what they're looking for; a minimum of jargon makes it easy to understand. Color-coded templates even make MLA and APA documentation easy.

It has just enough detail, with short chapters that include color-coded links sending students to more detail *if* they need more.

It's uniquely flexible for teachers. The two-books-in-one format allows you to teach from the rhetoric or from the readings, and there are explicit assignment sequences if you want them—or you can create your own. See the facing page for ways of teaching with this book.

What's New

39 new readings, 11 in the rhetoric and 28 in the anthology—including a new chapter of multi-genre texts.

2009 MLA and APA documentation guidelines and **documentation maps** showing where to look for publication information in common sources.

A new chapter on synthesizing ideas, helping students connect ideas in multiple sources and use them in their own writing. (Chapter 45)

A new chapter on mixing genres, showing how to combine a number of genres in a single text, as is done in much real-world writing. (Chapter 20)

A new chapter on writing as inquiry, helping students approach writing projects with curiosity and providing strategies to help them get beyond what they already know about their topic. (Chapter 21)

A new chapter on arguing, with strategies for articulating a position, giving good reasons and evidence, considering other positions, and more. (Chapter 32)

A new chapter on taking essay exams (Chapter 41)

Ways of Teaching with *The Norton Field Guide to Writing*

The Norton Field Guide is designed to give you both support and flexibility. It has clear assignment sequences if you want them, or you can create your own. If, for example, you assign a position paper, there's a full chapter. If you want students to use sources, add the appropriate research chapters. If you want them to submit a topic proposal or an annotated bibliography, add those chapters.

If you're a new teacher, the genre chapters offer explicit assignment sequences — and the color-coded links will remind you of other detail that you may want to bring in. The *Instructor's Manual* offers advice on creating a syllabus, responding to writing, and more.

If you teach with a rhetoric, you can organize your syllabus around the appropriate chapters in the *Field Guide*. Color-coded links will help you supplement with appropriate readings from the anthology.

If you base your course on the readings, you'll find more than 80 readings in this book. You can assign readings in particular genres in the anthology, or take a thematic approach (see below). Either way, you can focus your course on the readings, and color-coded links will refer students to writing guidelines elsewhere in the book.

If you focus on genres, there are complete chapters on 15 genres college students are often assigned. Color-coded links will help you bring in details about research or other writing strategies as you wish.

If you organize your course thematically, you can start with the Thematic Guide, which will lead you to readings on 18 themes. Each reading is followed by writing suggestions, or you can assign the chapter on generating ideas to get students thinking about a theme.

If you want students to do research, there are 8 chapters on the research process, along with guidelines and sample papers demonstrating MLA and APA documentation. If you want them writing particular genres, each genre chapter includes links to the research chapters.

If you teach online, much of the book is on the Web, with a Writer's Help Window that downloads into Word to give students access as they write.

Acknowledgments

Writing never takes place in isolation; from start to finish, it is always a collaborative venture. In writing our acknowledgments, we struggled thinking about whom to include and how far back we should go in recognizing the many people who have influenced what we do as writers and teachers, and as authors of this book. Even as we offer our gratitude here by naming those who have most directly contributed to making *The Norton Field Guide to Writing, with readings* a reality, we are aware that many others have been instrumental as well.

Marilyn Moller, the editor of the *Field Guide*, tops our list of those we want to thank, for her keen instincts, creative thinking, and unflagging assistance. She is one of the finest editors we've had the good fortune to work with. The quality of this book is due in large part to her knowledge of the field of composition, her formidable editing and writing skills, and her sometimes uncanny ability to see the future of the teaching of writing.

This edition has benefitted from the creative input and thoughtful suggestions of associate editor Ana Cooke. She graciously and steadfastly responded to questions, and helped to shepherd this edition to the end. We also want to thank Erin Granville for her steady editorial hand through revisions of this book. Her deft editing and insightful suggestions have been especially valuable for the new parts—and in fact have improved the entire book.

Many others have contributed. Thanks to project editor Rebecca Homiski for her energy, patience, and great skill. We thank Anna Palchik for the user-friendly (and award-winning) interior design and Debra Morton Hoyt for the whimsical cover. Jane Searle (and Diane O'Connor before her) transformed a scribbled-over manuscript into a finished product in record time—and to high standards. Katharine Ings copyedited and Nicole Balant proofread, both with great attention to detail. Mike Fleming and Fran Weinberg helped us update the guidelines for documenting sources—and did so in record time. Megan Jackson cleared text permissions, and Stephanie Romeo and Trish Marx researched and cleared permission for the images. Eileen Connell, Jack Lamb, and Cliff Landesman planned, designed, and produced the sensational website. Judy Voss edited the second-edition rhetoric into a concise Web-deliverable edition. Steve Dunn helped us all keep our eyes on the market. Thanks to all, and to Roby

Harrington, Drake McFeely, and Julia Reidhead for supporting this project in the first place.

We also want to acknowledge the generous support we've enjoyed at Wright State University and Arizona State University. Rich has many, many people at Wright State to thank for their support and assistance. Jane Blakelock has taught Rich most of what he knows about electronic text and writing on and for the Web and has assembled an impressive list of useful links for the book's website. Adrienne Cassel (now at Sinclair Community College) and Catherine Crowley read and commented on many drafts of the rhetoric. Peggy Lindsey shared her students' work and the idea of using charts to show how various genres might be organized. Stephanie Dickey, Brady Allen, Debbie Bertsch (now of Columbus State Community College), Vicki Burke, Jimmy Chesire, Carol Cornett, Byron Crews, Deborah Crusan, Sally DeThomas, Scott Geisel, Beth Klaisner, Nancy Mack, Marty Maner, Cynthia Marshall, Sarah McGinley, Michelle Metzner, Kristie Row, Bobby Rubin, Cathy Sayer, David Seitz, Caroline Simmons, Tracy Smith, Rick Strader, Mary Van Loveren, and A. J. Williams responded to drafts, submitted good models of student writing, contributed to the instructor's manual, and tested the *Field Guide* in their classes, providing support and sharing some of their best teaching ideas. Rich also thanks Henry Limouze, chair of the English Department, and Lynn Morgan and Becky Traxler, the secretaries to the writing programs. And thanks to the more than 200 graduate teaching assistants and 9,000 first-year students who class-tested various editions of the *Field Guide* and whose experience helped to shape it.

At Arizona State, Maureen wants to acknowledge the unwavering support of Neal A. Lester, chair of the English Department, and the assistance of Jason Diller, her former graduate research assistant, and Judy Holiday, her graduate mentee, for their reading suggestions. She thanks her colleagues, all exemplary teachers and mentors, for creating a supportive intellectual environment, especially Peter Goggin, Elenore Long, Paul Matsuda, Keith Miller, and Alice Robison. Elenore Long also deserves thanks for pointing out strong readings and for providing inspiration during the search for good models. Thanks also go to ASU instructors and first-year students who have used the *Field Guide* and have offered good suggestions—and to John Jarvis at Bay Path College for directing Maureen to excellent essays. Finally, Maureen wants to pay tribute to her students, who themselves are among her best teachers.

Thanks to the many teachers across the county who have reviewed various versions and offered valuable input and encouragement: Alan Ainsworth, Houston Community College; Jonathan Alexander, University of California at Irvine; Althea Allard, Community College of Rhode Island; James Allen, College of DuPage; Cathryn Amdahl, Harrisburg Area Community College; Jeff Andelora, Mesa Community College; Anne Beaufort, University of Washington, Tacoma; Sue Beebe, Texas State University; Patrick Bizzaro, East Carolina University; Kevin Brooks, North Dakota State University; Ron Brooks, Oklahoma State University; Cheryl Brown, Towson University; Gina Caison, University of Alabama, Birmingham; Susan Callender, Sinclair Community College; Beth Carroll, Appalachian State University; Jill Channing, Mitchell Community College; Ron Christiansen, Salt Lake Community College; Joanna Clark, Cisco Junior College; Susan Cochran-Miller, North Carolina State University at Raleigh Durham; Billye Currie, Samford University; Paul C. Davis, Northland Community and Technical College; David Dedo, Samford University; Pat Densby, San Jacinto College Central; Marvin Diogenes, Stanford University; Sarah Duerdan, Arizona State University; Russel Durst, University of Cincinnati; Sylvia Edwards, Longview Community College; Karen Fitts, West Chester University; Paul Formisano, University of New Mexico; Lloren A. Foster, Hampton University; Ivonne M. Garcia, Ohio State University; Anne Gervasi, DeVry University; Gregory Glau, Arizona State University; Emily Golson, University of Northern Colorado; Richard Hansen, California State Fresno; Susanmarie Harrington, University of Vermont; Chris Harris, University of Louisiana at Monroe; Lory Hawkes, DeVry Institute of Technology; Gary Hawkins, Warren Wilson College; Paul Heilker, Virginia Polytechnic Institute and State University; Hal Hellwig, Idaho State University; Michael Hennessy, Texas State University; Charlotte Hogg, Texas Christian University; Cheryl Huff, Germanna Community College; Maurice Hunt, Baylor University; Teresa James, South Florida Community College; Kim Jameson, Oklahoma City Community College; Peggy Jolly, University of Alabama, Birmingham; Mitzi Walker Jones, University of Arkansas, Fort Smith; Jeanne Kelly, Holmes Community College; Elizabeth Kessler, University of Houston; Rhonda Kyncl, University of Oklahoma; Sally Lahmon, Sinclair Community College; Erin Lebacqz, University of New Mexico; Paul Lynch, Purdue University; T. Michael Mackey, Community College of Denver; Magdalena Maczynska, Marymount Manhattan College; Leigh A. Martin, Community College of

Rhode Island; Deborah McCollister, Dallas Baptist University; Miles McCrimmon, J. Sargeant Reynolds Community College; Jeanne McDonald, Waubonsee Community College; Jacqueline McGrath, College of DuPage; Pat McQueeny, Johnson County Community College; Shellie Michael, Volunteer State Community College; Thomas Miller, University of Arizona; Bryan Moore, Arkansas State University; Mary Ellen Muesing, University of North Carolina, Charlotte; Roxanne Munch, Joliet Junior College; Terry Novak, Johnson & Wales University; Peggy Oliver, San Jacinto College; Amy Patrick, Western Illinois University; Ann Pearson, San Jacinto College; Irv Peckham, Louisiana State University; K. J. Peters, Loyola Marymount University; Deirdre Pettipiece, University of the Sciences; Tony Procell, El Paso Community College; Donna Qualley, Western Washington University; Daniela Ragusa, Southern Connecticut State University; Dana Resente, Montgomery County Community College; Nedra Reynolds, University of Rhode Island; Althea Rhodes, University of Arkansas, Fort Smith; Mauricio Rodriguez, El Paso Community College; Gardner Rogers, University of Illinois at Urbana-Champaign; DaRelle Rollins, Hampton University; Tony Russell, Purdue University; Matthew Samra, Kellogg Community College; Lisa L. Sandoval, Joliet Junior College; Lisa M. Schwerdt, California University of Pennsylvania; Michelle Sidler, Auburn University; Allison Smith, Middle Tennessee State University; William H. Smith, Weatherford College; Leah Sneider, University of New Mexico; Jeffrey Larsen Snodgrass, Prince George's Community College; Jean Sorensen, Grayson County College; Brady J. Spangenberg, Purdue University; Candace Stewart, Ohio University; Jennifer Stewart, Indiana University–Purdue University, Fort Wayne; Amy Ferdinandt Stolley, Purdue University; Mary Stripling, Dallas Baptist University; Martha Swearingen, University of the District of Columbia; Pat Szmania, Lone Star College–North Harris; Elyssa Tardiff, Purdue University; Linda Tetzlaff, Normandale Community College; John M. Thomson, Johnson County Community College; Monica Parrish Trent, Montgomery College, Rockville Campus; Griselda Valerio, University of Texas at Brownsville; Jarica Watts, University of Utah; Scott Weeden, Indiana University–Purdue University Fort Wayne; Candice Welhausen, University of New Mexico; Carol Westcamp, University of Arkansas, Fort Smith; Kristy Shuford White, Lurlene B. Wallace Community College; Barbara Whitehead, Hampton University; Melissa E. Whiting, University of Arkansas, Fort Smith; and Anne-Marie Yerks, University of Michigan. Thanks especially to Avon

Crismore's students at Indiana University–Purdue University Fort Wayne for their thoughtful (and well-written) evaluations.

The Norton Field Guide has also benefited from the good advice of writing teachers across the country, including (among many others) Maureen Mathison, Susan Miller, Tom Huckin, Gae Lyn Henderson, and Sundy Watanabe at the University of Utah; Christa Albrecht-Crane, Doug Downs, and Brian Whaley at Utah Valley State College; Anne Dvorak and Anya Morrissey at Longview Community University; Jeff Andelora at Mesa Community College; Robin Calitri at Merced College; Lori Gallinger, Rose Hawkins, Jennifer Nelson, Georgia Standish, and John Ziebell at the Community College of Southern Nevada; Stuart Blythe at Indiana University–Purdue University Fort Wayne; Janice Kelly at Arizona State University; Jeanne McDonald at Waubonsee Community College; Web Newbold, Mary Clark-Upchurch, Megan Auffart, Matt Balk, Edward James Chambers, Sarah Chavez, Desiree Dighton, Ashley Ellison, Theresa Evans, Keith Heller, Ellie Isenhart, Angela Jackson-Brown, Naoko Kato, Yuanyuan Liao, Claire Lutkewitte, Yeno Matuki, Casey McArdle, Tibor Munkacsi, Dani Nier-Weber, Karen Neubauer, Craig O'Hara, Martha Payne, Sarah Sandman, and Kellie Weiss at Ball State University.

We also want to acknowledge the help of the Norton travelers, the representatives who spend their days visiting faculty, showing and discussing the *Field Guide* and Norton's other fine textbooks. Thanks to Kim Bowers, Kathy Carlsen, Michelle Church, John Darger, Erin Lizer, Brita Mess, and all the other Norton travelers. And we'd especially like to thank Mike Wright, Katie Hannah, Doug Day, and Scott Berzon for promoting this book so enthusiastically and professionally.

It's customary to conclude by expressing gratitude to one's spouse and family, and for good reason. Drafting and revising the *Field Guide* over the years, Rich has enjoyed the loving support of his sons, Ben, Mickey, and Jonathan. Even as they went off to college, graduated, moved here and there and back, found and changed jobs, planned weddings—became adults, in other words—they have provided a strong, still center for Rich's life that has made projects like *The Norton Field Guide* possible. Barb, Rich's wife, is the genesis of whatever he does that's worthwhile and his ultimate reason for doing it. Maureen has enjoyed the loving and unconditional support of her spouse, Peter, to whom she offers her deep-hearted gratitude.

How to Use This Book

There's no one way to do anything, and writing is no exception. Some people need to do a lot of planning on paper; others write entire drafts in their heads. Some writers compose quickly and loosely, going back later to revise; others work on one sentence until they're satisfied with it, then move on to the next. And writers' needs vary from task to task, too: sometimes you know what you're going to write about and why, but need to figure out how to do it; other times your first job is to come up with a topic. *The Norton Field Guide to Writing* is designed to allow you to chart your own course as a writer—to offer you guidelines that suit your writing processes and needs. It is organized in seven parts:

1. **RHETORICAL SITUATIONS:** No matter what you're writing, it will always have some purpose, audience, genre, stance, and medium and design. This part will help you consider each of these elements.
2. **GENRES:** Use these chapters for help with specific kinds of writing, from abstracts to lab reports to memoirs and more. You'll find more detailed guidance for four especially common assignments: literacy narratives, analyzing texts, reporting information, and arguing a position.
3. **PROCESSES:** These chapters offer general advice for all writing situations—from generating ideas and text to drafting, revising and rewriting, compiling a portfolio—and more.
4. **STRATEGIES:** Use the advice in this part to develop and organize your writing—to write effective beginnings and endings, to guide readers through your text, and to use comparison, description, dialogue, and other strategies as appropriate.

5. **RESEARCH / DOCUMENTATION:** Use this section for advice on how to do research, work with sources, and compose and document research-based texts using MLA and APA styles.
6. **MEDIA / DESIGN:** This section offers guidance in designing your work and working with visuals, and in delivering what you write on paper, on screen, or in person.
7. **READINGS:** This section includes readings in 10 genres, and one chapter of texts that mix genres—60 readings in all that provide good examples of the kinds of writing you yourself may be assigned to do.

Ways into the Book

The Norton Field Guide gives you the writing advice you need, along with the flexibility to write in the way that works best for you. Here are some of the ways you can find what you need in the book.

Brief menus. Inside the front cover you'll find a list of all the chapters; start here if you are looking for a chapter on a certain kind of writing or a general writing issue. Inside the back cover is a menu of all the readings in the book.

Complete contents. Pages xix–xxxvii contain a detailed table of contents. Look here if you need to find a reading or a specific section in a chapter.

Guides to writing. If you know the kind of writing you need to do, you'll find guides to writing 15 common genres in Part 2. These guides are designed to help you through all the decisions you have to make—from coming up with a topic to organizing your materials to editing and proofreading your final draft.

Color-coding. The parts of this book are color-coded for easy reference: red for **RHETORICAL SITUATIONS**, green for **GENRES**, lavender for **PROCESSES**, orange for **STRATEGIES**, blue for **RESEARCH / DOCUMENTATION**, gold for **MEDIA / DESIGN**, and apple green for the **READINGS**. You'll find a key to the colors on the front cover flap and also at the foot of each left-hand page. When you see a word highlighted in a color, that tells you where you can find additional detail on the topic.

Glossary / index. At the back of the book is a combined glossary and index, where you'll find full definitions of key terms and topics, along with a list of the pages where everything is covered in detail.

Directories to MLA and APA documentation. A brief directory inside the back cover will lead you to guidelines on citing sources and composing a list of references or works cited. The documentation models are color-coded so you can easily see the key details.

The website. You can also start at **wwnorton.com/write/fieldguide.** There you'll find a quick-reference version of the book that downloads into Word, providing easy access to writing help—including guides to writing, MLA and APA guidelines, the glossary, the complete handbook, and more.

Ways of Getting Started

If you know your genre, simply turn to the appropriate genre chapter. There you'll find model readings, a description of the genre's Key Features, and a Guide to Writing that will help you come up with a topic, generate text, organize and write a draft, get response, revise, edit, and proofread. The genre chapters also point out places where you might need to do research, use certain writing strategies (comparison, description, and so on), design your text a certain way—and direct you to the exact pages in the book where you can find help doing so.

If you know your topic, you might start with some of the activities in Chapter 23, Generating Ideas and Text. From there, you might turn to Chapter 43, for help Finding Sources on the topic. When it comes time to narrow your topic and come up with a thesis statement, Chapter 30 can help. If you get stuck at any point, you might turn to Chapter 21, Writing as Inquiry; it provides tips that can get you beyond what you already know about your topic. If your assignment or your thesis defines your genre, turn to that chapter; if not, consult Chapter 3 for help determining the appropriate genre, and then turn to that genre chapter. The genre chapters point out places where you might need to do more research, use certain writing strategies, design your text a certain way—and direct you to the exact pages in the book where you can find help doing so.

Contents

Part 2 Genres *19*

Part 5 Doing Research *373*

Thematic Guide to the Readings

Childhood Memories

Class Issues

Death and Dying

Education and Schooling

Ethics

Food

Gender

History

Home and Family

Humor and Satire

Identity

Language and Literacy

Media and the Arts

Nature and the Environment

Politics

Race and Ethnicity

Science and Technology

World Cultures and Global Issues

part 1

Rhetorical Situations

Whenever we write, whether it's an email to a friend or a toast for a wedding, an English essay or a résumé, we face some kind of rhetorical situation. We have a **PURPOSE**, a certain **AUDIENCE**, a particular **STANCE**, a **GENRE**, and a **MEDIUM** to consider — and often as not a **DESIGN**. All are important elements that we need to think about carefully. The following chapters offer brief discussions of those elements of the rhetorical situation, along with questions that can help you make the choices you need to as you write. See also the fifteen **GENRES** chapters for guidelines for considering your rhetorical situation in each of these specific kinds of writing.

Rhetorical Situations

Purpose 1

All writing has a purpose. We write to explore our thoughts and emotions, to express ourselves, to entertain; we write to record words and events, to communicate with others, to try to persuade others to believe as we do or to behave in certain ways. In fact, we often have several purposes at the same time. We may write an essay in which we try to persuade an audience of something, but as we write, we may also be exploring our thoughts on the subject. Look, for example, at this passage from a 2002 *New York Times Magazine* essay by economist and editorial columnist Paul Krugman about the compensation of chief executive officers:

> Is it news that C.E.O.'s of large American corporations make a lot of money? Actually, it is. They were always well paid compared with the average worker, but there is simply no comparison between what executives got a generation ago and what they are paid today.
>
> Over the past 30 years most people have seen only modest salary increases: the average annual salary in America, expressed in 1998 dollars (that is, adjusted for inflation), rose from $32,522 in 1970 to $35,864 in 1999. That's about a 10 percent increase over 29 years—progress, but not much. Over the same period, however, according to *Fortune* magazine, the average real annual compensation of the top 100 C.E.O.'s went from $1.3 million—39 times the pay of an average worker—to $37.5 million, more than 1,000 times the pay of ordinary workers.
>
> The explosion in C.E.O. pay over the past 30 years is an amazing story in its own right, and an important one. But it is only the most spectacular indicator of a broader story, the reconcentration of income and wealth in the U.S. The rich have always been different from you and me, but they are far more different now than they were not long ago—indeed, they are as different now as they were when F. Scott Fitzgerald made his famous remark.
>
> —Paul Krugman, "For Richer"

Krugman is reporting information here, outlining how top business executives' pay has increased over the last thirty years. He is also making an argument, that their pay is far greater than it was not too long ago and that this difference between their income and the average worker's resembles the disparity that characterized the United States right before the Great Depression. (Krugman, writing for a magazine, is also using a style—dashes, contractions, rhetorical questions that he then answers—that strives to be entertaining while it informs and argues.)

Even though our purposes may be many, knowing our primary reason for writing can help us shape that writing and understand how to proceed with it. Our purpose can determine the genre we choose, our audience, even the way we design what we write.

Identify your purpose. While writing often has many purposes, we usually focus on one. When you get an assignment or see a need to write, ask yourself what the primary purpose of the writing task is: to entertain? to inform? to persuade? to demonstrate your knowledge or your writing ability? What are your own goals? What are your audience's expectations, and do they affect the way you define your purpose?

Thinking about Purpose

- ***What do you want your audience to do, think, or feel?*** How will they use what you tell them?
- ***What does this writing task call on you to do?*** Do you need to show that you have mastered certain content or skills? Do you have an assignment that specifies a particular STRATEGY or GENRE—to compare two things, perhaps, or to argue a position?
- ***What are the best ways to achieve your purpose?*** What kind of STANCE should you take? Should you write in a particular genre? Do you have a choice of MEDIUM, and does your text require any special format or DESIGN elements?

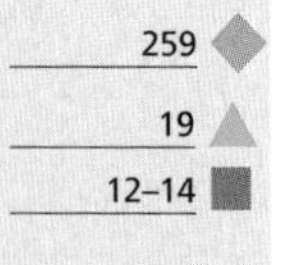
259
19
12–14
521

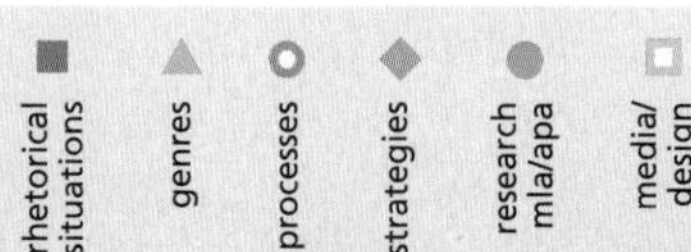

Audience 2

Who will read (or hear) what you are writing? A seemingly obvious but crucially important question. Your audience affects your writing in various ways. Consider a piece of writing as simple as a note left on the kitchen table:

> *Jon—*
> *Please take the chicken out to thaw,*
> *and don't forget to feed Annye.*
> *Remember: Dr. Wong at 4.*
> *Love,*
> *Mom*

On the surface, this brief note is a straightforward reminder to do three things. But in fact it is a complex message filled with compressed information for a specific audience. The writer (Mom) counts on the reader (her son) to know a lot that can be left unsaid. She expects that Jon knows that the chicken is in the freezer and needs to thaw in time to be cooked for dinner; she knows that he knows who Annye is (a pet?), what he or she is fed, and how much; she assumes that Jon knows who (and where) Dr. Wong is. She doesn't need to spell any of that out because she knows what Jon knows and what he needs to know—and in her note she can be brief. She understands her audience. Think how different such a reminder would be were it written to another audience—a babysitter, perhaps, or a friend helping out while Mom is out of town.

What you write, how much you write, how you phrase it, even your choice of **GENRE** (memo, essay, email, note, speech)—all are influenced by the audience you envision. And your audience will interpret your writing according to their expectations and experiences. 9–11

When you are a student, your teachers are most often your audience, so you need to be aware of their expectations and know the conventions (rules, often unstated) for writing in specific academic fields. You may make statements that seem obvious to you, not realizing that your instructors may consider them assertions that must be proved with evidence of one sort or another. Or you may write more or less formally than teachers expect. Understanding your audience's expectations—by asking outright, by reading materials in your field of study, by trial and error—is important to your success as a writer.

This point is worth dwelling on. You are probably reading this text for a writing course. As a student, you will be expected to produce essays with few or no errors. If as part of your job or among friends you correspond using email, you may question such standards; after all, much of the email you get at work or from friends is not grammatically perfect. But in a writing class, the instructor needs to see your best work. Whatever the rhetorical situation, your writing must meet the expectations of your audience.

Identify your audience. Audiences may be defined as *known*, *multiple*, or *unknown*. *Known audiences* can include people with whom you're familiar as well as people you don't know personally but whose needs and expectations you do know. You yourself are a known, familiar audience, and you write to and for yourself often. Class notes, to-do lists, reminders, and journals are all written primarily for an audience of one: you. For that reason, they are often in shorthand, full of references and code that you alone understand. Other known, familiar audiences include anyone you actually know—friends, relatives, teachers, classmates—and whose needs and expectations you understand. You can also know what certain readers want and need, even if you've never met them personally, if you write for them within a specific shared context. Such a known audience might include computer gamers who read instructions that you have posted on the Internet for beating a game; you don't know those people, but you know roughly what they know about the game and what they need to know, and you know how to write about it in ways they will understand.

You often have to write for *multiple audiences*. Business memos or reports may be written initially for a supervisor, but he or she may pass them along to others. Grant proposals are a good example: the National Cancer Institute website advises scientists applying for grants to bear in mind that the application may have six levels of readers—each, of course, with its own expectations and perspectives. Even writing for a class might involve multiple audiences: your instructor and your classmates.

Unknown audiences can be the most difficult to address since you can't be sure what they know, what they need to know, how they'll react. Such an audience could be your downstairs neighbor, whom you say hello to but with whom you've never had a real conversation. How will she respond to your letter asking her to sponsor you in an upcoming charity walk? Another unknown audience—perhaps surprisingly—might be many of your instructors, who want—and expect!—you to write in ways that are new to you. While you can benefit from analyzing any audience, you need to think most carefully about those you don't know.

Thinking about Audience

- ***Whom do you want to reach?*** To whom are you writing (or speaking)?
- ***What is your audience's background—their education and life experiences?*** It may be important for you to know, for example, whether your readers attended college, fought in a war, or have young children.
- ***What are their interests?*** What do they like? What motivates them? What do they care about?
- ***Is there any demographic information that you should keep in mind?*** Consider whether race, gender, sexual orientation, disabilities, occupations, religious beliefs, economic status, and so on should affect what or how you write. For example, writers for *Men's Health*, *InStyle*, and *Out* must consider the particular interests of each magazine's readers.
- ***What political circumstances may affect their reading?*** What attitudes—opinions, special interests, biases—may affect the way your audience reads your piece? Are your readers conservative, liberal, or middle of the road? Politics may take many other forms as well—retirees on a fixed income may object to increased school taxes, so a letter arguing for such an increase would need to appeal to them differently than would a similar letter sent to parents of young children.

- ***What does your audience already know—or believe—about your topic? What do you need to tell them? What is the best way to do so?*** Those retirees who oppose school taxes already know that taxes are a burden for them; they may need to know why schools are justified in asking for more money every few years when other government organizations do not. A good way to explain this may be with a bar graph showing how good schools with adequate funding benefit prop-
259 erty values. Consider which **STRATEGIES** will be effective—narrative, comparison, something else?
- ***What's your relationship with your audience, and how does it affect your language and tone?*** Do you know them, or not? Are they friends? Colleagues? Mentors? Adversaries? Strangers? Will they likely share your
15–17 **STANCE?** In general, you need to write more formally when you're addressing readers you don't know, and you may address friends and colleagues more informally than you would a boss.
- ***What does your audience need and expect from you?*** Your history professor, for example, may need to know how well you can discuss the economy of the late Middle Ages in order to assess your learning; that same professor may expect you to write a carefully reasoned argument, drawing conclusions from various sources, with a readily identifiable thesis in the first paragraph. Your boss, on the other hand, may need an informal email that briefly lists your sales contacts for the day; she may expect that you list the contacts in the order in which you saw them, that you clearly identify each one, and that you
19 give a few words about how well each contact went. What **GENRE** is most appropriate?
- ***What kind of response do you want?*** Do you want to persuade readers to do or believe something? To accept your information on a topic? To understand why an experience you once had matters to you?
- 521 ***How can you best appeal to your audience?*** Is there a particular **MEDIUM** that will best reach them? Are there any **DESIGN** requirements? (Elderly readers may need larger type, for instance.)

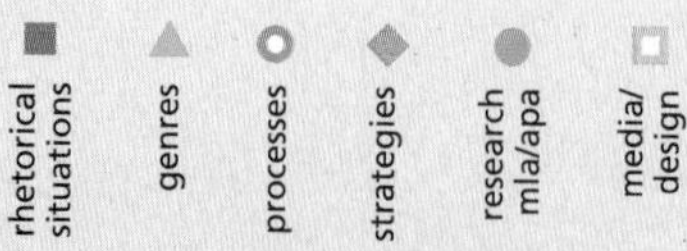

Genre 3

Genres are kinds of writing. Letters, profiles, reports, position papers, poems, Web pages, instructions, parodies — even jokes — are genres. Genres have particular conventions for presenting information that help writers write and readers read. For example, here is the beginning of a **PROFILE** of a mechanic who repairs a specific kind of automobile:

161–70

> Her business card reads Shirley Barnes, M.D., and she's a doctor, all right — a Metropolitan Doctor. Her passion is the Nash Metropolitan, the little car produced by Austin of England for American Motors between 1954 and 1962. Barnes is a legend among southern California Met lovers — an icon, a beacon, and a font of useful knowledge and freely offered opinions.

A profile offers a written portrait of someone or something that informs and sometimes entertains, often examining its subject from a particular angle — in this case, as a female mechanic who fixes Nash Metropolitans. While the language in this example is informal and lively ("she's a doctor, all right"), the focus is on the subject, Shirley Barnes, "M.D." If this same excerpt were presented as a poem, however, the new genre would change our reading:

> Her business card reads
> Shirley Barnes, M.D.,
> and she's a doctor, all right
> — a Metropolitan Doctor.
> Her passion is the Nash Metropolitan,
> the little car produced by Austin of England
> for American Motors between 1954 and 1962.
> Barnes is a legend
> among southern California Met lovers
> — an icon,

a beacon,
and a font of useful knowledge and
freely offered opinions.

The content and words haven't changed, but the presentation invites us to read not only to learn about Shirley Barnes but also to explore the significance of the words and phrases on each line, to read for deeper meaning and greater appreciation of language. The genre thus determines how we read and how we interpret what we read.

Genres help us write by establishing features for conveying certain kinds of information. They give readers clues about what sort of information they're likely to find and so help them figure out how to read ("Ah! A letter from Brit!" or "Thank goodness! I found the instructions for programming this DVD player"). At the same time, writers sometimes challenge genre conventions, reshaping them as communicative needs and technologies change. For example, computers have enabled us to add visuals to texts that we never before thought to illustrate.

19
Identify your genre. Does your writing situation call for a certain **GENRE**? A memo? A report? A proposal? A letter? Academic assignments generally specify the genre ("take a position," "analyze the text"), but if the genre isn't clear, ask your instructor.

Thinking about Genre

- ***What is your genre, and does it affect what content you can or should include?*** Objective information? Researched source material? Your own opinions? Personal experience?
- 259 133–42 ***Does your genre call for any specific*** **STRATEGIES?** Profiles, for example, usually include some narration; **LAB REPORTS** often explain a process.
- 171–79 ***Does your genre require a certain organization?*** Most **PROPOSALS**, for instance, first identify a problem and then offer a solution. Some genres leave room for choice. Business letters delivering good news might be organized differently than those making sales pitches.

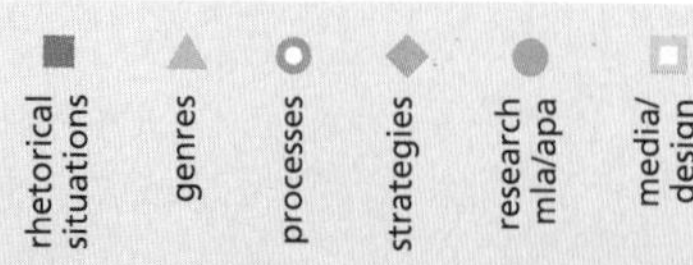

- ***Does your genre affect your tone?*** An abstract of a scholarly paper calls for a different **TONE** than a memoir. Should your words sound serious and scholarly? Brisk and to the point? Objective? Opinionated? Sometimes your genre affects the way you communicate your **STANCE.** 13 12–14
- ***Does the genre require formal (or informal) language?*** A letter to the mother of a friend asking for a summer job in her bookstore calls for more formal language than does an email to the friend thanking him for the lead.
- ***Do you have a choice of medium?*** Some genres call for print; others for an electronic medium. Sometimes you have a choice: a résumé, for instance, can be mailed (in which case it must be printed), or it may be emailed. Some teachers want reports turned in on paper; others prefer that they be emailed or posted to a class website. If you're not sure what **MEDIUM** you can use, ask. 521
- ***Does your genre have any design requirements?*** Some genres call for paragraphs; others require lists. Some require certain kinds of typefaces—you wouldn't use **Impact** for a personal narrative, nor would you likely use DrSeuss for an invitation to Grandma's sixty-fifth birthday party. Different genres call for different **DESIGN** elements. 521

4 Stance

Whenever you write, you have a certain stance, an attitude toward your topic. The way you express that stance affects the way you come across as a writer and a person. This email from a college student to his father, for example, shows a thoughtful, reasonable stance for a carefully researched argument:

> Hi Dad,
> I'll get right to the point: I'd like to buy a car. I saved over $2500 from working this summer, and I've found three different cars that I can get for under $2000. That'll leave me $400 to cover the insurance. I can park in Lot J, over behind Monte Hall, for $75 for both semesters. And I can earn gas and repair money by upping my hours at the cafeteria. It won't cost you any more, and if I have a car, you won't have to come and pick me up when I want to come home.
> Love,
> Michael

While such a stance can't guarantee that Dad will give permission, it's more likely to produce results than this version:

> Hi Dad,
> I'm buying a car. A guy in my Western Civ course has a cool Chevy he wants to get rid of. I've got $2500 saved from working this summer, it's mine, and I'm going to use it to get some wheels. Mom said you'd blow your top if I did, but I want this car.
> Michael

The writer of the first email respects his reader and offers reasoned arguments and evidence of research to convince him that buying a car is an action that will benefit them both. The writer of the second, by contrast, seems impulsive, ready to buy the first car that comes along, and

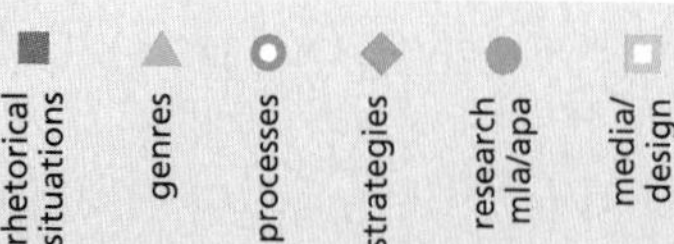

defiant—he's picking a fight. Each email reflects a certain stance that shows the writer as a certain kind of person dealing with a situation in a certain way and establishing a certain relationship with his audience.

Identify your stance. What is your attitude about your topic? Objective? Critical? Curious? Opinionated? Passionate? Indifferent? Your stance may be affected by your relationship to your **AUDIENCE.** How do you want them to see you? As a colleague sharing information? As a good student showing what you can do? As an advocate for a position? Often your stance is affected by your **GENRE:** for example, lab reports require an objective, unemotional stance that emphasizes the content and minimizes the writer's own attitudes. Memoir, by comparison, allows you to reveal your feelings about your topic. Your stance is also affected by your **PURPOSE,** as the two letters about cars show. Your stance in a piece written to entertain will likely differ from the stance you'd adopt to persuade. As a writer, you communicate your stance through your tone.

5–8

19

3–4

Tone is created through the words you use and the way you approach your subject and audience. For example, in an academic essay you would state your position directly—"*America's Next Top Model* reflects the values of American society today"—demonstrating a confident, assertive tone and stance. In contrast, using qualifiers like "might" or "I think" can give your writing a wishy-washy, uncertain tone: "I think *America's Next Top Model* might reflect some of the values of American society today." The following paragraph, from an essay analyzing a text, has a sarcastic tone that might be appropriate for a note to a friend, but that isn't right for an academic essay:

> In "Just Be Nice," Stephen M. Carter complains about a boy who wore his pants too low, showing his underwear. Is that really something people should worry about? We have wars raging and terrorism happening every day, and he wants to talk about how inconsiderate it is for someone to wear his pants too low? If by that boy pulling his pants up, the world would be a better place and the Iraq War would end, I'm sure everyone would buy a belt.

This writer clearly thinks Carter's example is trivial in comparison with the larger issues of the day, but her sarcastic tone belittles Carter's argument instead of answering it with a serious counterargument. Like every other element of writing, your tone must be appropriate for your rhetorical situation.

Just as you likely alter what you say depending on whether you're speaking to a boss, an instructor, a parent, or a good friend, so you need to make similar adjustments as a writer. It's a question of appropriateness: we behave in certain ways in various social situations, and writing is a social situation. You might sign an email to a friend with an *x* and an *o*, but in an email to your supervisor you'll likely sign off with a "Many thanks" or "Regards." To write well, you need to write with integrity, to say what you wish to say; yet you also must understand that in writing, as in speaking, your stance needs to suit your purpose, your relationship to your audience, the way in which you wish your audience to perceive you, and your medium. In writing as in other aspects of life, the Golden Rule applies: "Do unto audiences as you would have them do unto you." Address readers respectfully if you want them to respond to your words with respect.

Thinking about Stance

- ***What is your stance, and how can you best present it to achieve your purpose?*** If you're writing about something you take very seriously, be sure that your language and even your typeface reflect that seriousness. 3–4 Make sure your stance is appropriate to your **PURPOSE.**
- ***What tone will best convey your stance?*** Do you want to be seen as reasonable? Angry? Thoughtful? Gentle? Funny? Ironic? What aspects of your personality do you want to project? Check your writing for words that reflect that tone—and for ones that do not (and revise as necessary).
- ***How is your stance likely to be received by your audience?*** Your tone and 5–8 especially your attitude toward your **AUDIENCE** will affect how willing they are to take your argument seriously.
- ***Should you openly reveal your stance?*** Do you want or need to announce your own perspective on your topic? Will doing so help you reach your 283–99 audience, or would it be better to make your **ARGUMENT** without saying directly where you're coming from?

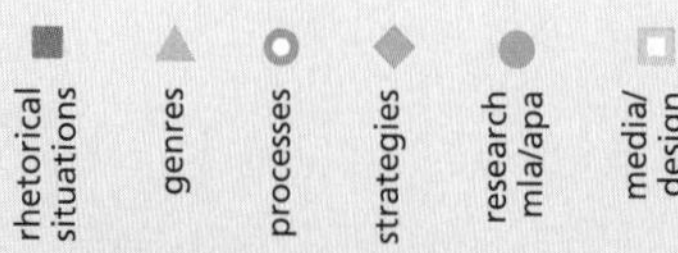

Media / Design 5

In its broadest sense, a *medium* is a go-between: a way for information to be conveyed from one person to another. We communicate through many media, verbal and nonverbal: our bodies (we catch someone's eye, wave, nod), our voices (we whisper, talk, shout, groan), and various technologies, including handwriting, print, telephone, radio, CD, film, and computer.

Each medium has unique characteristics that influence both what and how we communicate. As an example, consider this message: "I haven't told you this before, but I love you." Most of the time, we communicate such a message in person, using the medium of voice (with, presumably, help from eye contact and touch). A phone call will do, though most of us would think it a poor second choice, and a handwritten letter or note would be acceptable, if necessary. Few of us would break such news on a website or during a radio call-in program.

By contrast, imagine whispering the following sentence in a darkened room: "By the last decades of the nineteenth century, the territorial expansion of the United States had left almost all Indians confined to reservations." That sentence starts a chapter in a history textbook, and it would be strange indeed to whisper it into someone's ear. It is available in the medium of print, in the textbook, but it may also be read on a website, in promotional material for the book, or on a PowerPoint slide accompanying an oral presentation. Each medium has different uses and takes different forms, and each has distinctive characteristics. As you can see, we can choose various media depending on our purpose and audience. *The Norton Field Guide* focuses mostly on three media: **PRINT**, **SPOKEN**, and **ELECTRONIC**. 523–33 534–45 546–56

Because we now do most of our writing on computers, we are increasingly expected to pay close attention to the look of the material we write. No matter the medium, a text's *design* affects the way it is received and understood. A typed letter on official letterhead sends a different message than the same letter handwritten on pastel stationery, whatever the words on the page. Classic type sends a different message than *flowery italics*. Some 528–32 genres and media (and audiences) demand **PHOTOS, DIAGRAMS,** color. Some information is easier to explain—and read—in the form of a **PIE CHART** or a **BAR GRAPH** than in the form of a paragraph. Some reports and documents are so long and complex that they need to be divided into sections, which 526–28 are then best labeled with **HEADINGS.** Those are some of the elements to consider when you are thinking about how to design what you write.

Identify your media and design needs. Does your writing situation call for a certain medium and design? A printed essay? An oral report with visual aids? A website? Academic assignments often assume a particular medium and design, but if you're unsure about your options or the degree of flexibility you have, check with your instructor.

Thinking about Media

523–33 534–45 546–56

- ***What medium are you using—* PRINT? SPOKEN? ELECTRONIC?*—and how does it affect the way you will write your text?*** A printed résumé is usually no more than one page long; a scannable résumé sent via email has no length limits. An oral presentation should contain detailed information; accompanying PowerPoint slides should provide only an outline.

259

- ***Does your medium affect your organization and* STRATEGIES?** Long paragraphs are fine on paper but don't work well on the Web. On PowerPoint slides, phrases or key words work better than sentences. In print, you need to define unfamiliar terms; on the Web, you can sometimes just add a link to a definition found elsewhere.
- ***How does your medium affect your language?*** Some print documents require a more formal voice than spoken media; email often invites greater informality.
- ***Should you use a combination of media?*** Should you include audio or video in Web text? Do you need PowerPoint slides, handouts, or other visuals to accompany an oral presentation?

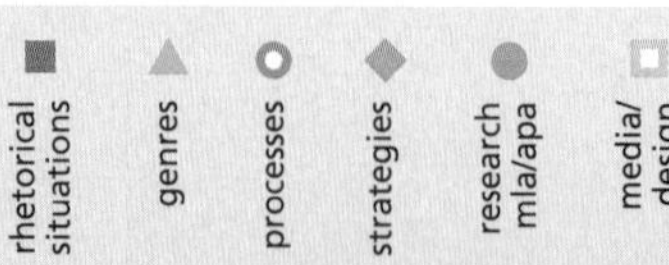

Thinking about Design

- ***What's the appropriate look for your* RHETORICAL SITUATION?** Should your text look serious? Whimsical? Personal? Something else? What design elements will suit your audience, purpose, genre, and medium? 1
- ***Does your text have any elements that need to be designed?*** Is there any information you would like to highlight by putting it in a box? Are there any key terms that should be boldfaced?
- ***What typeface(s) are appropriate*** to your audience, purpose, genre, and medium?
- ***Are you including any illustrations?*** Should you? Is there any information in your text that would be easier to understand as a chart or graph? Will your **AUDIENCE** expect or need any? 5–8
- ***Should you include headings?*** Would they help you organize your materials and help readers follow the text? Does your **GENRE** require them? 9–11

part 2

Genres

When we make a shopping list, we automatically write each item we need in a single column. When we email a friend, we begin with a salutation: "Hi, Brian." Whether we are writing a letter, a résumé, a lab report, or a proposal, we know generally what it should contain and what it should look like because we are familiar with each of those genres. Genres are kinds of writing, and texts in any given genre share goals and features—a proposal, for instance, generally starts out by identifying a problem and then suggests a certain solution. The chapters in this part provide guidelines for writing in fifteen common academic genres. First come detailed chapters on four genres often assigned in writing classes: **LITERACY NARRATIVES**, essays **ANALYZING TEXTS**, **REPORTS**, and **ARGUMENTS**, followed by brief chapters on **TEN OTHER GENRES** and one on **MIXING GENRES**.

Genres

Writing a Literacy Narrative 6

Narratives are stories, and we read and tell them for many different purposes. Parents read their children bedtime stories as an evening ritual. Preachers base their Sunday sermons on Bible stories to teach lessons about moral behavior. Grandparents tell how things used to be (sometimes the same stories year after year). Schoolchildren tell teachers that their dog ate their homework. College applicants write about significant moments in their lives. Writing students are often called upon to compose literacy narratives to explore their experiences with reading and writing. This chapter provides detailed guidelines for writing a literacy narrative. We'll begin with three good examples.

MARJORIE AGOSÍN

Always Living in Spanish: Recovering the Familiar, through Language

Marjorie Agosín, a Spanish professor at Wellesley College, wrote this literacy narrative for Poets & Writers *magazine in 1999. Originally written in Spanish, it tells of Agosín's Chilean childhood and her continuing connection to the Spanish language.*

In the evenings in the northern hemisphere, I repeat the ancient ritual that I observed as a child in the southern hemisphere: going out while the night is still warm and trying to recognize the stars as it begins to grow dark silently. In the sky of my country, Chile, that long and wide stretch of land that the poets blessed and dictators abused, I could eas-

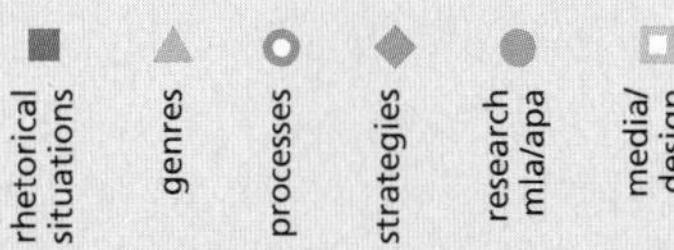

ily name the stars: the three Marias, the Southern Cross, and the three Lilies, names of beloved and courageous women.

But here in the United States, where I have lived since I was a young girl, the solitude of exile makes me feel that so little is mine, that not even the sky has the same constellations, the trees and the fauna the same names or sounds, or the rubbish the same smell. How does one recover the familiar? How does one name the unfamiliar? How can one be another or live in a foreign language? These are the dilemmas of one who writes in Spanish and lives in translation.

Since my earliest childhood in Chile I lived with the tempos and the melodies of a multiplicity of tongues: German, Yiddish, Russian, Turkish, and many Latin songs. Because everyone was from somewhere else, my relatives laughed, sang, and fought in a Babylon of languages. Spanish was reserved for matters of extreme seriousness, for commercial transactions, or for illnesses, but everyone's mother tongue was always associated with the memory of spaces inhabited in the past: the shtetl, the flowering and vast Vienna avenues, the minarets of Turkey, and the Ladino whispers of Toledo. When my paternal grandmother sang old songs in Turkish, her voice and body assumed the passion of one who was there in the city of Istanbul, gazing by turns toward the west and the east.

Destiny and the always ambiguous nature of history continued my family's enforced migration, and because of it I, too, became one who had to live and speak in translation. The disappearances, torture, and clandestine deaths in my country in the early seventies drove us to the United States, that other America that looked with suspicion at those who did not speak English and especially those who came from the supposedly uncivilized regions of Latin America. I had left a dangerous place that was my home, only to arrive in a dangerous place that was not: a high school in the small town of Athens, Georgia, where my poor English and my accent were the cause of ridicule and insult. The only way I could recover my usurped country and my Chilean childhood was by continuing to write in Spanish, the same way my grandparents had sung in their own tongues in diasporic sites.

The new and learned English language did not fit with the vis- 5
ceral emotions and themes that my poetry contained, but by writing in Spanish I could recover fragrances, spoken rhythms, and the passion of my own identity. Daily I felt the need to translate myself for the

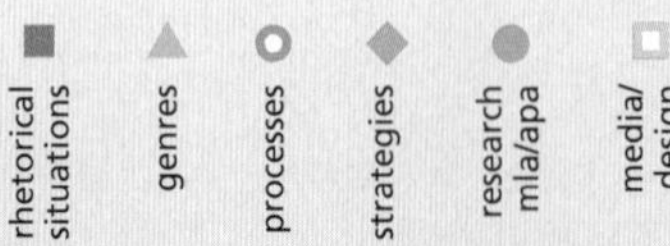

strangers living all around me, to tell them why we were in Georgia, why we are different, why we had fled, why my accent was so thick, and why I did not look Hispanic. Only at night, writing poems in Spanish, could I return to my senses, and soothe my own sorrow over what I had left behind.

This is how I became a Chilean poet who wrote in Spanish and lived in the southern United States. And then, one day, a poem of mine was translated and published in the English language. Finally, for the first time since I had left Chile, I felt I didn't have to explain myself. My poem, expressed in another language, spoke for itself . . . and for me.

Sometimes the austere sounds of English help me bear the solitude of knowing that I am foreign and so far away from those about whom I write. I must admit I would like more opportunities to read in Spanish to people whose language and culture is also mine, to join in our common heritage and in the feast of our sounds. I would also like readers of English to understand the beauty of the spoken word in Spanish, that constant flow of oxytonic and paraoxytonic syllables (*Vérde qué té quiéro vérde*),* the joy of writing — of dancing — in another language. I believe that many exiles share the unresolvable torment of not being able to live in the language of their childhood.

I miss that undulating and sensuous language of mine, those baroque descriptions, the sense of being and feeling that Spanish gives me. It is perhaps for this reason that I have chosen and will always choose to write in Spanish. Nothing else from my childhood world remains. My country seems to be frozen in gestures of silence and oblivion. My relatives have died, and I have grown up not knowing a young generation of cousins and nieces and nephews. Many of my friends were disappeared, others were tortured, and the most fortunate, like me, became guardians of memory. For us, to write in Spanish is to always be in active pursuit of memory. I seek to recapture a world lost to me on that sorrowful afternoon when the blue electric sky and the

* "*Vérde qué té quiéro vérde*" ("Green, how I want you, green") is the opening line of a famous Spanish poem that demonstrates the interplay of words with the main stress on the final syllable (oxytonic) and those with the main stress on next-to-last syllable (paroxytonic) in Spanish. [Editor's note]

Andean cordillera bade me farewell. On that, my last Chilean day, I carried under my arm my innocence recorded in a little blue notebook I kept even then. Gradually that diary filled with memoranda, poems written in free verse, descriptions of dreams and of the thresholds of my house surrounded by cherry trees and gardenias. To write in Spanish is for me a gesture of survival. And because of translation, my memory has now become a part of the memory of many others.

Translators are not traitors, as the proverb says, but rather splendid friends in this great human community of language.

Agosín's narrative uses vivid detail to bring her childhood in Chile to life for her readers. Her love for her homeland and its people is clear, as is the significance of her narrative — with her childhood home gone, to write in Spanish is a "gesture of survival."

RICHARD BULLOCK

How I Learned about the Power of Writing

I wrote this literacy narrative, about my own experience learning to read, as a model for my students in a first-year writing course.

When I was little, my grandmother and grandfather lived with us in a big house on a busy street in Willoughby, Ohio. My grandmother spent a lot of time reading to me. She mostly read the standards, like *The Little Engine That Could,* over and over and over again. She also let me help her plant African violets (I stood on a chair in her kitchen, carefully placing fuzzy violet leaves into small pots of soil) and taught me to tell time (again in her kitchen, where I watched the minute hand move slowly around the dial and tried in vain to see the hour hand move). All that attention and time spent studying the pages as Grandma read them again and again led me to start reading when I was around three years old.

My family was blue-collar, working-class, and — my grandmother excepted — not very interested in books or reading. But my parents took pride in my achievement and told stories about my precocious literacy,

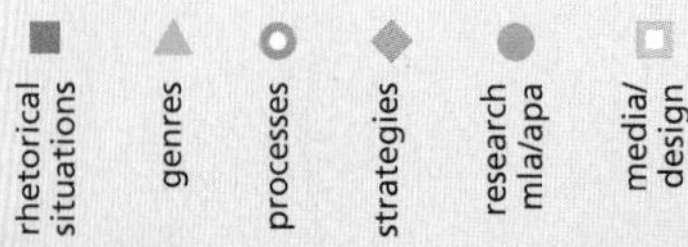

such as the time at a restaurant when the waitress bent over as I sat in my booster chair and asked, "What would you like, little boy?" I'm told I gave her a withering look and said, "I'd like to see a menu."

There was a more serious aspect to reading so young, however. At that time the murder trial of Dr. Sam Sheppard, a physician whose wife had been bludgeoned to death in their house, was the focus of lurid coverage in the Cleveland newspapers. Daily news stories recounted the grisly details of both the murder and the trial testimony, in which Sheppard maintained his innocence. (The story would serve as the inspiration for both *The Fugitive* TV series and the Harrison Ford movie of the same name.) Apparently I would get up early in the morning, climb over the side of my crib, go downstairs and fetch the paper, take it back upstairs to my crib, and be found reading about the trial when my parents got up. They learned that they had to beat me to the paper in the morning and remove the offending sections before my youthful eyes could see them.

The story of the Sheppard murder had a profound effect on me: it demonstrated the power of writing, for if my parents were so concerned that I not see certain things in print, those things must have had great importance. At the same time, adults' amazement that I could read was itself an inducement to continue: like any three-year-old, I liked attention, and if reading menus and the *Plain Dealer* would do it, well then, I'd keep reading.

5 As I got older, I also came to realize the great gift my grandmother had given me. While part of her motivation for spending so much time with me was undoubtedly to keep me entertained in a house isolated from other children at a time when I was too young for nursery school, another part of her motivation was a desire to shape me in a certain way. As the middle child in a large family in rural West Virginia, my grandmother had received a formal education only through the eighth grade, after which she had come alone to Cleveland to make a life for herself, working as a seamstress while reading the ancient Greeks and Etruscans on her own. She had had hopes that her daughter (my mother) would continue her education as she herself hadn't been able to, but Mom chose instead to marry Dad shortly after graduating from high school, and Dad hadn't even gotten that far—he had dropped out of school three days before graduation. So Grandma decided that I was going to be different, and she took over much of my preschool

life to promote the love of learning that she herself had always had. It worked, and at ninety she got to see me graduate from college, the first in our family to do so.

In my literacy narrative, the disconnect between my age and my ability to read provides a frame for several anecdotes. The narrative's significance comes through in the final paragraph, in which I explore the effects of my grandmother's motivation for teaching me.

SHANNON NICHOLS

"Proficiency"

In the following literacy narrative, Shannon Nichols, a student at Wright State University, describes her experience taking the standardized writing proficiency test that high school students in Ohio must pass to graduate. She wrote this essay for a college writing course, where her audience included her classmates and instructor.

The first time I took the ninth-grade proficiency test was in March of eighth grade. The test ultimately determines whether students may receive a high school diploma. After months of preparation and anxiety, the pressure was on. Throughout my elementary and middle school years, I was a strong student, always on the honor roll. I never had a GPA below 3.0. I was smart, and I knew it. That is, until I got the results of the proficiency test.

Although the test was challenging, covering reading, writing, math, and citizenship, I was sure I had passed every part. To my surprise, I did pass every part—except writing. "Writing! Yeah right! How did I manage to fail writing, and by half a point, no less?" I thought to myself in disbelief. Seeing my test results brought tears to my eyes. I honestly could not believe it. To make matters worse, most of my classmates, including some who were barely passing eighth-grade English, passed that part.

Until that time, I loved writing just as much as I loved math. It was one of my strengths. I was good at it, and I enjoyed it. If anything, I thought I might fail citizenship. How could I have screwed up writing? I surely spelled every word correctly, used good grammar, and even used big words in the proper context. How could I have failed?

Finally I got over it and decided it was no big deal. Surely I would pass the next time. In my honors English class I worked diligently, passing with an A. By October I'd be ready to conquer that writing test. Well, guess what? I failed the test again, again with only 4.5 of the 5 points needed to pass. That time I did cry, and even went to my English teacher, Mrs. Brown, and asked, "How can I get A's in all my English classes but fail the writing part of the proficiency test twice?" She couldn't answer my question. Even my friends and classmates were confused. I felt like a failure. I had disappointed my family and seriously let myself down. Worst of all, I still couldn't figure out what I was doing wrong.

I decided to quit trying so hard. Apparently—I told myself—the 5
people grading the tests didn't have the slightest clue about what constituted good writing. I continued to excel in class and passed the test on the third try. But I never again felt the same love of reading and writing.

This experience showed me just how differently my writing could be judged by various readers. Obviously all my English teachers and many others enjoyed or at least appreciated my writing. A poem I wrote was put on television once. I must have been a pretty good writer. Unfortunately the graders of the ninth-grade proficiency test didn't feel the same, and when students fail the test, the state of Ohio doesn't offer any explanation.

After I failed the test the first time, I began to hate writing, and I started to doubt myself. I doubted my ability and the ideas I wrote about. Failing the second time made things worse, so perhaps to protect myself from my doubts, I stopped taking English seriously. Perhaps because of that lack of seriousness, I earned a 2 on the Advanced Placement English Exam, barely passed the twelfth-grade proficiency test, and was placed in developmental writing in college. I wish I knew why I failed that test because then I might have written what was expected on the second try, maintained my enthusiasm for writing, and continued to do well.

Nichols's narrative focuses on her emotional reaction to failing a test that she should have passed easily. The contrast between her demonstrated writing ability and her repeated failures creates a tension that captures readers' attention. We want to know what will happen to her.

For five more literacy narratives, see CHAPTER 54.

Key Features / Literacy Narratives

A well-told story. As with most narratives, those about literacy often set up some sort of situation that needs to be resolved. That need for resolution makes readers want to keep reading. We want to know whether Nichols ultimately will pass the proficiency test. Some literacy narratives simply explore the role that reading or writing played at some time in someone's life—assuming, perhaps, that learning to read or write is a challenge to be met.

Vivid detail. Details can bring a narrative to life for readers by giving them vivid mental images of the sights, sounds, smells, tastes, and textures of the world in which your story takes place. The details you use when describing something can help readers picture places, people, and events; dialogue can help them hear what is being said. We get a picture of Agosín's Chilean childhood when she writes of the "blue electric sky" and her "little blue notebook" in which she described her "house surrounded by cherry trees and gardenias." Similarly, we can picture a little boy standing on a stool planting African violets—and hear a three-year-old's exasperation through his own words: "I'd like to see a menu." Dialogue can help bring a narrative to life.

Some indication of the narrative's significance. By definition, a literacy narrative tells something the writer remembers about learning to read or write. In addition, the writer needs to make clear why the incident matters to him or her. You may reveal its significance in various ways. Nichols does it when she says she no longer loves to read or write. Agosín points out that she writes in Spanish because "nothing else from my childhood world remains . . . To write in Spanish is for me a gesture of survival." The trick is to avoid tacking onto the end a brief statement about your narrative's significance as if it were a kind of moral of the story. My narrative would be less effective if, instead of discussing my grandmother's background and my graduation, I had simply said, "She taught me to be a lifelong reader."

A GUIDE TO WRITING LITERACY NARRATIVES

Choosing a Topic

In general, it's a good idea to focus on a single event that took place during a relatively brief period of time. For example:

- any early memory about writing or reading that you recall vividly
- someone who taught you to read or write
- a book or other text that has been significant for you in some way
- an event at school that was interesting, humorous, or embarrassing
- a writing or reading task that you found (or still find) especially difficult or challenging
- a memento that represents an important moment in your literacy development (perhaps the start of a **LITERACY PORTFOLIO**) 257–58
- the origins of your current attitudes about writing or reading
- learning to write instant messages, learning to write email appropriately, learning to construct a website, creating and maintaining a Facebook page

Make a list of possible topics, and then choose one that you think will be interesting to you and to others — and that you're willing to share with others. If several seem promising, try them out on a friend or classmate. Or just choose one and see where it leads; you can switch to another if need be. If you have trouble coming up with a topic, try **FREEWRITING, LISTING, CLUSTERING,** or **LOOPING.** 219–22

Considering the Rhetorical Situation

PURPOSE Why do you want to tell this story? To share a memory with others? To fulfill an assignment? To teach a lesson? To explore your past learning? Think about the reasons for your choice and how they will shape what you write. 3–4

5–8

AUDIENCE Are your readers likely to have had similar experiences? Would they tell similar stories? How much explaining will you have to do to help them understand your narrative? Can you assume that they will share your attitudes toward your story, or will you have to work at making them see your perspective? How much about your life are you willing to share with this audience?

12–14

STANCE What attitude do you want to project? Affectionate? Neutral? Critical? Do you wish to be sincere? serious? humorously detached? self-critical? self-effacing? something else? How do you want your readers to see you?

15–17

MEDIA / DESIGN Will your narrative be in print? presented orally? on a website? Would photos, charts, or other illustrations help you present your subject? Is there a typeface that conveys the right tone? Do you need headings?

Generating Ideas and Text

Good literacy narratives share certain elements that make them interesting and compelling for readers. Remember that your goals are to tell the story as clearly and vividly as you can and to convey the meaning the incident has for you today. Start by writing out what you remember about the setting and those involved, perhaps trying out some of the methods in the chapter on **GENERATING IDEAS AND TEXT**. You may also want to **INTERVIEW** a teacher or parent who figures in your narrative.

219–25
394–95

Describe the setting. Where does your narrative take place? List the places where your story unfolds. For each place, write informally for a few minutes, **DESCRIBING** what you remember:

324–32

- ***What do you see?*** If you're inside, what color are the walls? What's hanging on them? What can you see out any windows? What else do you see? Books? Lined paper? Red ink? Are there people? Places to sit? A desk or a table?

- *What do you hear?* A radiator hissing? Leaves rustling? The wind howling? Rain? Someone reading aloud? Shouts? Cheers? Children playing? Music? The zing of an instant message arriving?
- *What do you smell?* Sweat? Perfume? Incense? Food cooking?
- *How and what do you feel?* Nervous? Happy? Cold? Hot? A scratchy wool sweater? Tight shoes? Rough wood on a bench?
- *What do you taste?* Gum? Mints? Graham crackers? Juice? Coffee?

Think about the key people. Narratives include people whose actions play an important role in the story. In your literacy narrative, you are probably one of those people. A good way to develop your understanding of the people in your narrative is to write about them:

- *Describe each person in a paragraph or so.* What do the people look like? How do they dress? How do they speak? Quickly? Slowly? With an accent? Do they speak clearly, or do they mumble? Do they use any distinctive words or phrases? You might begin by **DESCRIBING** their movements, their posture, their bearing, their facial expressions. Do they have a distinctive scent? 324–32
- *Recall (or imagine) some characteristic dialogue.* A good way to bring people to life and move a story along is with **DIALOGUE**, to let readers hear them rather than just hearing about them. Try writing six to ten lines of dialogue between two people in your narrative. If you can't remember an actual conversation, make up one that could have happened. (After all, you are telling the story, and you get to decide how it is to be told.) Try to remember (and write down) some of the characteristic words or phrases that the people in your narrative used. 333–37

Write about "what happened." At the heart of every good **NARRATIVE** is the answer to the question "What happened?" The action in a literacy narrative may be as dramatic as winning a spelling bee or as subtle as a conversation between two friends; both contain action, movement, or change that the narrative tries to capture for readers. A good story dramatizes the action. Try **SUMMARIZING** the action in your narrative in a paragraph — try to capture what happened. Use active and specific verbs (*pondered, shouted, laughed*) to describe the action as vividly as possible.

343–51
360–61

Consider the significance of the narrative. You need to make clear the ways in which any event you are writing about is significant for you now. Write a page or so about the meaning it has for you. How did it change or otherwise affect you? What aspects of your life now can you trace to that event? How might your life have been different if this event had not happened or had turned out differently? Why does this story matter to you?

Ways of Organizing a Literacy Narrative

223–24

Start by **OUTLINING** the main events in your narrative. Then think about how you want to tell the story. Don't assume that the only way to tell your story is just as it happened. That's one way—starting at the beginning of the action and continuing to the end. But you could also start in the middle—or even at the end. Shannon Nichols, for example, could have begun her narrative by telling how she finally passed the proficiency test and then gone back to tell about the times she tried to pass it, even as she was an A student in an honors English class. Several ways of organizing a narrative follow.

[Chronologically, from beginning to end]

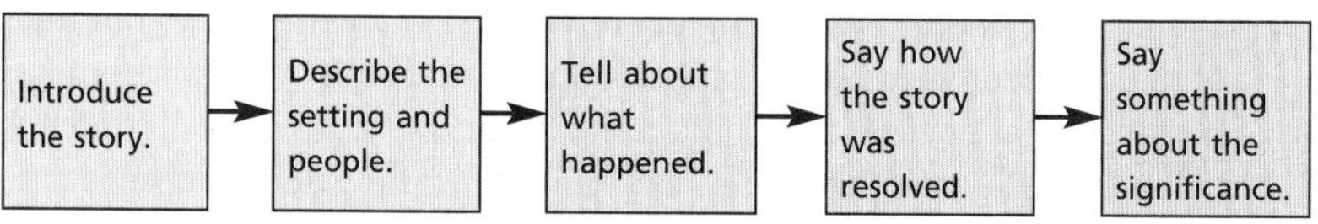

[Beginning in the middle]

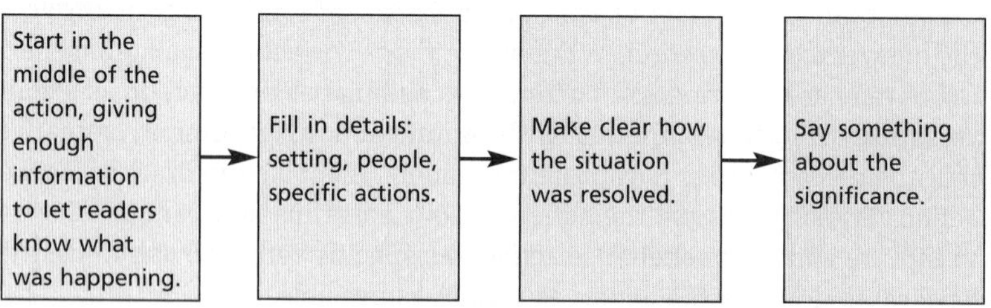

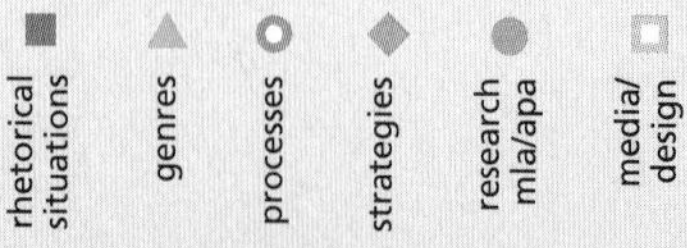

[Beginning at the end]

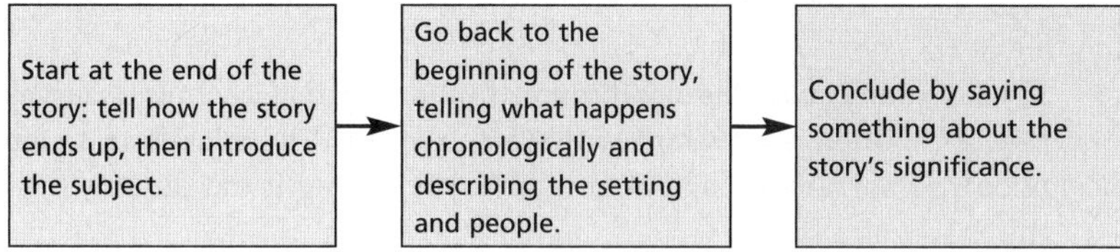

Start at the end of the story: tell how the story ends up, then introduce the subject.
Go back to the beginning of the story, telling what happens chronologically and describing the setting and people.
Conclude by saying something about the story's significance.

Writing Out a Draft

Once you have generated ideas and thought about how you want to organize your narrative, it's time to begin **DRAFTING.** Do this quickly—try to write a complete draft in one sitting, concentrating on getting the story on paper or screen and on putting in as much detail as you can. Some writers find it helpful to work on the beginning or ending first. Others write out the main event first and then draft the beginning and ending. 226–28

Draft a beginning. A good narrative grabs readers' attention right from the start. Here are some ways of beginning; you can find more advice in the chapter on **BEGINNING AND ENDING.** 261–71

- ***Jump right in.*** Sometimes you may want to get to the main action as quickly as possible. Nichols, for example, begins as she takes the ninth-grade proficiency test for the first time.
- ***Describe the context.*** You may want to provide any background information at the start of your narrative, as I decided to do, beginning by explaining how my grandmother taught me to read.
- ***Describe the setting, especially if it's important to the narrative.*** Agosín begins by describing the constellations in her native Chile.

Draft an ending. Think about what you want readers to read last. An effective **ENDING** helps them understand the meaning of your narrative. Here are some possibilities: 266–70

- ***End where your story ends***. It's up to you to decide where a narrative ends. Mine ends several years after it begins, with my graduation from college.
- ***Say something about the significance of your narrative.*** Nichols observes that she no longer loves to write, for example. The trick is to touch upon the narrative's significance without stating it too directly, like the moral of a fable.
- ***Refer back to the beginning.*** My narrative ends with my grandmother watching me graduate from college; Nichols ends by contemplating the negative effects of failing the proficiency test.
- ***End on a surprising note.*** Agosín catches our attention when she tells us of the deaths and disappearances of her friends and relatives.

272–73

Come up with a title. A good **TITLE** indicates something about the subject of your narrative—and makes readers want to take a look. Nichols's title states her subject, "Proficiency," but she also puts the word in quotes, calling it into question in a way that might make readers wonder—and read on. I focus on the significance of my narrative: "How I Learned about the Power of Writing." Agosín makes her title an expression of her sense of identity: "Always Living in Spanish."

Considering Matters of Design

You'll probably write your narrative in paragraph form, but think about the information you're presenting and how you can design it to enhance your story and appeal to your audience.

524–25

- What would be an appropriate **TYPEFACE**? Something serious, like Times Roman? Something whimsical, like Comic Sans? Something else?

526–27

- Would it help your readers if you added **HEADINGS** in order to divide your narrative into shorter sections?

528–32

- Would photographs or other **VISUALS** show details better than you can describe them with words alone? If you're writing about learning to read, for example, you might scan in an image of one of the first books you read in order to help readers picture it. Or if your topic is learning to write, you could include something you wrote.

Getting Response and Revising

The following questions can help you study your draft with a critical eye. **GETTING RESPONSE** from others is always good, and these questions 235–36 can guide their reading, too. Make sure they know your purpose and audience.

- Do the **TITLE** and first few sentences make readers want to read on? 272–73 If not, how else might you **BEGIN**? 261–66
- Does the narrative move from beginning to end clearly? Does it flow, and are there effective **TRANSITIONS**? Does the narrative get sidetracked 277 at any point?
- Is anything confusing?
- Is there enough detail, and is it interesting? Is there enough information about the setting and the people? Can readers picture the characters and sense what they're like as people? Would it help to add some **DIALOGUE**, so that readers can "hear" them? Will they be able to 333–37 imagine the setting?
- Have you made the situation meaningful enough to make readers wonder and care about what will happen?
- Do you narrate any actions clearly? vividly? Does the action keep readers engaged?
- Is the significance of the narrative clear?
- Is the **ENDING** satisfying? What are readers left thinking? 266–70

The preceding questions should identify aspects of your narrative you need to work on. When it's time to **REVISE**, make sure your text appeals 236–39 to your audience and achieves your purpose as successfully as possible.

Editing and Proofreading

Readers equate correctness with competence. Once you've revised your draft, follow these guidelines for **EDITING** a narrative:

- 343–51 Make sure events are **NARRATED** in a clear order and include appro-
277 priate time markers, **TRANSITIONS**, and summary phrases to link the parts and show the passing of time.
- Be careful that verb tenses are consistent throughout. If you write your narrative in the past tense ("he *taught* me how to use a computer"), be careful not to switch to the present ("So I *look* at him and *say* . . . ") along the way.
- Check to see that verb tenses correctly indicate when an action took place. If one action took place before another action in the past, for example, you should use the past perfect tense: "I forgot to dot my *i*'s, a mistake I *had made* many times."
- 333–37 Punctuate **DIALOGUE** correctly. Whenever someone speaks, surround the speech with quotation marks ("No way," I said.). Periods and commas go inside quotation marks; exclamation points and question marks go inside if they're part of the quotation, outside if they're part of the whole sentence:

  INSIDE Opening the door, Ms. Cordell announced, "Pop quiz!"
  OUTSIDE It wasn't my intention to announce "I hate to read"!
- 245–46 **PROOFREAD** your finished narrative carefully before turning it in.

Taking Stock of Your Work

- How well do you think you told the story?
- What did you do especially well?
- What could still be improved?
- How did you go about coming up with ideas and generating text?

- How did you go about drafting your narrative?
- Did you use photographs or any other graphics? What did they add? Can you think of graphics you might have used?
- How did others' responses influence your writing?
- What would you do differently next time?

IF YOU NEED MORE HELP

See also MEMOIRS (Chapter 15), a kind of narrative that focuses more generally on a significant event from your past, and REFLECTIONS (Chapter 18), a kind of essay for thinking about a topic in writing. See Chapter 28 if you are required to submit your literacy narrative as part of a writing PORTFOLIO.

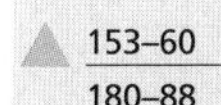
153–60
180–88

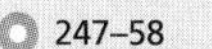
247–58

7 Analyzing a Text

Both *Time* and *U.S. News and World Report* cover the same events, but each magazine interprets them differently. All toothpaste ads claim to make teeth "the whitest." Saddam Hussein was supporting terrorists—or he wasn't, depending on which politician is speaking. Those are but three examples that demonstrate why we need to be careful, analytical readers of magazines and newspapers, ads, political documents, even textbooks. Not only does text convey information, but it also influences how and what we think. We need to read, then, to understand not only what texts say but also how they say it. Because understanding how texts say what they say is so crucial, assignments in many disciplines ask you to analyze texts. You may be asked to analyze sensory imagery in James Joyce's story "Araby" for a literature class or, for an art history course, to analyze the use of color and space in Edward Hopper's painting *Nighthawks*. In a statistics course, you might analyze a set of data—a numerical text—to find the standard deviation from the mean. This chapter offers detailed guidelines for writing an essay that closely examines a text both for what it says and for how it does so, with the goal of demonstrating for readers how—and how well—the text achieves its effects. We'll begin with three good examples.

GINIA BELLAFANTE

In the 24 World, Family Is the Main Casualty

In this 2007 analysis of the TV show 24, *Ginia Bellafante, a reporter at the* New York Times, *explores the show's depiction of family and relationships.*

The frenetic, labyrinthine, exhausting counterterrorism drama *24* concludes its sixth year on Monday night with its ratings slipping and its

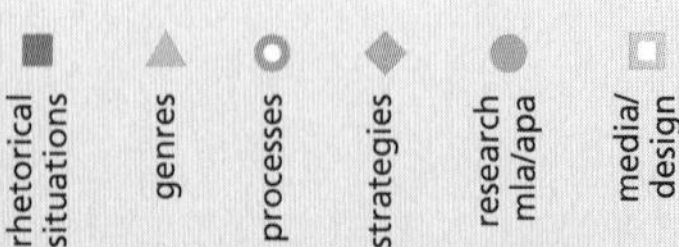

fans in revolt. With each season of the series transpiring over a single day, this one, detractors lament, has felt like 70. The producers themselves have acknowledged the challenges of maintaining the story line's intensity and focus. Recently in his blog on *24*, the humorist Dave Barry expressed a wish for Congressional hearings into the show's crimes against narrative cohesiveness.

Until two weeks ago I had included myself among the dissenters, complaining that digressions and strange forays into cold war nostalgia had subsumed the larger plot and proclaiming, to the walls in my living room, that *24* ought to become *12* — or *8* or *6*. But during Hour 21, Agent Jack Bauer's father, Phillip (played by the gifted James Cromwell), re-emerged to subject members of his family to renewed acts of twisted venality. And the effect was intense and chilling, a reminder that *24* has always sustained its tension by operating in two genres, not one, deploying the conventions of domestic horror in the language of an apocalyptic thriller.

Since it first appeared in 2001, *24* has successfully woven the terrors of intimate life through its narrative of an America facing potential annihilation. Parents kill children. Husbands abuse wives. Sisters try to kill sisters. Wives fire husbands — or stab them, as Martha Logan, ex-wife of Charles Logan, the former president, did earlier this year, plunging a knife into his shoulder as recompense for his treacheries, both personal and civic.

Discussions of *24* have long concentrated on its depiction of torture — elaborate to the point of parody this season — as the source of its controversy. But it is the show's treatment of family as an impossible and even dangerous illusion that truly challenges our complacency. The anxious gloom of watching *24* comes not from wondering whether the world will blow up (obviously it won't; Jack Bauer — played by Kiefer Sutherland — is protection against all that) but from knowing that the bonds that hold people together will eventually be imperiled or destroyed, perfidy and neglect so often the forces.

The introduction of Phillip Bauer early in the season quickly estab- 5
lished that Jack did not inherit his rectitude from his father. Shortly after he appeared, Phillip suffocated his son Graem, forced his daughter-in-law to endanger the lives of federal agents, and threatened Jack. When he reappeared, weeks later, Phillip was kidnapping his grandson, Josh, for the second time in a single day.

Parenthood, untouchably sacrosanct in so much of our culture, is on *24* a grotesquely compromised institution. During Season 4 we witnessed the show's defense secretary subject his son to torture for refusing to divulge information that might help track down a terrorist. At the same time we observed the director of the Counter Terrorist Unit labor to thwart a nuclear attack despite the deterioration of her mentally disturbed daughter in a nearby room.

That each child was portrayed as a petulant nuisance made it easier to see that the country's security imperatives had to come first. The perverse brilliance of *24* lies, at least in some part, in its capacity to elicit our sympathies for heinous miscalculations of judgment. In the end we feel less for the troubled girl than we do for her beleaguered mother, who after all has been making sound decisions every step of the way.

The most enduring relationships on *24* are not between parents and children, boyfriends and girlfriends, spouses or siblings, but between individuals and their governments and causes. And in this way the show seems committed not to the politics of the left or right, but to a kind of quasi-totalitarianism in which patriotism takes precedence over everything else and private life is eroded, undermined, demeaned. Privacy isn't even a viable concept in a world in which there is no taco stand, phone booth, laptop, or S.U.V. that isn't immediately accessible to the advanced surveillance systems of the ever-vigilant Counter Terrorist Unit.

Human connection is forever suffocated. Totalitarianism, Hannah Arendt, wrote, "bases itself on loneliness, on the experience of not belonging to the world at all." And above and beyond everything else, the universe of *24* is a very lonely place.

Friendship can barely be said to exist beyond the parameters of 10
bureaucracy: the offices of the Los Angeles division of the unit and the halls of the White House. And when men and women become involved, it is not only with each other but also with the greater American purpose. Ordinary social intercourse simply doesn't exist. The idea that two people might sit down for a cup of coffee is as contrary to the show's internal logic as the idea that polar bears might someday learn to sing.

On *24* the choice to forfeit all that and respond to your country's call is never the wrong choice, no matter how regrettable the personal consequences. Five seasons ago Jack was a married man who played chess with his teenage daughter. Since then he has lost his wife (at the

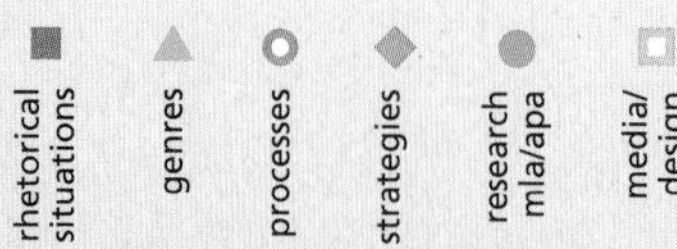

hands of a unit mole), his daughter (to his own emotional inattention), and various girlfriends to his unfailing devotion to eradicating the state's enemies, whatever the cost. He has killed colleagues who have impeded his pursuit of justice, lost his identity, and acquired a heroin addiction combating drug lords. The price of a safe world is considerable, *24* tells us: love and the rest of it mortgaged for some other lifetime.

Bellafante analyzes the depiction of relationships on 24 *and concludes that on the show, "human connection is forever suffocated." She cites several plotlines and events to support this interpretation, painting a bleak picture of the show's family relationships, and suggests that the show is making a larger statement about what we sacrifice for duty.*

WILLIAM SAFIRE

A Spirit Reborn

Just before the first anniversary of September 11, 2001, New York Times *columnist William Safire analyzed the Gettysburg Address for what it meant to Americans after 9/11.*

Abraham Lincoln's words at the dedication of the Gettysburg cemetery will be the speech repeated at the commemoration of September 11 by the governor of New York and by countless other speakers across the nation.

The lips of many listeners will silently form many of the famous phrases. "Four score and seven years ago"—a sonorous way of recalling the founding of the nation eighty-seven years before he spoke—is a phrase many now recite by rote, as is "the last full measure of devotion."

But the selection of this poetic political sermon as the oratorical centerpiece of our observance need not be only an exercise in historical evocation, nonpolitical correctness, and patriotic solemnity. What makes this particular speech so relevant for repetition on this first anniversary of the worst bloodbath on our territory since Antietam Creek's waters ran red is this: now, as then, a national spirit rose from the ashes of destruction.

Here is how to listen to Lincoln's all-too-familiar speech with new ears.

In those 236 words, you will hear the word *dedicate* five times. 5 The first two times refer to the nation's dedication to two ideals mentioned in the Declaration of Independence, the original ideal of "liberty" and the ideal that became central to the Civil War: "that all men are created equal."

The third, or middle, *dedication* is directed to the specific consecration of the site of the battle of Gettysburg: "to dedicate a portion of that field as a final resting place." The fourth and fifth times Lincoln repeated *dedicate* reaffirmed those dual ideals for which the dead being honored fought: "to the unfinished work" and then "to the great task remaining before us" of securing freedom and equality.

Those five pillars of dedication rested on a fundament of religious metaphor. From a president not known for his piety—indeed, often criticized for his supposed lack of faith—came a speech rooted in the theme of national resurrection. The speech is grounded in conception, birth, death, and rebirth.

Consider the barrage of images of birth in the opening sentence. The nation was "conceived in liberty" and "brought forth"—that is, delivered into life—by "our fathers" with all "created" equal. (In the nineteenth century, both "men" and "fathers" were taken to embrace women and mothers.) The nation was born.

Then, in the middle dedication, to those who sacrificed themselves, 10 come images of death: "final resting place" and "brave men, living and dead."

Finally, the nation's spirit rises from this scene of death: "that this nation, under God, shall have a new birth of freedom." Conception, birth, death, rebirth. The nation, purified in this fiery trial of war, is resurrected. Through the sacrifice of its sons, the sundered nation would be reborn as one.

An irreverent aside: All speechwriters stand on the shoulders of orators past. Lincoln's memorable conclusion was taken from a fine oration by the Reverend Theodore Parker at an 1850 Boston antislavery convention. That social reformer defined the transcendental "idea of freedom" to be "a government of all the people, by all the people, for all the people."

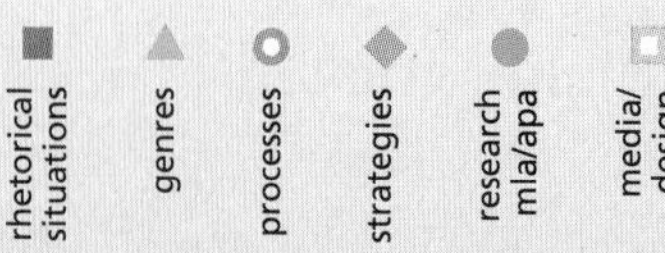

Lincoln, thirteen years later, dropped the "alls" and made the phrase his own. (A little judicious borrowing by presidents from previous orators shall not perish from the earth.) In delivering that final note, the Union's defender is said to have thrice stressed the noun "people" rather than the prepositions "of," "by," and "for." What is to be emphasized is not rhetorical rhythm but the reminder that our government's legitimacy springs from America's citizens; the people, not the rulers, are sovereign. Not all nations have yet grasped that.

Do not listen on September 11 only to Lincoln's famous words and comforting cadences. Think about how Lincoln's message encompasses but goes beyond paying "fitting and proper" respect to the dead and the bereaved. His sermon at Gettysburg reminds "us the living" of our "unfinished work" and "the great task remaining before us"—to resolve that this generation's response to the deaths of thousands of our people leads to "a new birth of freedom."

Safire's analysis focuses on patterns of specific words and images—he identifies dedicate *as a key term and analyzes how its meaning changes and develops each time it is used. He shows how Lincoln shaped his text around images of birth, death, and resurrection to assert that although a nation's soldiers die, their deaths permit the rebirth of the nation. In doing so, Safire builds an argument linking Lincoln's words to current circumstances.*

DOUG LANTRY

"Stay Sweet As You Are": An Analysis of Change and Continuity in Advertising Aimed at Women

Doug Lantry wrote this analysis of three print ads for a first-year writing course at the University of Akron.

Magazine advertisements aimed at American women have a long history of pushing things like makeup, mouthwash, soap, and other products that reinforce men's roles in women's lives. The concept of personal hygiene has been used to convey the message that "catching" a man or becoming a wife is a woman's ultimate goal, and in advertisements from the 1920s, 1930s, and 1950s this theme can be traced through verbal and visual content.

For example, a 1922 ad for Resinol soap urges women to "make that dream come true" by using Resinol (see Fig. 1). The dream is marriage. The premise is that a bad complexion will prevent marriage even if a woman has attributes like wit and grace, which the ad identifies as positive. Blotchy skin, the ad says, will undermine all that. The word *repellent* is used for emphasis and appears in the same sentence as the words *neglected* and *humiliated*, equating the look of the skin with the state of the person within. Of course, Resinol can remedy the condition, and a paragraph of redemption follows the paragraph about being repellent. A treatment program is suggested, and the look and feel of "velvety" skin are only "the first happy effects," with eventual marriage (fulfillment) implied as the ultimate result of using Resinol soap.

Visual content supports the mostly verbal ad. In a darkened room, a lone woman peers dreamily into a fireplace, where she sees an apparition of herself as a bride in a white veil, being fulfilled as a person by marriage to a handsome man. She lounges in a soft chair, where the glow of the image in the fireplace lights her up and warms her as much as the comforting fire itself. A smaller image shows the woman washing with Resinol, contentedly working her way toward clear skin and marriage over a water-filled basin suggestive of a vessel of holy water. This image is reinforced by her closed eyes and serene look and by the ad's suggestion that "right living" is a source of a good complexion.

A somewhat less innocent ad appeared more than a decade later, in 1934 (see Fig. 2). That ad, for Lux soap, like the one for Resinol, prescribes a daily hygiene regimen, but it differs significantly from the Resinol message in that it never mentions marriage and uses a clear-skinned movie star as proof of Lux's effectiveness. Instead of touting marriage, Lux teaches that "a girl who wants to break hearts simply must have a tea-rose complexion." Romance, not marriage, is the woman's goal, and competition among women is emphasized because "girls who want to make new conquests . . . [are] *sure* to win out!" by using Lux. Lux's pitch is more sophisticated than Resinol's, appealing to a more emancipated woman than that of the early 1920s and offering a kind of evidence based on science and statistics. The text cites "9 out of 10 glamorous Hollywood stars" and scientists who explain that Lux slows aging, but it declines to cite names, except that of Irene

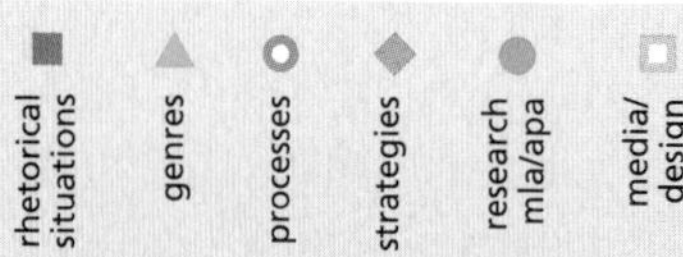

Make that dream come true
WHAT woman lives who has not at some time enjoyed the vision of herself a bride. For many the dream has been fulfilled. Don't allow a bad complexion to place you among the others!
Your beauty of feature, becoming dress, graceful bearing, keen wit, can be completely overshadowed by a blotchy or otherwise unattractive skin. But there is no excuse for submission to such a condition, when to correct it is so easy.
Usually all that nature requires to make a clear pleasing complexion is right living—and—proper, regular cleansing of the skin. It is this knowledge that has made Resinol Soap a favorite in thousands of homes where it is now in daily use.
If you are neglected and humiliated because of a red, oily, or otherwise repellent skin, begin today the following treatment:
Gently work the profuse foamy lather of Resinol Soap well into the pores with the finger tips. It rinses easily and completely with a little clear warm water. A dash of cold water to close the pores completes the treatment. Now see how velvety your skin looks and feels—how invigorated it is—and what a delicate glow it has. These are only the first happy effects of this delightful toilet soap.
At all drug and toilet goods counters. May we send you a free trial? Write now. Dept. 5-A, Resinol, Baltimore, Md.
Resinol Soap
Resinol Soap

Fig. 1. 1922 Resinol soap ad.

"Girls who know this secret always win out"
says Irene Dunne
1
YEARS AGO MY LOVELY SOUTHERN GRANDMOTHER FIRST TAUGHT ME THAT A GIRL WHO WANTS TO BREAK HEARTS SIMPLY MUST HAVE A TEAROSE COMPLEXION
RKO-RADIO STAR
2
3
SO MANY GIRLS have asked Irene Dunne how to make themselves more attractive . . . how to win admiration . . . romance.
Here this lovely star tells you! And her beauty method is so simple . . . so easy to try . . . regular, everyday care with exquisitely gentle Lux Toilet Soap.
Do follow her advice! See how much clearer, softer *your* skin becomes . . . how that extra-lovely complexion wins hearts—and *holds* them!
9 out of 10 glamorous Hollywood stars . . . countless girls the country over . . . have *proved* what this fragrant, white soap does for the skin. Is yours just an "average" complexion? Don't be content—start today—have the *added beauty* Lux Toilet Soap brings.
NOW THAT I'M ON THE SCREEN I REALIZE MORE THAN EVER THE FASCINATION THERE IS IN PEARLY-SMOOTH SKIN. I FOLLOW MY LUX TOILET SOAP BEAUTY TREATMENT REGULARLY EVERY DAY.
IT'S REALLY AMAZING HOW QUICKLY JUST THIS SIMPLE CARE BRINGS TEMPTING NEW BEAUTY TO THE SKIN. TRY IT-YOU GIRLS WHO WANT TO MAKE NEW CONQUESTS! YOU'RE SURE TO WIN OUT!
Precious Elements in this Soap—*Scientists say:*
"Skin grows old-looking through the gradual loss of certain elements Nature puts in skin to keep it youthful. Gentle Lux Toilet Soap, so readily soluble, *actually contains* such precious elements—checks their loss from the skin."
LUX TOILET SOAP
For EVERY Type of Skin… *dry…oily…"in-between"*
YOU can have the Charm men can't resist

Fig. 2. 1934 Lux soap ad.

Dunne, the ad's star. The unnamed stars and scientists give the ad an air of untruthfulness, and this sense is deepened by the paradox of the ad's title: "Girls who know this secret always win out." If Lux is a secret, why does it appear in a mass-media publication?

Like Resinol, Lux urges women to seek love and fulfillment by 5
enhancing their outward beauty and suggests that clear skin means having "the charm men can't resist."

The Lux ad's visual content, like Resinol's, supports its verbal message. Several demure views of Irene Dunne emphasize her "pearly-smooth skin," the top one framed by a large heart shape. In all the photos, Dunne wears a feathery, feminine collar, giving her a birdlike appearance: she is a bird of paradise or an ornament. At the bottom of the ad, we see a happy Dunne being cuddled and admired by a man.

The visual and verbal message is that women should strive, through steps actually numbered in the ad, to attain soft, clear skin and hence charm and hence romance. Not surprisingly, the ad uses the language of battle to describe the effects of clear skin: girls who use Lux will "make new conquests!" and "win out!" Similar themes are developed for a younger audience in a 1954 ad for Listerine mouthwash (see Fig. 3). This time the target is no longer grown women but teenage girls: "If you want to win the boys . . . Stay Sweet As You Are!" Because attracting men would be inappropriate for teenagers, boys are the catch of the day in the Listerine ad. The idea of staying sweet means on the surface that girls should have nice breath, but the youthful context of the ad means that for women to be attractive they must stay young and "stay adorable," preferably with the girlish innocence of a teenager. The consequences of not staying sweet are clear: if you don't use Listerine every morning, every night, and before every date, "you're headed for boredom and loneliness." If you do use Listerine, there are "good times, good friends, and gaiety ahead."

Like Lux, Listerine relies on science as well as sex. With talk of "the bacterial fermentation of proteins," research, and clinical tests, the mouthwash props up its romantic and sexual claims by proclaiming scientific facts. Listerine is "4 times better than any tooth paste," the ad proclaims. "With proof like this, it's easy to see why Listerine belongs in your home."

Visuals contribute to the message, as in the other ads. The central image is a photo of a perky, seemingly innocent teenage girl playing records on a portable phonograph. A vision of midcentury American femininity, she wears a fitted sweater, a scarf tied at the neck (like a wrapped present?), and a full, long skirt. She sits on the floor, her legs hidden by the skirt; she could be a cake decoration. Leaning forward slightly, she looks toward the reader, suggesting by her broad smile and submissive posture that perhaps kissing will follow when she wins the boys with her sweet breath. The record player affirms the ad's teenage target.

The intended consumers in the Resinol, Lux, and Listerine ads are 10
women, and the message of all three ads is that the product will lead

IF YOU WANT TO WIN THE BOYS . . .

Stay Sweet As You Are!

There are good times, good friends, and gaiety ahead if you do. And laughter and love . . . and marriage almost before you know it. But if you don't . . . you're headed for boredom and loneliness.

And it's so easy to stay sweet . . . stay adorable . . . if you let Listerine Antiseptic look after your breath. Every morning. Every night. And especially before every date when you want to be at your best. Listerine instantly stops bad breath, and keeps it stopped for hours, usually . . . *four times better than any tooth paste.*

No Tooth Paste Kills Odor Germs Like This . . . Instantly

Listerine Antiseptic does for you what no tooth paste does. Listerine instantly kills bacteria . . . by millions—stops bad breath instantly, and usually for hours on end.

You see, far and away the most common cause of offensive breath is the bacterial fermentation of proteins which are always present in the mouth. *And research shows that your breath stays sweeter longer, depending upon the degree to which you reduce germs in the mouth.*

Listerine Clinically Proved Four Times Better Than Tooth Paste

No tooth paste, of course, is antiseptic. Chlorophyll does not kill germs—but Listerine kills bacteria by millions, gives you lasting antiseptic protection against bad breath.

Is it any wonder Listerine Antiseptic in recent clinical tests averaged at least four times more effective in stopping bad breath odors than the chlorophyll products or tooth pastes it was tested against? With proof like this, it's easy to see why Listerine belongs in your home. Every morning . . . every night . . . before every date, make it a habit to always gargle Listerine, the most widely used antiseptic in the world.

LISTERINE ANTISEPTIC STOPS BAD BREATH

4 times better than any tooth paste

Every week 2 different shows, Radio & Television—"THE ADVENTURES OF OZZIE & HARRIET" See your paper for times and stations

A Product of The Lambert Company

Fig. 3. 1954 Listerine mouthwash ad.

to—and is required for—romantic or matrimonial success. Each ad implies that physical traits are paramount in achieving this success, and the ads' appearance in widely circulated magazines suggests that catching a man (whether or not she marries him) is the ultimate goal of every American woman. While there is a kind of progress over time, the ads' underlying assumptions remain constant. There is evidence of women's increasing sophistication, illustrated in the later ads' use of science and "objective" proof of the products' effectiveness. Women's development as individuals can also be seen in that marriage is not presupposed in the later ads, and in the case of Lux a single woman has a successful career and apparently has her pick of many partners.

Still, one theme remains constant and may be seen as a continuing debilitating factor in women's struggle for true equality in the world of sex roles: pleasing men is the prerequisite for happiness. Despite apparent advances on other levels, that assumption runs through all three ads and is the main selling point. The consumer of Resinol, Lux, and Listerine is encouraged to objectify herself, to become more physically attractive not for her own sake but for someone else's. The women in all three ads are beautifying themselves because they assume they must "make new conquests," "win the boys," and "make that dream come true."

Lantry summarizes each ad clearly and focuses his analysis on a theme running through all three ads: the concept that to find happiness, a woman must be physically attractive to men. He describes patterns of images and language in all three ads as evidence.

For five more textual analyses, see CHAPTER 55.

Key Features / Textual Analysis

A summary of the text. Your readers may not know the text you are analyzing, so you need to include it or tell them about it before you can analyze it. Because Safire's text is so well-known, he describes it only briefly as "Abraham Lincoln's words at the dedication of the Gettysburg cemetery." Texts that are not so well-known require a more detailed summary. Lantry includes the texts—and images—he analyzes and also describes them in detail.

Attention to the context. Texts don't exist in isolation: they are influenced by and contribute to ongoing conversations, controversies, or debates, so to understand the text, you need to understand the larger context. Bellafante opens by describing fans' critical response to the sixth season of 24. Safire notes the source of the phrase "of the people, by the people, for the people" and is clearly writing in the context of the United States after 9/11.

A clear interpretation or judgment. Your goal in analyzing a text is to lead readers through careful examination of the text to some kind of interpretation or reasoned judgment, generally announced clearly in a thesis statement. When you interpret something, you explain what you think it means, as Lantry does when he argues that the consumers of the three beauty products are encouraged to "objectify" themselves. He might instead have chosen to judge the effectiveness of the ads, perhaps noting that they promise the impossible, that no mouthwash, soap, or other product can guarantee romantic "success."

Reasonable support for your conclusions. Written analysis of a text is generally supported by evidence from the text itself and sometimes from other sources. The writer might support his or her interpretation by quoting words or passages from a written text or referring to images in a visual text. Safire, for example, looks at Lincoln's repetition of the word "dedicate" in the Gettysburg Address as a way of arguing that the speech was still relevant in 2002, on the anniversary of the 9/11 attacks. Lantry examines patterns of both language and images in his analysis of the three ads. Bellafante describes several scenes and plotlines from 24. Note that the support you offer for your interpretation need only be "reasonable"—there is never any one way to interpret something.

A GUIDE TO WRITING TEXTUAL ANALYSES

Choosing a Text to Analyze

Most of the time, you will be assigned a text or a type of text to analyze: a poem in a literature class, the work of a political philosopher in a political science class, a speech in a history or communications course, a painting or sculpture in an art class, a piece of music in a music theory course. If you must choose a text to analyze, look for one that suits the demands of the assignment—one that is neither too large or complex to analyze thoroughly (a Dickens novel or a Beethoven symphony is probably too big) nor too brief or limited to generate sufficient material (a ten-second TV news brief or a paragraph from *Fast Food Nation* would probably be too small). You might also choose to analyze three or four texts by examining elements common to all. Be sure you understand what the assignment asks you to do, and ask your instructor for clarification if you're not sure.

Considering the Rhetorical Situation

PURPOSE Why are you analyzing this text? To demonstrate that you understand it? To persuade readers that the text demonstrates a certain point? Or are you using the text as a way to make some other point? 3–4

AUDIENCE Are your readers likely to know your text? How much detail will you need to supply? 5–8

STANCE What interests you about your analysis? Why? What do you know or believe about your topic, and how will your own beliefs affect your analysis? 12–14

MEDIA / DESIGN Are you writing an essay for a class? To be published in a journal or magazine? Something for the Web? If you are analyzing a visual text, you will probably need to include an image of the text. 15–17

Generating Ideas and Text

In analyzing a text, your goal is to understand what it says, how it works, and what it means. To do so, you may find it helpful to follow a certain sequence: read, respond, summarize, analyze, and draw conclusions from your analysis.

Read to see what the text says. Start by reading carefully, to get a sense
353 of what it says. This means first skimming to **PREVIEW THE TEXT**, reread-
354–55 ing for the main ideas, then questioning and **ANNOTATING.**

354 Consider your **INITIAL RESPONSE.** Once you have a sense of what the text says, what do you think? What's your reaction to the argument, the tone, the language, the images? Do you find the text difficult? puzzling? Do you agree with what the writer says? Disagree? Agree *and* disagree? Your reaction to a text can color your analysis, so start by thinking about how you react—and why. Consider both your intellectual and any emotional reactions. Identify places in the text that trigger or account for those reactions. If you think that you have no particular reaction or response, try to articulate why. Whatever your response, think about what accounts for it.

416–17 Next, consolidate your understanding of the text by **SUMMARIZING** (or,
324–32 if it's a visual text, **DESCRIBING**) what it says in your own words. You may
223–24 find it helpful to **OUTLINE** its main ideas. See, for instance, how Lantry carefully described what a soap ad he was analyzing shows and says. Some of this analysis ended up in his essay.

> Several demure views of Irene Dunne emphasize her "pearly-smooth skin," the top one framed by a large heart shape. In all the photos, Dunne wears a feathery, feminine collar, giving her a birdlike appearance: she is a bird of paradise or an ornament. At the bottom of the ad, we see a happy Dunne being cuddled and admired by a man.

Decide what you want to analyze. Having read the text carefully, think about what you find most interesting or intriguing, and why. Does the language interest you? The imagery? The structure? The argument? The larger context? Something else? You might begin your analysis by exploring what attracted your notice.

Study how the text works. Texts are made up of several components—words, sentences, images, even punctuation. Visual texts might be made up of images, lines, angles, color, light and shadow, and sometimes words. All these elements can be used in various ways. To analyze them, look for patterns in the way they're used and try to decide what those patterns reveal about the text. How do they affect its message? See the sections on THINKING ABOUT HOW THE TEXT WORKS and IDENTIFYING PATTERNS for specific guidelines on examining patterns this way.

358–60

361–63

Then write a sentence or two describing the patterns you've discovered and how they contribute to what the text says.

Analyze the argument. Every text makes an argument. Both verbal and visual texts make certain assertions and provide some kind of support for those claims. An important part of understanding any text is to recognize its argument—what the writer or artist wants the audience to believe, feel, or do. Consider the text's purpose and audience, identify its thesis, and decide how convincingly it supports that thesis. See the section on ANALYZING THE ARGUMENT for help doing so.

364

Then write a sentence or two summarizing the argument the text makes, along with your reactions to or questions about that argument.

Think about the larger context. Texts are always part of larger, ongoing conversations. To analyze a text's role in its LARGER CONTEXT, you may need to do additional RESEARCH to determine where the text was originally published, what else was happening or being discussed at the time the text was published or created, and whether or not the text responded directly to other ideas or arguments.

365–66

373

Then write a sentence or two describing the larger context surrounding the text and how that context affects your understanding of the text.

Consider what you know about the writer or artist. What you know about the person who created a text can influence your understanding of that text. His or her CREDENTIALS, other work, reputation, stance, and beliefs are all useful windows into understanding a text.

401

Then write a sentence or two summarizing what you know about the writer and how that information affects your understanding of the text.

Come up with a thesis. When you analyze a text, you are basically ARGUING that the text should be read in a certain way. Once you've studied the text thoroughly, you need to identify your analytical goal: do you

283–99

want to show that the text has a certain meaning? Uses certain techniques to achieve its purposes? Tries to influence its audience in particular ways? Relates to some larger context in some significant manner? Should be taken seriously—or not? Something else? Come up with a tentative 273–75 **THESIS** to guide your thinking and analyzing—but be aware that your thesis may change as you continue to work.

Ways of Organizing a Textual Analysis

Examine the information you have to see how it supports or complicates your thesis. Look for clusters of related information that you can use to 223–24 structure an **OUTLINE.** Your analysis might be structured in at least two ways. You might, as Safire does, discuss patterns or themes that run through the text. Alternatively, you might analyze each text or section of text separately, as Bellafante and Lantry do. Following are graphic representations of some ways of organizing a textual analysis.

[Thematically]

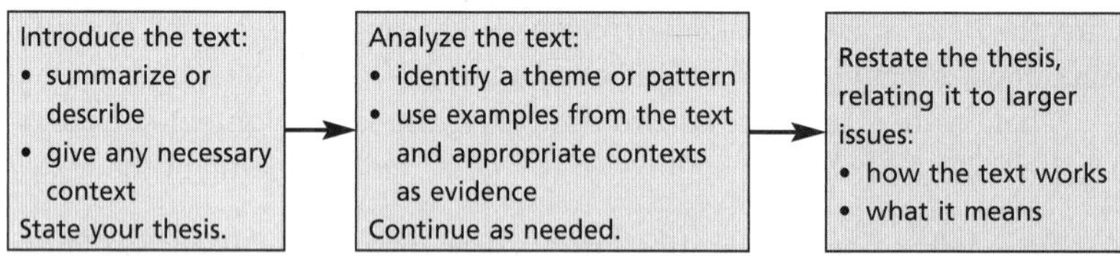

[Part by part, or text by text]

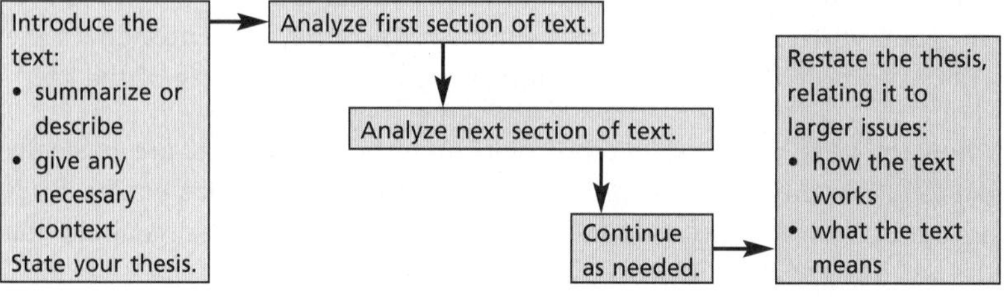

Writing Out a Draft

In drafting your analysis, your goal should be to integrate the various parts into a smoothly flowing, logically organized essay. However, it's easy to get bogged down in the details. Consider writing one section of the analysis first, then another and another until you've drafted the entire middle; then draft your beginning and ending. Alternatively, start by summarizing the text and moving from there to your analysis and then to your ending. However you do it, you need to support your analysis with evidence: from the text itself (as Lantry's analysis of advertisements and Bellafante's analysis of *24* do), or from **RESEARCH** on the larger context of the text (as Safire does). 373

Draft a beginning. The beginning of an essay that analyzes a text generally has several tasks: to introduce or summarize the text for your readers, to offer any necessary information on the larger context, and to present your thesis.

- ***Summarize the text.*** If the text is one your readers don't know, you need to give a brief **SUMMARY** early on that introduces it to them and shows that you understand it fully. For example, Lantry begins each analysis of a soap advertisement with a brief summary of its content. 416–17
- ***Provide a context for your analysis.*** If there is a larger context that is significant for your analysis, you might mention it in your introduction. Safire does this when he frames his analysis of the Gettysburg Address as a "centerpiece" of 9/11 commemorations.
- ***Introduce a pattern or theme.*** If your analysis centers on a certain pattern of textual or contextual elements, you might begin by describing it, as Bellafante does when she writes of *24* as "deploying the conventions of domestic horror in the language of an apocalyptic thriller."
- ***State your thesis.*** Lantry ends his first paragraph by stating the **THESIS** of his analysis: "The concept of personal hygiene has been used to convey the message that 'catching' a man or becoming a wife is a woman's 273–75

ultimate goal, and in advertisements from the 1920s, 1930s, and 1950s this theme can be traced through verbal and visual content."

261–71

- See Chapter 29 for more advice on **BEGINNING AND ENDING.**

Draft an ending. Think about what you want your readers to take away from your analysis, and end by getting them to focus on those thoughts.

- ***Restate your thesis — and say why it matters.*** Lantry, for example, ends by pointing out that "one theme remains constant" in all the ads he analyzes: that "pleasing men is the prerequisite for happiness."
- ***Say something about the implications of your findings.*** If your analysis has any general implications, you might end by stating them as Safire does: "[Lincoln's] sermon at Gettysburg reminds 'us the living' of our 'unfinished work' and 'the great task remaining before us' — to resolve that this generation's response to the deaths of thousands of our people leads to 'a new birth of freedom.' "

261–71

- See Chapter 29 for more advice on ways of **BEGINNING AND ENDING.**

272–73

Come up with a title. A good **TITLE** indicates something about the subject of your analysis — and makes readers want to see what you have to say about it. Bellafante's title makes her point that *24* depicts family relationships as unsustainable. And Lantry's title uses an eye-catching headline from one ad with a clear statement of his essay's content: " 'Stay Sweet As You Are': An Analysis of Change and Continuity in Advertising Aimed at Women."

Considering Matters of Design

425–27

526–27

- If you cite written text as evidence, be sure to set long quotations and **DOCUMENTATION** according to the style you're using.
- If your essay is lengthy, consider whether **HEADINGS** would make your analysis easier for readers to follow.
- If you're analyzing a visual text, you may need to include a reproduction, along with a caption identifying it.

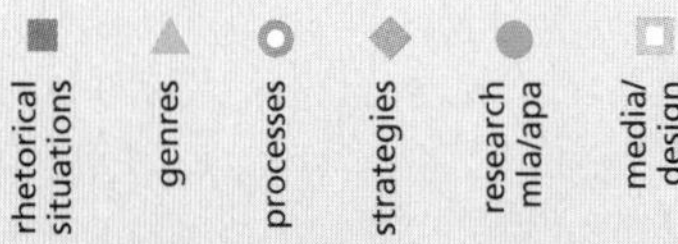

Getting Response and Revising

The following questions can help you and others study your draft with a critical eye. Make sure that anyone you ask to read and **RESPOND** to your text knows your purpose and audience. 235–36

- Is the **BEGINNING** effective? Does it make a reader want to continue? 261–66
- Does the introduction provide an overview of your analysis and conclusions? Is your **THESIS** clear? 273–75
- Is the text described or **SUMMARIZED** clearly and sufficiently? 416–17
- Is the analysis well organized and easy to follow? Do the parts fit together coherently? Does it read like an essay rather than a collection of separate bits of analysis?
- Does each part of the analysis relate to the thesis?
- Is anything confusing or in need of more explanation?
- Are all **QUOTATIONS** accurate and correctly **DOCUMENTED**? 410–13 425–27
- Is it clear how the analysis leads to the interpretation? Is there adequate **EVIDENCE** to support the interpretation? 287–93
- Does the **ENDING** make clear what your findings mean? 266–70

Then it's time to **REVISE**. Make sure your text appeals to your audience and achieves your purpose as successfully as possible. 236–39

Editing and Proofreading

Readers equate correctness with competence. Once you've revised your draft, edit carefully:

- Is your **THESIS** clearly stated? 273–75
- Check all **QUOTATIONS**, **PARAPHRASES**, and **SUMMARIES** for accuracy and form. Be sure that each has the required **DOCUMENTATION**. 408–19 425–27

- Make sure that your analysis flows clearly from one point to the next and that you use **TRANSITIONS** 277 to help readers move through your text.
- 245–46 **PROOFREAD** your finished analysis carefully before turning it in.

Taking Stock of Your Work

Take stock of what you've written and learned by writing out answers to these questions:

- How did you go about analyzing the text? What methods did you use—and which ones were most helpful?
- How did you go about drafting your essay?
- How well did you organize your written analysis? What, if anything, could you do to make it easier to read?
- Did you provide sufficient evidence to support your analysis?
- What did you do especially well?
- What could still be improved?
- Did you use any visuals, and if so, what did they add? Could you have shown the same thing with words?
- How did other readers' responses influence your writing?
- What would you do differently next time?
- Are you pleased with your analysis? What did it teach you about the text you analyzed? Did it make you want to study more works by the same writer or artist?

> **IF YOU NEED MORE HELP**
>
> **See also Chapter 14 on LITERARY ANALYSES 143–52 if you are analyzing a work of poetry, fiction, or drama. See Chapter 28 if you are required to submit your analysis as part of a writing PORTFOLIO. 247–58**

Reporting Information 8

Many kinds of writing report information. Newspapers report on local and world events; textbooks give information about biology, history, writing; websites provide information about products (jcrew.com), people (johnnydepp.com), institutions (smithsonian.org). We write out a lot of information ourselves, from a note we post on our door saying we've gone to choir practice to an essay we're assigned to write for a history class, reporting what we've learned about the state of U.S. diplomacy in the days before the bombing of Pearl Harbor. This chapter focuses on reports that are written to inform readers about a particular topic. Very often this kind of writing calls for some kind of research: you need to know your subject in order to report on it! When you write to report information, you are the expert. Before offering guidelines for writing essays that inform, we'll begin with three good examples.

SUSAN STELLIN

The Inevitability of Bumps

In this article, which appeared in the New York Times *in 2007, reporter and travel writer Susan Stellin explains the causes of turbulence and its effects on airplanes and passengers.*

People who fly a lot tend to be nonchalant about the experience—until the plane hits a patch of choppy air. Then, as cups start skidding across tray tables and luggage jostles overhead, even some frequent fliers admit to gripping the armrest with fear.

"Logically and rationally, I know that planes are designed to withstand pretty severe amounts of turbulence before anything bad would happen," said Lawrence Mosselson, who works for a commercial real estate company in Toronto and flies about 50 times a year. "And yet I find that at the first sign of any turbulence, I'm almost paralyzed in my seat."

Industry experts say turbulence rarely causes substantial damage to an aircraft, especially as systems to detect and respond to it have improved. Most of the injuries caused by turbulence, they say, could have been prevented by a decidedly low-tech measure: a seat belt.

"The airplane is designed to take a lot more aggressive maneuvering than we are," said Nora Marshall, chief of aviation survival factors at the National Transportation Safety Board. "We see people getting injured in turbulent events because they're not restrained."

Because of the way the safety board defines an accident—an 5
event involving substantial damage to the aircraft, a death, or a serious injury—the agency has officially investigated 94 accidents in the past decade involving turbulence as a cause or factor. Almost all were classified as accidents because 119 people (mostly flight attendants) suffered serious injuries, ranging from broken bones to a ruptured spleen. Only one of the accidents involved substantial damage to the aircraft.

The safety board attributed one death to turbulence over that time. In 1997, a Japanese passenger on a United Airlines flight from Tokyo to Honolulu was jolted out of her seat when the plane encountered turbulence; she suffered fatal injuries when she hit the armrest on the way back down. According to Ms. Marshall, who participated in the investigation, the woman was not wearing her seat belt, perhaps because the announcement advising passengers to keep seat belts fastened while the seat belt sign was off was not translated into Japanese.

That announcement is required by the Federal Aviation Administration. But Ms. Marshall said most passenger injuries still involve people seated without being buckled in. Including minor injuries, like a cut or a twisted ankle, safety board data indicates that about 50 people a year suffer turbulence-related injuries. But that is only the number of accidents the agency investigates, so the true figure is higher.

Now for the reassuring part: the plane should be able to handle the turbulence.

"People really shouldn't be too concerned about the airplane having difficulty in turbulence — it's designed for turbulence," said Jeff Bland, senior manager for commercial airplane loads and dynamics at Boeing, adding that structural failures because of turbulence are rare.

Although there have been airplane crashes where turbulence was 10 a factor, accidents typically involve multiple factors so it is often impossible to say that turbulence caused a crash. Industry and safety officials agree that such accidents have become unlikely as more has been learned about turbulence.

According to Mr. Bland, aircraft manufacturers have been collecting data since the 1970s to determine the maximum stress that planes experience in turbulence, and they then design aircraft to withstand one and a half times that. In fact, a video clip available on YouTube shows Boeing's test of the wing of a 777; using cables, the wing is bent upward about 24 feet at the tip before it breaks.

Systems to detect and respond to turbulence have also improved, including the technology that automatically adjusts to lateral gusts of wind. And Boeing's 787 aircraft will have a new vertical gust suppression system to minimize the stomach-churning sensation of the plane suddenly dropping midair.

Pilots say those drops are typically no more than 50 feet — not the hundreds of feet many passengers perceive. They also emphasize that avoiding turbulence is mostly a matter of comfort, not safety.

"The mistake that everybody makes is thinking of turbulence as something that's necessarily abnormal or dangerous," said Patrick Smith, a commercial pilot who also writes a column called "Ask the Pilot" for Salon.com. "For lack of a better term, turbulence is normal."

A variety of factors can cause turbulence, which is essentially a dis- 15
turbance in the movement of air. Thunderstorms, the jet stream, and mountains are some of the more common natural culprits, while what is known as wake turbulence is created by another plane. "Clear air turbulence" is the kind that comes up unexpectedly; it is difficult to detect because there is no moisture or particles to reveal the movement of air.

Pilots rely on radar, weather data, and reports from other aircraft to spot turbulence along their route, then can avoid it or at least minimize its effect by slowing down, changing altitude, or shifting course. But even with advances in technology, it is not always possible to predict rough air.

"We still don't have a really good means in the cockpit of seeing turbulence up ahead," said Terry McVenes, a pilot who serves as executive air safety chairman for the Air Line Pilots Association. "Sometimes we can prepare ourselves; other times it does sneak up on us."

Yet that has not deterred some fearful fliers from trying to gauge whether they are going to have a bumpy ride. Peter Murray, a computer network administrator from Lansing, Michigan, created TurbulenceForecast.com to offer nervous fliers like himself a way to view potential turbulence along their flight path.

At the time, he was frequently flying to Baltimore to visit his girlfriend and would sometimes change his flight if it looked as if he would encounter choppy air. "I have never been in anything that could even be considered light turbulence because I could avoid it so well," he said.

But for those unable to avoid a shaky situation, technology also 20
offers more ways to cope. That is why Tim Johnson, a frequent flier who works for a satellite phone company in Washington, posted a question on the forums at Flyertalk.com asking other travelers about their favorite turbulence tunes. (His choice was the "Theme From *Rawhide*" on *The Blues Brothers* soundtrack. Other suggestions included "I Will Survive" by Gloria Gaynor and "Free Fallin' " by Tom Petty.)

"I was on an A340 and it was flying all over the place," Mr. Johnson said, recalling a particularly bumpy flight. "But something about that song had me laughing out loud."

At least these days, he added, "You've got a lot more tools to distract you."

That is, as long as your iPod does not fly out of your hand.

This report focuses on turbulence during airline flights and how it affects passengers. Stellin interviews various authorities—frequent fliers, a researcher at the National Transportation Safety Board, an engineer at Boeing, pilots—and defines several key terms to provide an in-depth account of her subject. Notice how she balances statistical information with anecdotes about passengers' reactions to turbulence.

JAMES FALLOWS

Throwing Like a Girl

In the following report, Atlantic Monthly *correspondent James Fallows explores the art of throwing a baseball and the misconceptions that lead to the phrase "throwing like a girl."*

Most people remember the 1994 baseball season for the way it ended—with a strike rather than a World Series. I keep thinking about the way it began. On opening day, April 4, Bill Clinton went to Cleveland and, like many Presidents before him, threw out a ceremonial first pitch. That same day Hillary Rodham Clinton went to Chicago and, like no First Lady before her, also threw out a first ball, at a Cubs game in Wrigley Field.

The next day photos of the Clintons in action appeared in newspapers around the country. Many papers, including the *New York Times* and the *Washington Post*, chose the same two photos to run. The one of Bill Clinton showed him wearing an Indians cap and warm-up jacket. The President, throwing lefty, had turned his shoulders sideways to the plate in preparation for delivery. He was bringing the ball forward from behind his head in a clean-looking throwing action as the photo was snapped. Hillary Clinton was pictured wearing a dark jacket, a scarf, and an oversized Cubs hat. In preparation for her throw she was standing directly facing the plate. A right-hander, she had the elbow of her throwing arm pointed out in front of her. Her forearm was tilted back, toward her shoulder. The ball rested on her upturned palm. As the picture was taken, she was in the middle of an action that can only be described as throwing like a girl.

The phrase "throwing like a girl" has become an embattled and offensive one. Feminists smart at its implication that to do something "like a girl" is to do it the wrong way. Recently, on the heels of the O. J. Simpson case, a book appeared in which the phrase was used to help explain why male athletes, especially football players, were involved in so many assaults against women. Having been trained (like most American boys) to dread the accusation of doing anything "like a girl," athletes were said to grow into the assumption that women were valueless, and natural prey.

I grant the justice of such complaints. I am attuned to the hurt caused by similar broad-brush stereotypes when they apply to groups I belong to—"dancing like a white man," for instance, or "speaking foreign languages like an American," or "thinking like a Washingtonian."

5 Still, whatever we want to call it, the difference between the two Clintons in what they were doing that day is real, and it is instantly recognizable. And since seeing those photos I have been wondering, Why, exactly, do so many women throw "like a girl"? If the motion were easy to change, presumably a woman as motivated and self-possessed as Hillary Clinton would have changed it. (According to her press secretary, Lisa Caputo, Mrs. Clinton spent the weekend before opening day tossing a ball in the Rose Garden with her husband, for practice.) Presumably, too, the answer to the question cannot be anything quite as simple as, Because they *are* girls.

A surprising number of people think that there is a structural difference between male and female arms or shoulders—in the famous "rotator cuff," perhaps—that dictates different throwing motions. "It's in the shoulder joint," a well-educated woman told me recently. "They're hinged differently." Someday researchers may find evidence to support a biological theory of throwing actions. For now, what you'll hear if you ask an orthopedist, an anatomist, or (especially) the coach of a women's softball team is that there is no structural reason why men and women should throw in different ways. This point will be obvious to any male who grew up around girls who liked to play baseball and became good at it. It should be obvious on a larger scale this summer, in broadcasts of the Olympic Games. This year [1996], for the first time, women's fast-pitch softball teams will compete in the Olympics. Although the pitchers in these games will deliver the ball underhand, viewers will see female shortstops, center fielders, catchers, and so on pegging the ball to one another at speeds few male viewers could match.

Even women's tennis is a constant if indirect reminder that men's and women's shoulders are "hinged" the same way. The serving motion in tennis is like a throw—but more difficult, because it must be coordinated with the toss of the tennis ball. The men in professional tennis serve harder than the women, because they are bigger and stronger. But women pros serve harder than most male amateurs have ever done, and the service motion for good players is the same for men and women

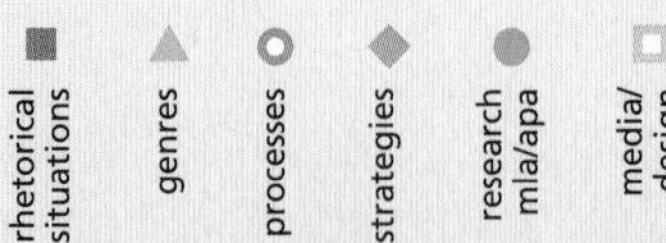

alike. There is no expectation in college or pro tennis that because of their anatomy female players must "serve like a girl." "I know many women who can throw a lot harder and better than the normal male," says Linda Wells, the coach of the highly successful women's softball team at Arizona State University. "It's not gender that makes the difference in how they throw."

At a superficial level it's easy to tick off the traits of an awkward-looking throw. The fundamental mistake is the one Mrs. Clinton appeared to be making in the photo: trying to throw a ball with your body facing the target, rather than rotating your shoulders and hips ninety degrees away from the target and then swinging them around in order to accelerate the ball. A throw looks bad if your elbow is lower than your shoulder as your arm comes forward (unless you're throwing sidearm). A throw looks really bad if, as the ball leaves your hand, your wrist is "inside your elbow"—that is, your elbow joint is bent in such a way that your forearm angles back toward your body and your wrist is closer to your head than your elbow is. Slow-motion film of big-league pitchers shows that when they release the ball, the throwing arm is fully extended and straight from shoulder to wrist. The combination of these three elements—head-on stance, dropped elbow, and wrist inside the elbow—mechanically dictates a pushing rather than a hurling motion, creating the familiar pattern of "throwing like a girl."

It is surprisingly hard to find in the literature of baseball a deeper explanation of the mechanics of good and bad throws. Tom Seaver's pitching for the Mets and the White Sox got him into the Hall of Fame, but his book *The Art of Pitching* is full of bromides that hardly clarify the process of throwing, even if they might mean something to accomplished pitchers. His chapter "The Absolutes of Pitching Mechanics," for instance, lays out these four unhelpful principles: "Keep the Front Leg Flexible!" "Rub Up the Baseball!" "Hide the Baseball!" "Get It Out, Get It Up!" (The fourth refers to the need to get the ball out of the glove and into the throwing hand in a quick motion.)

A variety of other instructional documents, from *Little League's* 10
Official How-to-Play Baseball Book to *Softball for Girls & Women*, mainly reveal the difficulty of finding words to describe a simple motor activity that everyone can recognize. The challenge, I suppose, is like that of writing a manual on how to ride a bike, or how to kiss. Indeed,

the most useful description I've found of the mechanics of throwing comes from a man whose specialty is another sport: Vic Braden made his name as a tennis coach, but he has attempted to analyze the physics of a wide variety of sports so that they all will be easier to teach.

Braden says that an effective throw involves connecting a series of links in a "kinetic chain." The kinetic chain, which is Braden's tool for analyzing most sporting activity, operates on a principle like that of crack-the-whip. Momentum builds up in one part of the body. When that part is suddenly stopped, as the end of the "whip" is stopped in crack-the-whip, the momentum is transferred to and concentrated in the next link in the chain. A good throw uses six links of chain, Braden says. The first two links involve the lower body, from feet to waist. The first motion of a throw (after the body has been rotated away from the target) is to rotate the legs and hips back in the direction of the throw, building up momentum as large muscles move body mass. Then those links stop—a pitcher stops turning his hips once they face the plate—and the momentum is transferred to the next link. This is the torso, from waist to shoulders, and since its mass is less than that of the legs, momentum makes it rotate faster than the hips and legs did. The torso stops when it is facing the plate, and the momentum is transferred to the next link—the upper arm. As the upper arm comes past the head, it stops moving forward, and the momentum goes into the final links—the forearm and wrist, which snap forward at tremendous speed.

This may sound arcane and jerkily mechanical, but it makes perfect sense when one sees Braden's slow-mo movies of pitchers in action. And it explains why people do, or don't, learn how to throw. The implication of Braden's analysis is that throwing is a perfectly natural action (millions and millions of people can do it), but not at all innate. A successful throw involves an intricate series of actions coordinated among muscle groups, as each link of the chain is timed to interact with the next. Like bike riding or skating, it can be learned by anyone—male or female. No one starts out knowing how to ride a bike or throw a ball. Everyone has to learn.

Fallows describes in detail what distinguishes a successful baseball throw from an awkward-looking one, concluding with the point that throwing a baseball effectively is a learned activity. He draws on various sources—including a

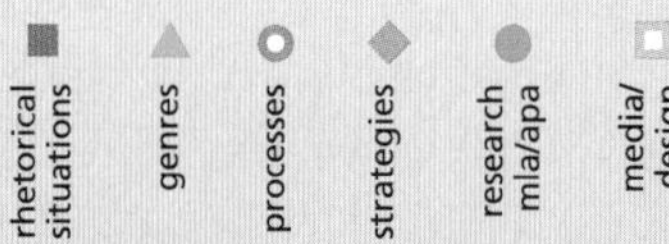

women's softball coach, a tennis coach, and his own observations — to support his claim. Notice how he establishes the context for his essay by focusing on the differences between the stances of the Clintons when photographed throwing a baseball.

JEFFREY DEROVEN

The Greatest Generation: The Great Depression and the American South

The following essay was written in 2001 by a student for a history course at the Trumbull Campus of Kent State University. It was first published in Etude and Techne, *a journal of Ohio college writing.*

Tom Brokaw called the folks of the mid-twentieth century the greatest generation. So why is the generation of my grandparents seen as this country's greatest? Perhaps the reason is not what they accomplished but what they endured. Many of the survivors feel people today "don't have the moral character to withstand a depression like that."[1] This paper will explore the Great Depression through the eyes of ordinary Americans in the most impoverished region in the country, the American South, in order to detail how they endured and how the government assisted them in this difficult era.

President Franklin D. Roosevelt (FDR) announced in 1938 that the American South "represented the nation's number one economic problem." He commissioned the National Emergency Council to investigate and report on the challenges facing the region. Though rich in physical and human resources, the southern states lagged behind other parts of the nation in economic development.[2]

Poor education in the South was blamed for much of the problem. Young children attending school became too costly for most families. In the Bland family, "when Lucy got to the sixth grade, we had to stop her because there was too much to do."[3] Overcrowding of schools, particularly in rural areas, lowered the educational standards. The short school terms further reduced effectiveness. As Mrs. Abercrombie recalls, "Me and Jon both went to school for a few months but that wa'n't enough for us to learn anything."[4] Without the proper education, the youth of the South entered the work force unprepared for the challenges before them.

Southern industries did not have the investment capital to turn their resources into commodities. Manufacturers were limited to producing goods in the textile and cigarette industries and relied heavily on the cash crops of cotton and tobacco for the economy. Few facilities existed in the South for research that might lead to the development of new industries. Hampered by low wages, low tax revenue, and a high interest rate, Southerners lacked the economic resources to compete with the vast industrial strength of the North. The National Emergency Council report concluded, "Penalized for being rural, and handicapped in its efforts to industrialize, the economic life of the South has been squeezed to a point where the purchasing power of the southern people does not provide an adequate market for its own industries nor an attractive market for those of the rest of the country."[5] The South had an untapped market for production and consumption. However, without adequate capital, it did not have the means to profit from them.

Southern industries paid their employees low wages, which led 5
to a low cost of living. "You could live very cheaply because . . . you couldn't make a great deal of money," remembers Rita Beline."[6] Most families did not have much left for themselves after bills and living expenses. "Nobody had much money, you know," recalls June Atchetce. "Everybody kind of lived at home, had gardens and raised their own produce, raised their own meat and had chickens and eggs and such as that." The needs of the families "were very small as far as purchases were concerned." What they could not grow, they did not have a need for, except for basic staples such as coffee, flour, sugar, and honey. To save on the cost of clothes, families "had a lot of hand-me-downs from the oldest to the baby. We did not throw them away. We patched them up and sent them down the line."[7] Luxury items, like radios, cost too much money, and "only the [aristocrats] had radios because the poor did not stay at home long enough to enjoy them."[8] The fact was that Southerners wanted modern consumer items but did not have the purchasing power to pay for them. "The people of the South need to buy, they want to buy, and they would buy—if they had the money."[9] Without paying laborers a fair wage, industry had

Franklin Delano Roosevelt (1882–1945)
Photo from Bettmann / Corbis

forced upon itself a lower living standard, thus perpetuating losses in local revenue resulting in a decline in purchasing power.[10]

The Federal government had to step in and help, as the National Emergency Council's report noted:

> Some of the South's credit difficulties have been slightly relieved in recent years . . . by the Public Works Administration, . . . the Works Progress Administration, [and] the Soil Conservation Service, [which] have brought desperately needed funds into the South.[11]

Along with other New Deal projects like the Tennessee Valley Authority (TVA) and the Civilian Conservation Corps [CCC], President Roosevelt was able to prime the pump into a seemingly dead Southern economy.

Other ways the federal government primed the pump was with the WPA [Works Progress Administration]. This New Deal measure gave jobs to those who wanted to work. Local governments benefited too. The WPA provided new roads, buildings, hospitals, and schools. Rita Beline remembers her "father came very short of money, . . . took a job with the WPA, in which he helped in building a road across a lagoon."[12] President Roosevelt knew "cheap wages mean low buying power."[13] The WPA ensured a fair wage for good work. Warren Addis remembers that "workers were tickled to death with it because it gave so many people jobs. It started out at eight cents an hour for common labor, and it finally went to thirty cents an hour."[14]

FDR also created the CCC. The concept of putting the American youth to work yielded an economic stimulus by having them send home twenty-five dollars a month. That money worked itself back into local economies as families spent the money on needed goods. Young men across the South "left home to go and do this work. They got paid a little bit of money, which they sent home to their families."[15] The CCC created recreation habitats as well. Jefferson Brock recalls, "They came and built brush poles for the fish to live in the lake near my cottage."[16] The CCC became an outlet for young men who could not find work in their hometowns. Jesse Brooks remembers:

> They did a great lot of good. For instance, they built Vogel State Park and raised the wall up on the national cemetery. Just put people to work. Gave them their pride back. A man's not going to feel very good about himself if he can't feed his family. So, that was the New Deal itself—to put people back to work and get the economy growing again.[17]

The South did not enjoy the United States' economic successes in 10
the early part of the twentieth century and in many ways was a third world country within our own nation. The federal action that fueled the Southern economy during the Great Depression changed the way of life for the better and helped Southerners endure a time of great despair. Programs like the TVA, WPA, and CCC planted the seeds for a prosperous future. I still do not know if they were the greatest generation, but they did overcome tremendous obstacles to bring forth other "greatest generations."

Notes

1. Allen Furline in Kenneth J. Bindas, "Oral History Project," Kent State University, Trumbull Campus, Trumbull, OH. Dr. Bindas has a collection of 476 oral-history interviews from western Georgia and eastern Alabama, from which the information for this paper is derived. (Hereafter cited in Notes as BOHP.)

2. David L. Carlton and Peter A. Coclanis, eds., *Confronting Southern Poverty in the Great Depression: The Report on Economic Conditions of the South with Related Documents* (New York: Bedford/St. Martin's Press, 1996), 92.

3. Vera Bland in BOHP.

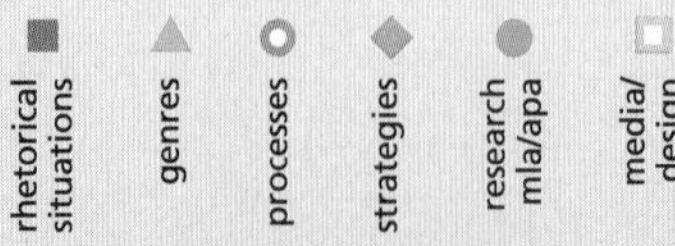

4. M. Abercrombie in BOHP.
5. Carlton and Coclanis, *Confronting Southern Poverty*, 76–78.
6. Rita Beline in BOHP.
7. June Romero Atchetce in BOHP.
8. Ruby Girley in BOHP.
9. Carlton and Coclanis, *Confronting Southern Poverty*, 78.
10. Ibid., 64–65.
11. Ibid., 73.
12. Rita Beline in BOHP.
13. David M. Kennedy, *Freedom from Fear: The American People in Depression and War, 1929–1945* (New York: Oxford University Press, 1999), 346.
14. Warren Addis in BOHP.
15. Jane Berry in BOHP.
16. Jefferson Brock in BOHP.
17. Jesse Brooks in BOHP.

DeRoven's essay reports information about how the American South got through the Great Depression. His information is based on both library research and recorded interviews with people who lived through the period he describes. He documents his sources according to The Chicago Manual of Style, *the preferred style in history classes.*

For five more reports, see CHAPTER 56.

Key Features / Reports

A tightly focused topic. The goal of this kind of writing is to inform readers about something without digressing—and without, in general, bringing in the writer's own opinions. All three examples focus on a particular topic—air turbulence, throwing a baseball, and the Great Depression in the American South—and present information about the topics evenhandedly.

Accurate, well-researched information. Reports usually require some research. The kind of research depends on the topic. Library research to locate scholarly sources may be necessary for some topics—DeRoven, for example, uses an archive available only at his university's library. Other topics may require field research—interviews, observations, and so on. Fallows interviewed two coaches in addition to reading several books on pitching baseballs.

Various writing strategies. Presenting information usually requires various organizing patterns—defining, comparing, classifying, explaining processes, analyzing causes and effects, and so on. Stellin explains the causes of turbulence and its effects; Fallows explains the process governing throwing a baseball and classifies different ways of throwing. DeRoven analyzes some of the causes of the Great Depression in the South.

Clear definitions. Reports need to provide clear definitions of any key terms that their audience may not know. Stellin defines three types of air turbulence as well as what constitutes an accident.

Appropriate design. Reports often combine paragraphs with information presented in lists, tables, diagrams, and other illustrations. When

Wake turbulence was captured in this photo of a British Airways flight descending through thin clouds near London last July.

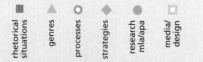

you're presenting information, you need to think carefully about how to design it — numerical data, for instance, can be easier to understand and remember in a table than in a paragraph. Often a photograph can bring a subject to life, as does the photo on page 72, which accompanied "The Inevitability of Bumps." The caption provides important information that is explained more fully in the essay itself.

A GUIDE TO WRITING REPORTS

Choosing a Topic

If you are working with an assigned topic, see if you can approach it from an angle that interests you. If you get to choose your topic, the following guidelines should help:

If you get to choose. What interests you? What do you wish you knew more about? The possible topics for informational reports are limitless, but the topics that you're most likely to write well on are those that engage you. They may be academic in nature or reflect your personal interests or both. If you're not sure where to begin, here are some places to start:

- an intriguing technology: hybrid cars, cell phones, roller coasters
- sports: soccer, snowboarding, ultimate Frisbee, basketball
- an important world event: 9/11, the fall of Rome, the Black Death
- a historical period: the African diaspora, the Middle Ages, the Ming dynasty, the Great Depression
- a common object: hooded sweatshirts, gel pens, mascara, Post-it notes
- a significant environmental issue: Arctic oil drilling, the Clean Air Act, mercury and the fish supply
- the arts: hip-hop, outsider art, the J. Paul Getty Museum, Savion Glover, Mary Cassatt

220–21 **LIST** a few possibilities, and then choose one that you'd like to know more about—and that your audience might find interesting, too. You might start out by phrasing your topic as a question that your research will attempt to answer. For example:

> How is Google different from Yahoo!?
>
> How was the Great Pyramid constructed?
>
> Why did the World Trade Center towers collapse on themselves rather than fall sideways?
>
> What kind of training do football referees receive?

If your topic is assigned. Some assignments are specific: "Explain the physics of roller coasters." If, however, your assignment is broad—"Explain some aspect of the U.S. government"—try focusing on a more limited topic within the larger topic: federalism, majority rule, political parties, states' rights. Even if an assignment seems to offer little flexibility, your task is to decide how to research the topic—and sometimes even narrow topics can be shaped to fit your own interests and those of your audience.

Considering the Rhetorical Situation

3–4 **PURPOSE** Why are you presenting this information? To teach readers about the subject? To demonstrate your research and writing skills? For some other reason?

5–8 **AUDIENCE** Who will read this report? What do they already know about the topic? What background information do they need in order to understand it? Will you need to define any terms? What do they want or need to know about it? Why should they care? How can you attract their interest?

12–14 **STANCE** What is your own attitude toward your subject? What interests you most about it? What about it seems important?

MEDIA / DESIGN What medium are you using? What is the best way to present the information? Will it all be in paragraph form, or is there information that is best presented as a chart or a table? Do you need headings? Would diagrams, photographs, or other illustrations help you explain the information? 15–17

Generating Ideas and Text

Good reports share certain features that make them useful and interesting to readers. Remember that your goal is to present information clearly and accurately. Start by exploring your topic.

Explore what you already know about your topic. Write out whatever you know or want to know about your topic, perhaps by **FREEWRITING, LISTING**, or **CLUSTERING.** Why are you interested in this topic? What questions do you have about it? Such questions can help you decide what you'd like to focus on and how you need to direct your research efforts. 219–22

Narrow your topic. To write a good report, you need to narrow your focus—and to narrow your focus, you need to know a fair amount about your subject. If you are assigned to write on a subject like biodiversity, for example, you need to know what it is, what the key issues are, and so on. If you do, you can simply list or brainstorm possibilities, choose one, and start your research. If you don't know much about the subject, though, you need to do some research to discover focused, workable topics. This research may shape your thinking and change your focus. Start with **SOURCES** that can give you a general sense of the subject, such as an encyclopedia entry, a magazine article, an Internet site, perhaps an interview with an expert. Your goal at this point is simply to find out what issues your topic might include and then to focus your efforts on an aspect of the topic you will be able to cover. 384–99

Come up with a tentative thesis. Once you narrow your topic, write out a statement that explains what you plan to report or explain. A good **THESIS** is potentially interesting (to you and your readers) and limits your 273–75 topic enough to make it manageable. Stellin presents her thesis, that plane accidents caused by turbulence "have become more unlikely as more has been learned about turbulence," after establishing a context for passengers' concern about it. DeRoven lays out exactly what will be discussed, using a format acceptable in some disciplines but frowned on in others: "This paper will explore the Great Depression through the eyes of ordinary Americans in the most impoverished region in the country, the American South, in order to detail how they endured and how the government assisted them in this difficult era." At this point, however, you need only a tentative thesis that will help focus any research you do.

Do any necessary research, and revise your thesis. To focus your
223–24 research efforts, **OUTLINE** the aspects of your topic that you expect to dis-
375–83 cuss. Identify any aspects that require additional research and **DEVELOP A RESEARCH PLAN.** Expect to revise your outline as you do your research, since more information will be available for some aspects of your topic than others, some may prove irrelevant to your topic, and some may turn out to be more than you need. You'll need to revisit your tentative thesis once you've done any research, to finalize your statement.

Ways of Organizing a Report

Reports can be organized in various ways. Here are three common ones:

[Reports on topics that are unfamiliar to readers]

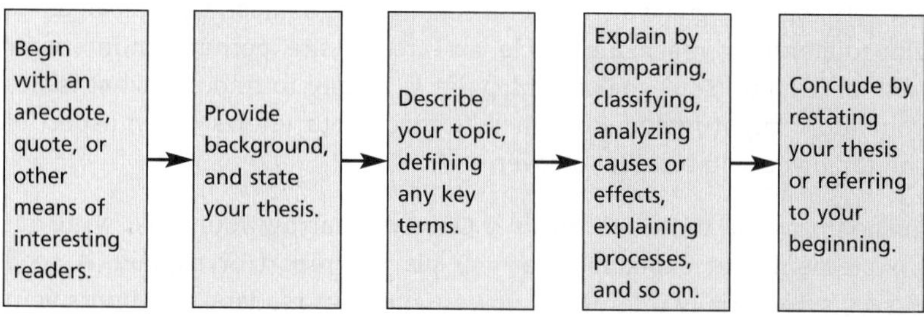
Begin with an anecdote, quote, or other means of interesting readers.
Provide background, and state your thesis.
Describe your topic, defining any key terms.
Explain by comparing, classifying, analyzing causes or effects, explaining processes, and so on.
Conclude by restating your thesis or referring to your beginning.

[Reports on an event]

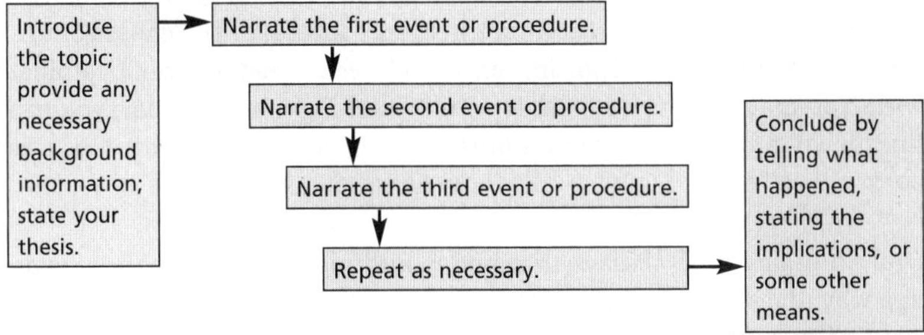

[Reports that compare and contrast]

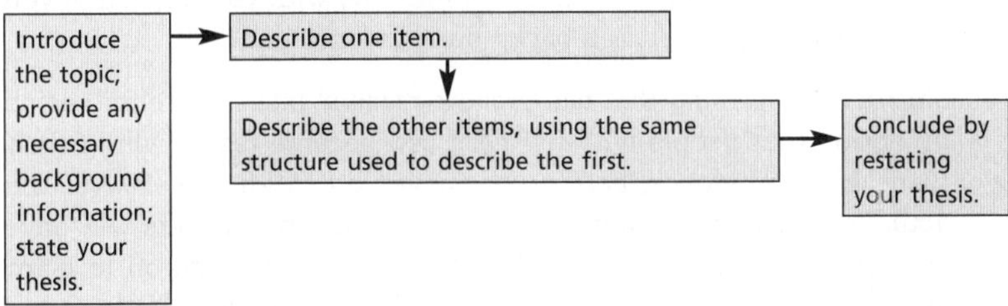

Many reports use a combination of organizational structures; don't be afraid to use whatever method of organization best suits your material and your purpose.

Writing Out a Draft

Once you have generated ideas and thought about how you want to organize your report, it's time to start **DRAFTING.** Do this quickly—try to write a complete draft in one sitting, concentrating on getting the report on paper or screen and on putting in as much detail as you can.

226–28

338–42
278–82
306–13

Writing that reports information often calls for certain writing strategies. The report on throwing a baseball, for example, **EXPLAINS THE PROCESS** of throwing, whereas the report on turbulence **ANALYZES THE CAUSES** of turbulence. When you're reporting on a topic your readers aren't familiar with, you may wish to **COMPARE** it with something more familiar; you can find useful advice on these and other writing strategies in Part 4 of this book.

261–66

Draft a beginning. Essays that report information often need to begin in a way that will get your audience interested in the topic. Here are a few ways of **BEGINNING**:

- ***Simply state your thesis.*** DeRoven begins his essay about "the greatest generation" this way. Opening with a thesis works well when you can assume your readers have enough familiarity with your topic that you don't need to give detailed background information.
- ***Start with something that will provoke readers' interest.*** Stellin begins by noting that people who fly often can become fearful when their plane hits turbulence, before she moves on to an overview of the actual safety risks involved. She knows that most readers will have experienced air turbulence and will likely want to read on to learn about how pilots and aircraft manufacturers—and other passengers—deal with it.
- ***Begin with an illustrative example.*** Fallows uses the contrasting photographs of the Clintons throwing baseballs as a way of defining "throwing like a girl."

266–70

Draft an ending. Think about what you want your readers to read last. An effective **ENDING** leaves them thinking about your topic.

- ***Summarize your main points.*** This is a good way to end when you've presented several key points you want readers to remember. DeRoven ends this way, summarizing the South's poverty and the government's successful actions to alleviate it.

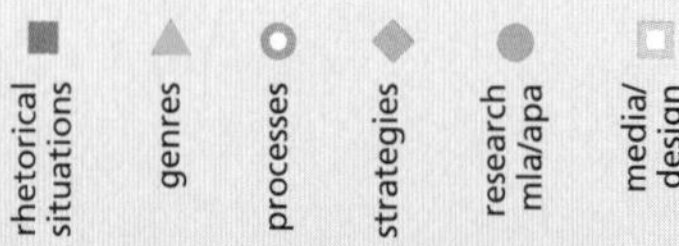

- ***Point out the implications of your report.*** Although Stellin's report on turbulence is reassuring, she ends by acknowledging that many air travelers still find rough air unsettling and describes some of their ways of coping.
- ***Frame your report by referring to its introduction.*** DeRoven begins and ends his report by mentioning "the greatest generation."
- ***Tell what happened.*** If you are reporting on an event, you could conclude by telling how it turns out.

Come up with a title. You'll want a title that tells readers something about your subject—and makes them want to know more. Stellin, for instance, gets our interest in her report on turbulence with the title "The Inevitability of Bumps," which generates interest first by its ambiguity (Is this about skin? Roads?) and then by its relevance to anyone who flies. See the chapter on **GUIDING YOUR READER** for tips on coming up with titles that are informative and enticing enough to make readers wish to read on. 272–77

Considering Matters of Design

You'll probably write your report in paragraph form, but think about the information you're presenting and how you can design and format it to make it as easy as possible for your readers to understand. You might ask yourself these questions:

- What is an appropriate **TYPEFACE**? Something serious like Times Roman, something traditional like `Courier`, something else? 524–25
- Would it help your readers if you divided your report into shorter sections and added **HEADINGS**? 526–27
- Is there any information that would be easier to follow in a **LIST**? 525–26
- Could any of your information be summarized in a **TABLE**? 528–32

- Do you have any data that readers would more easily understand in 528–30 the form of a bar **GRAPH**, line graph, or pie chart?
- 528–32 Would **ILLUSTRATIONS**—diagrams, photos, drawings, and so on—help you explain anything in your report?

Getting Response and Revising

The following questions can help you study your draft with a critical eye. 235–36 **GETTING RESPONSE** from others is always good, and these questions can guide their reading, too. Make sure they know your purpose and audience.

- 272–73 Do the **TITLE** and opening sentences get readers' interest? If not, how might they do so?
- 3–4 What information does this text provide, and for what **PURPOSE**?
- Does the introduction explain why this information is being presented? Does it place the topic in a larger context?
- Are all key terms defined?
- Do you have any questions? Is more information or explanation needed? Where might an example help you understand something?
- 528–32 Is any information presented **VISUALLY**, with a chart, graph, table, drawing, or photograph? If so, is it clear how these illustrations relate to the larger text? Is there any text that would be more easily understood if it were presented visually?
- Does the organization help make sense of the information? Does the 259 text include description, comparison, or any other writing **STRATEGIES**? Does the topic or rhetorical situation call for any particular strategies?
- 408–19 425–27 If the report cites any sources, are they **QUOTED, PARAPHRASED,** or **SUMMARIZED** effectively (and with appropriate **DOCUMENTATION**)?
- 266–70 Does the report **END** in a satisfying way? What are readers left thinking?

These questions should identify aspects on your report you need to work on. When it's time to **REVISE**, make sure your report appeals to your audience and achieves your purpose as successfully as possible. 236–39

Editing and Proofreading

Readers equate correctness with the writer's competence. Once you've revised your draft, follow these guidelines for **EDITING** a report: 242–45

- Check your use of key terms. Repeating key words is acceptable in reports; synonyms for unfamiliar words may confuse readers while the repetition of key words or the use of clearly identified pronouns can be genuinely helpful.
- Check your use of **TRANSITIONS** to be sure you have them where you need them. 277
- If you have included **HEADINGS**, make sure they're parallel in structure and consistent in design. 526–27
- Make sure that any photos or other **ILLUSTRATIONS** have captions, that charts and graphs have headings—and that all are referred to in the main text. Have you used white space effectively to separate sections of your report and to highlight graphic elements? 528–32
- Check any **DOCUMENTATION** to see that it follows the appropriate style without mistakes. 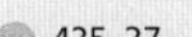 425–27
- **PROOFREAD** and spell-check your report carefully. 245–46

Taking Stock of Your Work

- How well did you convey the information? Is it complete enough for your audience's needs?
- What strategies did you rely on, and how did they help you achieve your purpose?

- How well did you organize the report?
- How did you go about researching the information for this piece?
- How did you go about drafting this piece?
- Did you use any tables, graphs, diagrams, photographs, illustrations, or other graphics effectively?
- How did others' responses influence your writing?
- What did you do especially well?
- What could still be improved?
- What would you do differently next time?

247–58
111–15
133–42
161–70

IF YOU NEED MORE HELP

See Chapter 28 if you are required to submit your report in a writing PORTFOLIO. See also Chapter 10 on ABSTRACTS if your report requires one; Chapter 13 on LAB REPORTS, a kind of report written in the sciences; and Chapter 16 on PROFILES, a report based on firsthand research.

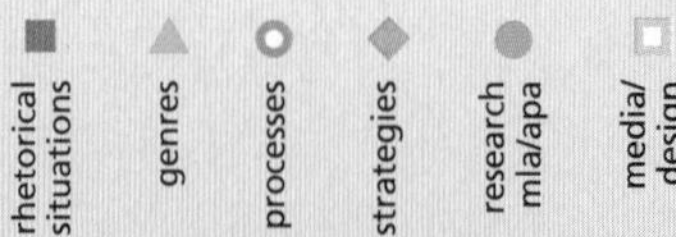

Arguing a Position 9

Everything we say or do presents some kind of argument, takes some kind of position. Often we take overt positions: "Everyone in the United States is entitled to affordable health care." "The university needs to offer more language courses." "Sean Combs shouldn't have gone into acting." Some scholars claim that everything makes some kind of argument, from yellow ribbons that honor U.S. troops to a yellow smiley face, which might be said to argue for a good day. In college course work, you are constantly called on to argue positions: in an English class, you may argue for a certain interpretation of a poem; in a business course, you may argue for the merits of a flat tax; in a linguistics class, you may argue that English should not be made the official language of the United States. All of those positions are arguable—people of goodwill can agree or disagree with them and present reasons and evidence to support their positions. This chapter provides detailed guidelines for writing an essay that argues a position. We'll begin with three good examples.

GARY TAUBES

What If It's All Been a Big Fat Lie?

In this text, science writer Gary Taubes argues that the root of the so-called obesity epidemic is our consumption of carbohydrates. It first appeared in the New York Times *in 2002.*

One of the reasonably reliable facts about the obesity epidemic is that it started around the early 1980s. According to Katherine Flegal, an epidemiologist at the National Center for Health Statistics, the percentage of obese Americans stayed relatively constant through the 1960s and 1970s at 13 percent to 14 percent and then shot up by 8 percentage points in the 1980s. By the end of that decade, nearly one in four Americans was obese. That steep rise, which is consistent through all segments of American society and which continued unabated through the 1990s, is the singular feature of the epidemic. Any theory that tries to explain obesity in America has to account for that. Meanwhile, overweight children nearly tripled in number. And for the first time, physicians began diagnosing Type 2 diabetes in adolescents. Type 2 diabetes often accompanies obesity. It used to be called adult-onset diabetes and now, for the obvious reason, is not.

So how did this happen? The orthodox and ubiquitous explanation is that we live in what Kelly Brownell, a Yale psychologist, has called a "toxic food environment" of cheap fatty food, large portions, pervasive food advertising and sedentary lives. By this theory, we are at the Pavlovian mercy of the food industry, which spends nearly $10 billion a year advertising unwholesome junk food and fast food. And because these foods, especially fast food, are so filled with fat, they are both irresistible and uniquely fattening. On top of this, so the theory goes, our modern society has successfully eliminated physical activity from our daily lives. We no longer exercise or walk up stairs, nor do our children bike to school or play outside, because they would prefer to play video games and watch television. And because some of us are obviously predisposed to gain weight while others are not, this explanation also has a genetic component—the thrifty gene. It suggests that storing extra calories as fat was an evolutionary advantage to our Paleolithic ancestors, who had to survive frequent famine. We then inherited these "thrifty" genes, despite their liability in today's toxic environment.

This theory makes perfect sense and plays to our puritanical prejudice that fat, fast food, and television are innately damaging to our humanity. But there are two catches. First, to buy this logic is to accept that the copious negative reinforcement that accompanies obesity—both socially and physically—is easily overcome by the constant bombardment of food advertising and the lure of a supersize bargain meal. And second, as Flegal points out, little data exist to support any of this. Certainly none of it explains what changed so significantly to start the epidemic. Fast-food consumption, for example, continued to grow steadily through the 70s and 80s, but it did not take a sudden leap, as obesity did.

As far as exercise and physical activity go, there are no reliable data before the mid-80s, according to William Dietz, who runs the division of nutrition and physical activity at the Centers for Disease Control; the 1990s data show obesity rates continuing to climb, while exercise activity remained unchanged. This suggests the two have little in common. Dietz also acknowledged that a culture of physical exercise began in the United States in the 70s—the "leisure exercise mania," as Robert Levy, director of the National Heart, Lung and Blood Institute, described it in 1981—and has continued through the present day.

As for the thrifty gene, it provides the kind of evolutionary ration- 5
ale for human behavior that scientists find comforting but that simply cannot be tested. In other words, if we were living through an anorexia epidemic, the experts would be discussing the equally untestable "spendthrift gene" theory, touting evolutionary advantages of losing weight effortlessly. An overweight homo erectus, they'd say, would have been easy prey for predators.

It is also undeniable, note students of Endocrinology 101 [the science behind the idea that carbohydrates cause obesity], that mankind never evolved to eat a diet high in starches or sugars. "Grain products and concentrated sugars were essentially absent from human nutrition until the invention of agriculture," Ludwig says, "which was only 10,000 years ago." This is discussed frequently in the anthropology texts but is mostly absent from the obesity literature, with the prominent exception of the low-carbohydrate-diet books.

What's forgotten in the current controversy is that the low-fat dogma itself is only about 25 years old. Until the late 70s, the accepted wisdom was that fat and protein protected against overeating by making you sated, and that carbohydrates made you fat. In *The Physiology of Taste*, for instance, an 1825 discourse considered among the most famous books ever written about food, the French gastronome Jean Anthelme Brillat-Savarin says that he could easily identify the causes of obesity after 30 years of listening to one "stout party" after another proclaiming the joys of bread, rice, and (from a "particularly stout party") potatoes. Brillat-Savarin describes the roots of obesity as a natural predisposition conjuncted with the "floury and feculent substances which man makes the prime ingredients of his daily nourishment." He added that the effects of this fecula—i.e., "potatoes, grain, or any kind of flour"—were seen sooner when sugar was added to the diet.

This is what my mother taught me 40 years ago, backed up by the vague observation that Italians tended toward corpulence because they ate so much pasta. This observation was actually documented by Ancel Keys, a University of Minnesota physician who noted that fats "have good staying power," by which he meant they are slow to be digested and so lead to satiation, and that Italians were among the heaviest populations he had studied. According to Keys, the Neopolitans, for instance, ate only a little lean meat once or twice a week, but ate bread and pasta every day for lunch and dinner. "There was no evidence of nutritional deficiency," he wrote, "but the working-class women were fat."

By the 70s, you could still find articles in the journals describing high rates of obesity in Africa and the Caribbean where diets contained almost exclusively carbohydrates. The common thinking, wrote a former director of the Nutrition Division of the United Nations, was that the ideal diet, one that prevented obesity, snacking, and excessive sugar consumption, was a diet "with plenty of eggs, beef, mutton, chicken, butter, and well-cooked vegetables." This was the identical prescription Brillat-Savarin put forth in 1825.

Few experts now deny that the low-fat message is radically over- 10
simplified. If nothing else, it effectively ignores the fact that unsaturated fats, like olive oil, are relatively good for you: they tend to elevate your good cholesterol, high-density lipoprotein (H.D.L.), and lower your bad cholesterol, low-density lipoprotein (L.D.L.), at least in comparison to the effect of carbohydrates. While higher L.D.L. raises your heart-disease risk, higher H.D.L. reduces it.

What this means is that even saturated fats—a k a, the bad fats—are not nearly as deleterious as you would think. True, they will elevate your bad cholesterol, but they will also elevate your good cholesterol. In other words, it's a virtual wash. As Walter Willett, chairman of the department of nutrition at the Harvard School of Public Health, explained to me, you will gain little to no health benefit by giving up milk, butter, and cheese and eating bagels instead.

But it gets even weirder than that. Foods considered more or less deadly under the low-fat dogma turn out to be comparatively benign if you actually look at their fat content. More than two-thirds of the fat in a porterhouse steak, for instance, will definitively improve your cholesterol profile (at least in comparison with the baked potato next to it); it's true that the remainder will raise your L.D.L., the bad stuff, but it will also boost your H.D.L. The same is true for lard. If you work out the numbers, you come to the surreal conclusion that you can eat lard straight from the can and conceivably reduce your risk of heart disease. . . .

After 20 years steeped in a low-fat paradigm, I find it hard to see the nutritional world any other way. I have learned that low-fat diets fail in clinical trials and in real life, and they certainly have failed in my life. I have read the papers suggesting that 20 years of low-fat recommendations have not managed to lower the incidence of heart disease in this country, and may have led instead to the steep increase in obesity and Type 2 diabetes. I have interviewed researchers whose computer models have calculated that cutting back on the saturated fats in my diet to the levels recommended by the American Heart Association would not add more than a few months to my life, if that. I have even lost considerable weight with relative ease by giving up carbohydrates on my test diet, and yet I can look down at my eggs and sausage and still imagine the imminent onset of heart disease and obesity, the latter assuredly to be caused by some bizarre rebound phenomena the likes of which science has not yet begun to describe.

This is the state of mind I imagine that mainstream nutritionists, researchers and physicians must inevitably take to the fat-versus-carbohydrate controversy. They may come around, but the evidence will have to be exceptionally compelling. Although this kind of conversion may be happening at the moment to John Farquhar, who is a professor of health research and policy at Stanford University and has worked in this field for more than 40 years. When I interviewed Farquhar in April, he explained why low-fat diets might lead to weight gain and low-carbohydrate diets might lead to weight loss, but he made me promise not to say he believed they did. He attributed the cause of the obesity epidemic to the "force-feeding of a nation." Three weeks later, after reading an article on Endocrinology 101 by David Ludwig in the *Journal of the American Medical Association*, he sent me an e-mail message asking the not-entirely-rhetorical question, "Can we get the low-fat proponents to apologize?"

Taubes offers evidence from many sources to support his argument that fat is actually better for you than carbohydrates. His matter-of-fact, objective tone helps readers take his unorthodox argument seriously. Because this text appeared in the New York Times, *Taubes does not document his sources—standard practice in journalism.*

LAWRENCE LESSIG

Some Like It Hot

This essay on electronic piracy appeared in Wired *magazine in March 2004. Lawrence Lessig is an authority on copyright law. He teaches at Stanford Law School, where he founded its Center for Internet and Society.*

If piracy means using the creative property of others without their permission, then the history of the content industry is a history of piracy. Every important sector of big media today—film, music, radio, and cable TV—was born of a kind of piracy. The consistent story is how each generation welcomes the pirates from the last. Each generation—until now.

The Hollywood film industry was built by fleeing pirates. Creators and directors migrated from the East Coast to California in the early twentieth century in part to escape controls that film patents granted the inventor Thomas Edison. These controls were exercised through the Motion Pictures Patents Company, a monopoly "trust" based on Edison's creative property and formed to vigorously protect his patent rights.

California was remote enough from Edison's reach that filmmakers like Fox and Paramount could move there and, without fear of the law, pirate his inventions. Hollywood grew quickly, and enforcement of federal law eventually spread west. But because patents granted their holders a truly "limited" monopoly of just seventeen years (at that time), the patents had expired by the time enough federal marshals appeared. A new industry had been founded, in part from the piracy of Edison's creative property.

Meanwhile, the record industry grew out of another kind of piracy. At the time that Edison and Henri Fourneaux invented machines for

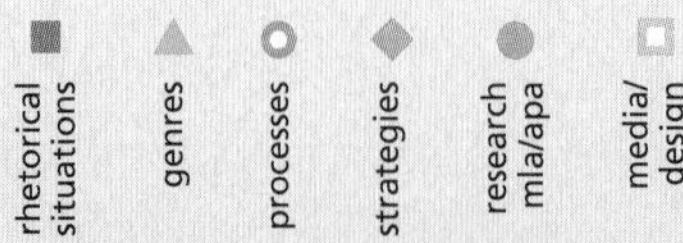

reproducing music (Edison the phonograph; Fourneaux the player piano), the law gave composers the exclusive right to control copies and public performances of their music. Thus, in 1900, if I wanted a copy of Phil Russel's 1899 hit, "Happy Mose," the law said I would have to pay for the right to get a copy of the score, and I would also have to pay for the right to perform it publicly.

5 But what if I wanted to record "Happy Mose" using Edison's phonograph or Fourneaux's player piano? Here the law stumbled. If I simply sang the piece into a recording device in my home, it wasn't clear that I owed the composer anything. And more important, it wasn't clear whether I owed the composer anything if I then made copies of those recordings. Because of this gap in the law, I could effectively use someone else's song without paying the composer anything. The composers (and publishers) were none too happy about this capacity to pirate.

In 1909, Congress closed the gap in favor of the composer and the recording artist, amending copyright law to make sure that composers would be paid for "mechanical reproductions" of their music. But rather than simply granting the composer complete control over the right to make such reproductions, Congress gave recording artists a right to record the music, at a price set by Congress, after the composer allowed it to be recorded once. This is the part of copyright law that makes cover songs possible. Once a composer authorizes a recording of his song, others are free to record the same song, so long as they pay the original composer a fee set by the law. So, by limiting musicians' rights—by partially pirating their creative work—record producers and the public benefit.

A similar story can be told about radio. When a station plays a composer's work on the air, that constitutes a "public performance." Copyright law gives the composer (or copyright holder) an exclusive right to public performances of his work. The radio station thus owes the composer money.

But when the station plays a record, it is not only performing a copy of the *composer's* work. The station is also performing a copy of the *recording artist's* work. It's one thing to air a recording of "Happy Birthday" by the local children's choir; it's quite another to air a recording of it by the Rolling Stones or Lyle Lovett. The recording artist is adding to the value of the composition played on the radio station.

Both photos from Bettmann / Corbis

And if the law were perfectly consistent, the station would have to pay the artist for his work, just as it pays the composer.

But it doesn't. This difference can be huge. Imagine you compose a piece of music. You own the exclusive right to authorize public performances of that music. So if Madonna wants to sing your song in public, she has to get your permission.

Imagine she does sing your song, and imagine she likes it a lot. 10
She then decides to make a recording of your song, and it becomes a top hit. Under today's law, every time a radio station plays your song, you get some money. But Madonna gets nothing, save the indirect effect on the sale of her CDs. The public performance of her recording is not a "protected" right. The radio station thus gets to pirate the value of Madonna's work without paying her a dime.

No doubt, one might argue, the promotion artists get is worth more than the performance rights they give up. Maybe. But even if that's the case, this is a choice that the law ordinarily gives to the creator. Instead, the law gives the radio station the right to take something for nothing.

Cable TV, too: When entrepreneurs first started installing cable in 1948, most refused to pay the networks for the content that they hijacked and delivered to their customers—even though they were basically selling access to otherwise free television broadcasts. Cable companies were thus Napsterizing broadcasters' content, but more egregiously than anything Napster ever did—Napster never charged for the content it enabled others to give away.

Broadcasters and copyright owners were quick to attack this theft. As then Screen Actors Guild president Charlton Heston put it, the cable outfits were "free riders" who were "depriving actors of compensation."

Copyright owners took the cable companies to court. Twice the Supreme Court held that the cable companies owed the copyright owners nothing. The debate shifted to Congress, where almost thirty years later it resolved the question in the same way it had dealt with phonographs and player pianos. Yes, cable companies would have to pay for the content that they broadcast, but the price they would have to pay was not set by the copyright owner. Instead, lawmakers set the price so that the broadcasters couldn't veto the emerging technologies of cable. The companies thus built their empire in part upon a piracy of the value created by broadcasters' content.

As the history of film, music, radio, and cable TV suggest, even if 15
some piracy is plainly wrong, not all piracy is. Or at least not in the sense that the term is increasingly being used today. Many kinds of piracy are useful and productive, either to create new content or foster new ways of doing business. Neither our tradition, nor any tradition, has ever banned all piracy.

This doesn't mean that there are no questions raised by the latest piracy concern—peer-to-peer file sharing. But it does mean that we need to understand the harm in P2P sharing a bit more before we condemn it to the gallows.

Like the original Hollywood, P2P sharing seeks to escape an overly controlling industry. And like the original recording and radio industries, it is simply exploiting a new way of distributing content. But unlike cable TV, no one is selling the content that gets shared on P2P services. This difference distinguishes P2P sharing. We should find a way to protect artists while permitting this sharing to survive.

Much of the "piracy" that file sharing enables is plainly legal and good. It provides access to content that is technically still under copyright but that is no longer commercially available — in the case of music, some four million tracks. More important, P2P networks enable sharing of content that copyright owners want shared, as well as work already in the public domain. This clearly benefits authors and society.

Moreover, much of the sharing — which is referred to by many as piracy — is motivated by a new way of spreading content made possible by changes in the technology of distribution. Thus, consistent with the tradition that gave us Hollywood, radio, the music industry, and cable TV, the question we should be asking about file sharing is how best to preserve its benefits while minimizing (to the extent possible) the wrongful harm it causes artists.

The question is one of balance, weighing the protection of the law 20
against the strong public interest in continued innovation. The law should seek that balance, and that balance will be found only with time.

Lessig argues that the "piracy" that Napster and other peer-to-peer music-sharing services are accused of is similar to that practiced by every other electronic medium in the last one hundred years. He offers a clear definition of piracy and carefully supports his assertions with historical evidence for each one.

JOANNA MACKAY

Organ Sales Will Save Lives

In this essay, written for a class on ethics and politics in science, MIT student Joanna MacKay argues that the sale of human organs should be legal.

There are thousands of people dying to buy a kidney and thousands of people dying to sell a kidney. It seems a match made in heaven. So why are we standing in the way? Governments should not ban the sale of human organs; they should regulate it. Lives should not be wasted; they should be saved.

About 350,000 Americans suffer from end-stage renal disease, a state of kidney disorder so advanced that the organ stops functioning altogether. There are no miracle drugs that can revive a failed kidney, leaving dialysis and kidney transplantation as the only possible treatments (McDonnell and Mallon).

Dialysis is harsh, expensive, and, worst of all, only temporary. Acting as an artificial kidney, dialysis mechanically filters the blood of a patient. It works, but not well. With treatment sessions lasting three hours, several times a week, those dependent on dialysis are, in a sense, shackled to a machine for the rest of their lives. Adding excessive stress to the body, dialysis causes patients to feel increasingly faint and tired, usually keeping them from work and other normal activities.

Kidney transplantation, on the other hand, is the closest thing to a cure that anyone could hope for. Today the procedure is both safe and reliable, causing few complications. With better technology for confirming tissue matches and new anti-rejection drugs, the surgery is relatively simple.

5 But those hoping for a new kidney have high hopes indeed. In the year 2000 alone, 2,583 Americans died while waiting for a kidney transplant; worldwide the number of deaths is around 50,000 (Finkel 27). With the sale of organs outlawed in almost every country, the number of living donors willing to part with a kidney for free is small. When no family member is a suitable candidate for donation, the patient is placed on a deceased donors list, relying on the organs from people dying of old age or accidents. The list is long. With over 60,000 people in line in the United States alone, the average wait for a cadaverous kidney is ten long years.

Daunted by the low odds, some have turned to an alternative solution: purchasing kidneys on the black market. For about $150,000, they can buy a fresh kidney from a healthy, living donor. There are no lines, no waits. Arranged through a broker, the entire procedure is carefully planned out. The buyer, seller, surgeons, and nurses are flown to a predetermined hospital in a foreign country. The operations are performed, and then all are flown back to their respective homes. There is no follow-up, no paperwork to sign (Finkel 27).

The illegal kidney trade is attractive not only because of the promptness, but also because of the chance at a living donor. An organ from a cadaver will most likely be old or damaged, estimated to function for about ten years at most. A kidney from a living donor can last over twice as long. Once a person's transplanted cadaverous kidney stops functioning, he or she must get back on the donors list, this time probably at the end of the line. A transplanted living kidney, however, could last a person a lifetime.

While there may seem to be a shortage of kidneys, in reality there is a surplus. In third world countries, there are people willing to do anything for money. In such extreme poverty these people barely have enough to eat, living in shacks and sleeping on dirt floors. Eager to pay off debts, they line up at hospitals, willing to sell a kidney for about $1,000. The money will go towards food and clothing, or perhaps to pay for a family member's medical operation (Goyal et al. 1590–1). Whatever the case, these people need the money.

There is certainly a risk in donating a kidney, but this risk is not great enough to be outlawed. Millions of people take risks to their health every day for money, or simply for enjoyment. As explained in *The Lancet*, "If the rich are free to engage in dangerous sports for pleasure, or dangerous jobs for high pay, it is difficult to see why the poor who take the lesser risk of kidney selling for greater rewards . . . should be thought so misguided as to need saving from themselves" (Radcliffe-Richards et al. 1951). Studies have shown that a person can live a healthy life with only one kidney. While these studies might not apply to the poor living under strenuous conditions in unsanitary environments, the risk is still theirs to take. These people have decided that their best hope for money is to sell a kidney. How can we deny them the best opportunity they have?

Some agree with Pope John Paul II that the selling of organs is 10
morally wrong and violates "the dignity of the human person" (qtd. in Finkel 26), but this is a belief professed by healthy and affluent individuals. Are we sure that the peasants of third world countries agree? The morals we hold are not absolute truths. We have the responsibility to protect and help those less fortunate, but we cannot let our own ideals cloud the issues at hand.

In a legal kidney transplant, everybody gains except the donor. The doctors and nurses are paid for the operation, the patient receives a new kidney, but the donor receives nothing. Sure, the donor will have the warm, uplifting feeling associated with helping a fellow human being, but this is not enough reward for most people to part with a piece of themselves. In an ideal world, the average person would be altruistic enough to donate a kidney with nothing expected in return. The real world, however, is run by money. We pay men for donating sperm, and we pay women for donating ova, yet we expect others to give away an entire organ for no compensation. If the sale of organs were allowed, people would have a greater incentive to help save the life of a stranger.

While many argue that legalizing the sale of organs will exploit the poorer people of third world countries, the truth of the matter is that this is already the case. Even with the threat of a $50,000 fine and five years in prison (Finkel 26), the current ban has not been successful in preventing illegal kidney transplants. The kidneys of the poor are still benefiting only the rich. While the sellers do receive most of the money promised, the sum is too small to have any real impact on their financial situation. A study in India discovered that in the long run, organ sellers suffer. In the illegal kidney trade, nobody has the interests of the seller at heart. After selling a kidney, their state of living actually worsens. While the $1,000 pays off one debt, it is not enough to relieve the donor of the extreme poverty that placed him in debt in the first place (Goyal et al. 1591).

These impoverished people do not need stricter and harsher penalties against organ selling to protect them, but quite the opposite. If the sale of organs were made legal, it could be regulated and closely monitored by the government and other responsible organizations. Under a regulated system, education would be incorporated into the application process. Before deciding to donate a kidney, the seller should know the details of the operation and any hazards involved. Only with an understanding of the long-term physical health risks can a person make an informed decision (Radcliffe-Richards et al. 1951).

Regulation would ensure that the seller is fairly compensated. In the illegal kidney trade, surgeons collect most of the buyer's money in return for putting their careers on the line. The brokers arranging the procedure also receive a modest cut, typically around ten percent. If the entire practice were legalized, more of the money could be directed towards the person who needs it most, the seller. By eliminating the middleman and allowing the doctors to settle for lower prices, a regulated system would benefit all those in need of a kidney, both rich and poor. According to Finkel, the money that would otherwise be spent on dialysis treatment could not only cover the charge of a kidney transplant at no cost to the recipient, but also reward the donor with as much as $25,000 (32). This money could go a long way for people living in the poverty of third world countries.

Critics fear that controlling the lawful sale of organs would be too 15
difficult, but could it be any more difficult than controlling the unlawful sale of organs? Governments have tried to eradicate the kidney market for decades to no avail. Maybe it is time to try something else. When "desperately wanted goods" are made illegal, history has shown that there is more opportunity for corruption and exploitation than if

those goods were allowed (Radcliffe-Richards et al. 1951). (Just look at the effects of the prohibition of alcohol, for example.) Legalization of organ sales would give governments the authority and the opportunity to closely monitor these live kidney operations.

Regulation would also protect the buyers. Because of the need for secrecy, the current illegal method of obtaining a kidney has no contracts and, therefore, no guarantees. Since what they are doing is illegal, the buyers have nobody to turn to if something goes wrong. There is nobody to point the finger at, nobody to sue. While those participating in the kidney market are breaking the law, they have no other choice. Without a new kidney, end-stage renal disease will soon kill them. Desperate to survive, they are forced to take the only offer available. It seems immoral to first deny them the opportunity of a new kidney and then to leave them stranded at the mercy of the black market. Without laws regulating live kidney transplants, these people are subject to possibly hazardous procedures. Instead of turning our backs, we have the power to ensure that these operations are done safely and efficiently for both the recipient and the donor.

Those suffering from end-stage renal disease would do anything for the chance at a new kidney, take any risk or pay any price. There are other people so poor that the sale of a kidney is worth the profit. Try to tell someone that he has to die from kidney failure because selling a kidney is morally wrong. Then turn around and try to tell another person that he has to remain in poverty for that same reason. In matters of life and death, our stances on moral issues must be reevaluated. If legalized and regulated, the sale of human organs would save lives. Is it moral to sentence thousands to unnecessary deaths?

Works Cited

Finkel, Michael. "This Little Kidney Went to Market." *New York Times Magazine* 27 May 2001: 26+. Print.

Goyal, Madhav, Ravindra L. Mehta, Lawrence J. Schneiderman, and Ashwini R. Sehgal. "Economic and Health Consequences of Selling a Kidney in India." *Journal of the American Medical Association* 288.13 (2002): 1589–92. Print.

McDonnell, Michael B., and William K. Mallon. "Kidney Transplant." *eMedicine Health*. WebMD, 18 Aug. 2008. Web. 30 Nov. 2008.

Radcliffe-Richards, J., A.S. Daar, R.D. Guttmann, R. Hoffenberg, I. Kennedy, M. Lock, R.A. Sells, and N. Tilney. "The Case for Allowing Kidney Sales." *The Lancet* 351.9120 (1998): 1950–2. Print.

MacKay clearly states her position at the beginning of her text: "Governments should not ban the sale of human organs; they should regulate it." Her argument appeals to her readers' value of fairness; when kidney sales are legalized and regulated, both sellers and buyers will benefit from the transaction. MacKay uses MLA style to document her sources.

For six more arguments, see CHAPTER 57.

Key Features / Arguments

A clear and arguable position. At the heart of every argument is a claim with which people may reasonably disagree. Some claims are not arguable because they're completely subjective, matters of taste or opinion ("I hate sauerkraut"), because they are a matter of fact ("The first *Star Wars* movie came out in 1977"), or because they are based on belief or faith ("There is life after death"). To be arguable, a position must reflect one of at least two points of view, making reasoned argument necessary: Internet file sharing should (or should not) be considered fair use; selling human organs should be legal (or illegal). In college writing, you will often argue not that a position is correct but that it is plausible—that it is reasonable, supportable, and worthy of being taken seriously.

Necessary background information. Sometimes we need to provide some background on a topic we are arguing so that readers can understand what is being argued. MacKay establishes the need for kidney donors before launching her argument for legalizing the selling of organs; Taubes describes the rise in obesity before he takes a position on its cause.

Good reasons. By itself, a position does not make an argument; the argument comes when a writer offers reasons to back the position up. There are many kinds of good reasons. Lessig makes his argument by comparing, showing many examples of so-called piracy in other media. Taubes points out that people didn't evolve to eat refined grains and that data show carbohydrates to be more fattening than fat. MacKay bases her argument in favor of legalizing the sale of human organs on the fact that kidney transplants save lives and that regulation would protect impoverished people who currently sell their organs on the black market.

Convincing evidence. It's one thing to give reasons for your position. You then need to offer evidence for your reasons: facts, statistics, expert testimony, anecdotal evidence, case studies, textual evidence. All three arguments use a mix of these types of evidence. MacKay cites statistics about Americans who die from renal failure to support her argument for legalizing organ sales; Lessig offers facts from the history of the broadcast media to support his argument for file sharing.

Appeals to readers' values. Effective arguers try to appeal to readers' values and emotions. Both MacKay and Lessig appeal to basic values—MacKay to the value of compassion, Lessig to the value of fairness. These are deeply held values that we may not think about very much and as a result may see as common ground we share with the writers. And some of MacKay's evidence appeals to emotion—her descriptions of people dying from kidney disease and of poor people selling their organs are likely to evoke an emotional response in many readers.

A trustworthy tone. Arguments can stand or fall on the way readers perceive the writer. Very simply, readers need to trust the person who's making the argument. One way of winning this trust is by demonstrating that you know what you're talking about. Lessig offers plenty of facts to show his knowledge of copyright history—and he does so in a self-assured tone. There are many other ways of establishing yourself (and your argument) as trustworthy—by showing that you have some experience with your subject, that you're fair, and of course that you're honest.

Careful consideration of other positions. No matter how reasonable and careful we are in arguing our positions, others may disagree or offer counterarguments or hold other positions. We need to consider those other views and to acknowledge and, if possible, refute them in our writ-

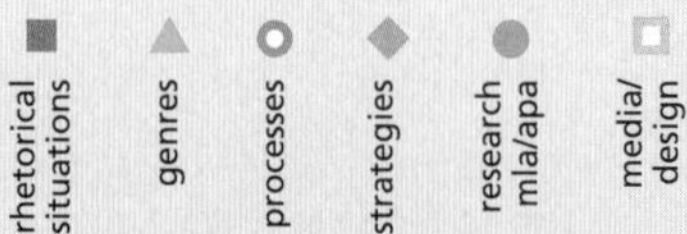

ten arguments. MacKay, for example, acknowledges that some believe that selling one's organs is unethical, but she counters that it's usually healthy, affluent people who say this—not people who need the money they could get by selling one.

A GUIDE TO WRITING ARGUMENTS

Choosing a Topic

A fully developed argument requires significant work and time, so choosing a topic in which you're interested is very important. Students find that widely debated topics such as "animal rights" or "gun control" can be difficult to write on because they seldom have a personal connection to them. Better topics include those that

- interest you right now,
- are focused, but not too narrowly,
- have some personal connection to your life.

One good way to **GENERATE IDEAS** for a topic that meets those three criteria is to explore your own roles in life. 219–25

Start with your roles in life. On a piece of paper, make four columns with the headings "Personal," "Family," "Public," and "School." Then **LIST** the roles you play that relate to it. Here is a list one student wrote: 220–21

Personal	*Family*	*Public*	*School*
gamer	son	voter	college student
dog owner	younger brother	homeless-shelter volunteer	work-study employee
old-car owner	grandson	American	dorm resident
male		resident of Ohio	primary-education major
white			
middle-class			

Identify issues that interest you. Think, then, about issues or controversies that may concern you as a member of one or more of those groups. For instance, as a primary-education major, this student cares about the controversy over whether kids should be taught to read by phonics or by whole language methods. As a college student, he cares about the costs of a college education. Issues that stem from these subjects could include the following: Should reading be taught by phonics or whole language? Should college cost less than it does?

Pick four or five of the roles you list. In five or ten minutes, identify issues that concern or affect you as a member of each of those roles. It might help to word each issue as a question starting with *Should*.

Frame your topic as a problem. Most position papers address issues that are subjects of ongoing debate—their solutions aren't easy, and people disagree on which ones are best. Posing your topic as a problem can help you think about the topic, find an issue that's suitable to write about, and find a clear focus for your essay.

For example, if you wanted to write an argument on the lack of student parking at your school, you could frame your topic as one of several problems: What causes the parking shortage? Why are the university's parking garages and lots limited in their capacity? What might alleviate the shortage?

Choose one issue to write about. Remember that the issue should be interesting to you and have some connection to your life. It is a tentative choice; if you find later that you have trouble writing about it, simply go back to your list of roles or issues and choose another.

Considering the Rhetorical Situation

3–4 **PURPOSE** Do you want to persuade your audience to do or think something? Change their minds? Consider alternative views? Accept your position as plausible—see that you have thought carefully about an issue and researched it appropriately?

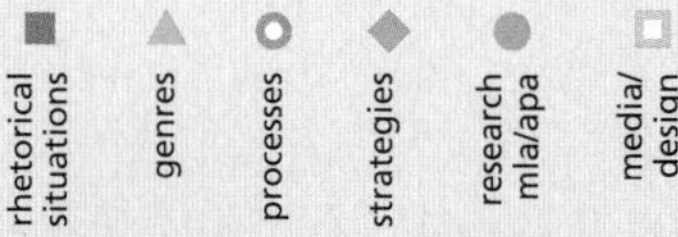

AUDIENCE Who is your intended audience? What do they likely know and believe about this issue? How personal is it for them? To what extent are they likely to agree or disagree with you? Why? What common ground can you find with them? 5–8

STANCE How do you want your audience to perceive you? As an authority on your topic? As someone much like them? As calm? Reasonable? Impassioned or angry? Something else? What's your attitude toward your topic, and why? 12–14

MEDIA / DESIGN What media will you use, and how do your media affect your argument? If you're writing on paper, does your argument call for photos or charts? If you're giving an oral presentation, should you put your reasons and support on slides? If you're writing on the Web, should you add links to counterarguments? 15–17

Generating Ideas and Text

Most essays that successfully argue a position share certain features that make them interesting and persuasive. Remember that your goal is to stake out a position and convince your readers that it is plausible.

Explore what you already know about the issue. Write out whatever you know about the issue by freewriting or as a **LIST** or **OUTLINE**. Why are you interested in this topic? What is your position on it at this point, and why? What aspect do you think you'd like to focus on? Where do you need to focus your research efforts? This activity can help you discover what more you need to learn. Chances are you'll need to learn a lot more about the issue before you even decide what position to take. 220–21 223–24

Do some research. At this point, try to get an overview. Start with one **GENERAL SOURCE** of information that will give you a sense of the ins and outs of your issue, one that isn't overtly biased. *Time*, *Newsweek*, and other national weekly newsmagazines can be good starting points on current 388

issues; encyclopedias are better for issues that are not so current. For some
394–95 issues, you may need to **INTERVIEW** an expert. For example, one student who wanted to write about chemical abuse of animals at 4H competitions interviewed an experienced show competitor. Use your overview source to find out the main questions raised about your issue and to get some idea about the various ways in which you might argue it.

Explore the issue strategically. Most issues may be argued from many different perspectives. You'll probably have some sense of the different views that exist on your issue, but you should explore multiple perspectives before deciding on your position. The following methods are good ways of exploring issues:

- 314–23 As a matter of **DEFINITION.** What is it? How should it be defined? How can *organic* or *genetically modified food* be defined? How do proponents of *organic food* define it—and how do they define *genetically modified food?* How do advocates of *genetically modified food* define it—and how do they define *organic?* Considering such definitions is one way to identify different perspectives on the topic.
- 300–305 As a matter of **CLASSIFICATION.** Can the issue be further divided? What categories might it be broken into? Are there different kinds and different ways of producing organic foods and genetically modified foods? Do different subcategories suggest particular positions or perhaps a way of supporting a certain position? Are there other ways of categorizing foods?
- 306–13 As a matter of **COMPARISON.** Is one subject being considered better than another? Is organic food healthier or safer than genetically modified food? Is genetically modified food healthier or safer than organic? Is the answer somewhere in the middle?
- 338–42 As a matter of **PROCESS.** Should somebody do something? What? Should people buy and eat more organic food? More genetically modified food? Should they buy and eat some of each?

Reconsider whether the issue can be argued. Is this issue worth discussing? Why is it important to you and to others? What difference will
283–99 it make if one position or another prevails? Is it **ARGUABLE?** At this point, you want to be sure that your topic is worth arguing about.

Draft a thesis. Having explored the possibilities, decide your position, and write it out as a complete sentence. For example:

> Pete Rose should not be eligible for the Hall of Fame.
>
> Reading should be taught using a mix of whole language and phonics.
>
> Genetically modified foods should be permitted in the United States.

Qualify your thesis. Rather than taking a strict pro or con position, in most cases you'll want to **QUALIFY YOUR POSITION**—in certain circumstances, with certain conditions, with these limitations, and so on. This is not to say that we should settle, give in, sell out; rather, it is to say that our position may not be the only "correct" one and that other positions may be valid as well. **QUALIFYING YOUR THESIS** also makes your topic manageable by limiting it. For example:

285

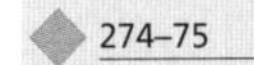
274–75

> Pete Rose should not be eligible for the Hall of Fame, though he should be permitted to contribute to major league baseball in other ways.
>
> Reading should be taught using a mix of phonics and whole language, but the needs of individual students, not a philosophy, should be the primary focus.
>
> Genetically modified foods should be permitted in the United States if they are clearly labeled as such.

Come up with good reasons. Once you have a thesis, you need to come up with good **REASONS** to convince your readers that it's plausible. Write out your position, and then list several reasons. For instance, if your thesis is that Pete Rose should not be eligible for the Hall of Fame, two of your reasons might be:

286–87

> He bet on professional games, an illegal practice.
>
> Professional athletes' gambling on the outcome of games will cause fans to lose faith in professional sports.

Think about which reasons are best for your purposes: Which seem the most persuasive? Which are most likely to be accepted by your audience? Which seem to matter the most now? If your list of reasons is short or you think you'll have trouble developing them enough to write an appropriate essay, this is a good time to rethink your topic—before you've invested too much time in it.

Develop support for your reasons. Next, you have to come up with 287–93 EVIDENCE to support your reasons: facts, statistics, examples, testimony by authorities and experts, anecdotal evidence, scenarios, case studies and observation, and textual evidence.

What counts as evidence varies across audiences. Statistical evidence may be required in certain disciplines but not in others; anecdotes may be accepted as evidence in some courses but not in engineering. Some audiences will be persuaded by emotional appeals while others will not. For example, if you argue that Pete Rose should be eligible for the Baseball Hall of Fame because he's one of the greatest baseball players of all time, you could support that reason with *facts*: he played well in five different positions during his career. Or you could support it with *statistics*: Rose holds Major League records for the most career hits, most games played, and most career at bats. *Expert testimony* might include a plea on his behalf by former President Jimmy Carter, who wrote in 1995, "Pete Rose should at least be declared eligible for later consideration" for election to the Hall of Fame.

Identify other positions. Now, think about positions that differ from yours and about the reasons people are likely to give for those positions. Be careful to represent their points of view as accurately and fairly as you can. Then decide whether you need to acknowledge or refute the position.

Acknowledging other positions. Some positions can't be refuted, but still 294 you need to ACKNOWLEDGE potential doubts, concerns, and objections to show that you've considered them. Doing so shows that you've considered other perspectives. For example, in an essay arguing that vacations are necessary to maintain good health, medical writer Alina Tugend acknowledges that "in some cases, these trips—particularly with entire families in tow—can be stressful in their own way. The joys of a holiday can also include lugging around a ridiculous amount of paraphernalia, jet-lagged children sobbing on airplanes, hotels that looked wonderful on the Web but are in reality next to a construction site." Tugend qualifies her assertions to moderate her position and make her stance appear reasonable.

Refuting other positions. State the position as clearly and as fairly as you can, and then REFUTE it by showing why you believe it is wrong. Perhaps the reasoning is faulty, or the supporting evidence inadequate. Acknowledge the merits of the argument, if any, but emphasize its shortcomings. Avoid the FALLACY of attacking the person making the argument or bringing up a competing position that no one seriously entertains.

295

296–98

Ways of Organizing an Argument

Readers need to be able to follow the reasoning of your argument from beginning to end; your task is to lead them from point to point as you build your case. Sometimes you'll want to give all the reasons for your argument first, followed by discussion of any other positions. Alternatively, you might discuss each reason and any counterargument together.

[Reasons to support your argument, followed by counterarguments]

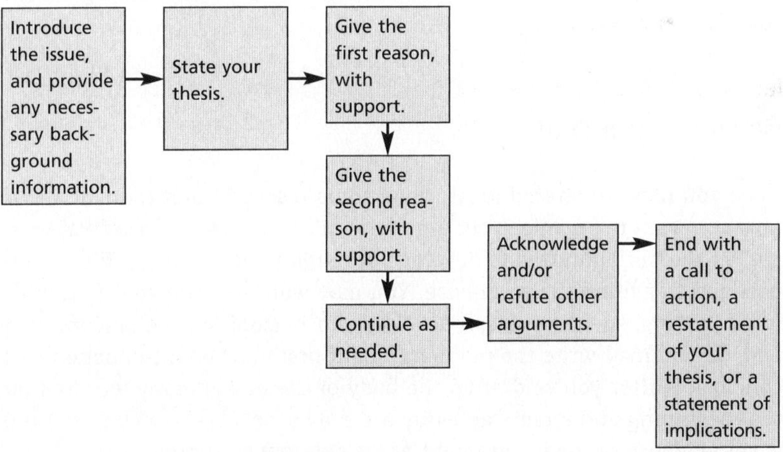

[Reason / counterargument, reason / counterargument]

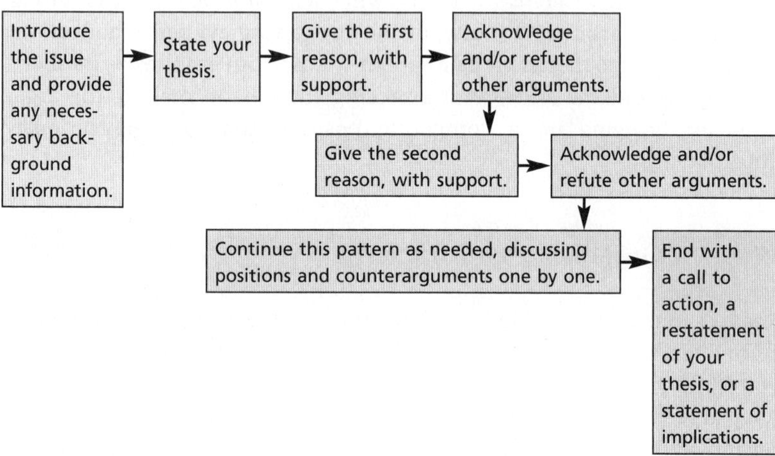

Consider the order in which you discuss your reasons. Usually what comes last is the most emphatic and what comes in the middle is the least emphatic, so you might want to put your most important or strongest reasons first and last.

Writing Out a Draft

Once you have generated ideas, done some research, and thought about how you want to organize your argument, it's time to start **DRAFTING.** 226–28 Your goal in the initial draft is to develop your argument—you can fill in support and transitions as you revise. You may want to write your first draft in one sitting, so that you can develop your reasoning from beginning to end. Or you may write the main argument first and the introduction and conclusion after you've drafted the body of the essay; many writers find that beginning and ending an essay are the hardest tasks they face. Here is some advice on how you might **BEGIN AND END** 261–71 your argument:

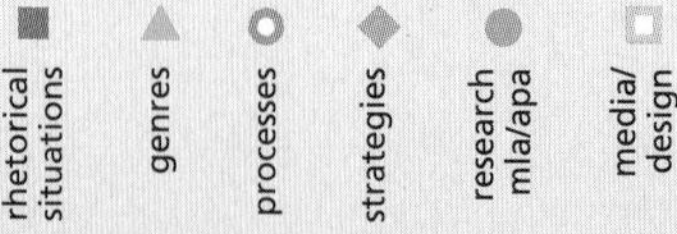

Draft a beginning. There are various ways to begin an argument essay, depending on your audience and purpose. Here are a few suggestions.

- *Offer background information.* You may need to give your readers information to help them understand your position. Taubes establishes that the obesity rate has risen in the past twenty years and states the conventional explanation before making his argument that carbohydrates, not fats, are to blame.
- *Define a key term.* You may need to show how you're using certain key words. Lessig, for example, defines piracy as "using the creative property of others without their permission" in his first sentence, a **DEFINITION** that is central to his argument. 314–23
- *Begin with something that will get readers' attention.* MacKay begins emphatically: "There are thousands of people dying to buy a kidney and thousands of people dying to sell a kidney . . . So why are we standing in the way?"
- *Explain the context for your position.* All arguments are part of a larger, ongoing conversation, so you might begin by showing how your position fits into the arguments others have made. Taubes does this in his second paragraph when he explains how scientists have traditionally explained the rise in obesity.

Draft an ending. Your conclusion is the chance to wrap up your argument in such a way that readers will remember what you've said. Here are a few ways of concluding an argument essay.

- *Summarize your main points.* Especially when you've presented a complex argument, it can help readers to **SUMMARIZE** your main point. MacKay sums up her argument with the sentence "If legalized and regulated, the sale of human organs would save lives." 416–17
- *Call for action.* Lessig does this when he concludes by saying the law should seek a balance between copyright law and the need for continued innovation.
- *Frame your argument by referring to the introduction.* MacKay does this when she ends by reiterating that selling organs benefits both seller and buyer.

Come up with a title. Most often you'll want your title to tell readers something about your topic—and to make them want to read on. MacKay's "Organ Sales Will Save Lives" tells us both her topic and position. Taubes's title is a little unclear until you read the first paragraph, but "What If It's All Been a Big Fat Lie" makes us want to read that paragraph.
272–77 See the chapter on **GUIDING YOUR READER** for more advice on composing a good title.

Considering Matters of Design

You'll probably write your essay in paragraph form, but think about the information you're presenting and how you can design it in such a way as to make your argument as easy as possible for your readers to understand. Think also about whether any visual elements would be more persuasive than plain words.

- 524–25 What would be an appropriate **TYPEFACE**? Something serious like Times Roman? Something traditional like `Courier`? Something else?
- Would it help your readers if you divided your argument into shorter
526–27 sections and added **HEADINGS**?
- If you're making several points, would they be easier to follow if you
525–26 set them off in a **LIST**?
- Do you have any supporting evidence that would be easier to under-
528–30 stand in the form of a bar **GRAPH**, line graph, or pie chart?
- 528–32 Would **ILLUSTRATIONS**—photos, diagrams, or drawings—add support for your argument?

Getting Response and Revising

At this point you need to look at your draft closely, and if possible
235–36 **GET RESPONSE** from others as well. Following are some questions for looking at an argument with a critical eye.

- Is there sufficient background or **CONTEXT**? 262–63
- Is the **THESIS** clear and appropriately qualified? 274–75
- Are the **REASONS** plausible? 286–87
- Is there enough **EVIDENCE** to support these reasons? Is that evidence appropriate? 287–93
- Have you cited enough **SOURCES**, and are these sources credible? 384–99
- Can readers follow the steps in your reasoning?
- Have you considered potential objections or **OTHER POSITIONS**? Are there any others that should be addressed? 294–95
- Are source materials **DOCUMENTED** carefully and completely, with in-text citations and a works cited or references section? 425–27

Next it's time to **REVISE**, to make sure your argument offers convincing evidence, appeals to readers' values, and achieves your purpose. 236–39

Editing and Proofreading

Readers equate correctness with competence. Once you've revised your draft, follow these guidelines for **EDITING** an argument: 241–45

- Check to see that your tone is appropriate and consistent throughout, reflects your **STANCE** accurately, and enhances the argument you're making. 12–14
- Be sure readers will be able to follow the argument; check to see you've provided **TRANSITIONS** and summary statements where necessary. 277
- Make sure you've smoothly integrated **QUOTATIONS**, **PARAPHRASES**, and **SUMMARIES** from source material into your writing and **DOCUMENTED** them accurately. 408–19 425–27
- Look for phrases such as "I think" or "I feel" and delete them; your essay itself expresses your opinion.
- Make sure that **ILLUSTRATIONS** have captions and that charts and graphs have headings—and that all are referred to in the main text. 528–32
- **PROOFREAD** and spell-check your essay carefully. 245–46

Taking Stock of Your Work

Take stock of what you've written by writing out answers to these questions:

- What did you do well in this piece?
- What could still be improved?
- How did you go about researching your topic?
- How did others' responses influence your writing?
- How did you go about drafting this piece?
- Did you use graphic elements (tables, graphs, diagrams, photographs, illustrations) effectively? If not, would they have helped?
- What would you do differently next time?
- What have you learned about your writing ability from writing this piece? What do you need to work on in the future?

247–58
125–32
143–52
171–79

IF YOU NEED MORE HELP

See Chapter 28 if you are required to submit your argument as part of a writing PORTFOLIO. See also Chapter 12 on EVALUATIONS, Chapter 14 on LITERARY ANALYSES, and Chapter 17 on PROPOSALS for advice on writing those specific types of arguments.

Abstracts 10

Abstracts are summaries written to give readers the gist of a report or presentation. Sometimes they are published in conference proceedings or databases. In some academic fields, you may be required to include an abstract in a **REPORT** or as a preview of a presentation you plan to give at an academic or professional conference. Abstracts are brief, typically 100–200 words, sometimes even shorter. Three common kinds are *informative abstracts*, *descriptive abstracts*, and *proposal abstracts*.

59–82

INFORMATIVE ABSTRACTS

Informative abstracts state in one paragraph the essence of a whole paper about a study or a research project. That one paragraph must mention all the main points or parts of the paper: a description of the study or project, its methods, the results, and the conclusions. Here is an example of the abstract accompanying a seven-page essay that appeared in 2002 in *The Journal of Clinical Psychology*:

> The relationship between boredom proneness and health-symptom reporting was examined. Undergraduate students (N = 200) completed the Boredom Proneness Scale and the Hopkins Symptom Checklist. A multiple analysis of covariance indicated that individuals with high boredom-proneness total scores reported significantly higher ratings on all five subscales of the Hopkins Symptom Checklist (Obsessive–Compulsive, Somatization, Anxiety, Interpersonal Sensitivity, and Depression). The results suggest that boredom proneness may be an important element to consider when assessing symptom reporting. Implications for determining the effects of boredom proneness on psychological- and physical-health symptoms, as well as the application in clinical settings, are discussed.
>
> —Jennifer Sommers and Stephen J. Vodanovich, "Boredom Proneness"

The first sentence states the nature of the study being reported. The next summarizes the method used to investigate the problem, and the following one gives the results: students who, according to specific tests, are more likely to be bored are also more likely to have certain medical or psychological symptoms. The last two sentences indicate that the paper discusses those results and examines the conclusion and its implications.

DESCRIPTIVE ABSTRACTS

Descriptive abstracts are usually much briefer than informative abstracts and provide much less information. Rather than summarizing the entire paper, a descriptive abstract functions more as a teaser, providing a quick overview that invites the reader to read the whole. Descriptive abstracts usually do not give or discuss results or set out the conclusion or its implications. A descriptive abstract of the boredom-proneness essay might simply include the first sentence from the informative abstract plus a final sentence of its own:

> The relationship between boredom proneness and health-symptom reporting was examined. The findings and their application in clinical settings are discussed.

PROPOSAL ABSTRACTS

Proposal abstracts contain the same basic information as informative abstracts, but their purpose is very different. You prepare proposal abstracts to persuade someone to let you write on a topic, pursue a project, conduct an experiment, or present a paper at a scholarly conference. This kind of abstract is not written to introduce a longer piece but rather to stand alone, and often the abstract is written before the paper itself. Titles and other aspects of the proposal deliberately reflect the theme of the proposed work, and you may use the future tense, rather than the past, to describe work not yet completed. Here is a possible proposal for doing research on boredom:

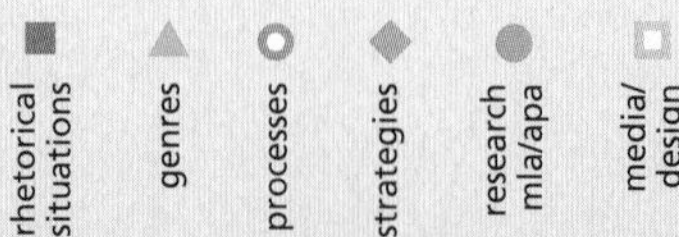

Undergraduate students will complete the Boredom Proneness Scale and the Hopkins Symptom Checklist. A multiple analysis of covariance will be performed to determine the relationship between boredom-proneness total scores and ratings on the five subscales of the Hopkins Symptom Checklist (Obsessive–Compulsive, Somatization, Anxiety, Interpersonal Sensitivity, and Depression).

Key Features / Abstracts

A summary of basic information. An informative abstract includes enough information to substitute for the report itself, a descriptive abstract offers only enough information to let the audience decide whether to read further, and a proposal abstract gives an overview of the planned work.

Objective description. Abstracts present information on the contents of a report or a proposed study; they do not present arguments about or personal perspectives on those contents. The informative abstract on boredom proneness, for example, offers only a tentative conclusion: "The results *suggest* that boredom proneness *may* be an important element to consider."

Brevity. Although the length of abstracts may vary, journals and organizations often restrict them to 120–200 words—meaning you must carefully select and edit your words.

A BRIEF GUIDE TO WRITING ABSTRACTS

Considering the Rhetorical Situation

PURPOSE Are you giving a brief but thorough overview of a completed study? Only enough information to create interest? Or a proposal for a planned study or presentation? 3–4

AUDIENCE For whom are you writing this abstract? What information about your project will your readers need? 5–8

12–14 **STANCE** Whatever your stance in the longer work, your abstract must be objective.

15–17 **MEDIA / DESIGN** How will you set your abstract off from the rest of the text? If you are publishing it online, will you devote a single page to it? What format does your audience require?

Generating Ideas and Text

Write the paper first, the abstract last. You can then use the finished work as the guide for the abstract, which should follow the same basic structure. *Exception:* You may need to write a proposal abstract months before the work it describes will be complete.

Copy and paste key statements. If you've already written the work, 274–75 highlight your **THESIS**, objective, or purpose; basic information on your methods; your results; and your conclusion. Copy and paste those sentences into a new document to create a rough version of your abstract.

416–17 **Pare down the information to key ideas.** **SUMMARIZE** the report, editing out any nonessential words and details. In your first sentence, introduce the overall scope of your study. Also include any other information that seems crucial to understanding your paper. Avoid phrases that add unnecessary words, such as "It is concluded that." In general, you probably won't want to use "I"; an abstract should cover ideas, not say what you think or will do.

Conform to any requirements. In general, an informative abstract should be at most 10 percent as long as the original and no longer than the maximum length allowed. Descriptive abstracts should be shorter still, and proposal abstracts should conform to the requirements of the organization calling for the proposal.

Ways of Organizing an Abstract

[An informative abstract]

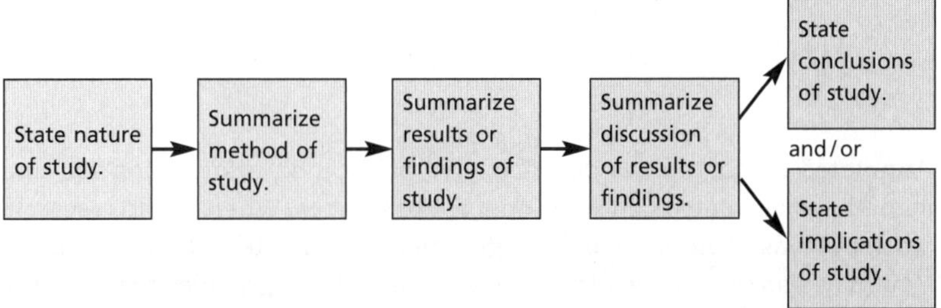
State nature of study.
Summarize method of study.
Summarize results or findings of study.
Summarize discussion of results or findings.
State conclusions of study.
and / or
State implications of study.

[A descriptive abstract]

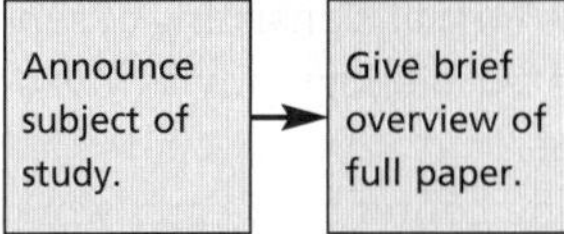
Announce subject of study.
Give brief overview of full paper.

[A proposal abstract]

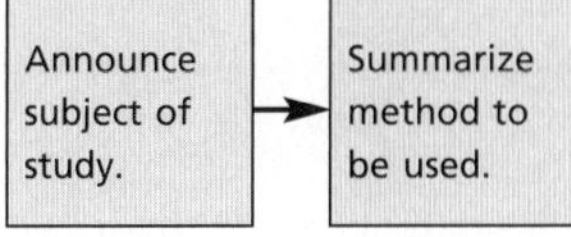
Announce subject of study.
Summarize method to be used.

IF YOU NEED MORE HELP

See Chapter 24 for guidelines on **DRAFTING,** Chapter 25 on **ASSESSING YOUR OWN WRITING,** Chapter 26 on **GETTING RESPONSE AND REVISING,** and Chapter 27 on **EDITING AND PROOFREADING.**

226–28
235–41
242–46

11 Annotated Bibliographies

Annotated bibliographies describe, give publication information for, and sometimes evaluate each work on a list of sources. When we do research, we may consult annotated bibliographies to evaluate potential sources. You may also be assigned to create annotated bibliographies to weigh the potential usefulness of sources and to document your search efforts so that teachers can assess your ability to find, describe, and evaluate sources. There are two kinds of annotations, *descriptive* and *evaluative*; both may be brief, consisting only of phrases, or more formal, consisting of sentences and paragraphs. Sometimes an annotated bibliography is introduced by a short statement explaining its scope.

Descriptive annotations simply summarize the contents of each work, without comment or evaluation. They may be very short, just long enough to capture the flavor of the work, like the following excerpt from a bibliography of books and articles on teen films, published in the *Journal of Popular Film and Television*.

MICHAEL BENTON, MARK DOLAN, AND REBECCA ZISCH

Teen Film$

In the introduction to his book *The Road to Romance and Ruin*, Jon Lewis points out that over half of the world's population is currently under the age of twenty. This rather startling fact should be enough to make most Hollywood producers drool when they think of the potential profits from a target movie audience. Attracting the largest demographic group is, after all, the quickest way to box-office success.

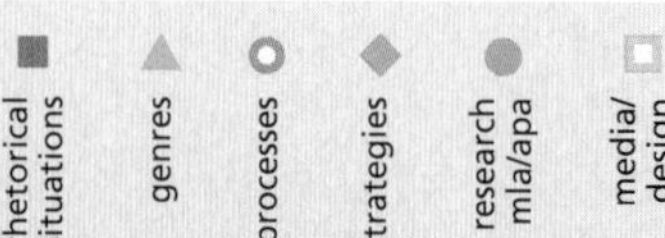

In fact, almost from its beginning, the film industry has recognized the importance of the teenaged audience, with characters such as Andy Hardy and locales such as Ridgemont High and the 'hood.

Beyond the assumption that teen films are geared exclusively toward teenagers, however, film researchers should keep in mind that people of all ages have attended and still attend teen films. Popular films about adolescents are also expressions of larger cultural currents. Studying the films is important for understanding an era's common beliefs about its teenaged population within a broader pattern of general cultural preoccupations.

This selected bibliography is intended both to serve and to stimulate interest in the teen film genre. It provides a research tool for those who are studying teen films and their cultural implications. Unfortunately, however, in the process of compiling this list we quickly realized that it was impossible to be genuinely comprehensive or to satisfy every interest.

Doherty, Thomas. *Teenagers and Teenpics: The Juvenilization of American Movies in the 1950s*. Boston: Unwin Hyman, 1988. Print.
Historical discussion of the identification of teenagers as a targeted film market.

Foster, Harold M. "Film in the Classroom: Coping with Teen Pics." *English Journal* 76.3 (1987): 86–88. Print.
Evaluation of the potential of using teen films such as *Sixteen Candles, The Karate Kid, Risky Business, The Flamingo Kid,* and *The Breakfast Club* to instruct adolescents on the difference between film as communication and film as exploitation.

Washington, Michael, and Marvin J. Berlowitz."Blaxploitation Films and High School Youth: Swat Superfly." *Jump Cut* 9 (1975): 23–24. Print.
Marxist reaction to the trend of youth-oriented black action films. Article seeks to illuminate the negative influences the films have on high school students by pointing out the false ideas about education, morality, and the black family espoused by the heroes in the films.

These annotations are purely descriptive; the authors express none of their own opinions. They describe works as "historical" or "Marxist" but do not indicate whether they're "good." The bibliography entries are documented in MLA style.

Evaluative annotations offer opinions on a source as well as describe it. They are often helpful in assessing how useful a source will be for your own writing. The following evaluative annotations are from a bibliography by Jessica Ann Olson, a student at Wright State University.

JESSICA ANN OLSON

Global Warming

Parmesan, Camille, and Hector Galbraith. "Executive Summary." *Observed Impacts of Global Climate Change in the U.S.* Pew Center on Global Climate Change, Nov. 2004. Web. 17 Jan. 2007.

This report summarizes recent scientific findings that document the impact changes in the climate have had on the distribution of plants and animals in the United States and on how they interact within their communities. For example, it explains how a shift has taken place in the blooming period for plants and the breeding period for animals caused by global warming. Because of changes in their geographic range, species may interact differently, possibly resulting in population declines. For example, the red fox is now found in areas dominated by the arctic fox and is threatening its survival. The report stresses that such shifts can harm the world's biodiversity. Plants and animals that are rare now face extinction. The annual cycle of carbon dioxide levels in the atmosphere has also changed, largely due to the lengthening of the growing season, affecting basic ecosystem processes. I did not find this report as helpful as other sources because its information is based only on observations made in the United States. The information appears reliable, though, because it is based on scientific evidence. This essay will be helpful to my essay because it focuses on how plants and animals are currently affected, such as their shifting communities and how they are clashing. I could use this to explain human changes by providing evidence of what is happening to other species. This source will not be as helpful in explaining the climate's effects on human biological function in particular, but it will provide some framework. For example, I could explain how the plants that help convert carbon dioxide into oxygen are being harmed and relate that to how the humans will suffer the consequences.

Gore, Al. *An Inconvenient Truth: The Planetary Emergency of Global Warming and What We Can Do About It.* New York: Rodale, 2006. Print.

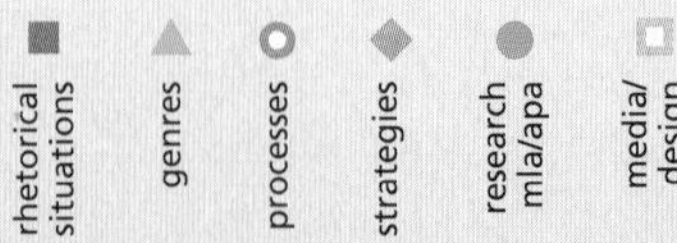

This publication, which is based on Gore's slide show on global warming, stresses the urgency of the global warming crisis. It centers on how the atmosphere is very thin and how greenhouse gases such as carbon dioxide are making it thicker. The thicker atmosphere traps more infrared radiation, causing warming of the Earth. Gore argues that carbon dioxide, which is created by burning fossil fuels, cutting down forests, and producing cement, accounts for eighty percent of greenhouse gas emissions. He includes several examples of problems caused by global warming. Penguins and polar bears are at risk because the glaciers they call home are quickly melting. Coral reefs are being bleached and destroyed when their inhabitants overheat and leave. Global warming is now affecting people's lives as well. For example, the highways in Alaska are only frozen enough to be driven on fewer than eighty days of the year. In China and elsewhere, record-setting floods and droughts are taking place. Hurricanes are on the rise. This source's goal is to inform its audience about the ongoing global warming crisis and to inspire change across the world. It is useful because it relies on scientific data that can be referred to easily and it provides a solid foundation for me to build on. For example, it explains how carbon dioxide is produced and how it is currently affecting plants and animals. This evidence could potentially help my research on how humans are biologically affected by global warming. It will also help me structure my essay, using its general information to lead into the specifics of my topic. For example, I could introduce the issue by explaining the thinness of the atmosphere and the effect of greenhouse gases, then focus on carbon dioxide and its effects on organisms.

These annotations not only describe the sources in detail, but also evaluate their usefulness for the writer's own project. They show that the writer understands the content of the sources and can relate it to her own anticipated needs as a researcher and writer.

Key Features / Annotated Bibliographies

A statement of scope. You need a brief introductory statement to explain what you're covering. The authors of the bibliography on teen films introduce their bibliography with three paragraphs establishing a context for the bibliography and announcing their purpose for compiling it.

Complete bibliographic information. Provide all the information about the source following one documentation system (MLA, APA, or another one) so that your readers or other researchers will be able to find each source easily.

A concise description of the work. A good annotation describes each item as carefully and objectively as possible, giving accurate information and showing that you understand the source. These qualities will help to build authority—for you as a writer and for your annotations.

Relevant commentary. If you write an evaluative bibliography, your comments should be relevant to your purpose and audience. The best way to achieve relevance is to consider what questions a potential reader might have about the sources. Your evaluation might also focus on the text's suitability as a source for your writing, as Olson's evaluative annotations do.

Consistent presentation. All annotations should follow a consistent pattern: if one is written in complete sentences, they should all be. Each annotation in the teen films bibliography, for example, begins with a phrase (not a complete sentence) characterizing the work.

A BRIEF GUIDE TO WRITING ANNOTATED BIBLIOGRAPHIES

Considering the Rhetorical Situation

3–4 **PURPOSE** Will your bibliography need to demonstrate the depth or breadth of your research? Will your readers actually track down and use your sources? Do you need or want to convince readers that your sources are good?

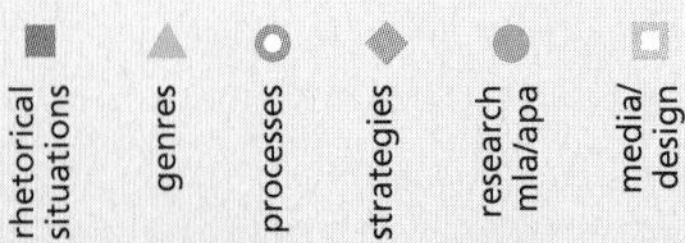

AUDIENCE For whom are you compiling this bibliography? What does your audience need to know about each source? 5–8

STANCE Are you presenting yourself as an objective describer or evaluator? Or are you expressing a particular point of view toward the sources you evaluate? 12–14

MEDIA / DESIGN If you are publishing the bibliography online, will you provide links from each annotation to the source itself? Online or off, do you need to distinguish the bibliographic information from the annotation by using a different font? 15–17

Generating Ideas and Text

Decide what sources to include. You may be tempted to include in a bibliography every source you find or look at. A better strategy is to include only those sources that you or your readers may find potentially useful in researching your topic. For an academic bibliography, you need to consider these qualities:

- *Appropriateness.* Is this source relevant to your topic? Is it a primary source or a secondary source? Is it aimed at an appropriate audience? General or specialized? Elementary, advanced, or somewhere in between?
- *Credibility.* Is the author reputable? Is the publication or publishing company reputable? Do its ideas more or less agree with those in other sources you've read?
- *Balance.* Does the source present enough evidence for its assertions? Does it show any particular bias? Does it present countering arguments fairly?
- *Timeliness.* Is the source recent enough? Does it reflect current thinking or research about the subject?

If you need help **FINDING SOURCES**, see Chapter 43. 384–99

MLA 428–76
APA 477–519

Compile a list of works to annotate. Give the sources themselves in whatever documentation style is required; see the guidelines for **MLA** and **APA** styles in Chapters 49 and 50.

Determine what kind of bibliography you need to write. Descriptive or evaluative? Will your annotations be in the form of phrases? Complete sentences? Paragraphs? The form will shape your reading and note taking. If you're writing a descriptive bibliography, your reading goal will be to understand and capture the writer's message as clearly as possible. If you're writing an evaluative bibliography, your annotations must also include your own comments on the source.

171–79

Read carefully. To write an annotation, you must understand the source's argument, but when you are writing an annotated bibliography as part of a **PROPOSAL**, you may have neither the time nor the need to read the whole text. Here's a way of quickly determining whether a source is likely to serve your needs:

- Check the publisher or sponsor (university press? scholarly journal? popular magazine? website sponsored by a reputable organization?).
- Read the preface (of a book), abstract (of a scholarly article), introduction (of an article in a nonscholarly magazine or a website).
- Skim the table of contents or the headings.
- Read the parts that relate specifically to your topic.

Research the writer, if necessary. If you are required to indicate the writer's credentials, you may need to do additional research. You may find information by typing the writer's name into a search engine or looking up the writer in *Contemporary Authors*. In any case, information about the writer should take up no more than one sentence in your annotation.

324–32

Summarize the work in a sentence or two. **DESCRIBE** it as objectively as possible: even if you are writing an evaluative annotation, you can evaluate the central point of a work better by stating it clearly first. *If you're writing a descriptive annotation, you're done.*

Establish criteria for evaluating sources. If you're **EVALUATING** sources for a project, you'll need to evaluate them in terms of their usefulness for your project, their **STANCE,** and their overall credibility.

125–32
12–14

Write a brief evaluation of the source. If you can generalize about the worth of the entire work, fine. You may find, however, that some parts are useful while others are not, and what you write should reflect that mix.

Be consistent—in content, sentence structure, and format.

- *Content.* Try to provide about the same amount of information for each entry; if you're evaluating, evaluate each source, not just some sources.
- *Sentence structure.* Use the same style throughout—complete sentences, brief phrases, or a mix.
- *Format.* Use one documentation style throughout; use consistent **TYPE** for each element in each entry—for example, italicize or underline all book titles.

524–25

Ways of Organizing an Annotated Bibliography

Depending on their purpose, annotated bibliographies may or may not include an introduction. Most annotated bibliographies cover a single topic and so are organized alphabetically by author's or editor's last name. When a work lacks a named author, alphabetize it by the first important word in its title. Consult the documentation system you're using for additional details about alphabetizing works appropriately.

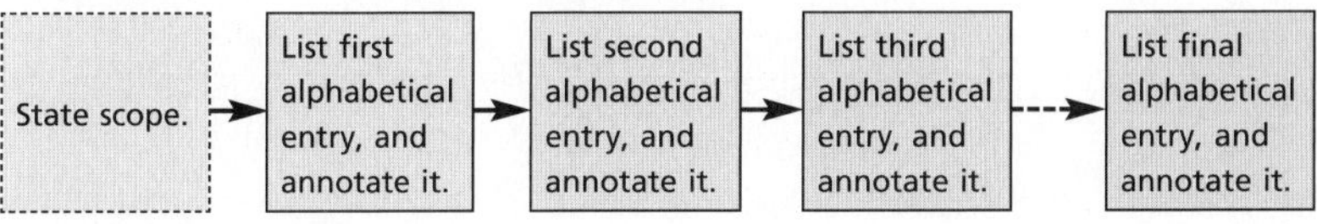
State scope.
List first alphabetical entry, and annotate it.
List second alphabetical entry, and annotate it.
List third alphabetical entry, and annotate it.
List final alphabetical entry, and annotate it.

Sometimes an annotated bibliography needs to be organized into several subject areas (or genres, periods, or some other category) and the entries are listed alphabetically within each category. For example, a bibliography about terrorism breaks down into subjects such as "Global Terrorism" and "Weapons of Mass Destruction."

[Multi-category bibliography]

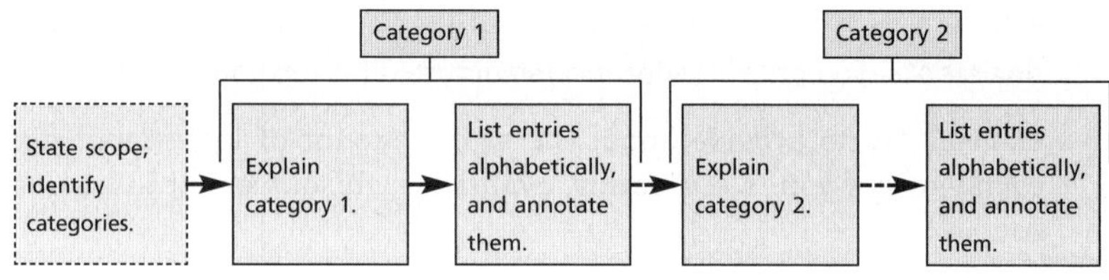

IF YOU NEED MORE HELP

See Chapter 24 for guidelines on **DRAFTING**, Chapter 25 on **ASSESSING YOUR OWN WRITING**, Chapter 26 on **GETTING RESPONSE AND REVISING**, and Chapter 27 on **EDITING AND PROOFREADING**. See Chapter 28 if you are required to submit your bibliography in a writing **PORTFOLIO**.

226–28
229–34
235–41
242–46
247–58

Evaluations 12

Consumer Reports evaluates cell phones and laundry detergents. The *Princeton Review* and *US News & World Report* evaluate colleges and universities. You probably consult such sources to make decisions, and you probably evaluate things all the time—when you recommend a film (or not) or a teacher (ditto). An evaluation is at bottom a judgment; you judge something according to certain criteria, supporting your judgment with reasons and evidence. You need to give your reasons for evaluating it as you do because often your evaluation will affect your audience's actions: they must see this movie, needn't bother with this book, should be sure to have the Caesar salad at this restaurant, and so on. In the following review, written for a first-year writing class at Wright State University, Ali Heinekamp offers her evaluation of the film *Juno*.

ALI HEINEKAMP

Juno: *Not Just Another Teen Movie*

It all starts with a chair, where Juno (Ellen Page) has unprotected sex with her best friend Bleeker (Michael Cera). Several weeks later, she's at a convenience store, buying a pregnancy test. Only sixteen, Juno faces the terrifying task of telling her parents that she is pregnant. With their support, Juno moves forward in her decision to give birth and give the child to Mark (Jason Bateman) and Vanessa (Jennifer Garner), a wealthy and seemingly perfect married couple looking to adopt. Although the situations *Juno*'s characters find themselves in and their dialogue may be criticized as unrealistic, the film, written by Diablo Cody and directed by Jason Reitman, successfully portrays the emotions of a teen being shoved into maturity way too fast.

Much of the time, *Juno* seems unrealistic because it seems to treat the impact of teen pregnancy so lightly. The consequences of Juno's pregnancy are sugar-coated to such an extent that in many cases, they are barely apparent. The film downplays the emotional struggle that a pregnant woman would feel in deciding to give birth and then put that child up for adoption, and it ignores the discomforts of pregnancy, such as mood swings and nausea.

Likewise, *Juno*'s dialogue is too good to be true — funny and clever, but unrealistic. For example, Juno tells Mark and Vanessa "If I could just have the thing and give it to you now, I totally would. But I'm guessing it looks probably like a sea monkey right now, and we should let it get a little cuter." At another point, talking about her absent mother, Juno says, "Oh, and she inexplicably mails me a cactus every Valentine's Day. And I'm like, 'Thanks a heap, coyote ugly. This cactus-gram stings even worse than your abandonment.' " As funny as they are, the creatively quirky one-liners often go a bit too far, detracting from both the gravity of Juno's situation and the film's believability.

But although the situations and dialogue are unrealistic, the emotional heart of the movie is believable — and moving. Despite the movie's lack of realism in portraying her pregnancy, Juno's vulnerability transforms her character and situation into something much more believable. Juno mentions at various times that her classmates stare at her stomach and talk about her behind her back, but initially she seems unconcerned with the negative attention. This façade falls apart, however, when Juno accuses Bleeker, the baby's father, of being ashamed of the fact that he and Juno have had sex. The strong front she is putting up drops when she bursts out, "At least you don't have to have the evidence under your sweater." This break in Juno's strength reveals her vulnerability and makes her character relatable and believable.

The juxtaposition of Juno's teenage quirks and the adult situation 5
she's in also remind us of her youth and vulnerability. As a result of the adult situation Juno finds herself in and her generally stoic demeanor, it's easy to see her as a young adult. But the film fills each scene with visual reminders that Juno is just a kid being forced into situations beyond her maturity level. At a convenience store, Juno buys a pregnancy test along with a licorice rope. She calls Women Now, an abortion clinic, on a phone that looks like a hamburger. And while she is giving birth, she wears long, brightly striped socks. These subtle visual

cues help us remember the reality of Juno's position as both physically an adult and emotionally an adolescent.

While the dialogue is too clever to be realistic, in the end it's carried by the movie's heart. Scott Tobias from the entertainment Web site *The A.V. Club* says it best when he writes that the colorful dialogue is often "too ostentatious for its own good, but the film's sincerity is what ultimately carries it across." In fact, intensely emotional scenes are marked by their *lack* of witty dialogue. For example, when Juno runs into Vanessa at the mall, Vanessa, reluctantly at first, kneels down to talk to the baby through Juno's stomach. Vanessa's diction while talking to the baby is so simple, so expected. She simply starts with, "Hi baby, it's me. It's Vanessa," and then continues, "I can't wait to meet you." This simple, everyday statement stands out in comparison to the rest of the well-crafted, humorous script. For her part, Juno simply stares admiringly at Vanessa. She doesn't have to say anything to transform the scene into a powerful one. Another scene in which the dialogue stops being clever is the one in which Juno and Bleeker lie in side by side in a hospital bed after Juno has given birth, Juno in tears and Bleeker lost in thought. They don't need to say anything for us to feel their pain at the realization that although the pregnancy is over, it will never truly be in the past. The absence of dialogue in scenes such as these actually contributes to their power. We finally see more than stoicism and sarcasm from Juno: we see caring and fear, which are feelings most would expect of a pregnant teen.

There has been much concern among critics that as a pregnant teenager, Juno doesn't present a good role model for teen girls. Worrying that teens may look up to Juno so much that being pregnant becomes "cool," Dana Stevens writes in *Slate*, "Let's hope that the teenage girls of America don't cast their condoms to the wind in hopes of becoming as cool as 16-year-old Juno MacGuff." But it is not Juno's pregnancy that makes her cool: it is her ability to overcome the difficult obstacles thrown at her, and that strength does make her a good role model. Another critic, Lisa Schwarzbaum from *Entertainment Weekly*, feels that the movie might have been more realistic had Juno chosen to go through with an abortion. It's true that Juno may have chosen the more difficult answer to a teen pregnancy, but she is far from alone in her decision. Perhaps Schwarzbaum underestimates teens in thinking that they would not be able to cope with the emotionally difficult situation Juno chooses. Again, in her strength, Juno is a role model for young women.

Although *Juno* is a comedy filled with improbable situations, exaggerations, and wit, its genuine emotion allows us to connect with and relate to the film. The reality of the characters' emotions in controversial and serious situations allows *Juno* to transcend its own genre. It reaches depths of emotion that are unusual for teenage comedies, proving that *Juno* is not just another teen movie.

Works Cited

Cody, Diablo. *Juno.* Dir. Jason Reitman. Perf. Ellen Page, Michael Cera, Jennifer Garner, Jason Bateman. Fox Searchlight, 2007. Film.

Schwarzbaum, Lisa. Rev. of *Juno*, dir. Jason Reitman. *EW.com.* Entertainment Weekly, 28 Nov. 2007. Web. 14 Apr. 2008.

Stevens, Dana. "Superpregnant: How *Juno* Is *Knocked Up* from the Girl's Point of View." Rev. of *Juno*, dir. Jason Reitman. *Slate.com*. Slate, 5 Dec. 2007. Web. 12 Apr. 2008.

Tobias, Scott. Rev. of *Juno*, dir. Jason Reitman. *The A. V. Club*. The Onion, 6 Dec. 2007. Web. 13 Apr. 2008.

For five more evaluations, see CHAPTER 58.

Heinekamp quickly summarizes Juno's *plot and then evaluates the film according to clearly stated criteria. In the process, she responds to several reviewers' comments, joining the critical conversation about the film. She documents her sources according to MLA style.*

Key Features / Evaluations

A concise description of the subject. You should include just enough information to let readers who may not be familiar with your subject understand what it is; the goal is to evaluate, not summarize. Heinekamp briefly describes *Juno*'s main plot points in her first paragraph, only providing what readers need to understand the context of her evaluation.

Clearly defined criteria. You need to determine clear criteria as the basis for your judgment. In reviews or other evaluations written for a broad audience, you can integrate the criteria into the discussion as reasons for

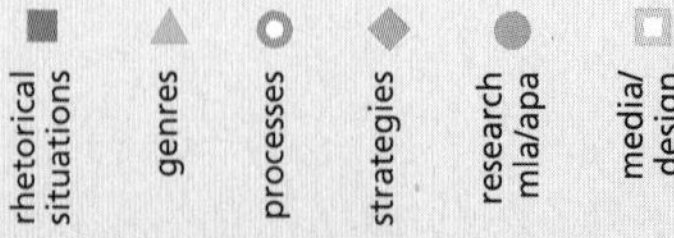

your assessment, as Heinekamp does in her evaluation of *Juno*. In more formal evaluations, you may need to announce your criteria explicitly. Heinekamp evaluates the film based on the power of its emotion and the realism of its situations, characters, and dialogue.

A knowledgeable discussion of the subject. To evaluate something credibly, you need to show that you know it yourself and that you've researched what other authoritative sources say. Heinekamp cites many examples from *Juno*, showing her knowledge of the film. She also cites reviews from three Internet sources, showing that she's researched others' views as well.

A balanced and fair assessment. An evaluation is centered on a judgment. Heinekamp concedes that *Juno*'s situations and dialogue are unrealistic, but she says it nevertheless "reaches depths of emotion that are unusual for teenage comedies." It is important that any judgment be balanced and fair. Seldom is something all good or all bad. A fair evaluation need not be all positive or all negative; it may acknowledge both strengths and weaknesses. For example, a movie's soundtrack may be wonderful while the plot is not. Heinekamp criticizes *Juno*'s too-witty dialogue and unrealistic situations, even as she appreciates its heart.

Well-supported reasons. You need to argue for your judgment, providing reasons and evidence. Heinekamp gives several reasons for her positive assessment of *Juno*—the believability of its characters, the intensely emotional scenes, the strength of the main character as a role model—and she supports these reasons with many quotations and examples from the film.

A BRIEF GUIDE TO WRITING EVALUATIONS

Choosing Something to Evaluate

You can more effectively evaluate a limited subject than a broad one: review certain dishes at a local restaurant rather than the entire menu; review one film or episode rather than all the films by Alfred Hitchcock or all eighty *Star Trek* episodes. The more specific and focused your subject, the better you can write about it.

Considering the Rhetorical Situation

3–4 **PURPOSE** Are you writing to affect your audience's opinion of a subject? Do you want to evaluate something to help others decide what to see, do, or buy?

5–8 **AUDIENCE** To whom are you writing? What will your audience already know about the subject? What will they expect to learn from your evaluation of it? Are they likely to agree with you or not?

12–14 **STANCE** How will you show that you have evaluated the subject fairly and appropriately? Think about the tone you want to use: should it be reasonable? Passionate? Critical?

15–17 **MEDIA / DESIGN** How will you deliver your evaluation? In print? Online? As a speech? Can you show an image or film clip? If you're submitting your text for publication, are there any format requirements?

Generating Ideas and Text

219–20 **Explore what you already know.** FREEWRITE to answer the following questions: What do you know about this subject or subjects like it? What are your initial or gut feelings, and why do you feel as you do? How does this subject reflect or affect your basic values or beliefs? How have others evaluated subjects like this?

Identify criteria. Make a list of criteria you think should be used to evaluate your subject. Think about which criteria will likely be important
5–8 to your AUDIENCE. You might find CUBING and QUESTIONING to be useful
222–23 processes for thinking about your topic.

Evaluate your subject. Study your subject closely to determine if it meets your criteria. You may want to list your criteria on a sheet of paper with space to take notes, or you may develop a grading scale for each criterion to help stay focused on it. Come up with a tentative judgment.

Compare your subject with others. Often, evaluating something involves **COMPARING AND CONTRASTING** 306–13 it with similar things. We judge movies in comparison with the other movies we've seen and french fries with the other fries we've tasted. Sometimes those comparisons can be made informally. For other evaluations, you may have to do research — to try on several pairs of jeans before buying any, for example — to see how your subject compares.

State your judgment as a tentative thesis statement. Your **THESIS STATEMENT** 273–75 should be one that balances both pros and cons. "*Fight Club* is a great film — but not for children." "Of the five sport-utility vehicles tested, the Toyota 4Runner emerged as the best in comfort, power, and durability, though not in styling or cargo capacity." Both of these examples offer a judgment but qualify it according to the writer's criteria.

Anticipate other opinions. I think Will Ferrell is a comic genius whose movies are first-rate. You think Will Ferrell is a terrible actor who makes awful movies. How can I write a review of his latest film that you will at least consider? One way is by **ACKNOWLEDGING** 294 other opinions — and **REFUTING** 295 those opinions as best I can. I may not persuade you to see Will Ferrell's next film, but I can at least demonstrate that by certain criteria he should be appreciated. You may need to **RESEARCH** 373 how others have evaluated your subject.

Identify and support your reasons. Write out all the **REASONS** 286–87 you can think of that will convince your audience to accept your judgment. Review your list to identify the most convincing or important reasons. Then review how well your subject meets your criteria and decide how best to **SUPPORT** 287–93 your reasons: through examples, authoritative opinions, statistics, or something else.

Ways of Organizing an Evaluation

Evaluations are usually organized in one of two ways. One way is to introduce what's being evaluated, followed by your judgment, discussing your criteria along the way. This is a useful strategy if your audience may not be familiar with your subject.

[Start with your subject]

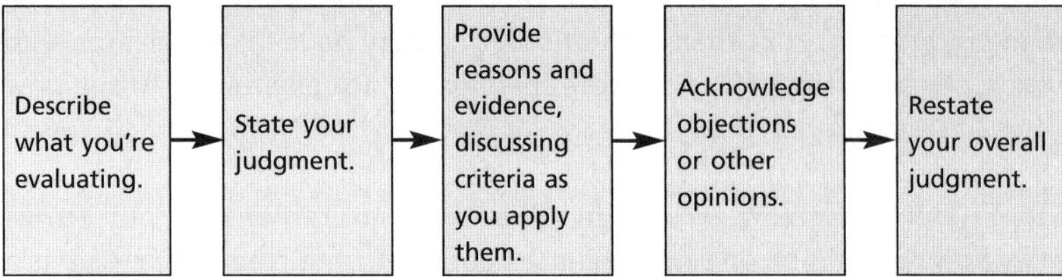
Describe what you're evaluating.
State your judgment.
Provide reasons and evidence, discussing criteria as you apply them.
Acknowledge objections or other opinions.
Restate your overall judgment.

You might also start by identifying your criteria and then follow with a discussion of how your subject meets or doesn't meet those criteria. This strategy foregrounds the process by which you reached your conclusions.

[Start with your criteria]

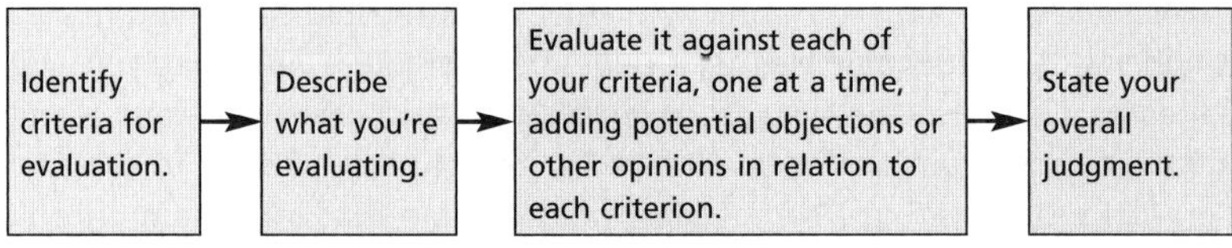
Identify criteria for evaluation.
Describe what you're evaluating.
Evaluate it against each of your criteria, one at a time, adding potential objections or other opinions in relation to each criterion.
State your overall judgment.

IF YOU NEED MORE HELP

See Chapter 24 for guidelines on DRAFTING, Chapter 25 on ASSESSING YOUR DRAFT, Chapter 26 on GETTING RESPONSE AND REVISING, and Chapter 27 on EDITING AND PROOFREADING. See Chapter 28 if you are required to submit your report in a writing PORTFOLIO.

226–28
229–34
235–41
242–46
247–58

Lab Reports 13

Lab reports describe the procedures and results of experiments in the natural sciences, the social sciences, and engineering. We write reports of lab work in school to show instructors that we have followed certain procedures, achieved appropriate results, and drawn accurate conclusions. On the job, lab reports not only describe what we did and what we learned; they may also present data and interpretations to attempt to persuade others to accept our hypotheses, and they become a record that others may refer to in the future. As an example, here is a lab report written by a student for a psychology class at Wittenberg University.

SARAH THOMAS

The Effect of Biofeedback Training on Muscle Tension and Skin Temperature

Purpose

The purpose of this lab was for subjects to train themselves to increase their skin temperature, measured on the index finger of their non-dominant hand, and to decrease their muscle tension, measured over the frontalis muscle, by using biofeedback training. This study is based on the research of Miller and Brucker (1979), which demonstrated that smooth muscles could experience operant conditioning.

Methods

Subjects

Seven subjects were used in this study: five female and two male. The subjects were the undergraduate students of Dr. Jo Wilson in her honors psychophysiology class at Wittenberg University in Springfield, Ohio. All subjects were in their early twenties.

Apparatus

Equipment used in this lab included an Apple Microlab system configured to measure (1) skin temperature through a thermode taped with paper surgical tape onto the index finger of the subjects' nondominant hand and (2) frontalis muscle tension via three electrodes placed over the frontalis. When subjects' skin temperatures were more than the means for the previous 90-second intervals, the computer emitted a tone. It also emitted a tone when muscle tension in the frontalis was less than the mean of the previous interval. See the procedure section for exact electrode placement specifications.

Materials

Materials used in this lab included paper surgical tape, alcohol to clean off the forehead, conducting gel, wire, electrode collars, and a chair.

Procedure

5 Upon arriving at the lab, the researchers turned on the Apple Microlab computer. With the aid of Dr. Wilson, subjects had either electrodes attached to their forehead or a thermode attached to the nondominant hand's index finger. The treatment order was random for each subject, and it was reversed for his or her second biofeedback session. The forehead was swiped with alcohol to clean the skin. Electrodes with conducting gel were placed over the frontalis muscle by putting the ground electrode in the center of the forehead and the white electrodes two inches on either side of the center of the forehead. Premeasured electrode collars allowed the researchers to place the conducting gel on the electrodes, peel off the backing on the collar, and place it on the subjects' forehead. The researchers still made sure the electrodes were placed properly. The wire running from the electrodes to the computer was then taped to the subjects' back so it would be out of the way. Subjects were then seated in a comfortable chair with their back to the computer.

Depending on the experimental condition, subjects were told to reduce their frontalis muscle tension by relaxing and even thinking of holding something warm in their hands. They were told that they would know they were meeting the goal when they heard a tone emitted by the computer.

Each session began with a 90-second baseline period, followed by fifteen 90-second trial periods. During each trial period, a tone was emitted by the computer each time the subjects' frontalis muscle tension was below their mean tension for the previous trial; the tone served as the rewarding stimulus in the operant conditioning paradigm.

When skin temperature was to be measured, a thermode was attached to the index finger of the subjects' nondominant hand with surgical tape. The wire running from the thermode to the computer was taped to the back of their hand so it would be out of their way. Then a 90-second baseline period occurred, followed by fifteen 90-second trial periods. During each trial period, a tone was emitted by the computer each time the subjects' skin temperature was above their mean temperature for the previous trial; once again, the tone served as the rewarding stimulus in the operant conditioning paradigm.

Results

The results of this lab were generally similar (Tables 1 and 2). All subjects demonstrated the ability to increase their skin temperature and decrease the tension in their frontalis muscle in at least one of their sessions. Five subjects were able to increase their skin temperature in both sessions; the same number decreased their muscle tension in both trials.

The majority of subjects (five) were able to both increase the skin 10
temperature of the index finger of their nondominant hand and decrease the tension of their frontalis muscle more during the second trial than the first.

Specifically, subject 7 had atypical results. This subject's overall average skin temperature was less than the baseline value; the subject's overall average muscle tension was more than the baseline value.

Discussion

The bulk of the data collected in this study validated the research of Neal Miller; the subjects appeared to undergo operant conditioning of their smooth muscles in order to relax their frontalis muscles and increase their skin temperatures. Subjects 3 and 6 each failed to do this in one session; subject 7 failed to do this several times. This finding is difficult to explain precisely. It is possible that for subjects 3 and 6, this

Table 1
Skin Temperature in Degrees Fahrenheit during Sessions 1 and 2

	Subject 1	Subject 2	Subject 3	Subject 4	Subject 5	Subject 6	Subject 7
Baseline, Session 1	75.2	77.3	78.5	74.3	78.0	67.7	75.1
Mean skin temp, Session 1	79.3	85.6	78.5	74.4	83.2	73.5	72.6
Mean minus baseline, Session 1	4.1	8.3	0.0	0.1	5.2	5.8	−2.5
Baseline, Session 2	77.9	80.1	69.5	80.9	67.2	73.7	88.0
Mean skin temp, Session 2	79.9	86.3	70.7	84.6	76.8	79.7	88.8
Mean minus baseline, Session 2	2.0	6.2	1.2	3.7	9.6	6.0	0.8
Overall average of mean skin temp minus baseline	3.1	7.3	0.6	1.9	7.4	5.9	−0.85

data was a fluke. For subject 7, it is likely that the subject was simply stressed due to outside factors before arriving for the first trials of EMG and skin temperature, and this stress skewed the data.

The effect of biofeedback training was generally greater as the operant conditioning became better learned. Learning was indicated by the finding that the majority of the subjects performed better on the second trials than on the first trials. This finding shows the effectiveness of

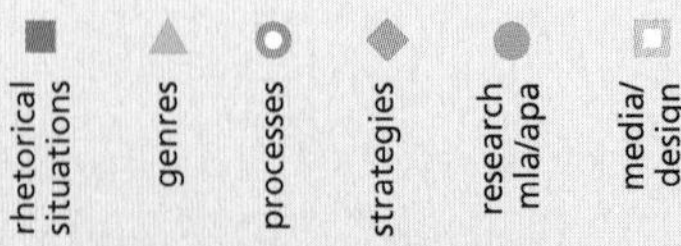

Table 2
EMG of the Frontalis Muscle in Microvolts for Sessions 1 and 2

	Subject 1	Subject 2	Subject 3	Subject 4	Subject 5	Subject 6	Subject 7
Baseline, Session 1	4.4	4.5	2.8	3.8	7.9	3.1	2.4
Mean EMG, Session 1	2.1	1.4	1.7	3.2	2.0	3.7	3.2
Baseline minus mean, Session 1	2.3	3.1	1.1	0.6	5.9	−0.6	−0.8
Baseline, Session 2	4.1	2.3	3.0	2.9	11.1	6.5	1.9
Mean EMG, Session 2	1.3	1.3	1.4	2.3	2.5	3.2	1.4
Baseline minus mean, Session 2	2.8	1.0	1.6	0.6	8.6	3.3	0.5
Overall average of mean EMG minus baseline	2.6	2.1	1.4	0.6	7.3	1.4	−0.15

biofeedback on reducing factors associated with stress, like muscle tension and low skin temperature; biofeedback's impact is even greater when it is administered over time. The implications of this information are without limits, especially for the treatment of a variety of medical disorders.

There were a few problems with this lab. The subjects all were at different levels of relaxation to begin with. It is impossible to determine the effects of outside events, like exams or other stresses, on their EMG and skin temperature levels. Skin temperature itself could have been altered by cold outside temperatures. Being in a lab may have altered the stress level of some subjects, and noises from outside the lab may have had an effect as well.

If this study were repeated, it would be a good idea to let sub- 15
jects simply be in the lab for a period of time before measures are taken. This would allow the effect of outside temperature to be minimized. It would also reduce the effect of getting used to the lab, decreasing the orienting response. Finally, it would also be good to do the experiment in a soundproof room.

Reference

Miller, N. E., & Brucker, B. S. (1979). A learned visceral response apparently independent of skeletal ones in patients paralyzed by spinal lesions. In N. Birnbaumer & H. D. Kimmel (Eds.), *Biofeedback and self-regulation* (pp. 287–304). Hillsdale, NJ: Erlbaum.

This report includes sections commonly part of lab reports in the natural and social sciences: purpose, method, results, discussion, and references. Some reports keep results and discussion in one section; some reports include an abstract; and some reports include one or more appendices containing tables, calculations, and other supplemental material, depending on the audience and publication. In this example, the author assumes that her audience understands basic terms used in the report, such as frontalis muscle and biofeedback.

Key Features / Lab Reports

An explicit title. Lab report titles should describe the report factually and explicitly to let readers know exactly what the report is about and to provide key words for indexes and search engines. Avoid phrases like "an Investigation into" or "a Study of" and titles that are clever or cute. Thomas's title, "The Effect of Biofeedback Training on Muscle Tension and Skin Temperature," clearly describes the report's subject and includes the key words needed for indexing (*biofeedback training, muscle tension, skin temperature*).

Abstract. Some lab reports include a one-paragraph, 100–200-word abstract, a summary of the report's purpose, method, and discussion.

Purpose. Sometimes called an "Introduction," this section describes the reason for conducting the study: Why is this research important, and why are you doing it? What has been done by others, and how does your work relate to previous work? What will your research tell us?

Methods. Here you describe how you conducted the study, including the materials and equipment you used and the procedures you followed. This is usually written as a narrative, explaining the process you followed in order to allow others to repeat your study, step-by-step. Your discussion should thoroughly describe the following:

- subjects studied and any necessary contextual information
- apparatus—equipment used, by brand and model number
- materials used
- procedures—including reference to the published work that describes any procedures you used that someone else had already followed; the techniques you used and any modifications you made to them; any statistical methods you used

Results and discussion. Here you analyze the results and present their implications, explain your logic in accepting or rejecting your initial hypotheses, relate your work to previous work in the field, and discuss the experiment's design and techniques and how they may have affected the results: what did you find out, and what does it mean? In longer reports, you may have two separate sections. "Results" should focus on the factual data you collected by doing the study; "Discussion" should speculate about what the study means: why the results turned out as they did, and what the implications for future studies may be.

References. List works cited in your report, alphabetized by author's last name and using the appropriate documentation style.

Appendices. Appendices are optional, presenting information that is too detailed for the body of the report.

Appropriate format. The design conventions for lab reports vary from discipline to discipline, so you'll need to check to see that yours meets the appropriate requirements. Find out whether any sections need to start their own page, whether you need to include a list of figures, whether you need to include a separate title page—and whether there are any other conventions you need to follow.

A BRIEF GUIDE TO WRITING LAB REPORTS

Considering the Rhetorical Situation

3–4 **PURPOSE** Why are you writing? To demonstrate your ability to follow the appropriate methods and make logical inferences? To persuade others that your hypotheses are sound and your conclusions believable? To provide a record of the experiment for others?

5–8 **AUDIENCE** Can you assume that your audience is familiar with the field's basic procedures? How routine were your procedures? Which procedures need to be explained in greater detail so your audience can repeat them?

12–14 **STANCE** Lab reports need to have an impersonal, analytical stance. Take care not to be too informal, and don't try to be cute.

15–17 **MEDIA / DESIGN** Are you planning to deliver your report in print or online? All lab reports have headings; choose a typeface that includes bold or italics so your headings will show clearly.

Generating Ideas and Text

Research your subject. Researchers do not work in isolation; rather, each study contributes to an ever-growing body of information, and you need to situate your work in that context. **RESEARCH** what studies 373 others have done on the same subject and what procedures they followed.

Take careful notes as you perform your study. A lab report must be repeatable. Another researcher should be able to duplicate your study exactly, using only your report as a guide, so you must document every method, material, apparatus, and procedure carefully. Break down procedures and activities into discrete parts, and record them in the order in which they occurred. **ANALYZE CAUSES AND EFFECTS;** think about whether 278–82 you should **COMPARE** your findings with other studies. Take careful notes 306–13 so that you'll be able to **EXPLAIN PROCESSES** you followed. 338–42

Draft the report a section at a time. You may find it easiest to start with the "Methods" or "Results" section first, then **DRAFT** the "Discussion," 226–28 followed by the "Purpose." Do the "Abstract" last.

- Write in complete sentences and paragraphs.
- Avoid using the first person *I* or *we*; keep the focus on the study and the actions taken.
- Use the active voice as much as possible ("the rats pushed the lever" rather than "the lever was pushed by the rats").
- Use the past tense throughout the report.
- Place subjects and verbs close together to make your sentences easy to follow.
- Use precise terms consistently throughout the report; don't alternate among synonyms.
- Be sure that each pronoun refers clearly to one noun.

Organizing a Lab Report

Lab reports vary in their details but generally include these sections:

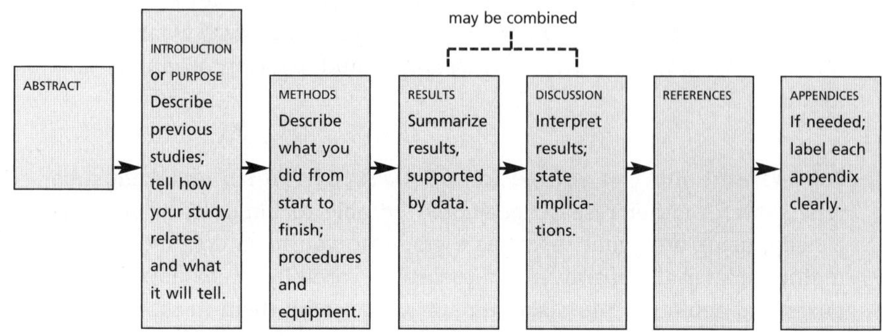
may be combined
ABSTRACT
INTRODUCTION or PURPOSE
Describe previous studies; tell how your study relates and what it will tell.
METHODS
Describe what you did from start to finish; procedures and equipment.
RESULTS
Summarize results, supported by data.
DISCUSSION
Interpret results; state implications.
REFERENCES
APPENDICES
If needed; label each appendix clearly.

229–34
235–41
242–46
247–58

IF YOU NEED MORE HELP

See Chapter 25 on **ASSESSING YOUR OWN WRITING**, Chapter 26 on **GETTING RESPONSE AND REVISING**, and Chapter 27 on **EDITING AND PROOFREADING**. See Chapter 28 if you are required to submit your report in a writing **PORTFOLIO**.

Literary Analyses **14**

Literary analyses are essays in which we examine literary texts closely to understand their messages, interpret their meanings, and appreciate their writers' techniques. You might read *Macbeth* and notice that Shakespeare's play contains a pattern of images of blood. You could explore the distinctive point of view in Ambrose Bierce's story "An Occurrence at Owl Creek Bridge." Or you could point out the differences between Stephen King's *The Shining* and Stanley Kubrick's screenplay based on that novel. In all these cases, you use specific analytical tools to go below the surface of the work to deepen your understanding of how it works and what it means. Here is a sonnet by the nineteenth-century English Romantic poet Percy Bysshe Shelley, followed by one student's analysis of it written for a literature course at Wright State University.

PERCY BYSSHE SHELLEY

Sonnet: "Lift not the painted veil which those who live"

Lift not the painted veil which those who live
Call Life: though unreal shapes be pictured there,
And it but mimic all we would believe
With colours idly spread,—behind, lurk Fear
And Hope, twin Destinies; who ever weave
Their shadows, o'er the chasm, sightless and drear.
I knew one who had lifted it—he sought,
For his lost heart was tender, things to love,
But found them not, alas! nor was there aught

The world contains, the which he could approve.
Through the unheeding many he did move,
A splendour among shadows, a bright blot
Upon this gloomy scene, a Spirit that strove
For truth, and like the Preacher found it not.

STEPHANIE HUFF

Metaphor and Society in Shelley's "Sonnet"

In his sonnet "Lift not the painted veil which those who live," Percy Bysshe Shelley introduces us to a bleak world that exists behind veils and shadows. We see that although fear and hope both exist, truth is dishearteningly absent. This absence of truth is exactly what Shelley chooses to address as he uses metaphors of grim distortion and radiant incandescence to expose the counterfeit nature of our world.

The speaker of Shelley's poem presents bold assertions about the nature of our society. In the opening lines of the poem, he warns the reader to "Lift not the painted veil which those who live / Call Life" (1–2). Here, the "painted veil" serves as a grim metaphor for life. More specifically, the speaker equates the veil with what people like to *call* life. In this sense, the speaker asserts that what we believe to be pure reality is actually nothing more than a covering that masks what really lies beneath. Truth is covered by a veil of falsehood and is made opaque with the paint of people's lies.

This painted veil does not completely obstruct our view, but rather distorts what we can see. All that can be viewed through it are "unreal shapes" (2) that metaphorically represent the people that make up this counterfeit society. These shapes are not to be taken for truth. They are unreal, twisted, deformed figures of humanity, people full of falsities and misrepresentations.

Most people, however, do not realize that the shapes and images seen through the veil are distorted because all they know of life is the veil—this life we see as reality only "mimic[s] all we would believe" (3), using "colours idly spread" (4) to create pictures that bear little resemblance to that which they claim to portray. All pure truths are covered up and painted over until they are mere mockeries. The lies that cloak the truth are not even carefully constructed, but are created idly, with little attention to detail. The paint is not applied carefully, but merely spread across the top. This idea of spreading brings to mind images of paint slopped on so heavily that the truth beneath becomes nearly impossible to find. Even the metaphor of color suggests only superficial beauty—"idly spread" (4)—rather than any sort of pure beauty that could penetrate the surface of appearances.

What really lies behind this facade are fear and hope, both of which 5
"weave / Their shadows, o'er the chasm, sightless and drear" (5–6). These two realities are never truly seen or experienced, though. They exist only as shadows. Just as shadows appear only at certain times of day, cast only sham images of what they reflect, and are paid little attention, so too do these emotions of hope and fear appear only as brief, ignored imitations of themselves when they enter the artificiality of this chasmlike world. Peering into a chasm, one cannot hope to make out what lies at the bottom. At best one could perhaps make out shadows and even that cannot be done with any certainty as to true appearance. The world is so large, so caught up in itself and its counterfeit ways, that it can no longer see even the simple truths of hope and fear. Individuals and civilizations have become sightless, dreary, and as enormously empty as a chasm.

This chasm does not include *all* people, however, as we are introduced to one individual, in line 7, who is trying to bring to light whatever truth may yet remain. This one person, who defies the rest of the world, is portrayed with metaphors of light, clearly standing out among the dark representations of the rest of mankind. He is first presented to us as possessing a "lost heart" (8) and seeking things to love. It is important that the first metaphor applied to him be a heart because this is the organ with which we associate love, passion, and purity. We associate it with brightness of the soul, making it the most radiant spot of the body. He is then described as a "splendour among shadows" (12), his purity and truth brilliantly shining through the darkness of the majority's falsehood. Finally, he is equated with "a bright blot / Upon this gloomy scene" (12–13), his own bright blaze of authenticity burning in stark contrast to the murky phoniness of the rest of the world.

These metaphors of light are few, however, in comparison to those of grim distortion. So, too, are this one individual's radiance and zeal too little to alter the warped darkness they temporarily pierce. This one person, though bright, is not bright enough to light up the rest of civilization and create real change. The light simply confirms the dark falsity that comprises the rest of the world. Shelley gives us one flame of hope, only to reveal to us what little chance it has under the suffocating veil. Both the metaphors of grim distortion and those of radiant incandescence work together in this poem to highlight the world's counterfeit nature.

For five more literary analyses, see CHAPTER 59.

Huff focuses her analysis on patterns in Shelley's imagery. In addition, she pays careful attention to individual words and to how, as the poem unfolds, they create a certain meaning. That meaning is her interpretation.

Key Features / Literary Analyses

An arguable thesis. A literary analysis is a form of argument; you are arguing that your analysis of a literary work is valid. Your thesis, then, should be arguable, as Huff's is: "[Shelley] uses metaphors of grim distortion and radiant incandescence to expose the counterfeit nature of our world." A mere summary—"Shelley writes about a person who sees reality and seeks love but never finds it"—would not be arguable and therefore is not a good thesis.

Careful attention to the language of the text. The key to analyzing a text is looking carefully at the language, which is the foundation of its meaning. Specific words, images, metaphors—these are where analysis begins. You may also bring in contextual information, such as cultural, historical, or biographical facts, or you may refer to similar texts. But the words, phrases, and sentences that make up the text you are analyzing are your primary source when dealing with texts. That's what literature teachers mean by "close reading": reading with the assumption that every word of a text is meaningful.

Attention to patterns or themes. Literary analyses are usually built on evidence of meaningful patterns or themes within a text or among several texts. These patterns and themes reveal meaning. In Shelley's poem, images of light and shadow and artifice and reality create patterns of meaning, while the poem's many half rhymes (*live/believe, love/approve*) create patterns of sound that may contribute to the overall meaning.

A clear interpretation. A literary analysis demonstrates the plausibility of its thesis by using evidence from the text and, sometimes, relevant contextual evidence to explain how the language and patterns found there support a particular interpretation. When you write a literary analysis, you show readers one way the text may be read and understood; that is your interpretation.

MLA style. Literary analyses usually follow MLA style. Even though Huff's essay has no works-cited list, it refers to line numbers using MLA style.

A BRIEF GUIDE TO WRITING LITERARY ANALYSES

Considering the Rhetorical Situation

PURPOSE What do you need to do? Show that you have examined the text carefully? Offer your own interpretation? Demonstrate a particular analytical technique? Or some combination? If you're responding to an assignment, does it specify what you need to do? 3–4

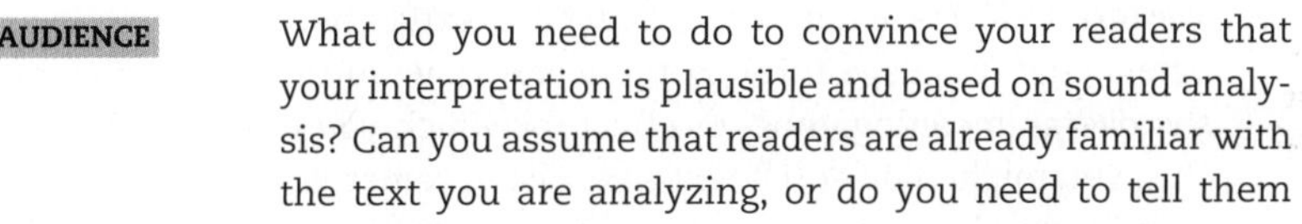

AUDIENCE What do you need to do to convince your readers that your interpretation is plausible and based on sound analysis? Can you assume that readers are already familiar with the text you are analyzing, or do you need to tell them about it? 5–8

STANCE How can you see your subject through interested, curious eyes—and then step back in order to see what your observations might *mean*? 12–14

MEDIA / DESIGN Will your analysis focus on a print text and take the form of a print text? If your subject is a visual or electronic medium, will you need to show significant elements in your analysis? Are you required to follow MLA or some other style? 15–18

Generating Ideas and Text

Look at your assignment. Does it specify a particular kind of analysis? Does it ask you to consider a particular theme? To use any specific critical approaches? Look for any terms that tell you what to do, words like *analyze*, *compare*, *interpret*, and so on.

Study the text with a critical eye. When we read a literary work, we often come away with a reaction to it: we like it, we hate it, it made us cry or laugh, it perplexed us. That may be a good starting point for a literary analysis, but students of literature need to go beyond initial reactions, to think about **HOW THE TEXT WORKS**: What does it *say*, and what does it *do*? What elements make up this text? How do those elements work together or fail to work together? Does this text lead you to think or feel a certain way? How does it fit into a particular context (of history, culture, technology, genre, and so on)?

358–60

Choose a method for analyzing the text. There are various ways to analyze your subject. Three common focuses are on the text itself, on your own experience reading it, and on other cultural, historical, or literary contexts.

- ***The text itself.*** Trace the development and expression of themes, characters, and language through the work. How do they help to create the overall meaning, tone, or effect for which you're arguing? To do this, you might look at the text as a whole, something you can understand from all angles at once. You could also pick out parts from the beginning, middle, and end as needed to make your case, **DEFINING** key terms, **DESCRIBING** characters and settings, and **NARRATING** key scenes. The example essay about the Shelley sonnet offers a text-based analysis that looks at patterns of images in the poem. You might also examine the same theme in several different works.

314–23
324–32
343–51

- ***Your own response as a reader.*** Explore the way the text affects you or develops meanings as you read through it from beginning to end. By doing such a close reading, you're slowing down the process to notice how one element of the text leads you to expect something, confirming earlier suspicions or surprises. You build your analysis on your experience of reading the text—as if you were pretending to drive somewhere for the first time, though in reality you know the way intimately. By closely examining the language of the text as you experience it, you explore how it leads you to a set of responses, both intellectual and emotional. If you were responding in this way to the Shelley poem, you might discuss how its first lines suggest that while life is an illusion, a veil, one might pull it aside and glimpse reality, however "drear."

- *Context.* Analyze the text as part of some **LARGER CONTEXT**—as part of a certain time or place in history or as an expression of a certain culture (how does this text relate to the time and place of its creation?), as one of many other texts like it, a representative of a genre (how is this text like or unlike others of its kind? how does it use, play with, or flout the conventions of the genre?). A context-based approach to the Shelley poem might look at Shelley's own philosophical and religious views and how they may have influenced the poem's characterization of the world we experience as illusory, a "veil." 365–66

Read the work more than once. Reading literature, watching films, or listening to speeches is like driving to a new destination: the first time you go, you need to concentrate on getting there; on subsequent trips, you can see other aspects—the scenery, the curve of the road, other possible routes—that you couldn't pay attention to earlier. When you experience a piece of literature for the first time, you usually focus on the story, the plot, the overall meaning. By experiencing it repeatedly, you can see how its effects are achieved, what the pieces are and how they fit together, where different patterns emerge, how the author crafted the work. To analyze a literary work, then, plan to read it more than once, with the assumption that every part of the text is there for a reason. Focus on details, even on a single detail that shows up more than once: Why is it there? What can it mean? How does it affect our experience of reading or studying the text? Also, look for anomalies, details that *don't* fit the patterns: Why are they part of the text? What can they mean? How do they affect the experience of the text? See the **READING STRATEGIES** chapter for several different methods for reading a text.  352–66

273–75 **Compose a strong thesis.** The **THESIS** of a literary analysis should be specific, limited, and open to potential disagreement. In addition, it should be analytical, not evaluative: avoid thesis statements that make overall judgments, such as a reviewer might do: "Virginia Woolf's *The Waves* is a failed experiment in narrative" or "No one has equaled the achievement of *The Matrix* trilogy." Rather, offer a way of seeing the text: "The choice presented in Robert Frost's 'The Road Not Taken' ultimately makes no difference"; "The plot of *The Matrix Reloaded* reflects the politics of America after 9/11."

Do a close reading. When you analyze a text, you need to find specific, brief passages that support your interpretation. Then you should interpret those passages in terms of their language, their context, or your reaction to them as a reader. To find such passages, you must read the text closely, questioning it as you go, asking, for example:

- What language provides evidence to support your thesis?
- What does each word (phrase, passage) mean exactly?
- Why does the writer choose *this* language, *these* words? What are the implications or connotations of the language? If the language is dense or difficult, why might the writer have written it that way?
- What images or metaphors are used? What is their effect on the meaning?
- 361–63 What **PATTERNS** of language, imagery, or plot do you see? If something is repeated, what significance does the repetition have?
- How does each word, phrase, or passage relate to what precedes and follows it?
- How does the experience of reading the text affect its meaning?
- 365–66 What words, phrases, or passages connect to a larger **CONTEXT**? What language demonstrates that this work reflects or is affected by that context?
- How do these various elements of language, image, and pattern support your interpretation?

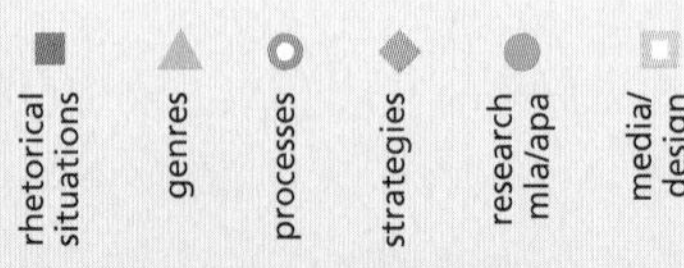

Your analysis should focus on analyzing and interpreting your subject, not simply summarizing or paraphrasing it. Many literary analyses also use the strategy of **COMPARING** two or more works. 306–13

Find evidence to support your interpretation. The parts of the text you examine in your close reading become the evidence you use to support your interpretation. Some think that we're all entitled to our own opinions about literature. And indeed we are. But when writing a literary analysis, we're entitled only to our own *well-supported* and *well-argued* opinions. When you analyze a text, you must treat it like any other **ARGUMENT**: 283–99 you need to discuss how the text creates an effect or expresses a theme, and then you have to show **EVIDENCE** 287–93 from the text — significant plot or structural elements; important characters; patterns of language, imagery, or action — to back up your argument.

Pay attention to matters of style. Literary analyses have certain conventions for using pronouns and verbs.

- In informal papers, it's okay to use the first person: "I believe Frost's narrator has little basis for claiming that one road is 'less traveled.'" In more formal essays, make assertions directly; claim authority to make statements about the text: "Frost's narrator has no basis for claiming that one road is 'less traveled.'"
- Discuss textual features in the present tense even if quotations from the text are in another tense: "When Nick finds Gatsby's body floating in the pool, he says very little about it: 'the laden mattress moved irregularly down the pool.'" Describe the historical context of the setting in the past tense: "In the 1920s, such estates as Gatsby's were rare."

Cite and document sources appropriately. Use **MLA** 428–76 citation and documentation style unless told otherwise. Format **QUOTATIONS** 410–13 properly, and use **SIGNAL PHRASES** 417–18 when need be.

Think about format and design. Brief essays do not require **HEADINGS**; 526–27 text divisions are usually marked by **TRANSITIONS** 277 between paragraphs. In longer papers, though, heads can be helpful.

Organizing a Literary Analysis

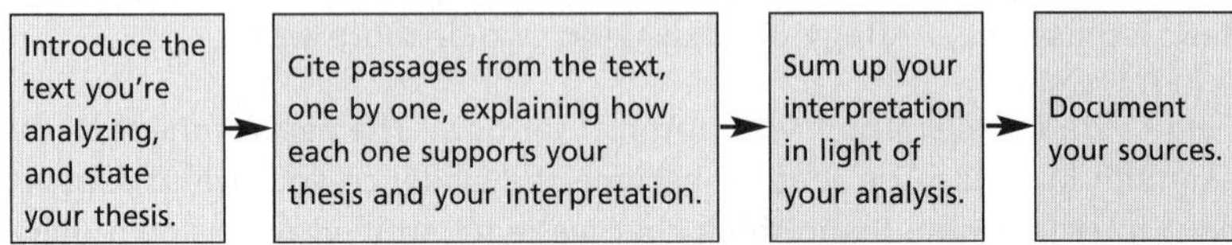

Document your sources.

226–28
229–34
235–41
242–46
247–58

IF YOU NEED MORE HELP

See Chapter 24 for guidelines on DRAFTING, Chapter 25 on ASSESSING YOUR OWN WRITING, Chapter 26 on GETTING RESPONSE AND REVISING, and Chapter 27 on EDITING AND PROOFREADING. See Chapter 28 if you are required to submit your analysis in a writing PORTFOLIO.

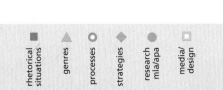

research mla/apa

Memoirs 15

We write memoirs to explore our past—about shopping for a party dress with Grandma, or driving a car for the first time, or breaking up with our first love. *Memoirs* focus on events and people and places that are important to us. We usually have two goals when we write a memoir: to capture an important moment and to convey something about its significance for us. The following example is from *All Over But the Shoutin'*, the 1997 autobiography by Rick Bragg, a former reporter for the *New York Times*. Bragg grew up in Alabama, and in this memoir he recalls when, as a teenager, he paid a final visit to his dying father.

RICK BRAGG

All Over But the Shoutin'

He was living in a little house in Jacksonville, Alabama, a college and mill town that was the closest urban center—with its stoplights and a high school and two supermarkets—to the country roads we roamed in our raggedy cars. He lived in the mill village, in one of those houses the mills subsidized for their workers, back when companies still did things like that. It was not much of a place, but better than anything we had ever lived in as a family. I knocked and a voice like an old woman's, punctuated with a cough that sounded like it came from deep in the guts, told me to come on in, it ain't locked. It was dark inside, but light enough to see what looked like a bundle of quilts on the corner of a sofa. Deep inside them was a ghost of a man, his hair and beard long and going dirty gray, his face pale and cut with deep grooves. I knew I was in the right house because my daddy's only real possessions, a velvet-covered board pinned with medals, sat inside a glass cabinet on a table. But this couldn't be him.

He coughed again, spit into a can and struggled to his feet, but stopped somewhere short of standing straight up, as if a stoop was all he could manage. "Hey, Cotton Top," he said, and then I knew. My daddy, who was supposed to be a still-young man, looked like the walking dead, not just old but damaged, poisoned, used up, crumpled up and thrown in a corner to die. I thought that the man I would see would be the trim, swaggering, high-toned little rooster of a man who stared back at me from the pages of my mother's photo album, the young soldier clowning around in Korea, the arrow-straight, good-looking boy who posed beside my mother back before the fields and mophandle and the rest of it took her looks. The man I remembered had always dressed nice even when there was no cornmeal left, whose black hair always shone with oil, whose chin, even when it wobbled from the beer, was always angled up, high.

I thought he would greet me with that strong voice that sounded so fine when he laughed and so evil when, slurred by a quart of corn likker, he whirled through the house and cried and shrieked, tormented by things we could not see or even imagine. I thought he would be the man and monster of my childhood. But that man was as dead as a man could be, and this was what remained, like when a snake sheds its skin and leaves a dry and brittle husk of itself hanging in the Johnson grass.

"It's all over but the shoutin' now, ain't it, boy," he said, and when he let the quilt slide from his shoulders I saw how he had wasted away, how the bones seemed to poke out of his clothes, and I could see how it killed his pride to look this way, unclean, and he looked away from me for a moment, ashamed.

5 He made a halfhearted try to shake my hand but had a coughing fit again that lasted a minute, coughing up his life, his lungs, and after that I did not want to touch him. I stared at the tops of my sneakers, ashamed to look at his face. He had a dark streak in his beard below his lip, and I wondered why, because he had never liked snuff. Now I know it was blood.

I remember much of what he had to say that day. When you don't see someone for eight, nine years, when you see that person's life red on their lips and know that you will never see them beyond this day, you listen close, even if what you want most of all is to run away.

"Your momma, she alright?" he said.

I said I reckon so.

"The other boys? They alright?"

I said I reckon so.

Then he was quiet for a minute, as if trying to find the words to a question to which he did not really want an answer.

"They ain't never come to see me. How come?"

I remember thinking, fool, why do you think? But I just choked down my words, and in doing so I gave up the only real chance I would ever have to accuse him, to attack him with the facts of his own sorry nature and the price it had cost us all. The opportunity hung perfectly still in the air in front of my face and fists, and I held my temper and let it float on by. I could have no more challenged him, berated him, hurt him, than I could have kicked some three-legged dog. Life had kicked his ass pretty good.

"How come?"

I just shrugged.

For the next few hours — unless I was mistaken, having never had one before — he tried to be my father. Between coughing and long pauses when he fought for air to generate his words, he asked me if I liked school, if I had ever gotten any better at math, the one thing that just flat evaded me. He asked me if I ever got even with the boy who blacked my eye ten years ago, and nodded his head, approvingly, as I described how I followed him into the boys' bathroom and knocked his dick string up to his watch pocket, and would have dunked his head in the urinal if the aging principal, Mr. Hand, had not had to pee and caught me dragging him across the concrete floor.

He asked me about basketball and baseball, said he had heard I had a good game against Cedar Springs, and I said pretty good, but it was two years ago, anyway. He asked if I had a girlfriend and I said, "One," and he said, "Just one?" For the slimmest of seconds he almost grinned and the young, swaggering man peeked through, but disappeared again in the disease that cloaked him. He talked and talked and never said a word, at least not the words I wanted.

He never said he was sorry.

He never said he wished things had turned out different.

He never acted like he did anything wrong.

Part of it, I know, was culture. Men did not talk about their feelings in his hard world. I did not expect, even for a second, that he would bare his soul. All I wanted was a simple acknowledgment that he was wrong, or at least too drunk to notice that he left his pretty wife and sons alone again and again, with no food, no money, no way to get any, short of begging, because when she tried to find work he yelled, screamed, refused. No, I didn't expect much.

After a while he motioned for me to follow him into a back room where he had my present, and I planned to take it and run. He handed me a long, thin box, and inside was a brand-new, well-oiled Remington .22 rifle. He said he had bought it some time back, just kept forgetting to give it to me. It was a fine gun, and for a moment we were just like anybody else in the culture of that place, where a father's gift of a gun to his son is a rite. He said, with absolute seriousness, not to shoot my brothers.

I thanked him and made to leave, but he stopped me with a hand on my arm and said wait, that ain't all, that he had some other things for me. He motioned to three big cardboard egg cartons stacked against one wall.

Inside was the only treasure I truly have ever known.

I had grown up in a house in which there were only two books, the 25
King James Bible and the spring seed catalog. But here, in these boxes, were dozens of hardback copies of everything from Mark Twain to Sir Arthur Conan Doyle. There was a water-damaged Faulkner, and the nearly complete set of Edgar Rice Burroughs's *Tarzan*. There was poetry and trash, Zane Grey's *Riders of the Purple Sage,* and a paperback with two naked women on the cover. There was a tiny, old copy of *Arabian Nights,* threadbare Hardy Boys, and one Hemingway. He had bought most of them at a yard sale, by the box or pound, and some at a flea market. He did not even know what he was giving me, did not recognize most of the writers. "Your momma said you still liked to read," he said.

There was Shakespeare. My father did not know who he was, exactly, but he had heard the name. He wanted them because they were pretty, because they were wrapped in fake leather, because they looked like rich folks' books. I do not love Shakespeare, but I still have those books. I would not trade them for a gold monkey.

"They's maybe some dirty books in there, by mistake, but I know you ain't interested in them, so just throw 'em away," he said. "Or at least, throw 'em away before your momma sees 'em." And then I swear to God he winked.

I guess my heart should have broken then, and maybe it did, a little. I guess I should have done something, anything, besides mumble

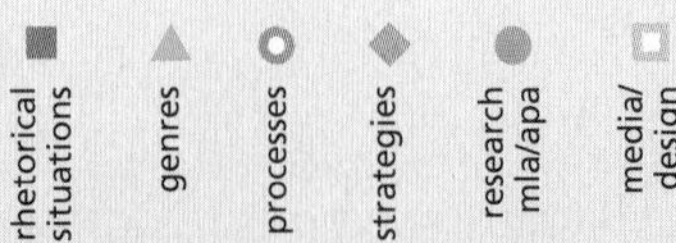

> "Thank you, Daddy." I guess that would have been fine, would not have betrayed in some way my mother, my brothers, myself. But I just stood there, trapped somewhere between my long-standing, comfortable hatred, and what might have been forgiveness. I am trapped there still.

Bragg's memoir illustrates all the features that make a memoir good: how the son and father react to each other creates the kind of suspense that keeps us reading; vivid details and rich dialogue bring the scene to life. His later reflections make the significance of that final meeting very clear.

For five more memoirs, see CHAPTER 60.

Key Features / Memoirs

A good story. Your memoir should be interesting, to yourself and others. It need not be about a world-shaking event, but your topic—and how you write about it—should interest your readers. At the center of most good stories stands a conflict or question to be resolved. The most compelling memoirs feature some sort of situation or problem that needs resolution. That need for resolution is another name for suspense. It's what makes us want to keep reading.

Vivid details. Details bring a memoir to life by giving readers mental images of the sights, sounds, smells, tastes, and textures of the world in which your story takes place. The goal is to show as well as tell, to take readers there. When Bragg describes a "voice like an old woman's, punctuated with a cough that sounded like it came from deep in the guts," we can hear his dying father ourselves. A memoir is more than simply a report of what happened; it uses vivid details and dialogue to bring the events of the past to life, much as good fiction brings to life events that the writer makes up or embellishes.

Clear significance. Memories of the past are filtered through our view from the present: we pick out some moments in our lives as significant, some as more important or vivid than others. Over time, our interpretations change, and our memories themselves change.

A good memoir conveys something about the significance of its subject. As a writer, you need to reveal something about what the incident means to you. You don't, however, want to simply announce the significance as if you're tacking on the moral of the story. Bragg tells us that he's "trapped between [his] long-standing, comfortable hatred, and what might have been forgiveness," but he doesn't come right out and say that's why the incident is so important to him.

A BRIEF GUIDE TO WRITING MEMOIRS

Choosing an Event to Write About

220–21

LIST several events or incidents from your past that you consider significant in some way. They do not have to be earthshaking; indeed, they may involve a quiet moment that only you see as important — a brief encounter with a remarkable person, a visit to a special place, a memorable achievement (or failure), something that makes you laugh whenever you think about it. Writing about events that happened at least a few years ago is often easier than writing about recent events because you can more easily step back and see those events with a clear perspective. To choose the event that you will write about, consider how well you can recall what happened, how interesting it will be to readers, and whether you want to share it with an audience.

Considering the Rhetorical Situation

3–4

PURPOSE What is the importance of the memory you are trying to convey? How will this story help your readers (and you yourself) understand you, as you were then and as you are now?

5–8

AUDIENCE Who are your readers? What do you want them to think of you after reading your memoir? How can you help them understand your experience?

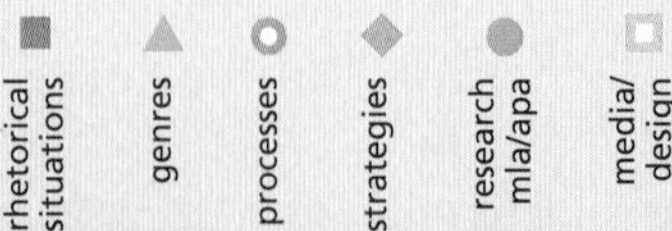

STANCE What impression do you want to give, and how can your words contribute to that impression? What tone do you want to project? Sincere? Serious? Humorous? Detached? Self-critical? 12–14

MEDIA / DESIGN Will your memoir be a print document? A speech? Will it be posted on a website? Will you include illustrations, audio or video clips, or other visual texts? 15–17

Generating Ideas and Text

Think about what happened. Take a few minutes to write out an account of the incident: **WHAT** happened, **WHERE** it took place, **WHO** else was involved, what was said, how you feel about it, and so on. Can you identify any tension or conflict that will make for a compelling story? If not, you might want to rethink your topic. 222–23

Consider its significance. Why do you still remember this event? What effect has it had on your life? What makes you want to tell someone else about it? Does it say anything about you? What about it might interest someone else? If you have trouble answering these questions, you should probably find another topic. But in general, once you have defined the significance of the incident, you can be sure you have a story to tell—and a reason for telling it.

Think about the details. The best memoirs connect with readers by giving them a sense of what it was like to be there, leading them to experience in words and images what the writer experienced in life. Spend some time **DESCRIBING** the incident, writing what you see, hear, smell, touch, and taste when you envision it. Do you have any photos or memorabilia or other **VISUAL** materials you might include in your memoir? Try writing out **DIALOGUE,** things that were said (or, if you can't recall exactly, things that might have been said). Look at what you come up with—is there detail enough to bring the scene to life? Anything that might be called vivid? If you don't have enough detail, you might reconsider whether you recall 324–32

528–32

333–37

enough about the incident to write about it. If you have trouble coming
219–21 up with plenty of detail, try **FREEWRITING, LISTING,** or **LOOPING.**

Ways of Organizing Memoirs

[Tell about the event from beginning to end]

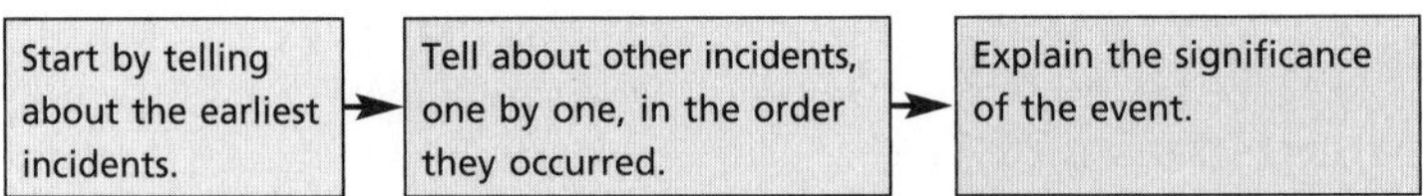

Start by telling about the earliest incidents.
Tell about other incidents, one by one, in the order they occurred.
Tell about earlier incidents, introducing key people and describing key places.
Explain the significance of the event.

[Start at the end and tell how the event came about]

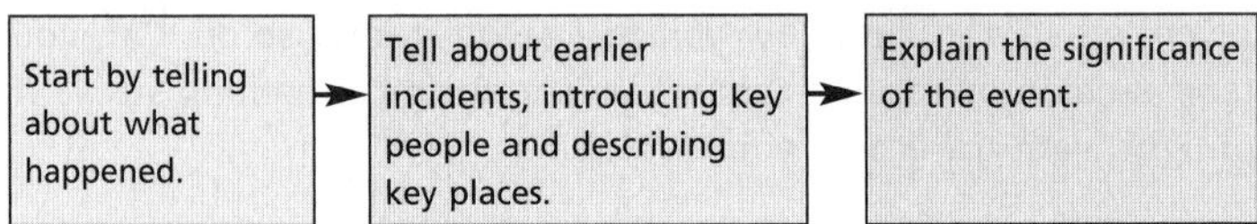

IF YOU NEED MORE HELP

226–28
229–34
235–41
242–46
247–58

See Chapter 24 for guidelines on **DRAFTING,** Chapter 25 on **ASSESSING YOUR OWN WRITING,** Chapter 26 on **GETTING RESPONSE AND REVISING,** and Chapter 27 on **EDITING AND PROOFREADING.** See Chapter 28 if you are required to submit your memoir in a writing **PORTFOLIO.**

Profiles 16

Profiles are written portraits — of people, places, events, or other things. We find profiles of celebrities, travel destinations, and offbeat festivals in magazines and newspapers, on radio and TV. A profile presents a subject in an entertaining way that conveys its significance, showing us something or someone that we may not have known existed or that we see every day but don't know much about. Here, for example, is a profile of a festival that takes place in the town where *Napoleon Dynamite* was filmed. It originally appeared in the *New York Times* in 2006.

LAURA M. HOLSON

Rural Idaho Town Seeks to Turn Film's Cult Status into Prosperity

The Big J Burger on State Street here could hardly be mistaken for a hip Hollywood club. But on Saturday afternoon, a 16-year-old wearing moon boots and a T-shirt with the slogan "Vote for Pedro" jumped out of his seat and began mixing it up on an improvised dance floor. With a boom box blaring behind him, he shimmied between the restaurant's tables to the 1999 dance hit "Canned Heat" while more than 100 people whooped and cheered.

The dancer, Bryan Demke, from Fort Worth, was recreating a pivotal moment from the 2004 cult movie *Napoleon Dynamite* which was filmed in Preston. And the crowd attending the second annual Napoleon Dynamite festival loved it. "You rock!" shouted a young girl, raising her cellphone to take a picture. "I love you, Napoleon!" added another, blowing the dancer a kiss.

"I thought the movie was stupid," said a smiling Craig Smith, who showed up with his brother Gordon and teenage son Kyle. "But that kid is killing me."

More than 300 people traveled from as far away as California and Connecticut for the chance to embrace their own inner Napoleon. The movie, written by the husband and wife team of Jared and Jerusha Hess, was directed by Mr. Hess, a native of Preston who lives in Salt Lake City. Now Preston, with a population of 5,000 in the mostly rural county, hopes to capitalize on the film's cult status.

5 Other towns have done the same and prospered. *Field of Dreams* turned little-known Dyersville, Iowa, into a tourist haven when that movie was released in 1989. Now about 65,000 people visit yearly. The Santa Ynez Valley in California became a popular vacation spot after *Sideways* was released two years ago. Even Metropolis, Illinois, experienced an increase in visitors after *Superman Returns* was released in theaters [in June 2006].

Preston, however, may be the unlikeliest backlot in recent memory. *Napoleon Dynamite* was filmed for $400,000, featured no Hollywood stars, and won no big awards. But the film, distributed by Fox Searchlight Pictures, struck a chord with moviegoers, particularly college students, garnering $44 million at the domestic box office.

"Some of the people here don't like it, but they are accepting it," said Penny Christensen, the executive director of the Preston Area Chamber of Commerce, who organized the first festival after 15,000 visitors stopped by her office last year asking for a map of the movie's sites. "I mean, why shouldn't we show off our town?"

Napoleon Dynamite is the story of an awkward small-town outsider trying to survive high school. He is a member of the Future Farmers of America (called F.F.A.) where he is milk taste-tester. He eats tater tots for lunch in the school cafeteria, plays tether ball, and dances alone in his bedroom after school. Napoleon finds newfound popularity after he shows off his Michael Jackson moves in the school auditorium, helping his friend, Pedro Sanchez, win the election for class president.

Gordon Smith, a fire sprinkler salesman, drove an hour and a half from his home in Utah to attend the festival with his daughter, Mariah. Like his brother Craig, he did not care for the movie at first, but it took on a new meaning after several viewings.

10 "I can relate to it," he said. "In high school it's the cool kids and everybody else. I was part of the 'everybody else' crowd. But in the

movie the geeks, like Napoleon, support each other. You know, there was a very good message."

The movie also made local stars of some of Mr. Hess's family friends, including Dale Critchlow, the 76-year-old cattle farmer who was signing photographs for fans lined up along State Street in downtown Preston on Saturday.

"I was putting hay in the barn when my daughter brought Jared over and said, 'Before you say no, listen to what he has to say,' " said Mr. Critchlow, recalling when Mr. Hess asked him to play Lyle in the film. "He said, 'I have a favor to ask. I want you to be in my movie.' I said, 'What do I have to do?' Jared said, 'Shoot a cow.' I said, 'Huh? O.K., I can do that.' "

Mr. Critchlow did not really shoot the cow and he was not paid for the scene. (None of the locals said they were paid.) Instead what he gained was celebrity.

"I have never had that kind of attention in my life," he said, as several onlookers listened intently. Just last week Mr. Critchlow said the cow's owner called and asked him to pose for a photograph, gun in hand, with the cow. The owner, he said, wants to sell the cow on the Internet.

While Mr. Critchlow was a favorite of autograph seekers on Saturday, fans at the festival dressed up as more recognizable characters from the film. (None of the main actors, including Jon Heder, who played Napoleon, attended.) At a look-alike contest held Saturday night at the Preston High School Auditorium, there were five Napoleons, two Rex Kwon Dos (a character who teaches Napoleon and his brother Kip self-defense), and one each of Pedro, Kip, and Deb, a classmate with a crush on Napoleon.

"If you don't get it, you just don't get it," said Ryan Grisso, who dressed up as Rex in red, white, and blue star-spangled pants, a patriotic kerchief on his head, and a blue knit shirt with the name "Rex" stitched on it (he came in second). On Friday Mr. Grisso arrived from San Francisco with his wife, Coline, and mother-in-law, Lila Ludahl McConnel, who lives 350 miles away in Caldwell, Idaho. He said they would have attended the festival last year but his wife was having a baby.

During the tater tot eating contest—where entrants were given one pound of the crispy potato lumps to down—Mr. Grisso's mother-in-law playfully slipped a few tots down the front of her green shirt. "I told them I wasn't playing to win," Ms. McConnel explained with a laugh after the shirt-stuffing was witnessed by a judge. "I know it's silly, but it's terribly fun."

A tater tot eating contest at the second annual Napoleon Dynamite festival.

But what is fun can be profitable too. Mr. Demke, the Napoleon impersonator, earns money performing at football and basketball games. What he liked best about being Napoleon was what any awkward teenager craves — the ability to speak without ridicule. In January Mr. Demke said he was performing at a basketball game between Oklahoma University and the University of Texas when an attractive woman wearing a tiara asked for a signed photograph. "I thought, 'What kind of idiot wears a tiara to a basketball game?' " he recalled.

So, channelling Napoleon, Mr. Demke posed the question. "She laughed," he said, then introduced herself as Jennifer Berry, the new Miss America. "I felt so stupid. She thought I was playing in character. I was grateful she was a fan of the movie."

But while visitors wholeheartedly embrace all that is *Napoleon* 20
Dynamite, some in Preston fear the movie portrayed them as backward and unsophisticated. And not everyone in the mostly Mormon town likes the throngs of tourists showing up to take photographs of their favorite movie sites.

"I thought it was funny, but I was concerned people would think it was a hick town," said Monte Henderson, a cattle farmer who was in the Happiness Is Scrapbooking store on Friday with his wife, Linda. "I have to admit I related to it, though. I mean, I was part of the F.F.A."

Ms. Henderson added: "I drive a school bus, and I can't tell you how many times we've had to tell the kids to reel their little rubber men in from out the window," referring to a scene where Napoleon threw a rubber doll attached to a string out a bus window and watched it bounce on the pavement.

If the festival thrives, it will be because of Ms. Christensen at the chamber. This year's attendance paled compared to last year's 6,000 attendees. Already the town is considering scrapping the $10 admission. That would be a boon to the likes of Tyra Andrews, winner of the tether ball game, who practiced all year and showed up at the festival with ten family members.

But what would really give the festival a jolt is the same thing many in Hollywood would like to see: a blockbuster sequel. (The studio has not decided whether to go ahead or not.) Joyce Williams, who owns Happiness Is Scrapbooking, said she recently was talking to a customer service representative from Hewlett-Packard who asked her where she lived. Ms. Williams said she told the agent "where *Napoleon Dynamite* was made."

"Oh, I know that place," the representative exclaimed. "My kids 25
love the movie. We'd love to come visit."

This profile starts with an unusual subject, a small-town festival that celebrates a cult film. The writer engages our interest with descriptions of several events, including a tater tot–eating contest and a look-alike contest, and interviews with several attendees and townspeople.

For five more profiles, see CHAPTER 61.

Key Features / Profiles

An interesting subject. The subject may be something unusual, or it may be something ordinary shown in an intriguing way. You might profile an interesting person (Dale Critchlow, for instance, the farmer who has a small role in *Napoleon Dynamite*), a place (the town of Preston itself, or, perhaps, Preston High School), or an event (a festival celebrating a cult film).

Any necessary background. A profile usually includes just enough information to let readers know something about the subject's larger context. Holson sums up the plot of *Napoleon Dynamite* in one brief paragraph and says very little about the town of Preston, only that it's a small town in "mostly rural" Idaho.

An interesting angle. A good profile captures its subject from a particular angle. Holson doesn't try to tell us everything about the Napoleon Dynamite festival; rather, she focuses on how the townspeople are reacting to their sudden fame from this small, quirky film. The complete schedule of events is irrelevant to Holson's goal: to show how *Napoleon Dynamite* has affected a rural Idaho town.

A firsthand account. Whether you are writing about a person, place, or event, you need to spend time observing and interacting with your subject. With a person, interacting means watching and conversing. Journalists tell us that "following the guy around," getting your subject to do something and talk about it at the same time, yields excellent material for a profile. When one writer met Theodor Geisel (Dr. Seuss) before profiling him, she asked him not only to talk about his characters but also to draw one — resulting in an illustration for her profile. With a place or event, interacting may mean visiting and participating, although sometimes you may gather even more information by playing the role of the silent observer.

Engaging details. You need to include details that bring your subject to life. These may include *specific information* ("More than 300 people traveled from as far away as California and Connecticut"); *sensory images* ("Ryan Grisso, who dressed up as Rex in red, white, and blue star-spangled pants, a patriotic kerchief on his head, and a blue knit shirt with the name 'Rex' stitched on it"); *figurative language* (visitors came "for the chance to embrace their own inner Napoleon"); *dialogue* ("I said, 'What do I have to do?' Jared said, 'Shoot a cow.' "); and *anecdotes* ("During the tater tot eating contest. . . . Mr. Grisso's mother-in-law playfully slipped a few tots down the front of her green shirt"). Choose details that show rather than tell — that let your audience see and hear your subject rather than merely read an abstract description of it. And be sure all the details create some *dominant impression* of your subject: the impression we get out of this festival, for example, is of a low-key, lighthearted event that nevertheless could contribute to the economy of the community.

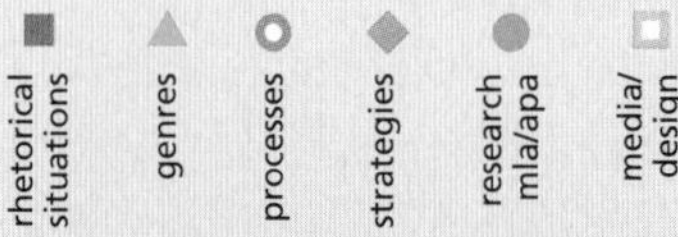

A BRIEF GUIDE TO WRITING PROFILES

Choosing a Suitable Subject

A person, a place, an event—whatever you choose, make sure it's something that arouses your curiosity and that you're not too familiar with. Knowing your subject too well can blind you to interesting details. **LIST** five to ten interesting subjects that you can experience firsthand. Obviously, you can't profile a person who won't be interviewed or a place or activity that can't be observed. So before you commit to a topic, make sure you'll be able to carry out firsthand research and not find out too late that the people you need to interview aren't willing or that places you need to visit are off-limits.

220–21

Considering the Rhetorical Situation

PURPOSE Why are you writing the profile? What angle will best achieve your purpose? How can you inform *and engage* your audience?

3–4

AUDIENCE Who is your audience? How familiar are they with your subject? What expectations of your profile might they have? What background information or definitions do you need to provide? How interested will they be—and how can you get their interest?

5–8

STANCE What view of your subject do you expect to present? Sympathetic? Critical? Sarcastic? Will you strive for a carefully balanced perspective?

12–14

MEDIA / DESIGN Will your profile be a print document? Will it be published on the Web? Will it be an oral presentation? Can (and should) you include images or any other visuals?

15–17

Generating Ideas and Text

Visit your subject. If you're writing about an amusement park, go there; if you're profiling the man who runs the carousel, make an appointment to meet and interview him. Get to know your subject—if you profile Ben and Jerry, sample the ice cream! Take along a camera if there's anything you might want to show visually in your profile. Find helpful hints for 394–96 **OBSERVING** and **INTERVIEWING** in the chapter on finding sources.

Explore what you already know about your subject. Why do you find this subject interesting? What do you know about it now? What do you expect to find out about it from your research? What preconceived ideas about or emotional reactions to this subject do you have? Why do you have them? It may be helpful to try some of the activities in the chapter 219–25 on **GENERATING IDEAS AND TEXT.**

If you're planning to interview someone, prepare questions. Holson likely asked townspeople such questions as, "How do you feel about the 394–95 festival? Did you like the movie?" See the **INTERVIEWING** guidelines in Chapter 43 for help with planning questions.

Do additional research. You may be able to write a profile based entirely on your field research. You may, though, need to do some library or 373 Web **RESEARCH** as well, to deepen your understanding, get a different perspective, or fill in gaps. Often the people you interview can help you find sources of additional information; so can the sponsors of events and those in charge of places. To learn more about a city park, for instance, contact the government office that maintains it.

Analyze your findings. Look for patterns, images, recurring ideas or phrases, and engaging details. Compare your preconceptions with your findings. Look for contrasts or discrepancies: between a subject's words and actions, between the appearance of a place and what goes on there, between your expectations and your research findings. Holson may have expected to meet *Napoleon Dynamite* fans—but not townspeople who don't support the festival. You may find the advice in the **READING STRATEGIES** chapter helpful here. 352–66

Come up with an angle. What's most memorable about your subject? What most interests you? What will interest your audience? Holson focuses on how *Napoleon Dynamite* has affected the people of Preston—whether they welcome the movie's fans, worry about how their town is perceived, or hope to make money off their town's unexpected fame. Sometimes you'll know your angle from the start; other times you'll need to look further into your topic. You might try **CLUSTERING, CUBING, FREEWRITING,** and **LOOPING,** activities that will help you look at your topic from many different angles. 219–22

Note details that support your angle. Use your angle to focus your research and generate text. Try **DESCRIBING** your subject as clearly as you can, **COMPARING** your subject with other subjects of its sort, writing **DIALOGUE** that captures your subject. Holson, for instance, quotes a local farmer who appeared in *Napoleon Dynamite* as saying, "I have never had that kind of attention in my life." Engaging details will bring your subject to life for your audience. Together, these details should create a dominant impression of your subject. 324–32 306–13 333–37

Ways of Organizing a Profile

[As a narrative]

One common way to organize a profile is by **NARRATING.** For example, if you are profiling a chess championship, you may write about it chronologically, creating suspense as you move from start to finish. 343–51

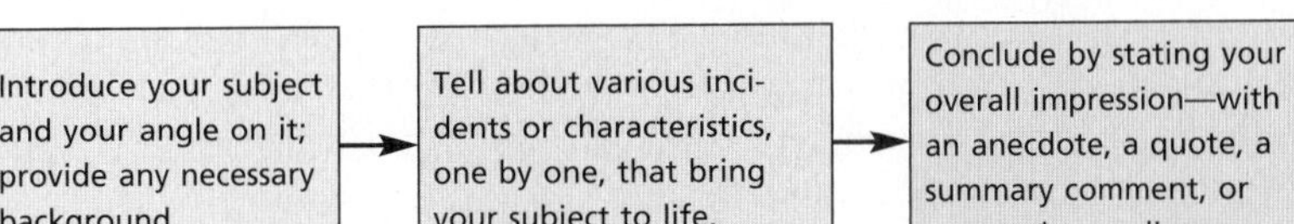

Introduce your subject and your angle on it; provide any necessary background.
Tell about various incidents or characteristics, one by one, that bring your subject to life.
Conclude by stating your overall impression—with an anecdote, a quote, a summary comment, or some other ending.

[As a description]

324–32

Sometimes you may organize a profile by **DESCRIBING**—a person or a place, for instance. The profile of the Napoleon Dynamite festival is organized this way.

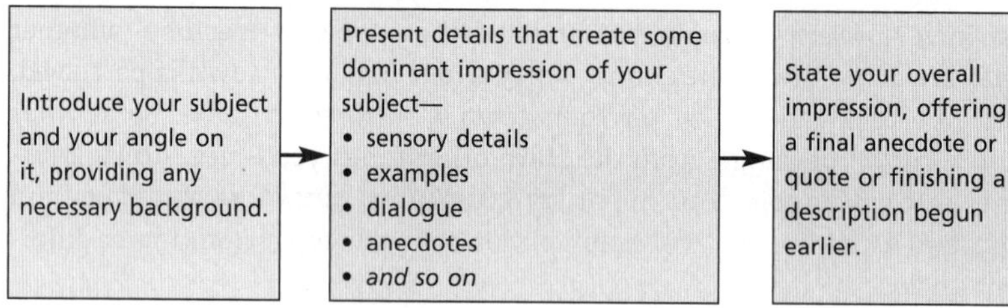

Introduce your subject and your angle on it, providing any necessary background.
Present details that create some dominant impression of your subject—
• sensory details
• examples
• dialogue
• anecdotes
• *and so on*
State your overall impression, offering a final anecdote or quote or finishing a description begun earlier.

226–28
229–34
235–41
242–46
247–58

IF YOU NEED MORE HELP

See Chapter 24 for guidelines on DRAFTING, Chapter 25 on ASSESSING YOUR OWN WRITING, Chapter 26 on GETTING RESPONSE AND REVISING, and Chapter 27 on EDITING AND PROOFREADING. See Chapter 28 if you are required to submit your profile in a writing PORTFOLIO.

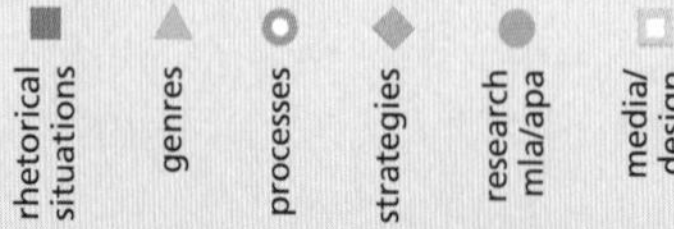

Proposals 17

Contractors bid on building projects. Musicians and educators apply for grants. Researchers seek funding. Student leaders call for lights on bike paths. You offer to pay half the cost of a car and insurance if your parents will pay the other half. Lovers propose marriage; friends propose sharing dinner and a movie. These are all examples of proposals: ideas put forward for consideration that say, "Here is a solution to a problem" or "This is what ought to be done." All proposals are arguments: when you propose something, you are trying to persuade others to see a problem in a particular way and to accept your solution to the problem. For example, here is a proposal for reducing the costs of college textbooks, written by an accounting professor at the University of Texas who is chairman of the university's Co-op Bookstore and himself a textbook author. It originally appeared on the Op-Ed page of the *New York Times* in August 2007.

MICHAEL GRANOF

Course Requirement: Extortion

By now, entering college students and their parents have been warned: textbooks are outrageously expensive. Few textbooks for semester-long courses retail for less than $120, and those for science and math courses typically approach $180. Contrast this with the $20 to $30 cost of most hardcover best sellers and other trade books.

Perhaps these students and their parents can take comfort in knowing that the federal government empathizes with them, and in an attempt to ease their pain Congress asked its Advisory Committee on Student Financial Assistance to suggest a cure for the problem. Unfortunately, though, the committee has proposed a remedy that would only worsen the problem.

The committee's report, released in May, mainly proposes strengthening the market for used textbooks—by encouraging college bookstores to guarantee that they will buy back textbooks, establishing online book swaps among students, and urging faculty to avoid switching textbooks from one semester to the next. The fatal flaw in that proposal (and similar ones made by many state legislatures) is that used books are the cause of, not the cure for, high textbook prices.

Yet there is a way to lighten the load for students in their budgets, if not their backpacks. With small modifications to the institutional arrangements between universities, publishers, and students, textbook costs could be reduced—and these changes could be made without government intervention.

Today the used-book market is exceedingly well organized and 5
efficient. Campus bookstores buy back not only the books that will be used at their university the next semester but also those that will not. Those that are no longer on their lists of required books they resell to national wholesalers, which in turn sell them to college bookstores on campuses where they will be required. This means that even if a text is being adopted for the first time at a particular college, there is almost certain to be an ample supply of used copies.

As a result, publishers have the chance to sell a book to only one of the multiple students who eventually use it. Hence, publishers must cover their costs and make their profit in the first semester their books are sold—before used copies swamp the market. That's why the prices are so high.

As might be expected, publishers do what they can to undermine the used-book market, principally by coming out with new editions every three or four years. To be sure, in rapidly changing fields like biology and physics, the new editions may be academically defensible. But in areas like algebra and calculus, they are nothing more than a transparent attempt to ensure premature textbook obsolescence. Publishers also try to discourage students from buying used books by bundling the text with extra materials like workbooks and CDs that

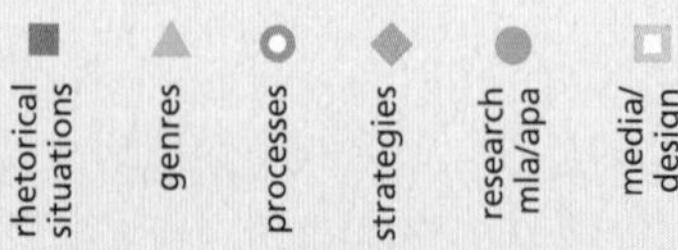

are not reusable and therefore cannot be passed from one student to another.

The system could be much improved if, first of all, colleges and publishers would acknowledge that textbooks are more akin to computer software than to trade books. A textbook's value, like that of a software program, is not in its physical form, but rather in its intellectual content. Therefore, just as software companies typically "site license" to colleges, so should textbook publishers.

Here's how it would work: A teacher would pick a textbook, and the college would pay a negotiated fee to the publisher based on the number of students enrolled in the class. If there were 50 students in the class, for example, the fee might be \$15 per student, or \$750 for the semester. If the text were used for ten semesters, the publisher would ultimately receive a total of \$150 (\$15 × 10) for each student enrolled in the course, or as much as \$7,500.

In other words, the publisher would have a stream of revenue 10
for as long as the text was in use. Presumably, the university would pass on this fee to the students, just as it does the cost of laboratory supplies and computer software. But the students would pay much less than the \$900 a semester they now typically pay for textbooks.

Once the university had paid the license fee, each student would have the option of using the text in electronic format or paying more to purchase a hard copy through the usual channels. The publisher could set the price of hard copies low enough to cover only its production and distribution costs plus a small profit, because it would be covering most of its costs and making most of its profit by way of the license fees. The hard copies could then be resold to other students or back to the bookstore, but that would be of little concern to the publisher.

A further benefit of this approach is that it would not affect the way courses are taught. The same cannot be said for other recommendations from the Congressional committee and from state legislatures, like placing teaching materials on electronic reserve, urging faculty to adopt cheaper "no frills" textbooks, and assigning mainly electronic textbooks. While each of these suggestions may have merit, they force faculty to weigh students' academic interests against their fiscal concerns and encourage them to rely less on new textbooks.

Neither colleges nor publishers are known for their cutting-edge innovations. But if they could slightly change the way they do business, they would make a substantial dent in the cost of higher education and provide a real benefit to students and their parents.

For five more proposals, see CHAPTER 62.

This proposal clearly defines the problem—some textbooks cost a lot—and explains why. It proposes a solution to the problem of high textbook prices and offers reasons why this solution will work better than others. Its tone is reasonable and measured, yet decisive.

Key Features / Proposals

A well-defined problem. Some problems are self-evident or relatively simple, and you would not need much persuasive power to make people act—as with the problem "This university discards too much paper." While some people might see nothing wrong with throwing paper away, most are likely to agree that recycling is a good thing. Other issues are controversial: some people see them as problems while others do not, such as this one: "Motorcycle riders who do not wear helmets risk serious injury and raise health-care costs for everyone." Some motorcyclists believe that wearing or not wearing a helmet is a personal choice; you would have to present arguments to convince your readers that not wearing a helmet is indeed a problem needing a solution. Any written proposal must establish at the outset that there is a problem—and that it's serious enough to require a solution.

A recommended solution. Once you have defined the problem, you need to describe the solution you are suggesting and to explain it in enough detail for readers to understand what you are proposing. Sometimes you might suggest several solutions, weigh their merits, and choose the best one.

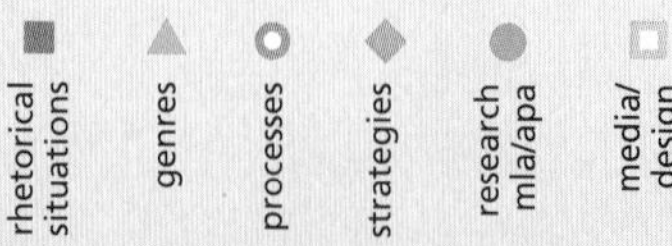

A convincing argument for your proposed solution. You need to convince readers that your solution is feasible—and that it is the best way to solve the problem. Sometimes you'll want to explain in detail how your proposed solution would work. See, for example, how the textbook proposal details the way a licensing system would operate.

Anticipate questions. You may need to consider any questions readers may have about your proposal—and to show how its advantages outweigh any disadvantages. Had the textbook proposal been written for college budget officers, it would have needed to anticipate and answer questions about the costs of implementing the proposed solution.

A call to action. The goal of a proposal is to persuade readers to accept your proposed solution. This solution may include asking readers to take action.

An appropriate tone. Since you're trying to persuade readers to act, your tone is important—readers will always react better to a reasonable, respectful presentation than to anger or self-righteousness.

A BRIEF GUIDE TO WRITING PROPOSALS

Deciding on a Topic

Choose a problem that can be solved. Complex, large problems, such as poverty, hunger, or terrorism, usually require complex, large solutions. Most of the time, focusing on a smaller problem or a limited aspect of a large problem will yield a more manageable proposal. Rather than tackling the problem of world poverty, for example, think about the problem faced by families in your community that have lost jobs and need help until they find employment.

Considering the Rhetorical Situation

3–4

PURPOSE Do you have a vested interest in the solution your readers adopt, or do you simply want to eliminate the problem, whatever solution might be adopted?

5–8

AUDIENCE How can you reach your readers? Do you know how receptive or resistant to change they are likely to be? Do they have the authority to enact your proposal?

12–14

STANCE How can you show your audience that your proposal is reasonable and should be taken seriously? How can you demonstrate your own authority and credibility?

15–17

MEDIA / DESIGN How will you deliver your proposal? In print? Online? As a speech? Would visuals help support your proposal?

Generating Ideas and Text

Explore potential solutions to the problem. Many problems can be solved in more than one way, and you need to show your readers that you've examined several potential solutions. You may develop solutions to your problem on your own; more often, though, you'll need to do **RESEARCH** to see how others have solved — or tried to solve — similar problems. Don't settle on a single solution too quickly — you'll need to **COMPARE** the advantages and disadvantages of several solutions in order to argue convincingly for one.

373

306–13

Decide on the most desirable solution(s). One solution may be head and shoulders above others — but be open to rejecting all the possible solutions on your list and starting over if you need to, or to combining two or more potential solutions in order to come up with an acceptable fix.

Think about why your solution is the best one. Why did you choose your solution? Why will it work better than others? What has to be done to enact it? What will it cost? What makes you think it can be done? Writing out answers to these questions will help you argue for your solution—to show that you have carefully and objectively outlined a problem, analyzed the potential solutions, and weighed their merits—and to show the reasons the solution you propose is the best.

Ways of Organizing a Proposal

You can organize a proposal in various ways, but always you will begin by establishing that there is a problem. You may then consider several solutions before recommending one particular solution. Sometimes, however, you might suggest only a single solution.

[Several possible solutions]

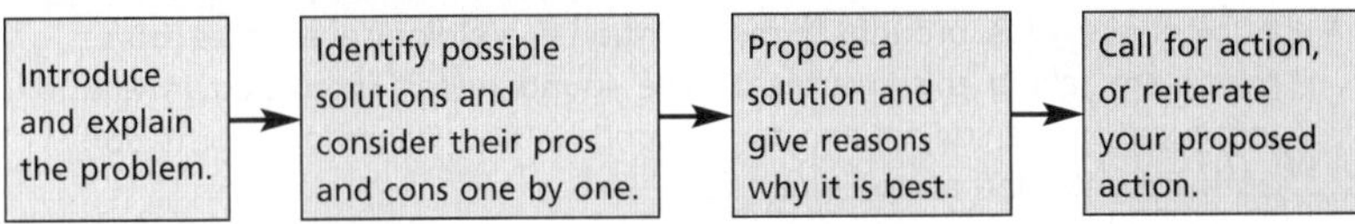

[A single solution]

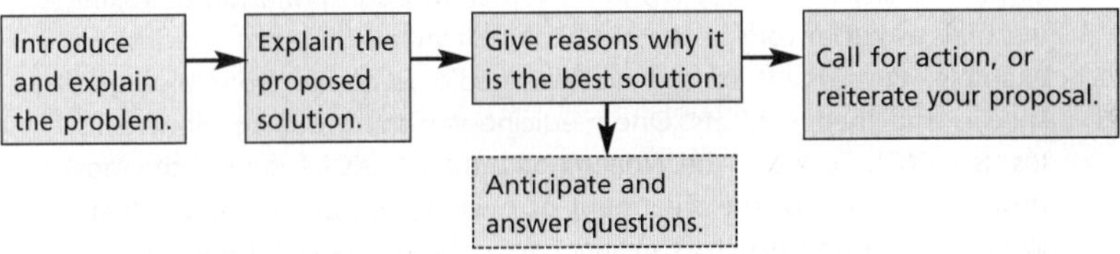

TOPIC PROPOSALS

Instructors often ask students to write topic proposals to ensure that their topics are appropriate or manageable. If you get your instructor's response to a good proposal before you write it, your finished product will likely be much better than if you try to guess the assignment's demands. Some

116–24 instructors may also ask for an **ANNOTATED BIBLIOGRAPHY** showing that appropriate sources of information are available—more evidence that the project can be carried out. Here a first-year student proposes a topic for an assignment in a writing course in which she has been asked to take a position on a global issue.

JENNIFER CHURCH

Biodiversity Loss and Its Effect on Medicine

The loss of biodiversity—the variety of organisms found in the world—is affecting the world every day. Some scientists estimate that we are losing approximately one hundred species per day and that more than a quarter of all species may vanish within fifty years. I recently had the issue of biodiversity loss brought to my attention in a biological sciences course that I am taking this quarter. I have found myself interested in and intrigued by the subject and have found an abundance of information both in books and on the Internet.

In this paper, I will argue that it is crucial for people to stop this rapid loss of our world's biodiversity. Humans are the number-one cause of biodiversity loss in the world. Whether through pollution or toxins, we play a crucial role in the extinction of many different species. For example, 80 percent of the world's medicine comes from biological species and their habitats. One medicine vanishing due to biodiversity loss is TAXOL. Found in the Wollemi pine tree, TAXOL is one of the most promising drugs for the treatment of ovarian and breast cancer. If the Wollemi pine tree becomes extinct, we will lose this potential cure.

I will concentrate primarily on biodiversity and its effects on the medical field. If we keep destroying the earth's biodiversity at the current rate, we may lose many opportunities to develop medicines we need to survive. The majority of my information will be found on the Internet, because there are many reliable Web sites from all around the world that address the issue of biodiversity loss and medicine.

Church defines and narrows her topic (from biodiversity loss to the impact of that loss on medicine), discusses her interest, outlines her argument, and discusses

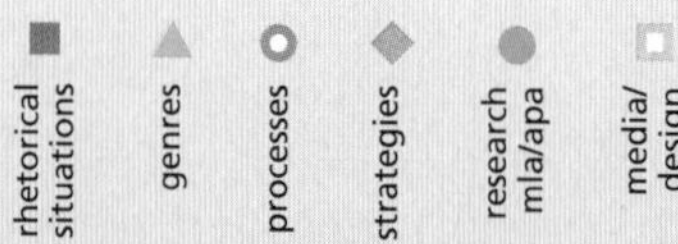

her research strategy. Her goal is to convince her instructor that she has a realistic writing project and a clear plan.

Key Features / Topic Proposals

You'll need to explain what you want to write about, why you want to explore it, and what you'll do with your topic. Unless your instructor has additional requirements, here are the features to include:

A concise discussion of the subject. Topic proposals generally open with a brief discussion of the subject, outlining any important areas of controversy or debate associated with it and clarifying the extent of the writer's current knowledge of it. In its first two paragraphs, Church's proposal includes a concise statement of the topic she wishes to address.

A clear statement of your intended focus. State what aspect of the topic you intend to write on as clearly as you can, narrowing your focus appropriately. Church does so by stating her intended topic—loss of biodiversity—and then showing how she will focus on the importance of biodiversity to the medical field.

A rationale for choosing the topic. Tell your instructor why this topic interests you and why you want to write about it. Church both states what made her interested in her topic and hints at a practical reason for choosing it: plenty of information is available.

Mention of resources. To show your instructor that you can achieve your goal, you need to identify the available research materials.

IF YOU NEED MORE HELP

See Chapter 24 for guidelines on **DRAFTING**, Chapter 25 on **ASSESSING YOUR OWN WRITING**, Chapter 26 on **GETTING RESPONSE AND REVISING**, and Chapter 27 on **EDITING AND PROOFREADING**. See Chapter 28 if you are required to submit your proposal in a writing **PORTFOLIO**.

226–28
229–34
235–41
242–46
247–58

18 Reflections

Sometimes we write essays just to think about something — to speculate, ponder, probe; to play with an idea, develop a thought; or simply to share something. Reflective essays are our attempt to think something through by writing about it and to share our thinking with others. If such essays make an argument, it is about things we care or think about more than about what we believe to be "true." Have a look at one example by Jonathan Safran Foer, a novelist who lives in Brooklyn. This essay originally appeared on the Op-Ed page of the *New York Times* in 2006.

JONATHAN SAFRAN FOER

My Life as a Dog

For the last twenty years, New York City parks without designated dog runs have permitted dogs to be off-leash from 9 p.m. to 9 a.m. Because of recent complaints from the Juniper Park Civic Association in Queens, the issue has been revisited. On December 5, the Board of Health will vote on the future of off-leash hours.

Retrievers in elevators, Pomeranians on No. 6 trains, bull mastiffs crossing the Brooklyn Bridge . . . it is easy to forget just how strange it is that dogs live in New York in the first place. It is about as unlikely a place for dogs as one could imagine, and yet 1.4 million of them are among us. Why do we keep them in our apartments and houses, always at some expense and inconvenience? Is it even possible, in a city, to provide a good life for a dog, and what is a "good life"? Does the health board's vote matter in ways other than the most obvious?

I adopted George (a Great Dane / Lab / pit / greyhound / ridgeback / whatever mix — a.k.a. Brooklyn shorthair) because I thought it would be fun. As it turns out, she is a major pain an awful lot of the time.

She mounts guests, eats my son's toys (and occasionally tries to eat my son), is obsessed with squirrels, lunges at skateboarders and Hasids,* has the savant-like ability to find her way between the camera lens and subject of every photo taken in her vicinity, backs her tush into the least interested person in the room, digs up the freshly planted, scratches the newly bought, licks the about-to-be-served, and occasionally relieves herself on the wrong side of the front door. Her head is resting on my foot as I type this. I love her.

Our various struggles — to communicate, to recognize and accom- 5
modate each other's desires, simply to coexist — force me to interact with something, or rather someone, entirely "other." George can respond to a handful of words, but our relationship takes place almost entirely outside of language. She seems to have thoughts and emotions, desires and fears. Sometimes I think I understand them; often I don't. She is a mystery to me. And I must be one to her.

Of course our relationship is not always a struggle. My morning walk with George is very often the highlight of my day — when I have my best thoughts, when I most appreciate both nature and the city, and in a deeper sense, life itself. Our hour together is a bit of compensation for the burdens of civilization: business attire, email, money, etiquette, walls, and artificial lighting. It is even a kind of compensation for language. Why does watching a dog be a dog fill one with happiness? And why does it make one feel, in the best sense of the word, human?

It is children, very often, who want dogs. In a recent study, when asked to name the ten most important "individuals" in their lives, 7- and 10-year-olds included two pets on average. In another study, 42 percent of 5-year-olds spontaneously mentioned their pets when asked, "Whom do you turn to when you are feeling, sad, angry, happy, or wanting to share a secret?" Just about every children's book in my local bookstore has an animal for its hero. But then, only a few feet away in the cookbook section, just about every cookbook includes recipes for cooking animals. Is there a more illuminating illustration of our paradoxical relationship with the nonhuman world?

In the course of our lives, we move from a warm and benevolent relationship with animals (learning responsibility through caring for

---

**Hasids*: a Jewish sect whose members dress distinctively. [Editor's note]

our pets, stroking and confiding in them) to a cruel one (virtually all animals raised for meat in this country are factory farmed — they spend their lives in confinement, dosed with antibiotics and other drugs).

How do you explain this? Is our kindness replaced with cruelty? I don't think so. I think in part it's because the older we get, the less exposure we have to animals. And nothing facilitates indifference or forgetfulness so much as distance. In this sense, dogs and cats have been very lucky: they are the only animals we are intimately exposed to daily.

Folk parental wisdom and behavioral studies alike generally view 10
the relationships children have with companion animals as beneficial. But one does not have to be a child to learn from a pet. It is precisely my frustrations with George, and the inconveniences she creates, that reinforce in me how much compromise is necessary to share space with other beings.

The practical arguments against off-leash hours are easily refuted. One doesn't have to be an animal scientist to know that the more a dog is able to exercise its "dogness" — to run and play, to socialize with other dogs — the happier it will be. Happy dogs, like happy people, tend not to be aggressive. In the years that dogs have been allowed to run free in city parks, dog bites have decreased 90 percent. But there is another argument that is not so easy to respond to: some people just don't want to be inconvenienced by dogs. Giving dogs space necessarily takes away space from humans.

We have been having this latter debate, in different forms, for ages. Again and again we are confronted with the reality — some might say the problem — of sharing our space with other living things, be they dogs, trees, fish, or penguins. Dogs in the park are a present example of something that is often too abstracted or far away to gain our consideration.

The very existence of parks is a response to this debate: earlier New Yorkers had the foresight to recognize that if we did not carve out places for nature in our cities, there would be no nature. It was recently estimated that Central Park's real estate would be worth more than $500 billion. Which is to say we are half a trillion dollars inconvenienced by trees and grass. But we do not think of it as an inconvenience. We think of it as balance.

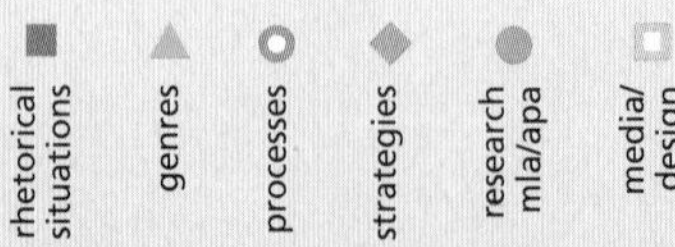

Living on a planet of fixed size requires compromise, and while we are the only party capable of negotiating, we are not the only party at the table. We've never claimed more, and we've never had less. There has never been less clean air or water, fewer fish or mature trees. If we are not simply ignoring the situation, we keep hoping for (and expecting) a technological solution that will erase our destruction, while allowing us to continue to live without compromise. Maybe zoos will be an adequate replacement for wild animals in natural habitats. Maybe we will be able to recreate the Amazon somewhere else. Maybe one day we will be able to genetically engineer dogs that do not wish to run free. Maybe. But will those futures make us feel, in the best sense of the word, human?

I have been taking George to Prospect Park twice a day for more 15
than three years, but her running is still a revelation to me. Effortlessly, joyfully, she runs quite a bit faster than the fastest human on the planet. And faster, I've come to realize, than the other dogs in the park. George might well be the fastest land animal in Brooklyn. Once or twice every morning, for no obvious reason, she'll tear into a full sprint. Other dog owners can't help but watch her. Every now and then someone will cheer her on. It is something to behold.

A vote regarding off-leash hours for dogs sparks Foer's reflection on the relationship between dogs and humans. He begins by thinking about his relationship with his own dog, then goes on to consider the paradoxical nature of our treatment of animals in general. From there, he moves into a larger discussion of the compromises we make to "share space with other beings." Finally, he brings his reflection back to the personal, describing the joy of watching his dog be herself, off-leash.

For five more reflections, see CHAPTER 63.

Key Features / Reflections

A topic that intrigues you. A reflective essay has a dual purpose: to ponder something you find interesting or puzzling and to share your thoughts with an audience. Your topic may be anything that interests you.

You might write about someone you have never met and are curious about, an object or occurrence that makes you think, a place where you feel comfortable or safe. Your goal is to explore the meaning that the person, object, event, or place has for you in a way that will interest others. One way to do that is by making connections between your personal experience and more general ones that readers may share. Foer writes about his experience with his dog, but in so doing he raises questions and offers insights about the way everyone relates to others, human and nonhuman alike.

Some kind of structure. A reflective essay can be structured in many ways, but it needs to *be* structured. It may seem to wander, but all its paths and ideas should relate, one way or another. The challenge is to keep your readers' interest as you explore your topic and to leave readers satisfied that the journey was pleasurable, interesting, and profitable. Foer brings his essay full-circle, introducing the vote on the off-leash law in his opening, then considering our complex relationship with dogs, and, after suggesting some of the compromises we make to share our world with other nonhuman living things, closing with an indelible image of the joy that freedom from a leash brings.

Specific details. You'll need to provide specific details to help readers understand and connect with your subject, especially if it's an abstract or unfamiliar one. Foer offers a wealth of details about his dog: "She mounts guests, eats my son's toys (and occasionally tries to eat my son), is obsessed by squirrels, lunges at skateboarders and Hasids." Anecdotes can bring your subject to life: "Once or twice every morning, for no obvious reason, she'll tear into a full sprint. Other dog owners can't help but watch her. Every now and then someone will cheer her on." Reflections may be about causes, such as why dogs make us feel more human; comparisons, such as when Foer compares animals as pets and as food; and examples: "virtually all animals raised for meat in this country are factory farmed."

A questioning, speculative tone. In a reflective essay, you are working toward answers, not providing them neatly organized and ready for consumption. So your tone is usually tentative and open, demonstrating a willingness to entertain, accept, and reject various ideas as your essay progresses from beginning to end. Foer achieves this tone by looking at people's relationships with dogs from several different perspectives as well as by asking questions for which he provides no direct answers.

A BRIEF GUIDE TO WRITING REFLECTIONS

Deciding on a Topic

Choose a subject you want to explore. Write a list of things that you think about, wonder about, find puzzling or annoying. They may be big things — life, relationships — or little things — quirks of certain people's behavior, curious objects, everyday events. Try **CLUSTERING** one or more of those things, or begin by **FREEWRITING** to see what comes to mind as you write.

221–22
219–20

Considering the Rhetorical Situation

PURPOSE What's your goal in writing this essay? To introduce a topic that interests you? Entertain? Provoke readers to think about something? What aspects of your subject do you want to ponder and reflect on? 3–4

AUDIENCE Who is the audience? How familiar are they with your subject? How will you introduce it in a way that will interest them? 5–8

STANCE What is your attitude toward the topic you plan to explore? Questioning? Playful? Critical? Curious? Something else? 12–14

MEDIA / DESIGN Will your essay be a print document? An oral presentation? Will it be posted on a website? Would it help to have any visuals? 15–17

Generating Ideas and Text

Explore your subject in detail. Reflections often include descriptive
324–32 details. Foer, for example, **DESCRIBES** the many ways he encounters dogs
in New York: "Retrievers in elevators, Pomeranians on No. 6 trains, bull
mastiffs crossing the Brooklyn Bridge." Those details provide a base
314–23 for the speculations to come. You may also make your point by **DEFINING,**
306–13 **COMPARING,** even **CLASSIFYING.** Virtually any organizing pattern will help you
300–305 explore your subject.

Back away. Ask yourself why your subject matters: why is it important
220–21 or intriguing or significant? You may try **LISTING** or **OUTLINING** possibilities,
223–24 or you may want to start **DRAFTING** to see where the writing takes your
226–28 thinking. Your goal is to think on paper (or screen) about your subject, to
play with its possibilities.

Think about how to keep readers with you. Reflections may seem loose
or unstructured, but they must be carefully crafted so that readers can fol-
273–75 low your train of thought. It's a good idea to sketch out a rough **THESIS** to
help focus your thoughts. You may not include the thesis in the essay
itself, but every part of the essay should in some way relate to it.

Ways of Organizing a Reflective Essay

Reflective essays may be organized in many ways because they mimic the way we think, associating one idea with another in ways that make sense but do not necessarily form a "logical" progression. In general, you might consider organizing a reflection using this overall strategy:

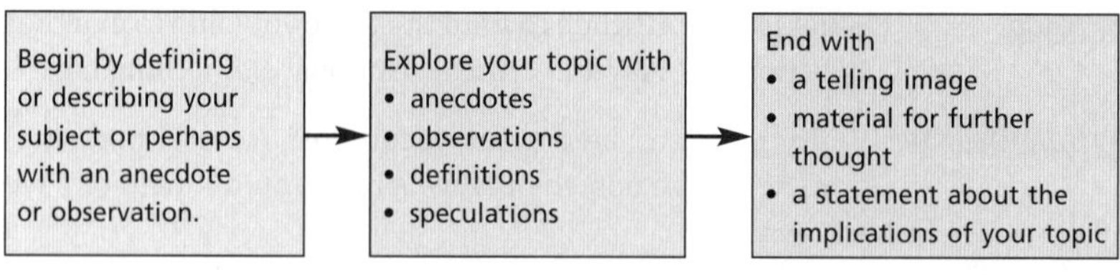

Begin by defining or describing your subject or perhaps with an anecdote or observation.
Explore your topic with
• anecdotes
• observations
• definitions
• speculations
End with
• a telling image
• material for further thought
• a statement about the implications of your topic

Another way to organize this type of essay is as a series of brief reflections that together create an overall impression:

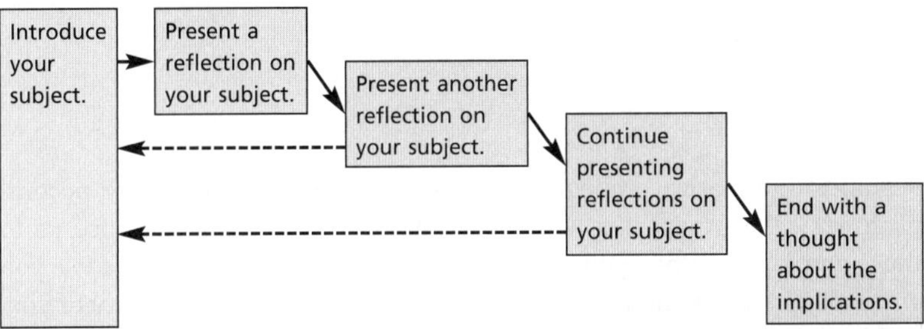

IF YOU NEED MORE HELP

See Chapter 24 for guidelines on DRAFTING, Chapter 25 on ASSESSING YOUR OWN WRITING, Chapter 26 on GETTING RESPONSE AND REVISING, and Chapter 27 on EDITING AND PROOFREADING. See Chapter 28 if you are required to submit your reflection in a writing PORTFOLIO.

226–28
229–34
235–41
242–46
247–58

19 Résumés and Job Letters

Résumés summarize our education, work experience, and other accomplishments for prospective employers. Application letters introduce us to those employers. When you send a letter and résumé applying for a job, you are making an argument for why that employer should want to meet you, and perhaps hire you. In a way, the two texts together serve as an advertisement selling your talents and abilities to someone who likely has to sift through many applications to decide whom to invite for an interview. That's why résumés and application letters require a level of care that few other documents do. In the same way, sending a thank-you letter following an interview completes your presentation of yourself to potential employers. Résumés, application letters, and thank-you letters are obviously very different genres—yet they share one common purpose and are done for the same audience. Thus, they are presented together in this chapter.

RÉSUMÉS

This chapter covers two kinds of résumés, print ones and scannable ones. *Print résumés* are presented on paper to be read by people. You usually design a print résumé to highlight key information typographically, using italic or bold type for headings, for instance. *Scannable résumés* can be delivered on paper or via email, but they are formatted to be read by a computer. Therefore, you need to use a single typeface without any bold or italics or even indents, and you need to write the résumé using keywords that you hope will match words found in the computer's job description database.

Following are two résumés—the first one print and the second one scannable—both written by a college student applying for an internship before his senior year.

Print Résumé

Samuel Praeger
28 Murphy Lane
Springfield, OH 45399
937-555-2640
spraeger22@webmail.com

name in boldface

OBJECTIVE To obtain an internship with a public relations firm

objective tailored to specific job sought

EDUCATION
Fall 2005–present

Wittenberg University, Springfield, OH
- B.A. in Psychology expected in May 2009
- Minor in East Asian Studies

EXPERIENCE

2007–present

Department of Psychology, Wittenberg University
Research Assistant
- Collect and analyze data
- Interview research participants

work experience in reverse chronological order

Summer 2007

Landis and Landis Public Relations, Springfield, OH
Events Coordinator
- Organized local charity events
- Coordinated database of potential donors
- Produced two radio spots for event promotion

Summers 2005, 2006

Springfield Aquatic Club, Springfield, OH
Assistant Swim Coach
- Instructed children ages 5–18 in competitive swimming

HONORS

2008 Psi Chi National Honor Society in Psychology

2006–2008 Community Service Scholarship, Wittenberg University

ACTIVITIES Varsity Swim Team, Ronald McDonald House Fund-raiser

SKILLS Microsoft Office; SPSS for Windows; Eudora Pro; PowerPoint; fluency in Japanese language

REFERENCES Available upon request

format to fill entire page

Scannable Résumé

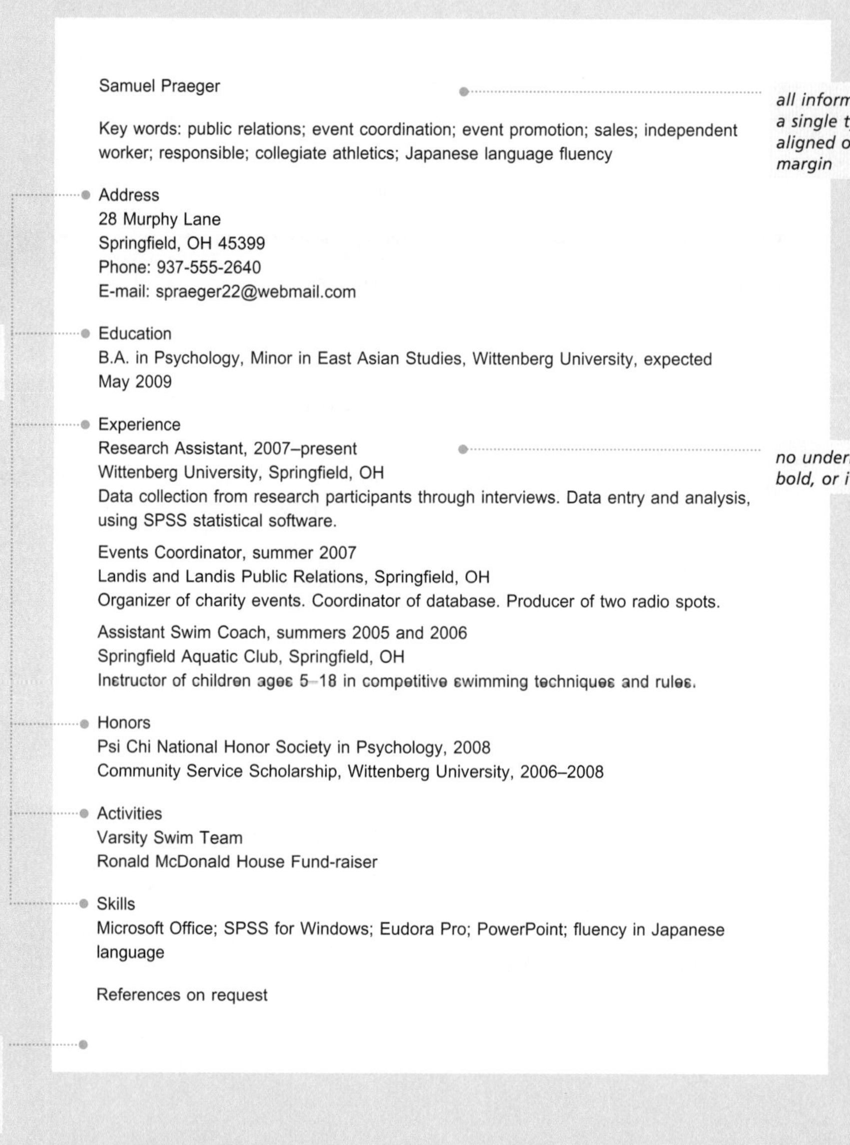
Samuel Praeger

Key words: public relations; event coordination; event promotion; sales; independent worker; responsible; collegiate athletics; Japanese language fluency

Address
28 Murphy Lane
Springfield, OH 45399
Phone: 937-555-2640
E-mail: spraeger22@webmail.com

Education
B.A. in Psychology, Minor in East Asian Studies, Wittenberg University, expected May 2009

Experience
Research Assistant, 2007–present
Wittenberg University, Springfield, OH
Data collection from research participants through interviews. Data entry and analysis, using SPSS statistical software.

Events Coordinator, summer 2007
Landis and Landis Public Relations, Springfield, OH
Organizer of charity events. Coordinator of database. Producer of two radio spots.

Assistant Swim Coach, summers 2005 and 2006
Springfield Aquatic Club, Springfield, OH
Instructor of children ages 5–18 in competitive swimming techniques and rules.

Honors
Psi Chi National Honor Society in Psychology, 2008
Community Service Scholarship, Wittenberg University, 2006–2008

Activities
Varsity Swim Team
Ronald McDonald House Fund-raiser

Skills
Microsoft Office; SPSS for Windows; Eudora Pro; PowerPoint; fluency in Japanese language

References on request

all information in a single typeface, aligned on left margin

key words to aid computer searching

no underlining, bold, or italics

printed on white paper; not folded or stapled

Samuel Praeger's résumé is arranged chronologically, and because he was looking for work in a certain field, the résumé is targeted, *focusing on his related work and skills and leaving out any references to high school (that he is in college allows readers to assume graduation from high school) or his past job as a house painter, which is not relevant. The print version describes his work responsibilities using action verbs to highlight what he actually did*—produced, instructed, *and so on*—*whereas the scannable version converts the verbs to nouns*—producer, instructor. *The scannable version is formatted in a single standard typeface, with no italics, boldfacing, or other typographic variation.*

Key Features / Résumés

An organization that suits your goals and experience. There are conventional ways of organizing a résumé but no one way. You can organize a résumé chronologically or functionally, and it can be targeted or not. A *chronological résumé* is the most general, listing pretty much all your academic and work experience from the most recent to the earliest. A *targeted résumé* will generally announce the specific goal up top, just beneath your name, and will offer information selectively, showing only the experience and skills relevant to your goal. A *functional résumé* is organized around various kinds of experience and is not chronological. You might write a functional résumé if you wish to demonstrate a lot of experience in more than one area and perhaps if you wish to downplay dates.

Succinct. A résumé should almost always be short—one page if at all possible. Entries should be parallel but do not need to be written in complete sentences—"Produced two radio spots," for instance, rather than "I produced two radio spots." *Print résumés* often use action verbs ("instructed," "produced") to emphasize what you accomplished; *scannable résumés* use nouns instead ("instructor," "producer").

A design that highlights key information. It's important for a résumé to look good and to be easy to scan. *On a print résumé,* typography, white space, and alignment matter. Your name should be bold at the top. Major sections should be labeled with headings, all of which should be in one slightly larger or bolder font. And you need to surround each section and the text as a whole with adequate white space to make the parts easy to read—and to make the entire document look professional. *On a scannable résumé*, you should use one standard typeface throughout and *not* use any italics, boldface, bullets, or indents.

A BRIEF GUIDE TO WRITING RÉSUMÉS

Considering the Rhetorical Situation

3–4 **PURPOSE** Are you seeking a job? An internship? Some other position? How will the position for which you're applying affect what you include on your résumé?

5–8 **AUDIENCE** What sort of employee is the company or organization seeking? What experience and qualities will the person doing the hiring be looking for?

12–14 **STANCE** What personal and professional qualities do you want to convey? Think about how you want to come across—as eager? polite? serious? ambitious?—and choose your words accordingly.

15–17 **MEDIA / DESIGN** Are you planning to send your résumé and letter on paper? As an email attachment? In a scannable format? Whatever your medium, be sure both documents are formatted appropriately and proofread carefully.

Generating Ideas and Text for a Résumé

Consider how you want to present yourself. Begin by gathering the information you will need to include. As you work through the steps of putting your résumé together, think about the method of organization that works best for your purpose—chronological, targeted, or functional.

- ***Contact information.*** At the top of your résumé, list your full name, a permanent address (rather than your school address), a permanent telephone number with area code, and your email address (which should sound professional; addresses like *hotbabe334@aol.com* do not make a good first impression on potential employers).
- ***Your education.*** Start with the most recent: degree, major, college attended, and minor (if any). You may want to list your GPA (if it's over 3.0) and any academic honors you've received. If you don't have much work experience, list education first.
- ***Your work experience.*** As with education, list your most recent job first and work backward. Include job title, organization name, city and state, start and end dates, and responsibilities. Describe them in terms of your duties and accomplishments. If you have extensive work experience in the area in which you're applying, list that first.
- ***Community service, volunteer, and charitable activities.*** Many high school students are required to perform community service, and many students participate in various volunteer activities that benefit others. List what you've done, and think about the skills and aptitudes that participation helped you develop or demonstrate.
- ***Other activities, interests, and abilities.*** What do you do for fun? What skills do your leisure activities require? (For example, if you play complicated games on the Internet, you probably have a high level of knowledge about computers. You should describe your computer skills in a way that an employer might find useful.)

Define your objective. Are you looking for a particular job for which you should create a targeted résumé? Are you preparing a generic chronological résumé to use in a search for work of any kind? Defining your objective as specifically as possible helps you decide on the form the résumé will take and the information it will include.

Choose contacts. Whether you list references on your résumé or offer to provide them on request, ask people to serve as references for you before you send out a résumé. It's a good idea to provide each reference with a one-page summary of relevant information about you (for example, give professors a list of courses you took with them, including the grades you earned and the titles of papers you wrote).

Choose your words carefully. Remember, your résumé is a sales document—you're trying to present yourself as someone worth a second look. Focus on your achievements, using action verbs that say what you've done. If, however, you're composing a scannable résumé, use nouns rather than verbs, and use terms that will function as key words. Key words help the computer match your qualifications to the organization's needs. People in charge of hiring search the database of résumés by entering key words relating to the job for which they are seeking applicants. Key words for a lab technician, for example, might include *laboratory, technician, procedures, subjects, experimental*—among many others. To determine what key words to list on your résumé, read job ads carefully, and use the same words the ads do—as long as they accurately reflect your experience. Be honest—employers expect truthfulness, and embellishing the truth can cause you to lose a job later.

Consider key design elements. Make sure your résumé is centered on the page and that it looks clean and clear. It's usually best to use a single, simple **FONT** (serif for print, sans serif for scannable) throughout and to print on white or off-white paper. Limit paper résumés to no more—and no less—than one full page. If you plan to send a scannable résumé or post it on a website, create a version that does *not* contain bullets, indents, italics, or underlining, since downloading can cause those elements to get lost or garbled.

524–25

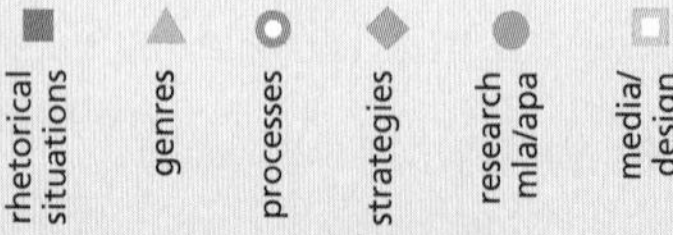

Edit and proofread carefully. Your résumé must be perfect. Show it to others, and proofread again. You don't want even one typo.

Ways of Organizing a Résumé

If you don't have much work experience or if you've just gone back to school to train for a new career, put education before work experience; if you have extensive work experience in the area in which you're applying, list work before education.

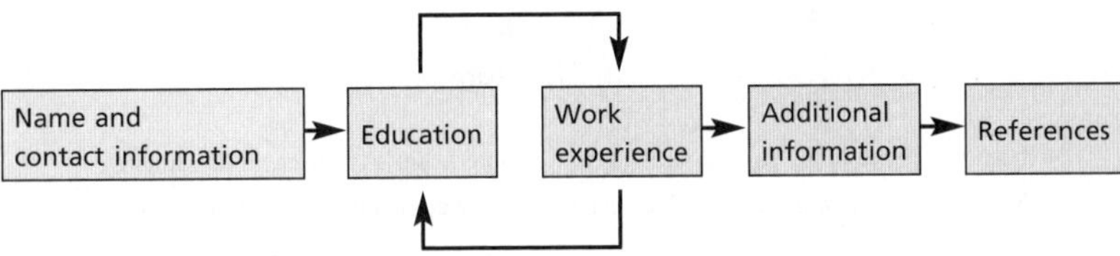

APPLICATION AND THANK-YOU LETTERS

The application letter argues that the writer should be taken seriously as a candidate for a job or some other opportunity. Generally, it is sent together with a résumé, so it doesn't need to give that much information. It does, however, have to make a favorable impression: the way it's written and presented can get you in for an interview—or not. On the following page is an application letter that Samuel Praeger wrote seeking a position at the end of his junior year. Praeger tailored his letter to one specific reader at a specific organization. The letter cites details, showing that it is not a generic application letter being sent to many possible employers. Rather, it identifies a particular position—the public relations internship—and stresses the fit between his credentials and the position. He also states his availability.

Application Letter

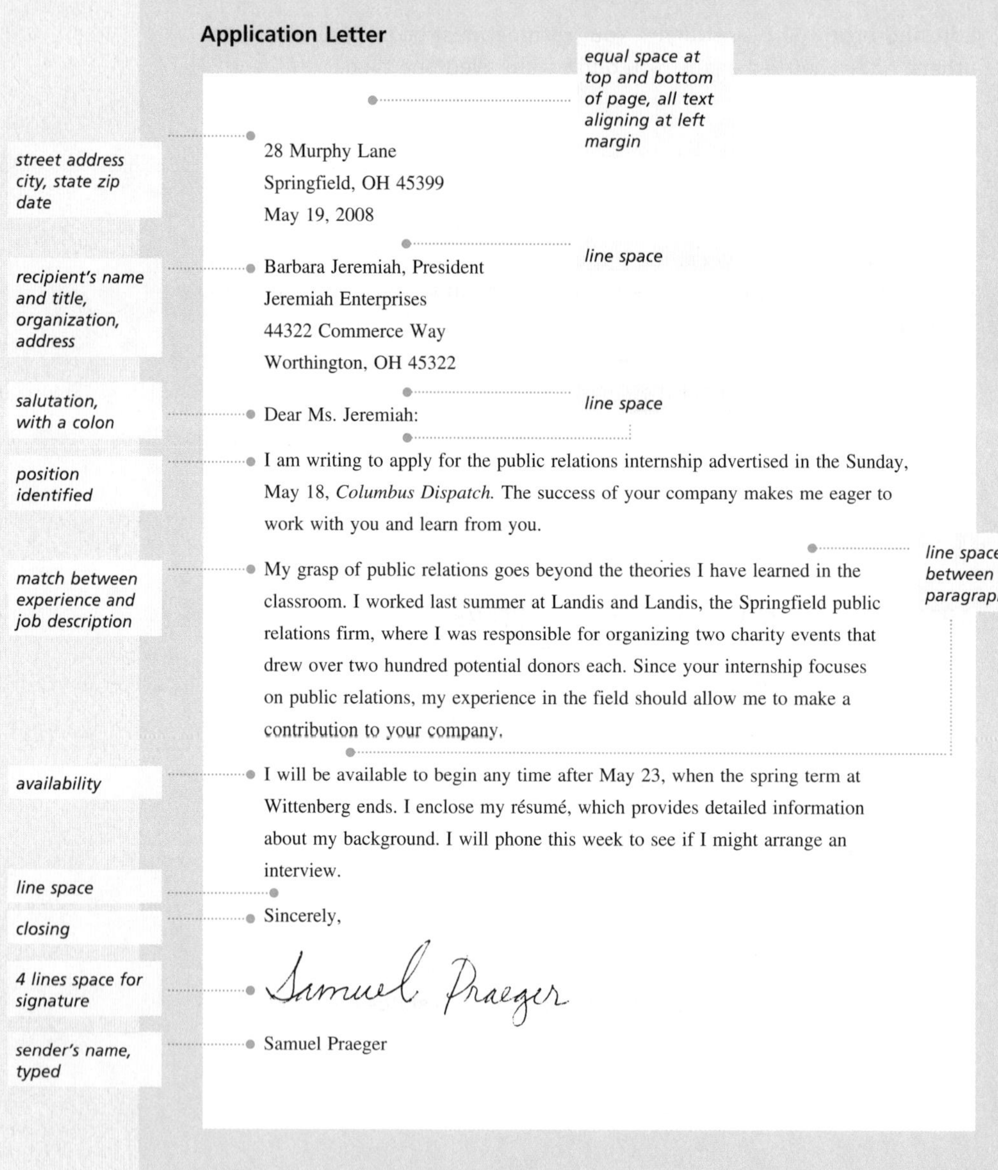
28 Murphy Lane
Springfield, OH 45399
May 19, 2008

Barbara Jeremiah, President
Jeremiah Enterprises
44322 Commerce Way
Worthington, OH 45322

Dear Ms. Jeremiah:

I am writing to apply for the public relations internship advertised in the Sunday, May 18, *Columbus Dispatch.* The success of your company makes me eager to work with you and learn from you.

My grasp of public relations goes beyond the theories I have learned in the classroom. I worked last summer at Landis and Landis, the Springfield public relations firm, where I was responsible for organizing two charity events that drew over two hundred potential donors each. Since your internship focuses on public relations, my experience in the field should allow me to make a contribution to your company.

I will be available to begin any time after May 23, when the spring term at Wittenberg ends. I enclose my résumé, which provides detailed information about my background. I will phone this week to see if I might arrange an interview.

Sincerely,

Samuel Praeger

Samuel Praeger

Thank-You Letter

equal space at top and bottom of page, all text aligning at left margin

28 Murphy Lane
Springfield, OH 45399
June 1, 2008

street address city, state zip date

one space

Barbara Jeremiah, President
Jeremiah Enterprises
44322 Commerce Way
Worthington, OH 45322

recipient's name and title, organization, address

one space

Dear Ms. Jeremiah:

salutation, with a colon

Thank you for the opportunity to meet with you yesterday. I enjoyed talking with you and meeting the people who work with you, and I continue to be very interested in becoming an intern with Jeremiah Enterprises.

thanks and confirmation of interest

line space between paragraphs

As we discussed, I worked with a public relations firm last summer, and since then I have completed three courses in marketing and public relations that relate directly to the work I would be doing as an intern.

brief review of qualifications

I enclose a list of references, as you requested.

enclosures

Thank you again for your time. I hope to hear from you soon.

repeat thanks

line space

Sincerely,

closing

Samuel Praeger

4 lines space for signature

Samuel Praeger

sender's name, typed

Sending a thank-you letter is a way of showing appreciation for an interview and restating your interest in the position. It also shows that you have good manners and understand proper business etiquette. On the previous page is a letter Samuel Praeger sent to the person who interviewed him for an internship, thanking the interviewer for her time and the opportunity to meet her, indicating his interest in the position, and reiterating his qualifications.

Key Features / Application and Thank-You Letters

A succinct indication of your qualifications. In an application letter, you need to make clear why you're interested in the position or the organization—and at the same time give some sense of why the person you're writing to should at least want to meet you. In a thank-you letter, you should remind the interviewer of your qualifications.

A reasonable and pleasing tone. When writing application and thank-you letters, you need to go beyond simply stating your accomplishments or saying thank-you. Through your words, you need to demonstrate that you will be the kind of employee the organization wants. Presentation is also important—your letter should be neat and error-free.

A conventional, businesslike format. Application and thank-you letters typically follow a prescribed format. The most common is the block format shown in the examples. It includes the writer's address, the date, the recipient's name and address, a salutation, the message, a closing, and a signature.

A BRIEF GUIDE TO WRITING JOB LETTERS

Generating Ideas and Text for Application and Thank-You Letters

Focus. Application and thank-you letters are not personal and should not be chatty. Keep them focused: when you're applying for a position, include only information relevant to the position. Don't make your audience wade through irrelevant side issues. Stay on topic.

State the reason for the letter. Unlike essays, which develop a thesis over several paragraphs, or emails, which announce their topic in a subject line, letters need to explicitly introduce their reason for being written, usually in the first paragraph. When you're applying for something or thanking someone, say so in the first sentence: "I am writing to apply for the Margaret Branscomb Peabody Scholarship for students majoring in veterinary science." "Thank you for meeting with me."

Think of your letter as an argument. When you're asking for a job, you're making an ARGUMENT. You're making a claim—that you're qualified for a certain position—and you need to support your claim with reasons and evidence. Praeger, for example, cites his education and his work experience—and he offers to supply references who will support his application.

283–99

Choose an appropriate salutation. If you know the person's name and title, use it: "Dear Professor Turnigan." If you don't know the person's title, one good solution is to address him or her by first and last name: "Dear Julia Turnigan." If, as sometimes happens, you must write to an unknown reader, your options include "To Whom It May Concern" and the more old fashioned "Dear Sir or Madam." Another option might be to omit the salutation completely in such situations and instead use a subject line, for example: "Subject: Public Relations Internship Application." Whenever possible, though, write to a specific person; call the organization and ask whom to write to. Once you've had an interview, write to your interviewer.

Proofread. Few writing situations demand greater perfection than professional letters—especially job letters. Employers receive dozens, sometimes hundreds, of applications, and often can't look at them all. Typos, grammar errors, and other forms of sloppiness prejudice readers against applicants: they're likely to think that if this applicant can't take the time and care to PROOFREAD, how badly does he or she want this position? To compete, strive for perfection.

245–46

Ways of Organizing an Application or Thank-You Letter

Application and thank-you letters should both follow a conventional organization, though you might vary the details somewhat. Here are two standard organizations.

[Application letter]

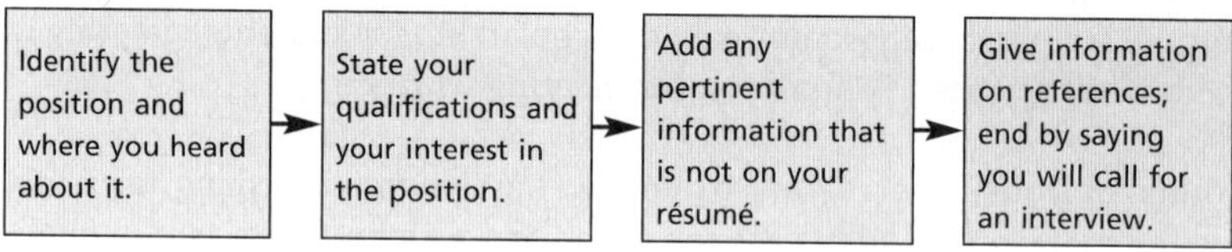

Identify the position and where you heard about it.

[Thank-you letter]

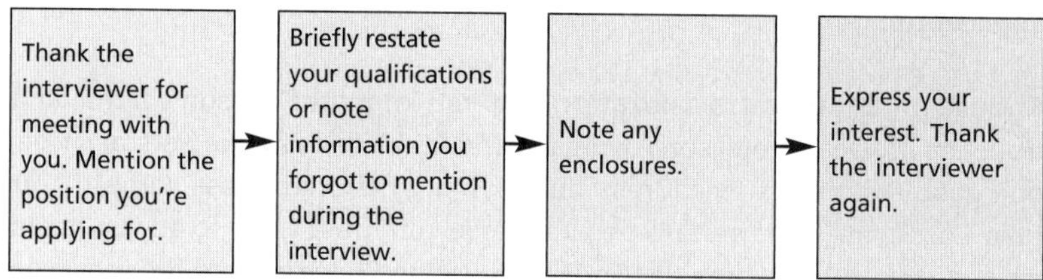

Thank the interviewer for meeting with you. Mention the position you're applying for.
Briefly restate your qualifications or note information you forgot to mention during the interview.
Note any enclosures.
Express your interest. Thank the interviewer again.

IF YOU NEED MORE HELP

226–28
229–34
235–41
242–46

See Chapter 24 for guidelines on **DRAFTING**, Chapter 25 on **ASSESSING YOUR OWN WRITING**, Chapter 26 on **GETTING RESPONSE AND REVISING**, and Chapter 27 on **EDITING**.

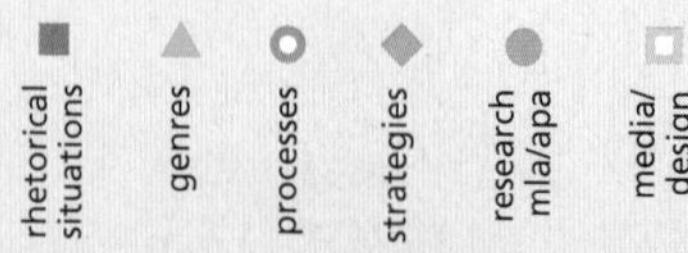

research mla/apa

Mixing Genres 20

Musicians regularly mix genres, blending, for instance, reggae, hip-hop, and jazz to create a unique sound. Like musicians, writers often combine different genres in a single text. An **EVALUATION** of mining practices might include a **PROFILE** of a coal company CEO. A **PROPOSAL** to start a neighborhood watch might begin with a **REPORT** on crime in the area. Here's a column that mixes genres written by Anna Quindlen for *Newsweek* magazine in 2007.

125–32
161–70
171–79
59–82

ANNA QUINDLEN

Write for Your Life

The new movie *Freedom Writers* isn't entirely about the themes the trailers suggest. It isn't only about gang warfare and racial tensions and tolerance. It isn't only about the difference one good teacher can make in the life of one messed-up kid. *Freedom Writers* is about the power of writing in the lives of ordinary people. That's a lesson everyone needs. The movie, and the book from which it was taken, track the education of a young teacher named Erin Gruwell, who shows up shiny-new to face a class of what are called, in pedagogical jargon, "at risk" students. It's a mixed bag of Latino, Asian, and black teenagers with one feckless white kid thrown in. They ignore, belittle, and dismiss her as she proffers lesson plans and reading materials seriously out of step with the homelessness, drug use, and violence that are the stuff of their precarious existences.

Textual Analysis

And then one day, she gives them all marbled composition books and the assignment to write their lives, ungraded, unjudged, and the world breaks open.

"My probation officer thinks he's slick; he swears he's an expert on gangs."

"Sorry, diary, I was going to try not to do it tonight, but the little baggy of white powder is calling my name."

"If you pull up my shirtsleeves and look at my arms, you will see 5 black and blue marks."

"The words 'Eviction Notice' stopped me dead in my tracks."

"When I was younger, they would lock me up in the closet because they wanted to get high and beat up on each other."

Ms. G, as the kids called her, embraced a concept that has been lost in modern life: writing can make pain tolerable, confusion clearer and the self stronger.

Report

How is it, at a time when clarity and strength go begging, that we have moved so far from everyday prose? Social critics might trace this back to the demise of letter writing. The details of housekeeping and child rearing, the rigors of war and work, advice to friends and family: none was slated for publication. They were communications that gave shape to life by describing it for others.

But as the letter fell out of favor and education became profes- 10 sionalized, with its goal less the expansion of the mind than the acquisition of a job, writing began to be seen largely as the purview of writers. Writing at work also became so stylistically removed from the story of our lives that the two seemed to have nothing in common. Corporate prose conformed to an equation: information × polysyllabic words + tortured syntax = aren't you impressed?

Reflection

And in the age of the telephone most communication became evanescent, gone into thin air no matter how important or heartfelt. Think of all those people inside the World Trade Center saying goodbye by phone. If only, in the blizzard of paper that followed the collapse of the buildings, a letter had fallen from the sky for every family member and friend, something to hold on to, something to read and reread. Something real. Words on paper confer a kind of immortality. Wouldn't all of us love to have a journal, a memoir, a letter, from those we have loved and lost? Shouldn't all of us leave a bit of that behind?

The age of technology has both revived the use of writing and provided ever more reasons for its spiritual solace. Emails are letters, after all, more lasting than phone calls, even if many of them r 2 cursory 4 u. And the physical isolation they and other arms-length cyber-advances create makes talking to yourself more important than ever. That's also what writing is: not just a legacy, but therapy. As the novelist Don DeLillo once said, "Writing is a form of personal freedom. It frees us from the mass identity we see in the making all around us. In the end, writers will write not to be outlaw heroes of some underculture but mainly to save themselves, to survive as individuals."

That's exactly what Gruwell was after when she got the kids in her class writing, in a program that's since been duplicated at other schools. Salvation and survival for teenagers whose chances of either seemed negligible. "Growing up, I always assumed I would either drop out of school or get pregnant," one student wrote. "So when Ms. G started talking about college, it was like a foreign language to me." Maybe that's the moment when that Latina girl began to speak that foreign language, when she wrote those words down. Today she has a college degree.

Argument

One of the texts Erin Gruwell assigned was *The Diary of a Young Girl* by Anne Frank. A student who balked at reading a book about 10
someone so different, so remote, went on to write: "At the end of the book, I was so mad that Anne died, because as she was dying, a part of me was dying with her." Of course Anne never dreamed her diary would be published, much less read by millions of people after her death at the hands of the Nazis. She wrote it for the same reason the kids who called themselves Freedom Writers wrote in those composition books: to make sense of themselves. That's not just for writers. That's for people.

Quindlen argues that writing helps us understand ourselves and our world. She uses several genres to help advance her argument—textual analysis of the film Freedom Writers, *a brief report on the decline of letter writing, and a reflection on the technologies we use to write. Together, these genres help her develop her argument that writing helps us "make sense of [our]selves."*

For five more multi-genre texts, see CHAPTER 64.

Key Features / Texts That Mix Genres

One primary genre. Your writing situation will often call for a certain genre that is appropriate for your purpose—an argument, a proposal, a report, a textual analysis, and so forth. Additional genres then play supporting roles. Quindlen's essay, for example, primarily argues a position and mixes in other genres, including report and reflection, to elaborate her argument and bring it to life.

A clear focus. A text that mixes genres approaches the topic several different ways, but each genre must contribute to your main point. One genre may serve as the introduction, and others may be woven throughout the text in other ways, but all must address some aspect of the topic and support the central claim. Quindlen's analysis of the film *Freedom Writers*, for example, supports her claim that writing is one way we learn about ourselves.

Careful organization. A text that combines several genres requires careful organization—the various genres must fit together neatly and clearly. Quindlen opens by analyzing the theme of *Freedom Writers*, noting that it's about "the power of writing in the lives of ordinary people." She then switches genres, reporting on how "we have moved so far from everyday prose" and then reflecting on the consequences of that move.

Clear transitions. When a text includes several genres, those genres need to be connected in some way. Transitions do that, and in so doing, they help readers make their way through the text. Transitions may include words such as "in addition" and "however," and they may also consist of phrases that sum up an idea and move it forward. See, for example, how Quindlen ends one paragraph by quoting Don DeLillo as saying that writers write "to save themselves, to survive as individuals" and then begins the next paragraph by referring to DeLillo's words, saying "That's exactly what Gruwell was after."

Some Typical Ways of Mixing Genres

It's possible to mix almost any genres together. Following are some of the most commonly mixed genres and how they combine with other genres.

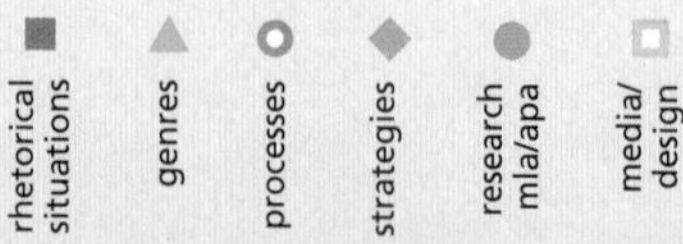

Memoirs. Sometimes a personal anecdote can help support an **ARGUMENT** or enhance a **REPORT**. Stories from your personal experience can help readers understand your motivations for arguing a certain position and can enhance your credibility as a writer. 83–110 59–82

Profiles. One way to bring a **REPORT** on an abstract topic to life is to include a profile of a person, place, or event. For example, if you were writing a report for your boss on the need to hire more sales representatives, including a profile of one salesperson's typical day might drive home the point that your sales force is stretched too thin. 59–82

Textual analyses. You might need to analyze a speech or other document as part of an **ARGUMENT**, especially on a historical or political topic. For instance, you might analyze speeches by Abraham Lincoln and Jefferson Davis if you're writing about the causes of the Civil War, or an advertisement for cigarettes if you're making an argument about teen smoking. 83–110

Evaluations. You might include an evaluation of something when you write a **PROPOSAL** about it. For example, if you were writing a proposal for additional student parking on your campus, you would need to evaluate the current parking facilities to discuss their inadequacy. 171–79

A BRIEF GUIDE TO WRITING TEXTS THAT MIX GENRES

Considering the Rhetorical Situation

PURPOSE Why are you writing this text? To inform? Persuade? Entertain? Explore an idea? Something else? What genres will help you achieve your purpose? 3–4

AUDIENCE Who are your readers? Which genres will help these readers understand your point? Will starting with a memoir or profile draw them in? Will some analysis help them 5–8 understand the topic? Will a profile make the topic less abstract or make them more sympathetic to your claim?

9–11
GENRE What is your primary genre? What other genres might support that primary genre?

12–14
STANCE What is your stance on your topic—objective? opinionated? something else? Will including a textual analysis or report help you establish an objective or analytical tone? Will some reflection or a brief memoir show your personal connection to your topic?

15–17
MEDIA / DESIGN Will your text be a print document? An oral presentation? Will it be published on the Web? Should you include illustrations? Audio or video clips? Do you need to present any information that would be best shown in a chart or graph?

Generating Ideas and Text

Identify your primary genre. If you're writing in response to an assignment, does it specify a particular genre? Look for key verbs that name specific genres—for example, *analyze*, *argue*, *evaluate*, and so on. Be aware that other verbs imply certain genres: *explain*, *summarize*, *review*, and *describe* ask for a report; *argue*, *prove*, and *justify* signal that you need to argue a position; and *evaluate* and *propose* specify evaluations and proposals.

3–4
5–8
If the choice of genre is up to you, consider your **PURPOSE** and **AUDIENCE** carefully to determine what genre is most appropriate. Consult the appropriate genre chapter to identify the key features of your primary genre and to generate ideas and text.

Determine if other genres would be helpful. As you write a draft, you may identify a need—for a beginning that grabs readers' attention, for a satisfying ending, for ways to make an abstract concept more concrete or to help in analyzing something. At this point, you may want to try mixing one or more genres within your draft. Determine what genre will help you achieve your purpose and consult the appropriate genre chapter for advice on writing in that genre. Remember, however, that you're mixing genres into your draft to support and enhance it—so your supporting genres may not be as developed as complete texts in that genre would be and may not include all the key features. For example, if you include a brief memoir as part of an argument, it should include a good story and vivid details—but its significance may well be stated as part of the argument, rather than revealed through the storytelling itself.

Integrate the genres. Your goal is to create a focused, unified, coherent text. So you need to make sure that your genres work together to achieve that goal. Make sure that each genre fulfills a purpose within the text—for example, that a textual analysis within an argument provides evidence to support your claim, or that the profile you include in a report provides a clear illustration of the larger subject. Also, use **TRANSITIONS** to help readers move from section to section in your text. 277

Multi-Genre Projects

Sometimes a collection of texts can together represent an experience or advance an argument. For example, you might document a trip to the Grand Canyon in an album that contains journal entries written during the trip, photographs, a map of northern Arizona showing the Canyon, postcards, an essay on the geology of the Canyon, and a souvenir coin stamped with an image of the Canyon. Each represents a different way of experiencing the Grand Canyon, and together they offer a multifaceted way to understand your trip.

You might also write in several different genres on the same topic. If you begin by **ARGUING** that the government should provide universal health care, for example, writing a **MEMOIR** about a time you were ill could help you explore a personal connection to the topic. Composing a **PROFILE** of a doctor might give you new insights into the issue, and writing a **PROPOSAL** for how universal health care could work might direct you to potential

283–99

153–60
161–70
171–79

solutions. You could assemble all these texts in a folder, with a title page and table of contents so that readers can see how it all fits together—or
546–56
you could create a **WEBSITE,** combining text, images, video, sound, and links to other sites.

226–28
229–34
261–71
272–77

IF YOU NEED MORE HELP

See Chapter 24 for guidelines on **DRAFTING,** Chapter 25 on **ASSESSING YOUR OWN WRITING,** Chapter 29 on **BEGINNING AND ENDING,** and Chapter 30 on **GUIDING YOUR READER.**

part 3

Processes

To create anything, we generally break the work down into a series of steps. We follow a recipe (or the directions on a box) to bake a cake; we break a song down into different parts and the music into various chords to arrange a piece of music. So it is when we write. We rely on various processes to get from a blank page to a finished product. The chapters that follow offer advice on some of these processes — from WRITING AS INQUIRY and GENERATING IDEAS to DRAFTING to GETTING RESPONSE to EDITING to COMPILING A PORTFOLIO, and more.

Processes

21 Writing as Inquiry

Sometimes we write to say what we think. Other times, however, we write in order to figure out what we think. Much of the writing you do in college will be the latter. Even as you learn to write, you will be writing to learn. This chapter is about writing with a spirit of inquiry—approaching writing projects with curiosity, moving beyond the familiar, keeping your eyes open, tackling issues that don't have easy answers. It's about starting with questions and going from there—and taking risks. As Mark Twain once said, "Sail away from the safe harbor. . . . Explore. Dream. Discover." This chapter offers strategies for doing just that with your writing.

Starting with Questions

The most important thing is to start with questions—with what you don't know rather than with what you do know. Your goal is to learn about your subject and then to learn more. If you're writing about a topic you know well, you want to expand on what you already know. In academic writing, good topics arise from important questions, issues, and problems that are already being discussed. As a writer, you need to find out what's being said about your topic and then see your writing as a way of entering that larger conversation.

So start with questions, and don't expect to find easy answers. If there were easy answers, there would be no reason for discussion—or for you to write. For purposes of inquiry, the best questions can't be answered by looking in a reference book. Instead, they are ones that help you explore what you think—and why. As it happens, many of the strategies in this book can help you ask questions of this kind. Following are some questions to get you started.

314–23 **How can it be DEFINED?** What is it, and what does it do? Look it up in a dictionary; check Wikipedia. Remember, though, that these are only starting points. How *else* can it be defined? What more is there to know about it? If your topic is being debated, chances are that its very definition is subject to debate. If, for instance, you're writing about gay marriage, how you define marriage will affect how you approach the topic.

324–32 **How can it be DESCRIBED?** What details should you include? From what vantage point should you describe your topic? If, for example, your topic were the physiological effects of running a marathon, what would those effects be—on the lungs, heart muscles, nerves, brain, and so on? How would you describe the physical experience of running over twenty-six miles from the runner's point of view?

338–42 **How can it be EXPLAINED?** What does it do? How does it work? If you were investigating the use of performance-enhancing drugs by athletes, for example, what exactly is the effect of these drugs? What makes them dangerous—and are they always dangerous or only in certain conditions? Why are they illegal—and should they be illegal?

306–13 **What can it be COMPARED with?** Again with the use of performance-enhancing drugs by athletes as an example, how does taking such supplements, or doping, compare with wearing high-tech footwear or uniforms? Does such a comparison make you see doping in a new light?

278–82 **What may have CAUSED it? What might be its EFFECTS?** Who or what does it affect? What causes hyperactivity in children, for example? What are the symptoms of hyperactivity? Are some children more likely than others to develop hyperactivity? Why? If children with hyperactive behavior are not treated, what might be the consequences? If they are treated with drugs, how might their lives as adults be affected?

300–305 **How can it be CLASSIFIED?** Is it a topic or issue that can be placed into categories of similar topics or issues? What categories can it be placed into? Are there legal and illegal performance-enhancing supplements (creatine and steroids, for instance), and what's the difference? Are some safe and others less safe? Classifying your topic in this way can help you consider its complexities.

How can it be ANALYZED? What parts can the topic be divided into? For example, if you were exploring the health effects of cell phone use, you might ask what evidence suggests that cell phone radiation causes cancer? What cancers are associated with cell phone use? What do medical experts and phone manufacturers say? How can cell phone users reduce their risk?

278–82

How can it be INTERPRETED? What does it really mean? How do you interpret it, and how does your interpretation differ from others? What evidence supports your interpretation, and what argues against it? Imagine you were exploring the topic of sports injuries among young women. Do these injuries reflect a larger cultural preoccupation with competition? A desire to win college scholarships? Something else?

38–58

What expectations does it raise? What will happen next? What makes you think so? If this happens, how will it affect those involved? For instance, will the governing bodies of professional sports require more blood testing than they do now? Will such tests be unfair to athletes taking drugs for legitimate medical needs?

What are the different POSITIONS on it? What controversies or disagreements exist, and what evidence is offered for the various positions? What else might be said? Are there any groups or individuals who seem especially authoritative? If so, you might want to explore what they have said.

83–110

What are your own feelings about it? What interests you about the topic? How much do you already know about it? For example, if you're an athlete, how do you feel about competing against others who may have taken supplements? If a friend has problems with drugs, do those problems affect your thinking about doping in sports? How do you react to what others say about the topic? What else do you want to find out?

Are there other ways to think about it? Is what seems true in this case also true in others? How can you apply this subject in another situation? Will what works in another situation also work here? What do you have to do to adapt it? Imagine you were writing about traffic fatalities. If replacing stop signs with roundabouts reduced traffic fatalities in England, could roundabouts also reduce accidents in the U.S.?

222–23 You can also start with the journalist's **QUESTIONS**: *Who? What? When? Where? Why? How?* Asking questions from these various perspectives can help you deepen your understanding of your topic by leading you to see it from many angles.

Keeping a Journal

One way to get into the habit of using writing as a tool for inquiry is to keep a journal. You can use a journal to record your observations, reactions, whatever you wish. Some writers find journals especially useful places to articulate questions or speculations. You may be assigned by teachers to do certain work in a journal, but in general, you can use a journal to write for yourself. Jot down ideas, speculate, digress—go wherever your thoughts lead you.

Keeping a Blog

You may also wish to explore issues or other ideas online in the form of 554–56 a **BLOG.** Most blogs have a comments section that allows others to read and respond to what you write, leading to potentially fruitful discussions. You can also include links to other websites, helping you connect various strands of thought and research. The blogs of others, along with online discussion forums and groups, may also be useful sources of opinion on your topic, but keep in mind that they probably aren't authoritative research sources. There are a number of search engines that can help you find blog posts related to specific topics, including Google Blog Search, Ice Rocket, Technorati, and Blog-Search. You can create your own blog on sites such as Blogger, LiveJournal, or Xanga.

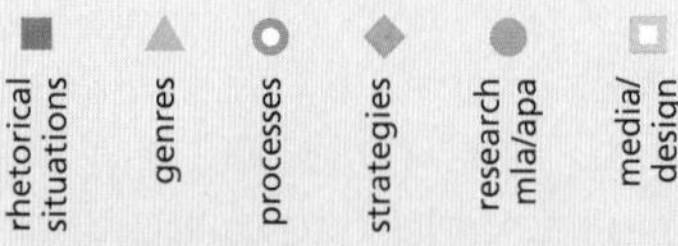

Collaborating 22

Whether you're working in a group, participating in a Listserv or wiki, or exchanging drafts with a classmate for peer review, you likely spend a lot of time collaborating with others. Even if you do much of your writing sitting alone at a computer, you probably get help from others at various stages in the writing process — and provide help as well. The fact is that two heads can be better than one — and learning to work well with a team is as important as anything else you'll learn in college. This chapter offers some guidelines for collaborating successfully with other writers.

Some Ground Rules for Working in a Group

- Make sure everyone is facing everyone else and is physically part of the group. Doing that makes a real difference in the quality of the interactions — think how much better conversation works when you're sitting around a table than it does when you're sitting in a row.
- Thoughtfulness, respect, and tact are key, since most writers (as you know) are sensitive and need to be able to trust those commenting on their work. Respond to the writing of others as you would like others to respond to yours.
- Each meeting needs an agenda — and careful attention paid to time. Appoint one person as timekeeper to make sure all necessary work gets done in the available time.
- Appoint another person to be group leader or facilitator. That person needs to make sure everyone gets a chance to speak, no one dominates the discussion, and the group stays on task.

- Appoint a third member of the group to keep a record of the group's discussion. He or she should jot down the major points as they come up and afterward write a **SUMMARY** of the discussion that the group members approve.

416–17

Group Writing Projects

Creating a document with a team is common in business and industry and in some academic fields as well. Collaboration of this kind presents new challenges and different kinds of responsibilities. Here are some tips for making group projects work well:

- ***Define the task as clearly as possible,*** and make sure everyone understands and agrees with the stated goals.
- ***Divide the task into parts.*** Decide which parts can be done by individuals, which can be done by a subgroup, and which need to be done by everyone together.
- ***Assign each group member certain tasks.*** Try to match tasks to each person's skills and interests, and divide the work equally.
- ***Establish a deadline for each task.*** Allow time for unforeseen problems before the project deadline.
- ***Try to accommodate everyone's style of working.*** Some people value discussion; others want to get right down to the writing. There's no best way to get work done; everyone needs to be conscious that his or her way is not the only way.
- ***Work for consensus—not necessarily total agreement.*** Everyone needs to agree that the plan is doable and appropriate—if not exactly the way you would do it if you were working alone.
- ***Make sure everyone performs.*** In some situations, your instructor may help, but in others the group itself may have to develop a way to make sure that the work gets done well and fairly. During the course of the project, it's sometimes helpful for each group member to write an assessment both of the group's work and of individual members' contributions.

Online Collaboration

Sometimes you'll need or want to work with one or more people online. Working together online offers many advantages, including the ability to collaborate without being in the same place at the same time. Nonetheless, working online presents some challenges that differ from those of face-to-face group work. When sharing writing or collaborating with others online, consider the following suggestions:

- As with all online communication, remember that you need to choose your words carefully to avoid flaming another group member or inadvertently hurting someone's feelings. Without facial expressions, gestures, and other forms of body language and without tone of voice, your words carry all the weight.
- Remember that the **AUDIENCE** for what you write may well extend beyond your group—your work might be forwarded to others, so there is no telling who else might read it. 5–8
- Decide as a group how best to deal with the logistics of exchanging drafts and comments. You can cut and paste text directly into email, send it as an attachment to a message, or post it to a newsgroup or course bulletin board. You may need to use a combination of methods, depending on each group member's access to equipment and software.

Writing Conferences

Conferences with instructors or writing tutors can be an especially helpful kind of collaboration. These one-on-one sessions often offer the most strongly focused assistance you can get—and truly valuable instruction. Here are some tips for making the most of conference time:

- *Come prepared.* Bring all necessary materials, including the draft you'll be discussing, your notes, any outlines—and, of course, any questions.
- *Be prompt.* Your instructor or tutor has set aside a block of time for you, and once that time is up, there's likely to be another student writer waiting.

- ***Listen carefully, discuss your work seriously, and try not to be defensive.*** Your instructor or tutor is only trying to help you produce the best piece possible. If you sense that your work is being misunderstood, explain what you're trying to say. Don't get angry! If a sympathetic reader who's trying to help can't understand what you mean, maybe you haven't conveyed your meaning well enough.
- ***Take notes.*** During the conference, jot down key words and suggestions. Immediately afterward, flesh out your notes so you'll have a complete record of what was said.
- ***Reflect on the conference.*** Afterward, think about what you learned. What do you have to do now? Think about questions you will ask at your next conference.

Generating Ideas and Text 23

All good writing revolves around ideas. Whether you're writing a job-application letter, a sonnet, or an essay, you'll always spend time and effort generating ideas. Some writers can come up with a topic, put their thoughts in order, and flesh out their arguments in their heads; but most of us need to write down our ideas, play with them, tease them out, and examine them from some distance and from multiple perspectives. This chapter offers activities that can help you do just that. *Freewriting*, *looping*, *listing*, and *clustering* can help you explore what you know about a subject; *cubing* and *questioning* nudge you to consider a subject in new ways; and *outlining*, *letter-writing*, *journal-keeping*, and *discovery drafting* offer ways to generate a text.

Freewriting

An informal method of exploring a subject by writing about it, freewriting ("writing freely") can help you generate ideas and come up with materials for your draft. Here's how to do it:

1. Write as quickly as you can without stopping for 5–10 minutes (or until you fill a page or screen).
2. If you have a subject to explore, write it at the top of the page and then start writing, but if you stray, don't worry—just keep writing. If you don't have a subject yet, just start writing and don't stop until the time is up. If you can't think of anything to say, write that ("I can't think of anything to say") again and again until you do—and you will!
3. Once the time is up, read over what you've written, and underline passages that interest you.

4. Then write some more, starting with one of those underlined passages as your new topic. Repeat the process until you've come up with a usable topic.

Looping

Looping is a more focused version of freewriting; it can help you explore what you know about a subject. You stop, reflect on what you've written, and then write again, developing your understanding in the process. It's good for clarifying your knowledge and understanding of a subject and finding a focus. Here's what you do:

1. Write for 5–10 minutes, jotting down whatever you know about your subject. This is your first loop.
2. Read over what you wrote, and then write a single sentence summarizing the most important or interesting idea. You might try completing one of these sentences: "I guess what I was trying to say was . . . " or "What surprises me most in reading what I wrote is . . . ." This will be the start of another loop.
3. Write again for 5–10 minutes, using your summary sentence as your beginning and your focus. Again, read what you've written, and then write a sentence capturing the most important idea—in a third loop.

Keep going until you have enough understanding of your topic to be able to decide on a tentative focus—something you can write about.

Listing

Some writers find it useful to keep lists of ideas that occur to them while they are thinking about a topic. Follow these steps:

1. Write a list of potential ideas about a topic, leaving space to add ideas that might occur to you later. Don't try to limit your list—include anything that interests you.

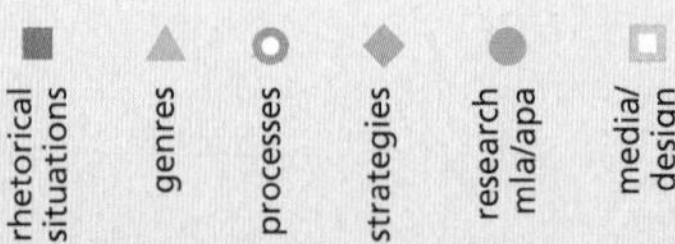

2. Look for relationships among the items on your list: what patterns do you see?
3. Finally, arrange the items in an order that makes sense for your purpose and can serve as the beginning of an outline for your writing.

Clustering

Clustering is a way of generating and connecting ideas visually. It's useful for seeing how various ideas relate to one another and for developing subtopics. The technique is simple:

1. Write your topic in the middle of a sheet of paper and circle it.
2. Write ideas relating to that topic around it, circle them, and connect them to the central circle.

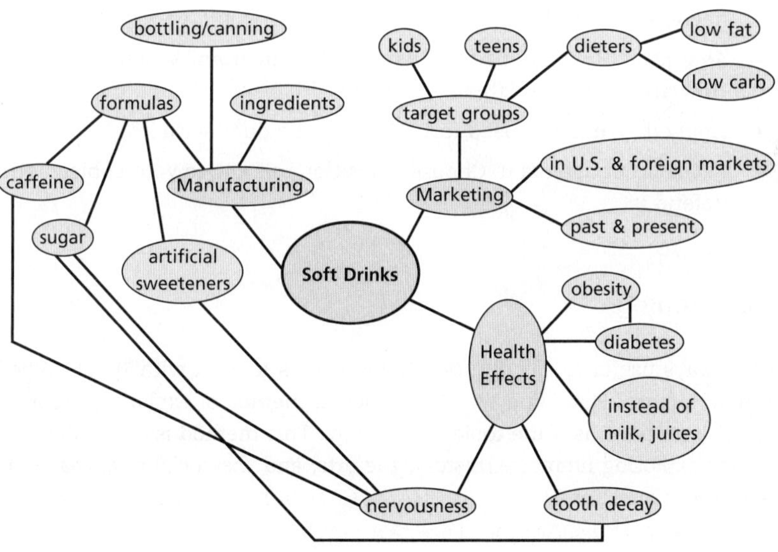

3. Write down ideas, examples, facts, or other details relating to each idea, and join them to the appropriate circles.
4. Keep going until you can't think of anything else relating to your topic.

You should end up with various ideas about your topic, and the clusters will allow you to see how they relate to one another. In the example cluster on the topic of "soft drinks" from page 221, note how some ideas link not only to the main topic or related topics but also to other ideas.

Cubing

A cube has six sides. You can examine a topic as you might a cube, looking at it in these six ways:

- 324–32 **DESCRIBE** it. What's its color? Shape? Age? Size? What's it made of?
- 306–13 **COMPARE** it to something else. What is it similar to or different from?
- Associate it with other things. What does it remind you of? What connections does it have to other things? How would you **CLASSIFY** it? 300–315
- 278–82 **ANALYZE** it. How is it made? Where did it come from? Where is it going? How are its parts related?
- Apply it. What is it used for? What can be done with it?
- 83–110 **ARGUE** for or against it. Choose a position relating to your subject, and defend it.

Questioning

211–14 It's always useful to ask **QUESTIONS.** One way is to start with What? Who? When? Where? How? and Why? A particular method of exploring a topic is to ask questions as if the topic were a play. This method is especially useful for exploring literature, history, the arts, and the social sciences. Start with these questions:

- ***What?*** What happens? How is it similar to or different from other actions?
- ***Who?*** Who are the actors? Who are the participants, and who are the spectators? How do the actors affect the action, and how are they affected by it?
- ***When?*** When does the action take place? How often does it happen? What happens before, after, or at the same time? Would it be different at another time? Does the time have historical significance?
- ***Where?*** What is the setting? What is the situation, and what makes it significant?
- ***How?*** How does the action occur? What are the steps in the process? What techniques are required? What equipment is needed?
- ***Why?*** Why did this happen? What are the actors' motives? What end does the action serve?

Outlining

You may create an *informal outline* by simply listing your ideas and numbering them in the order in which you want to write about them. You might prefer to make a *working outline*, to show the hierarchy of relationships among your ideas. While still informal, a working outline distinguishes your main ideas and your support, often through simple indentation:

First main idea
  Supporting evidence or detail
  Supporting evidence or detail
Second main idea
  Supporting evidence or detail
  Supporting evidence or detail

A *formal outline* shows the hierarchy of your ideas through a system of indenting, numbering, and lettering. Remember that when you divide a point into more specific subpoints, you should have at least two of them—you can't divide something into only one part. Also, try to keep items at each level parallel in structure. Formal outlines work this way:

Thesis statement

- I. First reason
  - A. Supporting evidence
    - 1. Detail of evidence
    - 2. Detail of evidence
  - B. Supporting evidence
- II. Another reason

Writing out a formal outline can be helpful when you're dealing with a complex subject; as you revise your drafts, though, be flexible and ready to change your outline as your understanding of your topic develops.

Letter Writing

Sometimes the prospect of writing a report or essay can be intimidating. You may find that simply explaining your topic to someone will help you get started. In that case, write a letter to someone you know—your best friend, a parent or grandparent, a sibling—in which you discuss your subject. Explain it in terms that your reader can understand. Use the unsent letter to rehearse your topic; make it a kind of rough draft that you can then revise and develop to suit your actual audience.

Keeping a Journal

Some writers find that writing in a journal helps them generate ideas. Jotting down ideas, thoughts, feelings, or the events of your day can provide a wealth of topics, and a journal can also be a good place to explore what you think and why you think as you do.

Discovery Drafting

Some writers do best by jumping in and writing. Here are the steps to take if you're ready to write a preliminary **DRAFT**: 226–28

1. Write your draft quickly, in one sitting if possible.
2. Assume that you are writing to discover what you want to say and how you need to say it — and that you will make substantial revisions in a later part of the process.
3. Don't worry about grammatical or factual correctness — if you can't think of a word, leave a blank to fill in later. If you're unsure of a date or spelling, put a question mark in parentheses as a reminder to check it later. Just write.

IF YOU NEED MORE HELP

See also each of the GENRE chapters for specific stategies for generating text in each genre. 19

24 Drafting

At some point, you need to write out a draft. By the time you begin drafting, you've probably written quite a bit—in the form of notes, lists, outlines, and other kinds of informal writing. This chapter offers some hints on how to write a draft—and reminds you that as you draft, you may well need to get more information, rethink some aspect of your work, or follow new ideas that occur to you as you write.

Establishing a Schedule with Deadlines

Don't wait until the last minute to write. Computers crash, printers jam. Life intervenes in unpredictable ways. You increase your chances of success immensely by setting and meeting **DEADLINES**: Research done by ____ ; rough draft done by ____ ; revisions done by ____ ; final draft edited, proofread, and submitted by ____ . How much time you need varies with each writing task—but trying to compress everything into twenty-four or forty-eight hours before the deadline is asking for trouble.

375

Getting Comfortable

When are you at your best? When do you have your best ideas? For major writing projects, consider establishing a schedule that lets you write when you stand the best chance of doing good work. Schedule breaks for exercise and snacks. Find a good place to write, a place where you've got a good surface on which to spread out your materials, good lighting, a comfortable chair, and the right tools (pen, paper, computer) for the job. Often, however, we must make do: you may have to do your drafting in a busy computer lab or classroom. The trick is to make yourself as comfortable as you can manage. Sort out what you *need* from what you *prefer*.

Starting to Write

All of the above advice notwithstanding, don't worry so much about the trappings of your writing situation that you don't get around to writing. Write. Start by **FREEWRITING**, start with a first sentence, start with awful writing that you know you'll discard later—but write. That's what gets you warmed up and going.

219–20

Write quickly in spurts. Write quickly with the goal of writing a complete draft, or a complete section of a longer draft, in one sitting. If you need to stop in the middle, jot down some notes about where you were headed when you stopped so that you can easily pick up your train of thought when you begin again.

Break down your writing task into small segments. Big projects can be intimidating. But you can always write one section or, if need be, one paragraph or even a single sentence—and then another and another. It's a little like dieting. If I think I need to lose twenty pounds, I get discouraged and head for the doughnuts; but if I decide that I'll lose one pound and I lose it, well, I'll lose another—*that* I can do.

Expect surprises. Writing is a form of thinking; the words you write lead you down certain roads and away from others. You may end up somewhere you didn't anticipate. Sometimes that can be a good thing—but sometimes you can write yourself into a dead end or out onto a tangent. Just know that this is natural, part of every writer's experience, and it's okay to double back or follow a new path that opens up before you.

Expect to write more than one draft. A first sentence, first page, or first draft represents your attempt to organize into words your thoughts, ideas, feelings, research findings, and more. It's likely that some of that first try will not achieve your goals. That's okay—having writing on paper or on screen that you can change, add to, and cut means you're part of the way there. As you revise, you can fill in gaps and improve your writing and thinking.

Dealing with Writer's Block

You may sit down to write but find that you can't — nothing occurs to you; your mind is blank. Don't panic; here are some ways to get started writing again:

- Think of the assignment as a problem to be solved. Try to capture that problem in a single sentence: "How do I . . . ?" "What is the best way to . . . ?" "What am I trying to do in . . . ?" Think of a solution to the problem, and then stop thinking about it. If you can't solve it, do something else; give yourself time. Many of us find the solution in the shower, after a good night's sleep.
- Stop trying: take a walk, take a shower, do something else. Come back in a half hour, refreshed.
- 219–21 Get a fresh piece of paper and **FREEWRITE,** or try **LOOPING** or **LISTING.** What are you trying to say? Just let whatever comes come — you may write yourself out of your box.
- 221–22 Try a different medium: try **CLUSTERING,** or draw a chart of what you want to say; draw a picture; doodle.
- 373 Do some **RESEARCH** on your topic to see what others have said about it.
- Talk to someone about what you are trying to do; if there's a writing 235–41 center at your school, talk to a tutor: **GET RESPONSE.** If there's no one to talk to, talk to yourself. It's the act of talking — using your mouth instead of your hands — that can free you up.

IF YOU NEED MORE HELP

219–25
229–34
235–41

See the chapter on GENERATING IDEAS AND TEXT if you find you need more material. And once you have a draft, see the chapters on ASSESSING YOUR OWN WRITING and GETTING RESPONSE AND REVISING for help evaluating your draft.

Assessing Your Own Writing 25

In school and out, our work is continually assessed by others. Teachers determine whether our writing is strong or weak; supervisors decide whether we merit raises or promotions; even friends and relatives size up the things we do in various ways. As writers, we need to assess our work—to step back and see it with a critical eye. By developing standards of our own and being conscious of the standards others use, we can assess—and shape—our writing, making sure it does what we want it to do. This chapter will help you assess your own written work.

Assessing the Writing You Do for Yourself

We sometimes write not for an audience but for ourselves—to generate ideas, reflect, make sense of things. The best advice on assessing such writing is *don't*. If you're writing to explore your thoughts, understand a subject, record the events of your day, or just for the pleasure of putting words on paper, shut off your internal evaluator. Let the words flow without worrying about them. Let yourself wander without censoring yourself or fretting that what you're writing is incorrect or incomplete or incoherent. That's okay.

One measure of the success of personal writing is its length. **FREEWRITING, LISTING, CUBING, JOURNAL KEEPING,** and other types of informal writing are like warm-up exercises to limber you up and get you thinking. 219–25 If you don't give those writing exercises enough time and space, they may not do what you want them to. I've found, for example, that my students' best insights most often appear at the end of their journal entries. Had they stopped before that point, they never would have had those good ideas.

A way to study the ideas in your personal writing is to highlight useful patterns in different colors. For example, journal entries usually involve some questioning and speculating, as well as summarizing and paraphrasing. Try color coding each of these, sentence by sentence, phrase by phrase: yellow for summaries or paraphrases, green for questions, blue for speculations. Do any colors dominate? If, for example, your text is mostly yellow, you may be restating the course content too much and perhaps need to ask more questions. If you're generating ideas for an essay, you might assign colors to ideas or themes to see which ones are most promising.

Assessing the Writing You Do for Others

What we write for others must stand on its own because we usually aren't present when it is read—we rarely get to explain to readers why we did what we did and what it means. So we need to make our writing as good as we can before we submit, post, display, or publish it. It's a good idea to assess your writing in two stages, first considering how well it meets the needs of your particular rhetorical situation, then studying the text itself to check its focus, argument, and organization. Sometimes some simple questions can get you started:

What works?
What still needs work?
Where do you need to say more (or less)?

Considering the Rhetorical Situation

3–4

PURPOSE What is your purpose for writing? If you have multiple purposes, list them, and then note which ones are the most important. How does your draft achieve your purpose(s)? If you're writing for an assignment, what are the requirements of the assignment and does your draft meet those requirements?

AUDIENCE To whom are you writing? What do those readers need and expect, as far as you can tell? Does your draft answer their needs? Do you define any terms and explain any concepts they won't know? 5–8

GENRE What is the genre, and what are the key features of that genre? Does your draft include each of those features? 9–11

STANCE Is it clear where you stand on your topic? Does your writing project the personality, voice, and tone that you want? Look at the words you use—how do they represent you as a person? 12–14

MEDIA / DESIGN At this point, your text is not likely to be designed, but think about the medium (print? spoken? electronic?) and whether your writing suits it. What design requirements can you anticipate? Lists? Headings? Charts? Visuals? 15–17

Examining the Text Itself

Look carefully at your text to see how well it says what you want it to say. Start with the broadest aspect, its focus, and then examine its reasons and evidence, organization, and clarity, in that order. If your writing lacks focus, the revising you'll do to sharpen the focus is likely to change everything else; if it needs more reasons and evidence, the organization may well change.

Consider your focus. Your writing should have a clear point, and every part of the writing should support that point. Here are some questions that can help you see if your draft is adequately focused:

- What is your **THESIS**? Even if it is not stated directly, you should be able to summarize it for yourself in a single sentence. 273–75
- Is your thesis narrow or broad enough to suit the needs and expectations of your audience?
- How does the **BEGINNING** focus attention on your main point? 261–66

- Does each paragraph support or develop that point? Do any paragraphs or sentences stray from your focus?
- 267–70 Does the **ENDING** leave readers thinking about your main point? Is there another way of concluding the essay that would sharpen your focus?

Consider the support you provide for your argument. Your writing needs to give readers enough information to understand your points, follow your
283–99 **ARGUMENT,** and see the logic of your thinking. How much information is enough will vary according to your audience. If they already know a lot about your subject or are likely to agree with your point of view, you may need to give less detail. If, however, they are unfamiliar with your topic or are skeptical about your views, you will probably need to provide much more information to help them understand your position.

- 286–93 What **REASONS** and **EVIDENCE** do you give to support your thesis? Where might more information be helpful or useful?
- 314–23 What key terms and concepts do you **DEFINE?** Are there any other terms your readers might need to have explained?
- 324–32 Where might you include more **DESCRIPTION** or other detail?
- 306–13 Do you make any **COMPARISONS?** Especially if your readers will not be familiar with your topic, it can help to compare it with something more familiar.
- 343–51 If you include **NARRATIVE,** how is it relevant to your point?
- 259 See Part 4 for other useful **STRATEGIES.**

Consider the organization. As a writer, you need to lead readers through your text, carefully structuring your material so that they will be able to follow your argument.

- 223–24 Analyze the structure by **OUTLINING** it. An informal outline will do since you mainly need to see the parts, not the details.
- Does your genre require an abstract, a works-cited list, or any other elements?

- What **TRANSITIONS** help readers move from idea to idea and paragraph to paragraph? 277
- Would **HEADINGS** help orient readers? 526–27

Check for clarity. Nothing else matters if readers can't understand what you write. So clarity matters. Following are some questions that can help you see whether your meaning is clear and your text is easy to read:

- Does your **TITLE** announce the subject of your text and give some sense of what you have to say? If not, would it strengthen your argument if the title were more direct? 272–73
- Do you state your **THESIS** directly? If not, how will readers understand your main point? Try stating your thesis outright, and see if it makes your argument easier to follow. 273–75
- Does your **BEGINNING** tell readers what they need to understand your text, and does your **ENDING** help them make sense of what they've just read? 261–71
- How does each paragraph relate to the ones before and after? Do you make those relationships clear—or do you need to add **TRANSITIONS**? 277
- Do you vary your sentences? If all the sentences are roughly the same length and follow the same subject-verb-object pattern, your text probably lacks any clear emphasis and might even be difficult to read.
- Are **VISUALS** clearly labeled, positioned near the text they relate to, and referred to clearly in the text? 528–32
- If you introduce materials from other **SOURCES**, have you clearly distinguished quoted, paraphrased, or summarized ideas from your own? 408–19
- Have a look at the words you use. Concrete words are generally easier to understand than abstract words. If you use too many abstract words, consider changing some of them to concrete terms. Do you **DEFINE** all the words that your readers may not know? 314–23
- Does your punctuation make your writing more clear, or less? Incorrect punctuation can make writing difficult to follow or, worse, change

the intended meaning. As a best-selling punctuation manual reminds us, there's a considerable difference between "eats, shoots, and leaves" and "eats shoots and leaves."

Thinking about Your Process

Your growth as a writer depends on how well you understand what you do when you write, so that you can build on good habits. After you finish a writing project, considering the following questions can help you see the process that led to its creation—and find ways to improve the process next time.

- How would you tell the story of your thinking? Try writing these sentences: "When I first began with my topic, I thought ______________. But, as I did some thinking, writing, and research about the topic, my ideas changed and I thought ______________."
- At some point in your writing, did you have to choose between two or more alternatives? What were they, and how did you choose?
- What was the most difficult problem you faced while writing? How did you go about trying to solve it?
- Whose advice did you seek while researching, organizing, drafting, revising, and editing? What advice did you take, and what did you ignore? Why?

Getting Response and Revising 26

If we want to learn to play a song on the guitar, we play it over and over again until we get it right. If we play basketball or baseball, we likely spend hours shooting foul shots or practicing a swing. Writing works the same way. Making our meaning clear can be tricky, and you should plan on revising and if need be rewriting in order to get it right. When we speak with someone face-to-face or on the phone or text message a friend, we can get immediate response and adjust or restate our message if we've been misunderstood. When we write, that immediate response is missing, so we need to seek out responses from readers to help us revise. This chapter includes a list of things for those readers to consider, along with various strategies for susequent revising and rewriting.

Getting Response

Sometimes the most helpful eyes belong to others: readers you trust, including trained writing-center tutors. They can often point out problems (and strengths) that you simply cannot see in your own work. Ask your readers to consider the specific elements in the list below, but don't restrict them to those elements. Caution: If a reader says nothing about any of these elements, don't be too quick to assume that you needn't think about them yourself.

- What did you think when you first saw the **TITLE**? Is it interesting? Informative? Appropriate? Will it attract other readers' attention? 272–73
- Does the **BEGINNING** grab readers' attention? If so, how does it do so? Does it give enough information about the topic? Offer necessary background information? How else might the piece begin? 261–66
- Is there a clear **THESIS**? What is it? 273–75

- 284 Is there sufficient **SUPPORT** for the thesis? Is there anywhere you'd like to have more detail? 425–27 Is the supporting material sufficiently **DOCUMENTED**?
- Does the text have a clear pattern of organization? Does each part relate to the thesis? Does each part follow from the one preceding it? Was the text easy to follow? How might the organization be improved?
- 267–70 Is the **ENDING** satisfying? What did it leave you thinking? How else might it end?
- 12–14 What is the writer's **STANCE**? Can you tell the writer's attitude toward the subject and audience? What words convey that attitude? Is it consistent throughout?
- 1 How well does the text address the rest of its **RHETORICAL SITUATION**? 5–8 Does it meet the needs and expectations of its **AUDIENCE**? Where might 3–4 readers need more information, guidance, or clarification? Does it 9–11 achieve its **PURPOSE**? Does every part of the text help achieve the purpose? Could anything be cut? Should anything be added? Does the text meet the requirements of its **GENRE**? Should anything be added, deleted, or changed to meet those requirements?

Revising

Once you have studied your draft with a critical eye and, if possible, gotten responses from other readers, it's time to revise. Major changes may be necessary, and you may need to generate new material or do some rewriting. But assume that your draft is good raw material that you can revise to achieve your purposes. Revision should take place on several levels, from global (whole-text issues) to particular (the details). Work on your draft in that order, starting with the elements that are global in nature and gradually moving to smaller, more particular aspects. This allows you to use your time most efficiently and take care of bigger issues first. In fact, as you deal with the larger aspects of your writing, many of the smaller ones will be taken care of along the way.

375 **Give yourself time to revise.** When you have a due date, set **DEADLINES** for yourself that will give you time—preferably several days but as much

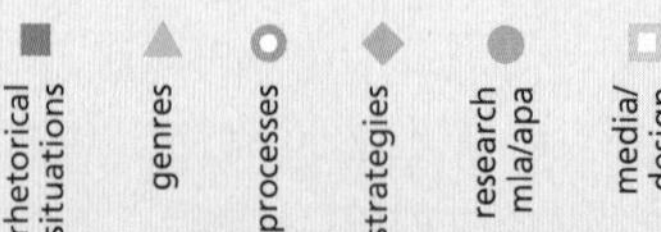

as your schedule permits — to work on the text before it has to be delivered. Also, get some distance. Often when you're immersed in a project, you can't see the big picture because you're so busy creating it. If you can, get away from your writing for a while and think about something else. When you return to it, you're more likely to see it freshly. If there's not time to put a draft away for several days or more, even letting it sit overnight or for a few hours can help.

As you revise, assume that nothing is sacred. Bring a critical eye to all parts of a draft, not only to those parts pointed out by your reviewers. Content, organization, sentence patterns, individual words — all are subject to improvement. Be aware that a change in one part of the text may require changes in other parts.

At the same time, don't waste energy struggling with writing that simply doesn't work; you can always discard it. Look for the parts of your draft that do work — the parts that match your **PURPOSE** and say what you want to say. Focus your efforts on those bright spots, expanding and developing them. 3–4

Revise to sharpen your focus. Examine your **THESIS** to make sure it matches your **PURPOSE** as you now understand it. Read each paragraph to ensure that it contributes to your main point; you may find it helpful to **OUTLINE** your draft to help you see all the parts. One way to do this is to print out a copy of your draft, highlight or underline one sentence in each paragraph that expresses the paragraph's main idea, and cross out everything else. Examine the sentences that remain: Does one state the thesis of the entire essay? Do the rest relate to the thesis? Are they in the best order? If not, you need to either modify the parts of the draft that don't advance your thesis or revise your thesis to reflect your draft's focus and to rearrange your points so they advance your discussion more effectively. 273–75 3–4 223–24

Read your **BEGINNING AND ENDING** carefully; make sure that the first paragraphs introduce your topic and provide any needed contextual information and that the final paragraphs provide a satisfying conclusion. 261–71

Revise to strengthen the argument. If readers find some of your claims unconvincing, you need to provide more information or more support. You may need to define terms you've assumed they will understand, offer

additional examples, or provide more detail by describing, explaining
259 processes, adding dialogue, or using some other **STRATEGIES.** Make sure you show as well as tell! You might try freewriting, clustering, or other ways
219–25 of **GENERATING IDEAS AND TEXT.** If you need to provide additional evidence,
373 you might need to do additional **RESEARCH.**

Revise to improve the organization. If you've outlined your draft, number each paragraph, and make sure each one follows from the one before. If anything seems out of place, move it, or if necessary, cut it completely.
277 Check to see if you've included appropriate **TRANSITIONS** or **HEADINGS** to
526–27 help readers move through the text, and add them as needed. Check to
9–11 make sure your text meets the requirements of the **GENRE** you're writing in.

Revise for clarity. Be sure readers will be able to understand what you're
272–73 saying. Look closely at your **TITLE** to be sure it gives a sense of what
273–75 the text is about, and at your **THESIS** to be sure readers will recognize your main point. If you don't state a thesis directly, consider whether you should. Be sure you provide any necessary background information
314–23 and **DEFINE** any key terms. Make sure you've integrated any **QUOTATIONS,**
408–19 **PARAPHRASES,** or **SUMMARIES** into your text clearly. Be sure all paragraphs are focused around one main point and that the sentences in each paragraph contribute to that point. Finally, consider whether there are any
528–30 data that would be more clearly presented in a **CHART, TABLE,** or **GRAPH.**

One way to test whether your text is clear is to switch audiences: say what you're trying to say as if you were talking to an eight-year-old. You probably don't want to write that way, but the act of explaining your ideas to a young audience or readers who know nothing about your topic can help you discover any points that may be unclear.

Read and reread—and reread. Take some advice from writing theorist Donald Murray:

> Nonwriters confront a writing problem and look away from the text to rules and principles and textbooks and handbooks and models. Writers look at the text, knowing that the text itself will reveal what needs to be done and what should not yet be done or may never be done.

> The writer reads and rereads and rereads, standing far back and reading quickly from a distance, moving in close and reading slowly line by line, reading again and again, knowing that the answers to all writing problems lie within the evolving text.
>
> —Donald Murray, *A Writer Teaches Writing*

Rewriting

Some writers find it useful to try rewriting a draft in various ways or from various perspectives just to explore possibilities. Try it! If you find that your original plan works best for your purpose, fine. But you may find that another way will work better. Especially if you're not completely satisfied with your draft, consider the following ways of rewriting. Experiment with your rhetorical situation:

- Rewrite your draft from different points of view, through the eyes of different people perhaps or through the eyes of an animal or even from the perspective of an object. See how the text changes (in the information it presents, its perspective, its voice).
- Rewrite for a different **AUDIENCE**. How might an email detailing a recent car accident be written to a friend, the insurance adjuster, a parent? 5–8
- Rewrite in a different **STANCE**. If the first draft was temperate and judicious, be extreme; if it was polite, be more direct. If the first draft was in standard English, rewrite it in the language your relatives use. 12–14
- Rewrite the draft in a different **GENRE** or **MEDIUM**. Rewrite an essay as a letter, story, poem, speech. Which genre and medium work best to reach your intended audience and achieve your purpose? 9–11 15–17

Ways of rewriting a narrative

- Rewrite one scene completely in **DIALOGUE**. 333–37
- Start at the end of the story and work back to the beginning, or start in the middle and fill in the beginning as you work toward the end.

Ways of rewriting a textual analysis

306–13

- **COMPARE** the text you're analyzing with another text (which may be in a completely different genre—film, TV, song lyrics, computer games, poetry, fiction, whatever).
- Write a parody of the text you're analyzing. Be as silly and as funny as you can while maintaining the structure of the original text. Alternatively, write a parody of your analysis, using evidence from the text to support an outrageous analysis.

Ways of rewriting a report

5–8

- Rewrite for a different **AUDIENCE.** For example, explain a concept to your grandparents; describe the subject of a profile to a visitor from another planet.
- Be silly. Rewrite the draft as if for *The Daily Show* or *The Onion*, or rewrite it as if it were written by Bart Simpson.

Ways of rewriting an argument

83–110

- Rewrite taking another **POSITION.** Argue as forcefully for that position as you did for your actual one, acknowledging and refuting your original position. Alternatively, write a rebuttal to your first draft from the perspective of someone with different beliefs.

343–51

- Rewrite your draft as a **STORY**—make it real in the lives of specific individuals. (For example, if you were writing about abortion rights, you could write a story about a young pregnant woman trying to decide what she believes and what to do.) Or rewrite the argument as a fable or parable.
- Rewrite the draft as a letter responding to a hostile reader, trying at least to make him or her understand what you have to say.
- Rewrite the draft as an angry letter to someone, or as a table-thumping dinner-with-the-relatives discussion. Write from the most extreme position possible.

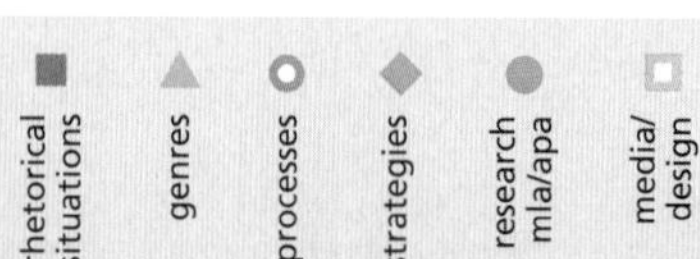

- Write an **ANALYSIS** of your argument in which you identify, as carefully and as neutrally as you can, the various positions people hold on the issue. 278–82

Once you've rewritten a draft in any of these ways, see whether there's anything you can use. Read each draft, considering how it might help you achieve your purpose, reach your audience, convey your stance. Revise your actual draft to incorporate anything you think will make your text more effective, whether it's other **GENRES** or a different perspective. 19

27 Editing and Proofreading

Your ability to produce clear, error-free writing shows something about your ability as a writer and also leads readers to make assumptions about your intellect, work habits, even your character. Readers of job-application letters and résumés, for example, may reject applications if they contain a single error for no other reason than it's an easy way to narrow the field of potential candidates. In addition, they may well assume that applicants who present themselves sloppily in an application will do sloppy work on the job. This is all to say that you should edit and proofread your work carefully.

Editing

Editing is the stage when you work on the details of your paragraphs, sentences, words, and punctuation to make your writing as clear, precise, correct—and effective—as possible. Your goal is not to achieve "perfection" (whatever that may be) so much as to make your writing as effective as possible for your particular purpose and audience. Check a good writing handbook for detailed advice, but the following guidelines can help you check your drafts systematically for some common errors with paragraphs, sentences, and words.

Editing paragraphs

275–76

- Does each paragraph focus on one point? Does it have a **TOPIC SENTENCE** that announces that point, and if so, where is it located? If it's not the first sentence, should it be? If there's no clear topic sentence, should there be one?

- Does every sentence in the paragraph relate to the main point of that paragraph? If any sentences do not, consider whether they should be deleted, moved, or revised.
- Is there enough detail to develop the paragraph's main point? How is the point developed — as a narrative? a definition? some other **STRATEGY**? 259
- Where have you placed the most important information — at the beginning? the end? in the middle? The most emphatic spot is at the end, so in general that's where to put information you want readers to remember. The second most emphatic spot is at the beginning.
- Are any paragraphs especially long or short? Consider breaking long paragraphs if there's a logical place to do so — maybe an extended example should be in its own paragraph, for instance. If you have paragraphs of only a sentence or two, see if you can add to them or combine them with another paragraph.
- Check the way your paragraphs fit together. Does each one follow smoothly from the one before? Do you need to add any **TRANSITIONS** or other links? 277
- Does the **BEGINNING** paragraph catch readers' attention? In what other ways might you begin your text? 261–66
- Does the final paragraph provide a satisfactory **ENDING**? How else might you conclude your text? 267–70

Editing sentences

- Is each sentence complete? Does it have someone or something (the subject) performing some sort of action or expressing a state of being (the verb)? Does each sentence begin with a capital letter and end with a period, question mark, or exclamation point?
- Check your use of the active voice ("The choir sang 'Amazing Grace.' ") and the passive (" 'Amazing Grace' was sung by the choir.") Some kinds of writing call for the passive voice, and sometimes it is more appropriate than the active voice, but in general, you'll do well to edit out any use of the passive voice that's not required.

- Check for parallelism. Items in a list or series should be parallel in form—all nouns (lions, tigers, bears), all verbs (hopped, skipped, jumped), all clauses (he came, he saw, he conquered), and so on.
- Do many of your sentences begin with *it* or *there*? Sometimes these words help introduce a topic, but too often they make your text vague or even conceal needed information. Why write "There are reasons we voted for him" when you can say "We had reasons to vote for him"?
- Are your sentences varied? If they all start with a subject or are all the same length, your writing might be dull and maybe even hard to read. Try varying your sentence openings by adding **TRANSITIONS**, introductory **PHRASES**, or dependent **CLAUSES**. Vary sentence lengths by adding detail to some or combining some sentences.

277
Glossary

- Make sure you've used commas correctly. Is there a comma after each introductory element? ("After an interview, you should send a thank-you note. However, an email note is generally frowned upon.") Do commas set off nonrestrictive elements—parts that aren't needed to understand the sentence? ("He always drives Dodges, which are made in America.") Are compound sentences connected with a comma? ("I'll eat broccoli steamed, but I prefer it roasted.")

Editing words

- Are you sure of the meaning of every word? Use a dictionary; be sure to look up words whose meanings you're not sure about. And remember your audience—do you use any terms they'll need to have **DEFINED**?

314–23

- Is any of your language too general or vague? Why write that you competed in a race, for example, if you could say you ran the 4 × 200 relay?
- What about the **TONE**? If your **STANCE** is serious (or humorous or critical or something else), make sure that your words all convey that tone.

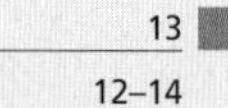
13
12–14

- Do all pronouns have clear antecedents? If you write "he" or "they" or "it" or "these," will readers know whom or what the words refer to?
- Have you used any clichés—expressions that are used so frequently that they are no longer fresh? "Live and let live," avoiding something

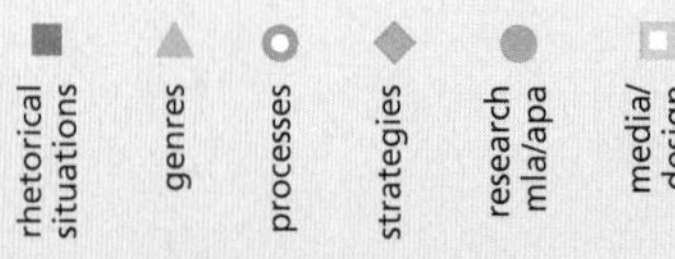

"like the plague," and similar expressions are so predictable that your writing will almost always be better off without them.

- Be careful with language that refers to others. Make sure that your words do not stereotype any individual or group. Mention age, gender, race, religion, sexual orientation, and so on only if they are relevant to your subject. When referring to an ethnic group, make every effort to use the terms members of the group prefer.
- Edit out language that might be considered sexist. Do you say "he" when you mean "he and she"? Have you used words like *manpower* or *policeman* to refer to people who may be female? If so, substitute less gendered words such as *personnel* or *police officer*. Do your words reflect any gender stereotypes—for example, that all engineers are male, or all nurses female? If you mention someone's gender, is it even necessary? If not, eliminate the unneeded words.
- How many of your verbs are forms of *be* and *do*? If you rely too much on these words, try replacing them with more specific verbs. Why write "She did a story" when you could say "She wrote a story"?
- Do you ever confuse *its* and *it's*? Use *it's* when you mean *it is* or *it has*. Use *its* when you mean *belonging to it*.

Proofreading

Proofreading is the final stage of the writing process, the point where you clean up your work to present it to your readers. Proofreading is like checking your appearance in a mirror before going into a job interview: being neat and well groomed looms large in creating a good first impression, and the same principle applies to writing. Misspelled words, missing pages, mixed-up fonts, and other lapses send a negative message about your work—and about you. Most readers excuse an occasional error, but by and large readers are an intolerant bunch: too many errors will lead them to declare your writing—and maybe your thinking—flawed. There goes your credibility. So proofread your final draft with care to ensure that your message is taken as seriously as you want it to be.

Up to this point, you've been told *not* to read individual words on the page and instead to read for meaning. Proofreading demands the opposite: you must slow down your reading so that you can see every word, every punctuation mark.

- Use your computer's grammar checker and spelling checker, but only as a first step, and know that they're not very reliable. Computer programs don't read writing; instead, they rely on formulas and banks of words, so what they flag (or don't flag) as mistakes may or may not be accurate. If you were to write, "Sea you soon," *sea* would not be flagged as misspelled because it is a word and it's spelled correctly even though it's the wrong word in that sentence.
- To keep your eyes from jumping ahead, place a ruler or piece of paper under each line as you read. Use your finger or a pencil as a pointer.
- Some writers find it helpful to read the text one sentence at a time, beginning with the last sentence and working backward.
- Read your text out loud to yourself—or better, to others, who may *hear* problems you can't see. Alternatively, have someone else read your text aloud to you while you follow along on the page or screen.
- Ask someone else to read your text. The more important the writing is, the more important this step.
- If you find a mistake after you've printed out your text and are unable to print out a corrected version, make the change as neatly as possible in pencil or pen.

Compiling a Portfolio 28

Artists maintain portfolios of their work to show gallery owners, collectors, and other potential buyers. Money managers work with investment portfolios of stocks, bonds, and various mutual funds. And often as part of a writing class, student writers compile portfolios of their work. As with a portfolio of paintings or drawings, a portfolio of writing includes a writer's best work and, sometimes, preliminary and revised drafts of that work, along with a statement by the writer articulating why he or she considers it good. The *why* is as important as the work, for it provides you with an occasion for assessing your overall strengths and weaknesses as a writer. This chapter offers guidelines to help you compile both a *writing portfolio* and a *literacy portfolio*, a project that writing students are sometimes asked to complete as part of a literacy narrative.

Considering the Rhetorical Situation

As with the writing you put in a portfolio, the portfolio itself is generally intended for a particular audience but could serve a number of different purposes. It's a good idea, then, to consider these and the other elements of your rhetorical situation when you begin to compile a portfolio.

PURPOSE Why are you creating this portfolio? To create a record of your writing? As the basis for a grade in a course? To organize your research? To explore your literacy? For something else? 3–4

AUDIENCE Who will read your portfolio? What will your readers expect it to contain? How can you help them understand the context or occasion for each piece of writing you include? 5–8

9–11 **GENRE** What genres of writing should the portfolio contain? Do you want to demonstrate your ability to write one particular type of writing or in a variety of genres? Will your statement about the portfolio be in the form of a letter or an essay?

12–14 **STANCE** How do you want to portray yourself in this portfolio? What items should you include to create this impression? What stance do you want to take in your written assessment of its contents? Thoughtful? Enthusiastic? Something else?

15–17 **MEDIA / DESIGN** Will your portfolio be in print? Or will it be electronic? Whichever medium you use, how can you help readers navigate its contents? What design elements will be most appropriate to your purpose and medium?

A WRITING PORTFOLIO

What to Include in a Writing Portfolio

A portfolio developed for a writing course typically contains examples of your best work in that course, including any notes, outlines, preliminary drafts, and so on, along with your own assessment of your performance in that course. You might include any of the following items:

- freewriting, outlines, and other work you did to generate ideas
- drafts, rough and revised
- in-class writing assignments
- source material—copies of articles, websites, observation notes, interview transcripts, and other evidence of your research
- tests and quizzes
- responses to your drafts
- conference notes, error logs, lecture notes, other course materials
- reflections on your work

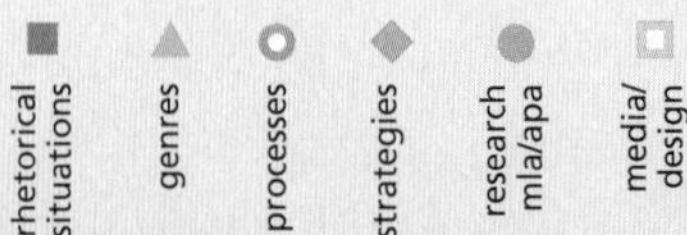

What you include will vary depending on what your instructor asks for. You may be asked to include three of your best papers or everything you've written. You may also be asked to choose certain items for evaluation or perhaps to show work in several different genres. In any case, you will need to choose, and to do that you will need to have criteria for making your choices. Don't base your decision solely on grades (unless grades are one criterion); your portfolio should reflect *your* assessment of your work, not your instructor's. What do you think is your best work? Your most interesting work? Your most ambitious work? Whatever criteria you use, you are the judge.

Organizing a Portfolio

Your instructor may provide explicit guidelines for organizing your portfolio. If not, here are some guidelines. If you set up a way to organize your writing at the start of the course, you'll be able to keep track of it throughout the course, making your job at term's end much easier. Remember that your portfolio presents you as a writer, presumably at your best. It should be neat, well organized, and easy to navigate.

Paper portfolios. Choose something in which to gather your work. You might use a two-pocket folder, a three-ring binder, or a file folder, or you may need a box, basket, or some other container to accommodate bulky or odd-shaped items. You might also put your drafts on a computer disk, with each file clearly named.

Label everything. Label each piece at the top of the first page, specifying the assignment, the draft, and the date: "Proposal, Draft 1, 2/12/08"; "Text Analysis, Final Draft, 10/10/08"; "Portfolio Self-Assessment, Final Draft, 12/11/08"—and so on. Write this information neatly on the page, or put it on a Post-it note. For each assignment, arrange your materials chronologically, with your earliest material (freewriting, for example) on the bottom, and each successive item (source materials, say, then your outline, then your first draft, and so on) on top of the last, ending with your final draft on top. That way readers can see how your writing progressed from earliest work to final draft.

Electronic portfolios. You might also create an electronic portfolio, or e-portfolio, that includes a home page with links to your portfolio's contents. There are several tools that can help you create an e-portfolio:

- ***Online tools.*** Several websites offer free tools to help you create a preformatted e-portfolio. For example, Google provides templates you can use to build an e-portfolio, uploading documents, images, and videos from your computer.
- ***Blogging tools.*** You can create an e-portfolio using a blogging platform, like WordPress, which allows you to upload files and create a network of linked pages. Readers can then comment on your e-portfolio, just as they might on your blog entries.
- ***Wikis.*** Wiki-based e-portfolios differ from blog-based ones in the level of interactivity they allow. In addition to commenting, readers may—if you allow them—make changes and add information. PBWiki is one free provider, as is WikiSpaces, although WikiSpaces pages may contain advertisements.
- ***Courseware.*** Your school may use a courseware system, such as Blackboard or Web CT, that allows you to create a portfolio of your work.
- ***Web-authoring programs.*** If you're interested in constructing a Web-based e-portfolio, you can do so using a program such as Adobe Dreamweaver and Microsoft FrontPage or a tool such as Tripod Site Builder or Yahoo! Geocities' HTML editor.

It's also possible to create an electronic portfolio using Microsoft Word, Excel, or PowerPoint. The programs available for your use and the requirements for posting your portfolio on the Web vary from school to school and instructor to instructor; ask your instructor or your school's help desk for assistance (and see the chapter on **ELECTRONIC TEXT** for general guidance).

546–56

Most electronic portfolio tools help you to first create a basic home page that includes your name, the portfolio's title, links to the various sections of the portfolio, and an introduction. Before you start creating pages and links, though, you should create a map to organize your portfolio and then add your files to the portfolio, following the map. Here's a sample map for a writing course e-portfolio that includes three major assignments (a literacy narrative, a textual analysis, and a film evaluation), and an overall self-assessment of the portfolio's contents. Each box represents a different page; each line represents a link.

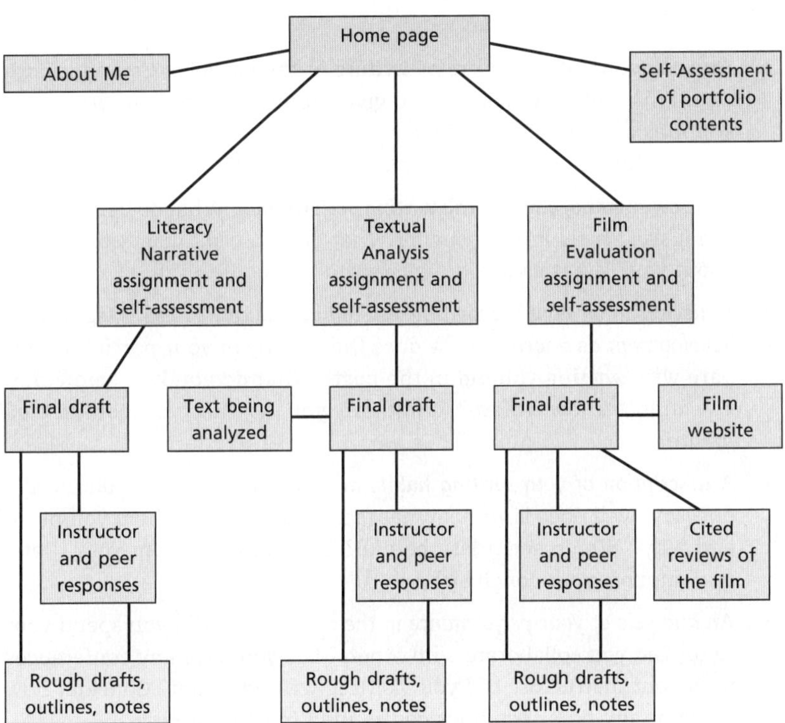

Reflecting on Your Writing Portfolio

The most important part of your portfolio is your written statement reflecting on your work. This is an occasion to step back from the work at hand and examine it with a critical eye. It is also an opportunity to assess your work and to think about what you're most proud of, what you most enjoyed doing, what you want to improve. It's your chance to think about and say what you've learned. Some instructors may ask you to write out your assessment in essay form; others will want you to put it in letter form, which usually allows for a more relaxed and personal tone. Whatever form it takes, your statement should cover the following ground:

- ***An evaluation of each piece of writing in the portfolio.*** Consider both strengths and weaknesses, and give examples from your writing to support what you say. What would you change if you had more time? Which is your favorite piece, and why? Your least favorite?
- ***An assessment of your overall writing performance.*** What do you do well? What still needs improvement? What do you *want* your work to say about you? What *does* your work say about you?
- ***A discussion of how the writing you did in this course has affected your development as a writer.*** How does the writing in your portfolio compare with writing you did in the past? What do you know now that you didn't know before? What can you do that you couldn't do before?
- ***A description of your writing habits and process.*** What do you usually do? How well does it work? What techniques seem to help you most, and why? Which seem less helpful? Cite passages from your drafts that support your conclusions.
- ***An analysis of your performance in the course.*** How did you spend your time? Did you collaborate with others? Did you have any conferences with your instructor? Did you visit the writing center? Consider how these or any other activities contributed to your success.

A Sample Self-Assessment

Here is a letter written by Nathaniel Cooney as part of his portfolio for his first-year writing class at Wright State University.

2 June 2008

Dear Reader,

It is my hope that in reading this letter, you will gain an understanding of the projects contained in this portfolio. I enclose three works that I have submitted for an introductory writing class at Wright State University, English 102, Writing in Academic Discourse: an informative report, an argument paper, and a genre project based largely on the content of the argument paper. I selected the topics of these works for two reasons: First, they address issues that I believe to be relevant in terms of both the intended audience (peers and instructors of the course) and the times when they were published. Second, they speak to issues that are important to me personally. Below I present general descriptions of the works, along with my review of their strengths and weaknesses.

My purpose in writing the informative report "Higher Standards in Education Are Taking Their Toll on Students" was to present a subject in a factual manner and to support it with well-documented research. My intent was not to argue a point. However, because I chose a narrowly focused topic and chose information to support a thesis, the report tends to favor one side of the issue over the other. Because as a student I have a personal stake in the changing standards in the formal education system, I chose to research recent changes in higher education and their effects on students. Specifically, I examine students' struggles to reach a standard that seems to be moving farther and farther beyond their grasp.

I believe that this paper could be improved in two areas. The first is a bias that I think exists because I am a student presenting information from the point of view of a student. It is my hope, however, that my inclusion of unbiased sources lessens this problem somewhat and, furthermore, that it presents the reader with a fair and accurate collection of facts and examples that supports the thesis. My second area of concern is the overall balance in the paper between outside sources supporting my own thoughts and outside sources supporting opposing points of view. Rereading the paper, I notice many places where I may have worked too hard to include sources to support my ideas. I do not necessarily see that as a bad thing, however, because, as I stated earlier, the outside sources work to counterbalance my own bias and provide the reader with additional information. I do think, though, that the paper might be improved if I were to reach a better balance between the amount of space dedicated to the expression of my ideas and the amount of space dedicated to the presentation of source materials.

The second paper, "Protecting Animals That Serve," is an argument intended not only to take a clear position on an issue but also to argue for that position and convince the reader that it is a valid one. That issue is the need for legislation guaranteeing that certain rights of service animals be protected. I am blind and use a guide dog. Thus, this issue is especially important to me. During the few months that I have had him, my guide dog has already encountered a number of situations where intentional or negligent treatment by others has put him in danger. At the time I was writing the paper, a bill was being written in the Ohio House of Representatives that, if passed, would protect service animals and establish consequences for those who violated the law. The purpose of the paper, therefore, was to present the reader with information about service animals, establish the need for the legislation in Ohio and nationwide, and argue for passage of such legislation.

I think that the best parts of my argument are the introduction and the conclusion. In particular, I think that the conclusion does a good job of not only bringing together the various points, but also conveying the significance of the issue for me and for others. In contrast, I think that the area most in need of further attention is the body of the paper. While I think the content is strong, I believe the overall organization could be improved. The connections between ideas are unclear in places, particularly in the section that acknowledges opposing viewpoints. This may be due in part to the fact that I had difficulty understanding the reasoning behind the opposing argument.

The argument paper served as a starting point for the genre project, for which the assignment was to revise one paper written for this class in a different genre. My genre project consists of a poster and a brochure. As it was for the argument paper, my primary goal was to convince my audience of the importance of a particular issue and viewpoint—specifically, to convince my audience to support House Bill 369, the bill being introduced in the Ohio Legislature that would create laws to protect the rights of service animals in the state.

Perhaps both the greatest strength and the greatest weakness of the genre project is my use of graphics. Because of my blindness, I was limited in my use of some graphics. Nevertheless, the pictures were carefully selected to capture the attention of readers, and, in part, to appeal to their emotions as they viewed and reflected on the material.

I noticed two other weaknesses in this project. First, I think that in my effort to include the most relevant information in the brochure, I may have included too many details. Because space is limited, brochures generally include only short, simple facts. Although I tried to keep the facts short and simple, I also tried to use the space that I had to provide as much supporting information as I could. This may have resulted in too much information, given the genre. Second, I dedicated one portion of the poster to a poem I wrote. While the thoughts it conveys are extremely important to me, I was somewhat unsatisfied with its style. I tried to avoid a simple rhyme scheme, but the words kept making their way back to that format. I kept the poem as it was on the advice of others, but I still believe that it could be better.

Despite its weakness, the poem also adds strength to the project in its last stanzas. There, I ask readers to take a side step for a moment, to consider what their lives would be like if they were directly affected by the issue, and to reflect on the issue from that perspective. I hope that doing so personalized the issue for readers and thus strengthened my argument.

I put a great deal of time, effort, and personal reflection into each project. While I am hesitant to say that they are finished and while I am dissatisfied with some of the finer points, I am satisfied with the overall outcome of this collection of works. Viewing it as a collection, I am also reminded that writing is an evolving process and that even if these works never become exactly what I envisioned them to be, they stand as reflections of my thoughts at a particular time in my life. In that respect, they need not be anything but what they already are, because what they are is a product of who I was when I wrote them. I hope that you find the papers interesting and informative and that as you read them, you, too, may realize their significance.

Respectfully,

Nathaniel J. Cooney

Nathaniel J. Cooney

Enclosures (3)

Cooney describes each of the works he includes and considers their strengths and weaknesses, citing examples from his texts to support his assessment.

A LITERACY PORTFOLIO

As a writing student, you may be asked to think back to the time when you first learned to read and write or to remember significant books or other texts you've read and perhaps to put together a portfolio that chronicles your development as a reader and writer. You may also be asked to put together a literacy portfolio as part of a written narrative assignment.

What you include in such a portfolio will vary depending on what you've kept over the years and what your family has kept. You may have all of your favorite books, stories you dictated to a preschool teacher, notebooks in which you practiced cursive writing. Or you may have almost nothing. What you have or don't have is unimportant in the end: what's important is that you gather what you can and arrange it in a way that shows how you think about your development and growth as a literate person. What has been your experience with reading and writing? What's your earliest memory of learning to write? If you love to read, what led you to love it? Who was most responsible for shaping your writing ability? Those are some of the questions you'll ask if you write a **LITERACY NARRATIVE**. You might also compile a literacy portfolio as a good way to generate ideas and text for that assignment.

21–37

What to Include in a Literacy Portfolio

- school papers
- drawings and doodles from preschool
- favorite books
- photographs you've taken
- drawings
- poems
- letters
- journals and diaries
- lists
- reading records or logs

- marriage vows
- legal documents
- speeches you've given
- awards you've received

Organizing a Literacy Portfolio

You may wish to organize your material chronologically, but there are other methods of organization to consider as well. For example, you might group items according to where they were written (at home, at school, at work), by genre (stories, poems, essays, letters, notes), or even by purpose (pleasure, school, work, church, and so on). Arrange your portfolio in the way that best conveys who you are as a literate person. Label each item you include, perhaps with a Post-it note, to identify what it is, when it was written or read, and why you've included it in your portfolio.

Reflecting on Your Literacy Portfolio

- Why did you choose each item?
- Is anything missing? Are there any other important materials that should be here?
- Why is the portfolio arranged as it is?
- What does the portfolio show about your development as a reader and writer?
- What patterns do you see? Are there any common themes you've read or written about? Any techniques you rely on? Any notable changes over time?
- What are the most significant items — and why?

part 4

Strategies

Whenever we write, we draw on many different strategies to articulate what we have to say. We may DEFINE key terms, DESCRIBE people or places, and EXPLAIN how something is done. We may COMPARE one thing to another. Sometimes we may choose a pertinent story to NARRATE, and we may even want to include some DIALOGUE. The chapters that follow offer advice on how to use these AND OTHER BASIC STRATEGIES for developing and organizing the texts you write.

Strategies

Beginning and Ending 29

Whenever we pick up something to read, we generally start by looking at the first few words or sentences to see if they grab our attention, and based on them we decide whether to keep reading. Beginnings, then, are important, both attracting readers and giving them some information about what's to come. When we get to the end of a text, we expect to be left with a sense of closure, of satisfaction—that the story is complete, our questions have been answered, the argument has been made. So endings are important, too. This chapter offers advice on how to write beginnings and endings.

Beginning

How you begin depends on your **RHETORICAL SITUATION**, especially your purpose and audience. Academic audiences generally expect your introduction to establish context, explaining how the text fits into some larger conversation, addresses certain questions, or explores an aspect of the subject. Most introductions also offer a brief description of the text's content, often in the form of a thesis statement. The following opening of an essay about "the greatest generation" does all of this: 1

> Tom Brokaw called the folks of the mid-twentieth century the greatest generation. So why is the generation of my grandparents seen as this country's greatest? Perhaps the reason is not what they accomplished but what they endured. Many of the survivors feel people today "don't have the moral character to withstand a depression like that." This paper will explore the Great Depression through the eyes of ordinary Americans in the most impoverished region in the country, the

> American South, in order to detail how they endured and how the government assisted them in this difficult era.
>
> —Jeffrey DeRoven, "The Greatest Generation: The Great Depression and the American South"

If you're writing for a nonacademic audience or genre—for a newspaper or a website, for example—your introduction may need to entice your readers to read on by connecting your text to their interests through shared experiences, anecdotes, or some other attention-getting device. Cynthia Bass, writing a newspaper article about the Gettysburg Address on its 135th anniversary, connects that date—the day her audience would read it—to Lincoln's address. She then develops the rationale for thinking about the speech and introduces her specific topic: debates about the writing and delivery of the Gettysburg Address:

> November 19 is the 135th anniversary of the Gettysburg Address. On that day in 1863, with the Civil War only half over and the worst yet to come, Abraham Lincoln delivered a speech now universally regarded as both the most important oration in U.S. history and the best explanation—"government of the people, by the people, for the people"—of why this nation exists.
>
> We would expect the history of an event so monumental as the Gettysburg Address to be well established. The truth is just the opposite. The only thing scholars agree on is that the speech is short—only ten sentences—and that it took Lincoln under five minutes to stand up, deliver it, and sit back down.
>
> Everything else—when Lincoln wrote it, where he wrote it, how quickly he wrote it, how he was invited, how the audience reacted—has been open to debate since the moment the words left his mouth.
>
> —Cynthia Bass, "Gettysburg Address: Two Versions"

Ways of Beginning

Explain the larger context of your topic. Most essays are part of an ongoing conversation, so you might begin by outlining the positions to which your writing responds, as the following example from an essay about prejudice does:

> The war on prejudice is now, in all likelihood, the most uncontroversial social movement in America. Opposition to "hate speech," formerly identified with the liberal left, has become a bipartisan piety. In the past year, groups and factions that agree on nothing else have agreed that the public expression of any and all prejudices must be forbidden. On the left, protesters and editorialists have insisted that Francis L. Lawrence resign as president of Rutgers University for describing blacks as "a disadvantaged population that doesn't have that genetic, hereditary background to have a higher average." On the other side of the ideological divide, Ralph Reed, the executive director of the Christian Coalition, responded to criticism of the religious right by calling a press conference to denounce a supposed outbreak of "name-calling, scapegoating, and religious bigotry." Craig Rogers, an evangelical Christian student at California State University, recently filed a $2.5 million sexual-harassment suit against a lesbian professor of psychology, claiming that anti-male bias in one of her lectures violated campus rules and left him feeling "raped and trapped."
>
> In universities and on Capitol Hill, in workplaces and newsrooms, authorities are declaring that there is no place for racism, sexism, homophobia, Christian-bashing, and other forms of prejudice in public debate or even in private thought. "Only when racism and other forms of prejudice are expunged," say the crusaders for sweetness and light, "can minorities be safe and society be fair." So sweet, this dream of a world without prejudice. But the very last thing society should do is seek to utterly eradicate racism and other forms of prejudice.
>
> —Jonathan Rauch, "In Defense of Prejudice"

State your thesis. Sometimes the best beginning is a clear **THESIS** stating your position, like the following statement in an essay arguing that under certain circumstances torture is necessary: 273–75

> It is generally assumed that torture is impermissible, a throwback to a more brutal age. Enlightened societies reject it outright, and regimes using it risk the wrath of the United States.
>
> I believe this attitude is unwise. There are situations in which torture is not merely permissible but morally mandatory. Moreover, these situations are moving from the realm of imagination to fact.
>
> —Michael Levin, "The Case for Torture"

Forecast your organization. You might begin by briefly outlining the way in which you will organize your text. The following example offers background on the subject and an analysis of immigration patterns in the United States, and describes the points that the writer's analysis will discuss:

> This paper analyzes the new geography of immigration during the twentieth century and highlights how immigrant destinations in the 1980s and 1990s differ from earlier settlement patterns. The first part of the analysis uses historical U.S. Census data to develop a classification of urban immigrant "gateways" that describes the ebb and flow of past, present, and likely future receiving areas. The remainder of the analysis examines contemporary trends to explore the recent and rapid settlement of the immigrant population in America's metropolitan gateways.
>
> —Audrey Singer, "The Rise of New Immigrant Gateways"

Offer background information. If your readers may not know as much as you do about your topic, giving them information to help them understand your position can be important, as David Guterson does in an essay on the Mall of America:

> Last April, on a visit to the new Mall of America near Minneapolis, I carried with me the public-relations press kit provided for the benefit of reporters. It included an assortment of "fun facts" about the mall: 140,000 hot dogs sold each week, 10,000 permanent jobs, 44 escalators and 17 elevators, 12,750 parking places, 13,300 short tons of steel, $1 million in cash disbursed weekly from 8 automatic-teller machines. Opened in the summer of 1992, the mall was built on the 78-acre site of the former Metropolitan Stadium, a five-minute drive from the Minneapolis–St. Paul International Airport. With 4.2 million square feet of floor space—including twenty-two times the retail footage of the average American shopping center—the Mall of America was "the largest fully enclosed combination retail and family entertainment complex in the United States."
>
> —David Guterson, "Enclosed. Encyclopedic. Endured: The Mall of America"

Define key terms or concepts. The success of an argument often hinges on how key terms are **DEFINED.** 314–23 You may wish to provide definitions up front, as this page from an advocacy website, *Health Care without Harm,* does in a report on the hazards of fragrances in health-care facilities:

> To many people, the word "fragrance" means something that smells nice, such as perfume. We don't often stop to think that scents are chemicals. Fragrance chemicals are organic compounds that volatilize, or vaporize into the air—that's why we can smell them. They are added to products to give them a scent or to mask the odor of other ingredients. The volatile organic chemicals (VOCs) emitted by fragrance products can contribute to poor indoor air quality (IAQ) and are associated with a variety of adverse health effects.
>
> —Health Care without Harm, "Fragrances"

Connect your subject to your readers' interests or values. You'll always want to establish common ground with your readers, and sometimes you may wish to do so immediately, in your introduction, as in this example:

> We all want to feel safe. Most Americans lock their doors at night, lock their cars in parking lots, try to park near buildings or under lights, and wear seat belts. Many invest in expensive security systems, carry pepper spray or a stun gun, keep guns in their homes, or take self-defense classes. Obviously, safety and security are important issues in American life.
>
> —Andy McDonie, "Airport Security: What Price Safety?"

Start with something that will provoke readers' interest. Anna Quindlen opens an essay on feminism with the following eye-opening assertion:

> Let's use the F word here. People say it's inappropriate, offensive, that it puts people off. But it seems to me it's the best way to begin, when it's simultaneously devalued and invaluable.
>
> Feminist. Feminist, feminist, feminist.
>
> —Anna Quindlen, "Still Needing the F Word"

Start with an anecdote. Sometimes a brief **NARRATIVE** helps bring a topic to life for readers. See, for example, how an essay on the dozens, a type of verbal contest played by some African Americans, begins:

343–51

> Alfred Wright, a nineteen-year-old whose manhood was at stake on Longwood Avenue in the South Bronx, looked fairly calm as another teenager called him Chicken Head and compared his mother to Shamu the whale.
>
> He fingered the gold chain around his thin neck while listening to a detailed complaint about his sister's sexual abilities. Then he slowly

took the toothpick out of his mouth; the jeering crowd of young men quieted as he pointed at his accuser.

"He was so ugly when he was born," Wright said, "the doctor smacked his mom instead of him."

—John Tierney, "Playing the Dozens"

Ask a question. Instead of a thesis statement, you might open with a question about the topic your text will explore, as this study of the status of women in science does:

> Are women's minds different from men's minds? In spite of the women's movement, the age-old debate centering around this question continues. We are surrounded by evidence of de facto differences between men's and women's intellects—in the problems that interest them, in the ways they try to solve those problems, and in the professions they choose. Even though it has become fashionable to view such differences as environmental in origin, the temptation to seek an explanation in terms of innate differences remains a powerful one.
>
> —Evelyn Fox Keller, "Women in Science: A Social Analysis"

Jump right in. Occasionally you may wish to start as close to the key action as possible. See how one writer jumps right into his profile of a blues concert:

> Long Tongue, the Blues Merchant, strolls onstage. His guitar rides side-saddle against his hip. The drummer slides onto the tripod seat behind the drums, adjusts the high-hat cymbal, and runs a quick, off-beat tattoo on the tom-tom, then relaxes. The bass player plugs into the amplifier, checks the settings on the control panel, and nods his okay. Three horn players stand off to one side, clustered, lurking like brilliant sorcerer-wizards waiting to do magic with their musical instruments.
>
> —Jerome Washington, "The Blues Merchant"

Ending

Endings are important because they're the last words readers read. How
1 you end a text will depend in part on your **RHETORICAL SITUATION**. You may end by wrapping up loose ends, or you may wish to give readers some-

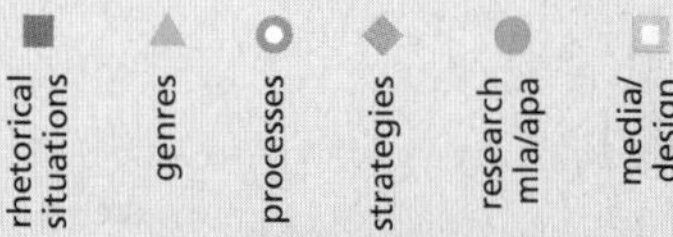

thing to think about. Some endings do both, as Cynthia Bass does in a report on the debate over the Gettysburg Address. In her two final paragraphs, she first summarizes the debate and then shows its implications:

> What's most interesting about the Lincoln-as-loser and Lincoln-as-winner versions is how they marshal the same facts to prove different points. The invitation asks Lincoln to deliver "a few appropriate remarks." Whether this is a putdown or a reflection of the protocol of the time depends on the "spin"—an expression the highly politicized Lincoln would have readily understood—which the scholar places on it.
>
> These diverse histories should not in any way diminish the power or beauty of Lincoln's words. However, they should remind us that history, even the history of something as deeply respected as the Gettysburg Address, is seldom simple or clear. This reminder is especially useful today as we watch expert witnesses, in an effort to divine what the founders meant by "high crimes and misdemeanors," club one another with conflicting interpretations of the same events, the same words, the same precedents, and the same laws.
>
> —Cynthia Bass, "Gettysburg Address: Two Versions"

Bass summarizes the dispute about Lincoln's Address and then moves on to discuss the role of scholars in interpreting historical events. Writing during the Clinton impeachment hearings, she concludes by pointing out the way in which expert government witnesses often offer conflicting interpretations of events to suit their own needs. The ending combines several strategies to bring various strands of her essay together, leaving readers to interpret her final words themselves.

Ways of Ending

Restate your main point. Sometimes you'll simply **SUMMARIZE** your central idea, as in this example from an essay arguing that we have no "inner" self and that we should be judged by our actions alone: 416–17

> The inner man is a fantasy. If it helps you to identify with one, by all means, do so; preserve it, cherish it, embrace it, but do not present it to others for evaluation or consideration, for excuse or exculpation, or, for that matter, for punishment or disapproval.

> Like any fantasy, it serves your purposes alone. It has no standing in the real world which we share with each other. Those character traits, those attitudes, that behavior—that strange and alien stuff sticking out all over you—*that's the real you!*
>
> —Willard Gaylin, "What You See Is the Real You"

Discuss the implications of your argument. The following conclusion of an essay on the development of Post-it notes leads readers to consider how failure sometimes leads to innovation:

> Post-it notes provide but one example of a technological artifact that has evolved from a perceived failure of existing artifacts to function without frustrating. Again, it is not that form follows function but, rather, that the form of one thing follows from the failure of another thing to function as we would like. Whether it be bookmarks that fail to stay in place or taped-on notes that fail to leave a once-nice surface clean and intact, their failure and perceived failure is what leads to the true evolution of artifacts. That the perception of failure may take centuries to develop, as in the case of loose bookmarks, does not reduce the importance of the principle in shaping our world.
>
> —Henry Petroski, "Little Things Can Mean a Lot"

343–51

End with an anecdote, maybe finishing a **NARRATIVE** that was begun earlier in your text or adding one that illustrates the point you are making See how Sarah Vowell uses a story to end an essay on students' need to examine news reporting critically:

> I looked at Joanne McGlynn's syllabus for her media studies course, the one she handed out at the beginning of the year, stating the goals of the class. By the end of the year, she hoped her students would be better able to challenge everything from novels to newscasts, that they would come to identify just who is telling a story and how that person's point of view affects the story being told. I'm going to go out on a limb here and say that this lesson has been learned. In fact, just recently, a student came up to McGlynn and told her something all teachers dream of hearing. The girl told the teacher that she was listening to the radio, singing along with her favorite song, and halfway

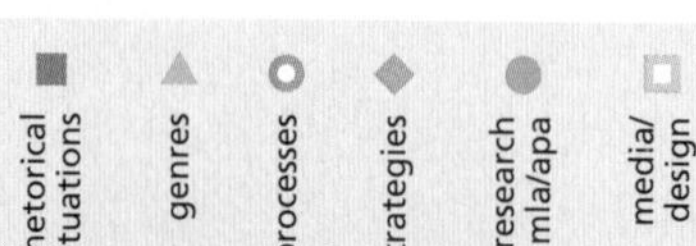

> through the sing-along she stopped and asked herself, "What am I singing? What do these words mean? What are they trying to tell me?" And then, this young citizen of the republic jokingly complained, "I can't even turn on the radio without thinking anymore."
>
> —Sarah Vowell, "Democracy and Things Like That"

Refer to the beginning. One way to bring closure to a text is to bring up something discussed in the beginning; often the reference adds to or even changes the original meaning. For example, Amy Tan opens an essay on her Chinese mother's English by establishing herself as a writer and lover of language who uses many versions of English in her writing:

> I am not a scholar of English or literature. I cannot give you much more than personal opinions on the English language and its variations in this country or others.
>
> I am a writer. And by that definition, I am someone who has always loved language. I am fascinated by language in daily life. I spend a great deal of my time thinking about the power of language—the way it can evoke an emotion, a visual image, a complex idea, or a simple truth. Language is the tool of my trade. And I use them all—all the Englishes I grew up with.

At the end of her essay, Tan repeats this phrase, but now she describes language not in terms of its power to evoke emotions, images, and ideas, but in its power to evoke "the essence" of her mother. When she began to write fiction, she says,

> [I] decided I should envision a reader for the stories I would write. And the reader I decided upon was my mother, because these were stories about mothers. So with this reader in mind—and in fact she did read my early drafts—I began to write stories using all the Englishes I grew up with: the English I spoke to my mother, which for lack of a better term might be described as "simple"; the English she used with me, which for lack of a better term might be described as "broken"; my translation of her Chinese, which could certainly be described as "watered down"; and what I imagined to be her translation of her Chinese if she could speak in perfect English, her internal language, and for that I sought to preserve the essence, but neither an English nor a

> Chinese structure. I wanted to capture what language ability tests can never reveal: her intent, her passion, her imagery, the rhythms of her speech and the nature of her thoughts.
>
> —Amy Tan, "Mother Tongue"

Note how Tan not only repeats "all the Englishes I grew up with", but also provides parallel lists of what those Englishes can do for her: "evoke an emotion, a visual image, a complex idea, or a simple truth" on the one hand, and, on the other, capture her mother's "intent, her passion, her imagery, the rhythms of her speech and the nature of her thoughts."

Propose some action, as in the following conclusion of a report on the consequences of binge drinking among college students:

> The scope of the problem makes immediate results of any interventions highly unlikely. Colleges need to be committed to large-scale and long-term behavior-change strategies, including referral of alcohol abusers to appropriate treatment. Frequent binge drinkers on college campuses are similar to other alcohol abusers elsewhere in their tendency to deny that they have a problem. Indeed, their youth, the visibility of others who drink the same way, and the shelter of the college community may make them less likely to recognize the problem. In addition to addressing the health problems of alcohol abusers, a major effort should address the large group of students who are not binge drinkers on campus who are adversely affected by the alcohol-related behavior of binge drinkers.
>
> —Henry Wechsler et al., "Health and Behavioral Consequences of Binge Drinking in College: A National Survey of Students at 140 Campuses"

Considering the Rhetorical Situation

As a writer or speaker, think about the message that you want to articulate, the audience you want to reach, and the larger context you are writing in.

3–4

PURPOSE Your purpose will affect the way you begin and end. If you're trying to persuade readers to do something, you may want to open by clearly stating your thesis and end by calling for a specific action.

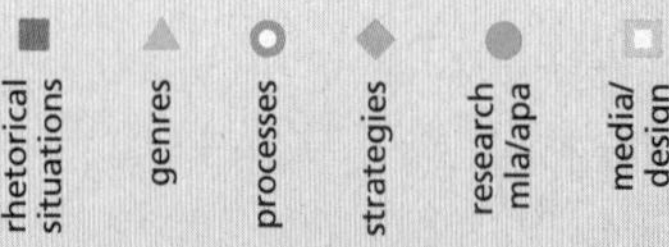

AUDIENCE Who do you want to reach, and how does that affect the way you begin and end? You may want to open with an intriguing fact or anecdote to entice your audience to read a profile, for instance, whereas readers of a report may expect it to conclude with a summary of your findings. 5–8

GENRE Does your genre require a certain type of beginning or ending? Arguments, for example, often provide a statement of the thesis near the beginning; proposals typically end with a call for some solution. 9–11

STANCE What is your stance, and can your beginning and ending help you convey that stance? For example, beginning an argument on the distribution of AIDS medications to underdeveloped countries with an anecdote may demonstrate concern for the human costs of the disease, whereas starting with a statistical analysis may suggest the stance of a careful researcher. Ending a proposal by weighing the advantages and disadvantages of the solution you propose may make you seem reasonable. 12–14

MEDIA / DESIGN Your medium may affect the way you begin and end. A Web text, for instance, may open with a home page listing a menu of the site—and giving readers a choice of where they will begin. With a print text, you get to decide how it will begin and end. 15–17

IF YOU NEED MORE HELP

See also the guides to writing in chapters 6–9 for ways of beginning and ending a LITERACY NARRATIVE, an essay ANALYZING TEXT, a REPORT, or an ARGUMENT.

33–34
55–56
78–79
107–8

30 Guiding Your Reader

Traffic lights, street signs, and lines on the road help drivers find their way. Readers need similar guidance—to know, for example, whether they're reading a report or an argument, an evaluation or a proposal. They also need to know what to expect: What will the report be about? What perspective will it offer? What will this paragraph cover? What about the next one? How do the two paragraphs relate to each other? When you write, you need to provide cues to help your readers navigate your text and understand the points you're trying to make. This chapter offers advice on guiding your reader and, specifically, on using *titles, thesis statements, topic sentences*, and *transitions*.

Titles

A title serves various purposes, naming a text and providing clues to the content. It also helps readers decide whether they want to read further, so it's worth your while to come up with a title that attracts interest. Some titles include subtitles. You generally have considerable freedom in choos-
1 ing a title, but always you'll want to consider the **RHETORICAL SITUATION** to be sure your title serves your purpose and appeals to the audience you want to reach.

Some titles simply announce the subject of the text:

"Black Men and Public Space"
"In the *24* World, Family Is the Main Casualty"
"Why Colleges Shower Their Students with A's"
The Greatest Generation

Some titles provoke readers or otherwise entice them to read:

"Kill 'Em! Crush 'Em! Eat 'Em Raw!"
"Thank God for the Atom Bomb"
"What Are Homosexuals For?"

Sometimes writers add a subtitle to explain or illuminate the title:

Aria: Memoir of a Bilingual Childhood
"Health and Behavioral Consequences of Binge Drinking in College: A National Survey of Students at 140 Campuses"
"From Realism to Virtual Reality: Images of America's Wars"

Sometimes when you're starting to write, you'll think of a title that helps you generate ideas and write. More often, though, a title is one of the last things you'll write, when you know what you've written and can craft a suitable name for your text.

Thesis Statements

A thesis identifies the topic of your text along with the claim you are making about it. A good thesis helps readers understand an essay. Working to create a sharp thesis can help you focus both your thinking and your writing. Here are three steps for moving from a topic to a thesis statement:

1. State your topic as a question. You may have an idea for a topic, such as "gasoline prices," "analysis of the Dove 'real women' ad campaign," or "famine." Those may be good topics, but they're not thesis statements, primarily because none of them actually makes a statement. A good way to begin moving from topic to thesis statement is to turn your topic into a question:

What causes fluctuations in gasoline prices?

Are ads picturing "real women" who aren't models effective?

What can be done to prevent famine in Africa?

2. Then turn your question into a position. A thesis statement is an assertion—it takes a stand or makes a claim. Whether you're writing a report or an argument, you are saying, "This is the way I see . . . " "My research shows . . . ," or "This is what I believe about . . . ." Your thesis statement announces your position on the question you are raising about your topic, so a relatively easy way of establishing a thesis is to answer your own question:

> Gasoline prices fluctuate for several reasons.
>
> Ads picturing "real women" instead of models are effective because women can easily identify with them.
>
> The most recent famine in Eritrea could have been avoided if certain measures had been taken.

3. Narrow your thesis. A good thesis is specific, guiding you as you write and showing your audience exactly what your essay will cover. The preceding thesis statements need to be qualified and focused—they need to be made more specific. For example:

> Gasoline prices fluctuate because of production procedures, consumer demand, international politics, and oil companies' policies.
>
> Dove skin-firming products' ad campaign featuring "real women" works because consumers can identify with the women's bodies and admire their confidence in displaying them.
>
> The 1984 famine in Eritrea could have been avoided if farmers had received training in more effective methods and had had access to certain technology and if Western nations had provided more aid more quickly.

222–23 A good way to narrow a thesis is to ask **QUESTIONS** about it: *Why* do gasoline prices fluctuate? *How* could the Eritrea famine have been avoided? The answers will help you craft a narrow, focused thesis.

4. Qualify your thesis. Sometimes you want to make a strong argument and to state your thesis bluntly. Often, however, you need to acknowledge that your assertions may be challenged or may not be unconditionally true. In those cases, consider limiting the scope of your thesis by adding to it such terms as *may*, *probably*, *apparently*, *very likely*, *sometimes*, and *often*.

> Gasoline prices *very likely* fluctuate because of production procedures, consumer demand, international politics, and oil companies' policies.
>
> Dove skin-firming products' ad campaign featuring "real women" may work because consumers can identify with the women's bodies and admire their confidence in displaying them.
>
> The 1984 famine in Eritrea could *probably* have been avoided if farmers had received training in more effective methods and had had access to certain technology and if Western nations had provided more aid more quickly.

Thesis statements are typically positioned at or near the end of a text's introduction, to let readers know at the outset what is being claimed and what the text will be aiming to prove. A thesis doesn't necessarily forecast your organization, which may be more complex than the thesis itself. For example, Carolyn Stonehill's research paper, "It's in Our Genes: The Biological Basis of Human Mating Behavior," contains this thesis statement:

> While cultural values and messages clearly play a part in the process of mate selection, the genetic and psychological predispositions developed by our ancestors play the biggest role in determining to whom we are attracted.

However, the paper that follows includes sections on "Women's Need to Find a Capable Mate" and "Men's Need to Find a Healthy Mate," in which the "genetic and psychological predispositions" are discussed, followed by sections titled "The Influence of the Media on Mate Selection" and "If Not Media, Then What?" which discuss "cultural values and messages." The paper delivers what the thesis delivers without following the order in which the thesis presents the topics.

Topic Sentences

Just as a thesis statement announces the topic and position of an essay, a topic sentence states the subject and focus of a paragraph. Good paragraphs focus on a single point, which is summarized in a topic sentence. Usually, but not always, the topic sentence begins the paragraph:

> *Graduating from high school or college is an exciting, occasionally even traumatic event.* Your identity changes as you move from being a high school teenager to a university student or a worker; your connection to home loosens as you attend school elsewhere, move to a place of your own, or simply exercise your right to stay out later. You suddenly find yourself doing different things, thinking different thoughts, fretting about different matters. As recent high school graduate T. J. Devoe puts it, "I wasn't really scared, but having this vast range of opportunity made me uneasy. I didn't know *what* was gonna happen." Jenny Petrow, in describing her first year out of college, observes, "It's a tough year. It was for all my friends."
>
> —Sydney Lewis, *Help Wanted: Tales from the First Job Front*

Sometimes the topic sentence may come at the end of the paragraph or even at the end of the preceding paragraph, depending on the way the paragraphs relate to one another. Other times a topic sentence will summarize or restate a point made in the previous paragraph, helping readers understand what they've just read as they move on to the next point. See how the linguist Deborah Tannen does this in the first paragraphs of an article on differences in men's and women's conversational styles:

> I was addressing a small gathering in a suburban Virginia living room—a women's group that had invited men to join them. Throughout the evening, one man had been particularly talkative, frequently offering ideas and anecdotes, while his wife sat silently beside him on the couch. Toward the end of the evening, I commented that women frequently complain that their husbands don't talk to them. This man quickly concurred. He gestured toward his wife and said, "She's the talker in our family." The room burst into laughter; the man looked puzzled and hurt. "It's true," he explained. "When I come home from work I have nothing to say. If she didn't keep the conversation going, we'd spend the whole evening in silence."
>
> *This episode crystallizes the irony that although American men tend to talk more than women in public situations, they often talk less at home.* And this pattern is wreaking havoc with marriage.
>
> —Deborah Tannen, "Sex, Lies, and Conversation: Why Is It So Hard for Men and Women to Talk to Each Other?"

Transitions

Transitions help readers move from thought to thought—from sentence to sentence, paragraph to paragraph. You are likely to use a number of transitions as you draft; when you're **EDITING,** you should make a point of checking transitions. Here are some common ones: 242–45

- ***To show causes and effects:*** accordingly, as a result, because, consequently, hence, so, then, therefore, thus
- ***To show comparisons:*** also, in the same way, like, likewise, similarly
- ***To show contrasts or exceptions:*** although, but, even though, however, in contrast, instead, nevertheless, nonetheless, on the contrary, on the one hand . . . on the other hand, still, yet
- ***To show examples:*** for example, for instance, indeed, in fact, of course, such as
- ***To show place or position:*** above, adjacent to, below, beyond, elsewhere, here
- ***To show sequence:*** again, also, and, and then, besides, finally, furthermore, last, moreover, next, too
- ***To show time:*** after, as soon as, at first, at the same time, before, eventually, finally, immediately, later, meanwhile, next, simultaneously, so far, soon, then, thereafter
- ***To signal a summary or conclusion:*** as a result, as we have seen, finally, in a word, in any event, in brief, in conclusion, in other words, in short, in the end, in the final analysis, on the whole, therefore, thus, to summarize

IF YOU NEED MORE HELP

See also Chapter 51 on PRINT TEXT for ways of creating visual signals for your readers. 523–33

31 Analyzing Causes and Effects

Analyzing causes helps us think about why something happened, whereas thinking about effects helps us consider what might happen. When we hear a noise in the night, we want to know what caused it. Children poke sticks into holes to see what will happen. Researchers try to understand the causes of diseases. Writers often have occasion to consider causes or effects as part of a larger topic or sometimes as a main focus: in a
171–79 **PROPOSAL,** we might consider the effects of reducing tuition or the causes
153–60 of recent tuition increases; in a **MEMOIR,** we might explore why the person we had a date with failed to show up. Often we can only speculate about probable causes or likely effects. In writing about causes and effects, then,
283–99 we are generally **ARGUING** for those we consider plausible or probable. This chapter will help you analyze causes and effects in writing—and to do so in a way that suits your rhetorical situation.

Determining Plausible Causes and Effects

What causes ozone depletion? Sleeplessness? Obesity? And what are their effects? Those are of course large, complex topics, but whenever you have reason to ask why something happened or what could happen, there will likely be several possible causes and just as many predictable effects. There may be obvious causes, though often they will be less important than others that are harder to recognize. (Eating too much may be an obvious cause of being overweight, but *why* people eat too much has several less obvious causes: portion size, advertising, lifestyle, and physiological disorders are only a few possibilities.) Similarly, short-term effects are often less important than long-term ones. (A stomachache may be an effect of eating too much candy, but the chemical imbalance that can result from consuming too much sugar is a much more serious effect.)

LISTING, CLUSTERING, and **OUTLINING** are useful processes for analyzing causes. And at times you might need to do some **RESEARCH** to identify possible causes or effects and to find evidence to support your analysis. When you've identified potential causes and effects, you need to analyze them. Which causes and effects are primary? Which seem to be secondary? Which are most relevant to your **PURPOSE** and are likely to convince your **AUDIENCE?** You will probably have to choose from several possible causes and effects for your analysis because you won't want or need to include all of them.

219–24
373
3–4
5–8

Arguing for Causes or Effects

Once you've identified several possible causes or predictable effects, you need to **ARGUE** that some are more plausible than others. You must provide convincing support for your argument because you cannot *prove* that X causes Y or that Y will be caused by Z; you can show only, with good reasons and appropriate evidence, that X is *likely* to cause Y or that Y will *likely* follow from Z. See, for example, how an essay on the psychological basis for risk taking speculates about two potential causes for the popularity of extreme sports:

283–99

> Studies now indicate that the inclination to take high risks may be hardwired into the brain, intimately linked to arousal and pleasure mechanisms, and may offer such a thrill that it functions like an addiction. The tendency probably affects one in five people, mostly young males, and declines with age. It may ensure our survival, even spur our evolution as individuals and as a species. Risk taking probably bestowed a crucial evolutionary advantage, inciting the fighting and foraging of the hunter-gatherer. . . .
>
> As psychologist Salvadore Maddi, PhD, of the University of California at Davis warns, "High-risk takers may have a hard time deriving meaning and purpose from everyday life." Indeed, this peculiar form of dissatisfaction could help explain the explosion of high-risk sports in America and other postindustrial Western nations. In unstable cultures, such as those at war or suffering poverty, people rarely seek out additional thrills. But in a rich and safety-obsessed country like America, land of guardrails, seat belts, and personal-injury lawsuits,

> everyday life may have become too safe, predictable, and boring for those programmed for risk taking.
>
> —Paul Roberts, "Risk"

Roberts suggests that genetics is one likely cause of extreme sports and that an American obsession with safety is perhaps a cause of their growing popularity. Notice, however, that he presents these as likely or possible, not certain, by choosing his words carefully: "studies now *indicate*"; "the inclination to take high risks *may* be hardwired"; "[R]isk taking *probably* bestowed a crucial evolutionary advantage"; "this . . . dissatisfaction *could help* explain." Like Roberts, you will almost always need to qualify what you say about causes and effects—to say that something *could explain* (rather than saying it "explains") or that it *suggests* (rather than "shows"). Plausible causes and effects can't be proved definitively, so you need to acknowledge that your argument is not the last word on the subject.

Ways of Organizing an Analysis of Causes and Effects

Your analysis of causes and effects may be part of a proposal or some other genre of writing, or you may write a text whose central purpose is to analyze causes or speculate about effects. While there are many ways to organize an analysis of causes and effects, three common ways are to state a cause and then discuss its effects, to state an effect and then discuss its causes, and to identify a chain of causes and effects.

Identify a cause and then discuss its effects. If you were writing about global warming, you might first show that many scientists fear it will have several effects, including drastic climate changes, the extinction of various kinds of plants, and elevated sea levels.

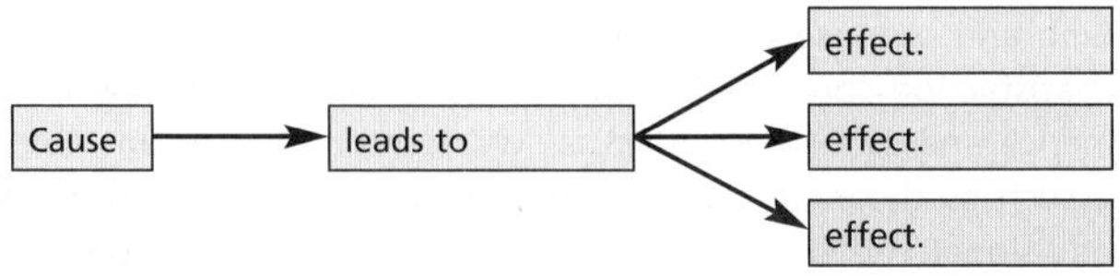

Identify an effect and then trace its causes. If you were writing about school violence, for example, you might argue that it is a result of sloppy dress, informal teacher-student relationships, low academic standards, and disregard for rules.

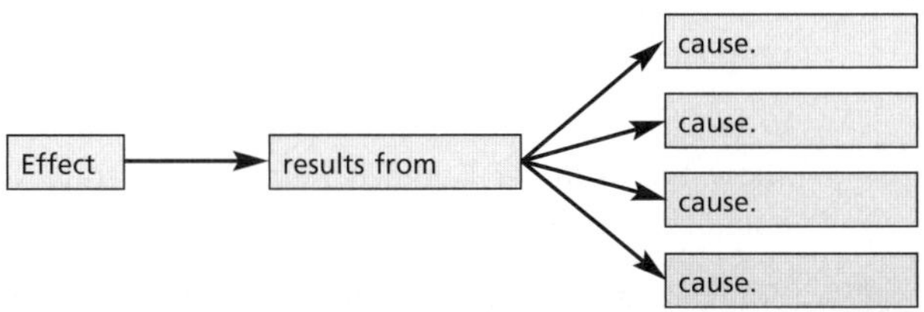

Identify a chain of causes and effects. You may sometimes discuss a chain of causes and effects. If you were writing about the right to privacy, for example, you might consider the case of Megan's law. A convicted child molester raped and murdered a girl named Megan; the crime caused New Jersey legislators to pass the so-called Megan's law (an effect), which requires that convicted sex offenders be publicly identified. As more states enact versions of Megan's law, concern for the rights of those who are identified is developing—the effect is becoming a cause of further effects.

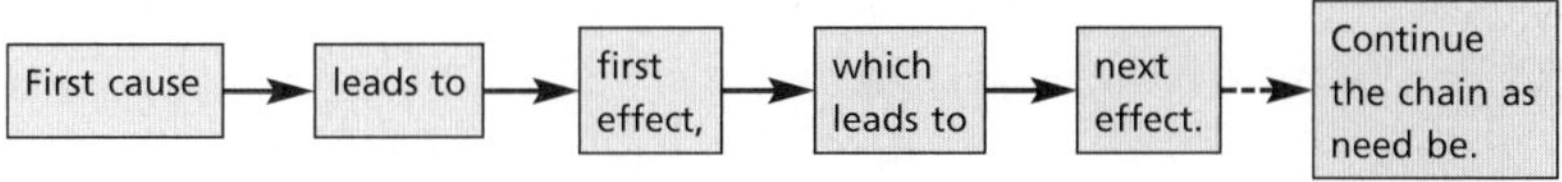

Considering the Rhetorical Situation

As a writer or speaker, you need to think about the message that you want to articulate, the audience you want to reach, and the larger context you are writing in.

PURPOSE Your purpose may be to analyze causes. But sometimes you'll have another goal that calls for such analysis—a business report, for example, might need to explain what caused a decline in sales.

3–4

5–8 **AUDIENCE** Who is your intended audience, and how will analyzing causes help you reach them? Do you need to tell them why some event happened or what effects resulted?

9–11 **GENRE** Does your genre require you to analyze causes? Proposals, for example, often need to consider the effects of a proposed solution.

12–14 **STANCE** What is your stance, and could analyzing causes or effects show that stance? Could it help demonstrate your seriousness or show that your conclusions are reasonable?

15–17 **MEDIA / DESIGN** You can rely on words to analyze causes, but sometimes a drawing will help readers *see* how causes lead to effects.

209–58

IF YOU NEED MORE HELP

See also the PROCESSES chapters for help generating ideas, drafting, and so on if you need to write an entire text whose purpose is to analyze causes or speculate about effects.

Arguing 32

Tennis fans argue about who's better, Venus or Serena. Political candidates argue that they have the most experience or best judgment. A toilet paper ad argues that you should "be kind to your behind." As you likely realize, we are surrounded by arguments, and much of the work you do as a college student requires you to read and write arguments. When you write a **LITERARY ANALYSIS**, for instance, you argue for a particular interpretation. In a **PROPOSAL**, you argue for a particular solution to a problem. Even a **PROFILE** argues that a subject should be seen in a certain way. This chapter offers advice on some of the key elements of making an argument, from developing an arguable thesis and identifying good reasons and evidence that supports those reasons to building common ground and dealing with viewpoints other than your own.

143–52
171–79
161–70

Reasons for Arguing

We argue for many reasons, and they often overlap: to convince others that our position on a subject is reasonable, to influence the way they think about a subject, to persuade them to change their point of view or to take some sort of action. In fact, many composition scholars and teachers believe that all writing makes an argument.

As a student, you'll be called upon to make arguments continually: when you participate in class discussions, when you take an essay exam, when you post a comment to a Listserv or a blog. In all these instances, you are adding your opinions to some larger conversation, arguing for what you believe—and why.

Arguing Logically: Claims, Reasons, and Evidence

The basic building blocks of argument are claims, reasons, and evidence that supports those reasons. Using these building blocks, we can construct a strong logical argument.

Claims. Good arguments are based on arguable claims — statements that reasonable people may disagree about. Certain kinds of statements cannot be argued:

- ***Verifiable statements of fact.*** Most of the time, there's no point in arguing about facts like "The earth is round" or "George H. W. Bush is America's 41st president." Such statements contain no controversy, no potential opposition — and so no interest for an audience. However, you might argue about the basis of a fact. For example, until recently it was a fact that our solar system had nine planets, but when further discoveries led to a change in the definition of *planet*, Pluto no longer qualified.
- ***Issues of faith or belief.*** By definition, matters of faith cannot be proven or refuted. If you believe in reincarnation or don't believe there is an afterlife, there's no way I can convince you otherwise. However, in a philosophy or religion course you may be asked to argue, for example, whether or not the universe must have a cause.
- ***Matters of simple opinion or personal taste.*** If you think cargo pants are ugly, no amount of arguing will convince you to think otherwise. If you own every Beyoncé CD and think she's the greatest singer ever, you won't convince your Beatles-loving parents to like her too. If matters of taste are based on identifiable criteria, though, they may be
125–32 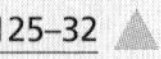 argued in an **EVALUATION**, where "Tom Cruise is a terrible actor" is more than just your opinion — it's an assertion you can support with evidence from his performances.

You may begin with an opinion: "I think wearing a helmet makes riding a bike more dangerous, not less." As it stands, that statement can't be considered a claim — it needs to be made more reasonable and informed. To do that, you might reframe it as a question — "Do bike riders who wear helmets get injured more often than those who don't?" — that may be answered as you do research and start to write. Your opinion or question should lead you to an arguable claim, however, one that could be challenged by another thoughtful person. In this case, for example, your research might lead you to a focused, qualified claim: *Contrary to common sense, wearing a helmet while riding a bicycle increases the chances of injury, at least to adult riders.*

Qualifying a claim. According to an old saying, there are two sides to every story. Much of the time, though, arguments don't sort themselves neatly into two sides, pro and con. No matter what your topic, your argument will rarely be a simple matter of being for or against; in most cases, you'll want to qualify your claim — that it is true in certain circumstances, with certain conditions, with these limitations, and so on. Qualifying your claim shows that you're reasonable and also makes your topic more manageable by limiting it. The following questions can help you qualify your claim.

- *Can it be true in some cases?* For example, most high school students should be urged to graduate, but students who cannot succeed there should be allowed to drop out.
- *Can it be true at some times or under certain circumstances?* For instance, cell phones and computer monitors should be recycled, but only by licensed, domestic recyclers.
- *Can it be true for some groups or individuals?* For example, nearly everyone should follow a low-carb diet, but some people, such as diabetics, should avoid it.

SOME WORDS FOR QUALIFYING A CLAIM

sometimes	nearly	it seems/seemingly
rarely	usually	some
in some cases	more or less	perhaps
often	for the most part	possibly
routinely		

Drafting a thesis statement. Once your claim is focused and appropriately qualified, it can form the core of your essay's **THESIS STATEMENT**, which announces your position and forecasts the path your argument will

273–75

follow. For example, here is the opening paragraph of an essay by the executive director of the National Congress of American Indians arguing that the remains of Native Americans should be treated with the same respect given to others. The author outlines the context of her argument and then presents her thesis (here, in italics):

> What if museums, universities and government agencies could put your dead relatives on display or keep them in boxes to be cut up and otherwise studied? What if you believed that the spirits of the dead could not rest until their human remains were placed in a sacred area? The ordinary American would say there ought to be a law—and there is, for ordinary Americans. *The problem for American Indians is that there are too many laws of the kind that make us the archeological property of the United States and too few of the kind that protect us from such insults.*
>
> —Susan Shown Harjo, "Last Rites for Indian Dead: Treating Remains Like Artifacts Is Intolerable"

Reasons. Your claim must be supported by reasons that your audience will accept. A reason can usually be linked to a claim with the word *because*:

CLAIM	+	*BECAUSE*	+	REASON
MP3 players harm society		*because*		they isolate users from other people.

Keep in mind that you likely have a further reason, a rule or principle that underlies the reason you link directly to your claim. In this argument, the underlying reason is that isolation from other people is bad. If your audience doesn't accept that principle, you may have to back it up with further reasons or evidence.

To come up with good reasons, start by stating your position and then answering the question *why*?

> **CLAIM:** MP3 players harm society. *Why?*
> **REASON:** (Because) They isolate users from other people. *Why?*
> **UNDERLYING REASON:** Isolation from other people is bad.

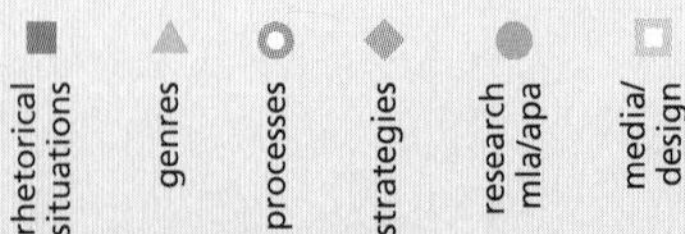

As you can see, this exercise can continue indefinitely as the underlying reasons grow more and more general and abstract. You can do the same with other positions:

> **CLAIM:** Smoking should be banned. *Why?*
> **REASON:** (Because) It is harmful to smokers and also to nonsmokers.
> **UNDERLYING REASON:** People should be protected from harmful substances.

Evidence. Evidence to support your reasons can come from various sources. In fact, you may need to use several kinds of evidence to persuade your audience that your claim is true. Some of the most common types of evidence include facts, statistics, examples, authorities, anecdotes, scenarios, case studies, textual evidence, and visuals.

Facts are ideas that are proven to be true. Facts can include observations or scholarly research (your own or someone else's), but they need to be accepted as true. If your audience accepts the facts you present, they can be powerful means of persuasion. For example, an essay on junk email offers these facts to demonstrate the seasonal nature of spam:

> The flow of spam is often seasonal. It slows in the spring, and then, in the month that technology specialists call "black September"—when hundreds of thousands of students return to college, many armed with new computers and access to fast Internet connections—the levels rise sharply.
>
> —Michael Specter, "Damn Spam"

Specter offers this fact with only a general reference to its origin ("technology specialists"), but given what most people know—or think they know—about college students, it rings true. A citation from a study published by a "technology specialist" would offer even greater credibility.

Statistics are numerical data, usually produced through research, surveys, or polls. Statistics should be relevant to your argument, as current as possible, accurate, and from a reliable source. An argument advocating that Americans should eat less meat presents these data to support the writer's contention that we eat far too much of it:

> Americans are downing close to 200 pounds of meat, poultry, and fish per capita per year (dairy and eggs are separate, and hardly insignificant), an increase of 50 pounds per person from 50 years ago. We each consume something like 110 grams of protein a day, about twice the federal government's recommended allowance; of that, about 75 grams come from animal protein. (The recommended level is itself considered by many dietary experts to be higher than it needs to be.) It's likely that most of us would do just fine on around 30 grams of protein a day, virtually all of it from plant sources.
>
> —Mark Bittman, "Rethinking the Meat-Guzzler"

Bittman's statistics demonstrate the extent to which Americans have increased their meat consumption over the last half-century, the proportion of our diets that comes from meat, and, by comparison, how much protein our bodies require—and summarize the heart of his argument in stark numeric terms.

Examples are specific instances that illustrate general statements. In a book on life after dark in Europe, a historian offers several examples to demonstrate his point that three hundred years ago, night—without artificial lighting—was treacherous:

> Even sure-footed natives on a dark night could misjudge the lay of the land, stumbling into a ditch or off a precipice. In Aberdeenshire, a fifteen-year-old girl died in 1739 after straying from her customary path through a churchyard and tumbling into a newly dug grave. The Yorkshireman Arthur Jessop, returning from a neighbor's home on a cold December evening, fell into a stone pit after losing his bearings.
>
> —A. Roger Ekirch, *At Day's Close: Night in Times Past*

Ekirch illustrates his point and makes it come alive for readers by citing two specific individuals' fates.

Authorities are experts on your subject. To be useful, authorities must be reputable, trustworthy, and qualified to address the subject. You should 400–403 **EVALUATE** any authorities you consult carefully to be sure they have the credentials necessary for readers to take them seriously. When you cite

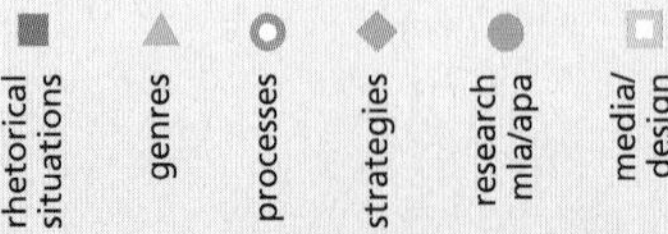

experts, you should clearly identify them and the origins of their authority in a **SIGNAL PHRASE,** as does the author of an argument that deforested land can be reclaimed: 417–18

> Reed Funk, professor of plant biology at Rutgers University, believes that the vast areas of deforested land can be used to grow millions of genetically improved trees for food, mostly nuts, and for fuel. Funk sees nuts used to supplement meat as a source of high-quality protein in developing-country diets.
>
> —Lester R. Brown, *Plan B 2.0: Rescuing a Planet under Stress and a Civilization in Trouble*

Brown cites Funk, an expert on plant biology, to support his argument that humans need to rethink the global economy in order to create a sustainable world. Without the information on Funk's credentials, though, readers would have no reason to take his proposal seriously.

Anecdotes are brief **NARRATIVES** that your audience will find believable and that contribute directly to your argument. Anecdotes may come from your personal experience or the experiences of others. In a speech almost two years after Hurricane Katrina devastated New Orleans, then-presidential candidate Barack Obama used an anecdote to personalize his criticism of the assistance given to the city's poor: 343–51

> Yes, parts of New Orleans are coming back to life. But we also know that over 25,000 families are still living in small trailers; that thousands of homes sit empty and condemned; and that schools and hospitals and firehouses are shuttered. We know that even though the streetcars run, there are fewer passengers; that even though the parades sound their joyful noise, there is too much violence in the shadows.
>
> To confront these challenges we have to understand that Katrina may have battered these shores—but it also exposed silent storms that have ravaged parts of this city and our country for far too long. The storms of poverty and joblessness; inequality and injustice.
>
> When I was down in Houston visiting evacuees a few days after Katrina, I met a woman in the Reliant Center who had long known these storms in her life.

> She told me, "We had nothing before the hurricane. Now we got less than nothing."
>
> We had nothing before the hurricane. Now we got less than nothing. I think about her sometimes. I think about how America left her behind. And I wonder where she is today.
>
> America failed that woman long before that failure showed up on our television screens. We failed her again during Katrina. And—tragically—we are failing her for a third time. That needs to change. It's time for us to restore our trust with her; it's time for America to rebuild trust with the people of New Orleans and the Gulf Coast.
>
> —Barack Obama, "Rebuilding Trust with New Orleans"

Obama uses the anecdote about the woman he met at the Reliant Center to make specific and personal his claim that the federal government neglected its duty to rebuild New Orleans as well as to reduce poverty and increase employment more generally.

Scenarios are hypothetical situations. Like anecdotes, "what if" scenarios can help you describe the possible effects of particular actions or offer new ways of looking at a particular state of affairs. For example, a mathematician presents this light-hearted scenario about Santa Claus in a tongue-in-cheek argument that Christmas is (almost) pure magic:

> Let's assume that Santa only visits those who are children in the eyes of the law, that is, those under the age of 18. There are roughly 2 billion such individuals in the world. However, Santa started his annual activities long before diversity and equal opportunity became issues, and as a result he doesn't handle Muslim, Hindu, Jewish and Buddhist children. That reduces his workload significantly to a mere 15% of the total, namely 378 million. However, the crucial figure is not the number of children but the number of homes Santa has to visit. According to the most recent census data, the average size of a family in the world is 3.5 children per household. Thus, Santa has to visit 108,000,000 individual homes. (Of course, as everyone knows, Santa only visits good children, but we can surely assume that, on an average, at least one child of the 3.5 in each home meets that criterion.)
>
> —Keith Devlin, "The Mathematics of Christmas"

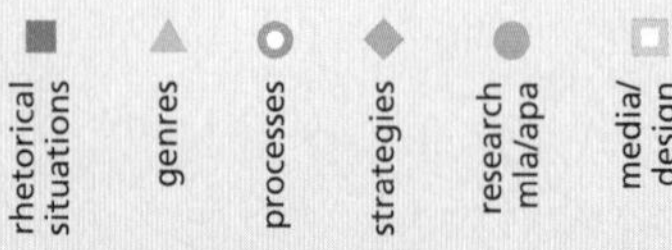

Devlin uses this scenario, as part of his mathematical analysis of Santa's yearly task, to help demonstrate that Christmas is indeed magical—because if you do the math, it's clear that Santa's task is physically impossible.

Case studies and observations feature detailed reporting about a subject. Case studies are in-depth, systematic examinations of an occasion, a person, or a group. For example, in arguing that class differences exist in the United States, sociologist Gregory Mantsios presents studies of three "typical" Americans to show "enormous class differences" in their lifestyles.

Observations offer detailed descriptions of a subject. Here's an observation of the emergence of a desert stream that flows only at night:

> At about 5:30 water came out of the ground. It did not spew up, but slowly escaped into the surrounding sand and small rocks. The wet circle grew until water became visible. Then it bubbled out like a small fountain and the creek began.
>
> —Craig Childs, *The Secret Knowledge of Water*

Childs presents this and other observations in a book that argues (among other things) that even in harsh, arid deserts, water exists, and knowing where to find it can mean the difference between life and death.

Textual evidence includes QUOTATIONS, PARAPHRASES, and SUMMARIES. Usually, the relevance of textual evidence must be stated directly, as excerpts from a text may carry several potential meanings. For example, here is an excerpt from a student essay analyzing the function of the raft in *Huckleberry Finn* as "a platform on which the resolution of conflicts is made possible": 408–19

> [T]he scenes where Jim and Huck are in consensus on the raft contain the moments in which they are most relaxed. For instance, in chapter twelve of the novel, Huck, after escaping capture from Jackson's Island, calls the rafting life "solemn" and articulates their experience as living "pretty high" (Twain 75–76). Likewise, subsequent to escaping the unresolved feud between the Grangerfords and Shepherdsons in chapter eighteen, Huck is unquestionably at ease on the raft: "I was

> powerful glad to get away from the feuds. . . . We said there warn't no home like a raft, after all. Other places do seem so cramped up and smothery, but a raft don't. You feel mighty free and easy and comfortable on a raft" (Twain 134).
>
> —Dave Nichols, "'Less All Be Friends': Rafts as Negotiating Platforms in Twain's *Huckleberry Finn*"

Huck's own words support Nichols's claim that he can relax on a raft. Nichols strengthens his claim by quoting evidence from two separate pages, suggesting that Huck's opinion of rafts pervades the novel.

Visuals can be a useful way of presenting evidence. Remember, though, 528–32 that charts, graphs, photos, drawings, and other **VISUAL TEXTS** seldom speak for themselves and thus must be explained in your text. Below, for example, is a photograph of a poster carried by demonstrators at the 2008 Beijing Summer Olympics, protesting China's treatment of Tibetans. If you were to use this photo in an essay, you would need to explain that the poster combines the image of a protester standing before a tank during the 1989 Tiananmen Square uprising with the Olympic logo, making clear to your readers that the protesters are likening China's treatment of Tibetans to its brutal actions in the past.

Choosing appropriate evidence. The kinds of evidence you provide to support your argument depends on your RHETORICAL SITUATION. If your purpose is, for example, to convince readers to accept the need for a proposed solution, you'd be likely to include facts, statistics, and anecdotes. If you're writing for an academic audience, you'd be less likely to rely on anecdotes, preferring authorities, textual evidence, statistics, and case studies instead. And even within academic communities different disciplines and genres may focus primarily on different kinds of evidence. If you're not sure what counts as appropriate evidence, ask your instructor for guidance.

1

Convincing Readers You're Trustworthy

For your argument to be convincing, you need to establish your own credibility with readers—to demonstrate your knowledge about your topic, to show that you and your readers share some common ground, and to show yourself to be evenhanded in the way you present your argument.

Building common ground. One important element of gaining readers' trust is to identify some common ground, some values you and your audience share. For example, to introduce a book arguing for the compatibility of science and religion, author Chet Raymo offers some common memories:

> Like most children, I was raised on miracles. Cows that jump over the moon; a jolly fat man that visits every house in the world in a single night; mice and ducks that talk; little engines that huff and puff and say, "I think I can"; geese that lay golden eggs. This lively exercise of credulity on the part of children is good practice for what follows—for believing in the miracle stories of traditional religion, yes, but also for the practice of poetry or science.
>
> —Chet Raymo, *Skeptics and True Believers: The Exhilarating Connection between Science and Religion*

Raymo presents childhood stories and myths that are part of many people's shared experiences to help readers find a connection between two realms that are often seen as opposed.

Incorporating other viewpoints. To show that you have carefully considered the viewpoints of others, including those who may agree or disagree with you, you should incorporate those viewpoints into your argument by acknowledging, accommodating, or refuting them.

Acknowledging other viewpoints. One essential part of establishing your credibility is to acknowledge that there are viewpoints different from yours and to represent them fairly and accurately. Rather than weakening your argument, acknowledging possible objections to your position shows that you've thought about and researched your topic thoroughly. For example, in an essay about his experience growing up homosexual, writer Andrew Sullivan acknowledges that not every young gay man or woman has the same experience:

> I should add that many young lesbians and homosexuals seem to have had a much easier time of it. For many, the question of sexual identity was not a critical factor in their life choices or vocation, or even a factor at all.
>
> —Andrew Sullivan, "What Is a Homosexual?"

Thus does Sullivan qualify his assertions, making his own stance appear to be reasonable.

Accommodating other viewpoints. You may be tempted to ignore views you don't agree with, but in fact it's important to acknowledge those views, to demonstrate that you are aware of them and have considered them carefully. You may find yourfself conceding that opposing views have some merit and qualifying your claim or even making them part of your own argument. See, for example, how a philosopher arguing that torture is sometimes "not merely permissible but morally mandatory" addresses a major objection to his position:

> The most powerful argument against using torture as a punishment or to secure confessions is that such practices disregard the rights of the individual. Well, if the individual is all that important—and he is—it is correspondingly important to protect the rights of individuals

> threatened by terrorists. If life is so valuable that it must never be taken, the lives of the innocents must be saved even at the price of hurting the one who endangers them.
>
> —Michael Levin, "The Case for Torture"

Levin folds his critics' argument into his own by acknowledging that the individual is indeed important and then asserting that if the life of one person is important, the lives of many people must be even more important.

Refuting other arguments. Often you may need to refute other arguments and make a case for why you believe they are wrong. Are the values underlying the argument questionable? Is the reasoning flawed? Is the evidence inadequate or faulty? For example, an essay arguing for the elimination of college athletics scholarships includes this refutation:

> Some argue that eliminating athletics scholarships would deny opportunity and limit access for many students, most notably black athletes. The question is, access to what? The fields of competition or an opportunity to earn a meaningful degree? With the six-year graduation rates of black basketball players hovering in the high 30-percent range, and black football players in the high 40-percent range, despite years of "academic reform," earning an athletics scholarship under the current system is little more than a chance to play sports.
>
> —John R. Gerdy, "For True Reform, Athletics Scholarships Must Go"

Gerdy bases his refutation on statistics showing that for more than half of African American college athletes, the opportunity to earn a degree by playing a sport is an illusion.

When you incorporate differing viewpoints, be careful to avoid the FALLACIES of attacking the person making the argument or refuting a competing position that no one seriously entertains. It is also important that you not distort or exaggerate opposing viewpoints. If *your* argument is to be persuasive, other arguments should be represented fairly. 296–98

Appealing to Readers' Emotions

Logic and facts, even when presented by someone reasonable and trustworthy, may not be enough to persuade readers. Many successful arguments include an emotional component that appeals to readers' hearts as well as to their minds. Advertising often works by appealing to its audience's emotions, as in this paragraph from a Volvo ad:

> Choosing a car is about the comfort and safety of your passengers, most especially your children. That's why we ensure Volvo's safety research examines how we can make our cars safer for everyone who travels in them — from adults to teenagers, children to babies. Even those who aren't even born yet.
>
> —Volvo.com

This ad plays on the fear that children — or a pregnant mother — may be injured or killed in an automobile accident.

Keep in mind that emotional appeals can make readers feel as though they are being manipulated and, consequently, less likely to accept an argument. For most kinds of academic writing, use emotional appeals sparingly.

Checking for Fallacies

Fallacies are arguments that involve faulty reasoning. It's important to avoid fallacies in your writing because they often seem plausible but are usually unfair or inaccurate and make reasonable discussion difficult. Here are some of the most common fallacies:

- ***Ad hominem*** arguments attack someone's character rather than addressing the issues. (*Ad hominem* is Latin for "to the man.") It is an especially common fallacy in political discourse and elsewhere: "Jack Turner has no business talking about the way we run things in this city. He's lived here only five years and is just another flaky liberal." The length of time Turner has lived in the city has no bearing on the

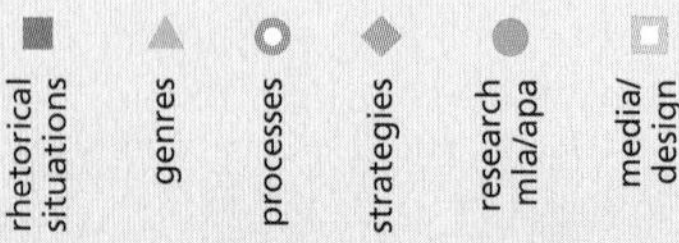

worth of his argument; neither does his political stance, which his opponent characterizes unfairly.

- ***Bandwagon appeals*** argue that because others think or do something, we should, too. For example, an advertisement for a rifle association suggests that "67 percent of voters support laws permitting concealed weapons. You should, too." It assumes that readers want to be part of the group and implies that an opinion that is popular must be correct.
- ***Begging the question*** is a circular argument. It assumes as a given what is trying to be proved, essentially supporting an assertion with the assertion itself. Consider this statement: "Affirmative action can never be fair or just because you cannot remedy one injustice by committing another." This statement begs the question because to prove that affirmative action is unjust, it assumes that it is an injustice.
- ***Either-or*** arguments, also called *false dilemmas*, are oversimplifications. Either-or arguments assert that there can be only two possible positions on a complex issue. For example, "Those who oppose our actions in this war are enemies of freedom" inaccurately assumes that if someone opposes the war in question, he or she opposes freedom. In fact, people might have many other reasons for opposing the war.
- ***False analogies*** compare things that resemble each other in some ways but not in the most important respects. For example: "Trees pollute the air just as much as cars and trucks do." Although it's true that plants emit hydrocarbons, and hydrocarbons are a component of smog, they also produce oxygen, whereas motor vehicles emit gases that combine with hydrocarbons to form smog. Vehicles pollute the air; trees provide the air that vehicles' emissions pollute.
- ***Faulty causality,*** also known as *post hoc, ergo propter hoc* (Latin for "after this, therefore because of this"), assumes that because one event followed another, the first event caused the second—for example, "Legalizing same-sex marriage in Sweden led to an increase in the number of children born to unwed mothers." The statement contains no evidence to show that the first event caused the second. The birth rate could have been affected by many factors, and same-sex marriage may not even be among them.

- ***Hasty generalizations*** are conclusions based on insufficient or inappropriately qualified evidence. This summary of a research study is a good example: "Twenty randomly chosen residents of Brooklyn, New York, were asked whether they found graffiti tags offensive; fourteen said yes, five said no, and one had no opinion. Therefore, 70 percent of Brooklyn residents find tagging offensive." In Brooklyn, a part of New York City with a population of over two million, twenty residents is far too small a group from which to draw meaningful conclusions. To be able to generalize, the researcher would have had to survey a much greater percentage of Brooklyn's population.
- ***Slippery slope*** arguments assert that one event will inevitably lead to another, often cataclysmic event without presenting evidence that such a chain of causes and effects will in fact take place. Here's an example: "If the state legislature passes this 2 percent tax increase, it won't be long before all the corporations in the state move to other states and leave thousands unemployed." According to this argument, if taxes are raised, the state's economy will be ruined — not a likely scenario, given the size of the proposed increase.

Considering the Rhetorical Situation

To argue effectively, you need to think about the message that you want to articulate, the audience you want to persuade, the effect of your stance, and the larger context you are writing in.

3–4 **PURPOSE** What do you want your audience to do? To think something? To act? To change their minds? To consider alternative views? To accept your position as plausible? To see that you have thought carefully about an issue and researched it appropriately?

5–8 **AUDIENCE** Who is your intended audience? What do they likely know and believe about your topic? How personal is it for them? To what extent are they likely to agree or disagree with you? Why? What common ground can you find with them?

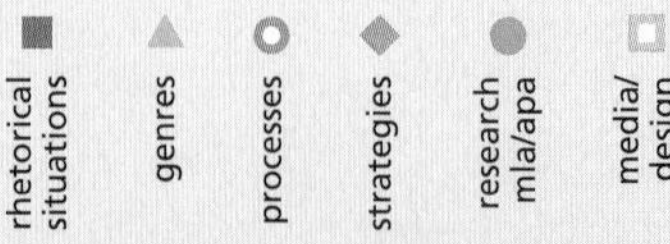

How will you incorporate other positions? What kind of evidence are they likely to accept?

GENRE What genre will help you achieve your purpose? A position paper? An evaluation? A review? A proposal? An analysis? 9–11

STANCE How do you want your audience to perceive you? As an authority on your topic? As someone much like them? As calm? Reasonable? Impassioned or angry? Something else? What's your attitude toward your topic, and why? What argument strategies will help you to convey that stance? 12–14

MEDIA / DESIGN What media will you use, and how do your media affect your argument? If you're writing on paper, does your argument call for photos or charts? If you're giving an oral presentation, should you put your reasons and support on slides? If you're writing on the Web, should you add links to sites representing other positions or containing evidence that supports your position? 15–17

33 Classifying and Dividing

Classification and division are ways of organizing information: various pieces of information about a topic may be classified according to their similarities, or a single topic may be divided into parts. We might classify different kinds of flowers as annuals or perennials, for example, and classify the perennials further as dahlias, daisies, roses, and peonies. We might also divide a flower garden into distinct areas: for herbs, flowers, and vegetables. Writers often use classification and division as ways of developing and organizing material. This book, for instance, classifies comparison, definition, description, and several other common ways of thinking and writing as strategies. It divides the information it provides about writing into seven parts: "Rhetorical Situations," "Genres," "Processes," and so on. Each part further divides its material into various chapters. Even if you never write a book, you will have occasion to classify and divide material 116–24 38–58 in **ANNOTATED BIBLIOGRAPHIES** and essays **ANALYZING TEXTS** and other kinds of writing. This chapter offers advice for classifying and dividing information for various writing purposes—and in a way that suits your own rhetorical situation.

Classifying

When we classify something, we group it with similar things. A linguist would classify French and Spanish and Italian as Romance languages, for example—and Russian, Polish, and Bulgarian as Slavic languages. In a hilarious (if totally phony) news story from *The Onion* about a church bake sale, the writer classifies the activities observed there as examples of the seven deadly sins:

> GADSDEN, AL—The seven deadly sins—avarice, sloth, envy, lust, gluttony, pride, and wrath—were all committed Sunday during the twice-annual bake sale at St. Mary's of the Immaculate Conception Church.
>
> —*The Onion,* "All Seven Deadly Sins Committed at Church Bake Sale"

The article goes on to categorize the participants' behavior in terms of the sins, describing one parishioner who commits the sin of pride by bragging about her cookies, others who commit the sin of envy by envying the popularity of the prideful parishioner's baked goods (the consumption of which leads to the sin of gluttony). In all, the article notes, "347 individual acts of sin were committed at the bake sale," and every one of them can be classified as one of the seven deadly sins.

Dividing

As a writing strategy, division is a way of breaking something into parts—and a way of making the information easy for readers to follow and understand. See how this example about children's ways of nagging divides their tactics into seven categories:

> James U. McNeal, a professor of marketing at Texas A&M University, is considered America's leading authority on marketing to children. In his book *Kids as Customers* (1992), McNeal provides marketers with a thorough analysis of "children's requesting styles and appeals." He [divides] juvenile nagging tactics into seven major categories. A *pleading* nag is one accompanied by repetitions of words like "please" or "mom, mom, mom." A *persistent* nag involves constant requests for the coveted product and may include the phrase "I'm gonna ask just one more time." *Forceful* nags are extremely pushy and may include subtle threats, like "Well, then, I'll go and ask Dad." *Demonstrative* nags are the most high risk, often characterized by full-blown tantrums in public places, breath

> holding, tears, a refusal to leave the store. *Sugar-coated* nags promise affection in return for a purchase and may rely on seemingly heartfelt declarations, like "You're the best dad in the world." *Threatening* nags are youthful forms of blackmail, vows of eternal hatred and of running away if something isn't bought. *Pity* nags claim the child will be heartbroken, teased, or socially stunted if the parent refuses to buy a certain item. "All of these appeals and styles may be used in combination," McNeal's research has discovered, "but kids tend to stick to one or two of each that prove most effective . . . for their own parents."
>
> —Eric Schlosser, *Fast Food Nation: The Dark Side of the All-American Meal*

Here the writer announces the division scheme of "seven major categories." Then he names each tactic and describes how it works. And notice the italics: each nagging tactic is italicized, making it easy to recognize and follow. Take away the italics, and the divisions would be less visible.

Creating Clear and Distinct Categories

When you classify or divide, you need to create clear and distinct categories. If you're writing about music, you might divide it on the basis of the genre (hip-hop, rock, classical, gospel), artist (male or female, group or solo), or instruments (violins, trumpets, bongos, guitars). These categories must be distinct, so that no information overlaps or fits into more than one category, and they must include every member of the group you're discussing. The simpler the criteria for selecting the categories, the better. The nagging categories in the example from *Fast Food Nation* are based on only one criterion: a child's verbal behavior.

Highlight your categories. Sometimes you may want to highlight your categories visually to make them easier to follow. Eric Schlosser does that by italicizing each category: the *pleading* nag, the *persistent* nag, the *forceful* nag, and so on. Other **DESIGN** elements—bulleted lists, pie charts, tables, images—might also prove useful.

524–32

See, for instance, how the humorist Dave Barry uses a two-column list to show two categories of males—"men" and "guys"—in his *Complete Guide to Guys*:

Men	*Guys*
Vince Lombardi	Joe Namath
Oliver North	Gilligan
Hemingway	Gary Larson
Columbus	Whichever astronaut hit the first golf ball on the moon
Superman	Bart Simpson
Doberman pinschers	Labrador retrievers
Abbott	Costello
Captain Ahab	Captain Kangaroo
Satan	Snidely Whiplash
The pope	Willard Scott
Germany	Italy
Geraldo	Katie Couric

—Dave Barry, *Dave Barry's Complete Guide to Guys: A Fairly Short Book*

Sometimes you might show categories visually, like the illustration on the following page from a news story about the many new varieties of Oreo cookies. In the article, the reporter David Barboza classifies Oreos with words:

> There is the Double Delight Oreo . . . , the Uh Oh Oreo (vanilla cookie with chocolate filling), Oreo Cookie Barz, Football Oreos, Oreos Cookies and Creme Pie, Oreos in Kraft Lunchables for kids, and Oreo cookies with a variety of cream fillings (mint, chocolate, coffee) and sizes (six-pack, twelve-pack, snack pack, and more).

DOUBLE DELIGHT MINT 'N CREME
Introduced in 2003

DOUBLE DELIGHT PEANUT BUTTER & CHOCOLATE
2003

DOUBLE DELIGHT COFFEE 'N CREME
2003

UH OH OREO
(Vanilla cookie, chocolate filling)
2003

CHOCOLATE CREME OREO
2001

FOOTBALL OREO
(Football design on biscuit)
Seasonal

DOUBLE STUFF
1974

ORIGINAL
1912

Piling on the Cookies
In the Oreo's first eight decades, Nabisco tried only a handful of variations on the original. But in recent years, it has stretched the line to more than two dozen by varying the size, the filling, the biscuit recipe—nearly everything but the brand name. Here are some examples now on store shelves.

—David Barboza, "Permutations Push Oreo Far Beyond Cookie Aisle"

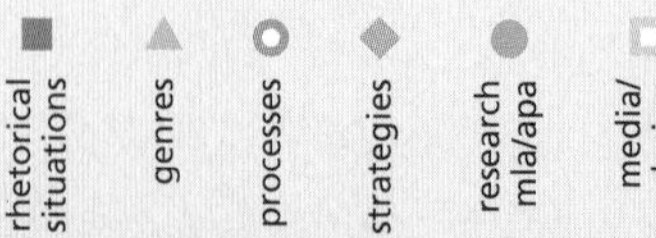

The illustration, for an article that shows Oreos to be a "hyperevolving, perpetually repackaged, category-migrating" cookie, makes that classification easy to see — and gets our attention in the first place.

Considering the Rhetorical Situation

As a writer or speaker, you need to think about the message that you want to articulate, the audience you want to reach, and the larger context you are writing in.

PURPOSE Your purpose for writing will affect how you classify or divide information. Dave Barry classifies males as "men" and "guys" to get a laugh, whereas J. Crew might divide sweaters into cashmere, wool, and cotton to help shoppers find and buy things from their website. 3–4

AUDIENCE What audience do you want to reach, and will classifying or dividing your material help them follow your discussion? 5–8

GENRE Does your genre call for you to categorize or divide information? A long report might need to be divided into sections, for instance. 9–11

STANCE Your stance may affect the way you classify information. Dave Barry classifies males as "men" and "guys" to reflect a humorist's stance; if he were a psychologist, he might categorize them as "Oedipal," "hormonal," and "libidinal." 12–14

MEDIA / DESIGN You can classify or divide in paragraph form, but sometimes a pie chart or list will show the categories better. 15–17

IF YOU NEED MORE HELP

See also CLUSTERING, CUBING, and LOOPING, three methods of generating ideas that can be especially helpful for classifying material. And see all the PROCESSES chapters for guidelines on drafting, revising, and so on if you need to write a classification essay. 220–22 209–58

34 Comparing and Contrasting

Comparing things looks at their similarities; contrasting them focuses on their differences. It's a kind of thinking that comes naturally and that we do constantly — for example, comparing Houston with Dallas, PCs with Macs, or three paintings by Renoir. And once we start comparing, we generally find ourselves contrasting — Houston and Dallas have differences as well as similarities.

As a student, you'll often be asked to compare and contrast paintings or poems or other things. As a writer, you'll have cause to compare and contrast in most kinds of writing. In a **PROPOSAL**, for instance, you will need to compare your solution with other possible solutions; or in an **EVALUATION**, such as a movie review, you might contrast the film you're reviewing with some other film. This chapter offers advice on ways of comparing and contrasting things for various writing purposes and for your own rhetorical situations.

171–79 ▲
125–32

Most of the time, we compare obviously similar things: cars we might purchase, three competing political philosophies, two versions of a film. Occasionally, however, we might compare things that are less obviously similar. See how John McMurtry, an ex–football player, compares football with war in an essay arguing that the attraction football holds for spectators is based in part on its potential for violence and injury:

> The family resemblance between football and war is, indeed, striking. Their languages are similar: "field general," "long bomb," "blitz," "take a shot," "front line," "pursuit," "good hit," "the draft," and so on. Their principles and practices are alike: mass hysteria, the art of intimidation, absolute command and total obedience, territorial aggression, censorship, inflated insignia and propaganda, blackboard maneuvers and strategies, drills, uniforms, marching bands, and train-

> ing camps. And the virtues they celebrate are almost identical: hyper-aggressiveness, coolness under fire, and suicidal bravery.
>
> —John McMurtry, "Kill 'Em! Crush 'Em! Eat 'Em Raw!"

McMurtry's comparison helps focus readers' attention on what he's arguing about football in part because it's somewhat unexpected. But the more unlikely the comparison, the more you might be accused of comparing apples and oranges. It's important, therefore, that the things we compare be legitimately compared—as is the case in the following comparison of the health of the world's richest and poorest people:

> World Health Organization (WHO) data indicate that roughly 1.2 billion people are undernourished, underweight, and often hungry. At the same time, roughly 1.2 billion people are overnourished and overweight, most of them suffering from excessive caloric intake and exercise deprivation. So while 1 billion people worry whether they will eat, another billion should worry about eating too much.
>
> Disease patterns also reflect the widening gap. The billion poorest suffer mostly from infectious diseases—malaria, tuberculosis, dysentery, and AIDS. Malnutrition leaves infants and small children even more vulnerable to such infectious diseases. Unsafe drinking water takes a heavier toll on those with hunger-weakened immune systems, resulting in millions of fatalities each year. In contrast, among the billion at the top of the global economic scale, it is diseases related to aging and lifestyle excesses, including obesity, smoking, diets rich in fat and sugar, and exercise deprivation, that cause most deaths.
>
> —Lester R. Brown, *Plan B 2.0: Rescuing a Planet Under Stress and a Civilization in Trouble*

While the two groups of roughly a billion people each undoubtedly have similarities, this selection from a book arguing for global action on the environment focuses on the stark contrasts.

Two Ways of Comparing and Contrasting

Comparisons and contrasts may be organized in two basic ways: block and point by point.

The block method. One way is to discuss separately each item you're comparing, giving all the information about one item and then all the information about the next item. A report on Seattle and Vancouver, for example, compares the firearm regulations in each city using a paragraph about Seattle and then a paragraph about Vancouver:

> Although similar in many ways, Seattle and Vancouver differ markedly in their approaches to the regulation of firearms. In Seattle, handguns may be purchased legally for self-defense in the street or at home. After a thirty-day waiting period, a permit can be obtained to carry a handgun as a concealed weapon. The recreational use of handguns is minimally restricted.
>
> In Vancouver, self-defense is not considered a valid or legal reason to purchase a handgun. Concealed weapons are not permitted. Recreational uses of handguns (such as target shooting and collecting) are regulated by the province, and the purchase of a handgun requires a restricted-weapons permit. A permit to carry a weapon must also be obtained in order to transport a handgun, and these weapons can be discharged only at a licensed shooting club. Handguns can be transported by car, but only if they are stored in the trunk in a locked box.
>
> —John Henry Sloan et al., "Handgun Regulations, Crime, Assaults, and Homicide: A Tale of Two Cities"

The point-by-point method. The other way to compare things is to focus on specific points of comparison. A later part of the Seattle-Vancouver study compares the two cities' gun laws and how they're enforced, discussing each point one at a time. (We've underlined each point.) The authors discuss one point, comparing the two cities; then they go on to the next point, again comparing the cities:

> Although they differ in their approach to firearm regulations, both cities aggressively enforce existing gun laws and regulations, and convictions for gun-related offenses carry similar penalties. For example, <u>the commission of a class A felony (such as murder or robbery) with a firearm</u> in Washington State adds a minimum of two years of confinement to the sentence for the felony. In the province of British Columbia, the same offense generally results in one to fourteen years of imprisonment in addition to the felony sentence. <u>Similar percent-</u>

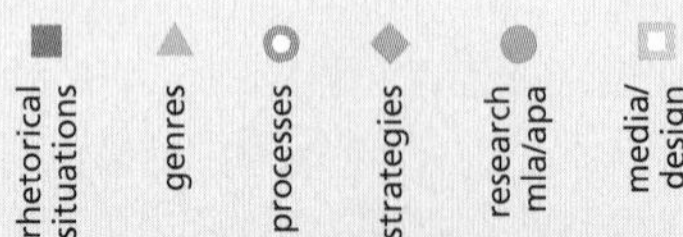

ages of homicides in both communities eventually lead to arrest and police charges. In Washington, under the Sentencing Reform Act of 1981, murder in the first degree carries a minimum sentence of twenty years of confinement. In British Columbia, first-degree murder carries a minimum sentence of twenty-five years, with a possible judicial parole review after fifteen years. Capital punishment was abolished in Canada during the 1970s. In Washington State, the death penalty may be invoked in cases of aggravated first-degree murder, but no one has been executed since 1963.

Using Graphs and Images to Present Comparisons

Some comparisons can be easier to understand if they're presented visually, as a **CHART, GRAPH,** or **ILLUSTRATION.** See how this chart shows comparative information about Vancouver and Seattle that can be easily understood at a glance and clearly categorized. It would be possible to show the same material in paragraph form, but it's much easier to see and read in this chart:

528–32

Seattle and Vancouver: Basic Demographic Information	*Seattle, Washington*	*Vancouver, British Columbia*
Population (1980)	493,846	430,826
Unemployment rate	5.8%	6.0%
High-school graduates	79.0%	66.0%
Median household income (U.S. dollars)	$16,254	$16,681

—John Henry Sloan et al., "Handgun Regulations, Crime, Assaults, and Homicide: A Tale of Two Cities"

The following bar graph, from an economics textbook, compares the incomes of various professions in the United States, both with one another and with the average U.S. income (defined as 100 percent). Again, it would be possible to write out this information in a paragraph—but it is much easier to understand it this way:

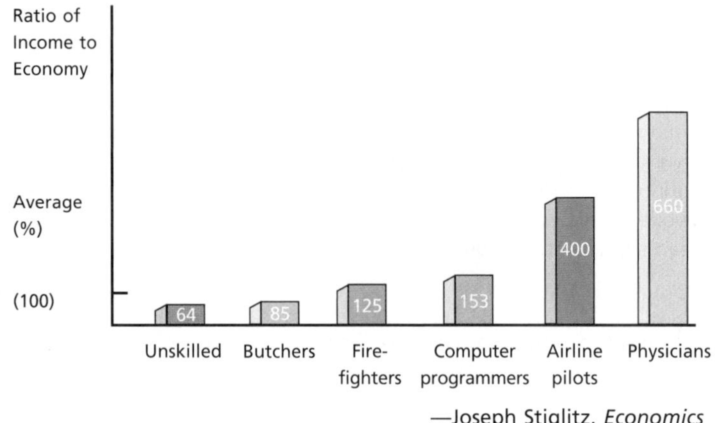

—Joseph Stiglitz, *Economics*

Sometimes photographs can make a comparison. The two photos below show a woman before and after she had her hair dyed. The caption suggests that the story is more complicated than the photos alone can tell, however; for the full story, we need words.

"GO BLONDE! 'I tried it before and it came out orange!'"

—iVillage.com

Using Figurative Language to Make Comparisons

Another way we make comparisons is with figurative language: words and phrases used in a nonliteral way to help readers see a point. Three kinds of figurative language that make comparisons are similes, metaphors, and analogies. When Robert Burns wrote that his love was "like a red, red rose," he was comparing his love with a rose and evoking an image—in this case, a simile—that helps us understand his feelings for her. A simile makes a comparison using *like* or *as*. In the following example, from an article in the food section of the *New York Times*, a restaurant critic uses several similes (underlined) to help us visualize an unusual food dish:

> Once upon a time, possibly at a lodge in Wyoming, possibly at a butcher shop in Maurice, Louisiana, or maybe even at a plantation in South Carolina, an enterprising cook decided to take a boned chicken, a boned duck, and a boned turkey, stuff them one inside the other like Russian dolls, and roast them. He called his masterpiece turducken. . . .
>
> A well-prepared turducken is a marvelous treat, a free-form poultry terrine layered with flavorful stuffing and moistened with duck fat. When it's assembled, it looks like a turkey and it roasts like a turkey, but when you go to carve it, you can slice through it like a loaf of bread. In each slice you get a little bit of everything: white meat from the breast; dark meat from the legs, duck, carrots, bits of sausage, bread, herbs, juices, and chicken, too.
>
> —Amanda Hesser, "Turkey Finds Its Inner Duck (and Chicken)"

Metaphors make comparisons without such connecting words as *like* or *as*. See how desert ecologist Craig Childs uses a metaphor to help us understand the nature of water during a flood in the Grand Canyon:

> Water splashed off the desert and ran all over the surface, looking for the quickest way down. It was too swift for the ground to absorb. When water flows like this, it will not be clean tap water. It will be a gravy of debris, snatching everything it finds.
>
> —Craig Childs, *The Secret Knowledge of Water*

Calling the water "a gravy of debris" allows us to see the murky liquid as it streams through the canyon.

Analogies are extended similes or metaphors that compare something unfamiliar with something more familiar. Arguing that corporations should not patent parts of DNA whose function isn't yet clear, a genetics professor uses the familiar image of a library to explain an unfamiliar concept:

> It's like having a library of books and randomly tearing pages out. You may know which books the pages came from but that doesn't tell you much about them.
>
> —Peter Goodfellow, quoted in John Vidal and John Carvel, "Lambs to the Gene Market"

Sometimes analogies are used for humorous effect as well as to make a point, as in this passage from a critique of history textbooks:

> Another history text—this one for fifth grade—begins with the story of how Henry B. Gonzalez, who is a member of Congress from Texas, learned about his own nationality. When he was ten years old, his teacher told him he was an American because he was born in the United States. His grandmother, however, said, "The cat was born in the oven. Does that make him bread?"
>
> —Frances FitzGerald, *America Revised: History Schoolbooks in the Twentieth Century*

The grandmother's question shows how an intentionally ridiculous analogy can be a source of humor—and can make a point memorably.

Considering the Rhetorical Situation

As a writer or speaker, you need to think about the message that you want to articulate, the audience you want to reach, and the larger context you are writing in.

3–4

PURPOSE Sometimes your purpose for writing will be to compare two or more things. Other times, you may want to compare several things for some other purpose—to compare your views with those of others in an argument essay, or to compare one text with another as you analyze them.

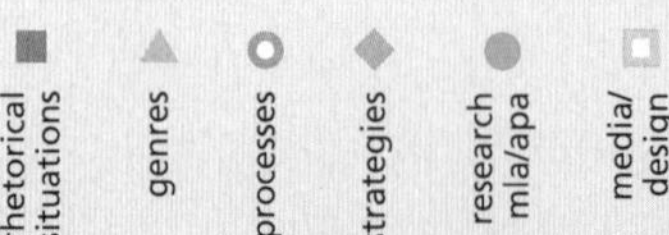

AUDIENCE Who is your audience, and will comparing your topic with a more familiar one help them to follow your discussion? 5–8

GENRE Does your genre require you to compare something? Evaluations often include comparisons—one book to another in a review, or ten different cell phones in *Consumer Reports*. 9–11

STANCE Your stance may affect any comparisons you make. How you compare two things—evenhandedly, or clearly favoring one over the other, for example—will reflect your stance. 12–14

MEDIA / DESIGN Some things you will want to compare with words alone (lines from two poems, for instance), but sometimes you may wish to make comparisons visually (two images juxtaposed on a page, or several numbers plotted on a line graph). 15–17

IF YOU NEED MORE HELP

See LOOPING and CUBING, two methods of generating ideas that can be especially helpful for comparing and contrasting. If you're writing an essay whose purpose is to compare two or more things, see also the PROCESSES chapters for help drafting, revising, and so on.

220–22
209–58

35 Defining

Defining something says what it is — and what it is not. A terrier, for example, is a kind of dog. A fox terrier is a small dog now generally kept as a pet but once used by hunters to dig for foxes. Happiness is a jelly doughnut, at least according to Homer Simpson. All of those are definitions. As writers, we need to define any terms our readers may not know. And sometimes you'll want to stipulate your own definition of a word in order to 283–99 set the terms of an **ARGUMENT** — as Homer Simpson does with a definition that's not found in any dictionary. This chapter details strategies for using definitions in your writing to suit your own rhetorical situations.

Formal Definitions

Sometimes to make sure readers understand you, you will need to provide a formal definition. If you are using a technical term that readers are unlikely to know or if you are using a term in a specific way, you need to say then and there what the word means. The word *mutual*, for example, has several dictionary meanings:

> **mu•tu•al . . .**
>
> **1a:** directed by each toward the other or the others <*mutual* affection> **b:** having the same feelings one for the other <they had long been *mutual* enemies> **c:** shared in common <enjoying their *mutual* hobby> **d:** joint
>
> **2:** characterized by intimacy
>
> **3:** of or relating to a plan whereby the members of an organization share in the profits and expenses; *specifically*: of, relating to, or taking the form of an insurance method in which the policyholders constitute the members of the insuring company
>
> — Merriam-Webster.com

The first two meanings are commonly understood and probably require no definition. But if you were to use *mutual* in the third sense, it might—depending on your audience. A general audience would probably need the definition; an audience from the insurance industry would not. A website that gives basic financial advice to an audience of non-specialists, for instance, offers a specific definition of the term *mutual fund*:

> *Mutual funds* are financial intermediaries. They are companies set up to receive your money and then, having received it, to make investments with the money.
>
> —Bill Barker, "A Grand, Comprehensive Overview to Mutual Funds Investing"

But even writers in specialized fields routinely provide formal definitions to make sure their readers understand the way they are using certain words. See how two writers define the word *stock* as it pertains to their respective (and very different) fields:

> Stocks are the basis for sauces and soups and important flavoring agents for braises. Admittedly, stock making is time consuming, but the extra effort yields great dividends.
>
> —Tom Colicchio, *Think Like a Chef*

> Want to own part of a business without having to show up at its office every day? Or ever? Stock is the vehicle of choice for those who do. Dating back to the Dutch mutual stock corporations of the sixteenth century, the modern stock market exists as a way for entrepreneurs to finance businesses using money collected from investors. In return for ponying up the dough to finance the company, the investor becomes a part owner of the company. That ownership is represented by stock—specialized financial "securities," or financial instruments, that are "secured" by a claim on the assets and profits of a company.
>
> —The Motley Fool, "Investing Basics: Stocks"

To write a formal definition

- Use words that readers are likely to be familiar with.
- Don't use the word being defined in the definition.

- Begin with the word being defined; include the general category to which the term belongs and the attributes that make it different from the others in that category.

For example:

Term	*General Category*	*Distinguishing Attributes*
Stock is	a specialized financial "security"	that is "secured" by a claim.
Photosynthesis is	a process	by which plants use sunlight to create energy.
Astronomers are	scientists	who study celestial objects and phenomena.
Adam Sandler,	a comedian,	has starred in several movies, including *Punch-Drunk Love* and *Click*.

Note that the category and distinguishing attributes cannot be stated too broadly; if they were, the definition would be too vague to be useful. It wouldn't be helpful in most circumstances, for example, to say, "Adam Sandler is a man who has acted" or "Photosynthesis is something having to do with plants."

Extended Definitions

Sometimes you need to provide a more detailed definition. Extended definitions may be several sentences long or several paragraphs long and may include pictures or diagrams. Sometimes an entire essay is devoted to defining a difficult or important concept. Here is one writer's extended definition of stem cells:

> By definition, a stem cell is an unspecialized cell that has the ability to divide and renew itself. Under certain conditions, it can generate large numbers of daughter cells and these go on to mature into cells with special functions, such as beating heart muscle or new bone to heal a fracture.

> Stem cells exist naturally in the body. They're in bone marrow and, although rare, in the blood stream. Stem cells also exist in other tissues and organs, such as the liver, pancreas, brain, and maybe even the heart.
>
> Currently, stem cells come from three sources: blastocysts, which are cells isolated from the inner cell mass of a three-to-five-day-old embryo grown in a petri dish in a lab, also called embryonic stem cells; cord blood cells, which are isolated from blood taken from an umbilical cord saved immediately after birth; and adult stem cells, which are collected from a person's own tissues.
>
> —"The Miracle of Stem Cells," *Cleveland Clinic Magazine*

That definition includes a description of the distinguishing features of stem cells and tells where they are found and where they come from. We can assume that it's written for a general audience, one that doesn't know anything about stem cells.

Abstract concepts often require extended definitions because by nature they are more complicated to define. There are many ways of writing an extended definition, depending in part on the term being defined and on your audience and purpose. The following examples show some of the methods that can be used for composing extended definitions of *democracy*.

Explore the word's origins. Where did the word come from? When did it first come into use? In the following example, from an essay considering what democracy means in the twenty-first century, the writer started by looking at the word's first known use in English. Though it's from an essay written for a first-year writing course and thus for a fairly general audience, it's a definition that might pique any audience's interest:

> According to the *Oxford English Dictionary*, the term *democracy* first appeared in English in a thirteenth-century translation of Aristotle's works—specifically, in his *Politics*, where he stated that the "underlying principle of democracy is freedom" and that "it is customary to say that only in democracies do men have a share in freedom, for that is what every democracy makes its aim." By the sixteenth century, the word was used much as it is now. One writer in 1586, for instance, defined it in this way: "where free and poore men being the greater number, are lords of the estate."
>
> —Susanna Mejía, "What Does Democracy Mean Now?"

Here's another example, this one written for a scholarly audience, from an essay about women, participation, democracy, and the information age:

> The very word *citizenship* carries with it a connotation of place, a "citizen" being, literally, the inhabitant of a city. Over the years the word has, of course, accumulated a number of associated meanings . . . and the word has come to stand in for such concepts as participation, equality, and democracy. The fact that the concept of locality is deeply embedded in the word *citizen* suggests that it is also fundamental to our current understanding of these other, more apparently abstract words.
>
> In Western thought, the concepts of citizenship, equality, and democracy are closely interlinked and can be traced back to a common source, in Athens in the fifth century B.C. Perhaps it is no accident that it was the same culture which also gave us, in its theater, the concept of the unity of time and space. The Greek city-state has been represented for centuries as the ideal model of democracy, with free and equal access for all citizens to decision making. Leaving aside, for the moment, the question of who was included, and who excluded from this notion of citizenship, we can see that the sense of place is fundamental to this model. Entitlement to participate in the democratic process is circumscribed by geography; it is the inhabitants of the geographical entity of the city-state, precisely defined and bounded, who have the rights to citizenship. Those who are not defined as inhabitants of that specific city-state are explicitly excluded, although, of course, they may have the right to citizenship elsewhere.
>
> —Ursula Huws, "Women, Participation, and Democracy in the Information Society"

Provide details. What are its characteristics? What is it made of? See how a historian explores the basic characteristics of democracy in a book written for an audience of historians:

> As a historian I am naturally disposed to be satisfied with the meaning which, in the history of politics, men have commonly attributed to the word—a meaning, needless to say, which derives partly from the experience and partly from the aspirations of mankind. So regarded, the term *democracy* refers primarily to a form of government, and it has always meant government by the many as opposed to government

by the one—government by the people as opposed to government by a tyrant, a dictator, or an absolute monarch. . . . Since the Greeks first used the term, the essential test of democratic government has always been this: the source of political authority must be and remain in the people and not in the ruler. A democratic government has always meant one in which the citizens, or a sufficient number of them to represent more or less effectively the common will, freely act from time to time, and according to established forms, to appoint or recall the magistrates and to enact or revoke the laws by which the community is governed.

—Carl Becker, *Modern Democracy*

Compare it with other words. How is this concept like other similar things? How does it differ? What is it *not* like? **COMPARE AND CONTRAST** it. 306–13 See how a political science textbook defines a *majoritarian democracy* by comparing its characteristics with those of a *consensual democracy*:

A majoritarian democracy is one

1. having only two major political parties, not many
2. having an electoral system that requires a bare majority to elect one clear winner in an election, as opposed to a proportional electoral system that distributes seats to political parties according to the rough share of votes received in the election
3. a strong executive (president or prime minister) and cabinet that together are largely independent of the legislature when it comes to exercising the executive's constitutional duties, in contrast to an executive and cabinet that are politically controlled by the parties in the legislature and therefore unable to exercise much influence when proposing policy initiatives.

—Benjamin Ginsberg, Theodore J. Lowi, and Margaret Weir, *We the People: An Introduction to American Politics*

And here's an example in which democracy is contrasted with various other forms of governments of the past:

Caesar's power derived from a popular mandate, conveyed through established republican forms, but that did not make his government

> any the less a dictatorship. Napoleon called his government a democratic republic, but no one, least of all Napoleon himself, doubted that he had destroyed the last vestiges of the democratic republic.
>
> —Carl Becker, *Modern Democracy*

Give examples. See how the essayist E. B. White defines democracy by giving some everyday examples of considerate behavior, humility, and civic participation—all things he suggests constitute democracy:

> It is the line that forms on the right. It is the don't in "don't shove." It is the hole in the stuffed shirt through which the sawdust slowly trickles; it is the dent in the high hat. Democracy is the recurrent suspicion that more than half of the people are right more than half of the time. . . . Democracy is a letter to the editor.
>
> —E. B. White, "Democracy"

White's definition is elegant because he uses examples that his readers will know. His characteristics—metaphors, really—define democracy not as a conceptual way of governing but as an everyday part of American life.

300–305

Classify it. Often it is useful to divide or **CLASSIFY** a term. The ways in which democracy unfolds are complex enough to warrant entire textbooks, of course, but the following definition, from a political science textbook, divides democracy into two kinds, representative and direct:

> A system of government that gives citizens a regular opportunity to elect the top government officials is usually called a representative democracy or republic. A system that permits citizens to vote directly on laws and policies is often called a direct democracy. At the national level, America is a representative democracy in which citizens select government officials but do not vote on legislation. Some states, however, have provisions for direct legislation through popular referendum. For example, California voters in 1995 decided to bar undocumented immigrants from receiving some state services.
>
> —Benjamin Ginsberg, Theodore J. Lowi, and Margaret Weir, *We the People: An Introduction to American Politics*

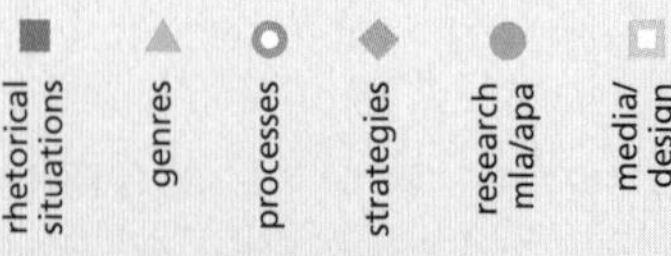

Stipulative Definitions

Sometimes a writer will stipulate a certain definition, essentially saying, "This is how I'm defining x." Such definitions are not usually found in a dictionary—and at the same time are central to the argument the writer is making. Here is one example, from an essay by Toni Morrison. Describing a scene from a film in which a newly arrived Greek immigrant, working as a shoe shiner in Grand Central Terminal, chases away an African American competitor, Morrison calls the scene an example of "race talk," a concept she then goes on to define:

> This is race talk, the explicit insertion into everyday life of racial signs and symbols that have no meaning other than pressing African Americans to the lowest level of the racial hierarchy. Popular culture, shaped by film, theater, advertising, the press, television, and literature, is heavily engaged in race talk. It participates freely in this most enduring and efficient rite of passage into American culture: negative appraisals of the native-born black population. Only when the lesson of racial estrangement is learned is assimilation complete. Whatever the lived experience of immigrants with African Americans—pleasant, beneficial, or bruising—the rhetorical experience renders blacks as noncitizens, already discredited outlaws.
>
> All immigrants fight for jobs and space, and who is there to fight but those who have both? As in the fishing ground struggle between Texas and Vietnamese shrimpers, they displace what and whom they can. Although U.S. history is awash in labor battles, political fights and property wars among all religious and ethnic groups, their struggles are persistently framed as struggles between recent arrivals and blacks. In race talk the move into mainstream America always means buying into the notion of American blacks as the real aliens. Whatever the ethnicity or nationality of the immigrant, his nemesis is understood to be African American.
>
> —Toni Morrison, "On the Backs of Blacks"

The following example is from a book review of Nancy L. Rosenblum's *Membership and Morals: The Personal Uses of Pluralism in America*, published in the *American Prospect*, a magazine for readers interested in political analysis. In it a Stanford law professor outlines a definition of "the democracy of everyday life":

> Democracy, in this understanding of it, means simply treating people as equals, disregarding social standing, avoiding attitudes of either deference or superiority, making allowances for others' weaknesses, and resisting the temptation to respond to perceived slights. It also means protesting everyday instances of arbitrariness and unfairness—from the rudeness of the bakery clerk to the sexism of the car dealer or the racism of those who vandalize the home of the first black neighbors on the block.
>
> —Kathleen M. Sullivan, "Defining Democracy Down"

Considering the Rhetorical Situation

As a writer or speaker, you need to think about the message that you want to articulate, the audience you want to reach, and the larger context you are writing in.

3–4 **PURPOSE** Your purpose for writing will affect any definitions you include. Would writing an extended definition help you explain something? Would stipulating definitions of key terms help you shape an argument? Could an offbeat definition help you entertain your readers?

5–8 **AUDIENCE** What audience do you want to reach, and are there any terms your readers are unlikely to know? Are there terms they might understand differently from the way you're defining them?

9–11 **GENRE** Does your genre require you to define terms? Chances are that if you're reporting information you'll need to define some terms, and some arguments rest on the way you define key terms.

12–14 **STANCE** What is your stance, and do you need to define key terms to show that stance clearly? How you define "fetus," for example, is likely to reveal your stance on abortion.

MEDIA / DESIGN Your medium will affect the form your definitions take. In a print text, you will need to define terms in your text; if you're giving a speech or presentation, you might also provide images of important terms and their definitions. In an electronic text, you may be able to define terms by linking to an online dictionary definition.

15–17

IF YOU NEED MORE HELP

See also the PROCESSES chapters for help generating ideas, drafting, revising, and so on if you are writing a whole essay dedicated to defining a term or concept.

209–58

36 Describing

When we describe something, we indicate what it looks like—and sometimes how it sounds, feels, smells, and tastes. Descriptive details are a way of showing rather than telling, of helping readers see (or hear, smell, and so on) what we're writing about—that the sky is blue, that Miss Havisham is wearing an old yellowed wedding gown, that the chemicals in the beaker have reacted and smell like rotten eggs. You'll have occasion to describe things in most of the writing you do—from describing a favorite hat in a **MEMOIR** to detailing a chemical reaction in a **LAB REPORT**. This chapter will help you work with description—and, in particular, help you think about the use of *detail*, about *objectivity and subjectivity*, about *vantage point*, about creating a clear *dominant impression*, and about using description to fit your rhetorical situation.

153–60
133–42

Detail

The goal of using details is to be as specific as possible, providing information that will help your audience imagine the subject or make sense of it. See, for example, how Nancy Mairs, an author with multiple sclerosis, describes the disease in clear, specific terms:

> During its course, which is unpredictable and uncontrollable, one may lose vision, hearing, speech, the ability to walk, control of bladder and/or bowels, strength in any or all extremities, sensitivity to touch, vibration, and/or pain, potency, coordination of movements—the list of possibilities is lengthy and, yes, horrifying. One may also lose one's sense of humor. That's the easiest to lose and the hardest to survive without.
>
> In the past ten years, I have sustained some of these losses. Characteristic of MS are sudden attacks, called exacerbations, followed by remissions, and these I have not had. Instead, my disease has been

> slowly progressive. My left leg is now so weak that I walk with the aid of a brace and a cane, and for distances I use an Amigo, a variation on the electric wheelchair that looks rather like an electrified kiddie car. I no longer have much use of my left hand. Now my right side is weakening as well. I still have the blurred spot in my right eye. Overall, though, I've been lucky so far.
>
> —Nancy Mairs, "On Being a Cripple"

Mairs's gruesome list demonstrates, through *specific details*, how the disease affects sufferers generally and her in particular. We know far more after reading this text than we do from the following more general description, from a National Multiple Sclerosis Society brochure:

> Multiple sclerosis is a chronic, unpredictable disease of the central nervous system (the brain, optic nerves, and spinal cord). It is thought to be an autoimmune disorder. This means the immune system incorrectly attacks the person's healthy tissue.
>
> MS can cause blurred vision, loss of balance, poor coordination, slurred speech, tremors, numbness, extreme fatigue, problems with memory and concentration, paralysis, and blindness. These problems may be permanent, or they may come and go.
>
> —National Multiple Sclerosis Society, *Just the Facts: 2003–2004*

Specific details are also more effective than labels, which give little meaningful information. Instead of saying that someone is a "moron" or "really smart," it's better to give details so that readers can understand the reasons behind the label: what does this person *do* or *say* that makes him or her deserve this label? See, for example, how the writer of a news story about shopping on the day after Thanksgiving opens with a description of a happy shopper:

> Last Friday afternoon, the day ritualized consumerism is traditionally at its most frenetic, Alexx Balcuns twirled in front of a full-length mirror at the Ritz Thrift Shop on West Fifty-seventh Street as if inhabited by the soul of Eva Gabor in *Green Acres*. Ms. Balcuns was languishing in a $795 dyed-mink parka her grandmother had just bought her. Ms. Balcuns is six.
>
> —Ginia Bellafante, "Staying Warm and Fuzzy during Uncertain Times"

The writer might simply have said, "A spoiled child admired herself in the mirror." Instead, she shows her subject twirling and "languishing" in a "$795 dyed-mink parka" and seemingly possessed by the soul of the actress Eva Gabor—all details that create a far more vivid description.

Sensory details help readers imagine sounds, odors, tastes, and physical sensations in addition to sights. In the following example, writer Scott Russell Sanders recalls sawing wood as a child. Note how visual details, odors, and even the physical sense of being picked up by his father mingle to form a vivid scene:

> As the saw teeth bit down, the wood released its smell, each kind with its own fragrance, oak or walnut or cherry or pine—usually pine because it was the softest, easiest for a child to work. No matter how weathered and gray the board, no matter how warped and cracked, inside there was this smell waiting, as of something freshly baked. I gathered every smidgen of sawdust and stored it away in coffee cans, which I kept in a drawer of the workbench. When I did not feel like hammering nails I would dump my sawdust on the concrete floor of the garage and landscape it into highways and farms and towns, running miniature cars and trucks along miniature roads. Looming as huge as a colossus, my father worked over and around me, now and again bending down to inspect my work, careful not to trample my creations. It was a landscape that smelled dizzyingly of wood. Even after a bath my skin would carry the smell, and so would my father's hair, when he lifted me for a bedtime hug.
>
> —Scott Russell Sanders, *The Paradise of Bombs*

Whenever you describe something, you'll select from many possible details you might use. Simply put, to exhaust all of the details to describe something is impossible—and would exhaust your readers as well. To focus your description, you'll need to determine the kinds of details that are appropriate for your subject. They will vary, depending on your **PURPOSE.** See, for example, how the details might differ in three different genres:

3–4
153–60

- *For a* **MEMOIR** *about an event*, you might choose details that are significant for you, that evoke the sights, sounds, and meaning of your event.

- *For a* **PROFILE**, you're likely to select details that will reinforce the dominant impression you want to give, that portray the event from the perspective you want readers to see. 161–70
- *For a* **LAB REPORT**, you need to give certain specifics—what equipment was used, what procedures were followed, what exactly were the results. 133–42

Deciding on a focus for your description can help you see it better, as you'll look for details that contribute to that focus.

Objectivity and Subjectivity

Descriptions can be written with objectivity, with subjectivity, or with a mixture of both. Objective descriptions attempt to be uncolored by personal opinion or emotion. Police reports and much news writing aim to describe events objectively; scientific writing strives for objectivity in describing laboratory procedures and results. See, for example, the following objective account of what happened at the World Trade Center on September 11, 2001:

> **World Trade Center Disaster—Tuesday, September 11, 2001**
>
> On Tuesday, September 11, 2001, at 8:45 a.m. New York local time, One World Trade Center, the north tower, was hit by a hijacked 767 commercial jet airplane loaded with fuel for a transcontinental flight. Two World Trade Center, the south tower, was hit by a similar hijacked jet eighteen minutes later, at 9:03 a.m. (In separate but related attacks, the Pentagon building near Washington, D.C., was hit by a hijacked 757 at 9:43 a.m., and at 10:10 a.m. a fourth hijacked jetliner crashed in Pennsylvania.) The south tower, WTC 2, which had been hit second, was the first to suffer a complete structural collapse, at 10:05 a.m., 62 minutes after being hit itself, 80 minutes after the first impact. The north tower, WTC 1, then also collapsed, at 10:29 a.m., 104 minutes after being hit. WTC 7, a substantial forty-seven-story office building in its own right, built in 1987, was damaged by the collapsing towers, caught fire, and later in the afternoon also totally collapsed.
>
> —"World Trade Center," GreatBuildingsOnline.com

Subjective descriptions, on the other hand, allow the writer's opinions and emotions to come through. A house can be described as comfortable, with a lived-in look, or as rundown and in need of a paint job and a new roof. Here's a subjective description of the planes striking the World Trade Center, as told by a woman watching from a nearby building:

> Incredulously, while looking out [the] window at the damage and carnage the first plane had inflicted, I saw the second plane abruptly come into my right field of vision and deliberately, with shimmering intention, thunder full-force into the south tower. It was so close, so low, so huge and fast, so intent on its target that I swear to you, I swear to you, I felt the vengeance and rage emanating from the plane.
>
> —Debra Fontaine, "Witnessing"

Advertisers regularly use subjective as well as objective description to sell their products, as this ad for a nicotine patch demonstrates. This ad

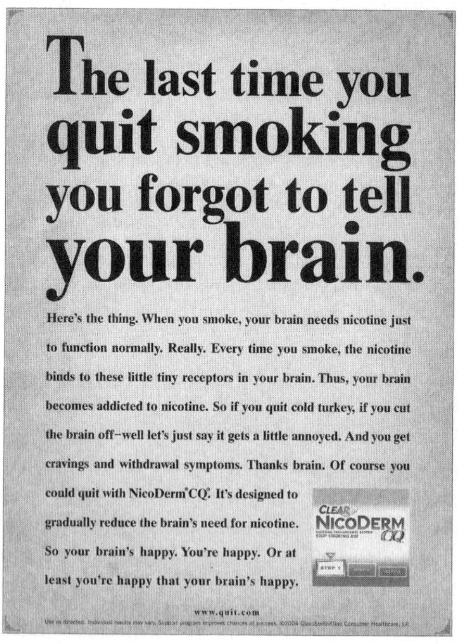

includes an objective description of what makes smoking addictive: "Every time you smoke, the nicotine binds to these little tiny receptors in your brain. Thus, your brain becomes addicted to nicotine." However, it also presents subjective descriptions of the effects of quitting ("if you cut the brain off—well let's just say it gets a little annoyed") and the results of buying and using the product: "So your brain's happy. You're happy. Or at least you're happy that your brain's happy."

Vantage Point

Sometimes you'll want or need to describe something from a certain vantage point. Where you locate yourself in relation to what you're describing will determine what you can perceive (and so describe) and what you can't. You may describe your subject from a *stationary vantage point*, from which you (and your readers) see your subject from one angle only, as if you were a camera. This description of one of three photographs that captured a woman's death records only what the camera saw from one angle at one particular moment:

> The first showed some people on a fire escape—a fireman, a woman and a child. The fireman had a nice strong jaw and looked very brave. The woman was holding the child. Smoke was pouring from the building behind them. A rescue ladder was approaching, just a few feet away, and the fireman had one arm around the woman and one arm reaching out toward the ladder.
>
> —Nora Ephron, "The Boston Photographs"

By contrast, this description of a drive to an Italian villa uses a *moving vantage point;* the writer recounts what he saw as he passed through a gate in a city wall, moving from city to country:

> La Pietra—"the stone"—is situated one mile from the Porta San Gallo, an entry to the Old City of Florence. You drive there along the Via Bolognese, twisting past modern apartment blocks, until you come to a gate, which swings open—and there you are, at the upper end of a long lane of cypresses facing a great ocher palazzo; with olive groves spreading out on both sides over an expanse of fifty-seven acres.

> There's something almost comically wonderful about the effect: here, the city, with its winding avenue; there, on the other side of a wall, the country, fertile and gray green.
>
> —James Traub, "Italian Hours"

The description of quarries below uses *multiple vantage points* to capture the quarries from many perspectives.

Dominant Impression

With any description, your aim is to create some dominant impression—the overall feeling that the individual details add up to. The dominant impression may be implied, growing out of the details themselves. For example, Scott Russell Sanders's memory of the smell of sawdust creates a dominant impression of warmth and comfort: the "fragrance . . . as of something freshly baked," sawdust "stored . . . away in coffee cans," a young boy "lifted . . . for a bedtime hug." Sometimes, though, a writer will inform readers directly of the dominant impression, in addition to describing it. In an essay about Indiana limestone quarries, Sanders makes the dominant impression clear from the start: "they are battlefields."

> The quarries will not be domesticated. They are not backyard pools; they are battlefields. Each quarry is an arena where violent struggles have taken place between machines and planet, between human ingenuity and brute resisting stone, between mind and matter. Waste rock litters the floor and brim like rubble in a bombed city. The ragged pits might have been the basements of vanished skyscrapers. Stones weighing tens of tons lean against one another at precarious angles, as if they have been thrown there by some gigantic strength and have not yet finished falling. Wrecked machinery hulks in the weeds, grimly rusting, the cogs and wheels, twisted rails, battered engine housings, trackless bulldozers and burst boilers like junk from an armored regiment. Everywhere the ledges are scarred from drills, as if from an artillery barrage or machine-gun strafing. Stumbling onto one of these abandoned quarries and gazing at the ruins, you might be left wondering who had won the battle, men or stone.
>
> —Scott Russell Sanders, *The Paradise of Bombs*

The rest of his description, full of more figurative language ("like rubble in a bombed city," "like junk from an armored regiment," "as if from an artillery barrage or machine-gun strafing") reinforces the direct "they are battlefields" statement.

Organizing Descriptions

You can organize descriptions in many ways. When your description is primarily visual, you will probably organize it spatially: from left to right, top to bottom, outside to inside. If your description uses the other senses, you may begin with the most significant or noteworthy feature and move outward from that center, as Ephron does, or you may create a chronological description of objects as you encounter them, as Traub does in his description of his drive on pages 329–30. You might even pile up details to create a dominant impression, as Sanders and Mairs do.

Considering the Rhetorical Situation

As a writer or speaker, you need to think about the message that you want to articulate, the audience you want to reach, and the larger context you are writing in.

PURPOSE Your purpose may affect the way you use description. If you're arguing that a government should intervene in another country's civil war, for example, describing the anguish of refugees from that war could make your argument more persuasive. If you're analyzing a painting, you will likely need to describe it. 3–4

AUDIENCE Who is your audience, and will they need detailed description to understand the points you wish to make? 5–8

GENRE Does your genre require description? A lab report generally calls for you to describe materials and results; a memoir about grandma should probably describe her—her smile, her dress, her apple pie. 9–11

12–14

STANCE The way you describe things can help you convey your stance. For example, the details you choose can show you to be objective (or not), careful or casual.

15–17

MEDIA / DESIGN Your medium will affect the form your description can take. In a print or spoken text, you will likely rely on words, though you may also include visuals. In an electronic text, you can easily provide links to visuals and so may need fewer words.

219–21
209–58

IF YOU NEED MORE HELP

See also FREEWRITING, CUBING, and LISTING, three methods of generating ideas that can be especially helpful for developing detailed descriptions. Sometimes you may be assigned to write a whole essay describing something: see the PROCESSES chapters for help drafting, revising, and so on.

Dialogue 37

Dialogue is a way of including people's own words in a text, letting readers hear those people's voices — not just what you say about them. **MEMOIRS** and **PROFILES** often include dialogue, and many other genres do as well: **LITERARY ANALYSES** often quote dialogue from the texts they analyze, and essays **ARGUING A POSITION** might quote an authoritative source as support for a claim. This chapter provides brief guidelines for the conventions of paragraphing and punctuating dialogue and offers some good examples of how you can use dialogue most effectively to suit your own rhetorical situations.

153–60
161–70
143–52
83–110

Why Add Dialogue?

Dialogue is a way of bringing in voices other than your own, of showing people and scenes rather than just telling about them. It can add color and texture to your writing, making it memorable. Most important, however, dialogue should be more than just colorful or interesting. It needs to contribute to your rhetorical purpose, to support the point you're making. See how dialogue is used in the following excerpt from a magazine profile of the Mall of America, how it gives us a sense of the place that the journalist's own words could not provide:

> Two pubescent girls in retainers and braces sat beside me sipping coffees topped with whipped cream and chocolate sprinkles, their shopping bags gathered tightly around their legs, their eyes fixed on the passing crowds. They came, they said, from Shakopee — "It's nowhere," one of them explained. The megamall, she added, was "a buzz at first, but now it seems pretty normal. 'Cept my parents are like Twenty Questions every time I want to come here. 'Specially since the shooting."

> On a Sunday night, she elaborated, three people had been wounded when shots were fired in a dispute over a San Jose Sharks jacket. "In the *mall*," her friend reminded me. "Right here at megamall. A shooting."
>
> "It's like nowhere's safe," the first added.
>
> —David Guterson, "Enclosed. Encyclopedic. Endured: The Mall of America"

Of course it was the writer who decided whom and what to quote, and Guterson deliberately chose words that capture the young shoppers' speech patterns, quoting fragments ("In the *mall*. . . . Right here at megamall. A shooting"), slang ("a buzz at first," "my parents are like Twenty Questions"), even contractions (*'cept*, *'specially*).

Integrating Dialogue into Your Writing

There are certain conventions for punctuating and paragraphing dialogue:

- ***Punctuating.*** Enclose each speaker's words in quotation marks, and put any end punctuation—periods, question marks, and exclamation marks—inside the closing quotation mark. Whether you're transcribing words you heard or making them up, you will sometimes need to add punctuation to reflect the rhythm and sound of the speech. In the last sentence of the example below, see how Chang-Rae Lee adds a comma after *well* and italicizes *practice* to show intonation—and attitude.
- ***Paragraphing.*** When you're writing dialogue that includes more than one speaker, start a new paragraph each time the speaker changes.
- ***Signal phrases.*** Sometimes you'll need to introduce dialogue with **SIGNAL PHRASES**—"I said," "she asked," and so on—to make clear who is speaking. At times, however, the speaker will be clear enough, and you won't need any signal phrases.

417–18

Here is a conversation between a mother and her son that illustrates each of the conventions for punctuating and paragraphing dialogue:

> "Whom do I talk to?" she said. She would mostly speak to me in Korean, and I would answer back in English.

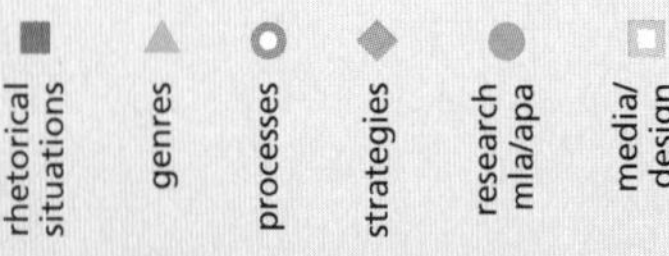

"The bank manager, who else?"
"What do I say?"
"Whatever you want to say."
"Don't speak to me like that!" she cried.
"It's just that you should be able to do it yourself," I said.
"You know how I feel about this!"
"Well, maybe then you should consider it *practice*," I answered lightly, using the Korean word to make sure she understood.

—Chang-Rae Lee, "Coming Home Again"

Interviews

Interviews are a kind of dialogue, with different conventions for punctuation. When you're transcribing an interview, give each speaker's name each time he or she speaks, starting a new line but not indenting, and do not use quotation marks. Here are a few lines from an *OnEarth* magazine interview that science journalist Kevin Krajick conducted with Paul Anastas, professor of green chemistry at Yale:

Krajik: Many people assume chemists are evil—they inevitably cause pollution.
Anastas: People don't know we have the option of doing things green. They think that in order to have cars, computers, and other modern conveniences, we need to generate all kinds of nasty poisons. Green chemistry is disproving that myth every day.
Krajik: What's really new about it?
Anastas: We're touching on something not done historically, which is to design molecules with an eye to consequences, right from the start. You go back to the basic chemical properties—volatility, electronic properties, boiling point. That way you can design a molecule to do exactly what you want. If you just try to deal with a particular hazardous outcome—cancer or poisoning or explosions—then you're addressing things piecemeal. If you go back down to the molecular architecture, you can address a wide range of issues.
Krajik: Has green chemistry actually taken hold anywhere?
Anastas: I could give you hundreds of examples of award-winning technologies, used by companies in the United States, the United Kingdom, Japan, Italy, that have eliminated literally billions of pounds of haz-

ardous substances. It goes from the way we make pharmaceuticals or electronics to the way we raise crops or paint the bottoms of boats. That said, for every one process or product that uses green chemistry, there may be a hundred or more that have yet to be considered. So 99 percent of the work is still left.

Krajik: Give me a few examples of things we're using now, or will be using soon.

Anastas: Sure. Polylactic acid is a plastic whose molecule is made from potatoes, corn, and other plant sources. Wal-Mart put in multimillion-pound orders a year ago for cups, soup containers, food packaging—it's just getting going. Arsenic in treated lumber has been recognized as a problem, and green chemistry has come up with a water-based alternative. There's also supercritical carbon dioxide—that is, CO2 put under high pressure so it becomes a fluid [in this form it does not contribute to greenhouse gas emissions]. It's now used in many processes that previously used some fairly toxic solvents. That includes decaffeinating coffee, which historically used methylene chloride, a cancer suspect that is also used for stripping paint.

—Kevin Krajik, "Q&A: Mastering the Molecule"

In preparing the interview for publication, Krajik had to add punctuation, which of course was not part of the oral conversation, and he probably deleted pauses and verbal expressions such as *um* and *uh*. At the same time, he kept informal constructions, such as incomplete sentences, which are typical answers to questions ("Sure.") to maintain the oral flavor of the interview and to reflect the professor's voice. Krajik may also have moved parts of the interview around, to eliminate repetition and keep related subjects together.

Considering the Rhetorical Situation

As a writer or speaker, you need to think about the message that you want to articulate, the audience you want to reach, and the larger context of your writing.

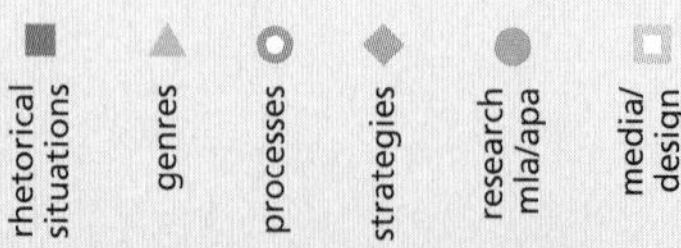

PURPOSE Your purpose will affect any use of dialogue. Dialogue can help bring a profile to life and make it memorable. Interviews with experts or first-hand witnesses can add credibility to a report or argument. 3–4

AUDIENCE Whom do you want to reach, and will dialogue help? Sometimes actual dialogue can help readers hear human voices behind facts or reason. 5–8

GENRE Does your genre require dialogue? If you're evaluating or analyzing a literary work, for instance, you may wish to include dialogue from that work. If you're writing a profile of a person or event, dialogue can help you bring your subject to life. Similarly, an interview with an expert can add credibility to a report or argument. 9–11

STANCE What is your stance, and can dialogue help you communicate that stance? For example, excerpts of an interview may allow you to challenge someone's views and make your own views clear. 12–14

MEDIA / DESIGN Your medium will affect the way you present dialogue. In a print text, you will present dialogue through written words. In an oral or electronic text, you might include actual recorded dialogue. 15–17

IF YOU NEED MORE HELP

See also the guidelines on INTERVIEWING EXPERTS for advice on setting up and recording interviews and those on QUOTING, PARAPHRASING, and SUMMARIZING for help deciding how to integrate dialogue into your text.

394–95
408–19

38 Explaining Processes

When you explain a process, you tell how something is (or was) done—how a bill becomes a law, how an embryo develops—or you tell someone how to do something—how to throw a curve ball, how to write a memoir. This chapter focuses on those two kinds of explanations, offering examples and guidelines for explaining a process in a way that works for your rhetorical situation.

Explaining a Process Clearly

Whether the process is simple or complex, you'll need to identify its key stages or steps and explain them one by one, in order. The sequence matters because it allows readers to follow your explanation; it is especially important when you're explaining a process that others are going to follow. Most often you'll explain a process chronologically, from start to finish. **TRANSITIONS**—words like *first*, *next*, *then*, and so on—are often necessary, therefore, to show readers how the stages of a process relate to one another and to indicate time sequences. Finally, you'll find that verbs matter; they indicate the actions that take place at each stage of the process.

277 

Explaining How Something Is Done

All processes consist of steps, and when you explain how something is done, you describe each step, generally in order, from first to last. Here, for example, is an explanation of how French fries are made, from an essay published in the *New Yorker:*

> Fast-food French fries are made from a baking potato like an Idaho russet, or any other variety that is mealy, or starchy, rather than waxy. The potatoes are harvested, cured, washed, peeled, sliced, and then blanched—cooked enough so that the insides have a fluffy texture but not so much that the fry gets soft and breaks. Blanching is followed by drying, and drying by a thirty-second deep fry, to give the potatoes a crisp shell. Then the fries are frozen until the moment of service, when they are deep-fried again, this time for somewhere around three minutes. Depending on the fast-food chain involved, there are other steps interspersed in this process. McDonald's fries, for example, are briefly dipped in a sugar solution, which gives them their golden-brown color; Burger King fries are dipped in a starch batter, which is what gives those fries their distinctive hard shell and audible crunch. But the result is similar. The potato that is first harvested in the field is roughly 80 percent water. The process of creating a French fry consists, essentially, of removing as much of that water as possible—through blanching, drying, and deep-frying—and replacing it with fat.
>
> —Malcolm Gladwell, "The Trouble with Fries"

Gladwell clearly explains the process of making French fries, showing us the specific steps—how the potatoes "are harvested, cured, washed, peeled, sliced," and so on—and using clear transitions—"followed by," "then," "until," "when"—and action verbs to show the sequence. His last sentence makes his stance clear, pointing out that the process of creating a French fry consists of removing as much of a potato's water as possible "and replacing it with fat."

Explaining How to Do Something

In explaining how to do something, you are giving instruction so that others can follow the process themselves. See how Martha Stewart explains the process of making French fries. She starts by listing the ingredients and then describes the steps:

> 4 medium baking potatoes
> 2 tablespoons olive oil
> $1\frac{1}{2}$ teaspoons salt
> $\frac{1}{4}$ teaspoon freshly ground pepper
> malt vinegar (optional)

1. Heat oven to 400 degrees. Place a heavy baking sheet in the oven. Scrub and rinse the potatoes well, and then cut them lengthwise into $\frac{1}{2}$-inch-wide batons. Place the potato batons in a medium bowl, and toss them with the olive oil, salt, and pepper.
2. When baking sheet is hot, about 15 minutes, remove from the oven. Place prepared potatoes on the baking sheet in a single later. Return to oven, and bake until potatoes are golden on the bottom, about 30 minutes. Turn potatoes over, and continue cooking until golden all over, about 15 minutes more. Serve immediately.

—Martha Stewart, *Favorite Comfort Food*

Coming from Martha Stewart, the explanation leaves out no details, giving a clear sequence of steps and descriptive verbs that tell us exactly what to do: "heat," "place," "scrub and rinse," and so on. After she gives the recipe, she even goes on to explain the process of *serving* the fries—"Serve these French fries with a bowl of malt vinegar"—and reminds us that "they are also delicious dipped in spicy mustard, mayonnaise, and, of course, ketchup."

Explaining a Process Visually

528–32

Some processes are best explained **VISUALLY**, with diagrams or photographs. See, for example, how a cookbook explains one process of shaping dough into a bagel—giving the details in words and then showing us in a drawing how to do it:

Roll each piece of dough on an unfloured counter into a 12-inch-long rope. Make a ring, overlapping the ends by 2 inches and joining them by pressing down and rolling on the overlap until it is the same thickness as the rest of the dough ring. There will be a 1-inch hole in the center.

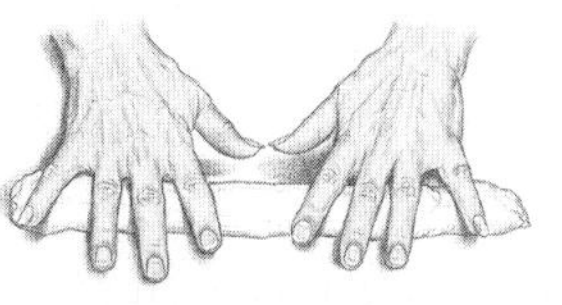

1. Rolling the dough into a 12-inch rope

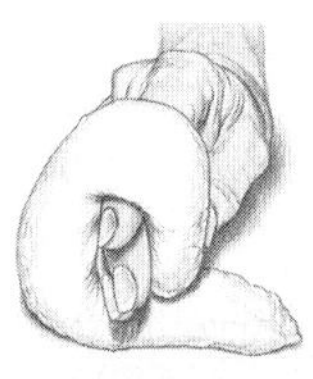

2. Making a ring by twisting one end of the dough over to overlap the other end by 2 inches

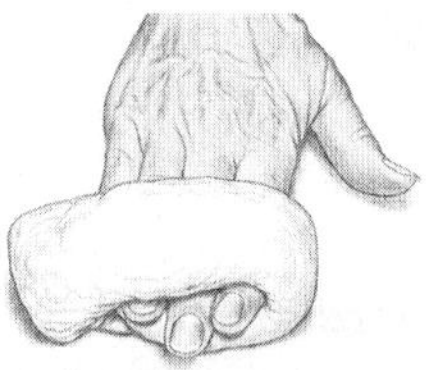

3. Pressing down and rolling the dough

—Rose Levy Beranbaum, *The Bread Bible*

Considering the Rhetorical Situation

As a writer or speaker, you need to think about the message that you want to articulate, the audience you want to reach, and the larger context you are writing in.

PURPOSE Your purpose for writing will affect the way you explain a process. If you're arguing that we should avoid eating fast food, you might explain the process by which chicken nuggets are made. But to give information about how to fry chicken, you would explain the process quite differently. 3–4

AUDIENCE Whom are you trying to reach, and will you need to provide any special background information? Can they be expected to be interested, or will you first need to interest them in the process? 5–8

9–11 **GENRE** Does your genre require you to explain a process? In a lab report, for example, you'll need to explain the processes used in the experiment. You might want to explain the process in a profile of an activity or the process of a solution you are proposing.

12–14 **STANCE** If you're giving directions for doing something, you'll want to take a straightforward "do this, then do that" perspective. If you're writing to entertain, you might want to take a clever or amusing stance.

15–17 **MEDIA / DESIGN** Your medium will affect the way you explain a process. In a print text or spoken text, you can use both words and images. On the Web, you may have the option of showing an animation of the process as well.

IF YOU NEED MORE HELP

See also **LAB REPORTS** if you need to explain the process by which an experiment is carried out; and **PROFILES** if you are writing about an activity that needs to be explained. See **NARRATING** for more advice on organizing an explanation chronologically. Sometimes you may be assigned to write a whole essay or report that explains a process; see **PROCESSES** for help drafting, revising, and so on.

133–42
161–70
343–51
209–58

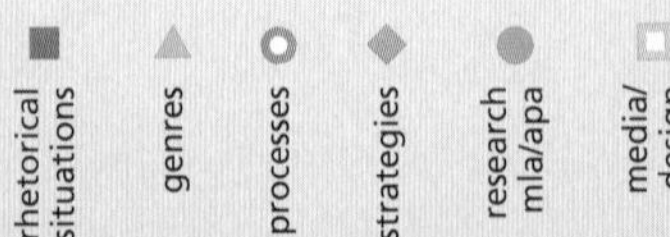

Narrating 39

Narratives are stories. As a writing strategy, a good narrative can lend support to most kinds of writing — in a **POSITION PAPER** arguing for Title IX compliance, for example, you might include a brief narrative about an Olympic sprinter who might never have learned to run without Title IX. Or you can bring a **PROFILE** of a favorite coach to life with an anecdote about a pep talk he or she once gave before a championship track meet. Whatever your larger writing purpose, you need to make sure that any narratives you add support that purpose — they should not be inserted simply to tell an interesting story. You'll also need to compose them carefully — to put them in a clear *sequence*, include *pertinent detail*, and make sure they are appropriate to your particular rhetorical situation.

83–110

161–70

Sequencing

When we write a narrative, we arrange events in a particular sequence. Writers typically sequence narratives in chronological order, reverse chronological order, or as a flashback.

Use chronological order. Often you may tell the story chronologically, starting at the beginning of an event and working through to the end, as Maya Angelou does in this brief narrative from an essay about her high school graduation:

> The school band struck up a march and all classes filed in as had been rehearsed. We stood in front of our seats, as assigned, and on a signal from the choir director, we sat. No sooner had this been accomplished than the band started to play the national anthem. We rose again and sang the song, after which we recited the pledge of allegiance. We

> remained standing for a brief minute before the choir director and the principal signaled to us, rather desperately I thought, to take our seats.
>
> —Maya Angelou, "Graduation"

Use reverse chronological order. You may also begin with the final action and work back to the first, as Aldo Leopold does in this narrative about cutting down a tree:

> Now our saw bites into the 1890s, called gay by those whose eyes turn cityward rather than landward. We cut 1899, when the last passenger pigeon collided with a charge of shot near Babcock, two counties to the north; we cut 1898, when a dry fall, followed by a snowless winter, froze the soil seven feet deep and killed the apple trees; 1897, another drouth year, when another forestry commission came into being; 1896, when 25,000 prairie chickens were shipped to market from the village of Spooner alone; 1895, another year of fires; 1894, another drouth year; and 1893, the year of "the Bluebird Storm," when a March blizzard reduced the migrating bluebirds to near zero.
>
> —Aldo Leopold, *A Sand County Almanac*

188–95

RÉSUMÉS are one genre where we generally use reverse chronological order, listing the most recent jobs or degrees first and then working backward. Notice, too, that we usually write these as narratives—telling what we have done rather than just naming positions we have held:

Sept. 2007–present	*Student worker*, Department of Information Management, Central State University, Wilberforce, OH. Compile data and format reports using Excel, Word, and university database programs.
June–Sept. 2007	*Intern*, QuestPro Corporation, West Louisville, KY. Assisted in development of software programs.
Sept. 2006–June 2007	*Bagger*, Ace Groceries, Elba, KY. Bagged customers' purchases.

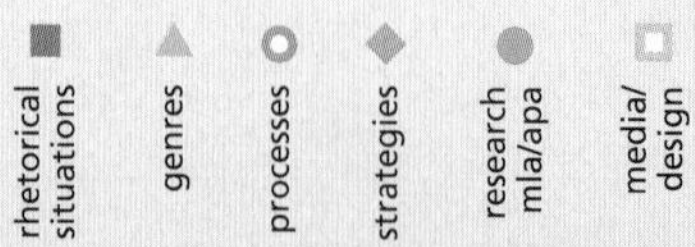

Use a flashback. You can sometimes put a flashback in the middle of a narrative, to tell about an incident that illuminates the larger narrative. Terry Tempest Williams does this in an essay about the startling incidence of breast cancer in her family: she recalls a dinnertime conversation with her father right after her mother's death from cancer, when she learned for the first time what caused all of the cancer in her family:

> Over dessert, I shared a recurring dream of mine. I told my father that for years, as long as I could remember, I saw this flash of light in the night in the desert. That this image had so permeated my being, I could not venture south without seeing it again, on the horizon, illuminating buttes and mesas.
>
> "You did see it," he said.
>
> "Saw what?" I asked, a bit tentative.
>
> "The bomb. The cloud. We were driving home from Riverside, California. You were sitting on your mother's lap. She was pregnant. In fact, I remember the date, September 7, 1957. We had just gotten out of the Service. We were driving north, past Las Vegas. It was an hour or so before dawn, when this explosion went off. We not only heard it, but felt it. I thought the oil tanker in front of us had blown up. We pulled over and suddenly, rising from the desert floor, we saw it, clearly, this golden-stemmed cloud, the mushroom. The sky seemed to vibrate with an eerie pink glow. Within a few minutes, a light ash was raining on the car."
>
> I stared at my father. This was new information to me.
>
> —Terry Tempest Williams, "The Clan of the One-Breasted Women"

Williams could have simply announced this information as a fact—but see how much more powerful it is when told in narrative form.

Use time markers. Time markers help readers follow a sequence of events. The most obvious time markers are those that simply label the time, as the narrative entries in a diary, journal, or log might. For example, here is the final part of the narrative kept in a diary by a doomed Antarctic explorer:

> WEDNESDAY, MARCH 21: Got within eleven miles of depot. Monday night; had to lay up all yesterday in severe blizzard. Today forlorn hope, Wilson and Bowers going to depot for fuel.

> MARCH 22 and 23: Blizzard bad as ever—Wilson and Bowers unable to start—tomorrow last chance—no fuel and only one or two [days] of food left—must be near the end. Have decided it shall be natural—we shall march for the depot with or without our effects and die in our tracks.
>
> THURSDAY, MARCH 29: Since the 21st we have had a continuous gale from W.S.W. and S.W. We had fuel to make two cups of tea apiece and bare food for two days on the 20th. Every day we have been ready to start for our depot eleven miles away, but outside the door of the tent it remains a scene of whirling drift. I do not think we can hope for any better things now. We shall stick it out to the end, but we are getting weaker, of course, and the end cannot be far. It seems a pity, but I do not think I can write more. . . .
>
> Last Entry: For God's sake look after our people.
>
> —Robert F. Scott, *Scott's Last Expedition: The Journals*

More often you will integrate time markers into the prose itself, as is done in this narrative about a woman preparing and delivering meals to workers at a cotton gin:

> She made her plans meticulously and in secret. <u>One early evening</u> to see if she was ready, she placed stones in two five-gallon pails and carried them three miles to the cotton gin. She rested a little, and then, discarding some rocks, she walked in the darkness to the sawmill five miles farther along the dirt road. <u>On her way back</u> to her little house and her babies, she dumped the remaining rocks along the path.
>
> <u>That same night</u> she worked into the early hours boiling chicken and frying ham. She made dough and filled the rolled-out pastry with meat. At last she went to sleep.
>
> <u>The next morning</u> she left her house carrying the meat pies, lard, an iron brazier, and coals for a fire. <u>Just before lunch</u> she appeared in an empty lot behind the cotton gin. <u>As the dinner noon bell rang</u>, she dropped the savors into boiling fat, and the aroma rose and floated over to the workers who spilled out of the gin, covered with white lint, looking like specters.
>
> —Maya Angelou, *Wouldn't Take Nothing for My Journey Now*

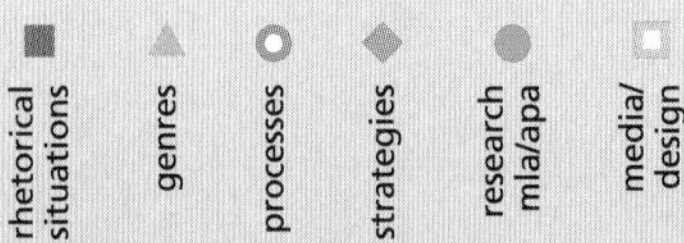

Use transitions. Another way to help readers follow a narrative is with **TRANSITIONS**, words like *first*, *then*, *meanwhile*, *at last*, and so on. See how the following paragraphs from Langston Hughes's classic essay about meeting Jesus use transitions (and time markers) to advance the action: 277

> Suddenly the whole room broke into a sea of shouting, as they saw me rise. Waves of rejoicing swept the place. Women leaped in the air. My aunt threw her arms around me. The minister took me by the hand and led me to the platform.
>
> When things quieted down, in a hushed silence, punctuated by a few ecstatic "Amens," all the new young lambs were blessed in the name of God. Then joyous singing filled the room. That night, for the last time in my life but one—for I was a big boy twelve years old—I cried.
>
> —Langston Hughes, "Salvation"

Including Pertinent Detail

When you include a narrative in your writing, you must decide which details you need—and which ones you don't need. For example, you don't want to include so much detail that the narrative distracts the reader from the larger text. You must also decide whether you need to include any background, to set the stage for the narrative. The amount of detail you include depends on your audience and purpose: How much detail does your audience need? How much detail do you need to make your meaning clear? In an essay on the suspicion African American men often face when walking at night, a journalist deliberately presents a story without setting the stage at all:

> My first victim was a woman—white, well dressed, probably in her late twenties. I came upon her late one evening on a deserted street in Hyde Park, a relatively affluent neighborhood in an otherwise mean, impoverished section of Chicago. As I swung onto the avenue behind her, there seemed to be a discreet, uninflammatory distance between us. Not so. She cast back a worried glance. To her, the youngish black

> man—a broad six feet two inches with a beard and billowing hair, both hands shoved into the pockets of a bulky military jacket—seemed menacingly close. After a few more quick glimpses, she picked up her pace and was soon running in earnest. Within seconds she disappeared into a cross street.
>
> —Brent Staples, "Black Men and Public Space"

Words like *victim* and phrases like "came upon her" lead us to assume the narrator is scary and perhaps dangerous. We don't know why he is walking on the deserted street because he hasn't told us: he simply begins with the moment he and the woman encounter each other. For his purposes, that's all the audience needs to know at first, and details of his physical appearance that explain the woman's response come later, after he tells us about the encounter. Had he given us those details at the outset, the narrative would not have been nearly so effective. In a way, Staples lets the story sneak up on us, as the woman apparently felt he had on her.

Other times you'll need to provide more background information, as an MIT professor does when she uses an anecdote to introduce an essay about young children's experiences with electronic toys. First the writer tells us a little about Merlin, the computer tic-tac-toe game that the children in her anecdote play with. As you'll see, the anecdote would be hard to follow without the introduction:

> Among the first generation of computational objects was Merlin, which challenged children to games of tic-tac-toe. For children who had only played games with human opponents, reaction to this object was intense. For example, while Merlin followed an optimal strategy for winning tic-tac-toe most of the time, it was programmed to make a slip every once in a while. So when children discovered strategies that allowed them to win and then tried these strategies a second time, they usually would not work. The machine gave the impression of not being "dumb enough" to let down its defenses twice. Robert, seven, playing with his friends on the beach, watched his friend Craig perform the "winning trick," but when he tried it, Merlin did not slip up and the game ended in a draw. Robert, confused and frustrated, threw Merlin into the sand and said, "Cheater. I hope your brains break." He was overheard by Craig and Greg, aged six and eight, who salvaged

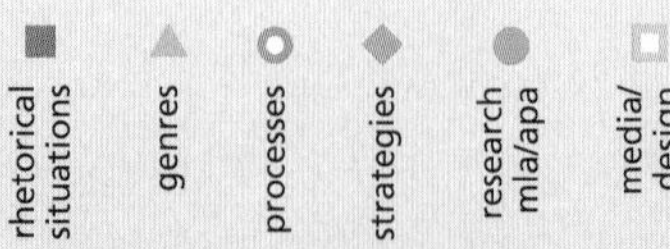

the by-now very sandy toy and took it upon themselves to set Robert straight. "Merlin doesn't know if it cheats," says Craig. "It doesn't know if you break it, Robert. It's not alive." Greg adds, "It's smart enough to make the right kinds of noises. But it doesn't really know if it loses. And when it cheats, it don't even know it's cheating." Jenny, six, interrupts with disdain: "Greg, to cheat you have to know you are cheating. Knowing is part of cheating."

—Sherry Turkle, "Cuddling Up to Cyborg Babies"

Opening and Closing with Narratives

Narratives are often useful as **BEGINNINGS** to essays and other kinds of writing. Everyone likes a good story, so an interesting or pithy narrative can be a good way to get your audience's attention. In the following introductory paragraph, a historian tells a gruesome but gripping story to attract our attention to a subject that might not otherwise merit our interest, bubonic plague: 261–66

In October 1347, two months after the fall of Calais, Genoese trading ships put into the harbor of Messina in Sicily with dead and dying men at the oars. The ships had come from the Black Sea port of Caffa (now Feodosiya) in the Crimea, where the Genoese maintained a trading post. The diseased sailors showed strange black swellings about the size of an egg or an apple in the armpits and groin. The swellings oozed blood and pus and were followed by spreading boils and black blotches on the skin from internal bleeding. The sick suffered severe pain and died quickly, within five days of the first symptoms. As the disease spread, other symptoms of continuous fever and spitting of blood appeared instead of the swellings or buboes. These victims coughed and sweated heavily and died even more quickly, within three days or less, sometimes in twenty-four hours. In both types everything that issued from the body—breath, sweat, blood from the buboes and lungs, bloody urine, and blood-blackened excrement—smelled foul. Depression and despair accompanied the physical symptoms, and before the end "death is seen seated on the face."

—Barbara Tuchman, "This Is the End of the World: The Black Death"

Imagine how different the preceding paragraph would be if it weren't in the form of a narrative. Imagine, for example, that Tuchman began by defining bubonic plague. Would that have gotten your interest? The piece was written for a general audience; how might it have been different if it had been written for scientists? Would they need (or appreciate) the story told here?

266–70 Narrative can be a good way of **ENDING** a text, too, by winding up a discussion with an illustration of the main point. Here, for instance, is a concluding paragraph from an essay on American values and Las Vegas weddings.

> I sat next to one . . . wedding party in a Strip restaurant the last time I was in Las Vegas. The marriage had just taken place; the bride still wore her dress, the mother her corsage. A bored waiter poured out a few swallows of pink champagne ("on the house") for everyone but the bride, who was too young to be served. "You'll need something with more kick than that," the bride's father said with heavy jocularity to his new son-in-law; the ritual jokes about the wedding night had a certain Panglossian character, since the bride was clearly several months pregnant. Another round of pink champagne, this time not on the house, and the bride began to cry. "It was just as nice," she sobbed, "as I hoped and dreamed it would be."
>
> —Joan Didion, "Marrying Absurd"

No doubt Didion makes her points about American values clearly and cogently in the essay. But concluding with this story lets us *see* (and hear) what she is saying about Las Vegas wedding chapels, which sell "'niceness,' the facsimile of proper ritual, to children who do not know how else to find it, how to make the arrangements, how to do it 'right.'"

Considering the Rhetorical Situation

As a writer or speaker, you need to think about the message that you want to articulate, the audience you want to reach, and the larger context you are writing in.

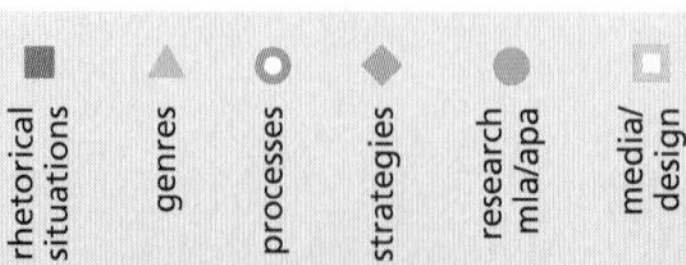

PURPOSE Your purpose will affect the way you use narrative. For example, in an essay about seat belt laws, you might tell about the painful rehabilitation of a teenager who was not wearing a seat belt and was injured in an accident in order to persuade readers that seat belt use should be mandatory. 3–4

AUDIENCE Whom do you want to reach, and do you have an anecdote or other narrative that will help them understand your topic or persuade them that your argument has merit? 5–8

GENRE Does your genre require you to include narrative? A memoir about an important event might be primarily narrative, whereas a reflection about an event might focus more on the significance of the event than on what happened. 9–11

STANCE What is your stance, and do you have any stories that would help you convey that stance? A funny story, for example, can help create a humorous stance. 12–14

MEDIA / DESIGN In a print or spoken text, you will likely be limited to brief narratives, perhaps illustrated with photos or other images. In an electronic text, you might have the option of linking to full-length narratives or visuals available on the Web. 15–17

IF YOU NEED MORE HELP

See also the PROCESSES chapters if you are assigned to write a narrative essay and need help drafting, revising, and so on. Two special kinds of narratives are LAB REPORTS (which use narrative to describe the steps in an experiment from beginning to end) and RÉSUMÉS (which essentially tell the story of the work we've done, at school and on the job).

209–58
133–42
188–95

40 Reading Strategies

We read newspapers and websites to learn about the events of the day. We read cookbooks to find out how to make brownies and textbooks to learn about history, chemistry, and other academic topics. We read short stories for pleasure—and, in literature classes, to analyze plot, setting, character, and theme. And as writers, we read our own drafts to make sure they say what we mean, and we proofread our final drafts to make sure they're correct. In other words, we read in various ways for many different purposes. This chapter offers a number of strategies for reading with a critical eye—from previewing a text to annotating as you read, identifying meaningful patterns, analyzing an argument, and more.

Reading Strategically

Academic reading is challenging because it makes several demands on you at once. Textbooks present new vocabulary and concepts, and picking out the main ideas can be difficult. Scholarly articles present content and arguments you need to understand, but they often assume readers already know key concepts and vocabulary and so don't generally provide background information. As you read more texts in an academic field and participate in its conversations, the reading will become easier, but in the meantime you can develop strategies that will help you to read carefully and critically.

Different texts require different kinds of effort. Some texts can be read fairly quickly, if you're reading to get a general overview. Most of the time, though, you need to read carefully, matching the pace of your reading to the difficulty of the text. To read with a critical eye, you can't be in too much of a hurry. You'll likely need to skim the text for an overview of the basic ideas and then go back to read carefully. And then you may read the text

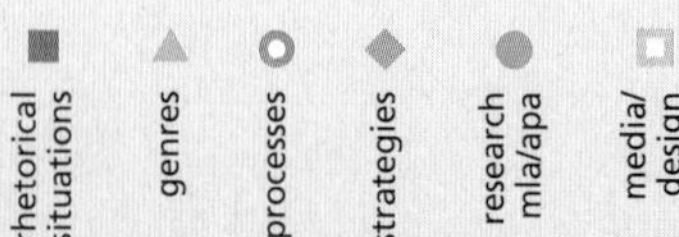

again. That is true for visual as well as verbal texts—you'll often need to get an overview of a text and then reread to pay close attention to its details.

Previewing a Text

It's usually a good idea to start by skimming a text: read the title and subtitle, any headings, the first and last paragraphs, the first sentences of all the other paragraphs. Study any illustrations and other visuals. Your goal is to get a sense of where the text is heading. At this point, don't stop to look up unfamiliar words; just underline them or put a mark in the margin, and look them up later.

Considering the Rhetorical Situation

PURPOSE What is the purpose? To entertain? Inform? Persuade readers to think something or take some action? 3–4

AUDIENCE Who is the intended audience? Are you a member of that group? If not, should you expect that you'll need to look up unfamiliar terms or concepts or that you'll run into assumptions you don't necessarily share? 5–8

GENRE What is the genre? Is it a report? An argument? An analysis? Something else? Knowing the genre can help you anticipate certain key features. 9–11

STANCE Who is the writer, and what is his or her stance? Critical? Curious? Opinionated? Objective? Passionate? Indifferent? Something else? Knowing the stance affects the way you understand a text, whether you're inclined to agree or disagree, to take it seriously, and so on. 12–14

MEDIA / DESIGN What is the medium, and how does it affect the way you read? If it's a print text, do you know anything about the publisher? If it's on the Web, who sponsors the site, and when was it last updated? Are there any design elements—such as headings, summaries, color, or boxes—that highlight key parts of the text? 15–17

Thinking about Your Initial Response

It's usually good to read a text first just to get a sense of it. Some readers find it helps to jot down brief notes about their first response to a text, noting their reaction and thinking a little about why they reacted as they did:

- *What are your initial reactions?* Describe both your intellectual reaction and any emotional reaction. Identify places in the text that caused you to react as you did. If you had no particular reaction, note that.
- *What accounts for your reaction?* Do you agree or disagree with the writer or have a different perspective? Why? Are your reactions rooted in personal experiences? Positions you hold? Particular beliefs? Some personal philosophy? As much as possible, you want to keep your opinions from coloring your analysis, so it's important to try to identify those opinions up front—and to give some thought to where they come from.

Annotating

Many readers find it helps to annotate as they read: highlighting key words, phrases, sentences; connecting ideas with lines or symbols; writing comments or questions in the margin; noting anything that seems noteworthy or questionable. Annotate as if you're having a conversation with the author, someone you take seriously but whose words you do not accept without question. Put your part of the conversation in the margin, asking questions, talking back: "What's this mean?" "So what?" "Says who?" "Where's evidence?" "Yes!" "Whoa!" or even ☺ or ☹. You may find it useful to annotate using text messaging shorthand: "intrstn," "mjr point". If you're using online sources, you may be able to copy them and annotate them electronically. If so, make your annotations a different color than the text itself.

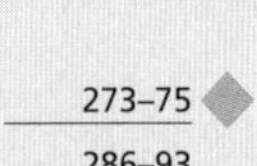
3–4
273–75
286–93

What you annotate depends on your **PURPOSE** or what you're most interested in. If you're analyzing an argument, you would probably underline any **THESIS STATEMENT** and then the **REASONS AND EVIDENCE** that support the statement. It might help to restate those ideas in your own words, in the margins—in order to put them in your own words, you need to understand them! If you are looking for meaningful patterns, you might highlight each pattern in a different color and write any questions or notes about it in that color. If you are analyzing a literary text to look for certain elements or themes or patterns, you might highlight key passages that demonstrate those things.

Annotating forces you to read for more than just the surface meaning. Especially when you are going to be writing about or responding to a text, annotating creates a record of things you may want to refer to.

There are some texts that you cannot annotate, of course: library books, materials you read on the Web, and so on. Then you will need to make notes elsewhere, and you might find it useful to keep a reading log for that purpose.

On pages 356–57 is an annotated passage from Lawrence Lessig's essay "Some Like It Hot," included in Chapter 9. These annotations rephrase key definitions, identify the essay's thesis and main ideas, ask questions, and comment on issues raised in the essay. Annotating the entire essay, which appears on pages 88–92, would provide a look at Lessig's ideas and a record of the experience of reading the essay—useful for both understanding it and analyzing it.

Playing the Believing and Doubting Game

One way to think about your response to a text is to **LIST** or **FREEWRITE** as many reasons as you can think of for believing what the writer says and then as many as you can for doubting it. First, write as if you agree with everything in the writer's argument; look at the world from his or her perspective, trying to understand the writer's premises and reasons for arguing as he or she does even if you strongly disagree. Then, write as if you doubt everything in the text: try to find every flaw in the argument, every possible way it can be refuted—even if you totally agree with it. Developed by writing theorist Peter Elbow, the believing and doubting game helps you consider new ideas and question ideas you already have—and at the same time see where you stand in relation to the ideas in the text you're reading. 219–21

Piracy—unauthorized use of the artistic work of others.

"Content industry"—new term. Film, music, and so on? Doesn't include books and magazines?

Thesis: "Big media" are all based on piracy.

Hollywood film industry started in order to avoid Edison's patents. What were they for? Cameras and projectors? Is this true?

Record-industry piracy.

Player pianos?

If piracy means using the creative property of others without their permission, then the history of the content industry is a history of piracy. Every important sector of big media today—film, music, radio, and cable TV—was born of a kind of piracy. The consistent story is how each generation welcomes the pirates from the last. Each generation—until now.

The Hollywood film industry was built by fleeing pirates. Creators and directors migrated from the East Coast to California in the early twentieth century in part to escape controls that film patents granted the inventor Thomas Edison. These controls were exercised through the Motion Pictures Patents Company, a monopoly "trust" based on Edison's creative property and formed to vigorously protect his patent rights.

California was remote enough from Edison's reach that filmmakers like Fox and Paramount could move there and, without fear of the law, pirate his inventions. Hollywood grew quickly, and enforcement of federal law eventually spread west. But because patents granted their holders a truly "limited" monopoly of just seventeen years (at that time), the patents had expired by the time enough federal marshals appeared. A new industry had been founded, in part from the piracy of Edison's creative property.

Meanwhile, the record industry grew out of another kind of piracy. At the time that Edison and Henri Fourneaux invented machines for reproducing music (Edison the phonograph; Fourneaux the player piano), the law gave composers the exclusive right to control copies and public performances of their music. Thus, in 1900, if I wanted a copy of Phil Russel's 1899 hit, "Happy Mose," the law said I would have to pay for the right to get a copy of the score, and I would also have to pay for the right to perform it publicly.

But what if I wanted to record "Happy Mose" using Edison's phonograph or Fourneaux's player piano? Here the law stumbled. If I simply sang the piece into a recording device in my home, it wasn't clear that I owed the composer anything. And more important, it wasn't clear whether I owed the composer anything if I then made copies of those recordings. Because of this gap in the law, I could effectively use someone else's song without paying the composer anything. The composers (and publishers) were none too happy about this capacity to pirate.

In 1909, Congress closed the gap in favor of the composer and the recording artist, amending copyright law to make sure that composers would be paid for "mechanical reproductions" of their music. But rather than simply granting the composer complete control over the right to make such reproductions, Congress gave recording artists a right to record the music, at a price set by Congress, after the composer allowed it to be recorded once. This is the part of copyright law that makes cover songs possible. Once a composer authorizes a recording of his song, others are free to record the same song, so long as they pay the original composer a fee set by the law. So, by limiting musicians' rights — by partially pirating their creative work —record producers and the public benefit.

—Lawrence Lessig, "Some Like It Hot"

Is copyright law different for books and other printed matter?

Partial piracy? Not sure about this — when artists use a song, they pay a fee but don't need permission. The composer doesn't have complete control. So it's piracy, but not completely?

Thinking about How the Text Works: What It Says, What It Does

Sometimes you'll need to think about how a text works, how its parts fit together. You may be assigned to analyze a text, or you may just need to make sense of a difficult text, to think about how the ideas all relate to one another. Whatever your purpose, a good way to think about a text's structure is by **OUTLINING** it, paragraph by paragraph. If you're interested in analyzing its ideas, look at what each paragraph *says*; if, on the other hand, you're concerned with how the ideas are presented, pay attention to what each paragraph *does*.

223–24

What it says. Write a sentence that identifies what each paragraph says. Once you've done that for the whole text, look for patterns in the topics the writer addresses. Pay attention to the order in which the topics are presented. Also look for gaps, ideas the writer has left unsaid. Such paragraph-by-paragraph outlining of the content can help you see how the writer has arranged ideas and how that arrangement builds an argument or develops a topic. Here, for example, is such an outline of Lawrence Lessig's essay (the left column refers to paragraph numbering noted in the full version of the essay on pages 88–92):

1	Every major type of media bases its development on piracy, the unauthorized use of artists' work.
2–3	To escape patents that restricted the copying of innovations in filmmaking, the movie industry moved from the East Coast to California.
4–5	Copyright law gave composers control over the performance of their music—but because it didn't cover the recording of music and the sale of copies of the recordings, it allowed piracy in the record industry.
6	Congress eventually changed the law, allowing musicians to record a song without the composer's permission if they paid the composer a fee.
7–11	When a radio station plays a song, it pays the composer but not the recording artist, thus pirating the artist's work.

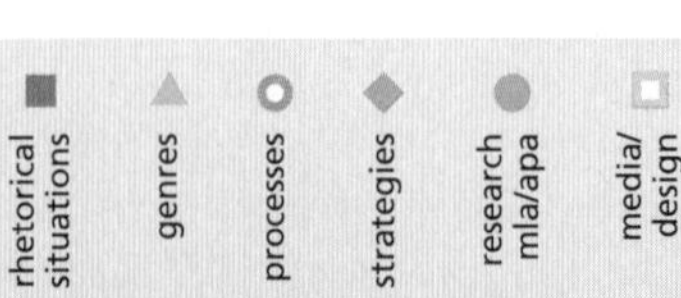

12, 13 Cable TV has pirated works, too, by paying networks nothing for their broadcasts—despite protests by broadcasters and copyright owners.

14 Congress eventually extended the copyright law to cable TV, forcing the cable companies to pay for their broadcasts at a price controlled by Congress in order to protect the innovations of the cable industry.

15 The history of the major media industries suggests that piracy is not necessarily "plainly wrong."

16, 17 Peer-to-peer file sharing, like the earlier media-industry innovations, is being used to share artistic content and avoid industry controls, but it differs from the early cable industry in that it is not selling any content.

18 P2P file sharing provides access to music that can no longer be purchased, music that copyright holders want to share, and music that is no longer copyrighted.

19 P2P file sharing, like the earlier innovations, is the result of new technology, and it raises similar questions: how can it best be used without penalizing the artists whose works are "pirated"?

20 Copyright law must balance the protection of artists' works with the innovation in technologies, a process that takes time.

What it does. Identify the function of each paragraph. Starting with the first paragraph, ask, What does this paragraph do? Does it introduce a topic? Provide background for a topic to come? Describe something? Define something? Entice me to read further? Something else? What does the second paragraph do? The third? As you go through the text, you may identify groups of paragraphs that have a single purpose. For an example, look at this functional outline of Lessig's essay (again, the numbers on the left refer to the paragraphs):

1 Defines the key term, *piracy*, and illustrates the thesis using the history of four media industries in the United States.

2–3 Tells the history of the first medium, film, by focusing on piracy as a major factor in its development.

4–6 Tells the history of the second medium, the recording industry, again by focusing on the role of piracy in its development.

7–11	Tells the history of the third medium, radio, focusing on the role of piracy in its development.
12–14	Tells the history of the fourth medium, cable TV, focusing on the role of piracy in its development.
15	Offers conclusions about piracy based on the similar roles played by piracy in the histories of the four media.
16–17	Compares the current controversy over piracy in peer-to-peer file sharing on the Internet with the role of piracy in the earlier media.
18	Describes the benefits of P2P file sharing.
19–20	Compares those benefits with those of the other media and offers a conclusion in the form of a problem to be solved.

Summarizing

416–17

Summarizing a text can help you both to see the relationships among its ideas and to understand what it's saying. When you **SUMMARIZE**, you restate a text's main ideas in your own words, leaving out most examples and other details. Here's a summary of Lawrence Lessig's essay:

> In his essay "Some Like It Hot," Lawrence Lessig argues that the development of every major media industry is based on piracy, the unauthorized use of artists' or inventors' work. First, the film industry flourished by evading restrictions on the copying of innovations in filmmaking. Then, the recording industry benefited from copyright laws that gave composers control over the performance of their music but not over the recording of it or the sale of the recordings. A law passed in 1909 in effect allows musicians to record a song without the composer's permission if they pay the composer a fee. According to Lessig, radio broadcasters benefit from piracy, too, every time they play a song recorded by someone other than the composer: they pay the composer a fee but not the recording artist. Finally, when it first started operating, cable TV benefited from piracy—by paying the networks nothing for their broadcasts. Congress eventually extended the copyright law, forcing cable companies to pay for the content they broadcast—but at a price controlled by Congress so that the networks wouldn't be able

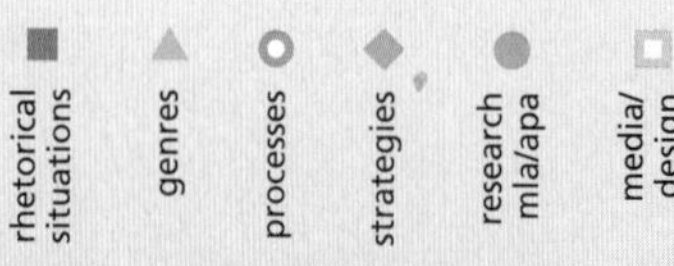

to drive the cable companies out of business. Peer-to-peer file sharing, like the early media industries, is being used to share artistic content and avoid industry controls on that sharing. It benefits the public by allowing access to music that is out of print, that copyright holders want to share, and that is no longer copyrighted. Therefore, Lessig argues, the public needs to figure out how to make file-sharing work without penalizing musicians by pirating their songs. Copyright law must balance the protection of artists' work with the encouragement of technological innovation.

Identifying Patterns

Look for notable patterns in the text: recurring words and their synonyms, as well as repeated phrases, metaphors and other images, and types of sentences. Some writers find it helps to highlight patterns in various colors. Does the author rely on any particular writing strategies: **NARRATION**? 343–51 **COMPARISON**? Something else? 306–13

It might be important to consider the kind of evidence offered: Is it more opinion than fact? Nothing but statistics? If many sources are cited, is the information presented in any predominant patterns: as **QUOTATIONS**? 408–19 **PARAPHRASES**? **SUMMARIES**? Are there repeated references to certain experts or sources?

In visual texts, look for patterns of color, shape, and line. What's in the foreground, and what's in the background? What's completely visible, partly visible, or invisible? In both verbal and visual texts, look for omissions and anomalies. What isn't there that you would expect to find? Is there anything that doesn't really fit in?

If you discover patterns, then you need to consider what, if anything, they mean in terms of what the writer is saying. What do they reveal about the writer's underlying premises and beliefs? What do they tell you about the writer's strategies for persuading readers to accept the truth of what he or she is saying?

See how color coding William Safire's essay on the Gettysburg Address reveals several patterns in the language Safire uses. In this excerpt from the essay, which appears in full in Chapter 7, religious references are colored yellow; references to a "national spirit," green; references to life, death, and rebirth, blue; and places where he directly addresses the reader, gray.

> But the selection of this poetic political sermon as the oratorical centerpiece of our observance need not be only an exercise. . . . now, as then, a national spirit rose from the ashes of destruction.
>
> Here is how to listen to Lincoln's all-too-familiar speech with new ears.
>
> In those 266 words, you will hear the word *dedicate* five times. . . .
>
> Those five pillars of dedication rested on a fundament of religious metaphor. From a president not known for his piety—indeed, often criticized for his supposed lack of faith—came a speech rooted in the theme of national resurrection. The speech is grounded in conception, birth, death, and rebirth.
>
> Consider the barrage of images of birth in the opening sentence. . . .
>
> Finally, the nation's spirit rises from this scene of death: "that this nation, under God, shall have a new birth of freedom." Conception, birth, death, rebirth. The nation, purified in this fiery trial of war, is resurrected. Through the sacrifice of its sons, the sundered nation would be reborn as one. . . .
>
> Do not listen on Sept. 11 only to Lincoln's famous words and comforting cadences. Think about how Lincoln's message encompasses but goes beyond paying "fitting and proper" respect to the dead and the bereaved. His sermon at Gettysburg reminds "us the living" of our "unfinished work" and "the great task remaining before us"—to resolve that this generation's response to the deaths of thousands of our people leads to "a new birth of freedom."

The color coding helps us to see patterns in Safire's language, just as Safire reveals patterns in Lincoln's words. He offers an interpretation of Lincoln's address as a "poetic political sermon," and the words he uses throughout support that interpretation. At the end, he repeats the assertion that Lincoln's address is a sermon, inviting us to consider it differently. Targeting different textual elements, such as commands to the reader ("Consider," "Do not listen," "Think about"), offers additional

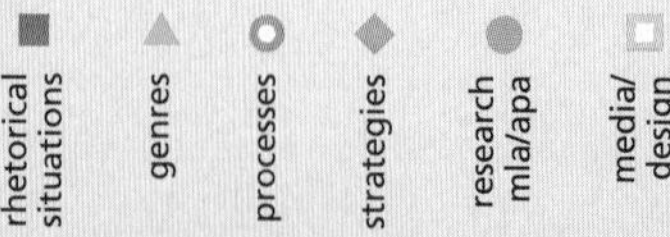

information on how Safire wishes to position himself in relation to his readers.

Count up the parts. This is a two-step process. First, you count things: how many of this, how many of that. Look for words, phrases, or sentences that seem important, or select a few typical paragraphs on which to focus. After you count, see what you can conclude about the writing. You may want to work with others, dividing up the counting.

- ***Count words.*** Count one-, two-, three-syllable words, repeated words, active and passive verbs, prepositions, jargon or specialized terms.
- ***Count sentences.*** Count the number of words in each sentence, the average number of words per sentence; figure the percentage of sentences above and below average. Count the number of sentences in each paragraph. Count the number of simple sentences, compound sentences, complex sentences, and fragments. Mark the distinct rhythms (tap out the beat as you read aloud). Count repeated phrases.
- ***Count paragraphs.*** Count the number of paragraphs, the average number of words and sentences per paragraph, the shortest and longest paragraphs. Consider the position of the longest and shortest paragraphs. Find parallel paragraph structures.
- ***Count images.*** List, circle, or underline verbal or visual images, similes, metaphors, and other figures of speech. Categorize them by meaning as well as type.

What do your findings tell you about the text? What generalizations can you make about it? Why did the author choose the words or images he or she used and in those combinations? What do those words tell you about the writer—or about his or her stance? Do your findings suggest a strategy, a plan for your analysis? For instance, Safire counts the number of times Lincoln uses *dedicate* and images of birth, death, and rebirth to argue something about Lincoln's speech and what it should mean to Safire's audience on the anniversary of 9/11.

Analyzing the Argument

All texts make some kind of argument, claiming something and then offering reasons and evidence as support for the claim. As a critical reader, you need to look closely at the argument a text makes—you need to recognize all the claims it makes, consider the support it offers for those claims, and decide how you want to respond. What do you think, and why? Here are some of the aspects of a text you'll need to consider when you analyze an argument:

- ***What is the claim?*** What is the main point the writer is trying to make? 273–75 Is there a clearly stated **THESIS**, or is it merely implied?
- 286–93 ***What support does the writer offer for the claim?*** What **REASONS** are given to support the claim? What **EVIDENCE** backs up those reasons? Facts? Statistics? Testimonials by authorities? Examples? Pertinent anecdotes? Are the reasons plausible and sufficient?
- ***How evenhandedly does the writer present the issues?*** Is there any mention of counterarguments? If so, how does the writer deal with them? 294–95 By **REFUTING** them? By **ACKNOWLEDGING** them and responding to them reasonably? Does the writer treat other arguments respectfully? Dismissively? Are his or her own arguments appropriately qualified?
- ***What authorities or sources of outside information does the writer use?*** How are they used? How credible are they? Are they in any way biased or otherwise unreliable? Are they current?
- ***How does the writer address you as the reader?*** Does the writer assume that readers know something about what is being discussed? Does his or her language include you or exclude you? (Hint: If you see the word *we*, do you feel included?) Do you sense that you and the author share any beliefs or attitudes?

296–98 **Check for fallacies.** **FALLACIES** are arguments that involve faulty reasoning. Because they often seem plausible, they can be persuasive. It is important, therefore, that you question the legitimacy of such reasoning when you run across it.

Considering the Larger Context

All texts are part of ongoing conversations with other texts that have dealt with the same topic. An essay arguing for handgun trigger locks is part of an ongoing conversation about gun control, which is itself part of a conversation on individual rights and responsibilities. Academic texts document their sources in part to show their relationship to the ongoing scholarly conversations on a particular topic. Academic reading usually challenges you to become aware of those conversations. And, in fact, any time you're reading to learn, you're probably reading for some larger context. Whatever your reading goals, being aware of that larger context can help you better understand what you're reading. Here are some specific aspects of the text to pay attention to:

- ***Who else cares about this topic?*** Especially when you're reading in order to learn about a topic, the texts you read will often reveal which people or groups are part of the conversation—and might be sources of further reading. For example, an essay describing the formation of Mammoth Cave could be of interest to geologists, spelunkers, travel writers, or tourists. If you're reading such an essay while doing research on the cave, you should consider how the audience addressed determines the nature of the information provided—and its suitability as a source for your research.
- ***Ideas.*** Does the text refer to any concepts or ideas that give you some sense that it's part of a larger conversation? An argument on airport security measures, for example, is part of larger conversations about government response to terrorism, the limits of freedom in a democracy, and the possibilities of using technology to detect weapons and explosives, among others.
- ***Terms.*** Is there any terminology or specialized language that reflects the writer's allegiance to a particular group or academic discipline? If you run across words like *false consciousness*, *ideology*, and *hegemony*, for example, you might guess the text was written by a Marxist scholar.

- *Citations.* Whom does the writer cite? Do the other writers have a particular academic specialty, belong to an identifiable intellectual school, share similar political leanings? If an article on politics cites Michael Moore and Barbara Ehrenreich in support of its argument, you might assume the writer holds liberal opinions; if it cites Rush Limbaugh and Sean Hannity, the writer is likely a conservative.

IF YOU NEED MORE HELP

400–403
229–34
235–41
242–46

See also the chapter on EVALUATING SOURCES for help analyzing the reliability of a text, and see the chapters on ASSESSING YOUR OWN WRITING, GETTING RESPONSE AND REVISING, and EDITING AND PROOFREADING for advice on reading your own writing.

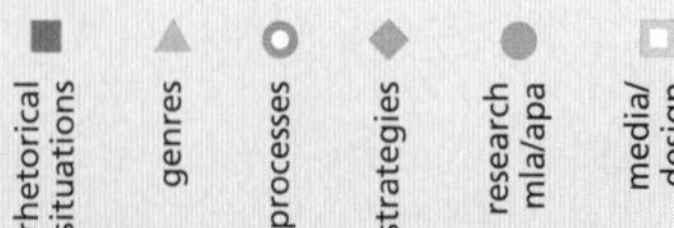

Taking Essay Exams 41

Essay exams present writers with special challenges. You must write quickly, on a topic presented to you on the spot, to show your instructor what you know about a specific body of information. This chapter offers advice on how to take essay exams.

Considering the Rhetorical Situation

PURPOSE In an essay exam, your purpose is to show that you have mastered certain material, and that you can analyze and apply it in an essay. You may need to make an argument, or simply to convey information on a topic. 3–4

AUDIENCE Will your course instructor be reading your exam, or a TA? Sometimes standardized tests are read by groups of trained readers. What specific criteria will your audience use to evaluate your writing? 5–8

GENRE Does the essay question specify or suggest a certain genre? In a literature course, you may need to write a compelling literary analysis of a passage. In a history course, you may need to write an argument for the significance of a key historical event. In an economics course, you may need to contrast the economies of the North and South before the Civil War. If the essay question doesn't specify a genre, look for key words such as *argue*, *evaluate*, or *explain*, which point to a certain genre. 9–11

12–14 **STANCE** In an essay exam, your stance is usually unemotional, thoughtful, and critical.

15–17 **MEDIA / DESIGN** Since essay exams are usually handwritten on lined paper or in an exam booklet, legible handwriting is a must.

Analyzing Essay Questions

Essay questions usually include key verbs that specify the kind of writing you'll need to do—argue a position, compare two texts, and so on. Following are some of the most common kinds of writing you'll be asked to do on an essay exam.

- *Analyze:* Break an idea, theory, text, or event into its parts and examine them. For example, a world history exam might ask you to **ANALYZE** 38–58 European imperialism's effect on Africa in the late nineteenth century, and discuss how Africans responded.
- *Apply:* Consider how an idea or concept might work out in practice. For instance, a film studies exam might ask you to apply the concept of auterism—a theory of film that sees the director as the primary creator, whose body of work reflects a distinct personal style—to two films by Robert Altman. An economics exam might ask you to apply the concept of opportunity costs to a certain supplied scenario.
- *Argue/prove/justify:* Offer reasons and evidence to support a position. A philosophy exam, for example, might ask you to **ARGUE** 283–99 whether or not all stereotypes contain a "kernel of truth," and whether believing a stereotype is ever justified.
- *Classify:* Group something into categories. For example, a marketing exam might ask you to **CLASSIFY** 300–305 shoppers in categories based on their purchasing behavior, motives, attitudes, or lifestyle patterns.

- *Compare / contrast:* Explore the similarities and/or differences between two or more things. An economics exam, for example, might ask you to **COMPARE** the effectiveness of patents and tax incentives in encouraging technological advances. 306–13

- *Critique:* **ANALYZE** and **EVALUATE** a text or argument, considering its strengths and weaknesses. For instance, an evolutionary biology exam might ask you to critique John Maynard Smith's assertion that "scientific theories say nothing about what is right, but only about what is possible" in the context of the theory of evolution. 38–58 125–32

- *Define:* Explain what a word or phrase means. An art history exam, for example, might ask you to **DEFINE** negative space, and to discuss the way various artists use it in their work. 314–23

- *Describe:* Tell about the important characteristics or features of something. For example, a sociology exam might ask you to **DESCRIBE** Erving Goffman's theory of the presentation of self in ordinary life, focusing on roles, props, and setting. 324–32

- *Evaluate:* Determine something's significance or value. A drama exam, for example, might ask you to **EVALUATE** the setting, lighting, and costumes in a filmed production of *Macbeth*. 125–32

- *Explain:* Provide reasons and examples to clarify an idea, argument, or event. For instance, a rhetoric exam might ask you to explain the structure of the African American sermon and discuss its use in writings of Frederick Douglass and Martin Luther King Jr.

- *Summarize / review:* Give the major points of a text or idea. A political science exam, for example, might ask you to **SUMMARIZE** John Stuart Mill's concept of utilitarianism and its relation to freedom of speech. 416–17

- *Trace:* Explain a sequence of ideas or order of events. For instance, a geography exam might ask you to trace the patterns of international migration since 1970, and discuss how these patterns differ from those of the 1870s.

Some Guidelines for Taking Essay Exams

Before the exam

- 354–55 *Read* over your class notes and course texts strategically, **ANNOTATING** them to keep track of details you'll want to remember.
- 215–16 *Collaborate* by forming a **STUDY GROUP** that meets throughout the term to help one another master the course content.
- *Review* key ideas, events, terms, and themes. Look for common 404–6 themes and **CONNECTIONS** in lecture notes, class discussions, and any readings — they'll lead you to important ideas.
- *Ask* your instructor about the form the exam will take: how long it will be, what kind of questions will be on it, how it will be evaluated, and so on. Working with a study group, write questions you think your instructor might ask, and then answer the questions together.
- 219–20 *Warm up* just before the exam by **FREEWRITING** for ten minutes or so to gather your thoughts.

During the exam

- *Scan the questions* to determine how much each part of the test counts and how much time you should spend on it. For example, if one essay is worth 50 points and two others are worth 25 points each, you'll want to spend half your time on the 50-point question.
- *Read over* the entire test before answering any questions. Start with the question you feel most confident answering, which may or may not be the first question on the test.
- *Don't panic.* Know yourself and your first reaction to the testing situation. Sometimes when I first read an essay question, my mind goes blank, but after a few moments, I start to recall the information I need.
- *Plan.* Although you won't have much time for revising or editing, you still need to plan and allow yourself time to make some last-minute

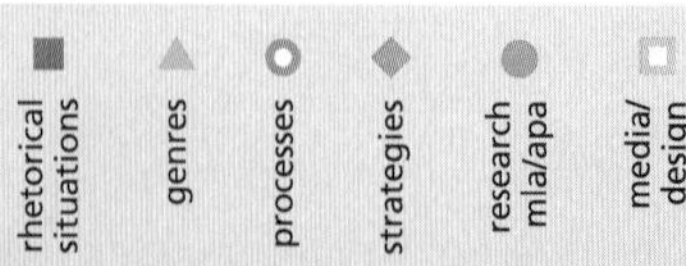

changes before you turn in the exam. So apportion your time. For a three-question essay test in a two-hour test period, you might divide your time like this:

Total Exam Time — 120 minutes

Generating ideas — 20 minutes (6–7 minutes per question)
Drafting — 85 minutes (45 for the 50-point question,
20 for each 25-point question)
Revising, editing, proofreading — 15 minutes

Knowing that you have built in time at the end of the exam period can help you remain calm as you write, as you can use that time to fill in gaps or reconsider answers you feel unsure about.

- *Jot down the main ideas* you need to cover in answering the question on scratch paper or on the cover of your exam book, number those ideas in the order you think makes sense — and you have an outline for your essay. If you're worried about time, plan to write the most important parts of your answers early on. If you don't complete your answer, refer your instructor to your outline to show where you were headed.
- *Turn the essay question into your introduction,* like this:

  Question: How did the outcomes of World War II differ from those of World War I?

  Introduction: The outcomes of World War II differed from those of World War I in three major ways: World War II affected more of the world and its people than World War I, distinctions between citizens and soldiers were eroded, and the war's brutality made it impossible for Europe to continue to claim cultural superiority over other cultures.

- *State your thesis explicitly,* provide **REASONS** and **EVIDENCE** to support your thesis, and use transitions to move logically from one idea to the next. Restate your main point in your conclusion. You don't want to give what one professor calls a "garbage truck answer," dumping everything you know into a blue book and expecting the instructor to sort it all out. 286–93

- ***Write on every other line*** and only on one side of each page so that you'll have room to make additions or corrections. If you're typing on a computer, double space.
- ***If you have time left, go over your exam,*** looking for ideas that need elaboration as well as for grammatical and punctuation errors.

After the exam. If your instructor doesn't return your exam, consider asking for a conference to go over your work so you can learn what you did well and where you need to improve—important knowledge to take with you into your next exam.

part 5

Doing Research

We do research all the time, for many different reasons. We search the Web for information about a new computer, ask friends about the best place to get coffee, try on several pairs of jeans before deciding which ones to buy. You have no doubt done your share of library research before now, and you probably have visited a number of schools' websites before deciding which college you wanted to attend. Research, in other words, is something you do every day. The following chapters offer advice on the kind of research you'll need to do for your academic work and, in particular, for research papers and other written documents.

Doing Research

Developing a Research Plan 42

When you need to do research, it's sometimes tempting to jump in and start looking for information right away. To do research well, however—to find appropriate sources and use them wisely—you need to work systematically. You need a research plan. This chapter will help you establish such a plan and then get started.

Establishing a Schedule

Doing research is complex and time-consuming, so it's good to establish a schedule for yourself. Research-based writing projects usually require you to come up with a topic (or to analyze the requirements of an assigned topic). You'll need to do preliminary research to come up with a research question to guide your research efforts. Once you do some serious, focused research to find the information you need, you'll be ready to turn your research question into a tentative thesis and sketch out a rough outline. After doing whatever additional research you need to fill in your outline, you'll write a draft—and get some response to that draft. Perhaps you'll need to do additional research before revising. Finally, you'll need to edit and proofread. And so you'll want to start by establishing a schedule, perhaps using the form on the next page.

Getting Started

Once you have a schedule, you can get started. The sections that follow offer advice on considering your rhetorical situation, coming up with a topic, and thinking about what you already know about it; doing prelim-

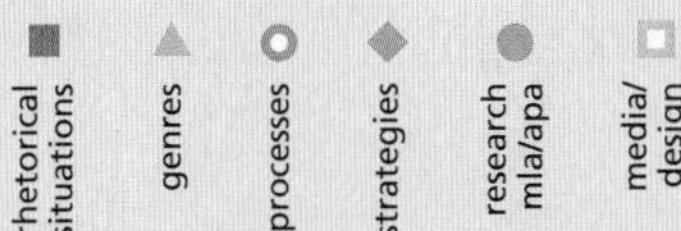

Scheduling a Research Project

	Complete by:
Analyze your rhetorical situation.	________
Choose a possible topic.	________
Do preliminary research.	________
Come up with a research question.	________
Schedule interviews and other field research.	________
Find and read library and Web sources.	________
Do any field research.	________
Come up with a tentative thesis and outline.	________
Write out a draft.	________
Get response.	________
Do any additional research.	________
Revise.	________
Prepare a list of works cited.	________
Edit.	________
Prepare the final draft.	________
Proofread.	________
Submit the final draft.	________

inary research, and creating a working bibliography; developing a research question, devising a tentative thesis and a rough outline, and keeping track of your sources. The chapters that follow offer guidelines for **FINDING SOURCES**, **EVALUATING SOURCES**, and **SYNTHESIZING IDEAS**.

384–99
400–405
404–7

Considering the Rhetorical Situation

As with any writing task, you need to start by considering your purpose, your audience, and the rest of your rhetorical situation:

PURPOSE Is this project part of an assignment—and if so, does it specify any one purpose? If not, what is your broad purpose? To inform? Argue? Entertain? A combination? 3–4

AUDIENCE To whom are you writing? What does your audience likely know about your topic, and is there any background information you'll need to provide? What opinions or attitudes do your readers likely hold? What kinds of evidence will they find persuasive? How do you want them to respond to your writing? 5–8

GENRE Are you writing to report on something? To compose a profile? To make a proposal? An argument? What are the requirements of your genre in terms of the number and kind of sources you must use? 9–11

STANCE What is your attitude toward your topic? What accounts for your attitude? How do you want to come across? Curious? Critical? Positive? Something else? 12–14

MEDIA / DESIGN What medium will you use? Print? Spoken? Electronic? Will you need to compose any charts, photographs, video, presentation software slides, or other visuals? 15–17

Coming Up with a Topic

If you need to choose a topic, consider your interests. What do you want to learn about? What do you have questions about? What topics from your courses have you found intriguing? What community, national, or global issues do you care about? If your topic is assigned, you still need to make sure you understand exactly what it asks you to do. Read the assignment carefully, looking for key words: does it ask you to **ANALYZE, COMPARE, EVALUATE, SUMMARIZE?** If the assignment offers broad guidelines but allows you to choose within them, identify the requirements and the range of possibilities, and define your topic within those constraints. For

278–82
306–13
125–32
416–17

example, in an American history course, your instructor might ask you to "discuss social effects of the Civil War." To define a suitable topic, you might choose to explore such topics as poverty among Confederate soldiers or former slaveholders, the migration of members of those groups to Mexico or northern cities, the establishment of independent black churches, the growth of sharecropping among former slaves, or the spread of the Ku Klux Klan—to name a few possibilities. Once you have
219–22
a broad topic, you might try **FREEWRITING, LOOPING, LISTING,** or **CLUSTERING** to find an angle to research.

Narrow the topic. As you consider possible topics, look to narrow your focus on a topic to make it specific enough for you to research and cover in a paper. For example:

> **Too general:** ethanol
>
> **Still too general:** ethanol and the environment
>
> **Better:** the potential environmental effects of increasing the use of gasoline mixed with ethanol

If you limit your topic, you can address it with specific information that you'll be more easily able to find and manage. In addition, a limited topic will be more likely to interest your audience than a broad subject that forces you to use abstract, general statements. For example, it's much harder to write well about "the environment" than it is to address a topic that covers a single environmental issue.

Think about what you know about your topic. Chances are you already know something about your topic, and articulating that knowledge can help you see possible ways to focus your topic or come up
219–22
with potential sources of information. **FREEWRITING, LISTING, CLUSTERING,** and **LOOPING** are all good ways of tapping your knowledge of your topic. Consider where you might find information about it: Have you read about it in a textbook? Heard stories about it on the news? Visited websites focused on it? Do you know anyone who knows about this topic?

Doing Some Preliminary Research

Doing some preliminary research can save you time in the long run. Scholarly sources usually focus on narrow, specialized aspects of subjects. To define the focus for your research, you first need to explore sources that will provide an overview of your topic.

One way to begin is to look at **REFERENCE WORKS** — sources that deal with the general topic and that include summaries or overviews of the scholarship in a field. General encyclopedias can give you some background, but they aren't suitable as sources for college work; use them as a starting point, to give you some basic information about your topic and help you see some of the paths you might follow. The same is true of the results you're likely to get from skimming websites on the subject. Discipline-specific encyclopedias can be more helpful, as they usually present subjects in much greater depth and provide more scholarly references that might suggest starting points for your research. Even if you know a lot about a subject, doing preliminary research can open you to new ways of seeing and approaching it, increasing your options for developing and narrowing your topic. 388–89

At this stage, pay close attention to the terms used to discuss your topic. These terms could be keywords that you can use to search for information on your topic in library catalogs, in databases, and on the Web.

Keeping a Working Bibliography

A working bibliography is a record of all the sources you consult. You should keep such a record so that you can find sources easily when you need them and then cite any that you use. You can keep a working bibliography on index cards or in a notebook, or in many cases you can print out or photocopy the data you find useful. To save time later, include all the bibliographic information you'll need to document the sources you use. If possible, follow the **DOCUMENTATION** style you'll use when you write. 425–27

On the next page is most of the basic information you'll want to include for each source in your working bibliography. Go to wwnorton.com/write/fieldguide for templates you can use to keep track of this information.

Information for a Working Bibliography

FOR A BOOK

Library call number
Author(s) or editor(s)
Title and subtitle
Publication information: city, publisher, year of publication
Other information: edition, volume number, translator, and so on
If your source is an essay in a collection, include its author, title, and page numbers.

FOR AN ARTICLE IN A PERIODICAL

Author(s)
Title and subtitle
Name of periodical
Volume number, issue number, date
Page numbers

FOR A WEB SOURCE

URL
DOI if provided
Author(s) or editor(s) if available
Name of site
Sponsor of site
Date site was first posted or last updated
Date you accessed site
If the source is an article or book reprinted on the Web, include its title, the title and publication information of the periodical or book where it was first published, and any page numbers.

FOR A SOURCE FROM AN ELECTRONIC DATABASE

Publication information for the source
Name of database
Item number, if there is one
Name of subscription service and its URL
Library where you accessed source
Date you accessed source

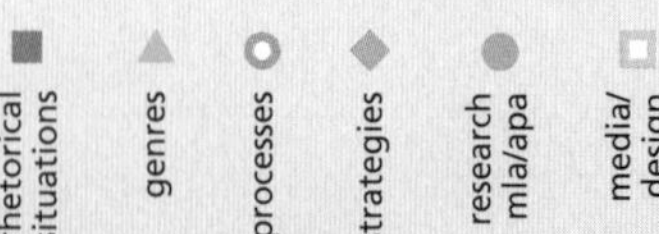

Coming Up with a Research Question

Once you've surveyed the territory of your topic, you'll likely find that your understanding of your topic has become broader and deeper. You may find that your interests have changed and your research has led to surprises and additional research. That's okay: as a result of exploring avenues you hadn't anticipated, you may well come up with a better topic than the one you'd started with. At some point, though, you need to come up with a research question — a specific question that you will then work to answer through your research.

To write a research question, review your analysis of the **RHETORICAL SITUATION**, to remind yourself of any time constraints or length considerations. Generate a list of questions beginning with *What? When? Where? Who? How? Why? Would? Could?* and *Should?* Here, for example, are some questions about the tentative topic "the potential environmental effects of increasing the use of gasoline mixed with ethanol": 1

> *What* are the environmental effects of producing and burning ethanol, gasoline, and diesel fuel?
>
> *When* was ethanol introduced as a gasoline additive?
>
> *Where* is ethanol produced, and how does this affect the energy costs of transporting it?
>
> *Who* will benefit from increased ethanol use?
>
> *How* much energy does producing ethanol require?
>
> *Why* do some environmental groups oppose the use of ethanol?
>
> *Would* other alternative energy sources be more energy-efficient?
>
> *Could* ethanol replace gasoline completely in passenger vehicles?
>
> *Should* ethanol use be increased?

Select one question from your list that you find interesting and that suits your rhetorical situation. Use the question to guide your research.

Drafting a Tentative Thesis

Once your research has led you to a possible answer to your research question, try formulating that answer as a tentative **THESIS**. You need not be 273–75 committed to the thesis; in fact, you should not be. The object of your research should be to learn about your topic, not to find information that simply supports what you already think you believe. Your tentative thesis may (and probably will) change as you learn more about your subject, consider the many points of view on it, and reconsider your topic and, perhaps, your goal: what you originally planned to be an informational report may become an argument, or the argument you planned to write may become a report. However tentative, a thesis allows you to move forward by clarifying your purpose for doing research. Here are some tentative thesis statements on the topic of ethanol:

> Producing ethanol uses more fossil fuels than burning it saves.
>
> The federal government should require the use of ethanol as a gasoline additive.
>
> Ethanol is a more environmentally friendly fuel than gasoline, but it's not as "green" as liquid propane gas.

As with a research question, a tentative thesis should guide your research efforts—but be ready to revise it as you learn still more about your topic. Research should be a process of inquiry in which you approach your topic with an open mind, ready to learn and possibly change. If you hold too tightly to a tentative thesis, you risk focusing only on evidence that supports your view, making your writing biased and unconvincing.

Creating a Rough Outline

223–24 After you've created a tentative thesis, write out a rough **OUTLINE** for your research paper. Your rough outline can be a simple list of topics you want to explore, something that will help you structure your research efforts and organize your notes and other materials. As you read your sources, you can use your outline to keep track of what you need to find and where the information you do find fits into your argument. Then you'll be able to see if you've covered all the ideas you intended to explore—or whether you need to rethink the categories on your outline.

Keeping Track of Your Sources

- ***Staple together copies and printouts of print materials.*** It's easy for individual pages to get shuffled or lost on a desk or in a backpack. Keep a stapler handy, and fasten pages together as soon as you copy them or print them out.
- ***Store website URLs*** as *favorites* (in Internet Explorer) or *bookmarks* (in Firefox).
- ***Label everything.*** Label your copies with the source's author and title.
- ***Highlight sections you plan to use.*** When you sit down to draft, your goal will be to find what you need quickly, so as soon as you decide you might use a source, highlight the paragraphs or sentences that you think you'll use. If your instructor wants copies of your sources to see how you used them, you've got them ready.
- ***Use your rough outline to keep track of what you've got.*** In the margin of each highlighted section, write the number or letter of the outline division to which the section corresponds. (It's a good idea to write it in the same place consistently so you can flip through a stack of copies and easily see what you've got.) Alternatively, attach sticky notes to each photocopy, using a different color for each main heading in your outline.
- ***Keep everything in a file folder or box.*** That way, even though your research material may not look organized, it will all be in one place—and if you highlight, number, and use sticky notes, your material will be organized and you'll be better prepared to write a draft. This folder or box will also serve you well if you are required to create a portfolio that includes your research notes, photocopies of sources, and drafts.

IF YOU NEED MORE HELP

See the guidelines on FINDING SOURCES once you're ready to move on to in-depth research and those on EVALUATING SOURCES for help thinking critically about the sources you find.

384–99
400–403

43 Finding Sources

To analyze media coverage of the 2008 Democratic National Convention, you examine news stories and blogs published at the time. To write an essay interpreting a poem by Maya Angelou, you study the poem and read several critical interpretations in literary journals. To write a report on career opportunities in psychology, you interview a graduate of your university who is working in a psychology clinic. In each of these cases, you go beyond your own knowledge to consult additional sources of information.

This chapter offers guidelines for locating a range of sources—print and online, general and specialized, published and firsthand. Keep in mind that as you do research, finding and **EVALUATING SOURCES** are two activities that usually take place simultaneously. So this chapter and the next one go hand in hand.

400–403

Kinds of Sources

Primary and secondary sources. Your research will likely lead you to both primary and secondary sources. *Primary sources* include historical documents, literary works, eyewitness accounts, field reports, diaries, letters, and lab studies, as well as any original research you do through interviews, observation, experiments, or surveys. *Secondary sources* include scholarly books and articles, reviews, biographies, textbooks, and other works that interpret or discuss primary sources. Novels and poems are primary sources; articles interpreting them are secondary sources. The

Declaration of Independence is a primary historical document; a historian's description of the events surrounding the Declaration's writing is secondary. A published report of scientific findings is primary; a critique of that report is secondary.

Whether a work is considered primary or secondary sometimes depends on your topic and purpose: if you're analyzing a poem, a critic's article interpreting the poem is a secondary source—but if you're investigating that critic's work, the article would be a primary source for your own study and interpretation.

Primary sources are useful because they offer subjects for firsthand study, whereas secondary sources can help you understand and evaluate primary source material.

Print and online sources. Some sources are available only in print; some are available only online. But many print sources are also available on the Web. You'll find print sources in your school's library, but chances are that many of the books in your library's reference section will also be available online. And when it comes to finding sources, it's likely that you'll *search* for most sources online, through the library's website (rather than through a commercial search engine, which may lead you to unreliable sources). In general, there are four kinds of sources you'll want to consult, each of which is discussed in this chapter:

- **GENERAL REFERENCE WORKS,** for encyclopedias, dictionaries, and the like 388
- **THE LIBRARY CATALOG,** for books 389–90
- **INDEXES AND DATABASES,** for periodicals 390–93
- **SEARCH ENGINES AND SUBJECT DIRECTORIES,** for material on the Web 393–94

On the next page is a sample search page from the catalog of one university library. This catalog, like most, allows you to search by book title, journal title, author, subject, call number, and keyword. In addition, the links at the top of the page permit you to search through various indexes and databases and take advantage of interlibrary loan (for materials that your library doesn't have) and various tutorials.

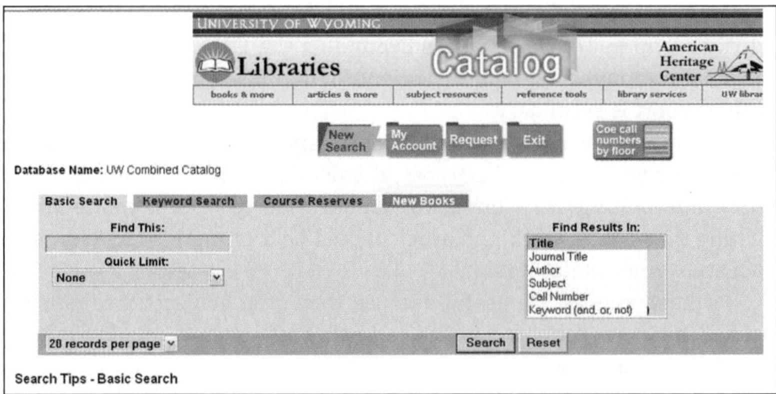

Part of a library catalog search page.

Searching Electronically

Whether you're searching for books, articles in periodicals, or material available on the Web, chances are you'll conduct much of your search electronically. Most materials produced since the 1980s can be found electronically, most library catalogs are online, and most periodical articles can be found by searching electronic indexes and databases. In each case, you can search for authors, titles, or subjects.

When you're searching for subjects, you'll need to come up with *keywords* that will lead you to the information you're looking for. Usually if you start with only one keyword, you'll end up with far too many results—tens of thousands of references when you're searching the Web—so the key to searching efficiently is to come up with keywords that will focus your searches on the information you need. Some search engines will let you enter more than one word and will identify only those sources that contain all the words you entered. Other search engines will let you type in more than one word and will identify those sources that contain at least one of those words but not necessarily all of them. Most search engines have "advanced search" options that will help you focus your research. Specific commands will vary among search engines and within databases, but here are some of the most common ones:

- Type quotation marks around words to search for an exact phrase—"Thomas Jefferson"—unless you're using a search engine that includes a field to search for exact phrases, in which case you won't need the quotation marks. If your exact-phrase search doesn't yield good results, try removing the quotation marks.
- Type AND to find sources that include more than one keyword: Jefferson AND Adams. Some search engines require a plus sign instead: +Jefferson+Adams.
- Type OR if you're looking for sources that include one of several terms: Jefferson OR Adams OR Madison.
- Type NOT to find sources *without* a certain word: Jefferson NOT Adams. Some search engines call for a minus sign (actually, a hyphen) instead: +Jefferson-Adams will result in sources in which the name Jefferson appears but the name Adams does not.
- Type an asterisk—or some other symbol—to search for words in different forms—teach* will yield sources containing *teacher* and *teaching*, for example. Check the search engine's search tips to find out what symbol to use.
- Some search engines allow you to ask questions in conversational language: What did Thomas Jefferson write about slavery?
- Be more general (*education Japan* instead of *secondary education Japan*) when you get too few sources; be more specific (*homeopathy* instead of *medicine*) when you get far too many sources.
- If you don't get results with one set of keywords, substitute synonyms (if *folk medicine* doesn't generate much information, try *home remedy*). Or look through the sources that turn up in response to other terms to see what keywords you might use in subsequent searches. Searching requires flexibility, in the words you use and the methods you try.

Reference Works

The reference section of your school's library is the place to find encyclopedias, dictionaries, atlases, almanacs, bibliographies, and other reference works in print. Many of these sources are also online and can be accessed from any computer that is connected to the Internet. Others are available only in the library. Remember, though, that whether in print or online, reference works are only a starting point, a place where you can get an overview of your topic.

General reference works. Consult encyclopedias for general background information on a subject, dictionaries for definitions of words, atlases for maps and geographic data, and almanacs for statistics and other data on current events. These are some works you might consult:

The New Encyclopaedia Britannica
The Columbia Encyclopedia
Webster's Third New International Dictionary
Oxford English Dictionary
National Geographic Atlas of the World
Statistical Abstract of the United States
The World Almanac and Book of Facts

Caution: Wikipedia is a popular online research tool, but since anyone can edit its entries, you can't be certain of its accuracy. Avoid using it.

Specialized reference works. You can also go to specialized reference works, which provide in-depth information on a single field or topic. These may also include authoritative bibliographies, leading you to more specific works. A reference librarian can refer you to specialized encyclopedias in particular fields; you'll find a list of some at wwnorton.com/write/fieldguide.

Bibliographies. Bibliographies provide an overview of what has been published on a topic, listing published works along with the information you'll need to find each work. Some are annotated with brief summaries of each work's contents. You'll find bibliographies at the end of scholarly articles and books, and you can also find book-length bibliographies, both in the reference section of your library and online. Check with a reference librarian for bibliographies on your research topic.

Books / Searching the Library Catalog

The library catalog is your primary source for finding books. Most library catalogs are computerized and can be accessed through the library's website. You can search by author, title, subject, or keyword. The image below shows the result of a keyword search for material on art in Nazi Germany. This search revealed that the library has nineteen books on

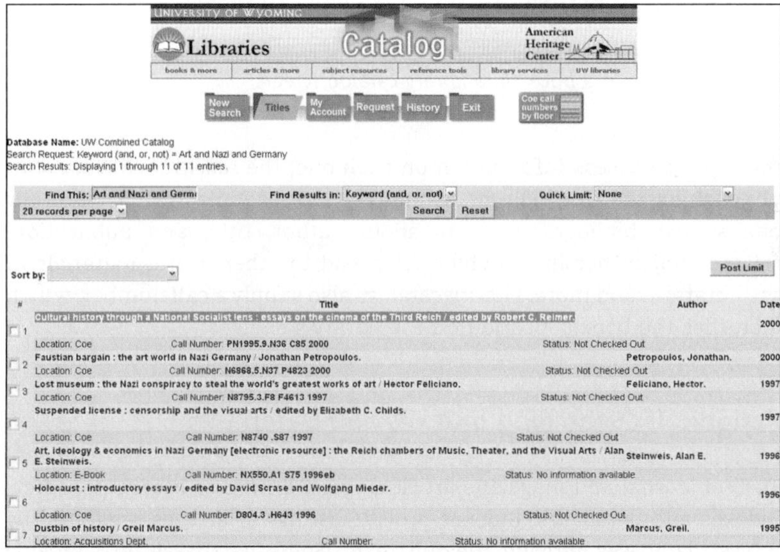

List of books on a library catalog screen.

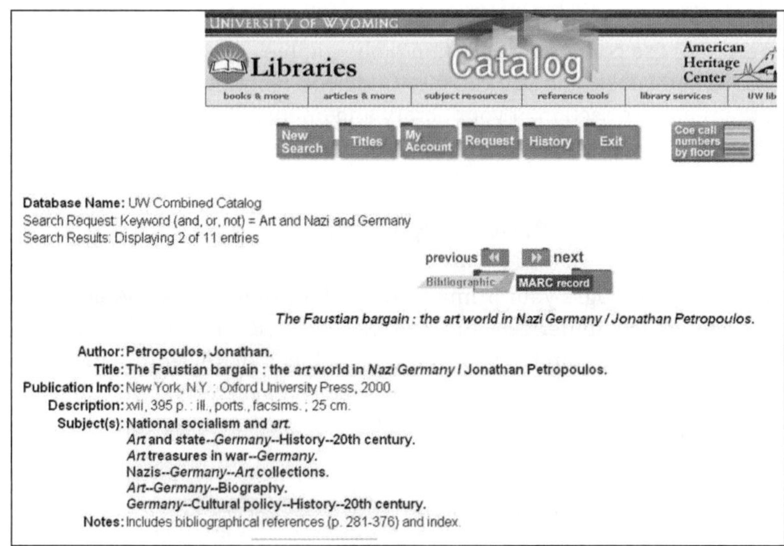

Information about a book on a library catalog screen.

the topic; to access information on each one, the researcher must simply click on the title. The image above shows detailed information for one source: bibliographic data about author, title, and publication; related subject headings (which may lead to other useful materials in the library) — and more. Library catalogs also supply a call number, which identifies the book's location on the library's shelves.

Periodicals / Searching Indexes and Databases

To find journal and magazine articles, you will need to search periodical indexes and databases. Indexes provide listings of articles organized by topics; databases provide the full texts. Some databases also provide indexes of bibliographic citations, so you can track down the actual articles. Some indexes are in print and can be found in the reference section of the library; many are online. Some databases are available for free; most of the more authoritative ones, however, are available only by subscription and so must be accessed through a library.

Print indexes. You'll need to consult print indexes to find articles published before the 1980s. Here are six useful ones:

The Readers' Guide to Periodical Literature (print, 1900–; online, 1983–)

Magazine Index (print, 1988–; online via InfoTrac, 1973–)

The New York Times Index (print and online, 1851–)

Humanities Index (print, 1974–; online, 1984–)

Social Sciences Index (print, 1974–; online, 1983–)

General Science Index (print, 1978–; online, 1984–)

General electronic indexes and databases. A reference librarian can help you determine which databases will be most helpful to you, but here are some useful ones:

Academic Search Complete is a multidisciplinary index and database containing the full text of articles in more than 4,400 journals and indexing of over 9,300 journals, with abstracts of their articles.

EBSCOhost provides interlinked databases of abstracts and full-text articles from a variety of periodicals.

FirstSearch offers access to more than 10 million full-text, full-image articles in dozens of databases covering many disciplines.

InfoTrac offers over 20 million full-text articles in a broad spectrum of disciplines and on a wide variety of topics from nearly 6,000 scholarly and popular periodicals, including the *New York Times*.

JSTOR archives scanned copies of entire publication runs of scholarly journals in many disciplines, but it does not include current issues of the journals.

LexisNexis Academic Universe contains full-text publications and articles from a large number of sources—newspapers, business and legal resources, medical texts, and reference sources such as *The World Almanac* and the Roper public opinion polls.

ProQuest provides access to full-text articles from thousands of periodicals and newspapers from 1986 to the present, with many entries updated daily, and a large collection of dissertations and theses.

SIRS Researcher contains records of articles from selected domestic and international newspapers, magazines, journals, and government publications.

Single-subject indexes and databases. These are just a sample of what's available; check with a reference librarian for indexes and databases in the subject you're researching.

America: History and Life indexes scholarly literature on the history of the United States and Canada.

BIOSIS Previews provides abstracts and indexes for more than 5,500 sources on biology, botany, zoology, environmental studies, and agriculture.

ERIC is the U.S. Department of Education's Educational Resource Information Center database.

Historical Abstracts includes abstracts of articles on the history of the world, excluding the United States and Canada, since 1450.

Humanities International Index contains bibliographic references to more than 1,700 journals dealing with the humanities.

MLA International Bibliography indexes scholarly articles on modern languages, literature, folklore, and linguistics.

PsychINFO indexes scholarly literature in a number of disciplines relating to psychology.

Web-based indexes and databases. The following are freely available on the Internet:

Infomine contains "useful Internet resources such as databases, electronic journals, electronic books, bulletin boards, mailing lists, online library card catalogs, articles, directories of researchers, and many other types of information."

Librarians' Internet Index is a searchable, annotated subject directory of more than 20,000 websites selected and evaluated by librarians for their usefulness to users of public libraries.

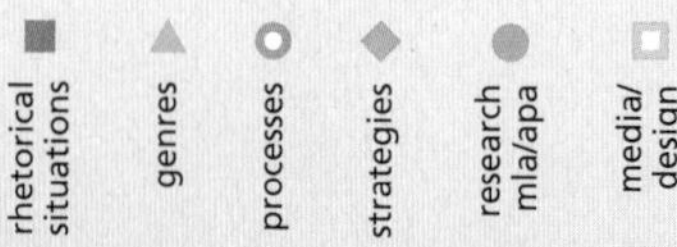

The World Wide Web Virtual Library is a catalog of websites on a wide range of subjects, compiled by volunteers with expertise in particular subject areas.

CSA Discovery Guides provide comprehensive information on current issues in biomedicine, engineering, the environment, the social sciences, and the humanities, with an overview of each subject, key citations with abstracts, and links to websites.

The Voice of the Shuttle: Web Site for Humanities Research offers information on subjects in the humanities, organized to mirror the way the humanities are organized for research and teaching as well as the way they are adapting to social, cultural, and technological changes.

The Library of Congress offers online access to information on a wide range of subjects, including academic subjects, as well as prints, photographs, and government documents.

JURIST is a university-based online gateway to authoritative legal instruction, information, scholarship, and news.

The Web

The Web provides access to countless sites containing information posted by governments, educational institutions, organizations, businesses, and individuals. Websites are different from other sources in several ways: (1) they often provide entire texts, not just citations of texts, (2) their content varies greatly in its reliability, and (3) they are not stable: what you see on a site today may be different (or gone) tomorrow. Anyone who wants to can post texts on the Web, so you need to **EVALUATE** carefully what you find there. 400–403

Because it is so vast and dynamic, finding what you want on the Web can be a challenge. The primary way of finding information on the Web is with a search engine. There are several ways of searching the Web:

- ***Keyword searches.*** Google, HotBot, AltaVista, Lycos, and Yahoo! all scan the Web looking for keywords that you specify.

- *Subject directories.* Google, Yahoo!, and some other search engines offer directories that arrange information by topics, much like a library cataloging system. Such directories allow you to broaden or narrow your search if you need to—for example, a search for "birds" can be broadened to "animals" or narrowed to "blue-footed booby."
- *Metasearches.* Copernic Agent, SurfWax, and Dogpile are metasearch engines that allow you to use several search engines simultaneously.
- *Academic searches.* You may find more suitable results for academic writing at Google Scholar (scholar.google.com), a search engine that finds scholarly literature, including peer-reviewed papers, technical reports, and abstracts, or at Scirus (scirus.com), which finds peer-reviewed documents on scientific, technical, and medical topics.

Each search engine and metasearch engine has its own protocols for searching; most have an "advanced search" option that will help you search more productively. Remember, though, that you need to be careful about evaluating sources that you find on the Web because the Web is unregulated and no one independently verifies the information posted on its sites.

Doing Field Research

Sometimes you'll need to do your own research, to go beyond the information you find in published sources and gather data by doing field research. Three kinds of field research you might want to consider are interviews, observations, and questionnaires.

Interviewing experts. Some kinds of writing—a profile of a living person, for instance—almost require that you conduct an interview. And sometimes you may just need to find information that you haven't been able to find in published sources. To get firsthand information on the experience of serving as a soldier in Iraq, you might interview your cousin who served a tour of duty there; to find current research on pesticide residues in food, you might need to interview a toxicologist. Whatever your goal, you can conduct interviews face-to-face, over the telephone, or by mail or email. In general, you will want to use interviews to find information you can't find elsewhere. Below is some advice on planning and conducting an interview.

Before the interview

1. Once you identify someone you want to interview, email or phone to ask for an appointment, stating your **PURPOSE** for the interview and what you hope to learn. 3–4
2. Once you've set up the appointment, send a note or email confirming the time and place. If you wish to record the interview, be sure to ask for permission to do so. If you plan to conduct the interview by mail or email, state when you will send your questions.
3. Write out questions. Plan questions that invite extended response: "What accounts for the recent spike in gasoline prices?" forces an explanation, whereas "Is the recent spike in gas prices a direct result of global politics?" is likely to elicit only a yes or a no.

At the interview

4. Record the full name of the person you interview, along with the date, time, and place of the interview; you'll need this information to cite and document the interview accurately.
5. Take notes, even if you are recording the interview.
6. Keep track of time: don't take more than you agreed to beforehand unless both of you agree to keep talking. End by saying thank you and offering to provide a copy of your final product.

After the interview

7. Flesh out your notes with details as soon as possible after the interview, while you still remember them. What did you learn? What surprised you? Summarize both the interviewee's words and your impressions.
8. Be sure to send a thank-you note or email.

Observation. Some writing projects are based on information you get by observing something. For a sociology paper, you may observe how students behave in large lectures. For an education course, you may observe one child's progress as a writer over a period of time. The following advice can help you conduct observations.

Before observing

3–4
1. Think about your research PURPOSE: What are you looking for? What do you expect to find? How will your presence as an observer affect what you observe? What do you plan to do with what you find?
2. If necessary, set up an appointment. You may need to ask permission of the people you wish to observe. Be honest and open about your goals and intentions; college students doing research assignments are often welcomed where others may not be.

While observing

3. You may want to divide each page of your notepaper down the middle vertically and write only on the left side of the page, reserving the right side for information you will fill in later.

324–27
4. Note DESCRIPTIVE DETAILS about the setting. What do you see? What do you hear? Do you smell anything? Get down details about color, shape, size, sound, and so on. Consider photographing or making a sketch of what you see.

324–32
5. Who is there, and what are they doing? DESCRIBE what they look like, and make notes about what they say. Note any significant demographic details—about gender, race, occupation, age, dress, and so on.
6. What is happening? Who's doing what? What's being said? Write down these kinds of NARRATIVE details.

343–51

After observing

7. As soon as possible after you complete your observations, use the right side of your pages to fill in gaps and note additional details.

278–82
8. ANALYZE your notes, looking for patterns. Did some things appear or happen more than once? Did anything stand out? Surprise or puzzle you? What did you learn?

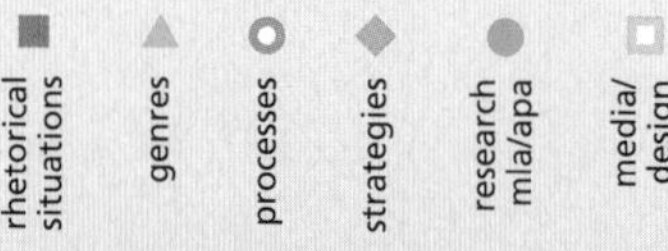

Questionnaires and surveys. Written or online questionnaires and surveys can provide information or opinions from a large number of people. For a political science course, you might conduct a survey to ask students who they plan to vote for. Or, for a marketing course, you might distribute a questionnaire asking what they think about an advertising campaign. The advice in this section will help you create useful questionnaires and surveys.

Define your goal. The goal of a questionnaire or survey should be limited and focused, so that every question will contribute to your research question. Also, people are more likely to respond to a brief, focused survey.

Define your sample. A survey gets responses from a representative sample of the whole group. The answers to these questions will help you define that sample:

1. Who should answer the questions? The people you contact should represent the whole population. For example, if you want to survey undergraduate students at your school, your sample should reflect your school's enrollment in terms of gender, year, major, age, ethnicity, and so forth.
2. How many people make up a representative sample? In general, the larger your sample, the more the answers will reflect those of the whole group. But if your population is small—200 students in a history course, for example—your sample must include a large percentage of that group.

Decide on a medium. Will you ask the questions face-to-face? Over the phone? On a website? By mail? Oral questionnaires work best for simple surveys or to gather impersonal information. You're more likely to get responses to more personal questions with written or Web-based questionnaires. **DESIGN** issues differ, depending on the medium: written or Web-based surveys should be neat and easy to read, while phone interviews may require well-thought-out scripts that anticipate possible answers and make it easy to record these answers. 521

Design good questions. The way you ask questions will determine the answers you get, so take care to write questions that are clear and unambiguous. Here are some typical question types:

- *Multiple-choice*

  What is your current age?

  ____ 15–20 ____ 21–25 ____ 26–30 ____ 31–35 ____ Other

- *Rating scale*

  How would you rate the service at the campus bookstore?

  ____ Excellent ____ Good ____ Fair ____ Poor

- *Agreement scale*

  How much do you agree with the following statements?

	Strongly Agree	Agree	Disagree	Strongly Disagree
The bookstore has sufficient numbers of textbooks available.	❒	❒	❒	❒
Staff at the bookstore are knowledgeable.	❒	❒	❒	❒
Staff at the bookstore are courteous and helpful.	❒	❒	❒	❒

- *Open-ended*

  How often do you visit the campus bookstore?

  How can the campus bookstore improve its service?

Include all potential alternatives when phrasing questions to avoid biasing the answers. And make sure each question addresses only one issue—for example, "bookstore staff are knowledgeable and courteous" could lead to the response "knowledgeable, agree; courteous, disagree."

When arranging questions, place easier ones at the beginning and harder ones near the end (but if the questions seem to fall into a natural order, follow it). Make sure each question asks for information you will need—if a question isn't absolutely necessary, omit it.

Include an introduction. Start by stating your survey's purpose and how the results will be used. It's also a good idea to offer an estimate of the time needed to complete the questions.

Test the survey or questionnaire. Make sure your questions elicit the kinds of answers you need by asking three or four people who are part of your target population to answer them. They can help you find unclear instructions, questions that aren't clear or that lack sufficient alternatives, or other problems that you should correct to make sure your results are useful. But if you change the questionnaire as a result of their responses, don't include their answers in your total.

IF YOU NEED MORE HELP

See EVALUATING SOURCES for help determining their usefulness. See also Chapter 46 for help TAKING NOTES on your sources.

400–403
408–9

44 Evaluating Sources

Searching the *Health Source* database for information on the incidence of meningitis among college students, you find seventeen articles. A Google search on the same topic produces over ten thousand hits. How do you decide which sources to read? This chapter presents advice on evaluating sources—first to determine whether a source is useful for your purposes and then to read with a critical eye the ones you choose.

Considering the Reliability of Print and Online Sources

Books and journals that have been published in print have most likely been evaluated by editors, publishers, or expert reviewers before publication. Magazines and newspapers have probably been fact-checked; not so most websites—anyone who wishes to post something on the Web can do so. In addition, Web sources come and go and are easily changed. So print sources (including journals available online) are always more stable and often more trustworthy.

Considering Whether a Source Serves Your Purpose

3–4 **Think about your PURPOSE.** Are you trying to persuade readers to believe or do something? To inform them about something? If the former, it will be especially important to find sources representing various stances; if the latter, you may need sources that are more factual or informative. Reconsider
5–8 your **AUDIENCE.** What kinds of sources will they find persuasive? If you're writing for readers in a particular field, what counts as evidence in that field? Following are some questions that can help you select useful sources:

- ***Is it relevant?*** How does the source relate to your purpose? What will it add to your work? Look at the title and at any introductory material—a preface, abstract, or introduction—to see what it covers.
- ***What are the author's credentials?*** What are the author's qualifications to write on the subject? Is he or she associated with a particular position on the issue? If the source is a book or a periodical, see whether it mentions other works this author has written. If it's a website, see whether an author is identified. If one is, you might do a Web search to see what else you can learn about him or her.
- ***What is the* STANCE?** Consider whether a source covers various points of view or advocates one particular point of view. Does its title suggest a certain slant? If it's a website, you might check to see whether it includes links to other sites of one or many perspectives. You'll want to consult sources with a variety of viewpoints. 12–14
- ***Who is the publisher?*** If it's a book, what kind of company published it; if an article, what kind of periodical did it appear in? Books published by university presses and articles in scholarly journals are reviewed by experts before they are published. Books and articles written for general audiences typically do not undergo rigorous review—and they may lack the kind of in-depth discussion that is useful for research.
- ***If it's a website, who is the sponsor?*** Is the site maintained by an organization? An interest group? A government agency? An individual? If the site doesn't give this information, look for clues in the URL: *edu* is used mostly by colleges and universities, *gov* by government agencies, *org* by nonprofit organizations, *mil* by the military, and *com* by commercial organizations.
- ***What is the level?*** Can you understand the material? Texts written for a general audience might be easier to understand but are not likely to be authoritative enough for academic work. Texts written for scholars will be more authoritative but may be hard to comprehend.
- ***When was it published?*** See when books and articles were published. Check to see when websites were last updated. (If the site lists no date, see if links to other sites still work.) Recent does not necessar-

ily mean better—some topics may require very current information whereas others may call for older sources.

- *Is it available?* Is it a source you can get hold of? If it's a book and your school's library doesn't have it, can you get it through interlibrary loan?
- *Does it include other useful information?* Is there a bibliography that might lead you to other sources? How current are the sources it cites?

Reading Sources with a Critical Eye

- 83–110 *What* **ARGUMENTS** *does the author make?* Does the author present a number of different positions, or does he or she argue for a particu-
283–99 lar position? Do you need to **ANALYZE THE ARGUMENT**?
- *How persuasive do you find the argument?* What reasons and evidence does the author provide in support of any position(s)? Are there citations or links—and if so, are they credible? Is any evidence presented without citations? Do you find any of the author's assumptions questionable? How thoroughly does he or she consider opposing arguments?
- 12–14 *What is the author's* **STANCE?** Does the author strive for objectivity, or does the language reveal a particular bias? Is the author associated with a special interest that might signal a certain perspective? Does he or she consider opposing views? Do the sources cited reflect multiple viewpoints, or only one?
- *Does the publisher bring a certain stance to the work?* Book publishers, periodicals, or websites that are clearly liberal or conservative or advance a particular agenda will likely express views reflecting their
12–14 **STANCE.**
- *Do you recognize ideas you've run across in other sources?* Does it leave out any information that other sources include?
- *Does this source support or challenge your own position—or does it do both?* Does it support your thesis? Offer a different argument alto-
104 gether? Does it represent a position you may need to **ACKNOWLEDGE** or

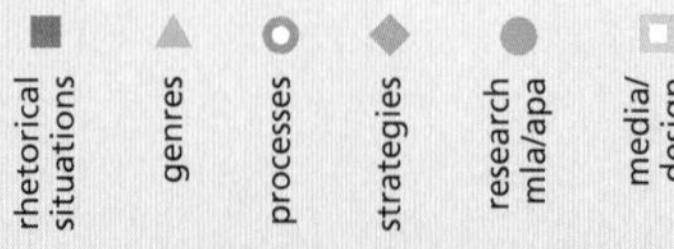

REFUTE? Don't reject a source that challenges your views; your sources should reflect a variety of views on your topic, showing that you've considered the subject thoroughly.

- *What can you tell about the intended* **AUDIENCE** *and* **PURPOSE**? Are you a member of the audience addressed—and if not, does that affect the way you interpret what you read? Is the main purpose to inform readers about a topic or to argue a certain point?

105
5–8
3–4

IF YOU NEED MORE HELP

See **QUOTING, PARAPHRASING, AND SUMMARIZING** for help in taking notes on your sources and deciding how to use them in your writing. See also **ACKNOWLEDGING SOURCES, AVOIDING PLAGIARISM** for advice on giving credit to the sources you use.

408–19
420–24

45 Synthesizing Ideas

38–58 To **ANALYZE** the works of a poet, you show how she uses similar images in three different poems to explore a recurring concept. To solve a crime, a detective studies several eyewitness accounts to figure out who did it. 306–13 To trace the history of photojournalism, a professor **COMPARES** the uses of photography during the Civil War and during the war in Vietnam. These are all cases where someone *synthesizes*—brings together material from two or more sources in order to generate new information or to support a new perspective. When you do research, you need to go beyond what your sources say; you need to use what they say to inspire and support *what you want to say*. This chapter focuses on how to synthesize ideas you find in other sources as the basis for your own ideas.

Reading for Patterns and Connections

Your task as a writer is to find as much information as you can on your topic—and then to sift through all that you have found to determine and support what you yourself will write. In other words, you'll need to synthesize ideas and information from the sources you've consulted to figure out first what arguments *you* want to make and then to provide support for those arguments.

When you synthesize, you group similar bits of information together, looking for patterns or themes or trends and trying to identify the key points. For example, researching the effectiveness of the SAT writing exam you find several sources showing that scores correlate directly with length and that a majority of U. S. colleges and universities have decided not to count the results of the test in their admission decisions. You can infer that the test is not yet seen as an effective measure of writing ability.

Here are some tips for reading to identify patterns and connections:

- Take notes and jot down a brief **SUMMARY** of each source to help you see relationships, patterns, and connections among your sources. Take notes on your own thoughts, too. 416–17
- Read all your sources with an open mind. Withhold judgment, even of sources that seem wrong-headed or implausible. Don't jump to conclusions.
- Pay attention to your first reactions. You'll likely have many ideas to work with, but your first thoughts can often lead somewhere that you will find interesting. Try **FREEWRITING**, **CLUSTERING**, or **LISTING** to see where they lead. 219–22
- Try to think creatively, and pay attention to thoughts that flicker at the edge of your consciousness, as they may well be productive.
- Be playful. Good ideas sometimes come when we let our guard down or take ideas to extremes just to see where they lead.

Ask yourself these questions about your sources:

- What sources make the strongest arguments? What makes them so strong?
- Do some arguments recur in several sources?
- Which arguments do you agree with? Disagree with? Of those you disagree with, which ones seem strong enough that you need to **ACKNOWLEDGE** them in your text? 294
- Are there any disagreements among your sources?
- Are there any themes you see in more than one source?
- Are any data—facts, statistics, examples—or experts cited in more than one source?

- What have you learned about your topic? How have your sources affected your thinking on your topic? Do you need to adjust your **RESEARCH QUESTION**? If so, how? 381
- Have you discovered new questions you need to investigate?
- Keep in mind your **RHETORICAL SITUATION**—have you found the information you need that will achieve your **PURPOSE,** appeal to your **AUDIENCE,** and suit your **GENRE** and **MEDIUM**? 1–17

What is likely to emerge from this questioning is a combination of big ideas—new ways of understanding your topic, insights into recent scholarship about it—and smaller ones—how two sources agree with one another but not completely, how the information in one source supports or undercuts the argument of another. These ideas and insights will become the basis for your own ideas, and for what *you* have to say about the topic.

Synthesizing Information to Support Your Own Ideas

59–82 If you're doing research to write a **REPORT**, your own ideas will be communicated primarily through the information you include from the sources you cite and how you organize that information. If you're writing a **TEXTUAL ANALYSIS,** your synthesis may focus on the themes, techniques, or other patterns you find. If you're writing a research-based **ARGUMENT,** on the other hand, your synthesis of sources must support that argument. No matter what your genre, the challenge is to synthesize information from your research to develop ideas about your topic and then to support those ideas. 38–58 83–110

Entering the Conversation

As you read and think about your topic, you will come to an understanding of the concepts, interpretations, and controversies relating to your topic—and you'll become aware that there's a larger conversation going on. When you begin to find connections among your sources, you will begin to see your own place in that conversation, to discover your own ideas, your own stance on your topic. This is the exciting part of a research project, for when you write out your own ideas on the topic, you will find yourself entering that conversation. Remember that your **STANCE** as an author needs to be clear: simply stringing together the words and ideas of others isn't enough. You need to show readers how your source materials relate to one another and to your thesis.

12–14

IF YOU NEED MORE HELP

See Chapter 46, QUOTING, PARAPHRASING, AND SUMMARIZING, for help in integrating source materials into your own text. See also Chapter 47 on ACKNOWLEDGING SOURCES, AVOIDING PLAGIARISM for advice on giving credit to the sources you cite.

408–19
420–24

46 Quoting, Paraphrasing, and Summarizing

In an oral presentation about the rhetoric of Abraham Lincoln, you quote a memorable line from the Gettysburg Address. For an essay on the Tet Offensive in the Vietnam War, you paraphrase arguments made by several commentators and summarize some key debates about that war. Like all writers, when you work with the ideas and words of others, you need to clearly distinguish those ideas and words from your own and give credit to their authors. This chapter will help you with the specifics of quoting, paraphrasing, and summarizing source materials that you wish to use in your writing.

Taking Notes

When you find material you think will be useful, take careful notes. How do you determine how much or how little to record? You need to write down enough information so that when you refer to it later, you will be reminded of the main points and have a precise record of where the information comes from.

- *Use index cards, a computer file, or a notebook,* labeling each entry with the information that will allow you to keep track of where it comes from—author, title, and the pages or the URL (or DOI). You needn't write down full bibliographic information (you can abbreviate the author's name and title) since you'll include that information in your **WORKING BIBLIOGRAPHY**.

379–80

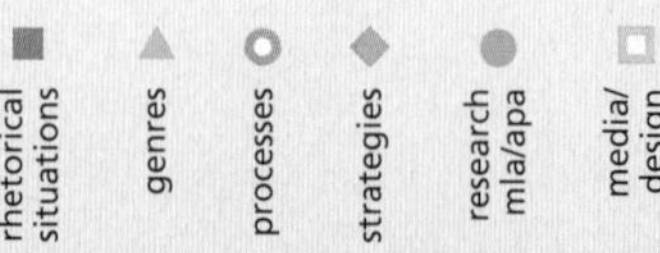

- *Take notes in your own words, and use your own sentence patterns.* If you make a note that is a detailed **PARAPHRASE**, label it as such so that you'll know to provide appropriate **DOCUMENTATION** if you use it. 413–16 425–27
- *If you find wording that you'd like to quote,* be sure to enclose it in quotation marks to distinguish your source's words from your own. Double-check your notes to be sure any quoted material is accurately quoted—and that you haven't accidentally **PLAGIARIZED** your sources. 420–24
- *Label each note with a subject heading.*

Here's an example of one writer's notes:

Dog Experiments Link Synth. Dyes and Bladder Cancer
Source: Steingraber, "Pesticides" (976)
—1938: pathbreaking experiments showed that dogs exposed to aromatic amines developed cancer of the bladder.
—aromatic amines: chemicals used in coal-derived synthetic dyes
—Mauve the first synthetic dye—invented in 1854—then synthetic dyes replaced most natural dyes made with plants
—Bladder cancer common among textile workers who used dyes
—Steingraber: "By the beginning of the twentieth century, bladder cancer rates among this group of workers had skyrocketed, and the dog experiments helped unravel this mystery."
—1921: ILO labels a.a. as carcinogenic (before experiments)
—Dog experiments also helped explain: early 20th century: metal workers, machinists, and workers in the tire industry developed bladder cancer—cutting oils contained aromatic amines to inhibit rust used a.a. accelerants.
—Sandra Steingraber: biologist and ecologist

Deciding Whether to Quote, Paraphrase, or Summarize

When it comes time to **DRAFT**, you'll need to decide *how* to use the sources you've found—in other words, whether to quote, paraphrase, or summa- 226–28

410–13 413–16 416–17

rize. You might follow this rule of thumb: **QUOTE** texts when the wording is worth repeating or makes a point so well that no rewording will do it justice, when you want to cite the exact words of a known authority on your topic, when his or her opinions challenge or disagree with those of others, or when the source is one you want to emphasize. **PARAPHRASE** sources that are not worth quoting but contain details you need to include. **SUMMARIZE** longer passages whose main points are important but whose details are not.

Quoting

417–18

Quoting a source is a way of weaving someone else's exact words into your text. You need to reproduce the source exactly, though you can modify it to omit unnecessary details (with ellipses) or to make it fit smoothly into your text (with brackets). You also need to distinguish quoted material from your own by enclosing short quotations in quotation marks, setting off longer quotes as a block, and using appropriate **SIGNAL PHRASES**.

428–76 477–519

Incorporate short quotations into your text, enclosed in quotation marks. If you are following **MLA STYLE,** this rule holds for four typed lines or fewer; if you are following **APA STYLE,** short means no more than forty words.

> Gerald Graff (2003) argues that colleges make the intellectual life seem more opaque than it needs to be, leaving many students with "the misconception that the life of the mind is a secret society for which only an elite few qualify" (p. 1).

If you are quoting three lines or less of poetry, run them in with your text, enclosed in quotation marks. Separate lines with slashes, leaving one space on each side of the slashes.

> Emma Lazarus almost speaks for the Statue of Liberty with the words inscribed on its pedestal: "Give me your tired, your poor, / Your huddled masses yearning to breathe free, / The wretched refuse of your teeming shore" (58).

Set off long quotations block style. If you are using MLA style, set off quotations of five or more typed lines by indenting the quote one inch (or ten spaces) from the left margin. If you are using APA style, indent quotes of forty or more words one-half inch (or five spaces) from the left margin. In either case, do not use quotation marks, and put any parenthetical citation *after* any end punctuation.

> Nonprofit organizations such as Oxfam and Habitat for Humanity rely on visual representations of the poor. What better way to get our attention, asks rhetorician Diana George:
>
>> In a culture saturated by the image, how else do we convince Americans that—despite the prosperity they see all around them—there is real need out there? The solution for most nonprofits has been to show the despair. To do that they must represent poverty as something that can be seen and easily recognized: fallen down shacks and trashed out public housing, broken windows, dilapidated porches, barefoot kids with stringy hair, emaciated old women and men staring out at the camera with empty eyes. (210)

If you are quoting four or more lines of poetry, they need to be set off block style in the same way.

Indicate any omissions with ellipses. You may sometimes delete words from a quotation that are unnecessary for your point. Insert three ellipsis marks (leaving a space before the first and after the last one) to indicate the deletion. If you omit a sentence or more in the middle of a quotation, put a period before the three ellipsis dots. Be careful not to distort the source's meaning, however.

> Faigley points out that Gore's "Information Superhighway" metaphor "associated the economic prosperity of the 1950s and . . . 1960s facilitated by new highways with the potential for vast . . . commerce to be conducted over the Internet" (253).
>
> According to Welch, "Television is more acoustic than visual. . . . One can turn one's gaze way from the television, but one cannot turn one's ears from it without leaving the area where the monitor leaks its aural signals into every corner" (102).

Indicate additions or changes with brackets. Sometimes you'll need to change or add words in a quote—to make the quote fit grammatically within your sentence, for example, or to add a comment. In the following example, the writer changes the passage "one of our goals" to fit the grammar of her sentences:

> Writing about the dwindling attention among some composition scholars to the actual teaching of writing, Susan Miller notes that "few discussions of writing pedagogy take it for granted that one of [their] goals is to teach how to write" (480).

Here's an example of brackets used to add explanatory words to a quotation:

> Barbosa observes that even Buarque's lyrics have long included "many a metaphor of *saudades* [yearning] so characteristic of *fado* music" (207).

A note about punctuating quotes. When you incorporate a quotation into your text, you have to think about the end punctuation in the quoted material and also about any punctuation you need to add when you insert the quote into your own sentence.

Periods and commas. With brief quotations, put periods or commas inside the quotation marks, except when you have a parenthetical citation at the end, in which case you put the period after the parentheses.

> "Country music," Tichi says, "is a crucial and vital part of the American identity" (23).

With long quotes set off block style, however, there are no quotation marks, so the period goes *before* the citation, as shown in the example on page 411.

Question marks and exclamation points. These go *inside* closing quotation marks if they are part of the quoted material but outside when they are not. If there's a parenthetical citation at the end, it immediately follows the closing quotation mark, and any punctuation that's part of your sentence comes after.

> Speaking at a Fourth of July celebration in 1852, Frederick Douglass asked, "What have I, or those I represent, to do with your national independence?" (35).

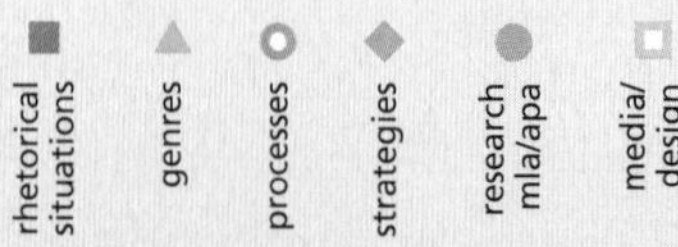

> Who can argue with W. Charisse Goodman's observation that media images persuade women that "thinness equals happiness and fulfillment" (53)?

Colons and semicolons. These always go outside the quotation marks.

> It's hard to argue with W. Charisse Goodman's observation that media images persuade women that "thinness equals happiness and fulfillment"; nevertheless, American women today are more overweight than ever (53).

Paraphrasing

When you paraphrase, you restate information from a source in your own words, using your own sentence structures. Paraphrase when the source material is important but the original wording is not. Because it includes all the main points of the source, a paraphrase is usually about the same length as the original.

Here is a paragraph about synthetic dyes and cancer, followed by three example paraphrases. The first two demonstrate some of the challenges of paraphrasing:

> **ORIGINAL SOURCE**
>
> In 1938, in a series of now-classic experiments, exposure to synthetic dyes derived from coal and belonging to a class of chemicals called aromatic amines was shown to cause bladder cancer in dogs. These results helped explain why bladder cancers had become so prevalent among dyestuffs workers. With the invention of mauve in 1854, synthetic dyes began replacing natural plant-based dyes in the coloring of cloth and leather. By the beginning of the twentieth century, bladder cancer rates among this group of workers had skyrocketed, and the dog experiments helped unravel this mystery. The International Labor Organization did not wait for the results of these animal tests, however, and in 1921 declared certain aromatic amines to be human carcinogens. Decades later, these dogs provided a lead in understanding why tire-industry workers, as well as machinists and metalworkers, also began

falling victim to bladder cancer: aromatic amines had been added to rubbers and cutting oils to serve as accelerants and antirust agents.

—Sandra Steingraber, "Pesticides, Animals, and Humans"

UNACCEPTABLE PARAPHRASE: WORDING TOO CLOSE

Now-classic experiments in 1938 showed that when dogs were exposed to aromatic amines, chemicals used in synthetic dyes derived from coal, they developed bladder cancer. Similar cancers were prevalent among dyestuffs workers, and these experiments helped to explain why. Mauve, a synthetic dye, was invented in 1854, after which cloth and leather manufacturers replaced most of the natural plant-based dyes with synthetic dyes. By the early twentieth century, this group of workers had skyrocketing rates of bladder cancer, a mystery the dog experiments helped to unravel. As early as 1921, though, before the test results proved the connection, the International Labor Organization had labeled certain aromatic amines carcinogenic. Even so, decades later many metalworkers, machinists, and tire-industry workers began developing bladder cancer. The animal tests helped researchers understand that rubbers and cutting oils contained aromatic amines as accelerants and antirust agents (Steingraber 976).

This paraphrase borrows too much of the language of the original or changes it only slightly, as the underlined words and phrases show.

UNACCEPTABLE PARAPHRASE: SENTENCE STRUCTURE TOO CLOSE

In 1938, several pathbreaking experiments showed that being exposed to synthetic dyes that are made from coal and belong to a type of chemicals called aromatic amines caused dogs to get bladder cancer. These results helped researchers identify why cancers of the bladder had become so common among textile workers who worked with dyes. With the development of mauve in 1854, synthetic dyes began to be used instead of dyes based on plants in the dyeing of leather and cloth. By the end of the nineteenth century, rates of bladder cancer among these workers had increased dramatically, and the experiments using dogs helped clear up this oddity. The International

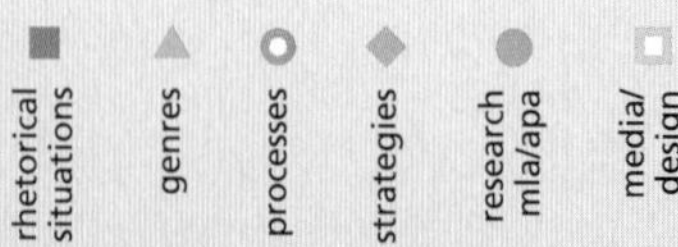

Labor Organization anticipated the results of these tests on animals, though, and in 1921 labeled some aromatic amines carcinogenic. Years later these experiments with dogs helped researchers explain why workers in the tire industry, as well as metalworkers and machinists, also started dying of bladder cancer: aromatic amines had been put into rubbers and cutting oils as rust inhibitors and accelerants (Steingraber 976).

This paraphrase uses original language but follows the sentence structure of Steingraber's text too closely.

ACCEPTABLE PARAPHRASE

Biologist Sandra Steingraber explains that pathbreaking experiments in 1938 demonstrated that dogs exposed to aromatic amines (chemicals used in coal-derived synthetic dyes) developed cancers of the bladder that were similar to cancers common among dyers in the textile industry. After mauve, the first synthetic dye, was invented in 1854, leather and cloth manufacturers replaced most natural dyes made from plants with synthetic dyes, and by the early 1900s textile workers had very high rates of bladder cancer. The experiments with dogs proved the connection, but years before, in 1921, the International Labor Organization had labeled some aromatic amines carcinogenic. Even so, years later many metalworkers, machinists, and workers in the tire industry started to develop unusually high rates of bladder cancer. The experiments with dogs helped researchers understand that the cancers were caused by aromatic amines used in cutting oils to inhibit rust and in rubbers as accelerants (976).

Some guidelines for paraphrasing

- ***Use your own words and sentence structure.*** It is acceptable to use some words from the original, but the phrasing and sentence structures should be your own.
- ***Put in quotation marks any of the source's original phrasing that you use.*** Quotation marks distinguish the source's phrases from your own.

- *Indicate the source of your paraphrase.* Although the wording may be yours, the ideas and information come from another source; be sure to name the author and include an **IN-TEXT CITATION** to avoid the possibility of **PLAGIARISM**.

MLA 432–38
APA 480–85
420–24

Summarizing

A summary states the main ideas found in a source concisely and in your own words. Unlike a paraphrase, a summary does *not* present all the details, so it is generally as brief as possible. Summaries may boil down an entire book or essay into a single sentence, or they may take a paragraph or more to present the main ideas. Here, for example, is a summary of the Steingraber paragraph:

> Steingraber explains that experiments with dogs demonstrated that aromatic amines, chemicals used in synthetic dyes, cutting oils, and rubber, cause bladder cancer (976).

In the context of an essay, the summary might take this form:

> Medical researchers have long relied on experiments using animals to expand understanding of the causes of disease. For example, biologist and ecologist Sandra Steingraber notes that in the second half of the nineteenth century, the rate of bladder cancer soared among textile workers. According to Steingraber, experiments with dogs demonstrated that synthetic chemicals in dyes used to color the textiles caused the cancer (976).

Some guidelines for summarizing

- *Include only the main ideas; leave out the details.* A summary should include just enough information to give the reader the gist of the original. It is always much shorter than the original, sometimes even as brief as one sentence.

- ***Use your own words.*** If you quote from the original, enclose the word or phrase in quotation marks.
- ***Indicate the source.*** Although the wording may be yours, the ideas and information come from another source. Name the author, either in a signal phrase or parentheses, and include an appropriate **IN-TEXT CITATION** to avoid the possibility of **PLAGIARISM**.

432–38 MLA
480–85 APA
420–24

Incorporating Source Materials into Your Text

You need to introduce quotations, paraphrases, and summaries clearly, usually letting readers know who the author is — and, if need be, something about his or her credentials. Consider this sentence:

> Professor and textbook author Elaine Tyler May argues that many high school history books are too bland to interest young readers (531).

The beginning ("Professor and textbook author Elaine Tyler May argues") functions as a *signal phrase*, telling readers who is making the assertion and why she has the authority to speak on the topic — and making clear that everything between the signal phrase and the parenthetical citation comes from that source. Since the signal phrase names the author, the parenthetical citation includes only the page number; had the author not been identified in the signal phrase, she would have been named in the parentheses:

> Even some textbook authors believe that many high school history books are too bland to interest young readers (May 531).

Signal phrases. A signal phrase tells readers who says or believes something. The verb you use can be neutral — *says* or *thinks* — or it can suggest something about the **STANCE** — the source's or your own. The example above referring to the textbook author uses the verb *claims*, suggesting that what she says is arguable (or that the writer believes it is). How would it change your understanding if the signal verb were *observes* or *suggests?*

12–14

SOME COMMON SIGNAL VERBS

acknowledges	claims	disagrees	observes
admits	comments	disputes	points out
advises	concludes	emphasizes	reasons
agrees	concurs	grants	rejects
argues	confirms	illustrates	reports
asserts	contends	implies	responds
believes	declares	insists	suggests
charges	denies	notes	thinks

Verb tenses. MLA and APA have different conventions regarding the verbs that introduce signal phrases. MLA requires present-tense verbs (*writes, asserts, notes*) in signal phrases to introduce a work you are quoting, paraphrasing, or summarizing.

> In *Poor Richard's Almanack*, Benjamin Franklin notes, "He that cannot obey, cannot command" (739).

If, however, you are referring to the act of writing or saying something rather than simply quoting someone's words, you might not use the present tense. The writer of the following sentence focuses on the year in which the source was written—therefore, the verb is necessarily in the past tense:

> Back in 1941, Kenneth Burke wrote that "the ethical values of work are in its application of the competitive equipment to cooperative ends" (316).

If you are following APA style, use the past tense or present-perfect tense to introduce sources composed in the past.

> Dowdall, Crawford, and Wechsler (1998) observed that women attending women's colleges are less likely to engage in binge drinking than are women who attend coeducational colleges (p. 713).

APA requires the present tense, however, to discuss the results of an experiment or to explain conclusions that are generally agreed on.

> The findings of this study suggest that excessive drinking has serious consequences for college students and their institutions.
>
> The authors of numerous studies agree that smoking and drinking among adolescents are associated with lower academic achievement.

IF YOU NEED MORE HELP

See the section on **ACKNOWLEDGING SOURCES, AVOIDING PLAGIARISM** for help in giving credit to the sources you use. See also the **SAMPLE RESEARCH PAPERS** to see how sources are cited in MLA and APA styles.

420–24
467–76 MLA
508–19 APA

47 Acknowledging Sources, Avoiding Plagiarism

Whenever you do research-based writing, you find yourself entering a conversation—reading what many others have had to say about your topic, figuring out what you yourself think, and then putting what you think in writing—"putting in your oar," as the rhetorician Kenneth Burke once wrote. As a writer, you need to *acknowledge* any words and ideas that come from others—to give credit where credit is due, to recognize the various authorities and many perspectives you have considered, to show readers where they can find your sources, and to situate your own arguments in the ongoing conversation. Using other people's words and ideas without acknowledgment is *plagiarism*, a serious academic and ethical offense. This chapter will show you how to acknowledge the materials you use and avoid plagiarism.

Acknowledging Sources

When you insert in your text information that you've obtained from others, your reader needs to know where your source's words or ideas begin and end. Therefore, you should introduce a source by naming the author in a **SIGNAL PHRASE,** and follow it with a brief parenthetical **IN-TEXT CITATION** or by naming the source in a parenthetical citation. (You need only a brief citation here, since your readers will find full bibliographic information in your list of **WORKS CITED** or **REFERENCES.**)

417–18
MLA 432–38
APA 480–85
MLA 439–67
APA 486–508

Sources that need acknowledgment. You almost always need to acknowledge any information that you get from a specific source. Material you should acknowledge includes the following:

- *Direct quotations.* Any quotations from another source must be enclosed in quotation marks, cited with brief bibliographic information in parentheses, and usually introduced with a signal phrase that tells who wrote it and provides necessary contextual information, as in the following sentence:

  > In a dissenting opinion on the issue of racial preferences in college admissions, Supreme Court justice Ruth Bader Ginsburg argues, "The stain of generations of racial oppression is still visible in our society, and the determination to hasten its removal remains vital" (*Gratz v. Bollinger*).

- *Arguable statements and information that may not be common knowledge.* If you state something about which there is disagreement or for which arguments can be made, cite the source of your statement. If in doubt about whether you need to give the source of an assertion, provide it. As part of an essay on "fake news" programs like *The Daily Show*, for example, you might make the following assertion:

  > The satire of *The Daily Show* complements the conservative bias of Fox News, since both have abandoned the stance of objectivity maintained by mainstream news sources, notes Michael Hoyt, executive editor of the *Columbia Journalism Review* (43).

  Others might argue with the contention that the Fox News Channel offers biased reports of the news, so the source of this assertion needs to be acknowledged. In the same essay, you might present information that should be cited because it's not widely known, as in this example:

  > According to a report by the Pew Research Center, 21 percent of Americans under thirty got information about the 2004 presidential campaign primarily from "fake news" and comedy shows like *The Daily Show* and *Saturday Night Live* (2).

- *The opinions and assertions of others.* When you present the ideas, opinions, and assertions of others, cite the source. You may have rewritten the concept in your own words, but the ideas were generated by someone else and must be acknowledged, as they are here:

> Social philosopher David Boonin, writing in the *Journal of Social Philosophy,* asserts that, logically, laws banning marriage between people of different races are not discriminatory since everyone of each race is affected equally by them. Laws banning same-sex unions are discriminatory, however, since they apply only to people with a certain sexual orientation (256).

- ***Any information that you didn't generate yourself.*** If you did not do the research or compile the data yourself, cite your source. This goes for interviews, statistics, graphs, charts, visuals, photographs—anything you use that you did not create. If you create a chart using data from another source, you need to cite that source.
- ***Collaboration with and help from others.*** In many of your courses and in work situations, you'll be called on to work with others. You may get help with your writing at your school's writing center or from fellow students in your writing courses. Acknowledging such collaboration or assistance, in a brief informational note, is a way of giving credit—and saying thank you. See guidelines for writing notes in the **MLA** and **APA** sections of this book.

439
486

Sources that don't need acknowledgment. Widely available information and common knowledge do not require acknowledgment. What constitutes common knowledge may not be clear, however. When in doubt, provide a citation, or ask your instructor whether the information needs to be cited. You generally do not need to cite the following sources:

- ***Information that most readers are likely to know.*** You don't need to acknowledge information that is widely known or commonly accepted as fact. For example, in a literary analysis, you wouldn't cite a source saying that Harriet Beecher Stowe wrote *Uncle Tom's Cabin;* you can assume your readers already know that. On the other hand, you should cite the source from which you got the information that the book was first published in installments in a magazine and then, with revisions, in book form, because that information isn't common knowledge. As you do research in areas you're not familiar with, be aware that what constitutes common knowledge isn't always clear; the history of the novel's publication would be known to Stowe scholars and would likely need no acknowledgment in an essay written for them. In this case, too, if you aren't sure whether to acknowledge information, do so.

- *Information and documents that are widely available.* If a piece of information appears in several sources or reference works or if a document has been published widely, you needn't cite a source for it. For example, the date when astronauts Neil Armstrong and Buzz Aldrin landed a spacecraft on the moon can be found in any number of reference works. Similarly, the Declaration of Independence and the Gettysburg Address are reprinted in thousands of sources, so the ones where you found them need no citation.
- *Well-known quotations.* These include such famous quotations as Lady Macbeth's "Out, damned spot!" and John F. Kennedy's "Ask not what your country can do for you; ask what you can do for your country." Be sure, however, that the quotation is correct; Winston Churchill is said to have told a class of schoolchildren, "Never, ever, ever, ever, ever, ever, ever give up. Never give up. Never give up. Never give up." His actual words, however, taken from a longer speech, are much different and begin "Never give in."
- *Material that you created or gathered yourself.* You need not cite photographs that you took, graphs that you composed based on your own findings, or data from an experiment or survey that you conducted—though you should make sure readers know that the work is yours.

A good rule of thumb: *when in doubt, cite your source.* You're unlikely to be criticized for citing too much—but you may invite charges of plagiarism by citing too little.

Avoiding Plagiarism

When you use the words or ideas of others, you need to acknowledge who and where the material came from; if you don't credit those sources, you are guilty of plagiarism. Plagiarism is often committed unintentionally—

as when a writer paraphrases someone else's ideas in language that is close to the original. It is essential, therefore, to know what constitutes plagiarism: (1) using another writer's words or ideas without in-text citation and documentation, (2) using another writer's exact words without quotation marks, and (3) paraphrasing or summarizing someone else's ideas using language or sentence structures that are too close to theirs.

408–9 To avoid plagiarizing, take careful **NOTES** as you do your research, clearly labeling as quotations any words you quote directly and being careful to use your own phrasing and sentence structures in paraphrases and 425–27 summaries. Be sure you know what source material you must **DOCUMENT**, APA 486–508 and give credit to your sources, both in the text and in a list of **REFERENCES** MLA 439–67 or **WORKS CITED**. Be especially careful with material found online—copying source material right into a document you are writing is all too easy to do. You must acknowledge information you find on the Web just as you must acknowledge all other source materials.

And you must recognize that plagiarism has consequences. Scholars' work will be discredited if it too closely resembles another's. Journalists found to have plagiarized lose their jobs, and students routinely fail courses or are dismissed from their school when they are caught cheating—all too often by submitting as their own essays that they have purchased from online "research" sites. If you're having trouble completing an assignment, seek assistance. Talk with your instructor, or if your school has a writing center, go there for advice on all aspects of your writing, including acknowledging sources and avoiding plagiarism.

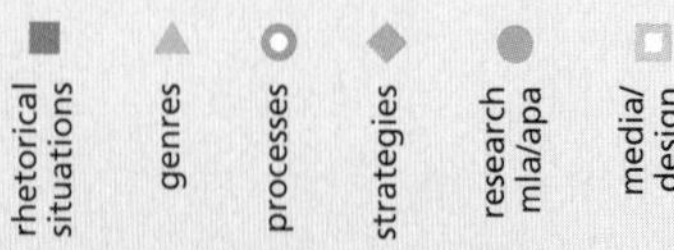

Documentation 48

In everyday life, we are generally aware of our sources: "I read it in the *Post*." "Amber told me it's your birthday." "If you don't believe me, ask Mom." Saying how we know what we know and where we got our information is part of establishing our credibility and persuading others to take what we say seriously.

The goal of a research project is to study a topic, combining what we learn from sources with our own thinking and then composing a written text. When we write up the results of a research project, we cite the sources we use, usually by quoting, paraphrasing, or summarizing, and we acknowledge those sources, telling readers where the ideas came from. The information we give about sources is called documentation, and we provide it not only to establish our credibility as researchers and writers but also so that our readers, if they wish to, can find the sources themselves.

Understanding Documentation Styles

The Norton Field Guide covers the documentation styles of the Modern Language Association (MLA) and the American Psychological Association (APA). MLA style is used chiefly in the humanities; APA is used mainly in the social sciences. Both are two-part systems, consisting of (1) brief in-text parenthetical documentation for quotations, paraphrases, or summaries and (2) more-detailed documentation in a list of sources at the end of the text. MLA and APA require that the end-of-text documentation provide the following basic information about each source you cite:

- author, editor, or organization providing the information
- title of work
- place of publication
- name of organization or company that published it
- date when it was published
- retrieval information for online sources

MLA and APA are by no means the only documentation styles. Many other publishers and organizations have their own style, among them the University of Chicago Press and the Council of Science Editors. We focus on MLA and APA here because those are styles that college students are often required to use. On the following page are examples of how the two parts—the brief parenthetical documentation in your text and the more detailed information at the end—correspond. The top of the next page shows the two parts according to the MLA system; the bottom, the two parts according to the APA system.

As the examples show, when you cite a work in your text, you can name the author either in a signal phrase or in parentheses. If you name the author in a signal phrase, give the page number(s) in parentheses; when the author's name is not given in a signal phrase, include it in the parentheses.

The examples here and throughout this book are color-coded to help you see the crucial parts of each citation: tan for author and editor, yellow for title, and gray for publication information: place of publication, name of publisher, date of publication, page number(s), medium of publication, and so on. Comparing the MLA and APA styles of listing works cited or references reveals some differences: MLA includes an author's first name while APA gives only initials; MLA puts the date at the end while APA places it right after the author's name; MLA requires the medium of publication while APA usually does not; MLA capitalizes most of the words in the title and subtitle while APA capitalizes only the first words and proper nouns of each. Overall, however, the styles provide similar information: each gives author, title, and publication data.

MLA Style

IN-TEXT DOCUMENTATION

As Lester Faigley puts it, "The world has become a bazaar from which to shop for an individual 'lifestyle' " (12).

As one observer suggests, "The world has become a bazaar from which to shop for an individual 'lifestyle' " (Faigley 12).

WORKS-CITED DOCUMENTATION

Faigley, Lester. *Fragments of Rationality: Postmodernity and the Subject of Composition*. Pittsburgh: U of Pittsburgh P, 1992. Print.

APA Style

IN-TEXT DOCUMENTATION

As Faigley (1992) suggested, "The world has become a bazaar from which to shop for an individual 'lifestyle'" (p. 12).

As one observer has noted, "The world has become a bazaar from which to shop for an individual 'lifestyle'" (Faigley, 1992, p. 12).

REFERENCE-LIST DOCUMENTATION

Faigley, L. (1992). *Fragments of rationality: Postmodernity and the subject of composition.* Pittsburgh, PA: University of Pittsburgh Press.

49 MLA Style

Modern Language Association style calls for (1) brief in-text documentation and (2) complete documentation in a list of works cited at the end of your text. The models in this chapter draw on the *MLA Handbook for Writers of Research Papers*, 7th edition (2009). Additional information is available at www.mla.org.

A DIRECTORY TO MLA STYLE

MLA In-Text Documentation 432

author title publication

Notes 439

MLA List of Works Cited 439

author title publication

MLA IN-TEXT DOCUMENTATION

Brief documentation in your text makes clear to your reader what you took from a source and where in the source you found the information.

408–19

In your text, you have three options for citing a source: **QUOTING, PARAPHRASING,** and **SUMMARIZING.** As you cite each source, you will need to decide whether or not to name the author in a signal phrase—"as Toni Morrison writes"—or in parentheses—"(Morrison 24)."

The first examples in this chapter show basic in-text citations of a work by one author. Variations on those examples follow. All of the examples are color-coded to help you see how writers using MLA style work authors and page numbers—and sometimes titles—into their texts. The examples also illustrate the MLA style of using quotation marks around titles of short works and italicizing titles of long works.

1. AUTHOR NAMED IN A SIGNAL PHRASE

If you mention the author in a signal phrase, put only the page number(s) in parentheses. Do not write *page* or *p.*

> McCullough describes John Adams as having "the hands of a man accustomed to pruning his own trees, cutting his own hay, and splitting his own firewood" (18).

> McCullough describes John Adams's hands as those of someone used to manual labor (18).

2. AUTHOR NAMED IN PARENTHESES

If you do not mention the author in a signal phrase, put his or her last name in parentheses along with the page number(s). Do not use punctuation between the name and the page number(s).

> Adams is said to have had "the hands of a man accustomed to pruning his own trees, cutting his own hay, and splitting his own firewood" (McCullough 18).

> One biographer describes John Adams as someone who was not a stranger to manual labor (McCullough 18).

Whether you use a signal phrase and parentheses or parentheses only, try to put the parenthetical citation at the end of the sentence or as close as possible to the material you've cited without awkwardly interrupting the sentence. Notice that in the first example above, the parenthetical reference comes after the closing quotation marks but before the period at the end of the sentence.

3. TWO OR MORE WORKS BY THE SAME AUTHOR

If you cite multiple works by one author, you have four choices. You can mention the author in a signal phrase and give the title and page reference in parentheses. Give the full title if it's brief; otherwise, give a short version.

> Kaplan insists that understanding power in the Near East requires "Western leaders who know when to intervene, and do so without illusions" (*Eastward* 330).

You can mention both author and title in a signal phrase and give only the page reference in parentheses.

> In *Eastward to Tartary*, Kaplan insists that understanding power in the Near East requires "Western leaders who know when to intervene, and do so without illusions" (330).

You can indicate author, title, and page reference only in parentheses, with a comma between author and title.

> Understanding power in the Near East requires "Western leaders who know when to intervene, and do so without illusions" (Kaplan, *Eastward* 330).

Or you can mention the title in a signal phrase and give the author and page reference in parentheses.

> *Eastward to Tartary* argues that understanding power in the Near East requires "Western leaders who know when to intervene, and do so without illusions" (Kaplan 330).

4. AUTHORS WITH THE SAME LAST NAME

If your works-cited list includes works by authors with the same last name, you need to give the author's first name in any signal phrase or the author's first initial in the parenthetical reference.

> Edmund Wilson uses the broader term *imaginative*, whereas Anne Wilson chooses the narrower adjective *magical*.
>
> *Imaginative* applies not only to modern literature (E. Wilson) but also to writing of all periods, whereas *magical* is often used in writing about Arthurian romances (A. Wilson).

5. AFTER A BLOCK QUOTATION

When quoting more than three lines of poetry, more than four lines of prose, or dialogue from a drama, set off the quotation from the rest of your text, indenting it one inch (or ten spaces) from the left margin. Do not use quotation marks. Place any parenthetical documentation *after* the final punctuation.

> In *Eastward to Tartary*, Kaplan captures ancient and contemporary Antioch for us:
>
> > At the height of its glory in the Roman-Byzantine age, when it had an amphitheater, public baths, aqueducts, and sewage pipes, half a million people lived in Antioch. Today the population is only 125,000. With sour relations between Turkey and Syria, and unstable politics throughout the Middle East,

author title publication

> Antioch is now a backwater—seedy and tumbledown, with relatively few tourists. I found it altogether charming. (123)

6. TWO OR MORE AUTHORS

For a work by two or three authors, name all the authors, either in a signal phrase or in the parentheses.

> Carlson and Ventura's stated goal is to introduce Julio Cortázar, Marjorie Agosín, and other Latin American writers to an audience of English-speaking adolescents (v).

For a work with four or more authors, you have the option of mentioning all their names or just the name of the first author followed by *et al.*, which means "and others."

> One popular survey of American literature breaks the contents into sixteen thematic groupings (Anderson, Brinnin, Leggett, Arpin, and Toth A19–24).

> One popular survey of American literature breaks the contents into sixteen thematic groupings (Anderson et al. A19–24).

7. ORGANIZATION OR GOVERNMENT AS AUTHOR

If the author is an organization, cite the organization either in a signal phrase or in parentheses. It's acceptable to shorten long names.

> The U.S. government can be direct when it wants to be. For example, it sternly warns, "If you are overpaid, we will recover any payments not due you" (Social Security Administration 12).

8. AUTHOR UNKNOWN

If you don't know the author of a work, as you won't with many reference books and with most newspaper editorials, use the work's title or a shortened version of the title in the parentheses (examples are on page 436).

The explanatory notes at the front of the literature encyclopedia point out that writers known by pseudonyms are listed alphabetically under those pseudonyms (*Merriam-Webster's* vii).

A powerful editorial in last week's paper asserts that healthy liver donor Mike Hurewitz died because of "frightening" faulty postoperative care ("Every Patient's Nightmare").

9. LITERARY WORKS

When referring to literary works that are available in many different editions, cite the page numbers from the edition you are using, followed by information that will let readers of any edition locate the text you are citing.

NOVELS

Give the page and chapter number.

In *Pride and Prejudice*, Mrs. Bennett shows no warmth toward Jane and Elizabeth when they return from Netherfield (105; ch. 12).

VERSE PLAYS

Give the act, scene, and line numbers; separate them with periods.

Macbeth continues the vision theme when he addresses the Ghost with "Thou hast no speculation in those eyes / Which thou dost glare with" (3.3.96–97).

POEMS

Give the part and the line numbers (separated by periods). If a poem has only line numbers, use the word *line(s)* in the first reference.

Whitman sets up not only opposing adjectives but also opposing nouns in "Song of Myself" when he says, "I am of old and young, of the foolish as much as the wise, / . . . a child as well as a man" (16.330–32).

One description of the mere in *Beowulf* is "not a pleasant place!" (line 1372). Later, the label is "the awful place" (1378).

10. WORK IN AN ANTHOLOGY

If you're citing a work that is included in an anthology, name the author(s) of the work, not the editor of the anthology—either in a signal phrase or in parentheses.

> "It is the teapots that truly shock," according to Cynthia Ozick in her essay on teapots as metaphor (70).
>
> In *In Short: A Collection of Creative Nonfiction*, readers will find both an essay on Scottish tea (Hiestand) and a piece on teapots as metaphors (Ozick).

11. SACRED TEXT

When citing sacred texts such as the Bible or the Qur'an, give the title of the edition used, and in parentheses give the book, chapter, and verse (or their equivalent), separated by periods. MLA style recommends that you abbreviate the names of the books of the Bible in parenthetical references.

> The wording from *The New English Bible* follows: "In the beginning of creation, when God made heaven and earth, the earth was without form and void, with darkness over the face of the abyss, and a mighty wind that swept over the surface of the waters" (Gen. 1.1–2).

12. MULTIVOLUME WORK

If you cite more than one volume of a multivolume work, each time you cite one of the volumes, give the volume *and* the page numbers in parentheses, separated by a colon.

> Sandburg concludes with the following sentence about those paying last respects to Lincoln: "All day long and through the night the unbroken line moved, the home town having its farewell" (4: 413).

If your works-cited list includes only a single volume of a multivolume work, the only number you need to give in your parenthetical reference is the page number.

13. TWO OR MORE WORKS CITED TOGETHER

If you're citing two or more works closely together, you will sometimes need to provide a parenthetical citation for each one.

> Tanner (7) and Smith (viii) have looked at works from a cultural perspective.

If the citation allows you to include both in the same parentheses, separate the references with a semicolon.

> Critics have looked at both *Pride and Prejudice* and *Frankenstein* from a cultural perspective (Tanner 7; Smith viii).

14. SOURCE QUOTED IN ANOTHER SOURCE

When you are quoting text that you found quoted in another source, use the abbreviation *qtd. in* in the parenthetical reference.

> Charlotte Brontë wrote to G. H. Lewes: "Why do you like Miss Austen so very much? I am puzzled on that point" (qtd. in Tanner 7).

15. WORK WITHOUT PAGE NUMBERS

For works without page numbers, give paragraph or section numbers if they appear in the source text; use the abbreviation *par.* or *sec.* If you are including the author's name in the parenthetical reference, add a comma.

> Russell's dismissals from Trinity College at Cambridge and from City College in New York City are seen as examples of the controversy that marked the philosopher's life (Irvine, par. 2).

16. AN ENTIRE WORK OR ONE-PAGE ARTICLE

If your text is referring to an entire work rather than a part of it or a one-page-long article, identify the author in a signal phrase or in parentheses. There's no need to include page numbers.

> Kaplan considers Turkey and Central Asia explosive.

> At least one observer considers Turkey and Central Asia explosive (Kaplan).

NOTES

Sometimes you may need to give information that doesn't fit into the text itself—to thank people who helped you, provide additional details, or refer readers to other sources not cited in your text. Such information can be given in a *footnote* (at the bottom of the page) or an *endnote* (on a separate page with the heading *Notes* just before your works-cited list. Put a superscript number at the appropriate point in your text, signaling to readers to look for the note with the corresponding number. If you have multiple notes, number them consecutively throughout your paper.

TEXT

This essay will argue that small liberal arts colleges should not recruit athletes and, more specifically, that giving student athletes preferential treatment undermines the larger educational goals.[1]

NOTE

[1]I want to thank all those who have contributed to my thinking on this topic, especially my classmates and my teachers Marian Johnson and Diane O'Connor.

MLA LIST OF WORKS CITED

A works-cited list provides full bibliographic information for every source cited in your text. The list should be alphabetized by authors' last names (or sometimes by editors' or translators' names). Works that do not have an identifiable author or editor are alphabetized by title, disregarding *A*, *An*, and *The*. See pages 475–76 for a sample works-cited list.

Books

BASIC FORMAT FOR A BOOK

For most books, you'll need to provide information about the author; the title and any subtitle; and the place of publication, publisher, and date. (You'll find this information on the book's title page and copyright page.) At the end of the citation provide the medium—Print.

Greenblatt, Stephen. *Will in the World: How Shakespeare Became Shakespeare*. New York: Norton, 2004. Print.

A FEW DETAILS TO NOTE

- **AUTHORS:** Include the author's middle name or initials, if any.
- **TITLES:** Capitalize the first and last words of titles, subtitles, and all principal words. Do not capitalize *a*, *an*, *the*, *to*, or any prepositions or coordinating conjunctions unless they begin a title or subtitle.
- **PLACE OF PUBLICATION:** If more than one city is given, use only the first.
- **PUBLISHER:** Use a short form of the publisher's name (Norton for W. W. Norton & Company, Princeton UP for Princeton University Press).
- **DATES:** If more than one year is given, use the most recent one.

1. ONE AUTHOR

Author's Last Name, First Name. *Title*. Publication City: Publisher, Year of publication. Medium.

Anderson, Curtis. *The Long Tail: Why the Future of Business Is Selling Less of More*. New York: Hyperion, 2006. Print.

When the title of a book itself contains the title of another book (or other long work), do not italicize that title.

Walker, Roy. *Time Is Free: A Study of* Macbeth. London: Dakers, 1949. Print.

When the title of a book contains the title of a short work, the title of the short work should be enclosed in quotation marks, and the entire title should be italicized.

Thompson, Lawrance Roger. *"Fire and Ice": The Art and Thought of Robert Frost*. New York: Holt, 1942. Print.

author title publication

Documentation Map (MLA)

Book

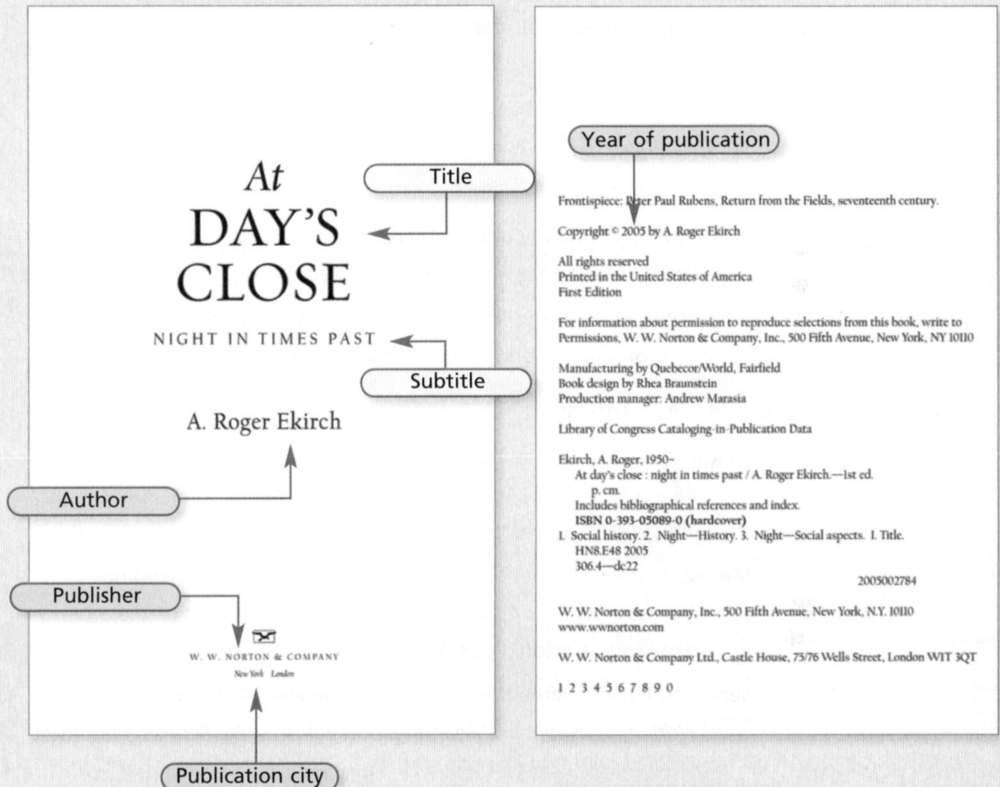

At
DAY'S
CLOSE

NIGHT IN TIMES PAST

A. Roger Ekirch

W. W. NORTON & COMPANY
New York London

Frontispiece: Peter Paul Rubens, Return from the Fields, seventeenth century.

Copyright © 2005 by A. Roger Ekirch

All rights reserved
Printed in the United States of America
First Edition

For information about permission to reproduce selections from this book, write to Permissions, W. W. Norton & Company, Inc., 500 Fifth Avenue, New York, NY 10110

Manufacturing by Quebecor/World, Fairfield
Book design by Rhea Braunstein
Production manager: Andrew Marasia

Library of Congress Cataloging-in-Publication Data

Ekirch, A. Roger, 1950–
At day's close : night in times past / A. Roger Ekirch.—1st ed.
p. cm.
Includes bibliographical references and index.
ISBN 0-393-05089-0 (hardcover)
1. Social history. 2. Night—History. 3. Night—Social aspects. I. Title.
HN8.E48 2005
306.4—dc22
2005002784

W. W. Norton & Company, Inc., 500 Fifth Avenue, New York, N.Y. 10110
www.wwnorton.com

W. W. Norton & Company Ltd., Castle House, 75/76 Wells Street, London WIT 3QT

1 2 3 4 5 6 7 8 9 0

439–47 for more on citing books MLA style

Author's Last Name, First Name. *Title: Subtitle*. Publication City: Publisher, Year of Publication. Medium.

Ekirch, A. Roger. *At Day's Close: Night in Times Past*. New York: Norton, 2005. Print.

2. TWO OR MORE WORKS BY THE SAME AUTHOR(S)

Give the author's name in the first entry, and then use three hyphens in the author slot for each of the subsequent works, listing them alphabetically by the first important word of each title.

Author's Last Name, First Name. *Title That Comes First Alphabetically*. Publication City: Publisher, Year of publication. Medium.

---. *Title That Comes Next Alphabetically*. Publication City: Publisher, Year of publication. Medium.

Kaplan, Robert D. *The Coming Anarchy: Shattering the Dreams of the Post Cold War*. New York: Random, 2000. Print.

---. *Eastward to Tartary: Travels in the Balkans, the Middle East, and the Caucasus*. New York: Random, 2000. Print.

3. TWO OR THREE AUTHORS

First Author's Last Name, First Name, Second Author's First and Last Names, and Third Author's First and Last Names. *Title*. Publication City: Publisher, Year of publication. Medium.

Malless, Stanley, and Jeffrey McQuain. *Coined by God: Words and Phrases That First Appear in the English Translations of the Bible*. New York: Norton, 2003. Print.

Sebranek, Patrick, Verne Meyer, and Dave Kemper. *Writers INC: A Guide to Writing, Thinking, and Learning*. Burlington: Write Source, 1990. Print.

4. FOUR OR MORE AUTHORS

You may give each author's name or the name of the first author only, followed by *et al.*, Latin for "and others."

First Author's Last Name, First Name, Second Author's First and Last Names, Third Author's First and Last Names, and Final Author's First and Last Names. *Title*. Publication City: Publisher, Year of publication. Medium.

author title publication

Anderson, Robert, John Malcolm Brinnin, John Leggett, Gary Q. Arpin, and Susan Allen Toth. *Elements of Literature: Literature of the United States*. Austin: Holt, 1993. Print.

Anderson, Robert, et al. *Elements of Literature: Literature of the United States*. Austin: Holt, 1993. Print.

5. ORGANIZATION OR GOVERNMENT AS AUTHOR

Sometimes the author is a corporation or government organization.

Organization Name. *Title*. Publication City: Publisher, Year of publication. Medium.

Diagram Group. *The Macmillan Visual Desk Reference*. New York: Macmillan, 1993. Print.

National Assessment of Educational Progress. *The Civics Report Card*. Princeton: ETS, 1990. Print.

6. ANTHOLOGY

Editor's Last Name, First Name, ed. *Title*. Publication City: Publisher, Year of publication. Medium.

Hall, Donald, ed. *The Oxford Book of Children's Verse in America*. New York: Oxford UP, 1985. Print.

If there is more than one editor, list the first editor last-name-first and the others first-name-first.

Kitchen, Judith, and Mary Paumier Jones, eds. *In Short: A Collection of Brief Creative Nonfiction*. New York: Norton, 1996. Print.

7. WORK(S) IN AN ANTHOLOGY

Author's Last Name, First Name. "Title of Work." *Title of Anthology*. Ed. Editor's First and Last Names. Publication City: Publisher, Year of publication. Pages. Medium.

Achebe, Chinua. "Uncle Ben's Choice." *The Seagull Reader: Literature*. Ed. Joseph Kelly. New York: Norton, 2005. 23–27. Print.

To document two or more selections from one anthology, list each selection by author and title, followed by the anthology editor(s)' names and the pages of the selection. Then include an entry for the anthology itself (see no. 6 on page 443).

Author's Last Name, First Name. "Title of Work." Anthology Editor's Last Name Pages.

Hiestand, Emily. "Afternoon Tea." Kitchen and Jones 65–67.

Ozick, Cynthia. "The Shock of Teapots." Kitchen and Jones 68–71.

Do not list the anthology separately if you're citing only one selection.

8. AUTHOR AND EDITOR

Start with the author if you've cited the text itself.

Author's Last Name, First Name. *Title*. Ed. Editor's First and Last Names. Publication City: Publisher, Year of publication. Medium.

Austen, Jane. *Emma*. Ed. Stephen M. Parrish. New York: Norton, 2000. Print.

Start with the editor if you've cited his or her work.

Editor's Last Name, First Name, ed. *Title*. By Author's First and Last Names. Publication City: Publisher, Year of publication. Medium.

Parrish, Stephen M., ed. *Emma*. By Jane Austen. New York: Norton, 2000. Print.

9. NO AUTHOR OR EDITOR

Title. Publication City: Publisher, Year of publication. Medium.

2008 New York City Restaurants. New York: Zagat, 2008. Print.

10. TRANSLATION

Start with the author to emphasize the work itself.

Author's Last Name, First Name. *Title*. Trans. Translator's First and Last Names. Publication City: Publisher, Year of publication. Medium.

Dostoevsky, Fyodor. *Crime and Punishment*. Trans. Richard Pevear and Larissa Volokhonsky. New York: Vintage, 1993. Print.

author title publication

Start with the translator to emphasize the translation.

Translator's Last Name, First Name, trans. *Title*. By Author's First and Last Names. Publication City: Publisher, Year of publication. Medium.

Pevear, Richard, and Larissa Volokhonsky, trans. *Crime and Punishment*. By Fyodor Dostoevsky. New York: Vintage, 1993. Print.

11. GRAPHIC NARRATIVE

Start with the name of the person whose contribution is most relevant to your research, and include labels to indicate each collaborator's role.

Author's Last Name, First Name, writer. *Title*. Illus. Artist's First and Last Names. Publication City: Publisher, Year of publication. Medium.

Pekar, Harvey, writer. *American Splendor: Bob and Harv's Comics*. Illus. R. Crumb. New York: Four Walls Eight Windows, 1996. Print.

Crumb, R., illus. *American Splendor: Bob and Harv's Comics*. By Harvey Pekar. New York: Four Walls Eight Windows, 1996. Print.

If the work was written and illustrated by the same person, format the entry like that of any other book.

12. FOREWORD, INTRODUCTION, PREFACE, OR AFTERWORD

Part Author's Last Name, First Name. Name of Part. *Title of Book*. By Author's First and Last Names. Publication City: Publisher, Year of publication. Pages. Medium.

Tanner, Tony. Introduction. *Pride and Prejudice*. By Jane Austen. London: Penguin, 1972. 7–46. Print.

13. MULTIVOLUME WORK

If you cite all the volumes of a multivolume work, give the number of volumes after the title.

Author's Last Name, First Name. *Title of Complete Work*. Number of vols. Publication City: Publisher, Year of publication. Medium.

Sandburg, Carl. *Abraham Lincoln: The War Years*. 4 vols. New York: Harcourt, 1939. Print.

If you cite only one volume, give the volume number after the title.

Sandburg, Carl. *Abraham Lincoln: The War Years*. Vol. 2. New York: Harcourt, 1939. Print.

14. ARTICLE IN A REFERENCE BOOK

Provide the author's name if the article is signed. If the reference work is well known, give only the edition and year of publication.

Author's Last Name, First Name. "Title of Article." *Title of Reference Book*. Edition number. Year of publication. Medium.

"Histrionics." *Merriam-Webster's Collegiate Dictionary.* 11th ed. 2003. Print.

If the reference work is less familiar or more specialized, give full publication information. If it has only one volume or is in its first edition, omit that information.

Author's Last Name, First Name. "Title of Article." *Title of Reference Book*. Ed. Editor's First and Last Name. Edition number. Number of vols. Publication City: Publisher, Year of publication. Medium.

Campbell, James. "The Harlem Renaissance." *The Oxford Companion to Twentieth-Century Poetry.* Ed. Ian Hamilton. Oxford: Oxford UP, 1994. Print.

15. BOOK IN A SERIES

Editor's Last Name, First Name, ed. *Title of Book*. By Author's First and Last Names. Publication City: Publisher, Year of publication. Medium. Series Title abbreviated.

author title publication

Wall, Cynthia, ed. *The Pilgrim's Progress*. By John Bunyan. New York: Norton, 2007. Print. Norton Critical Ed.

16. SACRED TEXT

If you have cited a specific edition of a religious text, you need to include it in your works-cited list.

Title. Editor's First and Last Names, ed. (if any) Publication City: Publisher, Year of publication. Medium.

The New English Bible with the Apocrypha. New York: Oxford UP, 1971. Print.

The Torah: A Modern Commentary. W. Gunther Plaut, ed. New York: Union of American Hebrew Congregations, 1981. Print.

17. EDITION OTHER THAN THE FIRST

Author's Last Name, First Name. *Title*. Name or number of ed. Publication City: Publisher, Year of publication. Medium.

Gibaldi, Joseph. *MLA Handbook for Writers of Research Papers*. 6th ed. New York: MLA, 2003. Print.

Hirsch, E. D., Jr., ed. *What Your Second Grader Needs to Know: Fundamentals of a Good Second-Grade Education*. Rev. ed. New York: Doubleday, 1998. Print.

18. REPUBLISHED WORK

Give the original publication date after the title, followed by the publication information of the republished edition.

Author's Last Name, First Name. *Title*. Year of original edition. Publication City: Current Publisher, Year of republication. Medium.

Bierce, Ambrose. *Civil War Stories*. 1909. New York: Dover, 1994. Print.

Periodicals

BASIC FORMAT FOR AN ARTICLE

For most articles, you'll need to provide information about the author, the article title and any subtitle, the periodical title, any volume or issue number, the date, inclusive page numbers, and the medium—Print.

Rancière, Jacques. "Why Emma Bovary Had to Be Killed."*Critical Inquiry* 34.2 (2009): 233–48. Print.

A FEW DETAILS TO NOTE

- **AUTHORS**: If there is more than one author, list the first author last-name-first and the others first-name-first.
- **TITLES**: Capitalize the first and last words of titles and subtitles and all principal words. Do not capitalize *a*, *an*, *the*, *to*, or any prepositions or coordinating conjunctions unless they begin a title or subtitle. For periodical titles, omit any initial *A*, *An*, or *The*.
- **DATES**: Abbreviate the names of months except for May, June, or July: Jan., Feb., Mar., Apr., Aug., Sept., Oct., Nov., Dec. Journals paginated by volume or issue call only for the year (in parentheses).
- **PAGES**: If an article does not fall on consecutive pages, give the first page with a plus sign (55+).

19. ARTICLE IN A JOURNAL

Author's Last Name, First Name. "Title of Article." *Title of Journal* Volume.Issue (Year): Pages. Medium.

Cooney, Brian C. "Considering *Robinson Crusoe*'s 'Liberty of Conscience' " in an Age of Terror." *College English* 69.3 (2007): 197–215. Print.

20. ARTICLE IN A JOURNAL NUMBERED BY ISSUE

Author's Last Name, First Name. "Title of Article." *Title of Journal* Issue (Year): Pages. Medium.

Flynn, Kevin. "The Railway in Canadian Poetry." *Canadian Literature* 174 (2002): 70–95. Print.

author title publication

Documentation Map (MLA)
Article in a Journal

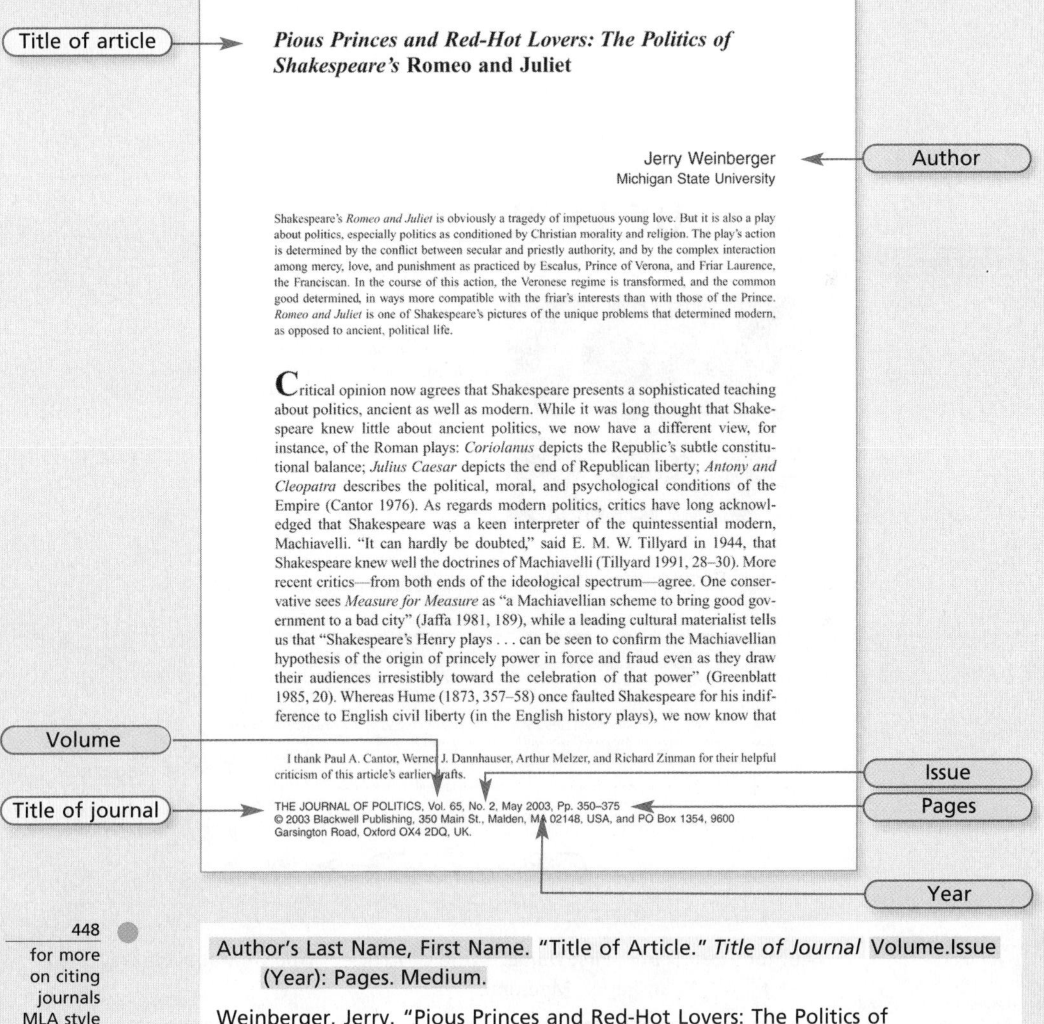

***Pious Princes and Red-Hot Lovers: The Politics of Shakespeare's* Romeo and Juliet**

Jerry Weinberger
Michigan State University

Shakespeare's *Romeo and Juliet* is obviously a tragedy of impetuous young love. But it is also a play about politics, especially politics as conditioned by Christian morality and religion. The play's action is determined by the conflict between secular and priestly authority, and by the complex interaction among mercy, love, and punishment as practiced by Escalus, Prince of Verona, and Friar Laurence, the Franciscan. In the course of this action, the Veronese regime is transformed, and the common good determined, in ways more compatible with the friar's interests than with those of the Prince. *Romeo and Juliet* is one of Shakespeare's pictures of the unique problems that determined modern, as opposed to ancient, political life.

Critical opinion now agrees that Shakespeare presents a sophisticated teaching about politics, ancient as well as modern. While it was long thought that Shakespeare knew little about ancient politics, we now have a different view, for instance, of the Roman plays: *Coriolanus* depicts the Republic's subtle constitutional balance; *Julius Caesar* depicts the end of Republican liberty; *Antony and Cleopatra* describes the political, moral, and psychological conditions of the Empire (Cantor 1976). As regards modern politics, critics have long acknowledged that Shakespeare was a keen interpreter of the quintessential modern, Machiavelli. "It can hardly be doubted," said E. M. W. Tillyard in 1944, that Shakespeare knew well the doctrines of Machiavelli (Tillyard 1991, 28–30). More recent critics—from both ends of the ideological spectrum—agree. One conservative sees *Measure for Measure* as "a Machiavellian scheme to bring good government to a bad city" (Jaffa 1981, 189), while a leading cultural materialist tells us that "Shakespeare's Henry plays . . . can be seen to confirm the Machiavellian hypothesis of the origin of princely power in force and fraud even as they draw their audiences irresistibly toward the celebration of that power" (Greenblatt 1985, 20). Whereas Hume (1873, 357–58) once faulted Shakespeare for his indifference to English civil liberty (in the English history plays), we now know that

I thank Paul A. Cantor, Werner J. Dannhauser, Arthur Melzer, and Richard Zinman for their helpful criticism of this article's earlier drafts.

THE JOURNAL OF POLITICS, Vol. 65, No. 2, May 2003, Pp. 350–375
© 2003 Blackwell Publishing, 350 Main St., Malden, MA 02148, USA, and PO Box 1354, 9600 Garsington Road, Oxford OX4 2DQ, UK.

448 for more on citing journals MLA style

Author's Last Name, First Name. "Title of Article." *Title of Journal* Volume.Issue (Year): Pages. Medium.

Weinberger, Jerry. "Pious Princes and Red-Hot Lovers: The Politics of Shakespeare's *Romeo and Juliet*." *Journal of Politics* 65.2 (2003): 350–75. Print.

Documentation Map (MLA)
Article in a Magazine

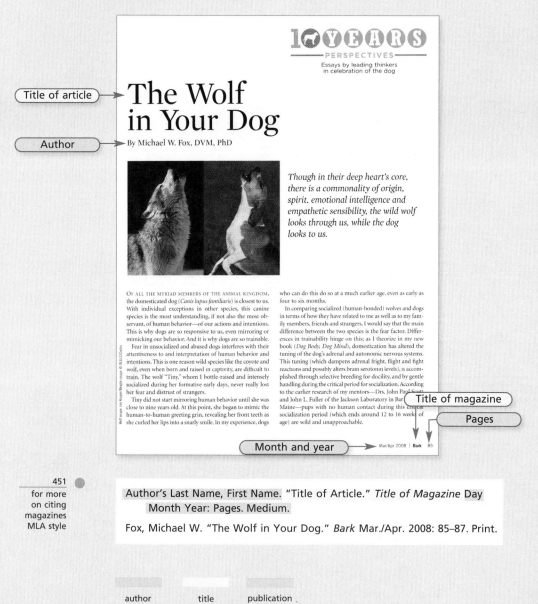

PERSPECTIVES

Essays by leading thinkers in celebration of the dog

Title of article → **The Wolf in Your Dog**

Author → By Michael W. Fox, DVM, PhD

Though in their deep heart's core, there is a commonality of origin, spirit, emotional intelligence and empathetic sensibility, the wild wolf looks through us, while the dog looks to us.

Wolf image: Jim Kruger/Beagle image: © DLILLC/Corbis

OF ALL THE MYRIAD MEMBERS OF THE ANIMAL KINGDOM, the domesticated dog (*Canis lupus familiaris*) is closest to us. With individual exceptions in other species, this canine species is the most understanding, if not also the most observant, of human behavior—of our actions and intentions. This is why dogs are so responsive to us, even mirroring or mimicking our behavior. And it is why dogs are so trainable.

Fear in unsocialized and abused dogs interferes with their attentiveness to and interpretation of human behavior and intentions. This is one reason wild species like the coyote and wolf, even when born and raised in captivity, are difficult to train. The wolf "Tiny," whom I bottle-raised and intensely socialized during her formative early days, never really lost her fear and distrust of strangers.

Tiny did not start mirroring human behavior until she was close to nine years old. At this point, she began to mimic the human-to-human greeting grin, revealing her front teeth as she curled her lips into a snarly smile. In my experience, dogs who can do this do so at a much earlier age, even as early as four to six months.

In comparing socialized (human-bonded) wolves and dogs in terms of how they have related to me as well as to my family members, friends and strangers, I would say that the main difference between the two species is the fear factor. Differences in trainability hinge on this; as I theorize in my new book (*Dog Body, Dog Mind*), domestication has altered the tuning of the dog's adrenal and autonomic nervous systems. This tuning (which dampens adrenal fright, flight and fight reactions and possibly alters brain serotonin levels), is accomplished through selective breeding for docility, and by gentle handling during the critical period for socialization. According to the earlier research of my mentors—Drs. John Paul Scott and John L. Fuller of the Jackson Laboratory in Bar Maine—pups with no human contact during this critical socialization period (which ends around 12 to 16 weeks of age) are wild and unapproachable.

Title of magazine

Pages

Month and year → Mar/Apr 2008 | **Bark** 85

451 for more on citing magazines MLA style

Author's Last Name, First Name. "Title of Article." *Title of Magazine* Day Month Year: Pages. Medium.

Fox, Michael W. "The Wolf in Your Dog." *Bark* Mar./Apr. 2008: 85–87. Print.

author title publication

21. ARTICLE IN A MAGAZINE

Author's Last Name, First Name. "Title of Article." *Title of Magazine* Day Month Year: Pages. Medium.

Walsh, Bryan. "Not a Watt to Be Wasted." *Time* 17 Mar. 2008: 46–47. Print.

For a monthly magazine, include only the month and year.

Fellman, Bruce. "Leading the Libraries." *Yale Alumni Magazine* Feb. 2002: 26–31. Print.

22. ARTICLE IN A DAILY NEWSPAPER

Author's Last Name, First Name. "Title of Article." *Name of Newspaper* Day Month Year: Pages. Medium.

Springer, Shira. "Celtics Reserves Are Whizzes vs. Wizards." *Boston Globe* 14 Mar. 2005: D4+. Print.

If you are documenting a particular edition of a newspaper, specify the edition (late ed., natl. ed., etc.) between the date and the section and page.

Svoboda, Elizabeth. "Faces, Faces Everywhere." *New York Times* 13 Feb. 2007, natl. ed.: D1+. Print.

23. UNSIGNED ARTICLE

"Title of Article." *Name of Publication* Day Month Year: Page(s). Medium.

"Being Invisible Closer to Reality." *Atlanta Journal-Constitution* 11 Aug. 2008: A3. Print.

24. EDITORIAL

"Title." Editorial. *Name of Publication* Day Month Year: Page. Medium.

"Gas, Cigarettes Are Safe to Tax." Editorial. *Lakeville Journal* 17 Feb. 2005: A10. Print.

25. LETTER TO THE EDITOR

Author's Last Name, First Name. "Title (if any)." Letter. *Name of Publication* Day Month Year: Page. Medium.

Festa, Roger. "Social Security: Another Phony Crisis." Letter. *Lakeville Journal* 17 Feb. 2005: A10. Print.

26. REVIEW

Author's Last Name, First Name. "Title (if any) of Review." Rev. of *Title of Work*, by Author's First and Last Names. *Title of Periodical* Day Month Year: Pages. Medium.

Frank, Jeffrey. "Body Count." Rev. of *The Exception*, by Christian Jungersen. *New Yorker* 30 July 2007: 86–87. Print.

Electronic Sources

BASIC FORMAT FOR AN ELECTRONIC SOURCE

Not every electronic source gives you all the data that MLA would like to see in a works-cited entry. Ideally, you will be able to list the author's name, the title, information about print publication, information about electronic publication (title of site, editor, date of first electronic publication and/or most recent revision, name of the publisher or sponsoring institution), date of access, the publication medium and, if necessary, a URL. Of those ten items, you will find seven in the following example.

Johnson, Charles W. "How Our Laws Are Made." *Thomas: Legislative Information on the Internet*. Lib. of Congress, 30 June 2003. Web. 21 June 2008.

A FEW DETAILS TO NOTE

- **AUTHORS OR EDITORS:** If there is more than one author or editor, list the first one last-name-first and the others first-name-first.
- **TITLES:** Capitalize titles and subtitles as you would for a print book or periodical.
- **PUBLISHER:** If the name of the publisher or sponsoring institution is unavailable, use *N.p.*
- **DATES:** Abbreviate the months as you would for a print periodical. Although MLA asks for the date when materials were first posted or

author title publication

most recently updated, you won't always be able to find that information; if it's unavailable, use *n.d.* You'll also find that it will vary—you may find only the year, not the day and month. The date you must include is the date on which you accessed the electronic source.

- **MEDIUM:** Indicate the medium—Web, Email, CD-ROM, and so on.
- **URL:** MLA assumes that readers can locate most sources on the Web by searching for the author, title, or other identifying information, so they don't require a URL for most online sources. When users can't locate the source without a URL, give the address of the website in angle brackets. When a URL won't fit on one line, break it only after a slash (and do not add a hyphen). If a URL is very long, consider giving the URL of the site's home or search page instead.

27. ENTIRE WEBSITE

For websites with an editor, compiler, director, narrator, or translator, follow the name with the appropriate abbreviation (*ed.*, *comp.*, *dir.*, *narr.*, *trans.*).

Author's Last Name, First Name. *Title of Website*. Publisher or Sponsoring Institution, Date posted or last updated. Medium. Day Month Year of access.

Zalta, Edward N., ed. *Stanford Encyclopedia of Philosophy*. Metaphysics Research Lab, Center for the Study of Language and Information, Stanford U, 2007. Web. 25 July 2008.

PERSONAL WEBSITE

Author's Last Name, First Name. Home page. Publisher or Sponsoring Institution, Date posted or last updated. Medium. Day Month Year of access.

Nunberg, Geoffrey. Home page. School of Information, U of California, Berkeley, 2009. Web. 13 Apr. 2009.

28. WORK FROM A WEBSITE

Author's Last Name, First Name. "Title of Work." *Title of Website.* Ed. Editor's First and Last Names. Sponsoring Institution, Date posted or last updated. Medium. Day Month Year of access.

Buff, Rachel Ida. "Becoming American." *Immigration History Research Center*. U of Minnesota, 24 Mar. 2008. Web. 4 Apr. 2008.

29. ONLINE BOOK OR PART OF A BOOK

Author's Last Name, First Name. "Title of Short Work." *Title of Long Work*. Original city of publication: Original publisher, Original year of publication. Original pages. *Title of Website or Database.* Medium. Day Month Year of access.

Anderson, Sherwood. "The Philosopher." *Winesburg, Ohio*. New York: B. W. Huebsch, 1919. N. pag. *Bartleby.com*. Web. 7 Apr. 2008.

30. ARTICLE IN AN ONLINE SCHOLARLY JOURNAL

If a journal does not number pages or if it numbers each article separately, use *n. pag.* in place of page numbers.

Author's Last Name, First Name. "Title of Article." *Title of Journal* Volume.Issue (Year): Pages. Medium. Day Month Year of access.

Gleckman, Jason. "Shakespeare as Poet or Playwright? The Player's Speech in *Hamlet*." *Early Modern Literary Studies* 11.3 (2006): n. pag. Web. 24 June 2008.

31. ARTICLE IN AN ONLINE NEWSPAPER

Author's Last Name, First Name. "Title of Article." *Title of Newspaper*. Publisher, Day Month Year. Medium. Day Month Year of access.

Banerjee, Neela. "Proposed Religion-Based Program for Federal Inmates Is Canceled." *New York Times*. New York Times, 28 Oct. 2006. Web. 24 June 2008.

author title publication

Documentation Map (MLA)
Work from a Website

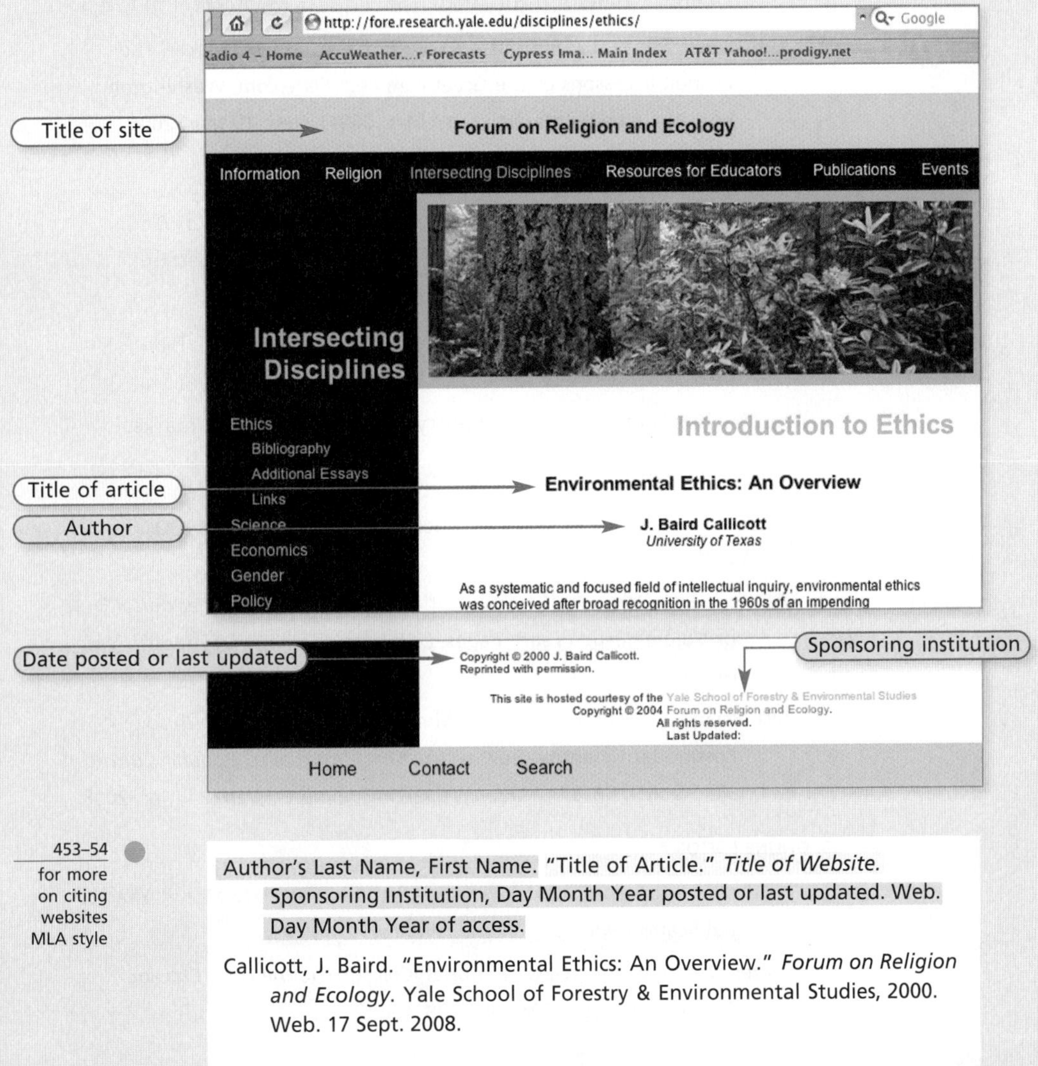

453–54 for more on citing websites MLA style

Author's Last Name, First Name. "Title of Article." *Title of Website.* Sponsoring Institution, Day Month Year posted or last updated. Web. Day Month Year of access.

Callicott, J. Baird. "Environmental Ethics: An Overview." *Forum on Religion and Ecology.* Yale School of Forestry & Environmental Studies, 2000. Web. 17 Sept. 2008.

32. ARTICLE IN AN ONLINE MAGAZINE

Author's Last Name, First Name. "Title of Article." *Title of Magazine*. Publisher, Date of publication. Medium. Day Month Year of access.

Landsburg, Steven E. "Putting All Your Potatoes in One Basket: The Economic Lessons of the Great Famine." *Slate.com*. Washington Post–Newsweek Interactive, 13 Mar. 2001. Web. 15 Mar. 2006.

33. BLOG ENTRY

Author's Last Name, First Name. "Title of Blog Entry." *Title of Blog*. Publisher or Sponsoring Institution, Day Month Year posted. Medium. Day Month Year of access.

Gladwell, Malcolm. "Enron and Newspapers." *Gladwell.com*. N.p., 4 Jan. 2007. Web. 26 Aug. 2008.

If the entry has no title, use "Blog entry" without quotation marks.

34. ARTICLE ACCESSED THROUGH AN ONLINE DATABASE

Many library subscription services, such as InfoTrac and EBSCO, provide access to texts for a fee.

Author's Last Name, First Name. "Title of Article." *Title of Periodical* Date or Volume.Issue (Year): Pages. *Database*. Medium. Day Month Year of access.

Ott, Brian L. " 'I'm Bart Simpson, Who the Hell Are You?': A Study in Postmodern Identity (Re)Construction." *Journal of Popular Culture* 37.1 (2003): 56–82. *Academic Search Complete*. Web. 24 Mar. 2008.

35. ONLINE EDITORIAL

"Title of Editorial." Editorial. *Title of Site*. Publisher, Day Month Year of publication. Medium. Day Month Year of access.

"Keep Drinking Age at 21." Editorial. *ChicagoTribune.com*. Chicago Tribune, 25 Aug. 2008. Web. 28 Aug. 2008.

author title publication

Documentation Map (MLA)

Article in a Database

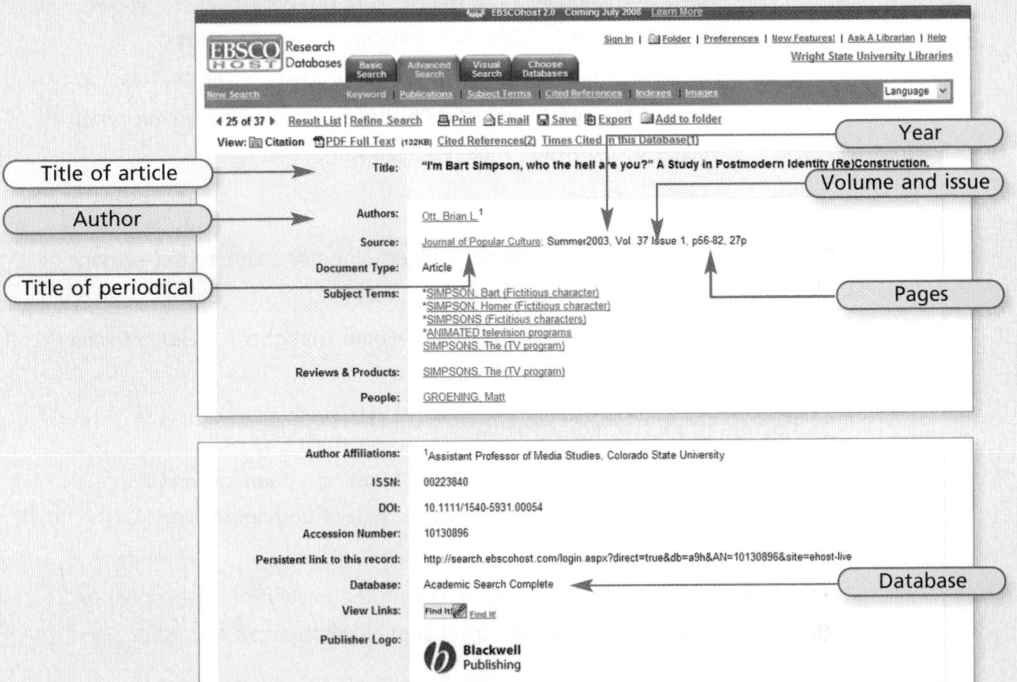

456 for more on citing an article in a database MLA style

Author's Last Name, First Name. "Title of Article." *Title of Periodical* Volume.Issue (Year): Pages. *Database*. Medium. Day Month Year of access.

Ott, Brian L. "'I'm Bart Simpson, Who the Hell Are You?' A Study in Postmodern Identity (Re)Construction." *Journal of Popular Culture* 37.1 (2003): 56–82. *Academic Search Complete*. Web. 24 Mar. 2008.

36. ONLINE REVIEW

Author's Last Name, First Name. "Title of Review." Rev. of *Title of Work*, by Author's First and Last Names. *Title of Website*. Publisher, Day Month Year posted. Medium. Day Month Year of access.

Foundas, Scott. "Heath Ledger Peers into the Abyss in *The Dark Knight*." Rev. of *The Dark Knight*, dir. Christopher Nolan. *VillageVoice.com*. Village Voice, 16 Jul. 2008. Web. 26 Aug. 2008.

37. EMAIL

Writer's Last Name, First Name. "Subject Line." Message to the author. Day Month Year of message. Medium.

Smith, William. "Teaching Grammar—Some Thoughts." Message to the author. 19 Nov. 2007. Email.

38. POSTING TO AN ELECTRONIC FORUM

Writer's Last Name, First Name. "Title of Posting." *Name of Forum*. Sponsoring Institution, Day Month Year of posting. Medium. Day Month Year of access.

Mintz, Stephen H. "Manumission During the Revolution." *H-Net List on Slavery*. Michigan State U, 14 Sept. 2006. Web. 18 Apr. 2009.

39. ARTICLE IN AN ONLINE REFERENCE WORK

"Title of Article." *Title of Reference Work*. Sponsor of work, Date of work. Medium. Day Month Year of access.

"Dubai." *MSN Encarta*. Microsoft Corporation, 2008. Web. 20 June 2008.

40. ENTRY IN A WIKI

"Title of Entry." *Title of Wiki*. Sponsoring Institution, Day Month Year updated. Medium. Day Month Year of access.

"Pi." *Wikipedia*. Wikimedia Foundation, 28 Aug. 2008. Web. 2 Sept. 2008.

author title publication

41. CD-ROM OR DVD-ROM

FOR A SINGLE-ISSUE CD-ROM

Title. Any pertinent information about the edition, release, or version. Publication City: Publisher, Year of publication. Medium.

Othello. Princeton: Films for the Humanities and Sciences, 1998. CD-ROM.

If you are citing only part of the CD-ROM or DVD-ROM, name the part as you would a part of a book.

"Snow Leopard." *Encarta Encyclopedia 2007*. Seattle: Microsoft, 2007. CD-ROM.

FOR A PERIODICAL ON A CD-ROM OR DVD-ROM

Author's Last Name, First Name. "Title of Article." *Title of Periodical* Date or Volume.Issue (Year): Page. Medium. *Database*. Database provider. Month Year of CD-ROM.

Hwang, Suein L. "While Many Competitors See Sales Melt, Ben & Jerry's Scoops Out Solid Growth." *Wall Street Journal* 25 May 1993: B1. CD-ROM. *ABI-INFORM*. ProQuest. June 1993.

42. PODCAST

Performer or Host's Last Name, First Name. "Title of Podcast." Host Host's First and Last Name. *Title of Program*. Sponsoring Institution, Day Month Year posted. Medium. Day Month Year of access.

Blumberg, Alex, and Adam Davidson. "The Giant Pool of Money." Host Ira Glass. *This American Life*. Chicago Public Radio, 9 May 2008. Web. 18 Sept. 2008.

Other Kinds of Sources (Including Online Versions)

Many of the sources in this section can be found online, and you'll find examples here for how to cite them. If there is no Web model here, start with the guidelines most appropriate for the source you need to cite, omit the original medium, and end your citation with the title of the website, italicized; the medium (Web); and the day, month, and year of access.

A FEW DETAILS TO NOTE

- **AUTHORS:** If there is more than one author, list the first author last-name-first and the others first-name-first. Do likewise if you begin an entry with performers, speakers, and so on.
- **TITLES:** Capitalize titles and subtitles as you would for a print book or periodical.
- **DATES:** Abbreviate the names of months as you would for a print periodical. Journals paginated by volume or issue need only the year (in parentheses).
- **MEDIUM:** Indicate the medium—Web, Lecture, Television, *Microsoft Word* file, MP3 file, PDF file, and so on.

43. ADVERTISEMENT

Product or Company. Advertisement. *Title of Periodical* Date or Volume.Issue (Year): Page. Medium.

Empire BlueCross BlueShield. Advertisement. *Fortune* 8 Dec. 2003: 208. Print.

ADVERTISEMENT ON THE WEB

Rolex. Advertisement. *Newsweek*. Newsweek, n.d. Web. 1 Apr. 2009.

44. ART

Artist's Last Name, First Name. *Title of Art*. Medium. Year. Institution, City.

Van Gogh, Vincent. *The Potato Eaters*. Oil on canvas. 1885. Van Gogh Museum, Amsterdam.

author title publication

ART ON THE WEB

Warhol, Andy. *Self-Portrait.* 1979. J. Paul Getty Museum, Los Angeles. *The Getty.* Web. 29 Mar. 2007.

45. CARTOON

Artist's Last Name, First Name. "Title of Cartoon (if titled)." Cartoon. *Title of Periodical* Date or Volume.Issue (Year): Page. Medium.

Chast, Roz. "The Three Wise Men of Thanksgiving." Cartoon. *New Yorker* 1 Dec. 2003: 174. Print.

CARTOON ON THE WEB

Horsey, David. Cartoon. *Seattle Post-Intelligencer.* Seattle Post-Intelligencer, 20 Apr. 2008. Web. 21 Apr. 2008.

46. DISSERTATION

Treat a published dissertation as you would a book, but after its title, add the abbreviation *Diss.*, the institution, and the date of the dissertation.

Author's Last Name, First Name. *Title*. Diss. Institution, Year. Publication City: Publisher, Year. Medium.

Goggin, Peter N. *A New Literacy Map of Research and Scholarship in Computers and Writing.* Diss. Indiana U of Pennsylvania, 2000. Ann Arbor: UMI, 2001. Print.

For unpublished dissertations, put the title in quotation marks and end with the degree-granting institution and the year.

Kim, Loel. "Students Respond to Teacher Comments: A Comparison of Online Written and Voice Modalities." Diss. Carnegie Mellon U, 1998. Print.

47. FILM, VIDEO, OR DVD

Title. Dir. Director's First and Last Names. Perf. Lead Actors' First and Last Names. Distributor, Year of release. Medium.

Casablanca. Dir. Michael Curtiz. Perf. Humphrey Bogart, Ingrid Bergman, and Claude Rains. Warner, 1942. Film.

To cite a particular person's work, start with that name.

Cody, Diablo, scr. *Juno*. Dir. Jason Reitman. Perf. Ellen Page, Michael Cera, Jennifer Garner, Jason Bateman. Fox Searchlight, 2007. DVD.

Cite a video clip on YouTube or a similar site as you would a short work from a website.

Director's Last Name, First Name, dir. "Title of Video." *Name of Website*. Sponsor of site, Day Month Year of release. Medium. Day Month Year of access.

PivotMasterDX, dir. "Bounce!" *YouTube*. YouTube, 14 June 2008. Web. 21 June 2008.

48. INTERVIEW

BROADCAST INTERVIEW

Subject's Last Name, First Name. Interview. *Title of Program*. Network. Station, City. Day Month Year. Medium.

Gates, Henry Louis, Jr. Interview. *Fresh Air*. NPR. WNYC, New York. 9 Apr. 2002. Radio.

author title publication

PUBLISHED INTERVIEW

Subject's Last Name, First Name. Interview. or "Title of Interview." *Title of Periodical* Date or Volume.Issue (Year): Pages. Medium.

Brzezinski, Zbigniew. "Against the Neocons." *American Prospect* Mar. 2005: 26–27. Print.

Stone, Oliver. Interview. *Esquire* Nov. 2004: 170. Print.

PERSONAL INTERVIEW

Subject's Last Name, First Name. Personal interview. Day Month Year.

Roddick, Andy. Personal interview. 17 Aug. 2008.

49. LETTER

UNPUBLISHED LETTER

Author's Last Name, First Name. Letter to the author. Day Month Year. Medium.

Quindlen, Anna. Letter to the author. 11 Apr. 2002. MS.

For the medium, use MS for a hand-written letter and TS for a typed one.

PUBLISHED LETTER

Letter Writer's Last Name, First Name. Letter to First and Last Names. Day Month Year of letter. *Title of Book*. Ed. Editor's First and Last Names. City: Publisher, Year of publication. Pages. Medium.

White, E. B. Letter to Carol Angell. 28 May 1970. *Letters of E. B. White*. Ed. Dorothy Lobarno Guth. New York: Harper, 1976. 600. Print.

50. MAP

Title of Map. Map. City: Publisher, Year of publication. Medium.

Toscana. Map. Milan: Touring Club Italiano, 1987. Print.

MAP ON THE WEB

"Portland, Oregon." Map. *Google Maps*. Google, 25 Apr. 2009. Web. 25 Apr. 2009.

51. MUSICAL SCORE

Composer's Last Name, First Name. *Title of Composition*. Year of composition. Publication City: Publisher, Year of publication. Medium. Series Information (if any).

Beethoven, Ludwig van. *String Quartet No. 13 in B Flat, Op. 130*. 1825. New York: Dover, 1970. Print.

52. SOUND RECORDING

Artist's Last Name, First Name. *Title of Long Work*. Other pertinent details about the artists. Manufacturer, Year of release. Medium.

Beethoven, Ludwig van. *Missa Solemnis*. Perf. Westminster Choir and New York Philharmonic. Cond. Leonard Bernstein. Sony, 1992. CD.

Whether you list the composer, conductor, or performer first depends on where you want to place the emphasis. If you are citing a specific song, put it in quotation marks before the name of the recording.

Brown, Greg. "Canned Goods." *The Live One*. Red House, 1995. MP3 file.

For a spoken-word recording, you may begin with the writer, speaker, or producer, depending on your emphasis.

Dale, Jim, narr. *Harry Potter and the Deathly Hallows*. By J.K. Rowling. Random House Audio, 2007. CD.

author title publication

53. ORAL PRESENTATION

Speaker's Last Name, First Name. "Title of Lecture." Sponsoring Institution. Site, City. Day Month Year. Medium.

Cassin, Michael. "Nature in the Raw—The Art of Landscape Painting." Berkshire Institute for Lifetime Learning. Clark Art Institute, Williamstown. 24 Mar. 2005. Lecture.

54. PAPER FROM PROCEEDINGS OF A CONFERENCE

Author's Last Name, First Name. "Title of Paper." *Title of Conference Proceedings*. Date, City. Ed. Editor's First and Last Names. Publication City: Publisher, Year. Pages. Medium.

Zolotow, Charlotte. "Passion in Publishing." *A Sea of Upturned Faces: Proceedings of the Third Pacific Rim Conference on Children's Literature*. 1986, Los Angeles. Ed. Winifred Ragsdale. Metuchen: Scarecrow P, 1989. 236–49. Print.

55. PERFORMANCE

Title. By Author's First and Last Names. Other appropriate details about the performance. Site, City. Day Month Year. Medium.

Take Me Out. By Richard Greenberg. Dir. Scott Plate. Perf. Caleb Sekeres. Dobama Theatre, Cleveland. 17 Aug. 2007. Performance.

56. TELEVISION OR RADIO PROGRAM

"Title of Episode." *Title of Program*. Other appropriate information about the writer, director, actors, etc. Network. Station, City, Day Month Year of broadcast. Medium.

"Tabula Rasa." *Criminal Minds*. Writ. Dan Dworkin. Dir. Steve Boyum. NBC. WCNC, Charlotte, 14 May 2008. Television.

TELEVISION OR RADIO ON THE WEB

"Bush's War." *Frontline*. Writ. and Dir. Michael Kirk. PBS, 24 Mar. 2008. *PBS.org*. Web. 10 Apr. 2009.

57. PAMPHLET, BROCHURE, OR PRESS RELEASE

Author's Last Name, First Name. *Title of Publication*. Publication City: Publisher, Year. Medium.

Bowers, Catherine. *Can We Find a Home Here? Answering Questions of Interfaith Couples*. Boston: UUA Publications, n.d. Print.

To cite a press release, include the day and month before the year.

58. LEGAL SOURCE

The name of a legal case is italicized in the text, but not in a works-cited entry.

Names of the first plaintiff and the first defendant. Volume Name Reference or page numbers of law report. Name of court. Year of decision. Source information for medium consulted.

District of Columbia v. Heller. 540 US 290. Supreme Court of the US. 2008. *Supreme Court Collection*. Legal Information Inst, Cornell U Law School, n.d. Web. 18 Mar. 2009.

For acts of law, include both the Public Law number and the Statutes at Large volume and page numbers.

Name of law. Public law number. Statutes at Large Volume Stat. Pages. Day Month Year enacted. Medium.

Military Commissions Act. Pub. L. 109-366. 120 Stat. 2083–2521. 17 Oct. 2006. Print.

author title publication

59. MP3 FILE, JPEG FILE, OR OTHER DIGITAL FILE

For scanned photos, downloaded songs, *Microsoft Word* documents, and other files stored on your computer, iPod, or other digital device, follow the guidelines for the type of work you are citing (art, sound recording, and so on) and give the file type as the medium. If you're not sure of the file type, call it a *Digital file.*

Conell, Lee. "Our Ancestors." 2009. *Microsoft Word* file.

Evans, Walker. *General Store, Moundville, Alabama*. 1936. Lib. of Congress, Washington. JPEG file.

Talking Heads. "Burning Down the House." *Speaking in Tongues*. Sire, 1983. Digital file.

How to Cite Sources That MLA Does Not Cover

To cite a source for which MLA does not provide guidelines, give any information readers will need in order to find it themselves—author; title, subtitle; publisher and/or sponsor; medium; dates; and any other pertinent information. In addition, you can look at models of sources similar to the one you are citing. You might want to try out your citation yourself, to be sure it will lead others to your source.

SAMPLE RESEARCH PAPER, MLA STYLE

Dylan Borchers wrote the following report for a first-year writing course. It is formatted according to the guidelines of the *MLA Handbook for Writers of Research Papers*, 7th edition (2009). While the MLA guidelines are used widely in literature and other disciplines in the humanities, exact documentation requirements may vary across disciplines and courses. If you're unsure about what your instructor wants, ask for clarification.

Put your last name and the page number in the upper-right corner of each page.

Center the title.

Double-space throughout.

1"

If you name the author of a source in a signal phrase, give the page numbers in parentheses.

1"

1/2"

1"

Borchers 1

Dylan Borchers

Professor Bullock

English 102, Section 4

31 March 2009

Against the Odds:

Harry S. Truman and the Election of 1948

"Thomas E. Dewey's Election as President Is a Foregone Conclusion," read a headline in the *New York Times* during the presidential election race between incumbent Democrat Harry S. Truman and his Republican challenger, Thomas E. Dewey. Earlier, *Life* magazine had put Dewey on its cover with the caption "The Next President of the United States" (qtd. in "1948 Truman-Dewey Election"). In a *Newsweek* survey of fifty prominent political writers, each one predicted Truman's defeat, and *Time* correspondents declared that Dewey would carry 39 of the 48 states (Donaldson 210). Nearly every major media outlet across the United States endorsed Dewey and lambasted Truman. As historian Robert H. Ferrell observes, even Truman's wife, Bess, thought he would be beaten (270).

The results of an election are not so easily predicted, as the famous photograph on page 2 shows. Not only did Truman win the election, but he won by a significant margin, with 303 electoral votes and 24,179,259 popular votes, compared to Dewey's 189 electoral votes and 21,991,291 popular votes (Donaldson 204-7). In fact, many historians and political analysts argue that Truman

Borchers 2

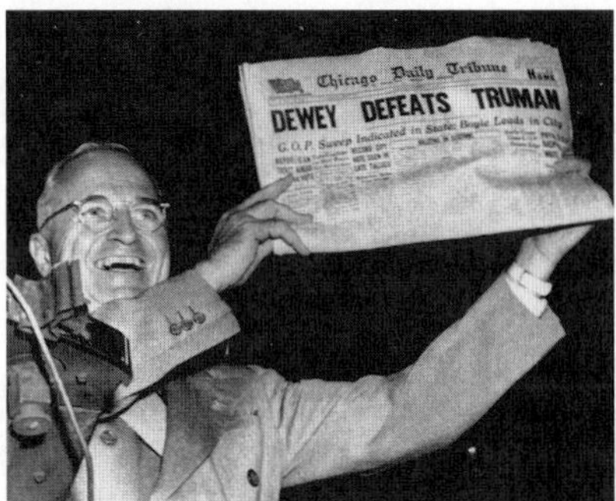

Fig. 1. President Harry S. Truman holds up an Election Day edition of the *Chicago Daily Tribune*, which mistakenly announced "Dewey Defeats Truman." St. Louis, 4 Nov. 1948 (Rollins).

Insert illustrations close to the text to which they relate. Label with figure number, caption, and parenthetical source citation.

would have won by an even greater margin had third-party Progressive candidate Henry A. Wallace not split the Democratic vote in New York State and Dixiecrat Strom Thurmond not won four states in the South (McCullough 711). Although Truman's defeat was heavily predicted, those predictions themselves, Dewey's passiveness as a campaigner, and Truman's zeal turned the tide for a Truman victory.

In the months preceding the election, public opinion polls predicted that Dewey would win by a large margin. Pollster Elmo Roper stopped polling in September, believing there was no reason to continue, given a seemingly inevitable Dewey landslide. Although the margin narrowed as the election drew near, the other

Indent paragraphs $\frac{1}{2}$ inch or 5 spaces.

Borchers 3

Give the author and page numbers in parentheses when no signal phrase is used.

pollsters predicted a Dewey win by at least 5 percent (Donaldson 209). Many historians believe that these predictions aided the president in the long run. First, surveys showing Dewey in the lead may have prompted some of Dewey's supporters to feel overconfident about their candidate's chances and therefore to stay home from the polls on Election Day. Second, these same surveys may have energized Democrats to mount late get-out-the-vote efforts ("1948 Truman-Dewey Election"). Other analysts believe that the overwhelming predictions of a Truman loss also kept at home some Democrats who approved of Truman's policies but saw a Truman loss as inevitable. According to political analyst Samuel Lubell, those Democrats may have saved Dewey from an even greater defeat (Hamby, *Man of the People* 465). Whatever the impact on the voters, the polling numbers had a decided effect on Dewey.

Historians and political analysts alike cite Dewey's overly cautious campaign as one of the main reasons Truman was able to achieve victory. Dewey firmly believed in public opinion polls. With all indications pointing to an easy victory, Dewey and his staff believed that all he had to do was bide his time and make no foolish mistakes. Dewey himself said, "When you're leading, don't talk" (qtd. in McCullough 672). Each of Dewey's speeches was well-crafted and well-rehearsed. As the leader in the race, he kept his remarks faultlessly positive, with the result that he failed to deliver a solid message or even mention Truman or any of Truman's policies. Eventually, Dewey began to be perceived as aloof and stuffy. One

If you quote text quoted in another source, cite that source in a parenthetical reference.

Borchers 4

observer compared him to the plastic groom on top of a wedding cake (Hamby, "Harry S. Truman"), and others noted his stiff, cold demeanor (McCullough 671-74).

If you cite 2 or more works closely together, give a parenthetical citation for each one.

As his campaign continued, observers noted that Dewey seemed uncomfortable in crowds, unable to connect with ordinary people. And he made a number of blunders. One took place at a train stop when the candidate, commenting on the number of children in the crowd, said he was glad they had been let out of school for his arrival. Unfortunately for Dewey, it was a Saturday ("1948: The Great Truman Surprise"). Such gaffes gave voters the feeling that Dewey was out of touch with the public.

Again and again through the autumn of 1948, Dewey's campaign speeches failed to address the issues, with the candidate declaring that he did not want to "get down in the gutter" (qtd. in McCullough 701). When told by fellow Republicans that he was losing ground, Dewey insisted that his campaign not alter its course. Even *Time* magazine, though it endorsed and praised him, conceded that his speeches were dull (McCullough 696). According to historian Zachary Karabell, they were "notable only for taking place, not for any specific message" (244). Dewey's numbers in the polls slipped in the weeks before the election, but he still held a comfortable lead over Truman. It would take Truman's famous whistle-stop campaign to make the difference.

Few candidates in U.S. history have campaigned for the presidency with more passion and faith than Harry Truman. In the autumn of 1948, he wrote to his sister, "It will be the greatest campaign any President ever made. Win, lose, or draw, people will know where I stand" (91). For thirty-three days, Truman traveled the nation, giving hundreds of speeches from the back of the *Ferdinand Magellan* railroad car. In the same letter, he described the pace: "We made about 140 stops and I spoke over 147 times, shook hands with at least 30,000 and am in good condition to start out again tomorrow for Wilmington, Philadelphia, Jersey City, Newark, Albany and Buffalo" (91). McCullough writes of Truman's campaign:

Set off quotations of 4 or more lines by indenting 1 inch (or 10 spaces).

> No President in history had ever gone so far in quest of support from the people, or with less cause for the effort, to judge by informed opinion. . . . As a test of his skills and judgment as a professional politician, not to say his stamina and disposition at age sixty-four, it would be like no other experience in his long, often difficult career, as he himself understood perfectly. More than any other event in his public life, or in his presidency thus far, it would reveal the kind of man he was. (655)

Put parenthetical references after final punctuation in a block quotation.

He spoke in large cities and small towns, defending his policies and attacking Republicans. As a former farmer and relatively late bloomer, Truman was able to connect with the public. He developed an energetic style, usually speaking from notes rather than from a prepared speech, and often mingled with the crowds that met his train. These crowds grew larger as the campaign

Borchers 6

progressed. In Chicago, over half a million people lined the streets as he passed, and in St. Paul the crowd numbered over 25,000. When Dewey entered St. Paul two days later, he was greeted by only 7,000 supporters ("1948 Truman-Dewey Election"). Reporters brushed off the large crowds as mere curiosity seekers wanting to see a president (McCullough 682). Yet Truman persisted, even if he often seemed to be the only one who thought he could win. By going directly to the American people and connecting with them, Truman built the momentum needed to surpass Dewey and win the election.

If you cite a work with no known author, use the title in your parenthetical reference.

The legacy and lessons of Truman's whistle-stop campaign continue to be studied by political analysts, and politicians today often mimic his campaign methods by scheduling multiple visits to key states, as Truman did. He visited California, Illinois, and Ohio 48 times, compared with 6 visits to those states by Dewey. Political scientist Thomas M. Holbrook concludes that his strategic campaigning in those states and others gave Truman the electoral votes he needed to win (61, 65).

The 1948 election also had an effect on pollsters, who, as Elmo Roper admitted, "couldn't have been more wrong" (qtd. in Karabell 255). *Life* magazine's editors concluded that pollsters as well as reporters and commentators were too convinced of a Dewey victory to analyze the polls seriously, especially the opinions of undecided voters (Karabell 256). Pollsters assumed that undecided voters would vote in the same proportion as decided voters -- and that turned out to be a false assumption (Karabell 258). In fact, the lopsidedness of the polls might have led voters who supported Truman to call themselves undecided out of an unwillingness to associate themselves with the losing side, further skewing the polls' results (McDonald, Glynn, Kim, and Ostman 152). Such errors led pollsters to change their methods significantly after the 1948 election.

In a work by 4 or more authors, either cite them all or name the first one followed by et al.

After the election, many political analysts, journalists, and historians concluded that the Truman upset was in fact a victory for the American people, who, the *New Republic* noted, "couldn't be ticketed by the polls, knew its own mind and had picked the rather unlikely but courageous figure of Truman to carry its banner" (qtd. in McCullough 715). How "unlikely" is unclear, however; Truman biographer Alonzo Hamby notes that "polls of scholars consistently rank Truman among the top eight presidents in American history" (*Man of the People* 641). But despite Truman's high standing, and despite the fact that the whistle-stop campaign is now part of our political landscape, politicians have increasingly imitated the style of the Dewey campaign, with its "packaged candidate who ran so as not to lose, who steered clear of controversy, and who made a good show of appearing presidential" (Karabell 266). The election of 1948 shows that voters are not necessarily swayed by polls, but it may have presaged the packaging of candidates by public relations experts, to the detriment of public debate on the issues in future presidential elections.

1"

Borchers 8

Works Cited

Donaldson, Gary A. *Truman Defeats Dewey*. Lexington: UP of Kentucky, 1999. Print.

Ferrell, Robert H. *Harry S. Truman: A Life*. Columbia: U of Missouri P, 1994. Print.

Hamby, Alonzo L., ed. "Harry S. Truman (1945-1953)." *AmericanPresident.org*. Miller Center of Public Affairs, U of Virginia, 11 Dec. 2003. Web. 17 Mar. 2009.

---. *Man of the People: A Life of Harry S. Truman*. New York: Oxford UP, 1995. Print.

Holbrook, Thomas M. "Did the Whistle-Stop Campaign Matter?" *PS: Political Science and Politics* 35.1 (2002): 59-66. Print.

Karabell, Zachary. *The Last Campaign: How Harry Truman Won the 1948 Election*. New York: Knopf, 2000. Print.

McCullough, David. *Truman*. New York: Simon & Schuster, 1992. Print.

McDonald, Daniel G., Carroll J. Glynn, Sei-Hill Kim, and Ronald E. Ostman. "The Spiral of Silence in the 1948 Presidential Election." *Communication Research* 28.2 (2001): 139-55. Print.

"1948: The Great Truman Surprise." *Media and Politics Online Projects: Media Coverage of Presidential Campaigns*. Dept. of Political Science and International Affairs, Kennesaw State U., 29 Oct. 2003. Web. 1 Apr. 2009.

Center the heading.

Double-space throughout.

Alphabetize the list by authors' last names or by title for works with no author.

Begin each entry at the left margin; indent subsequent lines ½ inch or 5 spaces.

If you cite more than one work by a single author, list them alphabetically by title, and use 3 hyphens instead of repeating the author's name after the first entry.

Check to be sure that every source you use is on the list of works cited.

"1948 Truman-Dewey Election." *Electronic Government Project: Eagleton Digital Archive of American Politics*. Eagleton Inst. of Politics, Rutgers, State U of New Jersey, 2004. Web. 19 Mar. 2009.

Rollins, Byron. Untitled photograph. "The First 150 Years: 1948." *AP History*. Associated Press, n.d. Web. 3 Apr. 2009.

Truman, Harry S. "Campaigning, Letter, October 5, 1948." *Harry S. Truman*. Ed. Robert H. Ferrell. Washington: CQ P, 2003. 91. Print.

APA Style 50

American Psychological Association (APA) style calls for (1) brief documentation in parentheses near each in-text citation and (2) complete documentation in a list of references at the end of your text. The models in this chapter draw on the *Publication Manual of the American Psychological Association*, 6th edition (2009). Additional information is available at www.apastyle.org.

A DIRECTORY TO APA STYLE

APA In-Text Documentation 480

author title publication

APA IN-TEXT DOCUMENTATION

Brief documentation in your text makes clear to your reader precisely what you took from a source and, in the case of a quotation, precisely where (usually, on which page) in the source you found the text you are quoting.

Paraphrases and summaries are more common than quotations in APA-style projects. The chapter on quoting, paraphrasing, and summarizing covers all three kinds of citations. It also includes a list of words you can use in signal phrases to introduce quotations, paraphrases, and summaries. As you cite each source, you will need to decide whether to name the author in a signal phrase—"as McCullough (2001) wrote"—or in parentheses—"(McCullough, 2001)."

The first examples in this chapter show basic in-text documentation for a work by one author. Variations on those examples follow. All of the examples are color-coded to help you see how writers using APA style work authors and page numbers—and sometimes titles—into their texts.

1. AUTHOR NAMED IN A SIGNAL PHRASE

If you are quoting, you must give the page number(s). You are not required to give the page number(s) with a paraphrase or a summary, but APA encourages you to do so, especially if you are citing a long or complex work; most of the models in this chapter do include page numbers. Check with your instructors to find out their preferences.

AUTHOR QUOTED

Put the date in parentheses right after the author's name; put the page in parentheses as close to the quotation as possible.

> McCullough (2001) described John Adams as having "the hands of a man accustomed to pruning his own trees, cutting his own hay, and splitting his own firewood" (p. 18).

author title publication

John Adams had "the hands of a man accustomed to pruning his own trees, cutting his own hay, and splitting his own firewood," according to McCullough (2001, p. 18).

Notice that in the first example, the parenthetical reference with the page number comes *after* the closing quotation marks but *before* the period at the end of the sentence.

AUTHOR PARAPHRASED

Put the date in parentheses right after the author's name; follow the date with the page.

McCullough (2001, p. 18) described John Adams's hands as those of someone used to manual labor.

John Adams's hands were those of a laborer, according to McCullough (2001, p. 18).

2. AUTHOR NAMED IN PARENTHESES

If you do not mention an author in a signal phrase, put his or her name, a comma, and the year of publication in parentheses as close as possible to the quotation, paraphrase, or summary.

AUTHOR QUOTED

Give the author, date, and page in one parentheses, or split the information between two parentheses.

Adams is said to have had "the hands of a man accustomed to pruning his own trees, cutting his own hay, and splitting his own firewood" (McCullough, 2001, p. 18).

One biographer (McCullough, 2001) has said John Adams had "the hands of a man accustomed to pruning his own trees, cutting his own hay, and splitting his own firewood" (p. 18).

AUTHOR PARAPHRASED OR SUMMARIZED

Give the author, date, and page in one parentheses toward the beginning or the end of the paraphrase.

> One biographer (McCullough, 2001, p. 18) described John Adams as someone who was not a stranger to manual labor.
>
> John Adams's hands were those of a laborer (McCullough, 2001, p. 18).

3. AUTHORS WITH THE SAME LAST NAME

If your reference list includes more than one person with the same last name, include initials in all documentation to distinguish the authors from one another.

> Eclecticism is common in contemporary criticism (J. M. Smith, 1992, p. vii).
>
> J. M. Smith (1992, p. vii) has explained that eclecticism is common in contemporary criticism.

4. AFTER A BLOCK QUOTATION

If a quotation runs forty or more words, set it off from the rest of your text and indent it one-half inch (or five spaces) from the left margin without quotation marks. Place the page number(s) in parentheses *after* the end punctuation.

> Kaplan (2000) captured ancient and contemporary Antioch for us:
>
>> At the height of its glory in the Roman Byzantine age, when it had an amphitheater, public baths, aqueducts, and sewage pipes, half a million people lived in Antioch. Today the population is only 125,000. With sour relations between Turkey and Syria, and unstable politics throughout the Middle East, Antioch is now a backwater—seedy and tumbledown, with relatively few tourists. (p. 123)
>
> Antioch's decline serves as a reminder that the fortunes of cities can change drastically over time.

author title publication

5. TWO AUTHORS

Always mention both authors. Use *and* in a signal phrase, but use an ampersand (&) in parentheses.

> Carlson and Ventura (1990, p. v) wanted to introduce Julio Cortázar, Marjorie Agosín, and other Latin American writers to an audience of English-speaking adolescents.
>
> According to the Peter Principle, "In a hierarchy, every employee tends to rise to his level of incompetence" (Peter & Hull, 1969, p. 26).

6. THREE OR MORE AUTHORS

In the first reference to a work by three to five persons, name all contributors. In subsequent references, name the first author followed by *et al.* Whenever you refer to a work by six or more contributors, name only the first author, followed by *et al.* Use *and* in a signal phrase, but use an ampersand (&) in parentheses.

> Faigley, George, Palchik, and Selfe (2004, p. xii) have argued that where there used to be a concept called *literacy*, today's multitude of new kinds of texts has given us *literacies*.
>
> It's easier to talk about a good movie than a good book (Sebranek, Meyer, & Kemper, 1990, p. 143).
>
> Peilen et al. (1990, p. 75) supported their claims about corporate corruption with startling anecdotal evidence.

7. ORGANIZATION OR GOVERNMENT AS AUTHOR

If an organization has a long name that is recognizable by its abbreviation, give the full name and the abbreviation the first time you cite the source. In subsequent citations, use only the abbreviation. If the organization does not have a familiar abbreviation, use the full name each time you refer to it. (See the next page for examples.)

FIRST CITATION

(American Psychological Association [APA], 2008)

SUBSEQUENT CITATIONS

(APA, 2008)

8. AUTHOR UNKNOWN

With reference books and newspaper editorials, among other things, you may not know the author of a work. Use the complete title if it is short; if it is long, use the first few words of the title under which the work appears in the reference list.

> *Webster's New Biographical Dictionary* (1988) identifies William James as "American psychologist and philosopher" (p. 520).
>
> A powerful editorial asserted that healthy liver donor Mike Hurewitz died because of "frightening" faulty postoperative care ("Every Patient's Nightmare," 2007).

9. TWO OR MORE WORKS CITED TOGETHER

If you need to cite multiple works in the same parentheses, list them in the same order that they appear in your reference list, separated by semicolons.

> Many researchers have argued that what counts as "literacy" is not necessarily learned at school (Heath, 1983; Moss, 2003).

10. SOURCE QUOTED IN ANOTHER SOURCE

When you need to cite a source that was quoted in another source, let the reader know that you used a secondary source by adding the words *as cited in*.

author title publication

During the meeting with the psychologist, the patient stated repeatedly that he "didn't want to be too paranoid" (as cited in Oberfield & Yasik, 2004, p. 294).

11. WORK WITHOUT PAGE NUMBERS

Instead of page numbers, some electronic works have paragraph numbers, which you should include (preceded by the abbreviation *para.*) if you are referring to a specific part of such a source. In sources with neither page nor paragraph numbers, refer readers to a particular part of the source if possible, perhaps indicating a heading and the paragraph under the heading.

Russell's dismissals from Trinity College at Cambridge and from City College in New York City have been seen as examples of the controversy that marked the philosopher's life (Irvine, 2006, para. 2).

12. AN ENTIRE WORK

You do not need to give a page number if you are directing readers' attention to an entire work. Identify the author in a signal phrase or in parentheses, and cite the year of publication in parentheses.

Kaplan (2000) considered Turkey and Central Asia explosive.

13. AN ENTIRE WEBSITE

When you are citing an entire website (and not a specific document within the website), give the URL in the text. You do not need to include the website in your reference list. To cite part of a website, see no. 20 on page 500.

Beyond providing diagnostic information, the website for the Alzheimer's Association includes a variety of resources for family and community support of patients suffering from Alzheimer's (http://www.alz.org).

14. PERSONAL COMMUNICATION

Cite email, telephone conversations, interviews, personal letters, messages from nonarchived discussion groups or message boards, and other personal texts as *personal communication*, along with the person's initial(s), last name, and the date. You do not need to include such personal communications in your reference list.

> The author and editors seriously considered alternative ways of demonstrating documentation styles (F. Weinberg, personal communication, November 14, 2007).

> L. Strauss (personal communication, December 6, 2006) told about visiting Yogi Berra when they both lived in Montclair, New Jersey.

NOTES

APA recognizes that there are instances when writers of research papers may need to use *content notes* to give an explanation or information that doesn't fit into the paper proper. To signal a content note, place a superscript numeral in your text at the appropriate point. Your readers will know to look for a note beginning with the same superscript numeral on a separate page with the heading *Notes*, after your paper but before the reference list. If you have multiple notes, number them consecutively throughout your paper. Indent the first line of each note five spaces, and set all subsequent lines flush left.

Here is an example showing text and an accompanying content note from a book called *In Search of Solutions: A New Direction in Psychotherapy* (2003).

TEXT WITH SUPERSCRIPT

> An important part of working with teams and one-way mirrors is taking the consultation break, as at Milan, BFTC, and MRI.[1]

author title publication

CONTENT NOTE

[1]It is crucial to note here that, while working within a team is fun, stimulating, and revitalizing, it is not necessary for successful outcomes. Solution-oriented therapy works equally well when working solo.

APA REFERENCE LIST

A reference list provides full bibliographic information for every source cited in your text with the exception of entire websites and personal communications. This list should be alphabetized by authors' (or editors') last names. Works that do not have an identifiable author or editor are alphabetized by title. See pages 518–19 for a sample reference list.

Books

BASIC FORMAT FOR A BOOK

For most books, you'll need to provide information about the author; the date of publication; the title and any subtitle; and the place of publication and publisher. You'll find this information on the book's title page and copyright page.

Diamond, J. (2005). *Collapse: How societies choose to fail or succeed.* New York, NY: Viking.

A FEW DETAILS TO NOTE

- **DATES:** If more than one year is given, use the most recent one.
- **TITLES:** Capitalize only the first word and proper nouns and proper adjectives in titles and subtitles.

- **PLACE OF PUBLICATION:** Give city followed by state (abbreviated) or country, if outside the United States (for example, Boston, MA; London, England; Toronto, Ontario, Canada). If more than one city is given, use the first. Do not include the state or country if the publisher is a university whose name includes it.
- **PUBLISHER:** Use a shortened form of the publisher's name (Little, Brown for Little, Brown and Company), but retain *Association*, *Books*, and *Press* (American Psychological Association, Princeton University Press).

1. ONE AUTHOR

Author's Last Name, Initials. (Year of publication). *Title*. Publication City, State or Country: Publisher.

Young, K. S. (1998). *Caught in the net: How to recognize the signs of Internet addiction—and a winning strategy for recovery*. New York, NY: Wiley.

2. TWO OR MORE WORKS BY THE SAME AUTHOR

If the works were published in different years, list them chronologically.

Lewis, B. (1995). *The Middle East: A brief history of the last 2,000 years.* New York, NY: Scribner.

Lewis, B. (2003). *The crisis of Islam: Holy war and unholy terror.* New York, NY: Modern Library.

If the works were published in the same year, list them alphabetically by title, adding "a," "b," and so on to the years.

Kaplan, R. D. (2000a). *The coming anarchy: Shattering the dreams of the post cold war.* New York, NY: Random House.

Kaplan, R. D. (2000b). *Eastward to Tartary: Travels in the Balkans, the Middle East, and the Caucasus.* New York, NY: Random House.

author title publication

Documentation Map (APA)

Book

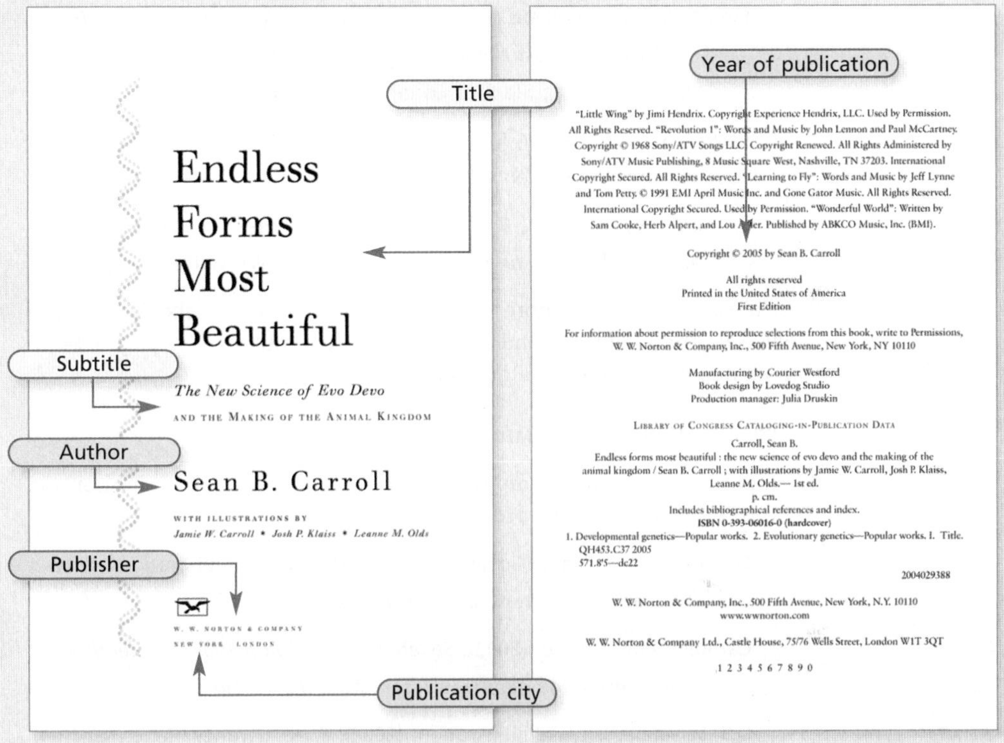

Endless Forms Most Beautiful

The New Science of Evo Devo

AND THE MAKING OF THE ANIMAL KINGDOM

Sean B. Carroll

WITH ILLUSTRATIONS BY

Jamie W. Carroll • Josh P. Klaiss • Leanne M. Olds

W. W. NORTON & COMPANY

NEW YORK LONDON

"Little Wing" by Jimi Hendrix. Copyright Experience Hendrix, LLC. Used by Permission. All Rights Reserved. "Revolution 1": Words and Music by John Lennon and Paul McCartney. Copyright © 1968 Sony/ATV Songs LLC. Copyright Renewed. All Rights Administered by Sony/ATV Music Publishing, 8 Music Square West, Nashville, TN 37203. International Copyright Secured. All Rights Reserved. "Learning to Fly": Words and Music by Jeff Lynne and Tom Petty. © 1991 EMI April Music Inc. and Gone Gator Music. All Rights Reserved. International Copyright Secured. Used by Permission. "Wonderful World": Written by Sam Cooke, Herb Alpert, and Lou Adler. Published by ABKCO Music, Inc. (BMI).

Copyright © 2005 by Sean B. Carroll

All rights reserved
Printed in the United States of America
First Edition

For information about permission to reproduce selections from this book, write to Permissions, W. W. Norton & Company, Inc., 500 Fifth Avenue, New York, NY 10110

Manufacturing by Courier Westford
Book design by Lovedog Studio
Production manager: Julia Druskin

LIBRARY OF CONGRESS CATALOGING-IN-PUBLICATION DATA

Carroll, Sean B.
Endless forms most beautiful : the new science of evo devo and the making of the animal kingdom / Sean B. Carroll ; with illustrations by Jamie W. Carroll, Josh P. Klaiss, Leanne M. Olds.— 1st ed.
p. cm.
Includes bibliographical references and index.
ISBN 0-393-06016-0 (hardcover)
1. Developmental genetics—Popular works. 2. Evolutionary genetics—Popular works. I. Title.
QH453.C37 2005
571.8'5—dc22
2004029388

W. W. Norton & Company, Inc., 500 Fifth Avenue, New York, N.Y. 10110
www.wwnorton.com

W. W. Norton & Company Ltd., Castle House, 75/76 Wells Street, London W1T 3QT

1 2 3 4 5 6 7 8 9 0

488, 490–93 for more on citing books APA style

Author's Last Name, Initials. (Year of publication). *Title: Subtitle.* Publication City, State or Country: Publisher.

Carroll, S. B. (2005). *Endless forms most beautiful: The new science of evo devo and the making of the animal kingdom.* New York, NY: Norton.

3. TWO OR MORE AUTHORS

For two to seven authors, use this format.

First Author's Last Name, Initials, Next Author's Last Name, Initials, & Final Author's Last Name, Initials. (Year of publication). *Title*. Publication City, State or Country: Publisher.

Leavitt, S. D., & Dubner, S. J. (2006). *Freakonomics: A rogue economist explores the hidden side of everything.* New York, NY: Morrow.

Sebranek, P., Meyer, V., & Kemper, D. (1990). *Writers INC: A guide to writing, thinking, and learning.* Burlington, WI: Write Source.

For a work by eight or more authors, name just the first six authors, followed by three ellipses, and end with the final author (see page 494 for an example from a journal article).

4. ORGANIZATION OR GOVERNMENT AS AUTHOR

Sometimes a corporation or government organization is both author and publisher. If so, use the word *Author* as the publisher.

Organization Name or Government Agency. (Year of publication). *Title*. Publication City, State or Country: Publisher.

Catholic News Service. (2002). *Stylebook on religion 2000: A reference guide and usage manual.* Washington, DC: Author.

U.S. Social Security Administration. (2008). *Social Security: Retirement benefits.* Washington, DC: Author.

5. AUTHOR AND EDITOR

Author's Last Name, Initials. (Year of edited edition). *Title.* (Editor's Initials Last Name, Ed.). Publication City, State or Country: Publisher. (Original work[s] published year[s])

Dick, P. F. (2008). *Five novels of the 1960s and 70s.* (J. Lethem, Ed.). New York, NY: Library of America. (Original works published 1964–1977)

author title publication

6. EDITED COLLECTION

First Editor's Last Name, Initials, Next Editor's Last Name, Initials, & Final Editor's Last Name, Initials. (Eds.). (Year of edited edition). *Title.* Publication City, State or Country: Publisher.

Raviv, A., Oppenheimer, L., & Bar-Tal, D. (Eds.). (1999). *How children understand war and peace: A call for international peace education.* San Francisco, CA: Jossey-Bass.

7. WORK IN AN EDITED COLLECTION

Author's Last Name, Initials. (Year of publication). Title of article or chapter. In Initials Last Name (Ed.), *Title* (pp. pages). Publication City, State or Country: Publisher.

Harris, I. M. (1999). Types of peace education. In A. Raviv, L. Oppenheimer, & D. Bar-Tal (Eds.), *How children understand war and peace: A call for international peace education* (pp. 46–70). San Francisco, CA: Jossey-Bass.

8. UNKNOWN AUTHOR

Title. (Year of publication). Publication City, State or Country: Publisher.

Webster's new biographical dictionary. (1988). Springfield, MA: Merriam-Webster.

If the title page of a work lists the author as *Anonymous*, treat the reference-list entry as if the author's name were Anonymous, and alphabetize it accordingly.

9. EDITION OTHER THAN THE FIRST

Author's Last Name, Initials. (Year). *Title* (name or number ed.). Publication City, State or Country: Publisher.

Burch, D. (2008). *Emergency navigation: Find your position and shape your course at sea even if your instruments fail* (2nd ed.). Camden, ME: International Marine/McGraw-Hill.

10. TRANSLATION

Author's Last Name, Initials. (Year of publication). *Title* (Translator's Initials Last Name, Trans.). Publication City, State or Country: Publisher. (Original work published Year)

Hugo, V. (2008). *Les misérables* (J. Rose, Trans.). New York, NY: Modern Library. (Original work published 1862)

11. MULTIVOLUME WORK

Author's Last Name, Initials. (Year). *Title* (Vols. numbers). Publication City, State or Country: Publisher.

Nastali, D. P. & Boardman, P. C. (2004). *The Arthurian annals: The tradition in English from 1250 to 2000* (Vols. 1–2). New York, NY: Oxford University Press USA.

ONE VOLUME OF A MULTIVOLUME WORK

Author's Last Name, Initials. (Year). *Title of whole work: Vol. number. Title of volume*. Publication City, State or Country: Publisher.

Spiegelman, A. (1986). *Maus: Vol. 1. My father bleeds history.* New York, NY: Random House.

12. ARTICLE IN A REFERENCE BOOK

UNSIGNED

Title of entry. (Year). In *Title of reference book* (Name or number ed., Vol. number, pp. pages). Publication City, State or Country: Publisher.

Macrophage. (2003). In *Merriam-Webster's collegiate dictionary* (10th ed., p. 698). Springfield, MA: Merriam-Webster.

author title publication

SIGNED

Author's Last Name, Initials. (Year). Title of entry. In *Title of reference book* (Vol. number, pp. pages). Publication City, State or Country: Publisher.

Wasserman, D. E. (2006). Human exposure to vibration. In *International encyclopedia of ergonomics and human factors* (Vol. 2, pp. 1800–1801). Boca Raton, FL: CRC.

Periodicals

BASIC FORMAT FOR AN ARTICLE

For most articles, you'll need to provide information about the author; the date; the article title and any subtitle; the periodical title; and any volume or issue number and inclusive page numbers. (APA also recommends including a DOI if one is available; for more on DOIs, see pages 499–500. For an example of a journal article that shows a DOI, see no. 21 on page 500.) Here is an example of a basic entry for an article in a journal.

Ferguson, N. (2005). Sinking globalization. *Foreign Affairs, 84*(2), 64–77.

A FEW DETAILS TO NOTE

- **AUTHORS**: List authors as you would for a book (see no. 1 on page 488 and no. 3 on page 490).
- **DATES**: For journals, give year only. For magazines and newspapers, give year followed by a comma and then month or month and day. Do not abbreviate months.
- **TITLES**: Capitalize only the first word and proper nouns and proper adjectives in titles and subtitles of articles. Capitalize the first and last words and all principal words of periodical titles. Do not capitalize *a*, *an*, *the*, or any prepositions or coordinating conjunctions unless they begin the title of the periodical.

- **VOLUME AND ISSUE:** For journals and magazines, give volume or volume and issue, as explained in more detail below. For newspapers, do not give volume or issue.
- **PAGES:** Use *p.* or *pp.* for a newspaper article but not for a journal or magazine article. If an article does not fall on consecutive pages, give all the page numbers (for example, 45, 75–77 for a journal or magazine; pp. C1, C3, C5–C7 for a newspaper).

13. ARTICLE IN A JOURNAL PAGINATED BY VOLUME

Author's Last Name, Initials. (Year). Title of article. *Title of Journal, volume*, pages.

Caspi, A., Sugden, K., Moffitt, T. E., Taylor, A., Craig, I. W., Harrington, H., . . . Poulton, R. (2003). Influence of life stress on depression: Moderation by a polymorphism in the 5-HTT gene. *Science, 301,* 386–389.

14. ARTICLE IN A JOURNAL PAGINATED BY ISSUE

Author's Last Name, Initials. (Year). Title of article. *Title of Journal, volume*(issue), pages.

Weaver, C., McNally, C., & Moerman, S. (2001). To grammar or not to grammar: That is *not* the question! *Voices from the Middle*, *8*(3), 17–33.

15. ARTICLE IN A MAGAZINE

If a magazine is published weekly, include the day and the month. If there are a volume number and an issue number, include them after the magazine title.

Author's Last Name, Initials. (Year, Month Day). Title of article. *Title of Magazine, volume*(issue), page(s).

Gregory, S. (2008, June 30). Crash course: Why golf carts are more hazardous than they look. *Time, 171*(26), 53.

author title publication

If a magazine is published monthly, include the month(s) only.

Fox, D. (2008, February). Did life begin in ice? Funky properties of frozen water may have made life possible. *Discover, 52*(2), 58–60.

16. ARTICLE IN A NEWSPAPER

If page numbers are consecutive, separate them with a dash. If not, separate them with a comma.

Author's Last Name, Initials. (Year, Month Day). Title of article. *Title of Newspaper*, p(p). page(s).

Schneider, G. (2005, March 13). Fashion sense on wheels. *The Washington Post*, pp. F1, F6.

17. ARTICLE BY AN UNKNOWN AUTHOR

IN A MAGAZINE

Title of article. (Year, Month Day). *Title of Periodical*, *volume*(issue), page(s).

Hot property: From carriage house to family compound. (2004, December). *Berkshire Living, 1*(1), 99.

IN A NEWSPAPER

Clues in salmonella outbreak. (2008, June 21). *New York Times*, p. A13.

18. REVIEW

IN A JOURNAL

Author's Last Name, Initials. (Date of publication). Title of review [Review of *Title of Work*, by Initials Last Name]. *Title of Periodical*, *volume*(issue), page(s).

Geller, J. L. (2005). The cock and bull of Augusten Burroughs [Review of *Running with scissors*, by A. Burroughs]. *Psychiatric Services, 56,* 364–365.

Documentation Map (APA)

Article in a Journal with DOI

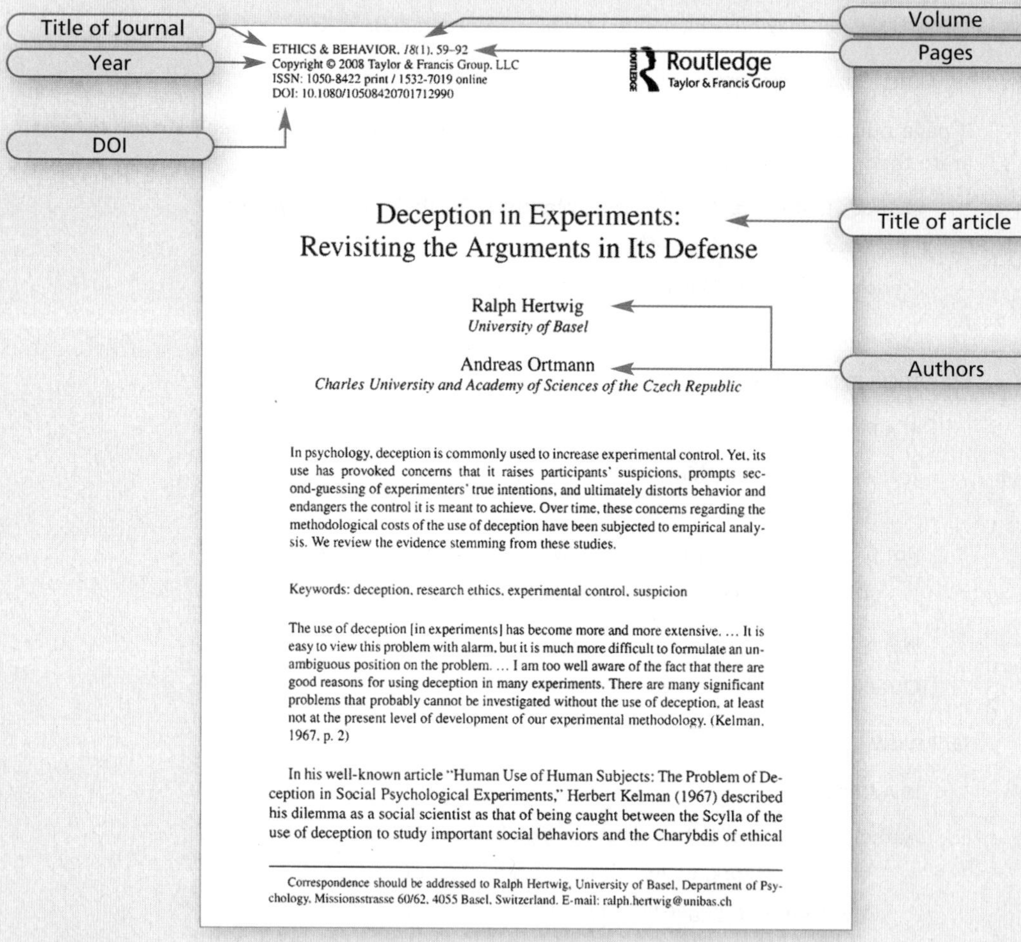

Deception in Experiments: Revisiting the Arguments in Its Defense

Ralph Hertwig
University of Basel

Andreas Ortmann
Charles University and Academy of Sciences of the Czech Republic

In psychology, deception is commonly used to increase experimental control. Yet, its use has provoked concerns that it raises participants' suspicions, prompts second-guessing of experimenters' true intentions, and ultimately distorts behavior and endangers the control it is meant to achieve. Over time, these concerns regarding the methodological costs of the use of deception have been subjected to empirical analysis. We review the evidence stemming from these studies.

Keywords: deception, research ethics, experimental control, suspicion

The use of deception [in experiments] has become more and more extensive. ... It is easy to view this problem with alarm, but it is much more difficult to formulate an unambiguous position on the problem. ... I am too well aware of the fact that there are good reasons for using deception in many experiments. There are many significant problems that probably cannot be investigated without the use of deception, at least not at the present level of development of our experimental methodology. (Kelman, 1967, p. 2)

In his well-known article "Human Use of Human Subjects: The Problem of Deception in Social Psychological Experiments," Herbert Kelman (1967) described his dilemma as a social scientist as that of being caught between the Scylla of the use of deception to study important social behaviors and the Charybdis of ethical

Correspondence should be addressed to Ralph Hertwig, University of Basel, Department of Psychology, Missionsstrasse 60/62, 4055 Basel, Switzerland. E-mail: ralph.hertwig@unibas.ch

494 for more on citing journals APA style

499–500 for more on DOIs

Author's Last Name, Initials. (Year). Title of article. *Title of Journal, volume*(issue), pages. DOI

Hertwig, R. & Ortmann, A. (2008). Deception in experiments: Revisiting the arguments in its defense. *Ethics & Behavior, 18,* 59–92. doi:10.1080/10508420701712990

author title publication

Documentation Map (APA)

Article in a Magazine

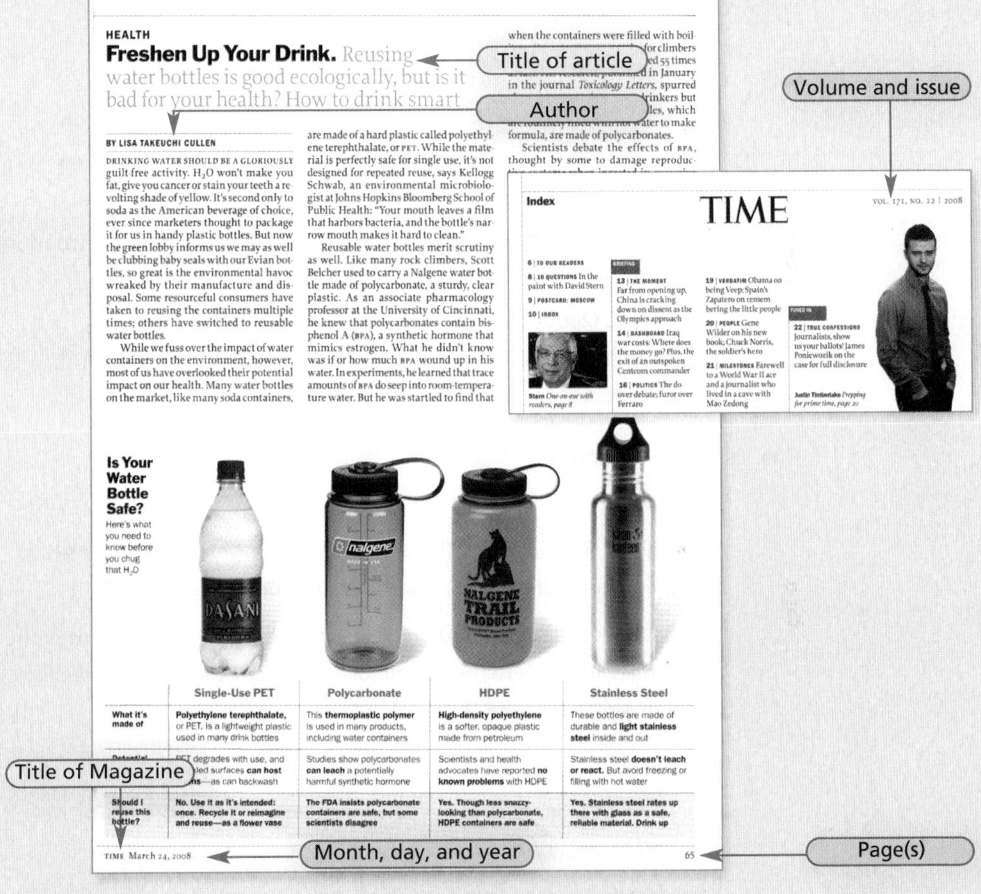

HEALTH

Freshen Up Your Drink. Reusing water bottles is good ecologically, but is it bad for your health? How to drink smart

BY LISA TAKEUCHI CULLEN

DRINKING WATER SHOULD BE A GLORIOUSLY guilt free activity. H_2O won't make you fat, give you cancer or stain your teeth a revolting shade of yellow. It's second only to soda as the American beverage of choice, ever since marketers thought to package it for us in handy plastic bottles. But now the green lobby informs us we may as well be clubbing baby seals with our Evian bottles, so great is the environmental havoc wreaked by their manufacture and disposal. Some resourceful consumers have taken to reusing the containers multiple times; others have switched to reusable water bottles.

While we fuss over the impact of water containers on the environment, however, most of us have overlooked their potential impact on our health. Many water bottles on the market, like many soda containers, are made of a hard plastic called polyethylene terephthalate, or PET. While the material is perfectly safe for single use, it's not designed for repeated reuse, says Kellogg Schwab, an environmental microbiologist at Johns Hopkins Bloomberg School of Public Health: "Your mouth leaves a film that harbors bacteria, and the bottle's narrow mouth makes it hard to clean."

Reusable water bottles merit scrutiny as well. Like many rock climbers, Scott Belcher used to carry a Nalgene water bottle made of polycarbonate, a sturdy, clear plastic. As an associate pharmacology professor at the University of Cincinnati, he knew that polycarbonates contain bisphenol A (BPA), a synthetic hormone that mimics estrogen. What he didn't know was if or how much BPA wound up in his water. In experiments, he learned that trace amounts of BPA do seep into room-temperature water. But he was startled to find that when the containers were filled with boil… for climbers … ed 55 times … in January in the journal *Toxicology Letters*, spurred … rinkers but … les, which … ater to make formula, are made of polycarbonates.

Scientists debate the effects of BPA, thought by some to damage reproduc-

Index

TIME

VOL. 171, NO. 12 | 2008

6 | TO OUR READERS

8 | 10 QUESTIONS In the paint with David Stern

9 | POSTCARD: MOSCOW

10 | INBOX

Stern *One-on-one with readers, page 8*

BRIEFING

13 | THE MOMENT Far from opening up, China is cracking down on dissent as the Olympics approach

14 | DASHBOARD Iraq war costs: Where does the money go? Plus, the exit of an outspoken Centcom commander

16 | POLITICS The do-over debate; furor over Ferraro

19 | VERBATIM Obama on being Veep; Spain's Zapatero on remembering the little people

20 | PEOPLE Gene Wilder on his new book; Chuck Norris, the soldier's hero

21 | MILESTONES Farewell to a World War II ace and a journalist who lived in a cave with Mao Zedong

TUNED IN

22 | TRUE CONFESSIONS Journalists, show us your ballots! James Poniewozik on the case for full disclosure

Justin Timberlake *Prepping for prime time, page 20*

Is Your Water Bottle Safe?

Here's what you need to know before you chug that H_2O

	Single-Use PET	Polycarbonate	HDPE	Stainless Steel
What it's made of	**Polyethylene terephthalate,** or PET, is a lightweight plastic used in many drink bottles	This **thermoplastic polymer** is used in many products, including water containers	**High-density polyethylene** is a softer, opaque plastic made from petroleum	These bottles are made of durable and **light stainless steel** inside and out
	…T degrades with use, and …led surfaces **can host** …**ns**—as can backwash	Studies show polycarbonates **can leach** a potentially harmful synthetic hormone	Scientists and health advocates have reported **no known problems** with HDPE	Stainless steel **doesn't leach or react.** But avoid freezing or filling with hot water
Should I reuse this bottle?	**No. Use it as it's intended: once. Recycle it or reimagine and reuse—as a flower vase**	**The FDA insists polycarbonate containers are safe, but some scientists disagree**	**Yes. Though less snazzy-looking than polycarbonate, HDPE containers are safe**	**Yes. Stainless steel rates up there with glass as a safe, reliable material. Drink up**

TIME March 24, 2008 65

494–95 for more on citing magazines APA style

Author's Last Name, Initials. (Year, Month Day). Title of article. *Title of Magazine*, *volume*(issue), page(s).

Cullen, L. T. (2008, March 24). Freshen up your drink: Reusing water bottles is good ecologically, but is it bad for your health? How to drink smart. *Time, 171*(12), 65.

IN A MAGAZINE

Brandt, A. (2003, October). Animal planet [Review of the book *Intelligence of apes and other rational beings*, by D. R. Rumb & D. A. Washburn]. *National Geographic Adventure, 5*(10), 47.

IN A NEWSPAPER

Morris, C. A. (2005, March 24). Untangling the threads of the Enron fraud [Review of the book *Conspiracy of fools: A true story*, by K. Eichenwald]. *The New York Times*, p. B9.

If the review does not have a title, include just the bracketed information about the work being reviewed.

Jarratt, S. C. (2000). [Review of the book *Lend me your ear: Rhetorical constructions of deafness*, by B. J. Brueggemann]. *College Composition and Communication, 52*, 300–302.

19. LETTER TO THE EDITOR

IN A JOURNAL

Author's Last Name, Initials. (Date of publication). Title of letter [Letter to the editor]. *Title of Periodical, volume*(issue), page(s).

Rosner, W. (2001). An extraordinarily inaccurate assay for free testosterone is still with us [Letter to the editor]. *Journal of Clinical Endocrinology and Metabolism, 86,* 2903.

IN A MAGAZINE

Jorrin, M. (2008, September 1). Mowing it [Letter to the editor]. *The New Yorker, 84*(36), 16.

IN A NEWSPAPER

Hitchcock, G. (2008, August 3). Save our species [Letter to the editor]. *San Francisco Chronicle,* p. P-3.

author title publication

Electronic Sources

BASIC FORMAT FOR AN ELECTRONIC SOURCE

Not every electronic source gives you all the data that APA would like to see in a reference entry. Ideally, you will be able to list author's or editor's name; date of first electronic publication or most recent revision; title of document; information about print publication if any; and retrieval information: DOI (Digital Object Identifier, a string of letters and numbers that identifies an online document) or URL (address of document or site). In some cases, additional information about electronic publication may be required (title of site, retrieval date, name of sponsoring institution). You will find most of those pieces of information in the following example.

> Johnson, C. W. (2000). How our laws are made. *Thomas: Legislative information on the Internet*. Retrieved March 5, 2007, from the Library of Congress website: http://thomas.loc.gov/home/holam.txt

A FEW DETAILS TO NOTE

- **AUTHORS:** List authors as you would for a print book or periodical.
- **TITLES:** For websites and electronic documents, articles, or books, capitalize titles and subtitles as you would for a book; capitalize periodical titles as you would for a print periodical.
- **DATES:** After the author, give the year of the document's original publication on the Web or of its most recent revision. If neither of those years is clear, use *n.d.* to mean "no date." For undated content or content that may change—like an "about us" statement or blog post—include the month (not abbreviated), day, and year that you retrieved the document. For content that's unlikely to change—like a published journal article or book excerpt—you don't need to include the retrieval date.
- **DOI OR URL:** A DOI provides a permanent link to an online document, so when it's available, include the DOI instead of the URL in the reference. A DOI is often found on the first page of an article, but

sometimes you'll need to click on a button labeled "Article" or "Cross-Ref" to find it. If you do not identify the sponsoring institution ("the Library of Congress website" in the example above), you do not need a colon before the URL or DOI. Don't include any punctuation at the end of the URL or DOI. If online material is presented in frames and no DOI is available, provide the URL of the home page or menu page. When a URL won't fit on one line, break the URL before most punctuation, but do not break *http://*.

20. WORK FROM A NONPERIODICAL WEBSITE

Author's Last Name, Initials. (Date of publication). Title of work. *Title of site*. DOI or Retrieved Month Day, Year (if necessary), from URL

Cruikshank, D. (2009, June 15). Unlocking the secrets and powers of the brain. *National Science Foundation*. Retrieved from http://www.nsf.gov /discoveries/disc_summ.jsp?cntn_id=114979&org=NSF

To cite an entire website, include the URL in parentheses in an in-text citation. Do not list the website in your list of references.

21. ARTICLE IN AN ONLINE PERIODICAL OR DATABASE

When available, include the volume number and issue number as you would for a print source. If no DOI has been assigned, provide the URL of the home page or menu page of the journal or magazine, even for articles that you access through a database.

AN ARTICLE IN AN ONLINE JOURNAL

Author's Last Name, Initials. (Year). Title of article. *Title of Journal, volume*(issue), pages. DOI or Retrieved from URL

Corbett, C. (2007). Vehicle-related crime and the gender gap. *Psychology, Crime & Law, 13*, 245–263. doi:10.1080/10683160600822022

author title publication

Documentation Map (APA)
Work from a Website

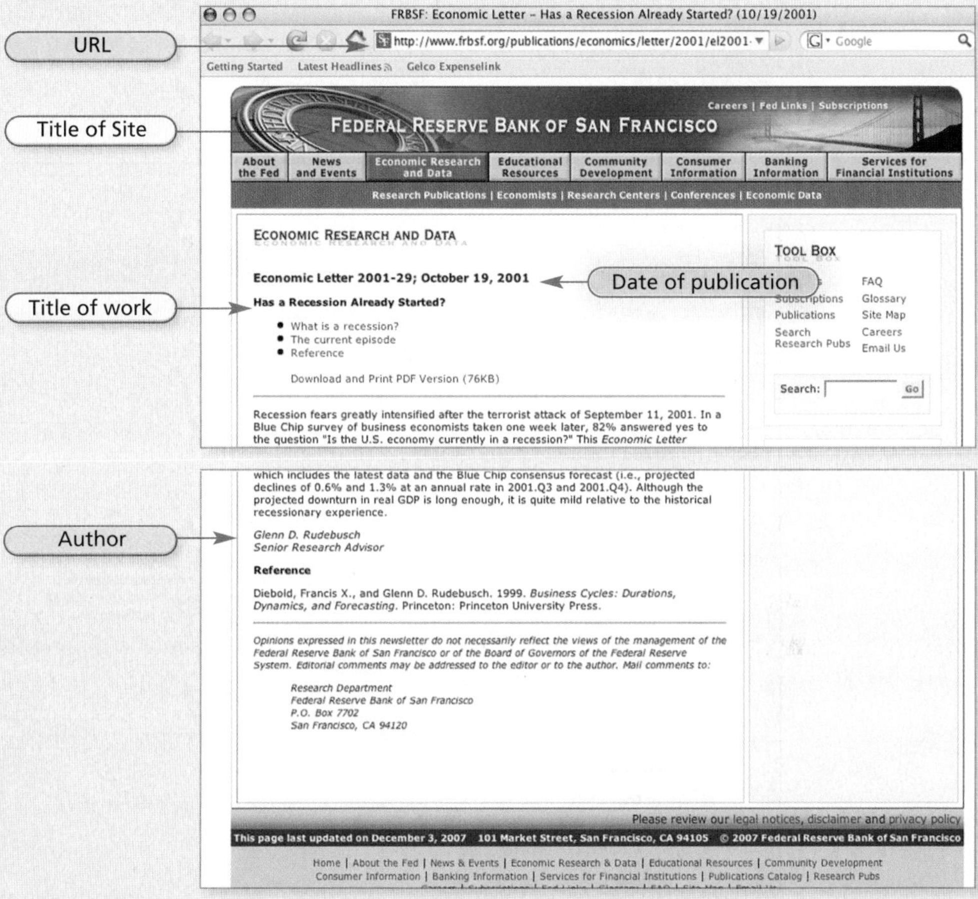

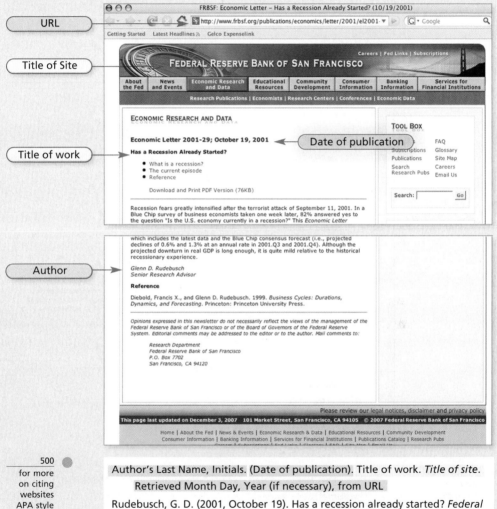

500 for more on citing websites APA style

Author's Last Name, Initials. (Date of publication). Title of work. *Title of site*. Retrieved Month Day, Year (if necessary), from URL

Rudebusch, G. D. (2001, October 19). Has a recession already started? *Federal Reserve Bank of San Francisco*. Retrieved April 3, 2008, from http://www.frbsf.org/publications/economics/letter/2001/el2001-29.html

Documentation Map (APA)
Article in a Database with DOI

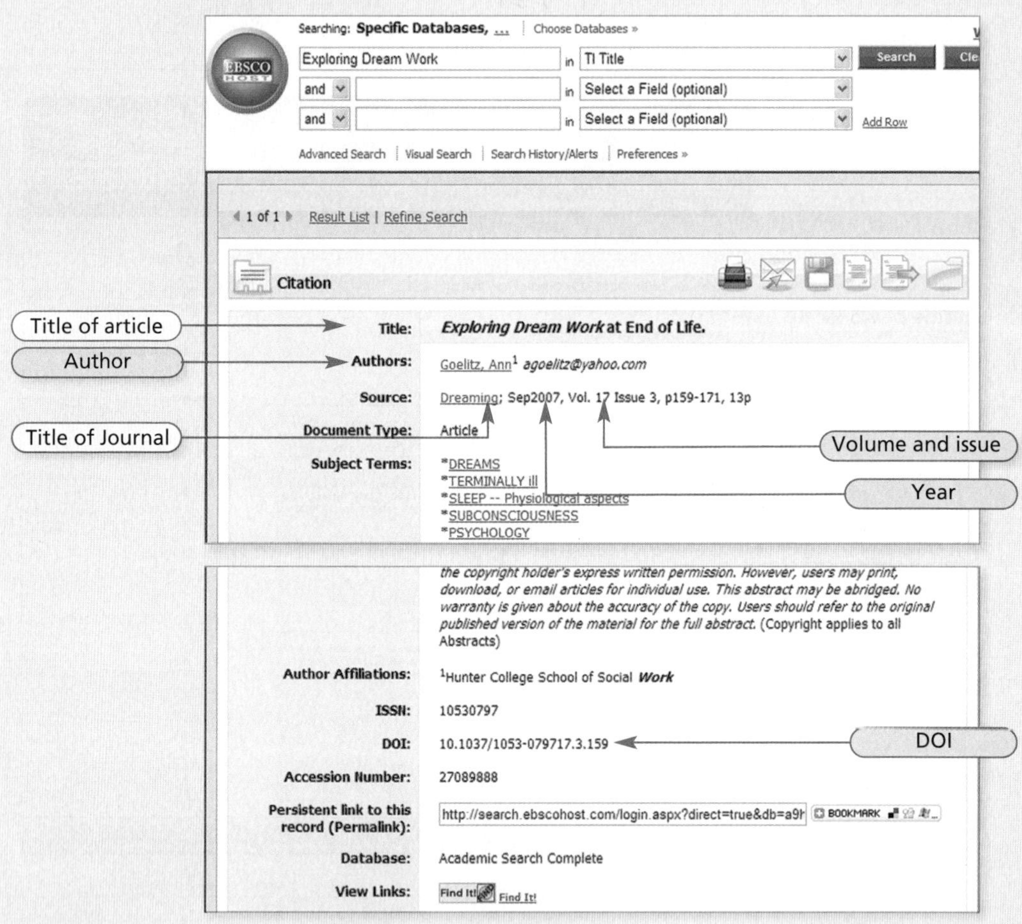

500, 503 for more on citing an article in a database APA style

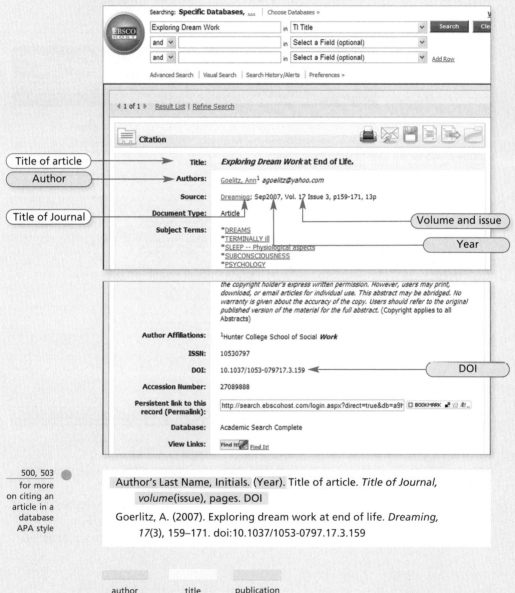

Author's Last Name, Initials. (Year). Title of article. *Title of Journal, volume*(issue), pages. DOI

Goerlitz, A. (2007). Exploring dream work at end of life. *Dreaming, 17*(3), 159–171. doi:10.1037/1053-0797.17.3.159

author title publication

AN ARTICLE IN AN ONLINE MAGAZINE

Author's Last Name, Initials. (Year, Month Day). Title of article. *Title of Magazine, volume*(issue). DOI or Retrieved Month Day, Year (if necessary), from URL

Bohannon, J. (2008, June 20). Slaying monsters for science. *Science, 320*(5883). doi:10.1126/science.320.5883.1592c

AN ARTICLE IN AN ONLINE NEWSPAPER

If the article can be found by searching the site, give the URL of the home page or menu page.

Author's Last Name, Initials. (Year, Month Day). Title of article. *Title of Newspaper*. Retrieved from URL

Collins, G. (2008, June 21). Vice is nice. *The New York Times*. Retrieved from http://www.nytimes.com

22. ARTICLE ONLY AVAILABLE THROUGH A DATABASE

Some sources, such as an out-of-print journal or rare book, can only be accessed through a database. When no DOI is provided, give either the name of the database or its URL.

Author's Last Name, Initials. (Year). Title of article. *Title of Journal, volume*(issue), pages. DOI or Retrieved from Name of database or URL

Simpson, M. (1972). Authoritarianism and education: A comparitive approach. *Sociometry 35*, 223–234. Retrieved from http://www.jstor.org

23. ARTICLE IN AN ONLINE REFERENCE WORK

For online reference works like dictionaries or encyclopedias, give the URL of the home page or menu page if no DOI is provided. (See next page for template and example.)

Author's Last Name, Initials. (Year). Title of entry. In *Title of reference work.* DOI or Retrieved from URL

Smith, R. L. (2008). Ecology. In *MSN Encarta.* Retrieved from http://encarta.msn.com

24. ELECTRONIC BOOK

Author's Last Name, Initials. (Year). *Title of book*. DOI or Retrieved from URL

TenDam, H. (n.d.). *Politics, civilization & humanity.* Retrieved from http://onlineoriginals.com/showitem.asp?itemID=46&page=2

For an electronic book based on a print version, include a description of the digital format in brackets after the book title.

Blain, M. (2009). *The sociology of terror: Studies in power, subjection, and victimage ritual* [Adobe Digital Editions version]. Retrieved from http://www.powells.com/sub/AdobeDigitalEditionsPolitics.html?sec_big_link=1

25. ELECTRONIC DISCUSSION SOURCE

If the name of the list to which to the message was posted is not part of the URL, include it after *Retrieved from*. The URL you provide should be for the archived version of the message or post.

Author's Last Name, Initials. (Year, Month Day). Subject line of message [Descriptive label]. Retrieved from URL

Baker, J. (2005, February 15). Re: Huffing and puffing [Electronic mailing list message]. Retrieved from American Dialect Society electronic mailing list: http://listserv.linguistlist.org/cgi-bin/wa?A2=ind0502C&L=ADS-L&P=R44

Do not include email or other nonarchived discussions in your list of references. Simply cite the sender's name in your text. See no. 14 on page 486 for guidelines on identifying such sources in your text.

author title publication

26. BLOG ENTRY

Author's Last Name, Initials. (Year, Month Day). Title of post [Web log post]. Retrieved from URL

Collins, C. (2009, August 19). Butterfly benefits from warmer springs? [Web log post]. Retrieved from http://www.intute.ac.uk/blog /2009/08/19/butterfly-benefits-from-warmer-springs/

27. ONLINE VIDEO

Last Name, Initials (Writer), & Last Name, Initials (Producer). (Year, Month Day posted). *Title* [Descriptive label]. Retrieved from URL

Coulter, J. (Songwriter & Performer), & Booth, M. S. (Producer). (2006, September 23). *Code Monkey* [Video file]. Retrieved from http://www.youtube.com/watch?v=v4Wy7gRGgeA

28. PODCAST

Writer's Last Name, Initials. (Writer), & Producer's Last Name, Initials. (Producer). (Year, Month Day). Title of podcast. *Title of website or program* [Audio podcast]. Retrieved from URL

Britt, M. A. (Writer & Producer). (2009, June 7). Episode 97: Stanley Milgram study finally replicated. *The Psych Files Podcast* [Audio podcast]. Retrieved from http://www.thepsychfiles.com/

Other Kinds of Sources

29. FILM, VIDEO, OR DVD

Last Name, Initials (Producer), & Last Name, Initials (Director). (Year). *Title* [Motion picture]. Country: Studio.

Wallis, H. B. (Producer), & Curtiz, M. (Director). (1942). *Casablanca* [Motion picture]. United States: Warner.

30. MUSIC RECORDING

Composer's Last Name, Initials. (Year of copyright). Title of song. On *Title of album* [Medium]. City, State or Country: Label.

Veloso, C. (1997). Na baixado sapateiro. On *Livros* [CD]. Los Angeles, CA: Nonesuch.

If the music is performed by someone other than the composer, put that information in brackets following the title. When the recording date is different from the copyright date, put it in parentheses after the label.

Cahn, S., & Van Heusen, J. (1960). The last dance [Recorded by F. Sinatra]. On *Sinatra reprise: The very good years* [CD]. Burbank, CA: Reprise Records. (1991)

31. PROCEEDINGS OF A CONFERENCE

Author's Last Name, Initials. (Year of publication). Title of paper. In *Proceedings Title* (pp. pages). Publication City, State or Country: Publisher.

Heath, S. B. (1997). Talking work: Language among teens. In *Symposium about Language and Society–Austin* (pp. 27–45). Austin: Department of Linguistics at the University of Texas.

32. TELEVISION PROGRAM

Last Name, Initials (Writer), & Last Name, Initials (Director). (Year). Title of episode [Descriptive label]. In Initials Last Name (Producer), *Series title*. City, State or Country: Network.

Mundy, C. (Writer), & Bernaro, E. A. (Director). (2007). In birth and death [Television series episode]. In E. A. Bernaro (Executive Producer), *Criminal minds.* New York, NY: NBC.

author title publication

33. SOFTWARE OR COMPUTER PROGRAM

Title and version number [Computer software]. (Year). Publication City, State or Country: Publisher.

The Sims 2: Holiday edition [Computer software]. (2005). Redwood City, CA: Electronic Arts.

34. DISSERTATION ABSTRACT

Author's Last Name, Initials. (Year). Title of dissertation. *Title of Source, volume*(issue), page(s).

Palenski, J. E. (1981). Running away: A sociological analysis. *Dissertation Abstracts International, 41*(12), 5251.

35. DISSERTATION

ACCESSED ONLINE

Author's Last Name, Initials. (Year). *Title of dissertation* (Doctoral dissertation). Retrieved from Name of database. (accession number)

Knapik, M. (2008). *Adolescent online trouble-talk: Help-seeking in cyberspace* (Doctoral dissertation). Retrieved from ProQuest Dissertation and Theses database. (AAT NR38024)

For a dissertation that you retrieve from the Web, include the name of institution after *Doctoral dissertation*. For example: (Doctoral dissertation, University of North Carolina). End your citation with *Retrieved from* and the URL.

UNPUBLISHED

Author's Last Name, Initials. (Year). *Title of dissertation* (Unpublished doctoral dissertation). Institution, City, State or Country.

Connell, E. (1996). *The age of experience: Edith Wharton and the "divorce question" in early twentieth-century America* (Unpublished doctoral dissertation). University of Virginia, Charlottesville.

36. TECHNICAL OR RESEARCH REPORT

Author's Last Name, Initials. (Year). *Title of report* (Report number). Publication City, State or Country: Publisher.

Elsayed, T., Namata, G., Getoor, L., & Oard., D. W. (2008). *Personal name resolution in email: A heuristic approach* (Report No. LAMP-TR-150). College Park: University of Maryland.

How to Cite Sources That APA Does Not Cover

To cite a source for which APA does not provide guidelines, look at models similar to the source you are citing. Give any information readers will need in order to find it themselves—author; date of publication; title; publisher; information about electronic retrieval (DOI or URL); and any other pertinent information. You might want to try your citation yourself, to be sure it will lead others to your source.

SAMPLE RESEARCH PAPER, APA STYLE

Carolyn Stonehill wrote the following paper for a first-year writing course. It is formatted according to the guidelines of the *Publication Manual of the American Psychological Association*, 6th edition (2009). While APA guidelines are used widely in linguistics and the social sciences, exact requirements may vary from discipline to discipline and course to course. If you're unsure about what your instructor wants, ask for clarification.

IT'S IN OUR GENES 1

Insert a shortened title in the upper-left corner of each page, including the title page. Place page numbers on the upper right.

It's in Our Genes:

The Biological Basis of Human Mating Behavior

Carolyn Stonehill

English 102, Section 22

Professor Bertsch

November 13, 2009

Center the full title, your name, the name and section number of the course, your instructor's name, and the date, unless your instructor requires different information.

Unless your instructor specifies another length, limit your abstract to 120 words or fewer.

APA requires 2 spaces after punctuation at the end of a sentence.

Abstract

While cultural values and messages certainly play a part in the process of mate selection, the genetic and psychological predispositions developed by our ancestors play the biggest role in determining to whom we are attracted. Women are attracted to strong, capable men with access to resources to help rear children. Men find women attractive based on visual signs of youth, health, and, by implication, fertility. While perceptions of attractiveness are influenced by cultural norms and reinforced by advertisements and popular media, the persistence of mating behaviors that have no relationship to societal realities suggests that they are part of our biological heritage.

It's in Our Genes:

The Biological Basis of Human Mating Behavior

Center the title.

Double-space the entire paper.

Consider the following scenario: It's a sunny afternoon on campus, and Jenny is walking to her next class. Out of the corner of her eye, she catches sight of her lab partner, Joey, parking his car. She stops to admire how tall, muscular, and stylishly dressed he is, and she does not take her eyes off him as he walks away from his shiny new BMW. As he flashes her a pearly white smile, Jenny melts, then quickly adjusts her skirt and smooths her hair.

Indent each new paragraph 5 to 7 spaces ($\frac{1}{2}$ inch).

This scenario, while generalized, is familiar: Our attraction to people—or lack of it—often depends on their physical traits. But why this attraction? Why does Jenny respond the way she does to her handsome lab partner? Why does she deem him handsome at all? Certainly Joey embodies the stereotypes of physical attractiveness prevalent in contemporary American society. Advertisements, television shows, and magazine articles all provide Jenny with signals telling her what constitutes the ideal American man. Yet she is also attracted to Joey's new sports car even though she has a new car herself. Does Jenny find this man striking because of the influence of her culture, or does her attraction lie in a more fundamental part of her constitution? Evolutionary psychologists, who apply principles of evolutionary biology to research on the human mind, would say that Jenny's responses in this situation are due largely to mating strategies developed by her prehistoric ancestors. Driven by the need to reproduce and propagate the species, these ancestors of ours formed patterns of mate selection so effective in providing for their needs and those of their offspring that they are mimicked even in today's society. While cultural values and messages clearly play a part in the process of mate selection, the genetic and psychological predispositions developed by our ancestors play the biggest role in determining to whom we are attracted.

Provide headings to help readers follow the organization.

Women's Need to Find a Capable Mate

Refer to authors by last name. In general, use the past tense or the present perfect in signal phrases.

Pioneering evolutionary psychologist Trivers (as cited in Allman, 1993) observed that having and rearing children requires women to invest far more resources than men because of the length of pregnancy, the dangers of childbirth, and the duration of infants' dependence on their mothers (p. 56). According to Fisher (as cited in Frank, 2001), one of the leading advocates of this theory, finding a capable mate was a huge preoccupation of all prehistoric reproductive women, and for good reason: "A female couldn't carry a baby in one arm and sticks and stones in the other arm and still feed and protect herself on the very dangerous open grasslands, so she began to need a mate to help her rear her young" (p. 85). So because of this it became advantageous for the woman to find a strong, capable man with access to resources, and it became suitable for the man to find a healthy, reproductively sound woman to bear and care for his offspring. According to evolutionary psychologists, these are the bases upon which modern mate selection is founded, and there are many examples of this phenomenon to be found in our own society.

One can see now why Jenny might be attracted by Joey's display of resources—his BMW. In our society, men with good job prospects, a respected social position, friends in high places, or any combination thereof have generally been viewed as more desirable mates than those without these things because they signal to women that the men have resources (Buss & Schmitt, 1993, p. 226). Compared with males, females invest more energy in bearing and raising children, so it is most advantageous for females to choose mates with easy access to resources, the better to provide for their children.

If the author is not named in a signal phrase, include the name in parentheses, along with the date and the page number.

Men's Need to Find a Healthy Mate

For men, reproductive success depends mainly on the reproductive fitness of their female counterpart: No amount of available resources can save a baby miscarried in the first month of gestation. Because of this need for a healthy mate, men have evolved a particular attraction "radar" that focuses on signs of a woman's health and youth, markers that are primarily visual (Weiten, 2001, p. 399). Present-day attractiveness ratings are based significantly on this primitive standard: "Some researchers have suggested that cross-cultural standards of beauty reflect an evolved preference for physical traits that are generally associated with youth, such as smooth skin, good muscle tone, and shiny hair" (Boyd & Silk, 2000, p. 625). This observation would explain why women of our time are preoccupied with plastic surgery, makeup, and—in Jenny's case—a quick hair check as a potential date

Use ampersands in parenthetical references—but use and *in signal phrases.*

If an author is named in a signal phrase, include the publication date in parentheses after the name.

approaches. As Cunningham, Roberts, Barbee, Druen, and Wu (1995) noted, "A focus on outer beauty may have stemmed from a need for desirable inner qualities," such as health, strength, and fertility, and "culture may build on evolutionary dynamics by specifying grooming attributes that signal successful adaptation" (pp. 262–263).

The Influence of the Media on Mate Selection

There is, however, a good deal of opposition to evolutionary theory. Some critics say that the messages fed to us by the media are a larger influence on the criteria of present-day mate selection than any sort of ancestral behavior. Advertisements and popular media have long shown Americans what constitutes a physically ideal mate: In general, youthful, well-toned, symmetrical features are considered more attractive than aging, flabby, or lopsided ones. Evolutionary psychologists argue that research has not determined what is cause and what is effect. Cosmides and Tooby (1997) offered the following analogy to show the danger of assigning culture too powerful a causal role:

Indent quotations of 40 or more words 5 to 7 spaces, about 1/2 inch from the left margin.

> For example, people think that if they can show that there is information in the culture that mirrors how people behave, then *that* is the cause of their behavior. So if they see that men on TV have trouble crying, they assume that their example is *causing* boys to be afraid to cry. But which is cause and which effect? Does the fact that men don't cry much on TV *teach* boys to not cry, or does it merely *reflect* the way boys normally develop? In the absence of research on the particular topic,

there is no way of knowing. ("Nature and Nurture: An Adaptationist Perspective," para. 16)

To cite a specific part of an unpaginated website, count paragraphs from the beginning of the document or, as is done here, from a major heading.

We can hypothesize, then, that rather than media messages determining our mating habits, our mating habits determine the media messages. Advertisers rely on classical conditioning to interest consumers in their products. For instance, by showing an image of a beautiful woman while advertising a beauty product, advertisers hope that consumers will associate attractiveness with the use of that particular product (Weiten, 2001). In order for this method to be effective, however, the images depicted in conjunction with the beauty product must be ones the general public already finds attractive, and an image of a youthful, clear-skinned woman would, according to evolutionary psychologists, be attractive for reasons of reproductive fitness. In short, what some call media influence is not an influence at all but merely a mirror in which we see evidence of our ancestral predispositions.

If Not Media, Then What?

Tattersall (2001), a paleoanthropologist at the American Museum of Natural History, offered another counterargument to the evolutionary theory of mate selection. First, he argued that the behavior of organisms is influenced not only by genetics, but also by economics and ecology working together (p. 663). Second, he argued that no comparisons can be made between modern human behavior and that of our evolutionary predecessors because the appearance of *Homo sapiens* presented a sudden, qualitative change from the Neanderthals — not a gradual evolution of behavioral traits:

> As a cognitive and behavioral entity, our species is truly unprecedented. Our consciousness is an emergent quality, not the result of eons of fine-tuning of a single instrument. And, if so, it is to this recently acquired quality of uniqueness, not to the hypothetical "ancestral environments," that we must look in the effort to understand our often unfathomable behaviors. (p. 665)

The key to Tattersall's argument is this "emergent quality" of symbolic thought; according to his theories, the ability to think symbolically is what separates modern humans from their ancestors and shows the impossibility of sexual selection behaviors having been passed down over millions of years. Our sexual preferences, Tattersall said, are a result of our own recent and species-specific development and have nothing whatsoever to do with our ancestors.

Opponents of the evolutionary theory, though, fail to explain how "unfathomable" mating behaviors can exist in our present society for no apparent or logical reason. Though medicine has advanced to the point where fertility can be medically enhanced, Singh (1993) observed that curvy women are still viewed as especially attractive because they are perceived to possess greater fertility — a perception that is borne out by several studies of female fertility, hormone levels, and waist-to-hip ratio (p. 304). Though more and more women are attending college and achieving high-paying positions, women are still "more likely than men to consider economic prospects a high priority in a mate" (Sapolsky, 2001–2002, p. 18). While cultural norms and economic conditions influence our taste in mates, as Singh (1993) showed in observing that "the degree of affluence of a society or of an ethnic group within a society may, to a large extent, determine the prevalence and admiration of fatness [of women]" (pp. 304–305), we still react to potential mates in ways determined in Paleolithic times. The key to understanding our mating behavior does not lie only in an emergent modern quality, nor does it lie solely in the messages relayed to us by society; rather, it involves as well the complex mating strategies developed by our ancestors.

Begin list of references on a new page; center the heading.

Alphabetize the list by author's last name.

Indent all lines after the first line of each entry 5 spaces or ½ inch.

Be sure every source listed is cited in the text; don't list sources consulted but not cited.

IT'S IN OUR GENES 10

References

Allman, W. F. (1993, July 19). The mating game. *U.S. News & World Report*, *115*(3), 56–63.

Boyd, R., & Silk, J. B. (2000). *How humans evolved.* (2nd ed.). New York, NY: Norton.

Buss, D. M., & Schmitt, D. P. (1993). Sexual strategies theory: An evolutionary perspective on human mating. *Psychological Review*, *100*(2), 204–232.

Cosmides, L., & Tooby, J. (1997). *Evolutionary psychology: A primer.* Retrieved February 2, 2009, from http://www.psych.ucsb.edu/research/cep/primer.html

Cunningham, M. R., Roberts, A. R., Barbee, A. P., Druen, P. B., & Wu, C.-H. (1995). "Their ideas of beauty are, on the whole, the same as ours": Consistency and variability in the cross-cultural perception of female physical attractiveness. *Journal of Personality and Social Psychology*, *68*, 261–279.

Frank, C. (2001, February). Why do we fall in — and out of — love? Dr. Helen Fisher unravels the mystery. *Biography*, 85–87, 112.

Sapolsky, R. M. (2001–2002, December–January). What do females want? *Natural History*, 18–21.

Singh, D. (1993). Adaptive significance of female physical attractiveness: Role of waist-to-hip ratio. *Journal of Personality and Social Behavior*, *65*, 293–307.

Tattersall, I. (2001). Evolution, genes, and behavior. *Zygon: Journal of Religion & Science, 36,* 657–666. Retrieved from the Psychology and Behavioral Sciences Collection database.

Weiten, W. (2001). *Psychology: Themes & variations* (5th ed.). San Bernardino, CA: Wadsworth.

part 6

Media / Design

Consciously or not, we design all the texts we write, choosing typefaces, setting up text as lists or charts, deciding whether to add headings — and then whether to center them or flush them left. Sometimes our genre calls for certain design elements — essays begin with titles, letters begin with salutations ("Dear Auntie Em"). Other times we design texts to meet the demands of particular audiences, formatting documentation in MLA or APA or some other style, setting type larger for young children, and so on. And always our designs will depend upon our medium. A memoir might take the form of an essay in a book, be turned into a bulleted list for a PowerPoint presentation, or include links to images or other pages if presented on a website. The chapters in this part offer advice for working with PRINT texts, SPOKEN texts, and ELECTRONIC texts.

Media / Design

Print Text 51

USA Today reports on a major news story with an article that includes a large photo and a colorful graph; the *New York Times* covers the same story with an article that is not illustrated but has a large headline and a pull quote highlighting one key point. Your psychology textbook includes many photos, tables, charts, and other visuals to help readers understand the subject matter. When you submit an essay for a class, you choose a typeface and you may make the type larger—or smaller—as need be. In all these instances, the message is in some way "designed." This chapter offers advice on designing print texts to suit your purpose, audience, genre, and subject. Much of the advice also holds for **ELECTRONIC TEXTS** and for visuals that accompany **SPOKEN TEXTS**.

546–56
534–45

Considering the Rhetorical Situation

As with all writing tasks, your rhetorical situation affects the way you design a print text.

PURPOSE Consider how you can design your text to help achieve your purpose. If you're reporting certain kinds of information, for instance, you may want to present some data in a chart or table; if you're trying to get readers to care about an issue, a photo or pull quote—a brief selection of text "pulled out" and reprinted in a larger typeface—might help you do so.

3–4

AUDIENCE Do you need to do anything designwise for your intended audience? Change the type size? Add headings? Tables? Color?

5–8

9–11 **GENRE** Does your genre have any design requirements? Must (or can) it have headings? Illustrations? Tables or graphs? A certain size paper?

12–14 **STANCE** How can your design reflect your attitude toward your audience and subject? Do you need a businesslike typeface, or a playful one? Will illustrations help you convey a certain tone?

Some Elements of Design

Whatever your text, you have various design decisions to make. What typeface(s) should you use? How should you arrange your text on the page? Should you include any headings? The following guidelines will help you consider each of these questions.

Type. You can choose from among many typefaces, and the one you choose will affect your text—how well readers can read it and how they
13 will perceive your **TONE** and **STANCE.** Times Roman will make a text look busi-
12–14 nesslike or academic; Comic Sans will make it look playful. For most academic writing, you'll want to use 10- or 11- or 12-point type, and you'll usually want to use a serif face (such as Times Roman or Bookman), which is generally easier to read than a sans serif face (such as Arial, Verdana, or Century Gothic). It's usually a good idea to use a serif face for your main text, reserving sans serif for headings and parts you want to highlight. Decorative typefaces (such as Magneto, Amaze, Chiller, and Jokerman) should be used sparingly and only when they're appropriate for your audi-
1 ence, purpose, and the rest of your **RHETORICAL SITUATION.** If you use more
526–27 than one typeface in a text, use each one consistently: one face for **HEADINGS,** one for captions, one for the main body of your text. And don't go overboard—you won't often have reason to use more than two or, at most, three typefaces in any one text.

Every typeface has regular, **bold**, and *italic* fonts. In general, choose regular for the main text, bold for major headings, and italic for titles of

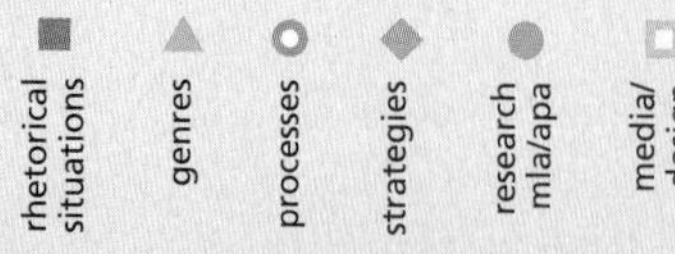

books and other long works and, occasionally, to emphasize words or brief phrases. Avoid italicizing or boldfacing entire paragraphs. If you are following **MLA**, **APA**, or some other style, be sure your use of fonts conforms to its requirements.

428–76
477–519

Finally, consider the line spacing of your text. Generally, academic writing is double-spaced, whereas **LETTERS** and **RÉSUMÉS** are usually single-spaced. Some kinds of **REPORTS** may call for single-spacing; check with your instructor if you're not sure. In addition, you'll often need to add an extra space to set off parts of a text—items in a list, for instance, or headings.

189–200
59–82

Layout. Layout is the way text is arranged on a page. An academic essay, for example, will usually have a title centered at the top, one-inch margins all around, and double-spacing. A text can be presented in paragraphs—or in the form of **LISTS**, **TABLES**, **CHARTS**, **GRAPHS**, and so on. Sometimes you need to include other elements as well: headings, images and other graphics, captions, lists of works cited.

525–26
528–30

Paragraphs. Dividing text into paragraphs focuses information for readers and helps them process the information by dividing it into manageable chunks. If you're writing a story for a newspaper with narrow columns, for example, you'll divide your text into shorter paragraphs than you would if you were writing an academic essay. In general, indent paragraphs five spaces when your text is double-spaced; either indent or skip a line between paragraphs that are single-spaced.

Lists. Put information into list form that you want to set off and make easily accessible. Number the items in a list when the sequence matters (in instructions, for example); use bullets when the order is not important. Set off lists with an extra line of space above and below, and add extra space between the items on a list if necessary for legibility. Here's an example:

> Darwin's theory of how species change through time derives from three postulates, each of which builds on the previous one:
>
> 1. The ability of a population to expand is infinite, but the ability of any environment to support populations is always finite.

2. Organisms within populations vary, and this variation affects the ability of individuals to survive and reproduce.
3. The variations are transmitted from parents to offspring.

—Robert Boyd and Joan B. Silk, *How Humans Evolved*

Do not set off text as a list unless there's a good reason to do so, however. Some lists are more appropriately presented in paragraph form, especially when they give information that is not meant to be referred to more than once. In the following example, there is no reason to highlight the information by setting it off in a list—and bad news is softened by putting it in paragraph form:

> I regret to inform you that the Scholarship Review Committee did not approve your application for a Board of Rectors scholarship, for the following reasons: your grade-point average did not meet the minimum requirements; your major is not among those eligible for consideration; and the required letter of recommendation was not received before the deadline.

Presented as a list, that information would be needlessly emphatic.

Headings. Headings make the structure of a text easier to follow and help readers find specific information. Some genres require standard headings—announcing an **ABSTRACT**, for example, or a list of **WORKS CITED**. Other times you will want to use headings to provide an overview of a section of text. You may not need any headings with brief texts, and when you do, you'll probably want to use one level at most, just to announce major topics. Longer texts and information-rich genres, such as pamphlets or detailed **REPORTS**, may require several levels of headings. If you decide to include headings, you will need to decide how to phrase them, what typefaces and fonts to use, and where to position them.

111–15
475–76
59–82

Phrase headings concisely. Make your headings succinct and parallel in structure. You might make all the headings nouns (**Mushrooms**), noun phrases (**Kinds of Mushrooms**), gerund phrases (**Recognizing Kinds of Mushrooms**), or questions (**How Do I Identify Mushrooms?**). Whatever form you decide on, use it consistently for each heading. Sometimes your phrasing will depend on your purpose. If you're simply helping readers find information, use brief phrases:

Head	**Forms of Social Groups among Primates**
Subhead	*Solitary Social Groups*
Subhead	*Monogamous Social Groups*

If you want to address your readers directly with the information in your text, consider writing your headings as questions:

How can you identify morels?
Where can you find morels?
How can you cook morels?

Make headings visible. Headings need to be visible, so consider setting them in bold, italics, or underline—or use a different typeface. For example, you could print your main text in a serif font like Times Roman and your headings in a sans serif font like Arial or make the headings larger than the regular text. When you have several levels of headings, use capitalization, bold, and italics to distinguish among the various levels:

First-Level Head
Second-Level Head
Third-level head

Be aware that APA and MLA formats expect headings to be in the same typeface as the main text; APA requires that each level of heading appear in a specific style: uppercase and lowercase, italicized uppercase and lowercase, and so on. If five levels of headings are needed, make the first heading all uppercase.

Position headings appropriately. If you're following **APA** or **MLA** format, center first-level headings. If you are not following a prescribed format, you get to decide where to position your headings: centered, flush with the left margin, or even alongside the text, in a wide left-hand margin. Position each level of head consistently throughout your text.

477–519
428–76

White space. Use white space to separate the various parts of a text. In general, use one-inch margins for the text of an essay or report. Unless you're following MLA or APA format, include space above headings, above and below lists, and around photos, graphs, and other images to set them apart from the rest of the text. See the two **SAMPLE RESEARCH PAPERS** in this book for examples of the formats required by MLA and APA.

MLA 467–76
APA 508–19

Visuals

Visuals can sometimes help you to make a point in ways that words alone cannot. Be careful, however, that any visuals you use contribute to your point—not simply act as decoration. This section discusses how to use photos, graphs, charts, tables, and diagrams effectively.

Select visuals that are appropriate for your rhetorical situation. There are various kinds of visuals: photographs, line graphs, bar graphs, pie charts, tables, diagrams, flowcharts, drawings, and more. Which ones you use, if any, will depend on your content, your **GENRE,** and your **RHETORICAL SITUATION.** A newspaper article on housing prices might include a bar graph or line graph, and also some photographs; a report on the same topic written for an economics class would probably have graphs but no photos. See the examples on the facing page, along with advice for using each one.

19
1

Some guidelines for using visuals

- Use visuals as an element of your text's content, one that is as important as your words to your message. Therefore, avoid clip art, which is primarily intended as decoration.
- Position visuals in your text as close as possible to your discussion of the topic to which they relate.
- Number all visuals, using a separate sequence for figures (photos, graphs, and drawings) and tables: *Figure 1, Figure 2; Table 1, Table 2.*
- Refer to the visual before it appears, identifying it and summarizing its point. For example: "As Figure 1 shows, Japan's economy grew dramatically between 1965 and 1980."

Photographs can support an argument, illustrate events and processes, present other points of view, and help readers "place" your information in time and space.

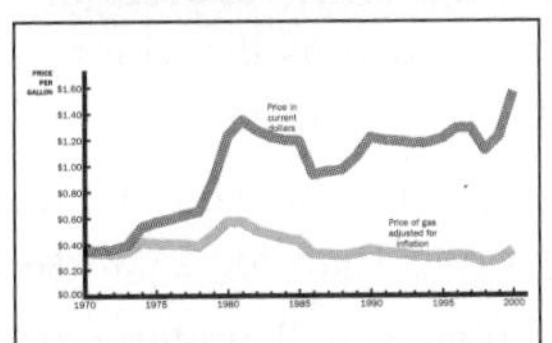

Line graphs are a good way of showing changes in data over time. Each line here shows a different set of data; plotting the two lines together allows readers to compare the data at different points in time.

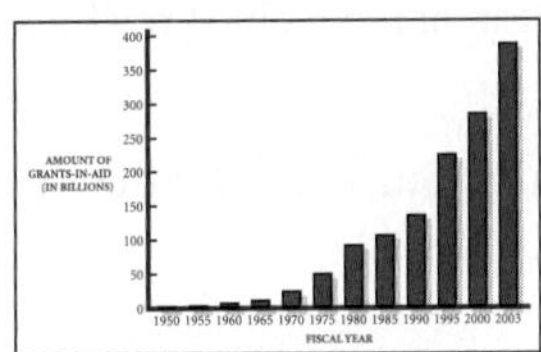

Bar graphs are useful for comparing quantitative data, measurements of how much or how many. The bars can be horizontal or vertical.

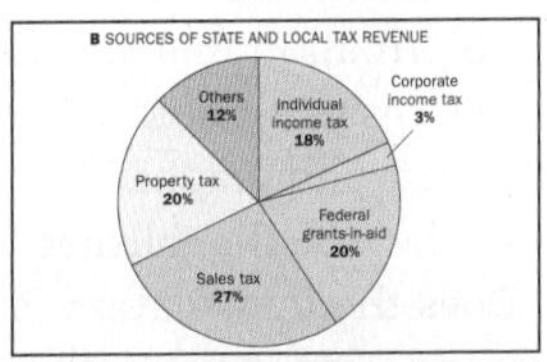

Pie charts can be used for showing how a whole is divided into parts or how something is apportioned.

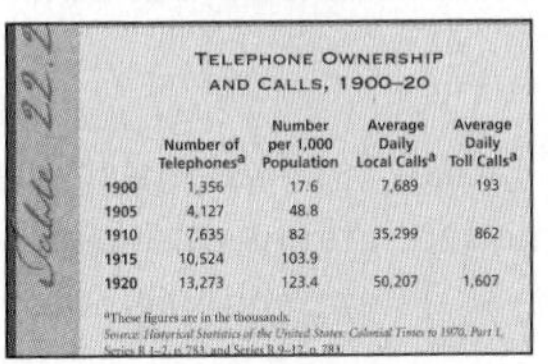

Table 22.2

TELEPHONE OWNERSHIP AND CALLS, 1900–20

	Number of Telephones[a]	Number per 1,000 Population	Average Daily Local Calls[a]	Average Daily Toll Calls[a]
1900	1,356	17.6	7,689	193
1905	4,127	48.8		
1910	7,635	82	35,299	862
1915	10,524	103.9		
1920	13,273	123.4	50,207	1,607

[a]These figures are in the thousands.
Source: Historical Statistics of the United States: Colonial Times to 1970, Part 1, Series R 1–2, p. 783, and Series R 9–12, p. 783.

Tables are useful for displaying information concisely, especially when several items are being compared.

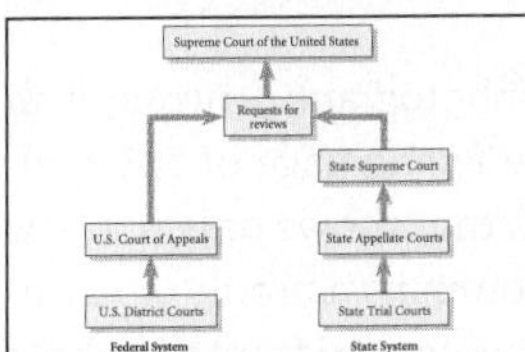

Diagrams, flowcharts, and drawings are ways of showing relationships and processes.

- Provide a title or caption for each visual to identify it and explain its significance for your text. For example: "Table 1. Japanese economic output, 1965–80."
- 425–27 **DOCUMENT** the source of any visuals you found in another source: "Figure 1. Two Tokyo shoppers display their purchases. (Ochiro, 1967)." Document any tables you create with data from another source. You need not document visuals you create yourself, such as drawings or photos, or data from your own experimental or field research.
- Obtain permission to use any visuals you found in another source that will appear in texts you publish in any form other than for a course.
- Label visuals clearly to ensure that your audience will understand what they show. For example, label each section of a pie chart to show what it represents.

When you choose visuals and integrate them into your texts, follow the same procedures you use with other source materials.

Evaluate visuals as you would any text. Make sure visuals relate directly to your subject, support your assertions, and add information that words alone can't provide as clearly or easily. Evaluate visuals as you would other source materials: Is the photographer named? Do charts and graphs identify the source of the data they portray? Where was the visual published? How was the visual used in its original context? Does the information in the visual match, complement, or contradict the information in your other sources?

Include any necessary source information. Make sure visuals are accompanied by background and citation information: graphs and tables should cite the source of the data they present, and captions of photos should identify the photographer and date.

Use visuals ethically. You may want to crop a photograph, cutting it to show only part. See, for example, the photo on the facing page of two children in medieval costumes and the cropped version that shows only the boy.

You might have reason to crop the photo to accompany a profile or memoir about the boy, but you would not want to eliminate the girl from the photo

in an account of their school's medieval festival. If you crop or otherwise alter a photograph, keep your **PURPOSE** in mind. 3–4

But altering photographs in a way that misrepresents someone or something is a serious breach of ethics. In 1997, when O. J. Simpson was arrested for the murder of his ex-wife, both *Time* and *Newsweek* used the same mug shot on their covers. *Time*, however, digitally darkened Simpson's skin, making him look "blacker." This sort of manipulation misleads readers, creating visual lies that can inappropriately influence how readers interpret both the text and the subject. If you alter a photo, be sure the image represents the subject accurately—and tell your readers how you have changed it.

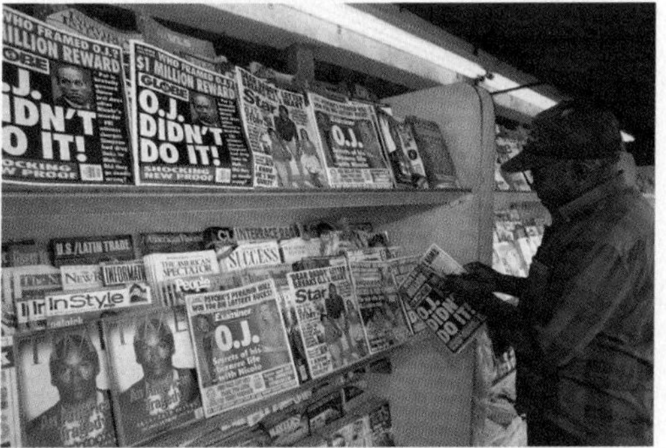

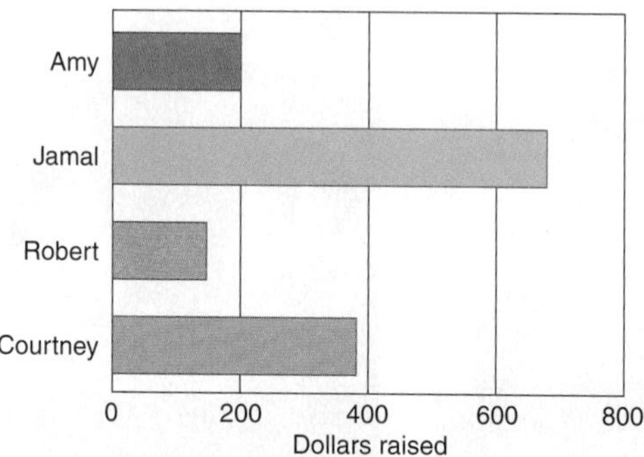

Fig. 1. Fund-raising results for the class gift.

Charts and graphs can mislead, too. Changing the scale on a bar graph, for example, can change the effect of the comparison, making the quantities being compared seem very similar or very different, as the two bar graphs of identical data show in figures 1 and 2.

Depending on the fund-raising goal implied by each bar graph ($800 or $5,000) and the increments of the dollars raised ($200 or $1,000), the two graphs send very different messages, though the dollars raised by each fund-raiser remain the same. Just as you shouldn't edit a quotation or a photograph in a way that might misrepresent its meaning, you should not present data in a way that could mislead readers.

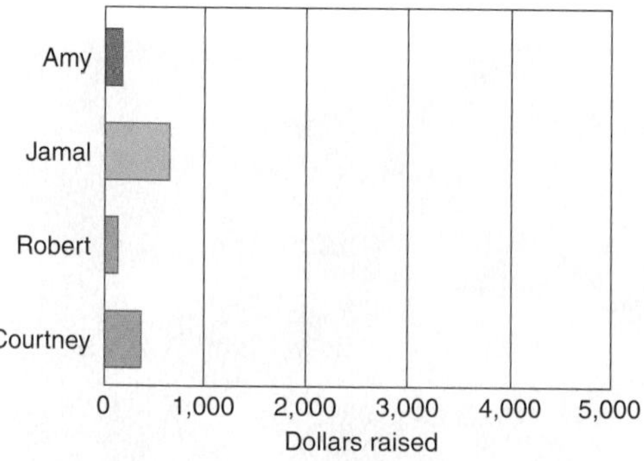

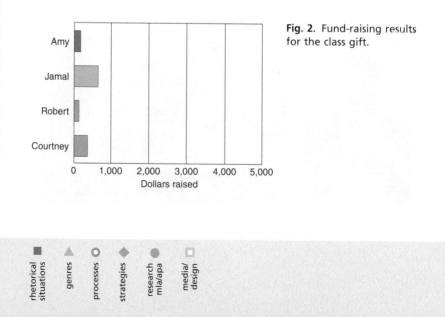

Fig. 2. Fund-raising results for the class gift.

Evaluating a Design

Does the design suit its PURPOSE? Do the typeface and any visuals help convey the text's message, support its argument, or present information? Is there any key information that should be highlighted in a list or chart?

3–4

How well does the design meet the needs of its AUDIENCE? Will the overall appearance of the text appeal to the intended readers? Is the typeface large enough for them to read? Are there headings to help them find their way through the text? Are there the kind of visuals they are likely to expect? Are the visuals clearly labeled and referred to in the main text so that readers know why they're there?

5–8

How well does the text meet the requirements of its GENRE? Can you tell by looking at the text that it is an academic essay, a lab report, a résumé? Do its typeface, margins, headings, and page layout meet the requirements of MLA, APA, or whatever style is being followed? Are visuals appropriately labeled and cited?

9–11
428–76
477–519

How well does the design reflect the writer's STANCE? Do the page layout and typeface convey the appropriate tone—serious, playful, adventuresome, conservative, and so on? Do the visuals reveal anything about the writer's position or beliefs? For instance, does the choice of visuals show any particular bias?

12–14

52 Spoken Text

In a marketing class, you give a formal presentation as part of a research project. As a candidate for student government, you deliver several speeches to various campus groups. At a good friend's wedding, you make a toast to the married couple. In school and out, you may be called on to speak in public, to compose and deliver spoken texts. This chapter offers guidelines to help you prepare and deliver effective spoken texts, along with the visual aids you often need to include. We'll start with two good examples.

ABRAHAM LINCOLN

Gettysburg Address

Given by the sixteenth president of the United States, at the dedication of the Gettysburg battlefield as a memorial to those who died in the Civil War, this is one of the most famous speeches ever delivered in the United States.

Four score and seven years ago our fathers brought forth on this continent, a new nation, conceived in Liberty, and dedicated to the proposition that all men are created equal.

Now we are engaged in a great civil war, testing whether that nation, or any nation so conceived and so dedicated, can long endure. We are met on a great battle-field of that war. We have come to dedicate a portion of that field, as a final resting place for those who here gave their lives that that nation might live. It is altogether fitting and proper that we should do this.

But, in a larger sense, we can not dedicate—we can not consecrate—we can not hallow—this ground. The brave men, living and dead, who struggled here, have consecrated it, far above our poor power to add or detract. The world will little note, nor long remember what we say here, but it can never forget what they did here. It is for us the living, rather, to be dedicated here to the unfinished work which they who fought here have thus far so nobly advanced. It is rather for us to be here dedicated to the great task remaining before us — that from these honored dead we take increased devotion to that cause for which they gave the last full measure of devotion — that we here highly resolve that these dead shall not have died in vain — that this nation, under God, shall have a new birth of freedom — and that government of the people, by the people, for the people, shall not perish from the earth.

You won't likely be called on to deliver such an address, but the techniques Lincoln used — brevity, rhythm, recurring themes — are ones you can use in your own spoken texts. The next example represents the type of spoken text we are sometimes called on to deliver at important occasions in the lives of our families.

JUDY DAVIS

Ours Was a Dad . . .

This short eulogy was given at the funeral of the writer's father, Walter Boock. Judy Davis lives in Davis, California, where she is the principal of North Davis Elementary School.

Elsa, Peggy, David, and I were lucky to have such a dad. Ours was a dad who created the childhood for us that he did not have for himself. The dad who sent us airborne on the soles of his feet, squealing with delight. The dad who built a platform in the peach tree so we could eat ourselves comfortably into peachy oblivion. The dad who assigned us chores and then did them with us. The dad who felt our pain when we skinned our knees.

Ours was the dad who took us camping, all over the U.S. and Canada, but most of all in our beloved Yosemite. The one who awed us with his ability to swing around a full pail of water without spilling a drop and let us hold sticks in the fire and draw designs in the night air with hot orange coals.

Our dad wanted us to feel safe and secure. On Elsa's eighth birthday, we acquired a small camping trailer. One very blustery night in Minnesota, Mom and Dad asleep in the main bed, David suspended in the hammock over them, Peggy and Elsa snuggled in the little dinette bed, and me on an air mattress on the floor, I remember the most incredible sense of well-being: our family all together, so snug, in that little trailer as the storm rocked us back and forth. It was only in the morning that I learned about the tornado warnings. Mom and Dad weren't sleeping; they were praying that when morning came we wouldn't find ourselves in the next state.

Ours was the dad who helped us with homework at the round oak table. He listened to our oral reports, taught us to add by looking for combinations of 10, quizzed us on spelling words, and when our written reports sounded a little too much like the *World Book* encyclopedia, he told us so.

Ours was the dad who believed our round oak table that seated 5
twelve when fully extended should be full at Thanksgiving. Dad called the chaplain at the airbase, asked about homesick boys, and invited them to join our family. Or he'd call International House in Berkeley to see if someone from another country would like to experience an American Thanksgiving. We're still friends with the Swedish couple who came for turkey forty-five years ago. Many people became a part of our extended family around that table. And if twelve around the table were good, then certainly fourteen would be better. Just last fall, Dad commissioned our neighbor Randy to make yet another leaf for the table. There were fourteen around the table for Dad's last Thanksgiving.

Ours was a dad who had a lifelong desire to serve. He delivered Meals on Wheels until he was eighty-three. He delighted in picking up the day-old doughnuts from Mr. Rollen's shop to give those on his route an extra treat. We teased him that he should be receiving those meals himself! Even after walking became difficult for him, he continued to drive and took along an able friend to carry the meals to the door.

Our family, like most, had its ups and downs. But ours was a dad who forgave us our human failings as we forgave him his. He died in peace, surrounded by love. Elsa, Peggy, David, and I were so lucky to have such a dad.

This eulogy, in honor of the writer's father, provides concrete and memorable details that give the audience a clear image of the kind of man he was. The repetition of the phrase "ours was a dad" provides a rhythm and unity that moves the text forward, and the use of short, conventional sentences makes the text easy to understand—and deliver.

Key Features / Spoken Text

A clear structure. Spoken texts need to be clearly organized so that your audience can follow what you're saying. The **BEGINNING** needs to engage their interest, make clear what you will be talking about, and perhaps forecast the central parts of your talk. The main part of the text should focus on a few main points and only as many as your listeners can be expected to handle. (Remember, they can't go back to reread!) The **ENDING** is especially important: it should leave your audience with something to remember, think about, or do. Davis ends as she begins, saying that she and her sisters and brother "were so lucky to have such a dad." Lincoln ends by challenging his audience to "the great task remaining before us . . . that we . . . resolve that these dead shall not have died in vain—that this nation, under God, shall have a new birth of freedom—and that government of the people, by the people, for the people, shall not perish from the earth."

261–66

266–70

Signpost language to keep your audience on track. You may need to provide cues to help your listeners follow your text, especially **TRANSITIONS** that lead them from one point to the next. Sometimes you'll also want to stop and **SUMMARIZE** a complex point to help your audience keep track of your ideas and follow your development of them.

277

416–17

A tone to suit the occasion. Lincoln spoke at a serious, formal event, the dedication of a national cemetery, and his address is formal and even solemn. Davis's eulogy is more informal in **TONE,** as befits a speech given

13

for friends and loved ones. In a presentation to a panel of professors, you probably would want to take an academic tone, avoiding too much slang and speaking in complete sentences. If you had occasion to speak on the very same topic to a neighborhood group, however, you would likely want to speak more casually.

Sound. Remember that spoken texts have the added element of sound. Be aware of how your words and phrases sound. Even if you're never called on to deliver a Gettysburg Address, you will find that repetition and parallel structure can lend power to a presentation, making it easier to follow—and more likely to be remembered. "We can not dedicate—we can not consecrate—we can not hallow": these are words said more than one hundred years ago, but who among us does not know where they're from? The repetition of "we can not" and the parallel forms of the three verbs are one reason they stay with us. These are structures any writer can use. See how the repetition of "ours was a dad" in Davis's eulogy creates a rhythm that engages listeners and at the same time unifies the text.

Visual aids. Sometimes you will want or need to use visuals—PowerPoint or other presentation software, transparencies, flip charts, and so on—to present certain information and to highlight key points.

Considering the Rhetorical Situation

As with any writing, you need to consider your purpose, audience, and the rest of your rhetorical situation:

3–4 **PURPOSE** What is your primary purpose? To inform? Persuade? Entertain? Evoke an emotional response? Something else?

5–8 **AUDIENCE** Think about whom you'll be addressing and how well you know your audience. Will they be interested, or will you need to get them interested? Are they likely to be friendly?

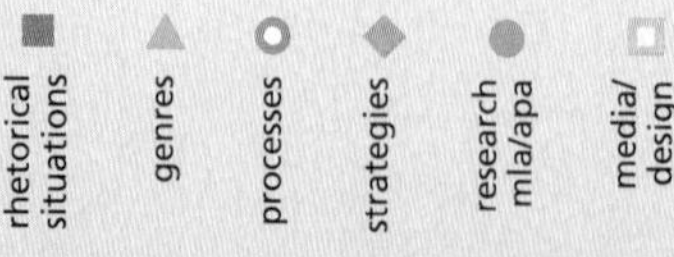

How can you get and maintain their attention, and how can you establish common ground? Will they know about your subject, or will you need to provide background and define key terms?

GENRE The genre of your text will affect the way you structure it. If you're making an argument, for instance, you'll need to consider counterarguments—and to anticipate questions from members of the audience who hold other opinions. If you're giving a report, you may have reason to prepare handouts with detailed information you don't have time to cover. 9–11

STANCE Consider the attitude you want to express—is it serious? thoughtful? passionate? well-informed? funny? something else?—and choose your words accordingly. 12–14

Delivering a Spoken Text

The success of a spoken text often hinges on how you deliver it. As you practice delivering your spoken texts, bear in mind the following points.

Speak clearly. When delivering a spoken text, your first goal is to be understood by your audience. If listeners miss important words or phrases because you don't form your words distinctly, your talk will not succeed. Make sure your pace matches your audience's needs—sometimes you may need to speak slowly to explain complex material; other times you may need to speed up to keep an audience's attention.

Pause for emphasis. In writing, you have white space and punctuation to show readers where an idea or discussion ends. When speaking, you need to be the one to pause to signal the end of a thought, to give listeners a moment to consider something you've said, or to get them ready for a surprising or amusing statement.

Try not to read your presentation. Speech textbooks often advise that you never read your speech. For some of us, though, that's just not possible. If you can speak well from notes or an outline, great—you're likely to do well. If you must have a complete text in front of you, though, try to write it as if you were talking. Then, practice by reading it into a tape recorder; listen for spots that sound as if you're reading, and work on your delivery to sound more relaxed.

Stand up straight, and look at your audience. Try to maintain some eye contact with your audience. If that's uncomfortable, fake it: pick a spot on the wall just above the head of a person in the last row of chairs, and focus on it. You'll appear as if you're looking at your audience even if you're not looking them in the eye. And if you stand up straight, you'll project the sense that you have confidence in what you're saying. If you appear to believe in your words, others will, too.

Use gestures for emphasis. If you're not used to speaking in front of a group, you may let your nervousness show by holding yourself stiffly, elbows tucked in. To overcome some of that nervousness, take some deep breaths, try to relax, move your arms as you would if you were talking to a friend. Use your hands for emphasis. Most public speakers use one hand to emphasize points and both to make larger gestures. Watch politicians on C-SPAN to see how people who speak on a regular basis use their hands and bodies as part of their overall delivery.

Practice. Practice, practice, and then practice some more. Pay particular attention to how much time you have—and don't go over your time limit. If possible, deliver your speech to an audience of friends to test their response.

Visual Aids

When you give an oral presentation, you'll often want or need to include some visuals to help listeners follow what you're saying. Especially when you're presenting complex information, it helps to let them see it as well as hear it. Remember, though, that visuals are a means of conveying information, not mere decoration.

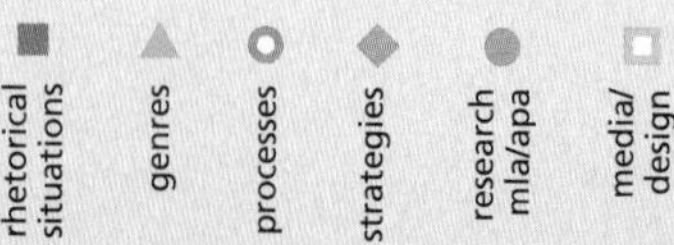

Deciding on the appropriate visual. Presentation software, overhead transparencies, flip charts, and posters are some of the most common kinds of visuals. Presentation software and overhead transparencies are useful for listing main points and for projecting illustrations, tables, and graphs. Overhead transparencies, like whiteboards and chalkboards, allow you to create visuals as you speak. Sometimes you'll want to distribute handouts to provide lists of works cited or copies of any slides you show.

Whatever you decide to use, make sure that the necessary equipment is available—and that it works. If at all possible, check out the room and the equipment before you give your presentation. If you bring your own equipment, make sure electrical outlets are in reach of your power cords.

Also make sure that your visuals will be seen. You may have to rearrange the furniture or the screen in the room to make sure everyone can see. And finally: *have a backup plan*. Computers fail; projector bulbs burn out; marking pens run dry. Whatever visuals you plan, have an alternative plan in case any of these things happen.

Using presentation software. Programs such as Microsoft PowerPoint allow you to create slides that you then project via a computer. These programs enable you to project graphs, charts, photographs, sound—and plain text. Here are some tips for using presentation software effectively:

- ***Use* LISTS *rather than paragraphs.*** Use slides to emphasize your main points, not to reproduce your talk onscreen. Be aware that you can project the list all at once or one item at a time. 525–26
- ***Don't put too much information on a slide.*** How many bulleted points you include will depend on how long each one is, but you want to be sure that you don't include more words than listeners will be able to read as you present each slide.
- ***Be sure your* TYPE *is large enough for your audience to read it.*** In general, you don't want to use any type smaller than 18 points, and you'll want something larger than that for headings. Projected slides are easier to read in sans serif fonts like Arial, Helvetica, and Tahoma instead of serif fonts like Times Roman. Avoid using all caps—all-capped text is hard to read. 524–25

Dewey
o Appeared overconfident
o Ran a lackluster, "safe" campaign
o Was perceived as stuffy and aloof
o Made several blunders
o Would not address issues

Truman
o Conducted whistle-stop campaign
o Made hundreds of speeches
o Spoke energetically
o Connected personally with voters
o Focused on key states

Slides made with presentation software.

- ***Choose colors carefully.*** Your text must contrast strongly with the background. Dark text on a light background is easier to read than the reverse. And remember that not everyone sees all colors; be sure your audience does not need to recognize colors in order to get your meaning. Red-green contrasts are especially hard to see and should be avoided.

- *Use bells and whistles sparingly, if at all.* Presentation software offers lots of decorative backgrounds, letters that fade in or dance across the screen, and, literally, bells and whistles. These can be more distracting than helpful; avoid using them unless they help you make your point.
- *Mark your text.* In your notes, mark each place where you need to click a mouse to call up the next slide.

The example on page 542 shows two slides from a PowerPoint presentation that Dylan Borchers created for an oral presentation based on his essay exploring the U.S. presidential election campaign of 1948. These slides offer an outline of Borchers' main points; the speech itself fills in the details. The design is simple and uncluttered, and the large font and high contrast between type and background make the slides easy to read, even from across a large room.

Overhead transparencies. Transparency slides can hold more information than slides created with presentation software, but someone must place each transparency on the projector one at a time. To minimize the number of slides you will need, you can place a lot of information on each transparency and use a blank sheet of paper to cover and reveal each point as you discuss it. Here are some tips for using transparencies effectively:

- *Use a white background and large type.* If you're typing your text, use black type. Use type that is at least 18 points, and use larger type for headings. As with presentation software, fonts like Arial and Tahoma are easiest to read from a distance. If you're making handwritten transparencies, you might write in several colors.
- *Write legibly and large.* If you want to write as you speak and have trouble writing in a straight line, place a sheet of lined paper under the blank slide. Use a blank sheet to cover any unused part of the slide so that you don't smudge the ink on the slide as you write.
- *Position slides carefully.* You might want to mark the top right corner of each transparency to make sure you put it where it needs to go on the projector. And have someplace to put the transparencies before and after you use them.

Dewey

- Appeared overconfident
- Ran a lackluster, "safe" campaign
- Was perceived as stuffy and aloof
- Made several blunders
- Would not address issues

Truman

- Conducted whistle-stop campaign
- Made hundreds of speeches
- Spoke energetically
- Connected personally with voters
- Focused on key states

An overhead transparency.

Compare the sample transparency slide shown above with the PowerPoint slides on page 542—you'll see that they provide identical information.

Handouts. When you want to give your audience information they can refer to later—reproductions of your visuals, bibliographic information about your sources, printouts of your slides—do so in the form of a handout. Refer to the handout in your presentation, but unless it includes material your audience needs to consult as you talk, don't distribute the handouts until you are finished because they can distract listeners from your presentation. Clearly label everything you give out, including your name and the date and title of the presentation.

IF YOU NEED MORE HELP

See also the guidelines in Chapter 51 on designing PRINT TEXT for additional help creating visuals. If you are working with a group, see Chapter 22 on COLLABORATING.

523–33
215–18

53 Electronic Text

College singing groups create websites to publicize their concerts and sell their CDs. Political commentators post their opinions on blogs; readers of the blogs post responses. Job seekers post scannable résumés. And for most of us, email and text messaging are parts of everyday life. In the future, you'll likely have occasion to write many other electronic texts. Such texts differ in a few obvious ways from print texts—websites open with home pages rather than with plain introductory paragraphs, for instance—but like print texts, they have certain key features and are composed in the context of particular rhetorical situations. This chapter offers some very basic advice for thinking about the rhetorical situations and key features of texts that you post online.

Considering the Rhetorical Situation

As with any writing task, you need to consider your particular rhetorical situation when you write something to post online. In fact, you may need to consider it especially carefully, since in most cases the makeup of an online audience is pretty much impossible to predict—there's often no telling who might read what you write or how efficient your readers' computer systems will be at dealing with different types and sizes of files.

3–4

PURPOSE Why are you writing? To fulfill an assignment? Answer a question? Find or provide information? Get in touch with someone? In email, you may want to state your topic, and even your purpose, in the subject line. On a website, you will need to make the site's purpose clear on its home page.

AUDIENCE What kind of readers are you aiming to reach, and what might they be expecting from you? What are they likely to know about your topic, and what information will you need to provide? What are their technical limitations—can they receive files the size of the one you want to send? If you're constructing a website, what kind of home page will appeal to your intended audience? 5–8

What do you want them to do? Read what you write? Forward what you write to others? Write something themselves? Remember, however, that you can never be sure where your original readers will forward your email or who will visit a website; don't put any writing online that you don't feel comfortable having lots of different people read.

GENRE Are you reporting information? Evaluating something? Arguing a point? Proposing an action? 9–11

STANCE What overall impression do you want to convey? If you're constructing a website for a group, how does the group wish to be seen? Should the site look academic? Hip? Professional? If you want to demonstrate a political stance, remember that the links you provide can help you to do so. (Remember too that if you want to show a balanced political stance, the links should reflect a range of different viewpoints.) 12–14

DESIGN Your medium will affect your design choices. If you're writing email, you'll want to format it to be as simple as possible—different colors and fonts are not necessarily recognized by every email program, so it's best to write in black type using a standard font. It's best also to keep your paragraphs short so readers can see each point without a lot of scrolling. If you're constructing a website, you'll need to create a consistent design scheme using color and type to signal key parts of the site. 15–17

Key Features / Email

Email is such a constant form of communicating that it can feel and read more like talking than writing. But writing it is, and it has certain features and conventions that readers expect and that writers need to be aware of.

An explicit subject line. Your subject line should state your topic clearly: "Reminder: emedia meeting at 2" rather than "Meeting" or "Hi" (though the latter is appropriate for informal messages to friends). People get so much email that they need to see a reason to read yours. In addition, most computer viruses are sent via unsolicited email messages, so many people—or their spam filters—delete all messages from unknown senders or with suspicious or vague subject lines. A clear subject line increases the chances that your message will be read.

A tone appropriate to the situation. Email messages should be written in the same tone you'd use if you were writing the same text on paper. You can be informal when writing to friends, but you should be more formal when writing to people you don't know, especially in professional or academic contexts (to your boss or your instructor). Be aware that your tone starts with your salutation (*Hi Lisa* to a friend, *Dear Professor Alikum* to a teacher). And of course your tone is reflected in the register and conventions of your writing. You can use email shorthand with friends (gtg, cul8r), but professional and academic email should observe professional and academic conventions (complete sentences, correct spelling and punctuation).

Brevity. Email works best when it's brief. Short paragraphs are easier to read on screen than long ones—you don't want readers to have to do too much scrolling to see the point you're trying to make. When you need to email a longer text, you may want to send it as an attachment that readers can open separately. If you don't know for sure whether your recipients will be able to open an attachment, check with them first before sending it.

Speed and reach. This one's not a textual feature as much as it is a reminder to be careful before you hit *send*. Email travels so fast—and can be so easily forwarded to people you never imagined would read what

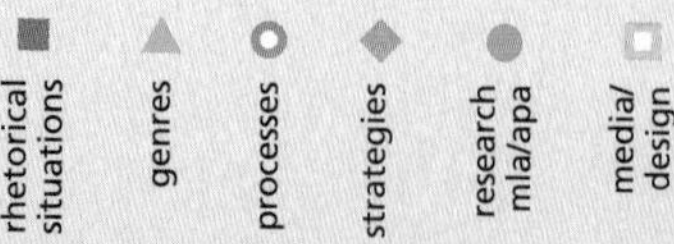

you've written — that you want to be good and sure that your email neither says something you'll regret later (don't send email when you're angry!) nor includes anything you don't want the whole world, or at least part of it, reading (don't put confidential or sensitive information in email).

Key Features / Websites

The writing you do for the Web differs from that which you do on paper in the way that you organize and present it — and in the way your readers will approach what you write. Here are some of the features that characterize most websites, along with general advice to help you think about each feature when you write for the Web.

A home page. The home page functions much like the first page of an essay, giving the name of the site, indicating something about its purpose, and letting readers know what they'll find on the site. It also gives the name of the site's author or sponsor and includes information about when the site was last updated. Plan the text for a home page so that it fits on one screen, and make it simple enough graphically that it downloads quickly.

A clear organizational structure. Web texts are presented as a number of separate pages, and when you compose a website you need to organize the pages so that readers can get to them. Unlike print text, in which the writer determines where a text begins and ends and what order it follows in between, most online texts are organized so that readers can choose which pages they'll look at and in what order. There's no sure way that you can know what sequence they'll follow. Here are three common ways of organizing a website:

As a sequence. A simple way to organize a site is as a linear sequence of pages.

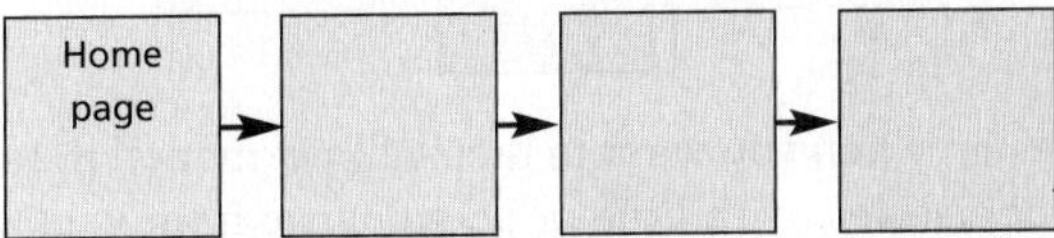

Use this organization if you want readers to view pages in a specific sequence. Though it still doesn't guarantee that they'll follow your sequence, it certainly increases the chances that they'll do so.

As a hierarchy. A hierarchical design groups related pages in the same way an outline organizes related topics in an essay.

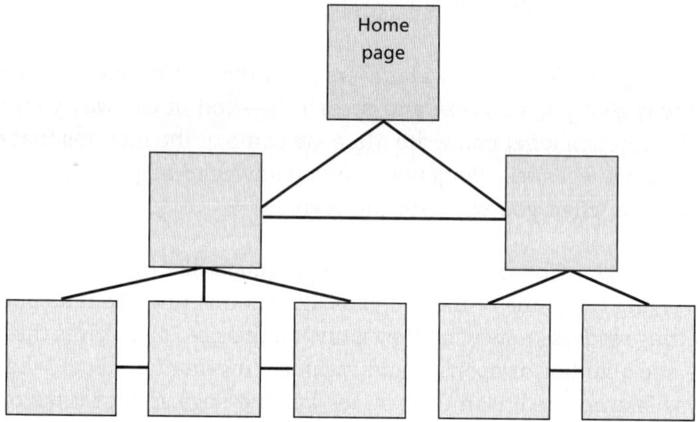

Use a hierarchy to guide readers through complex information while allowing them to choose what to read within categories.

As a web. A web design allows readers to view pages in just about any order they wish.

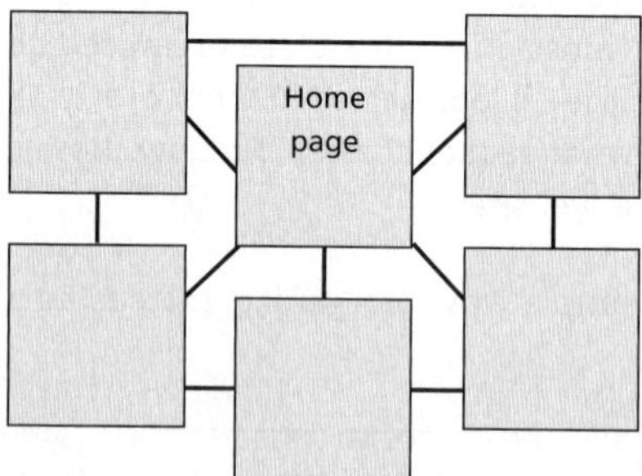

Use a web design when you want to present information that readers can browse for themselves, with little or no guidance from you.

An explicit navigation system. Just as a book has a table of contents, so a website has a navigation menu. The navigation menu shows what's on your site, usually in a menu of the main parts that readers can click on to get to the pages. The navigation menu should appear in the same place on every page. One item on the menu should be a button that lets readers return to the home page.

A consistent design. Design is important—for creating a visual tone for the site, highlighting features or information, and providing a clear focus and emphasis. You need to create a clear color scheme (all links in one color, for example, to distinguish them from the rest of the text) and a consistent **PAGE DESIGN** 524–28 (for example, a navigation bar at the top of each page and a background color that stays the same and doesn't detract from the content); in addition, you need to use **TYPE** 524–25 consistently (for example, one font for the main text, another for the headings).

You can also use color and type to create emphasis or to highlight particular types of information. Though you can't know which pages readers will go to, careful site design can help you control what's on the page they'll see first. You can also include **IMAGES** 528–32—drawings, photos, maps, and the like. Be sure, however, that the illustrations you include support or add to your point, that they are not mere decoration. Take care also that you don't include so many graphics that the site takes a long time to open.

Finally, your design should reflect the appropriate tone and **STANCE.** 12–14 Formal, informal, academic, whimsical, whatever—your choice of type and color and images can convey this stance.

Links. Websites include links among the pages on the site as well as to material elsewhere on the Web. Links allow you to bring material from other sources into your text—you can link to the definition of a key term, for instance, rather than defining it yourself, or you can link to a **SOURCE** 384–99 rather than summarizing or paraphrasing it. You can also provide a list of links to related sites. When you're writing a text for a website, you can link to some of the details, giving readers the choice of whether they want or need to see an illustration, detailed description, map, and so on. For example, page 552 shows how my literacy narrative (see pages 24–26) might look as a Web text.

Sample Web text, with links

Amanda K. Hartman was born in 1882 in West Virginia. She left home at 14 for Cleveland, Ohio, where she worked as a seamstress. In her 30s she married Frederick Hartman, a German immigrant. Together they had one child, Louise. After her husband's death in 1955, Amanda obtained a realtor's license and sold real estate for many years.

She read widely, preferring Greek and Roman history and philosophy. Between 1952 and 1956, she and her husband shared a large house with my parents, giving her ample opportunity to read to me. She taught me to read by reading to me for hours on end, every day. She died at the age of 93.

My family was blue-collar, working-class, and—my grandmother excepted—not very interested in books or reading. But my parents took pride in my achievement and told stories about my precocious literacy, such as the time at a restaurant when the waitress bent over as I sat in my booster chair and asked, "What would you like, little boy?" I'm told I gave her a withering look and said, "I'd like to see a menu."

There was a more serious aspect to reading so young, however. At that time the murder trial of Dr. Sam Sheppard, a physician whose wife had been bludgeoned to death in their house, was the focus of lurid coverage in the Cleveland newspapers. Daily news stories recounted the grisly details of both the murder and the trial testimony, in which Sheppard maintained his innocence. (The story would serve as the inspiration for the TV series and Harrison Ford movie, The Fugitive.)

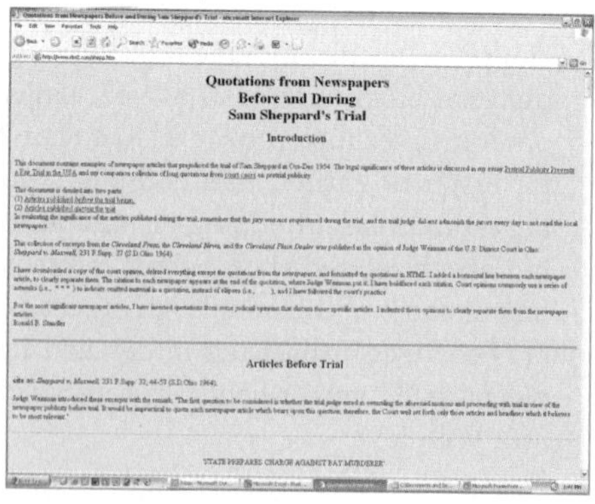

Quotations from Newspapers Before and During Sam Sheppard's Trial

Introduction

Articles Before Trial

How text on the Web links to details from other sources. As the text on the facing page shows, links from my narrative might include a brief biography of my grandmother, *Court TV*'s account of the Sheppard murder case, a site presenting excerpts of news coverage of the trial, and a poster from *The Fugitive*. Such links allow me to stay focused on my own narrative while offering readers the opportunity to explore issues mentioned in my story in as much depth as they want.

A Sample Site

Here and on page 554 are examples from a home page, a content page, and a linked page from a website created by Colleen James, a student at Illinois State University, as part of an online portfolio of work for a course in hypertext.

Home page

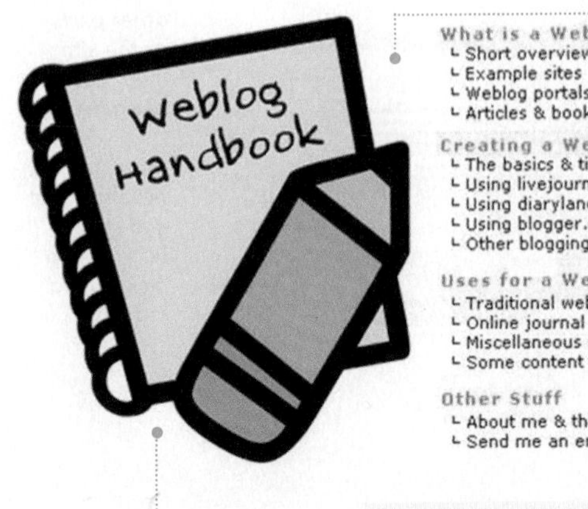

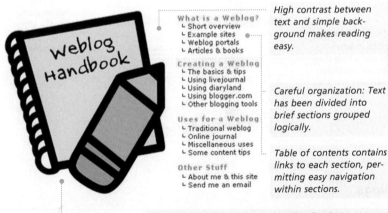

High contrast between text and simple background makes reading easy.

Careful organization: Text has been divided into brief sections grouped logically.

Table of contents contains links to each section, permitting easy navigation within sections.

Illustration and title clearly describe the site's contents.

Content page

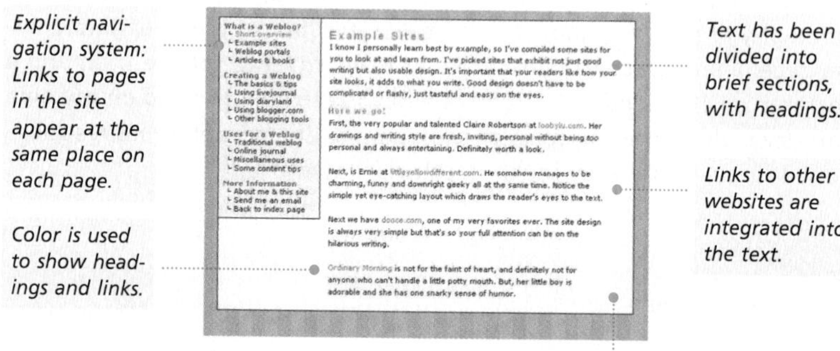

Explicit navigation system: Links to pages in the site appear at the same place on each page.

Color is used to show headings and links.

Text has been divided into brief sections, with headings.

Links to other websites are integrated into the text.

Background doesn't interfere with reading.

Linked page

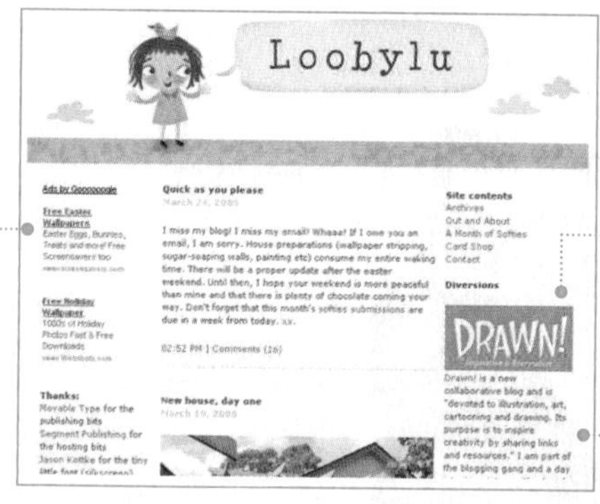

Consistent design helps readers know where they are and how to navigate the site.

Links to other parts of the site help readers navigate.

High contrast between text and simple background makes reading easy.

Blogs

Blogs are journals that are kept online. They generally include written entries, photos, links to other blogs or websites of interest to the writer (or "blogger"), and space for readers to post comments. Sites such as blogger.com, vox.com, or livejournal.com will walk you through the process of creating a blog. Julia Gilkinson's blog, below, created for her writing class at Edinboro University, consists of two columns: the larger, right-hand column contains her postings, each of which is titled and includes the date and time it was posted. Below each posting are comments readers have made in response to her post and a link inviting more comments. The left-hand column presents a list of Julia's postings and, under the heading "about me," a link to her profile. This blog consists entirely of class-related writing, but a similar structure can be used for virtually any blog content, whether personal or professional. In fact, many companies use blogs as their primary websites.

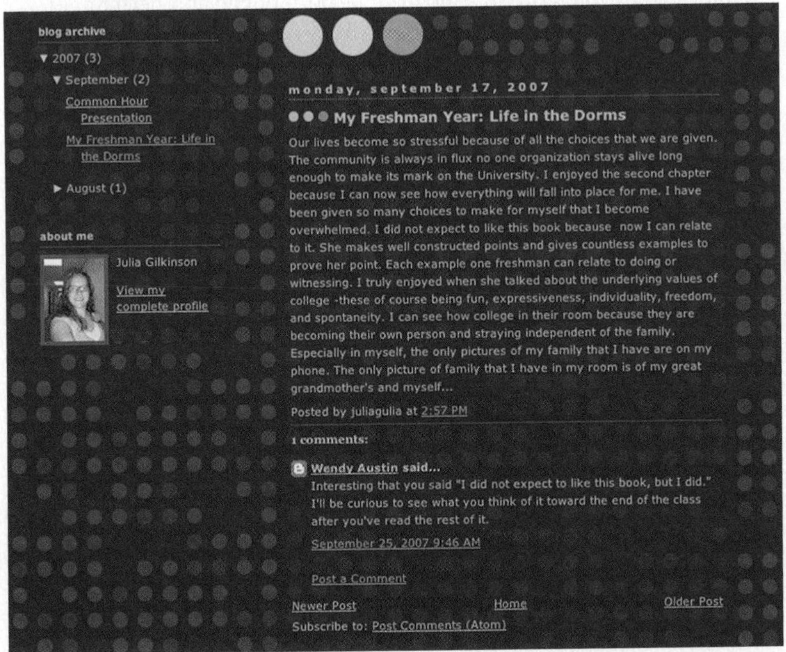

blog archive
▼ 2007 (3)
▼ September (2)
Common Hour Presentation
My Freshman Year: Life in the Dorms
► August (1)
about me
Julia Gilkinson
View my complete profile
monday, september 17, 2007
My Freshman Year: Life in the Dorms
Our lives become so stressful because of all the choices that we are given. The community is always in flux no one organization stays alive long enough to make its mark on the University. I enjoyed the second chapter because I can now see how everything will fall into place for me. I have been given so many choices to make for myself that I become overwhelmed. I did not expect to like this book because now I can relate to it. She makes well constructed points and gives countless examples to prove her point. Each example one freshman can relate to doing or witnessing. I truly enjoyed when she talked about the underlying values of college -these of course being fun, expressiveness, individuality, freedom, and spontaneity. I can see how college in their room because they are becoming their own person and straying independent of the family. Especially in myself, the only pictures of my family that I have are on my phone. The only picture of family that I have in my room is of my great grandmother's and myself...
Posted by juliagulia at 2:57 PM
1 comments:
Wendy Austin said...
Interesting that you said "I did not expect to like this book, but I did." I'll be curious to see what you think of it toward the end of the class after you've read the rest of it.
September 25, 2007 9:46 AM
Post a Comment
Newer Post
Home
Older Post
Subscribe to: Post Comments (Atom)

When you create or respond to a blog:

- Remember that, unlike entries in a private journal or diary, blog postings are public, so you shouldn't post anything that you wouldn't want your parents, friends, or employer to read. Some bloggers have forgotten that rule and paid serious consequences: for example, in 2002 Heather Armstrong criticized her employer on her blog, dooce.com. Her employer discovered her post and fired her, leading to the slang term *dooced:* fired for the contents of one's blog.
- Assume that what you post in a blog is permanent. Because your content is stored on a computer server and may be copied and pasted by others, it is likely to be available even if you edit or delete it. So your friends, family, and employer—anyone—may read a posting years in the future, even if the blog no longer exists.
- Since what you write in a blog will be both public and permanent, it's especially important to think twice before posting when you're angry or upset. In the heat of the moment, it's easy to write an entry or comment that you'll regret later. Give yourself some time to cool down before you post what will be immediately read by others.

IF YOU NEED MORE HELP

523–33
259

See Chapter 51, PRINT TEXT, for more information on text design elements, such as fonts and effective use of white space. When writing electronic texts, be aware that the way you use various STRATEGIES may change—for example, you may create a link to a dictionary definition of a term instead of defining it within the text.

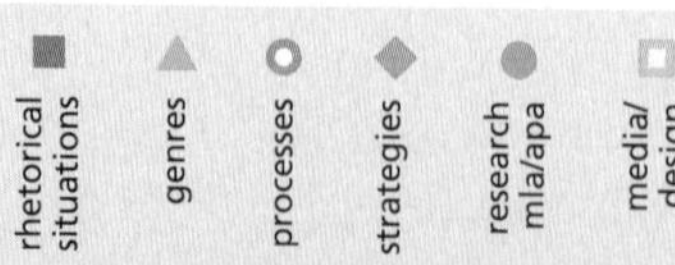

part 7

Readings

"Read, read, read. Read everything — trash, classics, good and bad, and see how they do it." So said the American writer William Faulkner, and on the following pages you will find an anthology of readings that show how Faulkner, Zora Neale Hurston, David Sedaris, Ruth Behar, Joan Didion, and many other writers "do it." Read on, and pay attention to how these writers use the KEY FEATURES and STRATEGIES that you yourself are learning to use. The anthology includes readings in ten GENRES and a chapter of readings that mix genres; you'll find a menu of the readings on the inside back cover of the book.

Readings

Literacy Narratives 54

See also:

TANYA BARRIENTOS

Se Habla Español

Tanya Barrientos is a columnist and feature writer for the Philadelphia Inquirer. *The following essay appeared in a 2004 issue of* Latina, *a bilingual magazine published by and for Latinas. It was adapted from an essay of the same title that was published in* Border-Line Personalities: A New Generation of Latinas Dish on Sex, Sass, and Cultural Shifting *(2004). In this piece, Barrientos recounts her struggles as a Latina who is not fluent in Spanish. She takes her title from a phrase often seen in store windows, announcing that "Spanish is spoken" there.*

THE MAN ON THE OTHER END of the phone line is telling me the classes I've called about are first-rate: native speakers in charge, no more than six students per group. I tell him that will be fine and yes, I've studied a bit of Spanish in the past. He asks for my name and I supply it, rolling the double "r" in "Barrientos" like a pro. That's when I hear the silent snag, the momentary hesitation I've come to expect at this part of the exchange. Should I go into it again? Should I explain, the way I have to half a dozen others, that I am Guatemalan by birth but *pura gringa* by circumstance?

This will be the sixth time I've signed up to learn the language my parents speak to each other. It will be the sixth time I've bought workbooks and notebooks and textbooks listing 501 conjugated verbs in alphabetical order, in hopes that the subjunctive tense will finally take root in my mind. In class I will sit across a table from the "native speaker," who will wonder what to make of me. "Look," I'll want to say (but never do). "Forget the dark skin. Ignore the obsidian eyes. Pretend I'm a pink-cheeked, blue-eyed blonde whose name tag says 'Shannon.'" Because that is what a person who doesn't innately know the difference between *corre, corra,* and *corrí* is supposed to look like, isn't it?

I came to the United States in 1963 at age 3 with my family and immediately stopped speaking Spanish. College-educated and seamlessly bilingual when they settled in west Texas, my parents (a psychology professor and an artist) wholeheartedly embraced the notion of the American melting pot. They declared that their two children would

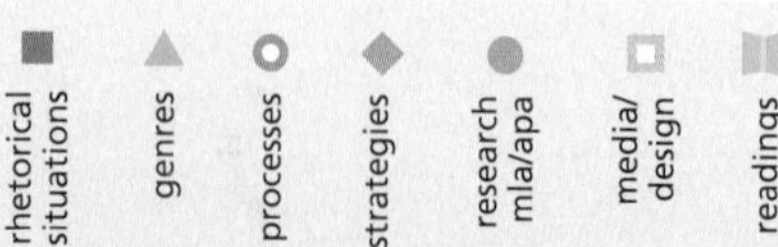

speak nothing but *inglés*. They'd read in English, write in English, and fit into Anglo society beautifully.

It sounds politically incorrect now. But America was not a hyphenated nation back then. People who called themselves Mexican Americans or Afro-Americans were considered dangerous radicals, while law-abiding citizens were expected to drop their cultural baggage at the border and erase any lingering ethnic traits.

To be honest, for most of my childhood I liked being the brown girl who defied expectations. When I was 7, my mother returned my older brother and me to elementary school one week after the school year had already begun. We'd been on vacation in Washington, D.C., visiting the Smithsonian, the Capitol, and the home of Edgar Allan Poe. In the Volkswagen on the way home, I'd memorized "The Raven," and I would recite it with melodramatic flair to any poor soul duped into sitting through my performance. At the school's office, the registrar frowned when we arrived.

"You people. Your children are always behind, and you have the nerve to bring them in late?"

"My children," my mother answered in a clear, curt tone, "will be at the top of their classes in two weeks."

The registrar filed our cards, shaking her head.

I did not live in a neighborhood with other Latinos, and the public school I attended attracted very few. I saw the world through the clear, cruel vision of a child. To me, speaking Spanish translated into being poor. It meant waiting tables and cleaning hotel rooms. It meant being left off the cheerleading squad and receiving a condescending smile from the guidance counselor when you said you planned on becoming a lawyer or a doctor. My best friends' names were Heidi and Leslie and Kim. They told me I didn't seem "Mexican" to them, and I took it as a compliment. I enjoyed looking into the faces of Latino store clerks and waitresses and, yes, even our maid and saying "*Yo no hablo español.*" It made me feel superior. It made me feel American. It made me feel white. I thought if I stayed away from Spanish, stereotypes would stay away from me.

Then came the backlash. During the two decades when I'd worked hard to isolate myself from the stereotype I'd constructed in my own head, society shifted. The nation changed its views on ethnic identity. College professors started teaching history through African American and Native American eyes. Children were told to forget about the melting pot and picture America as a multicolored quilt instead. Hyphens suddenly had muscle, and I was left wondering where I fit in.

The Spanish language was supposedly the glue that held the new Latino community together. But in my case it was what kept me apart. I felt awkward among groups whose conversations flowed in and out of Spanish. I'd be asked a question in Spanish and I'd have to answer in English, knowing this raised a mountain of questions. I wanted to call myself Latina, to finally take pride, but it felt like a lie. So I set out to learn the language that people assumed I already knew.

If I stayed away from Spanish, stereotypes would stay away from me.

After my first set of lessons, I could function in the present tense. "*Hola, Paco. ¿Qué tal? ¿Qué color es tu cuaderno? El mío es azul.*" My vocabulary built quickly, but when I spoke, my tongue felt thick inside my mouth — and if I needed to deal with anything in the future or the past, I was sunk. I enrolled in a three-month submersion program in Mexico and emerged able to speak like a sixth-grader with a solid C average. I could read Gabriel García Márquez with a Spanish-English dictionary at my elbow, and I could follow 90 percent of the melodrama on any given telenovela. But true speakers discover my limitations the moment I stumble over a difficult construction, and that is when I get the look. The one that raises the wall between us. The one that makes me think I'll never really belong. Spanish has become a litmus test showing how far from your roots you've strayed.

My bilingual friends say I make too much of it. They tell me that my Guatemalan heritage and unmistakable Mayan features are enough to legitimize my membership in the Latin American club. After all, not all Poles speak Polish. Not all Italians speak Italian. And as this nation grows more and more Hispanic, not all Latinos will share one language. But I don't believe them.

There must be other Latinas like me. But I haven't met any. Or, I should say, I haven't met any who have fessed up. Maybe they are secretly struggling to fit in, the same way I am. Maybe they are hiring tutors and listening to tapes behind locked doors, just like me. I wish we all had the courage to come out of our hiding places and claim our rightful spot in the broad Latino spectrum. Without being called hopeless gringas. Without having to offer apologies or show remorse.

If it will help, I will go first. 15

Aquí estoy. Spanish-challenged and *pura* Latina.

Engaging with the Text

1. Tanya Barrientos gives her article a Spanish **TITLE.** How does this prepare you for the subject of the article? What does this title lead you to believe about Barrientos's feelings about Spanish? Is that impression supported by the rest of the article? Why or why not? 272–73
2. Barrientos **BEGINS** her essay with an anecdote about signing up for a Spanish class. What is the effect of beginning with this anecdote? Does it attract your interest? How does it prepare you for the rest of the essay? 261–66
3. Barrientos tells of learning to read and write in Spanish. One key feature of a literacy narrative is an indication of the narrative's **SIGNIFICANCE.** For her, what is the significance of learning that language? Why is it so important to her? 32
4. Barrientos peppers her essay with Spanish words and phrases, without offering any English translation. What does this tell you about her **STANCE?** Would her stance seem different if she'd translated the Spanish? Why or why not? 12–14
5. ***For Writing.*** As Barrientos notes, language plays a big part in her identity. Think about the languages you speak. If you speak only English, think about what kind of accent you have. (If you think you don't have one, consider how you might sound to someone from a different region.) Does the language you speak or accent you have change according to the situation? Does it change according to how you perceive yourself? Write an essay **REFLECTING** on the way you speak and how it affects (or is affected by) your identity. 180–87

AMY TAN

Mother Tongue

Amy Tan is the author of novels, children's books, essays, and a memoir. Her work has appeared in McCall's, Atlantic Monthly, *the* New Yorker, *and other magazines. She is best known for her novel* The Joy Luck Club *(1989), which examines the lives of and the relationships between four Chinese American daughters and their mothers. The following selection was first delivered as a talk at a symposium on language in San Francisco in 1989.*

I AM NOT A SCHOLAR OF ENGLISH OR LITERATURE. I cannot give you much more than personal opinions on the English language and its variations in this country or others.

I am a writer. And by that definition, I am someone who has always loved language. I am fascinated by language in daily life. I spend a great deal of my time thinking about the power of language — the way it can evoke an emotion, a visual image, a complex idea, or a simple truth. Language is the tool of my trade. And I use them all — all the Englishes I grew up with.

Recently, I was made keenly aware of the different Englishes I do use. I was giving a talk to a large group of people, the same talk I had already given to half a dozen other groups. The nature of the talk was about my writing, my life, and my book, *The Joy Luck Club*. The talk was going along well enough, until I remembered one major difference that made the whole talk sound wrong. My mother was in the room. And it was perhaps the first time she had heard me give a lengthy speech, using the kind of English I have never used with her. I was saying things like, "The intersection of memory upon imagination" and "There is an aspect of my fiction that relates to thus-and-thus" — a speech filled with carefully wrought grammatical phrases, burdened, it suddenly seemed to me, with nominalized forms, past perfect tenses, conditional phrases, all the forms of standard English that I had learned in school and through books, the forms of English I did not use at home with my mother.

Just last week, I was walking down the street with my mother, and I again found myself conscious of the English I was using, the English I do use with her. We were talking about the price of new and used furniture and I heard myself saying this: "Not waste money that way." My husband was with us as well, and he didn't notice any switch in my English. And then I realized why. It's because over the twenty years we've been together I've often used the same kind of English with him, and sometimes he even uses it with me. It has become our language of intimacy, a different sort of English that relates to family talk, the language I grew up with.

So you'll have some idea of what this family talk I heard sounds 5
like, I'll quote what my mother said during a recent conversation which I videotaped and then transcribed. During this conversation, my mother was talking about a political gangster in Shanghai who had the same last name as her family's, Du, and how the gangster in his early years wanted to be adopted by her family, which was rich by comparison. Later, the gangster became more powerful, far richer than my mother's family, and one day showed up at my mother's wedding to pay his respects. Here's what she said in part:

"Du Yusong having business like fruit stand. Like off the street kind. He is Du like Du Zong — but not Tsung-ming Island people. The local people call putong, the river east side, he belong to that side local people. That man want to ask Du Zong father take him in like become own family. Du Zong father wasn't look down on him, but didn't take seriously, until that man big like become a mafia. Now important person, very hard to inviting him. Chinese way, came only to show respect, don't stay for dinner. Respect for making big celebration, he shows up. Mean gives lots of respect. Chinese custom. Chinese social life that way. If too important won't have to stay too long. He come to my wedding. I didn't see, I heard it. I gone to boy's side, they have YMCA dinner. Chinese age I was nineteen."

You should know that my mother's expressive command of English belies how much she actually understands. She reads the *Forbes* report, listens to *Wall Street Week*, converses daily with her stockbroker, reads all of Shirley MacLaine's books with ease — all kinds of things I can't begin to understand. Yet some of my friends tell me they understand 50 percent of what my mother says. Some say they understand 80 to 90 percent. Some say they understand none of it, as if she were speaking pure Chinese. But to me, my mother's English is perfectly clear, perfectly natural. It's my mother tongue. Her language, as I hear it, is vivid, direct, full of observation and imagery. That was the language that helped shape the way I saw things, expressed things, made sense of the world.

Lately, I've been giving more thought to the kind of English my mother speaks. Like others, I have described it to people as "broken" or "fractured" English. But I wince when I say that. It has always bothered me that I can think of no way to describe it other than "broken," as if it were damaged and needed to be fixed, as if it lacked a certain wholeness and soundness. I've heard other terms used, "limited English," for example. But they seem just as bad, as if everything is limited, including people's perceptions of the limited English speaker.

I know this for a fact, because when I was growing up, my mother's "limited" English limited *my* perception of her. I was ashamed of her English. I believed that her English reflected the quality of what she had to say. That is, because she expressed them imperfectly her thoughts were imperfect. And I had plenty of empirical evidence to support me: the fact that people in department stores, at banks, and at restaurants did not take her seriously, did not give her good service, pretended not to understand her, or even acted as if they did not hear her.

My mother has long realized the limitations of her English as well. 10
When I was fifteen, she used to have me call people on the phone to pretend I was she. In this guise, I was forced to ask for information or even to complain and yell at people who had been rude to her. One time it was a call to her stockbroker in New York. She had cashed out her small portfolio and it just so happened we were going to go to New York the next week, our very first trip outside California. I had to get on the phone and say in an adolescent voice that was not very convincing, "This is Mrs. Tan."

And my mother was standing in the back whispering loudly, "Why he don't send me check, already two weeks late. So mad he lie to me, losing me money."

And then I said in perfect English, "Yes, I'm getting rather concerned. You had agreed to send the check two weeks ago, but it hasn't arrived."

Then she began to talk more loudly. "What he want, I come to New York tell him front of his boss, you cheating me?" And I was trying to calm her down, make her be quiet, while telling the stockbroker, "I can't tolerate any more excuses. If I don't receive the check immediately, I am going to have to speak to your manager when I'm in New York next week." And sure enough, the following week there we were in front of this astonished stockbroker, and I was sitting there red-faced and quiet, and my mother, the real Mrs. Tan, was shouting at his boss in her impeccable broken English.

We used a similar routine just five days ago, for a situation that was far less humorous. My mother had gone to the hospital for an appointment, to find out about a benign brain tumor a CAT scan had revealed a month ago. She said she had spoken very good English, her best English, no mistakes. Still, she said, the hospital did not apologize when they said they had lost the CAT scan and she had come for nothing. She said they did not seem to have any sympathy when she told them she was anxious to know the exact diagnosis, since her husband and son had both died of brain tumors. She said they would not give her any more information until the next time and she would have to make another appointment for that. So she said she would not leave until the doctor called her daughter. She wouldn't budge. And when the doctor finally called her daughter, me, who spoke in perfect English — lo and behold — we had assurances the CAT scan would be found, promises that a conference call on Monday would be held, and apologies for any suffering my mother had gone through for a most regrettable mistake.

15 I think my mother's English almost had an effect on limiting my possibilities in life as well. Sociologists and linguists probably will tell you that a person's developing language skills are more influenced by peers. But I do think that the language spoken in the family, especially in immigrant families which are more insular, plays a large role in shaping the language of the child. And I believe that it affected my results on achievement tests, IQ tests, and the SAT. While my English skills

were never judged as poor, compared to math, English could not be considered my strong suit. In grade school I did moderately well, getting perhaps B's, sometimes B-pluses, in English and scoring perhaps in the sixtieth or seventieth percentile on achievement tests. But those scores were not good enough to override the opinion that my true abilities lay in math and science, because in those areas I achieved A's and scored in the ninetieth percentile or higher.

This was understandable. Math is precise; there is only one correct answer. Whereas, for me at least, the answers on English tests were always a judgment call, a matter of opinion and personal experience. Those tests were constructed around items like fill-in-the-blank sentence completion, such as, "Even though Tom was ______, Mary thought he was ______." And the correct answer always seemed to be the most bland combinations of thoughts, for example, "Even though Tom was shy, Mary thought he was charming," with the grammatical structure "even though" limiting the correct answer to some sort of semantic opposites, so you wouldn't get answers like, "Even though Tom was foolish, Mary thought he was ridiculous." Well, according to my mother, there were very few limitations as to what Tom could have been and what Mary might have thought of him. So I never did well on tests like that.

The same was true with word analogies, pairs of words in which you were supposed to find some sort of logical, semantic relationship — for example, "*Sunset* is to *nightfall* as ______ is to ______." And here you would be presented with a list of four possible pairs, one of which showed the same kind of relationship: *red* is to *stoplight*, *bus* is to *arrival*, *chills* is to *fever*, *yawn* is to *boring*. Well, I could never think that way. I knew what the tests were asking, but I could not block out of my mind the images already created by the first pair, "*sunset* is to *nightfall*" — and I would see a burst of colors against a darkening sky, the moon rising, the lowering of a curtain of stars. And all the other pairs of words — red, bus, stoplight, boring — just threw up a mass of confusing images, making it impossible for me to sort out something as logical as saying: "A sunset precedes nightfall" is the same as "a chill precedes a fever." The only way I would have gotten that answer right would have been to imagine an associative situation, for example, my being disobedient and staying out past sunset, catching a chill at night, which turns into feverish pneumonia as punishment, which indeed did happen to me.

I have been thinking about all this lately, about my mother's English, about achievement tests. Because lately I've been asked, as a writer, why there are not more Asian Americans represented in American literature. Why are there few Asian Americans enrolled in creative writing programs? Why do so many Chinese students go into engineering? Well, these are broad sociological questions I can't begin to answer. But I have noticed in surveys — in fact, just last week — that Asian students, as a whole, always do significantly better on math achievement tests than in English. And this makes me think that there are other Asian-American students whose English spoken in the home might also be described as "broken" or "limited." And perhaps they also have teachers who are steering them away from writing and into math and science, which is what happened to me.

Fortunately, I happen to be rebellious in nature and enjoy the challenge of disproving assumptions made about me. I became an English major my first year in college, after being enrolled as pre-med. I started writing nonfiction as a freelancer the week after I was told by my former boss that writing was my worst skill and I should hone my talents toward account management.

But it wasn't until 1985 that I finally began to write fiction. And at 20
first I wrote using what I thought to be wittily crafted sentences, sentences that would finally prove I had mastery over the English language. Here's an example from the first draft of a story that later made its way into *The Joy Luck Club*, but without this line: "That was my mental quandary in its nascent state." A terrible line, which I can barely pronounce.

Fortunately, for reasons I won't get into today, I later decided I should envision a reader for the stories I would write. And the reader I decided upon was my mother, because these were stories about mothers. So with this reader in mind — and in fact she did read my early drafts — I began to write stories using all the Englishes I grew up with: the English I spoke to my mother, which for lack of a better term might be described as "simple"; the English she used with me, which for lack of a better term might be described as "broken"; my translation of her Chinese, which could certainly be described as "watered down"; and what I imagined to be her translation of her Chinese if she could speak in perfect English, her internal language, and for that I sought to preserve the essence, but neither an English nor a Chinese structure. I wanted to capture what language ability tests can never reveal: her intent, her passion, her imagery, the rhythms of her speech and the nature of her thoughts.

Apart from what any critic had to say about my writing, I knew I had succeeded where it counted when my mother finished reading my book and gave me her verdict: "So easy to read."

Engaging with the Text

1. 261–66 Amy Tan **BEGINS** by announcing, "I am not a scholar of English. . . . I cannot give you much more than personal opinions on the English language and its variations in this country or others." How does this opening set up your expectations for the rest of the essay? Why do you think she chose to begin by denying her own authority?
2. Tan writes about the different "Englishes" she speaks. What categories 301–2 does she **DIVIDE** English into? Why are these divisions important to Tan? How does she say they affect her as a writer?
3. Tan wrote this essay for a literary journal. How does writing for a lit- 5–8 erary **AUDIENCE** affect the language she primarily uses in the essay? What kind of English do you think she believes her audience speaks? Why? Support your answer with quotations from the text.
4. 272–73 How does Tan's **TITLE** — "Mother Tongue" — affect the way you read her argument? What other titles might she have chosen?
5. ***For Writing.*** Explore the differences between the language you speak at home and the languages you use with friends, teachers, employers, 180–87 and so on. Write an essay that **REFLECTS** on the various languages you speak. If you speak only one language, consider the variations in the ways you speak it — at home, at work, at school, at church, wherever.

MARINA NEMAT

The Secondhand Bookseller

Marina Nemat was born in Tehran, Iran, in 1965. Following the 1979 Islamic Revolution, she was arrested at age sixteen for speaking out in a science class against the Ayatollah Khomeini's regime. She spent over two years as a political prisoner in the infamous Evin prison, where she was tortured and nearly executed, and fled Iran in 1991, settling with her husband and family in Canada. In December 2007, Nemat was awarded the first Human Dignity Prize by the European Parliament and the Cultural Association Europa. Detailing her early love of books, this selection from her memoir Prisoner of Tehran *(2007) takes place before censorship was imposed by the Islamic Revolution. For a review of* Prisoner of Tehran, *see p. 742.*

I DECIDED TO STAY OUT OF MY MOTHER'S WAY, and the best way to achieve this was to stay in my room as long as possible. Every day, as soon as I arrived home from school, I tiptoed to the kitchen to see if my mother was there. If she wasn't, I fixed myself a bologna sandwich, and if she was, I said a quick hello and then went to my room and waited for her to leave the kitchen. After eating, I stayed in my room, did my homework, and read the books I had borrowed from my school library. Most of these books were translations: *Peter Pan, Alice in Wonderland, The Little Mermaid, The Snow Queen, The Steadfast Tin Soldier, Cinderella, The Sleeping Beauty, Hansel and Gretel,* and *Rapunzel.* My school library was small, and soon I had read all its books not only once, but three or four times. A couple of times every night, my mother opened the door of my bedroom to see what I was doing and smiled when she found me reading. In a way, books had saved us both.

One day, I gathered all my courage and asked my mother if she would buy me books, and she said she could buy me only one book a month because books were expensive and we couldn't spend all our money on them. But one book a month wasn't enough. A few days later, when my mother and I were walking home after visiting her father, I noticed a small bookstore. The sign read: Secondhand Books. I knew "secondhand" meant cheap, but I didn't dare ask my mother to check it out.

One week later, when my mother told me it was time for us to visit my grandfather, I told her I wasn't feeling well, and she agreed to let me stay home. My father was at work. Not too long after Grandma's death, he had closed down his dance studio and had found a job at a division of the Ministry of Arts and Culture, working with folklore dance groups. He liked his new job and sometimes traveled to different countries with the dancers, young men and women who represented Iran at different international events. As soon as my mother left the house, I ran to my parents' bedroom and took my mother's spare house keys from the drawer of her dresser. I had saved all my chocolate-milk money for a week and hoped it would be enough for a book.

I ran to the secondhand bookstore. All day, the late-spring sun had shone on the black asphalt, creating quivering waves of heat, which rose into the air and pushed against me. When I arrived at the bookstore, drops of sweat were dripping down my forehead and into my eyes, making them burn. I wiped my face with my T-shirt, pushed open the glass door of the store, and stepped in. Once my eyes adjusted to the low level of light, I couldn't believe what I saw. All around me, piles of books were stacked on bookshelves up to the ceiling, leaving only narrow tunnels that disappeared into darkness. I was surrounded by thousands of books. The air was heavy with the scent of paper, of stories and dreams that lived in written words.

"Hello?" I called. 5

There was no answer.

"Hello?" I called again, a little louder this time.

From the depths of one of the book tunnels, a man's voice called, "How can I help you?" in a thick Armenian accent.

I took a step back, calling, "Where are you?"

Right in front of me, a gray shadow came into focus. I gasped. 10

The shadow laughed.

"I'm sorry, little girl. I didn't mean to scare you. What do you want?"

I had to remind myself to breathe.

"I . . . I want to buy a book."

"What book?"

I took all my money out of my pocket and showed the coins to the thin, old man standing in front of me.

"I have this much money. Doesn't matter what book, as long as it's good."

He smiled and ran his fingers through his gray hair.

"Why don't you go to the bakery next door and buy yourself a few donuts instead?"

"But I want a book. Isn't this money enough?"

"Young lady, the problem is that all my books are written in English. Do you speak English?"

"I'm very good in English. In school, we study English for an hour every day. I'm in the third grade."

"Okay, let's see what I can find for you," he said with a sigh and disappeared behind the book mountains.

I waited, wondering how he could possibly find anything in that mess, but he miraculously emerged from the dark clutter with a book.

"Here you go," he said, handing it to me. "*The Lion, the Witch, and the Wardrobe*. It's a wonderful book and the first one of a series."

I examined it. It had a blue-gray cover in the center of which was the picture of a lion with a boy and a girl sitting on its back. The lion had leaped into the air. The book looked old but was in reasonably good shape.

"How much does it cost?"

"Five tomans."

"But, I only have four!" I said, almost in tears.

"Four will do."

I thanked him, ecstatic, and ran home.

Three days later, I had read *The Lion, the Witch, and the Wardrobe* twice and had fallen in love with it. I wanted more. But only having two tomans saved, I wasn't sure if the man at the bookstore was going to be generous again, and I was afraid to ask my mother for money, so I decided to sell my pencil box to my friend Sarah. At the beginning of the school year, Sarah had asked me where I had bought the box, and I had told her that my mother had bought it at the big department store at the intersection of Shah and Pahlavi Avenues. But when Sarah's mother went to buy one like mine, they were sold out, and Sarah was very disappointed. It was a blue plastic box with a magnetic lock that clicked when you closed its lid. The next day, I caught up with Sarah on my way to school. She had large dark brown eyes, thick curly black hair that fell on her shoulders, and she owned a fancy watch, on the face of which was a picture of Cinderella with Prince Charming putting a glass slipper on her foot. Cinderella was sitting on a stool and had crossed one leg over the other, and her leg moved back and forth every second. Sarah's mother had bought the watch for her when they were vacationing in England. I asked her if she still wanted my pencil box, and she said she did. I told her I was willing to sell it to her. She wanted to know why, sounding rather suspicious. So I told her about the bookstore. She agreed to give me five tomans if I also gave her my scented eraser. I accepted her condition.

After school, it took Sarah and me less than five minutes to run to her house, which was on a narrow residential crescent where all houses had small yards and were surrounded by tall brick walls to provide privacy for the residents. I loved her street, because without cars, stores, vendors, and beggars, it was quiet. The air was filled with the mouthwatering fragrance of sautéed onions and garlic. One of the neighbors was probably making dinner. Sarah had a house key because both her parents worked and didn't return home until later in the day. She opened the door, and we stepped in her yard. On our right, a small flower bed overflowed with the reds, greens, and purples of geraniums and pansies.

I secretly wished to live in a house like Sarah's. Her mother, who worked at the bank and always wore elegant suits and very high-heeled shiny black shoes, was a small, round woman with short black hair. She hugged me whenever I went for a visit, telling me how wonderful it was to have me over. Sarah's father was an engineer and a big man, who always told funny jokes, laughed loudly, and recited beautiful old poems. Sarah's only brother, Sirus, was twelve, three years older than Sarah and me, and, unlike the rest of his family, was very shy. Sarah's house was always colored with noise and laughter.

I gave Sarah the pencil box, and she gave me the money. Then I called 35
my mother and told her that I was at Sarah's to help her with homework.

My mother didn't mind. I thanked Sarah and ran to the bookstore to find it as dark, dusty, and mysterious as my first visit. Again, the old man emerged from the darkness.

"Let me guess: you couldn't understand a word, and now you want your money back," he said, narrowing his eyes.

"No. I read it twice, and I loved it! I didn't understand a few words, but I used my father's dictionary. I'm here to buy the second book of the series. Do you have it? I sold my pencil box and my scented eraser to my friend, Sarah, so I have enough money this time."

The old man stared at me and didn't move. My heart sank. Maybe he didn't have the second book.

"So, do you have it?"

"Yes, I do. But . . . you don't have to pay for it; you can borrow it if you promise to take good care of it and return it when you have read it. Twice."

I thought of my angel. Maybe he was pretending to be an old man. I looked into the old man's eyes, and they seemed almost as dark, deep, and kind as the angel's eyes. I looked at the book; it was *Prince Caspian*.

"What's your name?" he asked.

"Marina. What's your name?"

"Albert," he answered.

Hmm. An angel named Albert.

From that day on, I went to visit Albert and to borrow books from him at least once a week.

Engaging with the Text

1. The note at the beginning of this selection tells us that when Marina Nemat was sixteen years old, she was persecuted for her beliefs and for speaking out at school by a regime that imposed strict censorship. Does that information affect your understanding of the text? If so, how?
2. Nemat uses **DIALOGUE** in her narrative when she describes her two encounters with the bookseller but not when she recounts her inter-

333–37

actions with other people. Why do you think she chose to rely on dialogue for these two scenes? What does this dialogue contribute to her narrative?

3. 28 Well-written literacy narratives typically include **VIVID DETAILS.** What details does Nemat include about the setting and people in her narrative? 330–31 Point to specific passages as examples. What **DOMINANT IMPRESSION** do they create in her descriptions of both the secondhand bookstore and of her friend Sarah's home?

4. Early in her narrative, Nemat observes that "In a way, books had saved us both," referring to herself and her mother. What role do you think books played in this part of Nemat's life? How might they have saved her later in her life under Ayatollah Khomeini's regime? What does 28 her observation reveal about the **SIGNIFICANCE** of the bookseller, and of books, in her life?

5. *For Writing.* Explore your earliest memory of securing reading material on your own. What kinds of reading material did you seek? Was it print or digital, or both? Where did you look for it — at a library? In a store? Online? Elsewhere? What attracted you to particular topics or genres? Did you have to resort to any of the kind of secrecy or sacrifice that Nemat did? 21–37 Write a **LITERACY NARRATIVE** in which you describe your hunt for reading material. Incorporate vivid detail and, if appropriate, dialogue, and be sure to give some indication of your story's significance.

MALCOLM X

Literacy Behind Bars

Best known as a militant black nationalist leader who rose to global fame as an advocate for Pan-Africanism (a movement that aims to unite all people of African descent), Malcolm X was born Malcolm Little in 1925. He replaced the name Little, which he considered a slave name, with the letter X to represent his lost African tribal name. Founder of the Muslim Mosque Inc. and the Organization of Afro-American Unity, Malcolm X was assassinated by political rivals on February 21, 1965. The following narrative comes from his autobiography, The Autobiography of Malcolm X *(1965), which he wrote with Alex Haley.*

MANY WHO TODAY HEAR ME somewhere in person, or on television, or those who read something I've said, will think I went to school far beyond the eighth grade. This impression is due entirely to my prison studies.

It had really begun back in the Charlestown Prison,* when Bimbi first made me feel envy of his stock of knowledge. Bimbi had always taken charge of any conversation he was in, and I had tried to emulate him. But every book I picked up had few sentences which didn't contain anywhere from one to nearly all of the words that might as well have been in Chinese. When I just skipped those words, of course, I really ended up with little idea of what the book said. So I had come to the Norfolk Prison Colony still going through only book-reading motions. Pretty soon, I would have quit even these motions, unless I had received the motivation that I did.

I saw that the best thing I could do was get hold of a dictionary — to study, to learn some words. I was lucky enough to reason also that I should try to improve my penmanship. It was sad. I couldn't even write in a straight line. It was both ideas together that moved me to request a dictionary along with some tablets and pencils from the Norfolk Prison Colony school.

**Charlestown Prison:* a prison near Boston, Massachusetts. [Editor's note]

Malcolm X, 1964.

I spent two days just riffling uncertainly through the dictionary's pages. I'd never realized so many words existed! I didn't know *which* words I needed to learn. Finally, just to start some kind of action, I began copying.

In my slow, painstaking, ragged handwriting, I copied into my tablet everything printed on that first page, down to the punctuation marks.

I believe it took me a day. Then, aloud, I read back, to myself, everything I'd written on the tablet. Over and over, aloud, to myself, I read my own handwriting.

I woke up the next morning, thinking about those words—immensely proud to realize that not only had I written so much at one time, but I'd written words that I never knew were in the world. Moreover, with a little effort, I also could remember what many of these words meant. I reviewed the words whose meanings I didn't remember. Funny thing, from the dictionary first page right now, that "aardvark" springs to my mind. The dictionary had a picture of it, a long-tailed, long-eared, burrowing African mammal, which lives off termites caught by sticking out its tongue as an anteater does for ants.

I was so fascinated that I went on—I copied the dictionary's next page. And the same experience came when I studied that. With every succeeding page, I also learned of people and places and events from history. Actually the dictionary is like a miniature encyclopedia. Finally the dictionary's A section had filled a whole tablet—and I went on into the B's. That was the way I started copying what eventually became the entire dictionary. It went a lot faster after so much practice helped me to pick up handwriting speed. Between what I wrote in my tablet, and writing letters, during the rest of my time in prison I would guess I wrote a million words.

I suppose it was inevitable that as my word-base broadened, I could for the first time pick up a book and read and now begin to understand what the book was saying. Anyone who has read a great deal can imagine the new world that opened. Let me tell you something: from then until I left that prison, in every free moment I had, if I was not reading in the library, I was reading on my bunk. You couldn't have gotten me out of books with a wedge. Between Mr. Muhammad's teachings, my correspondence, my visitors — usually Ella and Reginald — and my reading of books, months passed without my even thinking about being imprisoned. In fact, up to then, I never had been so truly free in my life.

As you can imagine, especially in a prison where there was heavy emphasis on rehabilitation, an inmate was smiled upon if he demonstrated an unusually intense interest in books. There was a sizable number of well-read inmates, especially the popular debaters. Some were said by many to be practically walking encyclopedias. They were almost celebrities. No university would ask any student to devour literature as I did when this new world opened to me, of being able to read and *understand*. 10

I read more in my room than in the library itself. An inmate who was known to read a lot could check out more than the permitted maximum number of books. I preferred reading in the total isolation of my own room.

When I had progressed to really serious reading, every night at about ten P.M. I would be outraged with the "lights out." It always seemed to catch me right in the middle of something engrossing.

Fortunately, right outside my door was a corridor light that cast a glow into my room. The glow was enough to read by, once my eyes adjusted to it. So when "lights out" came, I would sit on the floor where I could continue reading in that glow.

At one-hour intervals the night guards paced past every room. Each time I heard the approaching footsteps, I jumped into bed and feigned sleep. And as soon as the guard passed, I got back out of bed onto the floor area of that light-glow, where I would read for another fifty-eight minutes — until the guard approached again. That went on until three or four every morning. Three or four hours of sleep a night was enough for me. Often in the years in the streets I had slept less than that. [. . .]

I have often reflected upon the new vistas that reading opened to me. I knew right there in prison that reading had changed forever the course of my life. As I see it today, the ability to read awoke inside me some long dormant craving to be mentally alive. I certainly wasn't seeking any degree, the way a college confers a status symbol upon its students. My homemade education gave me, with every additional book 15

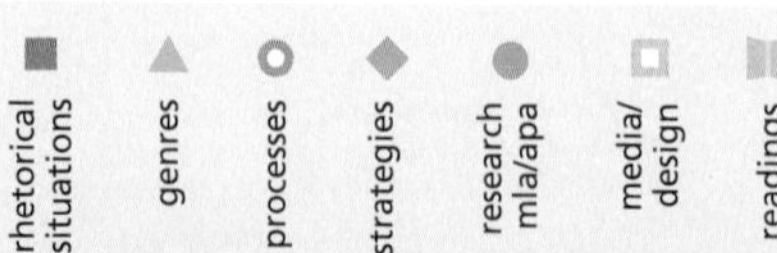

that I read, a little bit more sensitivity to the deafness, dumbness, and blindness that was afflicting the black race in America. Not long ago, an English writer telephoned me from London, asking questions. One was, "What's your alma mater?" I told him, "Books." You will never catch me with a free fifteen minutes in which I'm not studying something I feel might be able to help the black man. [. . .]

Every time I catch a plane, I have with me a book that I want to read — and that's a lot of books these days. If I weren't out here every day battling the white man, I could spend the rest of my life reading, just satisfying my curiosity — because you can hardly mention anything I'm not curious about. I don't think anybody ever got more out of going to prison than I did. In fact, prison enabled me to study far more intensively than I would have if my life had gone differently and I had attended some college. I imagine that one of the biggest troubles with colleges is there are too many distractions, too much panty-raiding, fraternities, and boola-boola and all of that. Where else but in a prison could I have attacked my ignorance by being able to study intensely sometimes as much as fifteen hours a day.

Engaging with the Text

1. In **DESCRIBING** how he felt after learning to read and write more fluently, Malcolm X states that even though he was in prison, he "never had been so truly free in [his] life." There is a certain irony that anyone would feel free while incarcerated. What does his narrative suggest about the relationship between literacy and freedom? 324–32
2. How would you characterize Malcolm X's **STANCE?** Where in his narrative is this stance made most explicit? Point to specific words and phrases that convey his stance. 12–14
3. As he describes his efforts to learn to read and write, do you think Malcolm X is **OBJECTIVE, SUBJECTIVE,** or a mixture of both? Give examples from the text to support your answer. Why do you think he chose to write that way? 327–29

28

4. Discuss the **SIGNIFICANCE** of Malcolm X's narrative, and by implication the significance of learning to read and write. What lessons does his experience teach us about the power of reading and writing?

21–37

5. ***For Writing.*** Malcolm X advocates reading as an excellent road to education, but a college education consists of far more than reading. Write a **LITERACY NARRATIVE** looking at the role that reading has played in your education so far. Consider the kinds of texts you've read — those you've been assigned to read, and also those you yourself have chosen to read. Consider also the other kinds of work you've done at school — lectures you've attended, exams you've taken, discussions you've participated in, essays you've written, blogs you've created. How important is reading compared with this other work?

ALISON BECHDEL

The Canary-Colored Caravan of Death

Alison Bechdel grew up in Lock Haven, Pennsylvania, where her parents, both high school English teachers, ran a funeral parlor that doubled as their family home. A graduate of Oberlin College, Bechdel applied to art schools and, failing to get in, took positions in various publishing companies. She went on to become an award-winning cartoonist. This selection is from Fun Home: A Family Tragicomic *(2006), which was named by* Time *magazine as number one of its 10 Best Books of the Year. In this graphic memoir, Bechdel narrates her childhood, moving back and forth between the years prior to and following her father's death, and explores her coming to understand her and her father's sexuality. Bechdel's work has appeared in* Ms., Slate, The Village Voice, *and* The Advocate.

TWO NIGHTS BEFORE MY FATHER DIED, I DREAMED THAT I WAS OUT AT THE BULLPEN WITH HIM. THERE WAS A GLORIOUS SUNSET VISIBLE THROUGH THE TREES.
DAD! C'MON! LET'S GO UP THE HILL AND SEE IT!

AT FIRST HE IGNORED ME. I RACED OVER THE VELVETY MOSS IN MY BARE FEET.
HURRY UP! IT'S AMAZING!

WHEN HE FINALLY GOT THERE, THE SUN HAD SUNK BEHIND THE HORIZON AND THE BRILLIANT COLORS WERE GONE.
YOU **MISSED** IT! GOD, IT WAS **BEAUTIFUL!**

IF THIS WAS A PREMONITORY DREAM, I CAN ONLY SAY THAT ITS CONDOLENCE-CARD ASSOCIATION OF DEATH WITH A SETTING SUN IS MAUDLIN IN THE EXTREME.

YET MY FATHER DID POSSESS A CERTAIN RADIANCE--

--PERHAPS DUE TO HIS HABIT OF EXCESSIVE, EVEN IDOLATROUS, SUNBATHING--
OFF TO CHURCH

--AND SO HIS DEATH HAD AN INEVITABLY DIMMING, CREPUSCULAR EFFECT. MY COUSIN EVEN POSTPONED HIS ANNUAL FIREWORKS DISPLAY THE NIGHT BEFORE THE FUNERAL.

WHY?
WELL, UH...OUT OF RESPECT FOR YOUR DAD.
I HAD BEEN HOPING FOR A MORE BLUNT RESPONSE, LIKE, "BECAUSE YOUR FATHER JUST DIED, YOU IDIOT."

MY NUMBNESS, ALONG WITH ALL THE MEALY-MOUTHED MOURNING, WAS MAKING ME IRRITABLE. WHAT WOULD HAPPEN IF WE SPOKE THE TRUTH?

I DIDN'T FIND OUT.

WHEN I THINK ABOUT HOW MY FATHER'S STORY MIGHT HAVE TURNED OUT DIFFERENTLY, A GEOGRAPHICAL RELOCATION IS USUALLY INVOLVED.

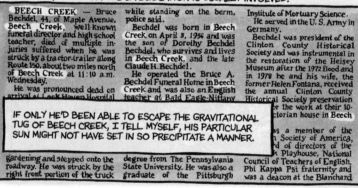

BEECH CREEK — Bruce Bechdel, 44, of Maple Avenue, Beech Creek, well-known funeral director and high school teacher, died of multiple injuries suffered when he was struck by a tractor-trailer along Route 150, about two miles north of Beech Creek at 11:10 a.m. Wednesday.

He was pronounced dead on arrival at Lock Haven Hospital

gardening and stepped onto the roadway. He was struck by the right front portion of the truck while standing on the berm, police said.

Bechdel was born in Beech Creek on April 8, 1936 and was the son of Dorothy Bechdel Bechdel, who survives and lives in Beech Creek, and the late Claude H. Bechdel.

He operated the Bruce A. Bechdel Funeral Home in Beech Creek and was also an English teacher at Bald Eagle-Nittany

degree from The Pennsylvania State University. He was also a graduate of the Pittsburgh Institute of Mortuary Science.

He served in the U. S. Army in Germany.

Bechdel was president of the Clinton County Historical Society and was instrumental in the restoration of the Heisey Museum after the 1972 flood and in 1978 he and his wife, the former Helen Fontana, received the annual Clinton County Historical Society preservation

r the work at their 10-

ctorian house in Beech

s a member of the

h Society of America,

rd of directors of the

k Playhouse, National Council of Teachers of English, Phi Kappa Psi fraternity and was a deacon at the Blanchard

IF ONLY HE'D BEEN ABLE TO ESCAPE THE GRAVITATIONAL TUG OF BEECH CREEK, I TELL MYSELF, HIS PARTICULAR SUN MIGHT NOT HAVE SET IN SO PRECIPITATE A MANNER.

PERHAPS THE PECULIAR TOPOGRAPHY REALLY DID EXERT SOME KIND OF PULL.

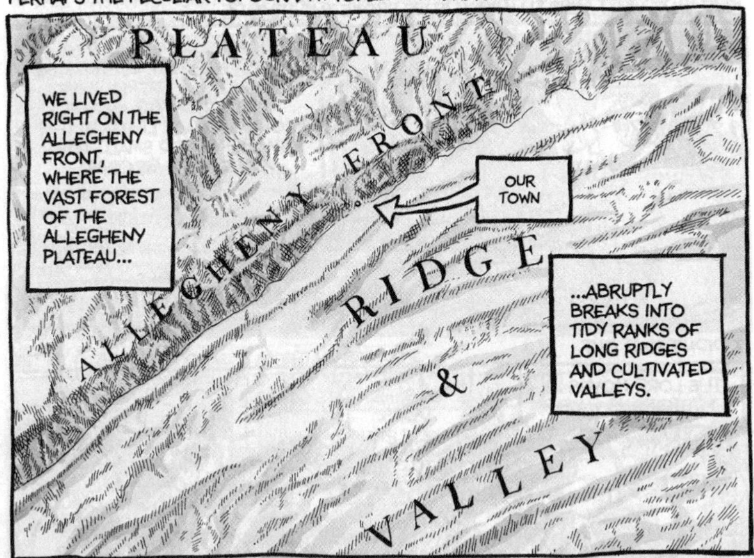

THE APPALACHIAN RIDGES--MANY LONGER THAN HADRIAN'S WALL--HISTORICALLY DISCOURAGED CULTURAL EXCHANGE. MY GRANDMOTHER, FOR EXAMPLE, WAS A BECHDEL EVEN BEFORE SHE MARRIED MY GRANDFATHER. AND IN OUR TOWN OF 800 SOULS, THERE WERE 26 BECHDEL FAMILIES LISTED IN THE PHONE BOOK.

THIS DESPITE THE FACT THAT PEOPLE COULD EASILY DRIVE AROUND THE MOUNTAINS BY THE TIME MY FATHER WAS A CHILD.

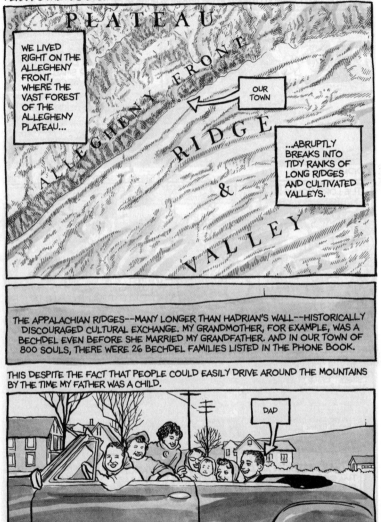

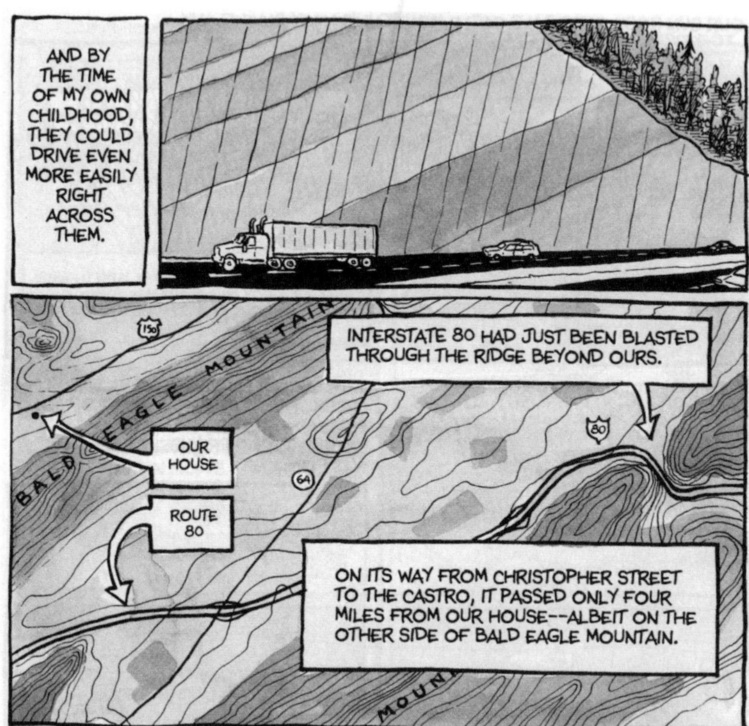

AND BY THE TIME OF MY OWN CHILDHOOD, THEY COULD DRIVE EVEN MORE EASILY RIGHT ACROSS THEM.
INTERSTATE 80 HAD JUST BEEN BLASTED THROUGH THE RIDGE BEYOND OURS.
150
BALD EAGLE MOUNTAIN
OUR HOUSE
ROUTE 80
64
80
ON ITS WAY FROM CHRISTOPHER STREET TO THE CASTRO, IT PASSED ONLY FOUR MILES FROM OUR HOUSE--ALBEIT ON THE OTHER SIDE OF BALD EAGLE MOUNTAIN.

THIS MASSIVE EARTHEN BERM EFFECTIVELY DEADENED ANY HINT OF NOISE FROM THE GLORIOUS THOROUGHFARE...

...EXCEPT ON STILL, HOT NIGHTS WHEN THE HUMIDITY WAS PARTIC-ULARLY CONDUCTIVE.

Christopher Street: a street in New York City. *The Castro*: a neighborhood in San Francisco. [Editor's note]

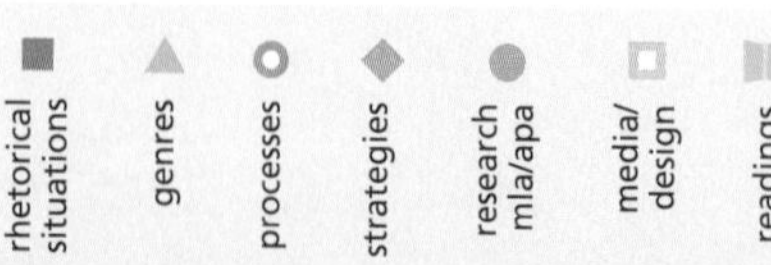

OUR SUN ROSE OVER BALD EAGLE MOUNTAIN'S HAZY BLUE FLANK.

(WE SAW LOTS OF SUNRISES IN 1974, THANKS TO THE ENERGY CRISIS AND THE YEAR-ROUND DAYLIGHT SAVINGS TIME IT ENTAILED.)

AND IT SET BEHIND THE STRIP MINE-POCKED PLATEAU...

...TYPICALLY WITH SOME DEGREE OF PYROTECHNIC SPLENDOR, DUE TO PARTICULATES FROM THE PRE-CLEAN AIR ACT PAPER MILL TEN MILES AWAY.

WITH SIMILAR PERVERSITY, THE SPARKLING CREEK THAT COURSED DOWN FROM THE PLATEAU AND THROUGH OUR TOWN WAS CRYSTAL CLEAR PRECISELY BECAUSE IT WAS POLLUTED.

MINE RUNOFF HAD LEFT THE WATER TOO ACIDIC TO SUPPORT LIFE OF ANY KIND.

I WAS INSPIRED TO POETRY MYSELF BY THESE PICTURESQUE SURROUNDINGS, AT THE AGE OF SEVEN.

I SHOWED IT TO MY FATHER, WHO IMPROVISED A SECOND STANZA ON THE SPOT.

LIMP WITH ADMIRATION, I ADDED HIS LINES TO MY TYPESCRIPT....

...THEN ILLUSTRATED THE PAGE WITH A MUDDY WATERCOLOR SUNSET.

IN THE FOREGROUND STANDS A MAN, MY SAD PROXY, GAZING ON THE UNTIMELY ECLIPSE OF HIS CREATIVE LIGHT.

SPRING
spring is very nice youknow
not a bit of ice or snow!
LiLACS tu lips and daffodils
peak their heads inthewindowsill.
I NEVER WROTE ANOTHER POEM. AND SOON, I ABANDONED COLOR TOO.

WE HAD A HUGE, OVERSIZE COLORING BOOK OF E.H. SHEPARD'S ILLUSTRATIONS FOR *THE WIND IN THE WILLOWS*.

DAD HAD READ ME BITS OF THE STORY FROM THE REAL BOOK. IN ONE SCENE, THE CHARMING SOCIOPATH MR. TOAD PURCHASES A GYPSY CARAVAN.

I WAS FILLING THIS IN ONE DAY WITH MY FAVORITE COLOR, MIDNIGHT BLUE.

WHAT ARE YOU DOING? THAT'S THE *CANARY-COLORED CARAVAN!*
Crayola
CRAYONS

IT WAS A CRAYONIC TOUR DE FORCE.

MY MOTHER'S TALENTS WERE NO LESS DAUNTING. ONCE I WENT WITH HER TO A HOUSE WHERE SHE ARGUED WITH A STRANGE MAN, AS IF SHE KNEW HIM INTIMATELY.

THIS WAS ACTING.

SHE COULD ALSO PLAY ASTONISHING THINGS ON THE PIANO, EVEN THE MUSIC FROM THE DOWNY COMMERCIAL ON TV.

SEVERAL YEARS AFTER DAD DIED, MOM WAS USING OUR OLD TAPE RECORDER TO REHEARSE FOR A PLAY. SHE READ FROM THE SCRIPT, LEAVING PAUSES WHERE IT WAS HER CHARACTER'S TURN TO SPEAK.

WHEN SHE CHECKED TO MAKE SURE THE MACHINE WAS RECORDING PROPERLY...

...SHE REALIZED THAT SHE WAS TAPING OVER MY FATHER'S VOICE.

IT'S JARRING TO HEAR MY FATHER SPEAK FROM BEYOND THE GRAVE.

BUT THE MOST ARRESTING THING ABOUT THE TAPE IS ITS EVIDENCE OF BOTH MY PARENTS AT WORK, INTENT AND SEPARATE.

THEIR RAPT IMMERSION EVOKES A FAMILIAR RESENTMENT IN ME.

IT'S CHILDISH, PERHAPS, TO GRUDGE THEM THE SUSTENANCE OF THEIR CREATIVE SOLITUDE.

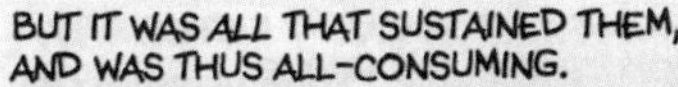
BUT IT WAS ALL THAT SUSTAINED THEM,
AND WAS THUS ALL-CONSUMING.

FROM THEIR EXAMPLE, I LEARNED
QUICKLY TO FEED MYSELF.

IT WAS A VICIOUS CIRCLE, THOUGH. THE MORE GRATIFICATION WE FOUND IN OUR OWN GENIUSES, THE MORE ISOLATED WE GREW.
OUR HOME WAS LIKE AN ARTISTS' COLONY. WE ATE TOGETHER, BUT OTHERWISE WERE ABSORBED IN OUR SEPARATE PURSUITS.
AND IN THIS ISOLATION, OUR CREATIVITY TOOK ON AN ASPECT OF COMPULSION.

Engaging with the Text

1. What are the various literacy practices that appear in Alison Bechdel's narrative? In your response, consider the creative activities depicted for all of her family members. How might exposure to these various creative endeavors have shaped Bechdel as an artist and writer? How  28 do these creative pastimes relate to the **SIGNIFICANCE** of her literacy narrative and to the medium she chose for it?

2. 324–27 330–31 Bechdel includes a great deal of descriptive **DETAIL** in her narrative — about her family, their work, the geography, and so on. What kinds of details does she show with images? What details does she provide with words? What **DOMINANT IMPRESSION** of her family do the details create?

3. 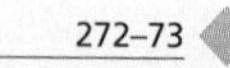 272–73 *Fun Home*, the **TITLE** of Bechdel's graphic memoir, refers both to the funeral home in which she grew up and to a fun house in an amusement park. Compare the characteristics of a fun house to those of Bechdel's home as she portrays it in this narrative. Why do you think 12–14 Bechdel selected this title? What does it reveal about her **STANCE** toward her childhood home?

4. Bechdel uses some challenging vocabulary in her text — "crepuscular," "berm," "rococo," "premonitory dream." What does her choice of 5–8 such words indicate about her expectations of her intended **AUDIENCE?**

5. ***For Writing.*** Rewrite Bechdel's piece using words alone. Compare your version with Bechdel's. What is lost when the images are removed? 306–13 283–99 What is gained? Write a paragraph that **COMPARES** the two versions and **ARGUES** for the effectiveness of one over the other.

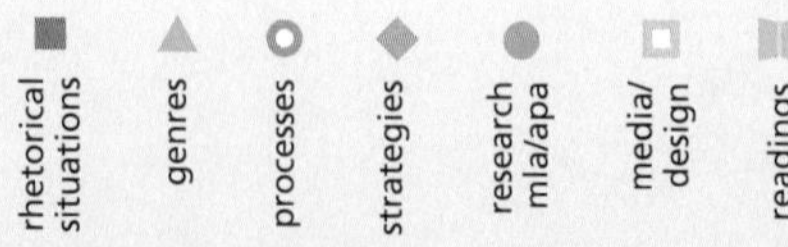

Textual Analyses 55

See also:

DENISE NOE

Parallel Worlds:
The Surprising Similarities (and Differences) of Country-and-Western and Rap

Denise Noe is the community editor for the newsmagazine Caribbean Star *and a writer whose essays have appeared in the* Atlanta Journal-Constitution *and elsewhere. She has also written widely on true crime. The following analysis appeared in 1995 in the* Humanist, *a magazine published by the American Humanist Association that covers such topics as politics, popular culture, science, and religion from a humanist perspective.*

IN ALL OF POPULAR MUSIC TODAY, there are probably no two genres that are more apparently dissimilar than country-and-western and rap: the one rural, white, and southern; the other urban, black, and identified with the two coasts ("New York style" versus "L.A. style"). Yet C&W and rap are surprisingly similar in many ways. In both C&W and rap, for example, lyrics are important. Both types of music tell stories, as do folk songs, and the story is much more than frosting for the rhythm and beat.

The ideologies espoused by these types of music are remarkably similar as well. We frequently stereotype country fans as simple-minded conservatives — "redneck," moralistic super-patriots à la Archie Bunker. But country music often speaks critically of mainstream American platitudes, especially in such highly charged areas as sexual morality, crime, and the Protestant work ethic.

The sexual ethos of C&W and rap are depressingly similar: the men of both genres are champion chauvinists. Country singer Hank Williams, Jr., declares he's "Going Hunting Tonight," but he doesn't need a gun since he's hunting the "she-cats" in a singles bar. Male rappers such as Ice-T, Ice Cube, and Snoop Doggy Dogg are stridently misogynist, with "bitches" and "hos" their trademark terms for half of humanity; their enthusiastic depictions of women raped and murdered are terrifying.

Indeed, the sexism of rap group NWA (Niggaz with Attitude) reached a real-life nadir when one member of the group beat up a woman he thought "dissed" them — and was praised for his brutality by the other members.

On a happier note, both rap and C&W feature strong female voices as well. Women rappers are strong, confident, and raunchy: "I want a man, not a boy / to approach me / Your lame game really insults me. . . . I've got to sit on my feet to come down to your level," taunt lady rappers Entice and Barbie at Too Short in their duet/duel, "Don't Fight the Feeling." Likewise, Loretta Lynn rose to C&W fame with defiant songs like "Don't Come Home a-Drinkin' with Lovin' on Your Mind" and "Your Squaw Is on the Warpath Tonight."

Country music can be bluntly honest about the realities of sex and 5
money — in sharp contrast to the "family values" rhetoric of the right. "Son of Hickory Hollow's Tramp" by Johnny Darrell salutes a mother who works as a prostitute to support her children. "Fancy" by Bobbie Gentry (and, more recently, Reba McEntire) describes a poverty-stricken woman's use of sex for survival and her rise to wealth on the ancient "gold mine." Both tunes are unapologetic about the pragmatic coping strategies of their heroines.

More startling than the resemblances in their male sexism and "uppity" women are the parallels between C&W and rap in their treatment of criminality. Country-and-western music is very far from a rigid law-and-order mentality. The criminal's life is celebrated for its excitement and clear-cut rewards — a seemingly promising alternative to the dull grind of day-to-day labor.

"Ain't got no money / Ain't got no job / Let's find a place to rob," sings a jaunty Ricky Van Shelton in "Crime of Passion." In "I Never Picked Cotton," Roy Clark is more subdued but still unrepentant when he says: "I never picked cotton / like my mother did and my sister did and my brother did / And I'll never die young / working in a coal mine like my daddy did." Waylon Jennings' "Good Ole Boys" boasts gleefully of having "hot-wired a city truck / turned it over in the mayor's yard."

Similarly, rap songs like "Gangsta, Gangsta" and "Dopeman" by NWA and "Drama" by Ice-T tell of the thrill and easy money offered by a life of crime. "Drama" records the dizzying high of the thief; "Gangsta,

Gangsta," the rush of adrenaline experienced by a murderer making a quick getaway. Of course, both C&W and rap songs do express the idea that in the long run crime doesn't pay. The sad narrator of Merle Haggard's "Mama Tried" "turned 21 in prison / doing life without parole," while the thief of Ice-T's "Drama" is forced to realize that "I wouldn't be here if I'd fed my brain / Got knowledge from schoolbooks / 'stead of street crooks / Now all I get is penitentiary hard looks."

Though both C&W and rap narrators are often criminals, their attitudes toward law enforcement differ radically. The Irish Rovers' "Wasn't That a Party?" ("that little drag race down on Main Street / was just to see if the cops could run") pokes light-hearted fun at the police, while the Bobby Fuller Four's "I Fought the Law and the Law Won" expresses the most common C&W attitude: an acceptance that criminals must be caught, even if you are one. Neither song displays any anger toward the police, who are, after all, just doing their job.

To rappers, on the other hand, cops are the enemy. Two of the most 10
notorious rap songs are Ice-T's "Cop Killer" and NWA's "Fuck tha Police" (which angrily asserts, "Some police think they have the authority to kill a minority"). Despite ample evidence of police brutality in the inner city, "Fuck tha Police" was almost certainly regarded by nonblack America as a paranoid shriek — until the world witnessed the infamous videotape of several of Los Angeles' finest brutally beating Rodney King while a dozen other "peace officers" nonchalantly looked on.

Interestingly, although the C&W view of law enforcement naturally sits better with the general public (certainly with the police themselves), the fact remains that country-and-western music contains a good deal of crime, violence, and casual sex. Yet it is easily accepted by white Americans while rap arouses alarm and calls for labeling. Why?

I believe there are three major reasons. The first, and simplest, is language. Rappers say "bitch," "ho," "fuck," and "motherfucker"; C&W artists don't. Country singers may say, "I'm in the mood to speak some French tonight" (Mary Chapin Carpenter, "How Do") or "There's two kinds of cherries / and two kinds of fairies" (Merle Haggard, "My Own Kind of Hat"), but they avoid the bluntest Anglo-Saxon terms.

A second reason is race. African-Americans have a unique history of oppression in this country, and rap reflects the inner-city African-

American experience. Then, too, whites expect angry, frightening messages from blacks and listen for them. Many blacks, on the other hand, hope for uplifting messages — and are dismayed when black artists seem to encourage or glorify the drug abuse and violence in their beleaguered communities. Thus, the focus on violence in rap — and the dismissal of same in C&W.

While the differing attitudes toward law enforcement are real enough, much of the difference between violence in country-and-western music and in rap lies not in the songs themselves but in the way they are heard. Thus, when Ice Cube says, "Let the suburbs see a nigga invasion / Point-blank, smoke the Caucasian," many whites interpret that as an incitement to violence. But when Johnny Cash's disgruntled factory worker in "Oney" crows, "Today's the day old Oney gets his," it's merely a joke. Likewise, when Ice Cube raps, "I've got a shotgun and here's the plot / Taking niggas out with the fire of buckshot" ("Gangsta, Gangsta"), he sends shudders through many African-Americans heartbroken by black-on-black violence; but when Johnny Cash sings of an equally nihilistic killing in "Folsom Prison Blues" — "Shot a man in Reno / just to watch him die" — the public taps its feet and hums along. . . . It's just a song, after all.

There is a third — and ironic — reason why rap is so widely attacked: 15
rap is actually closer to mainstream American economic ideology than country-and-western is. While C&W complains about the rough life of honest labor for poor and working-class people, rap ignores it almost entirely. "Work your fingers to the bone and what do you get?" asks Hoyt Axton in a satirical C&W song, then answers sardonically with its title: "Bony Fingers." Likewise, Johnny Paycheck's infamous "Take This Job and Shove It" is a blue-collar man's bitter protest against the rough and repetitive nature of his life's work. Work in C&W is hard and meaningless; it keeps one alive, but leaves the worker with little time or energy left to enjoy life.

Songs by female country singers reinforce this point in a different way; they insist that love (with sex) is more important than affluence. The heroine of Reba McEntire's "Little Rock" says she'll have to "slip [her wedding ring] off," feeling no loyalty to the workaholic husband who "sure likes his money" but neglects his wife's emotional and physical needs. Jeanne Pruett in "Back to Back" lampoons the trappings of wealth and proclaims, "I'd trade this mansion / for a run-down shack / and a man who don't believe in sleeping back to back."

Rap's protagonists, on the other hand, are shrewd, materialistic, and rabidly ambitious — although the means to their success are officially proscribed in our society. Not for them a "life that moves at a slower pace" (Alabama, "Down Home"); unlike the languorous hero of country-and-western, "catching these fish like they're going out of style" (Hank Williams, Jr., "Country State of Mind"), rap singers and rap characters alike are imbued with the great American determination to get ahead.

Rap's protagonists — drug dealers, burglars, armed robbers, and "gangstas" — live in a society where success is "a fistful of jewelry" (Eazy E, "No More ?s"), "Motorola phones, Sony color TVs" (Ice-T, "Drama"), where "without a BMW you're through" (NWA, "A Bitch Iz a Bitch"). In NWA's "Dopeman," sometimes cited as an antidrug song, the "Dopeman" is the archetypal American entrepreneur: clever, organized, ruthless, and not ruled by impulse — "To be a dopeman you must qualify / Don't get high off your own supply."

The proximity of rap to our success ethic arouses hostility because America is torn by a deep ideological contradiction: we proudly proclaim ourselves a moral (even religious) nation and tout our capitalist economic system. But the reality of a successful capitalist system is that it undermines conventional morality. A glance at the history books shows how our supposedly moral nation heaped rewards upon the aptly named "robber barons": the Rockefellers, Vanderbilts, Carnegies, and Morgans. The crack dealer is a contemporary version of the bootlegger — at least one of whom, Joe Kennedy, Sr., founded America's most famous political dynasty. (Indeed; I would not be surprised if history repeated itself and the son — or daughter — of a drug lord becomes this country's first African-American president.)

Capitalism is unparalleled in its ability to create goods and distribute services, but it is, like the hero of "Drama," "blind to what's wrong." The only real criterion of a person's worth becomes how much money she or he has — a successful crook is treated better than a poor, law-abiding failure. 20

In short, the laid-back anti-materialism of country-and-western can be dismissed with a shrug, but the rapper is attacked for that unforgivable sin: holding a mirror up to unpleasant truths. And one of them is that amoral ambition is as American as apple pie and the Saturday Night Special.*

Engaging with the Text

1. Denise Noe **ANALYZES** country-and-western and rap music, **COMPARING AND CONTRASTING** their lyrics and themes. What conclusions does she draw from her analysis? 38–58 306–13
2. Noe wrote this analysis for a magazine devoted to humanism, which it defines as a "naturalistic and democratic outlook informed by science, inspired by art, and motivated by compassion." How does she appeal to those values? How might her analysis differ had she written it for a business magazine?
3. What **EVIDENCE** does Noe offer to support her case about the similarities and differences between country-and-western and rap? What other kind of evidence might she have offered? 287–93
4. What kind of information about **CONTEXT** does Noe provide? Why is this contextual information important in her final analysis of the acceptance of rap and country-and-western music? 49–50
5. ***For Writing.*** Select two other genres of music that at first glance would seem as different as the two Noe writes about, and **ANALYZE** their lyrics, music, and contexts for any surprising similarities between them. Help readers understand the nature of the differences between the two genres. 38–58

**Saturday Night Special*: any cheap, easily obtained handgun. [Editor's note]

KATHARINE Q. SEELYE

Lurid Numbers on Glossy Pages!
(Magazines Exploit What Sells)

Katharine Q. Seelye is a veteran reporter for the New York Times, *where she has written widely on the environment and politics. The following article appeared in the* Times *in 2006.*

A **TRIP TO THE NEWSSTAND THESE DAYS** can be a dizzying descent into a blizzard of numbers. The March issue of *Elle Girl* promises readers "375 excuses to shop." *Harper's Bazaar* offers "783 new ideas to flatter you." *Marie Claire* trumpets not only "71 easy hair and makeup how-tos" but a mind-blowing "1,157 hot looks (all shapes, all sizes, all prices)."

Magazines, particularly the "service" publications aimed at women, have long used numbers as a selling point while helping readers divine what's in, what's hot, what's cool, what's not. But today, these totals, scores, and inventories seem both increasingly random and increasingly increasing, leaping exponentially beyond the sorry single digits of yesteryear to an incalculable proliferation of paths to a better you.

Glamour's March cover takes number-running to a new level, going full tilt with numerals in all cover lines, those blurbs meant to hook the reader at a glance: "7 reasons you will succeed at work," "15 shocking truths about women & food," "25 sexy little secrets of men's bodies," "25 cheap ways to make over your home," to a grand finale of "500 spring looks for all shapes & sizes!"

Men's magazines, too, are buying into the numbers racket.

Field & Stream gives guys "19 ways to get out alive" (Do you really 5
need more than one?) and "50 ways to get your late-season deer." *Blender*, the music magazine, offers "the 50 most awesomely dead rock stars." *Men's Health* boasts on its March cover: "2,143 sexy women confess what they want in bed." (Look closely — it's a poll, not interviews with 2,143 such women.)

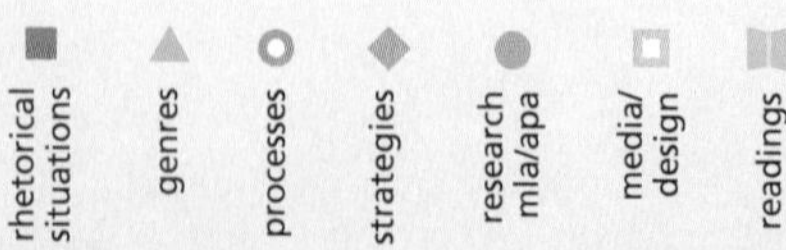

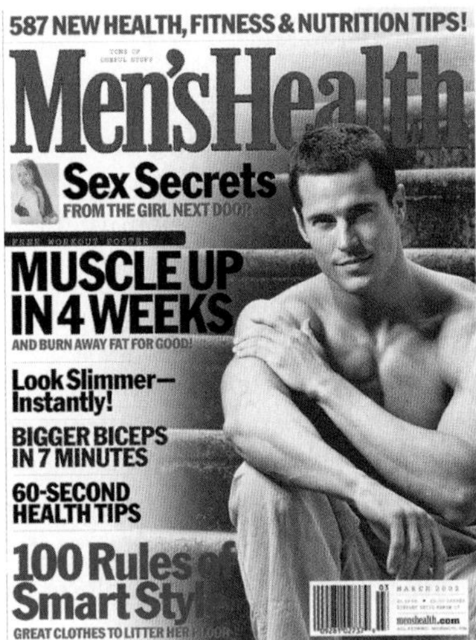

Men's Health *magazine, March 2003.*

It all adds up to an arms race at the newsstand. The escalating numbers reflect a new reality for monthly magazines as they struggle against hot-selling, celebrity-crazed weeklies and the Internet to maintain their traditional roles as guideposts in an aspirational society and as glossy vehicles for advertisers, particularly those in the multibillion-dollar cosmetics and fashion industries.

Editors sweat to find the perfect number, but admit there is no formula. As Craig Marks, the editor of *Blender,* put it, "It's all voodoo."

Yet certain patterns are evident. One is that bigger is better. "Size matters," Mr. Marks said.

Another is that odd numbers seem to be more believable than ever numbers. "The odd number really speaks to authenticity," said Ariel Foxman, editor of *Cargo.* "If it's odd, it can't be made up or shouldn't have been made up." (Editors insist that they use numbers that their writers actually find in their reporting.) And they said that the number 7 seemed to carry a certain appeal, while 13 is to be shunned.

The subject matter often dictates the size of the number. Cynthia 10
Leive, the editor of *Glamour,* said that if the subject was serious, numbers should be avoided. David Zinczenko, editor of *Men's Health,* said that smaller numbers were better for exercise tips, for example, because readers want something manageable. "Saying '35 best exercises' is too many," Mr. Zinczenko said. "But '789 great new tips for summer' is fine. That says value without saying work."

Most editors test their covers in focus groups in an endless search for the magic that will make their magazines fly off the shelves — and to avoid costly mistakes. And many find that numbers, while not solely responsible for a popular cover, are almost always written large on those that sell best.

Numbers jump out from the clutter of type on the newsstand. They draw the eye and quickly convey value and utility, helping monthlies in particular stay afloat in the rising ride of celebrity obsession.

"Today, the biggest force everyone is dealing with is celebrity magazines," said Kate White, editor of *Cosmopolitan*, the biggest monthly seller in the country. "You're not competing with other people's numbers, you're competing with Brad and Angelina and babies."

Sex still sells, of course, especially when mingled with celebrity. But behind the glamazons and smoldering cover girls, and often in front of them, stand the numbers.

Cosmo sizzles with a sleek Beyoncé Knowles. And in the upper left 15
quadrant, the portion of a magazine that is usually most visible on the newsstand and therefore is considered prime real estate, blares a numeric come-on: "60 sex skills."

That numbers-laden *Glamour* cover features a curvy Sarah Jessica Parker — ringed by numbers. Ms. Leive said that cover with numbers tested better than the same cover without numbers. She also said she used numbers in that case to give readers something to focus on against the busy background.

But numbers are more than a graphic device.

"The arms race took off because people are busy," Ms. Leive said. Numbers, she said, make certain stories "sound like what they are — a fun, quick, informative, quick, entertaining, quick read."

Bonnie Fuller set off the numbers craze a dozen years ago when she was the founding editor of *Marie Claire*.

Ms. Fuller, now the editorial director of American Media, which 20
publishes *Star* magazine, said she started to use numbers because readers shop from magazines and, as a reader, she wanted to look at more stuff; as an editor, she wanted to tell her readers what she had found.

"You're alerting readers that you have the expertise, you've honed down the massive amount of information out there, especially with the Internet, and you won't waste their time," she said.

Lesley Jane Seymour, the current editor of *Marie Claire,* said she periodically muses about dropping the magazine's signature gigantic number that anchors the bottom right of the cover. But readers in focus groups are saying no to zero.

"Readers say, 'I love the number,'" Ms. Seymour said. "It is one of the best-rated cover lines on the magazine. Do we go overboard? Yes, sometimes. But research shows numbers sell."

Compelling covers are essential for newsstand sales, one of the most cut-throat aspects of the publishing business.

"The newsstand market is a vicious one," said Scott Mowbray, edi- 25
torial director for Time4 Media, which oversees the Time Inc. enthusiast magazines, including *Field & Stream*. "But it's a very good discipline for editors. They're under tremendous pressure and they're using every tool they can and this approach, where you quantify the value, is working right now."

Newsstand sales are potentially more lucrative than subscriptions. They require no postage and the reader pays full price. The newsstand is where publishers find new customers. Home subscribers, by definition, already subscribe, probably at a discount. Printing subscription cards and stuffing them into magazines is cheaper than trolling for new subscribers through a direct mail campaign. And newsstand sales contribute to the rate base that publishers can charge for selling ads, said Martin S. Walker, a magazine consultant.

Still, newsstand sales have their own problems. Newsstands have become more crowded and promotional space at checkout counters more expensive, Mr. Walker said.

This new reality is what drove Glenda Bailey, editor of *Harper's Bazaar,* to start producing separate covers of her magazine, one for the newsstand and one for subscribers. The one on the newsstand has more numbers, Ms. Bailey said, because she is trying to capture new readers who may not know what the magazine has to offer; readers who get it at home already know and can take a more leisurely, if not less commercial, approach.

"On the newsstand, the cover is acting as a poster, an ad for what's inside," she said. "The loyal reader is looking for what makes the magazine exceptional."

Mr. Marks of *Blender* said he liked numbers because, like many men, 30
he likes to rank things. "We've done 'The 500 greatest songs since you were born,' and '1,001 songs to download' — in case someone did '1,000 songs,' we would have one more."

Jay Rocco, 27, who was thumbing through magazines in Times Square yesterday and who is a marketer for movies, is one of those guys. "I pay attention if there's a list, like the best restaurants," Mr. Rocco said. "Numbers definitely have an effect on me. I consider a point system to be a good filter and it lets me evaluate something really quickly."

Editors admit to some numbers burnout but say they do not dare drop them.

"It's such a powerful device, it works over and over and over again," said Isobel McKenzie-Price, editor of *All You,* which sells only on newsstands. "As an editor, I often think, 'I can't do this again.'" But, she said, there are so many drive-by readers, "that what's boring and old hat to us is new to them."

Kim France, editor of *Lucky,* the women's shopping magazine, which offers "774 instant wardrobe updates" in its March issue, said that despite some skepticism, numbers are resurgent. "Five or six years ago, there were a ton of numbers on covers and people doubted they were working because there were so many of them," Ms. France said. "Now there's a numbers creep again. People wouldn't go back to it if it didn't sell."

Engaging with the Text

38–58

1. According to Katharine Seelye's **TEXTUAL ANALYSIS,** what role do numbers serve on the covers of magazines? Why does she say that numbers are increasingly showing up on front covers? How much attention do you pay to numbers on a magazine cover when you are considering whether to buy it? Do you agree with Seelye's analysis — and if not, why not?

272–73
12–14

2. How does the **TITLE** of this article — "Lurid Numbers on Glossy Pages! (Magazines Exploit What Sells)" — reflect the author's **STANCE?** Is it an effective title? Why or why not?

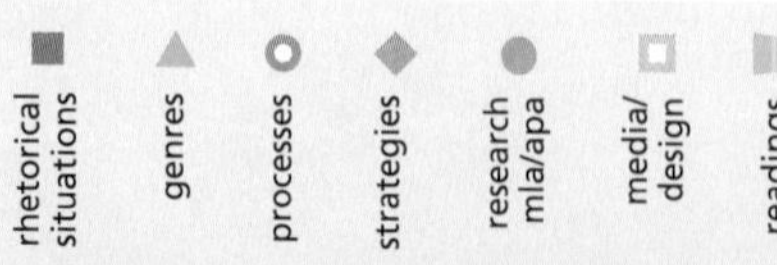

3. This article appeared in the business section of the *New York Times*. How has the **AUDIENCE** affected the way Seelye analyzes the magazine covers? How might she have analyzed the same covers for an article for the arts section of the *Times*? 5–8

4. Seelye incorporates numerous **QUOTATIONS** in her article, all of which seem to come from interviews. Why do you think Seelye chose to limit her research to interviews? Is this effective? What additional **SOURCES** could she have used, if any? 410–13 384–99

5. ***For Writing.*** Seelye focuses her analysis on one feature of popular magazine covers. Identify one other common feature — bold typefaces, photographs of famous people, bright colors, shocking quotations — and **ANALYZE** and **COMPARE** how that feature is used on several different magazines. What role does it serve and how is it related to the nature of the publication and its intended audience? Restrict your analysis to one kind of magazine (e.g., sports, teen, women's, fitness, gossip, music, news, science, computers), so that you can focus on how that practice functions for one kind of audience.

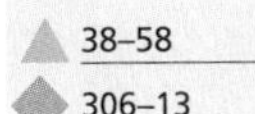

38–58 306–13

JAMES WOOD
Victory Speech

James Wood is a professor of literary criticism at Harvard University as well as a staff writer and book critic at the New Yorker. *Previously he served as the chief literary critic at the* Guardian *in London and as senior editor at the* New Republic. *His books of criticism include* How Fiction Works *(2008) and* The Irresponsible Self: On Laughter and the Novel *(2004). In addition, he is author of the novel* The Book Against God *(2003). In this essay, published in the* New Yorker *shortly after the 2008 presidential election, he turns his critical eye toward Barack Obama's speech on election night; for the full text of the speech,* *see p. 677.*

A THEATRE CRITIC ONCE MEMORABLY COMPLAINED of a bad play that it had not been a good night out for the English language. Among other triumphs, last Tuesday night was a very good night for the English language. A movement in American politics hostile to the possession and the possibility of words — it had repeatedly disparaged Barack Obama as "just a person words" — was not only defeated but embarrassed by a victory speech eloquent in echo, allusion, and counterpoint. No doubt many of us would have watched in tears if President-elect Obama had only thanked his campaign staff and shuffled off to bed; but his midnight address was written in a language with roots, and stirred in his audience a correspondingly deep emotion.

On Tuesday night, Obama returned to his cherished theme, the perfection of the Union. Any victorious election speech must turn campaign vinegar into national balm, must move from local conquest to national triumph, and Obama cunningly used this necessity to expand epically through American space and time. Behind his speech were the ghosts of Lincoln's First Inaugural, which moved anxiously over "every living heart and hearthstone all over this broad land," and his Second, which promised to "bind up the nation's wounds." Obama quoted from the end

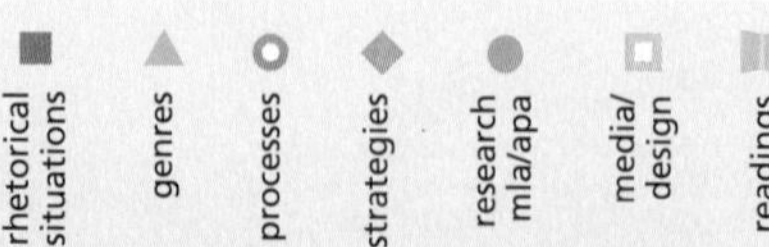

of the First Inaugural — "We are not enemies, but friends" — and the implication was clear: that the past eight years have been a kind of civil war.

Rhetorically, his speech sought to bind those wounds by binding us together. First, he moved through the people — young and old, rich and poor, gay and straight. Then he moved through the country — the back yards of Des Moines, the living rooms of Concord — ending, by way of the Gettysburg Address, with the earth: "from the millions of Americans who volunteered, and organized, and proved that, more than two centuries later, a government of the people, by the people and for the people has not perished from this Earth." And then he moved through time, using the epic novelist's trick of a heroine as old as the century. Ann Nixon Cooper, at the age of a hundred and six, had voted in Atlanta. Obama paused to imagine all that she had seen: woman suffrage, the "despair in the dust bowl, and Depression across the land"; the start of the Second World War, when "bombs fell on our harbor" (Pearl Harbor became simply "our harbor," which was Obama's way of reclaiming Hawaii from its recent alienation — his harbor and ours); and "the buses in Montgomery, the hoses in Birmingham, a bridge in Selma." At the end of each witnessed decade, Obama appended a quiet "Yes we can," extraordinarily moving in its sobriety. "Yes we can" had never been much more than a motivational vitamin, too close for comfort to Bob the Builder's "Yes we can!" But by attaching the phrase to the past tense, to achieved history, Obama stripped it of its bright futurity and invested it with a measure of uncertainty, as if intoning both "Yes we did" and an implied "Yes we may."

Besides Lincoln, Martin Luther King, Jr., was the speech's other founder. The allusions were deeper, and quieter, than the explicit reference to King's famous phrase about how "the arc of the moral universe is long, but it bends toward justice." (Obama said that we will put our hands "on the arc of history and bend it once more toward the hope of a better day.") When the President-elect warned that the road will be long, and that "we may not get there in one year or even one term, but America . . . I promise you — we as a people will get there," the word "promise" surely activated, however unconsciously, the rich narrative of exodus that found a culminating expression in King's last speech, in Memphis: "And I've seen the promised land. I may not get there with you." In the Memphis speech, King says that if God asked him which epoch he would like to inhabit he would want to go to Egypt in bondage, but also to Europe during the Reformation, and America when Lincoln signed the Emancipation Proclamation. Borrowing, perhaps, from King's epic radiations, Obama had Ann Nixon Cooper move through her American decades, then burst into world history:

> A man touched down on the moon, a wall came down in Berlin, a world was connected by our own science and imagination. And this year, in this election, she touched her finger to a screen, and cast her vote.

The language is plain but musical: the repeated "down" and the repeated "touched" enact the connection in they describe. And then, at the end, as Obama returned once more to the Union ("that out of many, we are one") and the promised land ("if our children should live to see the next century"), his language again invoked Lincoln ("and where we are met with cynicism and doubt, and those who tell us that we can't" — that archaic "are met with" taking us back, allusively, to the Gettysburg Address): "We are met on a great battlefield of that war."

Engaging with the Text

1. Typically, presidential victory speeches function to confirm values and build support across the country. Or in James Wood's words: "Any victorious election speech must turn campaign vinegar into national balm, must move from local conquest to national triumph." According to Wood, how does Obama's victory speech fulfill this function? Point to specific passages to support your response.
2. According to Wood, what figures from the past does Obama echo in his speech? What **EVIDENCE** does Wood provide to support his claim of these echoes?

287–93

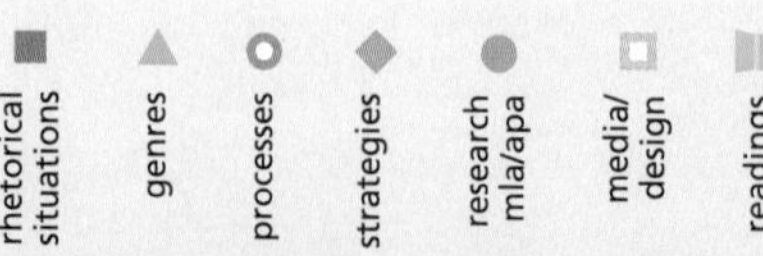

3. Wood observes of Obama's speech that: "Rhetorically, his speech sought to bind those wounds by binding us together." What does this statement reveal about Wood's **STANCE** toward the speech and the speaker? Point to other phrases that also reveal this stance.

12–14

4. Textual analyses generally include attention to the larger **CONTEXT** of the text. What contextual information does Wood provide? Do you think he offers enough? How might the amount of contextual information that's necessary be different for an audience reading the piece ten years from now?

49–50

5. ***For Writing.*** Read Obama's speech on p. 677 and decide whether you agree with Wood's analysis of it. Write an essay that either supports or refutes his interpretation using **TEXTUAL EVIDENCE** from both Wood's essay and Obama's speech to support your **ARGUMENT**.

291–92
83–110

GREGORY HOADLEY

Classic Nuance:
Simon Hall at Indiana University

A freelance writer and editor, Gregory Hoadley is a member of ArchNet, an international online community for architects, conservationists, planners, urban designers, and landscape architects. Hoadley is a frequent contributor to ArchNewsNow, *an online newsletter that covers topics in design and archictecture. This piece first appeared in* ArchNewsNow *in 2008. As you read, consider how buildings can be viewed productively as texts to be read and analyzed, and how specific details help to support this textual analysis of a physical structure.*

ACADEMIC ARCHITECTURE INVARIABLY PROJECTS AN IDENTITY about campus and community to building users and to the world beyond. Some institutions desire new buildings to be stand-alone statements, with ultramodern exteriors to symbolize the cutting-edge research to be conducted within. Yet in other cases, the architectural language established in surrounding precedents may be more appropriate, even for high-tech facilities. Simon Hall, a new $46.6 million interdisciplinary science building on the Indiana University campus, designed by Flad Architects of Madison, Wisconsin, inserts state-of-the-art research infrastructure in a building mass and exterior crafted to respond to their surroundings in the established vernacular of the historic Bloomington campus.

The interior of the 140,412-square-foot facility, dedicated in 2007, speaks to advanced scientific endeavor, featuring innovative spaces to support the realities of the collaborative research process. Yet the building exterior connects to its immediate location in Indiana University's Old Crescent, an area on the southwestern corner of campus listed on the National Register of Historic Places, containing a cluster of nine landmark buildings dating to the late 19th and early 20th centuries, all finished in locally quarried limestone, a hallmark of Bloomington campus architecture.

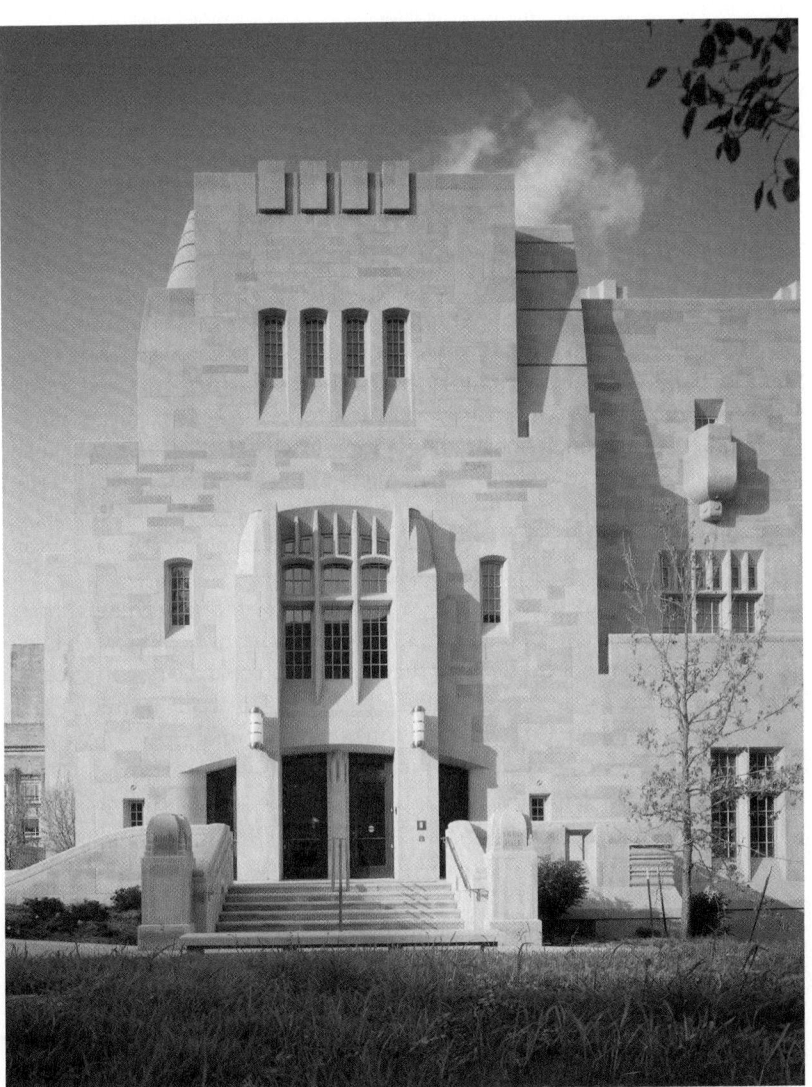

Exterior of Simon Hall.

In the case of Indiana University, the prized campus fabric was itself the signature identity to be projected and affirmed. The campus community felt that an earlier experiment with a concrete building by I. M. Pei (1982) didn't fit in with Bloomington's limestone context. Project challenges for Simon Hall included fitting state-of-the-art research facilities into the existing picturesque context, deeply imbued with powerful architectural imagery. A more brazen building would have interrupted the local texture of the limestone-clad vertical elevations, meandering pathways, and extensive foliage.

While interiors were programmed according to the needs of today's interdisciplinary research, the exterior and mass avoid dissonance with Simon Hall's surroundings, adjacent to a wooded expanse and completing a quadrangle with nearby historic structures. The concrete frame is finished in Indiana limestone, creating a wall that is over two feet thick and carved in the style of the neighboring neo-gothic and art moderne buildings. Figures of an *E. Coli* bacterium, a paramecium, maize, a fruit fly, and a mouse, all organisms with importance to the study of genetics, are sculpted into the façade.

The scale of the new building was kept in harmony with neighbor- 5
ing historic structures by placing 65,000 square feet of floor space below grade. The green roof that covers this buried lab provides open space at ground level but is designed to allow daylighting to areas located below grade. Subterranean tunnels also connect the building to the three nearby science facilities on the quad, ensuring easy interdisciplinary access to the new labs.

The interior plan is rooted in extensive consulting with eventual building users, and in the architect's ongoing comparative research into the design and use of existing scientific labs. Several design moves underpin Simon Hall's intention to create an interdisciplinary and collaborative research facility. Notably, the interior plan provides space for more than just versatile labs and high-tech devices, but also for the social interactions among researchers and visitors that enrich the research process.

Simon Hall houses 45 laboratories in three styles (low-hood intensive laboratories, high-hood intensive laboratories, and instrumentation

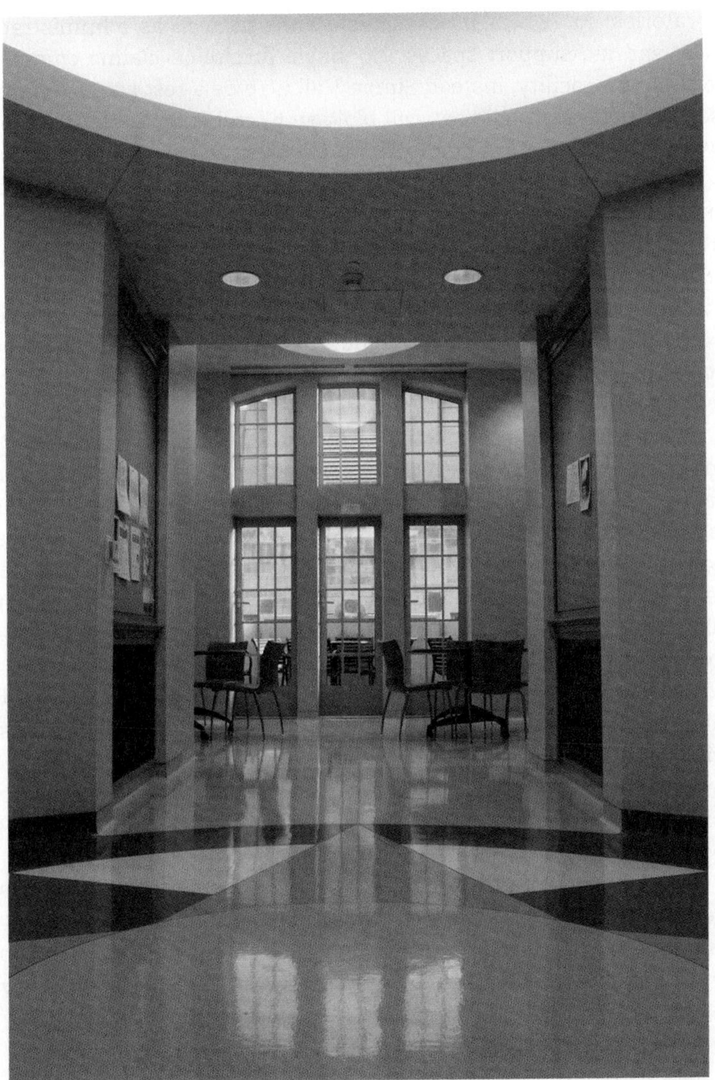

An informal gathering space opens onto a balcony.

laboratories) in 78% of its assignable area, as well as administrative, office, and lab support spaces. No single discipline claims ownership over the new facility; instead Simon Hall is to be a resource for Indiana researchers in such fields as cell biology, microbiology, molecular biology, genetics, analytical chemistry and biochemistry, and biophysics.

To meet the needs of interdisciplinary research, the modular and flexible labs can be quickly reconfigured to accommodate users from various backgrounds, while mechanical systems are designed to be adaptable to new machinery as building use evolves in the coming decades. High-tech equipment includes a high field nuclear magnetic resonance facility, a clean room for nanofabrication, a cryo-electric microscope, a bio-safety level 3 facility used for virology and bacteriology, and an X-ray crystallography suite.

Flad's own research on laboratory buildings found that the layout of non-research spaces can actually shape the productivity of those conducting research in a site. Plans with centrally located non-laboratory spaces provide nodes for informal interaction between building users, creating community and facilitating academic dialogue. In collaborative research environments, Flad found that project teams frequently make use of common spaces in buildings for problem-solving and coordination.

10 As such, Simon Hall has spaces designed for both formal and informal interaction, treating the social connections between researchers as a vital part of the research infrastructure. Impromptu meeting spaces are incorporated near stairwells, while a conference center provides a more formal meeting area along with a catering kitchen for staging light food services.

One design element that grew out of consultation with Indiana researchers was the placement of balconies near the labs, for taking in fresh air and short breaks during the long hours required at the lab in the research process. Finished in limestone, the balconies tie in with the language of the building exterior and that of Myers Hall, a 1930s art moderne science building next door.

Extensive use of glass interior walls enhances informal and planned interaction among research colleagues. This transparency also allows a

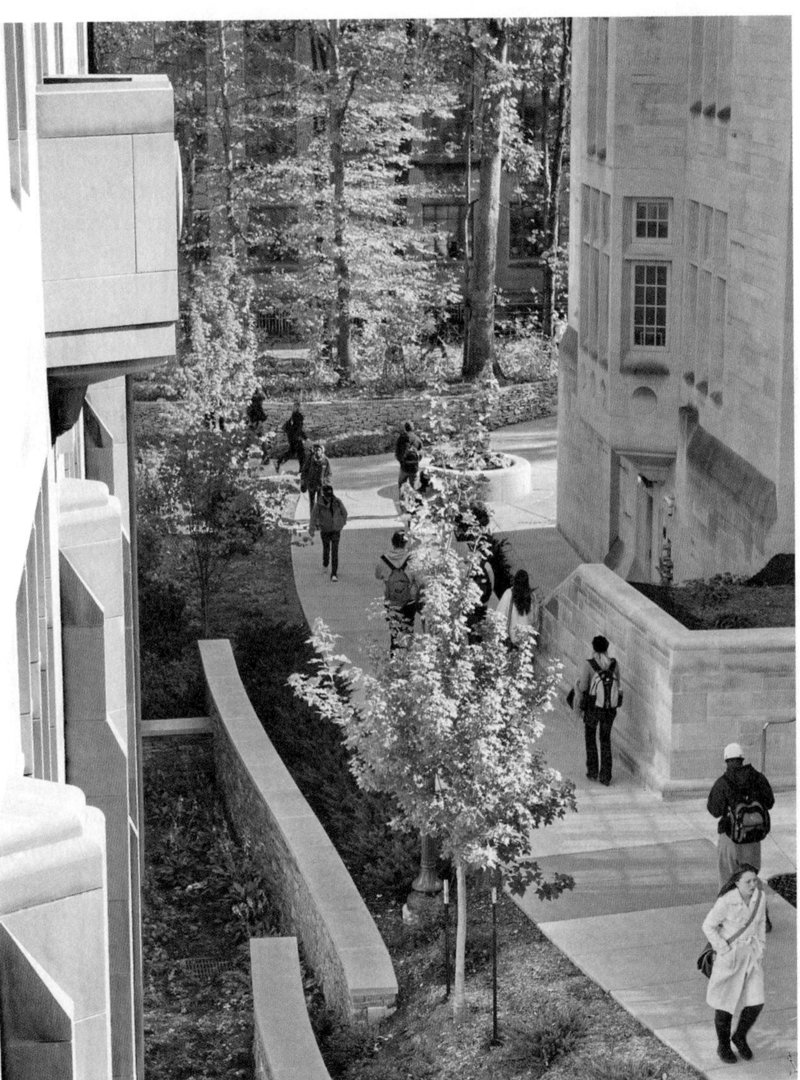

A network of outdoor spaces linked by a pedestrian circulation system.

high level of visibility to the scientific research practiced within, providing an outreach tool to visitors from the business community.

The new facility houses the Biocomplexity Institute and the Center for Genomics and Bioinformatics, along with the Linda and Jack Gill Center for Biomolecular Science and the Johnson Center for Entrepreneurship & Science Innovation, part of the Kelly School of Business, whose purpose is to link science emerging form the laboratories with business opportunities.

As David Black, AIA, design principal for Flad Architects, says, "You don't walk up to Simon Hall and say that it's a Flad building, or a David Black building; you say 'I'm at Indiana University.'" By inserting state-of-the-art technical facilities into a building envelope that responds to its architectural precedents, Simon Hall projects an image of both innovation and historical continuity for Indiana University science.

Engaging with the Text

1. Gregory Hoadley's analysis shows how inanimate objects, such as buildings, can project identities. What is the identity that Simon Hall 324–27 projects? What **DETAILS** does Hoadley include to reveal that identity? Can you think of any other kinds of objects that project identities? How do they accomplish this?
2. 266–70 261–66 How does Hoadley **END** his textual analysis of Simon Hall? How does this ending relate to his **BEGINNING**? How effective are his beginning and ending for framing his subject, Simon Hall?
3. 50 What **JUDGMENT** does Hoadley offer about the interior and exterior design of Simon Hall? What kinds of **SUPPORT** does he offer for his conclusions?
4. 5–8 Who is the primary **AUDIENCE** for this analysis? Point to places in the text (or the note preceding it) that provide evidence to support your answer. What other audiences might be interested in Hoadley's analysis?

5. ***For Writing.*** In his opening, Hoadley identifies two different approaches to designing architecture on college campuses. One seeks to demonstrate the cutting-edge nature of the research taking place on campus through ultra-contemporary exterior designs. The other seeks to create buildings that blend in with the design of other buildings on campus. **ANALYZE** one of the newest buildings on your campus. Which approach does it follow? Does it fit into the "vernacular" of your campus? If so, how? If not, why not? Write an essay analyzing both its exterior and interior to arrive at a conclusion about the identity the building projects and how that identity relates to the rest of campus. Include photographs of the building to support your analysis.

38–58

DIANA GEORGE

Changing the Face of Poverty: *Nonprofits and the Problem of Representation*

Diana George is a professor of English at Virgina Polytechnic Institute and State University. She has written widely on culture, writing, and visual representation. She is the editor of Kitchen Cooks, Plate Twirlers, and Troubadours *(1999), a collection of essays by writing program administrators;* Reading Culture *(with John Trimbur, 2006); and* Picturing Texts *(with Lester Faigley, Anna Palchik, and Cynthia Selfe, 2004). The following analysis comes from* Popular Literacy: Studies in Cultural Practices and Poetics *(2001). The endnotes are presented according to* The Chicago Manual of Style, *as they appeared in the original publication.*

> Constructively changing the ways the poor are represented in every aspect of life is one progressive intervention that can challenge everyone to look at the face of poverty and not turn away.
>
> — BELL HOOKS, *OUTLAW CULTURE*

ENCLOSED: No Address Labels to Use Up.
No Calendars to Look At.
No Petitions to Sign.

And No Pictures of Starving Children.

Text from the outer envelope of a 1998 Oxfam appeal.

AS I WRITE THIS, Thanksgiving is near. I am about to go out and fill a box with nonperishables for the annual St. Vincent de Paul food drive. Christmas lights already outline some porches. Each day my mailbox is stuffed with catalogs and bills and with appeals from the Native American

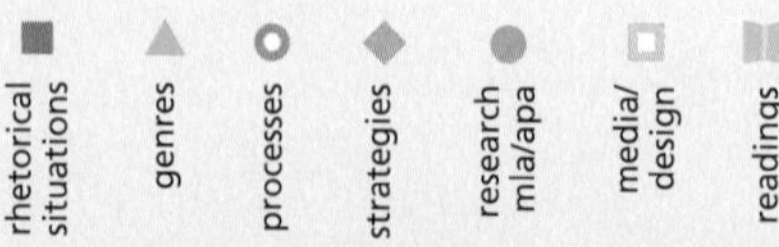

Scholarship Fund, the Salvation Army, WOJB — Voice of the Anishinabe, the Navaho Health Foundation, the Barbara Kettle Gundlach Shelter Home for Abused Women, Little Brothers Friends of the Elderly, Habitat for Humanity, and more. One *New Yorker* ad for *Children, Inc.* reads, "You don't have to leave your own country to find third-world poverty." Underneath the ad copy, from a black-and-white photo, a young girl in torn and ill-fitting clothes looks directly at the viewer. The copy continues, "In Appalachia, sad faces of children, like Mandy's, will haunt you. There are so many children like her — children who are deprived of the basic necessities right here in America."*

The Oxfam promise that I quote above — to use no pictures of starving children — is surely an attempt to avoid the emotional overload of such images as the one *Children, Inc.* offers. Still, those pictures — those representations of poverty — have typically been one way nonprofits have kept the poor before us. In a culture saturated by the image, how else do we convince Americans that — despite the prosperity they see all around them — there is real need out there? The solution for most nonprofits has been to show the despair. To do that they must represent poverty as something that can be seen and easily recognized: fallen down shacks and trashed out public housing, broken windows, dilapidated porches, barefoot kids with stringy hair, emaciated old women and men staring out at the camera with empty eyes. In such images, poverty is dirt and rags and helplessness. In mail, in magazines, and in newspapers, ads echoing these appeals must vie for our time, attention, and dollars with Eddie Bauer, Nordstrom's, The Gap, and others like them whose polished and attractive images fill our days.

In the pages that follow [. . .] I examine a particular representation of poverty — publicity videos produced by Habitat for Humanity — in order to suggest that reliance on stereotypes of poverty can, in fact, work against the aims of the organization producing them. [. . .]

*The copy here has been revised, with the author's permission, to reflect the more recent Children, Inc., ad. [Editor's note]

You don't have to leave your own country to find third-world poverty.

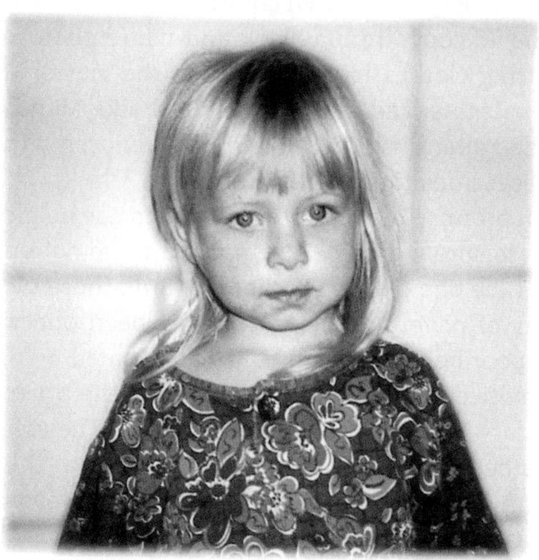

In Appalachia, sad faces of children, like Mandy's, will haunt you. There are so many children like her – children who are deprived of the basic necessities right here in America.

You can sponsor a boy or girl in need through Children, Inc. Just $24 a month will help provide clothing, shoes, school supplies and food as well as a feeling that someone cares. We'll send you the picture and story of the child you will be helping Please write, call or visit our website to enroll. Your help will mean so much.

Write to: Children, Inc., 4205 Dover Road, Dept.RB5M6, Richmond, VA 23221-3267 USA

❑ I wish to sponsor a ❑ boy, ❑ girl, in ❑ USA, ❑ Africa, ❑ Latin America, ❑ Middle East, ❑ Asia, ❑ Greatest need.

❑ I will give $24 a month ($288 a year). Enclosed is my gift for a full year ❑, the first month ❑.

❑ I can't sponsor, but I will help $________.

www.children-inc.org
1-800-538-5381

Children
INCORPORATED
Share in their future

Name

Address City State Zip Code

❑ Check or Money Order ❑ American Express ❑ Visa ❑ MasterCard

Card No. Expiration Date

U.S. gifts are fully tax deductible. Annual financial statements are available on request.

An ad for Children, Inc.

Habitat for Humanity: A Case in Point

I have chosen Habitat for Humanity publicity videos for my focus because Habitat is a popular and far-reaching nonprofit with affiliates not only in the United States but throughout the world. Its goal is not a modest one: Habitat for Humanity aims to eliminate poverty housing from the globe. More than that, Habitat puts housing into the hands of the people who will be housed — into the hands of the homeowners and their neighbors. This is not another program aimed at keeping people in what has become known as the poverty or welfare cycle.

To be very clear, then, I am not criticizing the work of Habitat for 5
Humanity. It is an organization that has done an amazing job of addressing what is, as cofounder Millard Fuller tells us again and again, a worldwide problem. What I would draw attention to, however, is how that problem of inadequate housing and its solution are represented, especially in publicity material produced and distributed by the organization, and how those representations can feed into the troubles that Habitat continues to have as it attempts to change the ways Americans think of helping others. What's more, the kinds of visual arguments Habitat and other nonprofits use to advocate for action or change have become increasingly common tools for getting the message to the public, and yet, I would argue, these messages too often fail to overturn cultural commonplaces that represent poverty as an individual problem that can be addressed on an individual basis. Habitat's catch phrase — A Hand Up, Not a Hand-Out — appeals to a nation that believes anyone can achieve economic security with just the right attitude and set of circumstances.

Habitat's basic program has a kind of elegance. Applicants who are chosen as homeowners put in sweat equity hours to build their home and to help build the homes of others chosen by Habitat. The organization then sells the home to the applicant at cost (that cost held down through Habitat's ability to provide volunteer labor and donated materials) and charges a small monthly mortgage that includes no interest. Unlike public assistance, which is raised or lowered depending on the recipient's circumstances, most Habitat affiliates do not raise mortgage payments when homeowners get better jobs or find themselves in better financial shape. And once the house is paid for, it belongs to the homeowner.

Obviously, in order to run a program like this one, Habitat must produce publicity appeals aimed at convincing potential donors to give time, money, and material. Print ads, public service television and radio spots, commercial appeals linked to products like Maxwell House coffee, and publicity videos meant to be played for churches, volunteer organizations, and even in-flight video appeals on certain airlines are common media for Habitat.

Habitat publicity videos are typically configured as problem-solution arguments. The problem is that too many people have inadequate shelter. The solution is community involvement in a program like Habitat for Humanity. The most common setup for these productions is an opening sequence of images — a visual montage — in which we see black-and-white shots of rural shacks, of men and women clearly in despair, and of thin children in ragged clothing. The voice-over narrative of one such montage tells us the story:

> Poverty condemns millions of people throughout the world to live in deplorable and inhuman conditions. These people are trapped in a cycle of poverty, living in places offering little protection from the rain, wind, and cold. Terrible sanitary conditions make each day a battle with disease and death. And, for this, they often pay over half their income in rent because, for the poor, there are no other choices. Daily, these families are denied a most basic human need: a decent place to live. The reasons for this worldwide tragedy are many. They vary from city to city, country to country, but the result is painfully the same whether the families are in New York or New Delhi.[1]

It is a compelling dilemma.

Organizations like Habitat for Humanity, in order to convey the seriousness of this struggle and, of course, to raise funds and volunteer support for their efforts in addressing it, must produce all sorts of publicity. And in that publicity they must tell us quickly what the problem is and what we can do to help. To do that, Habitat gives us a visual representation of poverty, a representation that mirrors the most common understandings of poverty in America.

Now, there is nothing inherently wrong with that representation 10
unless, of course, what you want to do (as Habitat does) is convince the American people to believe in the radical idea that those who have must care for the needs of others, not just by writing a check, but by enabling an entirely different lifestyle. For Americans, it is truly radical to think that our poorer neighbors might actually be allowed to buy a home at no interest and with the donated time and materials of others. It is a radical notion that such a program means that these neighbors then own that house and aren't obliged to do more than keep up with payments in order to continue owning it. And it is a radical idea that Habitat does this work not only in our neighborhoods (not isolated in low-income housing developments) but throughout the world. Habitat International truly believes that we are all responsible for partnering with our neighbors throughout the world so that everyone might eventually have, at least, a simple decent place to live. Like the philosophy behind many nonprofits, Habitat's is not a mainstream notion.

Still, that representation of poverty — clinging as it does to commonplaces drawn from FSA photographs in this century, from Jacob Riis's nineteenth-century photos of urban poverty, and from documentaries of Third World hunger — has serious limitations, which must be obvious to those who remember the moment that the Bush administration* confidently announced that, after looking everywhere, they had discovered no real hunger in the United States. And that myth that poverty cannot/does not actually exist in the heart of capitalism has once again been reinforced in the 1998 Heritage Foundation report in which Robert Rector echoed the perennial argument that there is little true poverty in this country ("Myth").[2] Heritage Foundation's finding

---

**Bush administration*: the administration of George H. W. Bush (1989–93). *FSA*: the Farm Security Administration, which hired such prominent photographers as Walker Evans and Dorothea Lange to document rural poverty in the 1930s. *Jacob Riis* (1849–1914): Danish American social reformer. [Editor's note] comes despite figures from the National Coalition for the Homeless ("Myths and Facts About Homelessness"), which tell us that in 1997 nearly one in five homeless people in twenty-nine cities across the United States was employed in a full- or part-time job.[3]

In her call for a changed representation of poverty in America, bell hooks argues that in this culture poverty "is seen as synonymous with depravity, lack and worthlessness." She continues, "I talked with young black women receiving state aid, who have not worked in years, about the issue of representation. They all agree that they do not want to be identified as poor. In their apartments they have the material possessions that indicate success (a VCR, a color television), even if it means that they do without necessities and plunge into debt to buy these items."[4] Hers is hardly a noble image of poverty, but it is a true one and one that complicates the job of an organization like Habitat that must identify "worthy" applicants. This phenomenon of poverty in the center of wealth, in a country with its national mythology of hearty individuals facing the hardness of the Depression with dignity and pride, is certainly a part of what Manning Marable challenges when he asks readers not to judge poverty in the United States by the standards of other countries. Writing of poverty among black Americans, Marable reminds us that "the process of impoverishment is profoundly national and regional."[5] It does little good to compare the impoverished of this country with Third World poverty or, for that matter, with Depression Era poverty.

The solution in these Habitat videos is just as visible and compelling a representation as is the problem. The solution, it seems, is a modern-day barn raising. In clip after clip, Habitat volunteers are shown lined up to raise walls, to hammer nails, to cut boards, to offer each other the "hand up not a hand out," as these publicity messages tell us again and again. Like the barn-raising scene from Peter Weir's *Witness*, framed walls come together against blue skies. People who would normally live in very different worlds come together to help a neighbor. It is all finished in record time: a week, even a day. Volunteers can come together quickly. Do something. Get out just as quickly.

The real trouble with Habitat's representation, then, is twofold: it tells us that the signs of poverty are visible and easily recognized. And

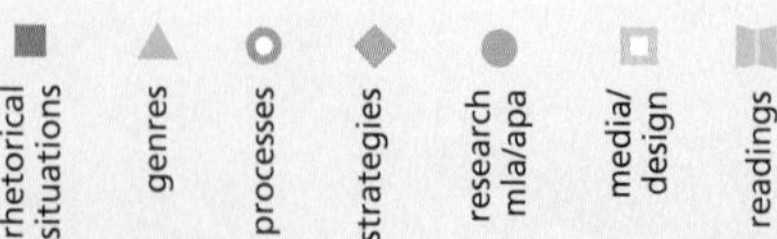

it suggests that one of the most serious results of poverty (inadequate shelter) can be addressed quickly with volunteer efforts to bring individuals up and out of the poverty cycle.

Of course, if Habitat works, what could be wrong with the representation? It is an organization so popular that it receives support from diametrically opposed camps. Newt Gingrich and Jesse Jackson have both pounded nails and raised funds for Habitat. This is what Millard Fuller calls the "theology of the hammer." People might not agree on political parties and they might not agree on how to worship or even what to worship, Fuller says, but they can all agree on a hammer. All can come together to build houses. Or, can they?

As successful as Habitat has been, it is an organization that continues to struggle with such issues as who to choose for housing, how to support potential homeowners, and how to convince affiliates in the United States to tithe a portion of their funds to the real effort of Habitat: eliminating poverty housing throughout the world, not just in the United States. And, even in the United States, affiliates often have trouble identifying "deserving" applicants or convincing local residents to allow Habitat homes to be built in their neighborhoods. There are certainly many cultural and political reasons for these problems, but I would suggest that the way poverty continues to be represented in this country and on tapes like those videos limits our understanding of what poverty is and how we might address it.

That limitation holds true for those caught in poverty as well as those wanting to help. What if, as a potential Habitat applicant, you don't recognize yourself or you refuse to recognize yourself in those representations? As Stanley Aronowitz points out in *The Politics of Identity*, that can happen very easily as class identities, in particular, have become much more difficult to pin down since World War II, especially with an expansion of consumer credit that allowed class and social status to be linked to consumption rather than to professions or even wages. In his discussion of how electronic media construct the *social imaginary*, Aronowitz talks of the working class with few media representations available to them as having fallen into a kind of "cultural homelessness."[6] How much more true is that of the impoverished in this country who may be neither homeless nor ragged, but are certainly struggling every day to feed their families, pay rent, and find jobs that pay more than what it costs for daycare?

I have been particularly interested in this last question because of a difficulty I mentioned earlier, that of identifying appropriate applicants for Habitat homes or even getting some of the most needy families of a given affiliate to apply for Habitat homes. When I showed the video *Building New Lives* to Kim Puuri, a Copper Country Habitat for Humanity homeowner and now member of the affiliate's Homeowner Selection Committee, and asked her to respond, she was very clear in what she saw as the problem:

> When I see those pictures I usually think of Africa or a third-world country and NOT the U.S. It's not that they can't be found here, it's just that you don't publicly see people that bad off other than street people. If they could gear the publicity more to the geographical areas, it may make more of an impact or get a better response from people. It would mean making several videos. It may not be so much of a stereotype, but an association between Habitat and the people they help. People viewing the videos and pictures see the conditions of the people and feel that their own condition may not be that bad and feel they probably wouldn't qualify.[7]

What this Habitat homeowner has noticed is very close to what Stuart Hall describes. That is, the problem with this image, this representation, is not that it is not real enough. The problem has nothing to do with whether or not these are images of poverty as it exists in the world. There is no doubt that this level of poverty does exist in this country and elsewhere despite the Heritage Foundation's attempts to demonstrate otherwise. The problem is that this representation of poverty is a narrow one and functions to narrow the ways we might respond to the poor who do not fit this representation.

The representation I have been discussing is one that insists on constructing poverty as an individual problem that can be dealt with by volunteers on an individual basis. That is the sort of representation common in this country, the sort of representation Paul Wellstone objects to in a recent call to action when he says "We can offer no sin-

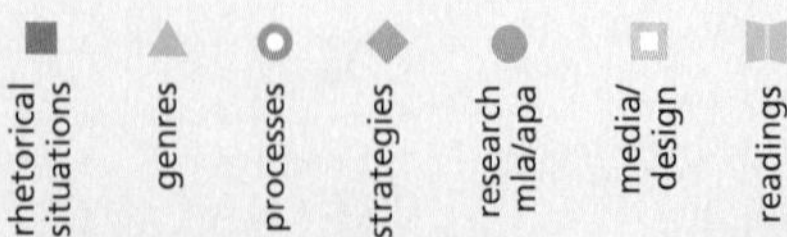

gle description of American poverty." What it takes to break through such a representation is first, as Hall suggests, to understand it as a representation, to understand it as a way of imparting meaning. And the only way to contest that representation, to allow for other meanings, other descriptions, is to know more about the many dimensions of poverty in America. "More than 35 million Americans — one out of every seven of our fellow citizens — are officially poor. More than one in five American children are poor. And the poor are getting poorer," Wellstone writes.[8] But we can be certain that much of that poverty is not the sort pictured in those black-and-white images. And if it doesn't *look* like poverty, then how do we address it? How do we identify those "deserving" our help?

Indeed, as Herbert Gans has suggested, the labels we have chosen 20
to place on the poor in this country often reveal more than anything "an ideology of undeservingness," by which we have often elided poverty and immorality or laziness or criminality. "By making scapegoats of the poor for fundamental problems they have not caused nor can change," Gans argues, "Americans can also postpone politically difficult and divisive solutions to the country's economic ills and the need to prepare the economy and polity for the challenges of the twenty-first century."[9] These are tough issues to confront and certainly to argue in a twenty-minute video presentation aimed at raising funds and volunteer support, especially when every piece of publicity must make a complex argument visible.

Notes

1. *Building New Lives* (Americus, Ga.: Habitat for Humanity International). This and other Habitat videos are directed primarily at potential volunteers for the organization or might be used to inform local residents about the work of Habitat.

2. Robert Rector, "The Myth of Widespread American Poverty," *The Heritage Foundation Backgrounder* (18 Sept. 1998), no. 1221. This publication is available on-line at <http://www.heritage.org/library/backgrounder/bg1221es.html>.

3. Cited in Barbara Ehrenreich, "Nickel and Dimed: On (Not) Getting By in America," *Harper's* (January 1999), 44. See also Christina Coburn Herman's *Poverty Amid Plenty: The Unfinished Business of Welfare Reform* NETWORK, A National Social Justice Lobby (Washington, D.C., 1999), from NETWORK's national Welfare Reform Watch Project, which reports that most studies of welfare use telephone surveys even though a substantial percentage of those needing aid do not have phone service (41 percent in the NETWORK survey had no operative phone) and, therefore, are not represented in most welfare reform reports. This report is available on-line at <http://www.network-lobby.org>.

4. bell hooks, "Seeing and Making Culture: Representing the Poor," *Outlaw Culture: Resisting Representations* (New York: 1994), 169.

5. Manning Marable, *How Capitalism Underdeveloped Black America* (Boston: South End Press, 1983), 54.

6. Stanley Aronowitz, *The Politics of Identity: Class, Culture, Social Movements* (New York: Routledge, 1992), 201.

7. Kim Puuri, personal correspondence with author.

8. Paul Wellstone, "If Poverty Is the Question," *Nation* (14 April 1997), 15.

9. Herbert J. Gans, *The War Against the Poor* (New York: Basic Books, 1995), 6–7.

Engaging with the Text

1. How, according to Diana George, is poverty represented by nonprofit agencies such as Habitat for Humanity? What problems does George identify as a result of such representation?
2. George opens her analysis with a bell hooks quote, followed by descriptions of how frequently she encounters charities near Thanksgiving. How do the quote by bell hooks and George's anecdote appeal to different **AUDIENCES**? 5–8
3. The Children, Inc. ad that George refers to is reprinted here on p. 624. What does George mean by the "emotional overload" of this image? Why do you think the Oxfam envelope promises not to include images like this?

4. What **PURPOSE** does George's textual analysis serve? Where is that purpose made explicit? What other purposes might her essay serve? 3–4

5. ***For Writing.*** Identify a print, TV, or Web ad aimed at influencing your opinion on a political or social issue. **ANALYZE** the visuals (drawings, pictures, photographs) and the accompanying words in the ad to describe how the issue is represented. How effectively does the ad meet its goals? Can you identify any problems with how the issue is represented that might undermine those goals? 38–58

56 Reports

See also:

SUSAN STELLIN
The Inevitability of Bumps 59

JAMES FALLOWS
Throwing Like a Girl 63

JEFFREY DeROVEN
The Greatest Generation 67

ELEANOR J. BADER

Homeless on Campus

Eleanor J. Bader is a freelance writer and an instructor in the English Department at Kingsborough Community College in Brooklyn, New York. She is also the co-author of Targets of Hatred: Anti-Abortion Terrorism *(2001). The following report appeared in 2004 in* The Progressive, *a liberal political magazine. As you read, notice how Bader effectively incorporates specific examples to support the information she reports.*

AESHA IS A TWENTY-YEAR-OLD at Kingsborough Community College in Brooklyn, New York. Until the fall of 2003, she lived with five people — her one-year-old son, her son's father, her sister, her mother, and her mother's boyfriend — in a three-bedroom South Bronx apartment. Things at home were fine until her child's father became physically abusive. Shortly thereafter, Aesha realized that she and her son had to leave the unit.

After spending thirty days in a temporary shelter, they landed at the city's emergency assistance unit (EAU). "It was horrible," Aesha says. "We slept on benches, and it was very crowded. I was so scared I sat on my bag and held onto the stroller day and night, from Friday to Monday." Aesha and her son spent several nights in the EAU before being sent to a hotel. Sadly, this proved to be a temporary respite. After a few days, they were returned to the EAU, where they remained until they were finally moved to a family shelter in Queens.

Although Aesha believes that she will be able to stay in this facility until she completes her associate's degree, the ordeal of being homeless has taken a toll on her and her studies. "I spend almost eight hours a day on the trains," she says. "I have to leave the shelter at 5:00 a.m. for the Bronx where my girlfriend watches my son for me. I get to her house around 7:00. Then I have to travel to school in Brooklyn — the last stop on the train followed by a bus ride — another two hours away."

Reluctantly, Aesha felt that she had no choice but to confide in teachers and explain her periodic absences. "They've all said that as long as I keep up with the work I'll be OK," she says. But that is not easy for Aesha or other homeless students.

Adriana Broadway lived in ten places, with ten different families, 5
during high school. A native of Sparks, Nevada, Broadway told the LeTendre Education Fund for Homeless Children, a scholarship program administered by the National Association for the Education of Homeless Children and Youth, that she left home when she was thirteen. "For five years, I stayed here and there with friends," she wrote on her funding application. "I'd stay with whoever would take me in and allow me to live under their roof."

Johnny Montgomery also became homeless in his early teens. He told LeTendre staffers that his mother threw him out because he did not get along with her boyfriend. "She chose him over me," he wrote. "Hard days and nights have shaped me." Much of that time was spent on the streets.

Asad Dahir has also spent time on the streets. "I've been homeless more than one time and in more than one country," Dahir wrote on his scholarship application. Originally from Somalia, he and his family fled their homeland due to civil war and ended up in a refugee camp in neighboring Kenya. After more than a year in the camp, he and his thirteen-year-old brother were resettled, first in Atlanta and later in Ohio. There, high housing costs once again rendered the pair homeless.

Broadway, Montgomery, and Dahir are three of the forty-four homeless students from across the country who have been awarded LeTendre grants since 1999. Thanks, in part, to these funds, all three have been attending college and doing well.

But few homeless students are so lucky. "Each year at our national conference, homeless students come forward to share their stories," says Jenn Hecker, the organizing director of the National Student Campaign Against Hunger and Homelessness. "What often comes through is shame. Most feel as though they should be able to cover their costs." Such students usually try to blend in and are reluctant to disclose either their poverty or homelessness to others on campus, she says. Hecker blames rising housing costs for the problem and cites a 2003 survey that found the median wage needed to pay for a two-bedroom apartment in the United States to be $15.21, nearly three times the federal minimum.

Even when doubled up, students in the most expensive states — 10
Massachusetts, California, New Jersey, New York, and Maryland — are scrambling. "In any given semester, there are four or five families where the head of household is in college," says Beth Kelly, a family service counselor at the Clinton Family Inn, a New York City transitional housing program run by Homes for the Homeless.

Advocates for the homeless report countless examples of students sleeping in their cars and sneaking into a school gym to shower and change clothes. They speak of students who couch surf or camp in the woods — bicycling or walking to classes — during temperate weather. Yet, for all the anecdotes, details about homeless college students are hazy.

"I wish statistics existed on the number of homeless college students," says Barbara Duffield, executive director of the National Association for the Education of Homeless Children and Youth. "Once state and federal responsibility to homeless kids stops — at the end of high school — it's as if they cease to exist. They fall off the map."

Worse, they are neither counted nor attended to.

"Nobody has ever thought about this population or collected data on them because nobody thinks they are a priority to study," says Martha Burt, principal research associate at the Urban Institute.

Critics say colleges are not doing enough to meet — or even recog- 15
nize — the needs of this group.

"The school should do more," says Aesha. "They have a child care center on my campus, but they only accept children two and up. It would have helped if I could've brought my son to day care at school." She also believes that the college should maintain emergency housing for homeless students.

"As an urban community college, our students are commuters," responds Uda Bradford, interim dean of student affairs at Kingsborough Community College. "Therefore, our student support services are developed within that framework."

"As far as I know, no college has ever asked for help in reaching homeless students," says Mary Jean LeTendre, a retired Department of Education administrator and creator of the LeTendre Education Fund. "Individual colleges have come forward to help specific people, but there is nothing systematic like there is for students in elementary and high school."

"There is a very low awareness level amongst colleges," Duffield adds. "People have this 'you can pull yourself up by your bootstraps' myth about college. There is a real gap between the myth and the reality for those who are trying to overcome poverty by getting an education." 20

Part of the problem is that the demographics of college attendance have changed. "Most educational institutions were set up to serve fewer, less diverse, more privileged students," says Andrea Leskes, a vice president with the Association of American Colleges and Universities. "As a result, we are not successfully educating all the students who come to college today. This means that nontraditional students — the older, returning ones as well as those from low income or other disenfranchised communities — often receive inadequate support services."

"It's not that colleges are not concerned, but attention today is not on serving the poor," says Susan O'Malley, chair of the faculty senate at the City University of New York. "It's not in fashion. During the 1960s, people from all over the country were going to Washington and making a lot of noise. The War on Poverty was influenced by this noise. Now the poor are less visible."

Mary Gesing, a counselor at Kirkwood Community College in Cedar Rapids, Iowa, agrees. "Nothing formal exists for this population, and the number of homeless students on campus is not tracked," she says. Because of this statistical gap, programs are not devised to accommodate homeless students or address their needs.

Despite these programmatic shortfalls, Gesing encounters two to three homeless students — often single parents — each semester. Some became homeless when they left an abuser. Others lost their housing because they could no longer pay for it due to a lost job, the termination of unemployment benefits, illness, the cessation of child support, or drug or alcohol abuse.

Kirkwood's approach is a "patchwork system," Gesing explains, and homeless students often drop out or fail classes because no one knows of their plight. "When people don't know who to come to for help they just fade away," she says.

"Without housing, access to a workspace, or access to a shower, 25
students' lives suffer, their grades suffer, and they are more likely to drop classes, if not withdraw entirely from school. I've seen it happen," says Amit Rai, an English professor at a large, public university in Florida. "If seen from the perspective of students, administrators would place affordable housing and full access to health care at the top of what a university should provide."

Yet for all this, individual teachers — as well as administrators and counselors — can sometimes make an enormous difference.

B.R., a faculty member who asked that neither her name nor school be disclosed, has allowed several homeless students to sleep in her office during the past decade. "Although there is no institutional interest or involvement in keeping these students enrolled, a few faculty members really care about the whole student and don't shy away from helping," she says.

One of the students she sheltered lived in the space for three months, whenever she couldn't stay with friends. Like Aesha, this student was fleeing a partner who beat her. Another student had been kicked out of the dorm because her stepfather never paid the bill. She applied for financial assistance to cover the cost, but processing took months. "This student stayed in my office for an entire semester," B.R. says.

A sympathetic cleaning woman knew what was going on and turned a blind eye to the arrangement. "Both students showered in the dorms and kept their toothbrushes and cosmetics in one of the two department bathrooms which I gave them keys to," B.R. adds. "The administration never knew a thing. Both of the students finished school and went on to become social workers. They knew that school would be their saving grace, that knowledge was the only thing that couldn't be snatched."

Engaging with the Text

3–4

1. What do you think is the **PURPOSE** of this report? How does this purpose affect the way the report is written? Point to examples from the text in your response.

59–82

2. This piece basically **REPORTS** on the general topic of homeless college students. What is the author's specific point? How do you know? How else could she have made her point explicit?

266–70

3. Eleanor Bader **ENDS** her essay with a powerful quote from one of her informants, a teacher she calls B.R.: "[The students] knew that school would be their saving grace, that knowledge was the only thing that couldn't be snatched." What does B.R. mean by this observation? In what ways can an education help such students, and in what ways might it be misleading to think that an education alone will solve all of the problems these students face?

343–51

4. Consider the amount of **NARRATIVES** in this report. Why do you think Bader includes so many? What other kinds of support does she include, if any? What additional kinds of support might she have used to help accomplish her purpose?

59–82

5. ***For Writing.*** You may not be aware of services that are readily available on your campus. Find out what services are available at your school, and do some research on one of those services to learn who uses it and whether they're satisfied with it or think it could be improved. Write a **REPORT** on your findings. As an alternative, you may want to deliver your report as a website.

JONATHAN KOZOL

Fremont High School

An educator, activist, and writer, Jonathan Kozol is known for his work as an advocate for social justice and public education. Currently on the editorial board of Greater Good Magazine, *Kozol is the author of over a dozen books, including* The Shame of the Nation: The Restoration of Apartheid Schooling in America *(2005), from which the following selection is taken. In this piece, Kozol reports on one of the many schools he studied to write this book.*

FREMONT HIGH SCHOOL IN LOS ANGELES enrolls almost 5,000 students on a three-track schedule, with about 3,300 in attendance at a given time. The campus "sprawls across a city block, between San Pedro Street and Avalon Boulevard in South Central Los Angeles," the *Los Angeles Times* observes. A "neighborhood fortress, its perimeter protected by an eight-foot steel fence topped by spikes," the windows of the school are "shielded from gunfire by thick screens." According to teachers at the school, the average ninth grade student reads at fourth or fifth grade level. Nearly a third read at third grade level or below. About two thirds of the ninth grade students drop out prior to twelfth grade.

There were 27 homerooms for the first-year students, nine homerooms for seniors at the time I visited in spring of 2003. Thirty-five to 40 classrooms, nearly a third of all the classrooms in the school, were located in portables. Some classes also took place in converted storage closets — "windowless and nasty," said one of the counselors — or in converted shop rooms without blackboards. Class size was high, according to a teacher who had been here for six years and who invited me into her tenth grade social studies class. Nearly 220 classes had enrollments ranging between 33 and over 40 students. The class I visited had 40 students, almost all of whom were present on the day that I was there.

Unlike the staggered luncheon sessions I observed at Walton High, lunch was served in a single sitting to the students in this school. "It's physically impossible to feed 3,300 kids at once," the teacher said. "The line for kids to get their food is very long and the entire period lasts only 30 minutes. It takes them 15 minutes just to walk there from their classes and get through the line. They get 10 minutes probably to eat their meals. A lot of them don't try. You've been a teacher, so you can imagine what it does to students when they have no food to eat for an entire day. The schoolday here at Fremont is eight hours long."

For teachers, too, the schedule sounded punishing. "I have six classes every day, including my homeroom," she said. "I've had *more* than 40 students in a class some years. My average class this year is 36. I see more than 200 students every day. Classes start at seven-thirty. I don't usually leave until four or four-thirty. . . . "

High school students, when I meet them first, are often more reluc- 5
tant than the younger children are to open up their feelings and express their personal concerns; but hesitation on the part of students did not prove to be a problem in this class at Fremont High. The students knew I was a writer (they were told this by their teacher) and they took no time in getting down to matters that were on their minds.

"Can we talk about the bathrooms?" asked a student named Mireya.

In almost any classroom there are certain students who, by force of the directness or unusual sophistication of their way of speaking, tend to capture your attention from the start. Mireya later spoke insightfully of academic problems, at the school, but her observations on the physical and personal embarrassments she and her schoolmates had to undergo cuts to the heart of questions of essential dignity or the denial of such dignity that kids in squalid schools like this one have to deal with.

Fremont High School, as court papers document, has "15 fewer bathrooms than the law requires." Of the limited number of bathrooms that are working in the school, "only one or two . . . are open and unlocked for girls to use." Long lines of girls are "waiting to use the bathrooms," which are generally "unclean" and "lack basic supplies," including toilet paper. Some of the classrooms "do not have air-conditioning," so that students "become red-faced and unable to concentrate" during "the extreme heat of summer." The rats observed by children in their elementary schools proliferate at Fremont High as well. "Rats in eleven . . . classrooms," maintenance records of the school report. "Rat droppings" are recorded "in the bins and drawers" of the high school's kitchen. "Hamburger buns" are being "eaten off [the] bread-delivery rack," school records note.

No matter how many times I read these tawdry details in court filings and depositions, I'm always surprised again to learn how often these unsanitary physical conditions are permitted to continue in a public school even after media accounts describe them vividly. But hearing of these conditions in Mireya's words was even more unsettling, in part because this student was so fragile-seeming and because the need even to speak of these indignities in front of me and all the other students seemed like an additional indignity.

"The problem is this," she carefully explained. "You're not allowed 10
to use the bathroom during lunch, which is a 30-minute period. The only time that you're allowed to use it is between your classes." But "this is a huge building," she went on. "It has long corridors. If you have one class at one end of the building and your next class happens to be way down at the other end, you don't have time to use the bathroom and still get to class before it starts. So you go to your class and then you ask permission from your teacher to go to the bathroom and the teacher tells you, 'No. You had your chance between the periods. . . .'

"I feel embarrassed when I have to stand there and explain it to a teacher."

"This is the question," said a wiry-looking boy named Edward, leaning forward in his chair close to the door, a little to the right of where I stood. "Students are not animals, but even animals need to relieve themselves sometimes. We're in this building for eight hours. What do they think we're supposed to do?"

"It humiliates you," said Mireya, who went on to make the interesting statement that "the school provides solutions that don't actually work," and this idea was taken up by other students in describing course requirements within the school. A tall black student, for example, told me that she hoped to be a social worker or a doctor but was programmed into "Sewing Class" this year. She also had to take another course, called

"Life Skills," which she told me was a very basic course — "a retarded class," to use her words — that "teaches things like the six continents," which she said she'd learned in elementary school.

When I asked her why she had to take these courses, she replied that she'd been told they were required, which reminded me of the response the sewing teacher I had met at Roosevelt Junior High School gave to the same question. As at Roosevelt, it turned out that this was not exactly so. What was required was that high school students take two courses in an area of study that was called "the Technical Arts," according to the teacher. At schools that served the middle class or upper middle class, this requirement was likely to be met by courses that had academic substance and, perhaps, some relevance to college preparation. At Beverly Hills High School, for example, the technical arts requirement could be fulfilled by taking subjects such as residential architecture, the designing of commercial structures, broadcast journalism, advanced computer graphics, a sophisticated course in furniture design, carving and sculpture, or an honors course in engineering research and design. At Fremont High, in contrast, this requirement was far more likely to be met by courses that were basically vocational.

Mireya, for example, who had plans to go to college, told me that 15
she had to take a sewing class last year and now was told she'd been assigned to take a class in hair-dressing as well. When I asked the teacher why Mireya could not skip these subjects and enroll in classes that would help her to pursue her college aspirations, she replied, "It isn't a question of what students want. It's what the school may have available. If all the other elective classes that a student wants to take are full, she has to take one of these classes if she wants to graduate."

A very small girl named Obie who had big blue-tinted glasses tilted up across her hair interrupted then to tell me with a kind of wild gusto that she took hair-dressing *twice*! When I expressed surprise that this was possible, she said there were two levels of hair-dressing offered here at Fremont High. "One is in hair-styling," she said. "The other is in braiding."

Mireya stared hard at this student for a moment and then suddenly began to cry. "I don't *want* to take hair-dressing. I did not need sewing

either. I knew how to sew. My mother is a seamstress in a factory. I'm trying to go to college. I don't need to sew to go to college. My mother sews. I hoped for something else."

"What would you rather take?" I asked.

"I wanted to take an AP class," she answered.

Mireya's sudden tears elicited a strong reaction from one of the boys 20 who had been silent up to now. A thin and dark-eyed student, named Fortino, with long hair down to his shoulders who was sitting on the left side of the classroom, he turned directly to Mireya.

"Listen to me," he said. "The owners of the sewing factories need laborers. Correct?"

"I guess they do," Mireya said.

"It's not going to be their own kids. Right?"

"Why not?" another student said.

"So they can grow beyond themselves," Mireya answered quietly. 25 "But we remain the same."

"You're ghetto," said Fortino, "so we send you to the factory." He sat low in his desk chair, leaning on one elbow, his voice and dark eyes loaded with a cynical intelligence. "You're ghetto — so you sew!"

"There are higher positions than these," said a student named Samantha.

"You're ghetto," said Fortino unrelentingly to her. "So sew!"

Mireya was still crying.

Several students spoke then of a problem about frequent substitute 30 teachers, which was documented also in court papers. One strategy for staffing classes in these three- and four-track schools when substitutes could not be found was to assign a teacher who was not "on track" — that is, a teacher who was on vacation — to come back to school and fill in for the missing teacher. "Just yesterday I was subbing [for] a substitute who was subbing for a teacher who never shows up," a teacher told the ACLU lawyers. "That's one scenario. . . . "

Obie told me that she stopped coming to class during the previous semester because, out of her six teachers, three were substitutes. "Come on now! Like — hello? We live in a rich country? Like the richest country in the world? Hello?"

The teacher later told me that three substitutes in one semester, if the student's words were accurate, would be unusual. But "on average, every student has a substitute teacher in at least one class. Out of 180 teacher-slots, typically 25 or so cannot be filled and have to be assigned to substitutes."

Hair-dressing and sewing, it turned out, were not the only classes students at the school were taking that appeared to have no relevance to academic education. A number of the students, for example, said that they were taking what were known as "service classes" in which they would sit in on an academic class but didn't read the texts or do the lessons or participate in class activities but passed out books and did small errands for the teachers. They were given half-credits for these courses. Students received credits, too, for jobs they took outside of school, in fast-food restaurants for instance, I was told. How, I wondered, was a credit earned or grade determined for a job like this outside of school? "Best behavior and great customer service," said a student who was working in a restaurant, as she explained the logic of it all to ACLU lawyers in her deposition.

The teacher gave some other examples of the ways in which the students were shortchanged in academic terms. The year-round calendar, she said, gave these students 20 fewer schooldays than the students who attended school on normal calendars receive. In compensation, they attended classes for an extra hour, up until three-thirty, and students in the higher grades who had failed a course and had to take a make-up class remained here even later, until six, or sometimes up to nine.

"They come out of it just totally glassed-over," said the teacher, and, 35
as one result, most teachers could not realistically give extra homework to make up for fewer days of school attendance and, in fact, because the kids have been in school so long each day, she said, "are likely to give less."

Students who needed to use the library to do a research paper for a class ran into problems here as well, because, as a result of the tight scheduling of classes, they were given no free time to use the library except at lunch, or for 30 minutes after school, unless a teacher chose to bring a class into the library to do a research project during a class period. But this was frequently impossible because the library was often closed when it was being used for other purposes such as administration of examinations, typically for "make-up tests," as I was told. "It's been closed now for a week because they're using it for testing," said Samantha.

"They were using it for testing last week also," said Fortino, who reported that he had a research paper due for which he had to locate 20 sources but had make no progress on it yet because he could not get into the library.

"You have to remember," said the teacher, "that the school's in session all year long, so if repairs need to be made in wiring or something like that in the library, they have to do it while the kids are here. So at those times the library is closed. Then, if there's testing taking place in there, the library is closed. And if an AP teacher needs a place to do an AP prep, the library is closed. And sometimes when the teachers need a place to meet, the library is closed." In all, according to the school librarian, the library closed more than a quarter of the year.

During a meeting with a group of teachers later in the afternoon, it was explained to me in greater detail how the overcrowding of the building limited course offerings for students. "Even when students *ask* to take a course that interests them and teachers want to teach it," said one member of the faculty — she gave the example of a class in women's studies she said she would like to teach — "the physical shortages of space repeatedly prevent this." Putting students into service classes, on the other hand, did not require extra space. So, instead of the enrichment students might have gained from taking an elective course that had some academic substance, they were obliged to sit through classes in which they were not enrolled and from which they said that they learned virtually nothing.

Mireya had asked her teacher for permission to stay in the room 40
with us during my meeting with the other teachers and remained right to the end. At five p.m., as I was about to leave the school, she stood beside the doorway of the classroom as the teacher, who was giving me a ride, assembled all the work she would be taking home.

"Why is it," she asked, "that students who do not need what we need get so much more? And we who need it so much more get so much less?"

I told her I'd been asking the same question now for nearly 40 years and still had no good answer. She answered, maturely, that she did not think there was an answer.

Engaging with the Text

272–73

1. The **TITLE** of the book in which this essay appears is *The Shame of the Nation: The Restoration of Apartheid Schooling in America*. How does this piece illuminate and support the book title? Based on your reading of this report, what is the "shame of the nation" and how is "apartheid schooling" taking place in the United States even though schools were legally desegregated over thirty years ago?

3–4

2. What is the **PURPOSE** of Jonathan Kozol's report? What do you think Kozol hopes will happen because of his report? Given this purpose, who is the most important audience for this piece?

71–72
287–93

3. How does Kozol demonstrate that his information is **ACCURATE** and **WELL RESEARCHED**? What kinds of **EVIDENCE** does he use to support his points? To what degree do you find his information accurate?

266–70

4. Re-read the final three paragraphs of Kozol's report. How effective is this **ENDING**? Do you think Kozol believes there is no answer to Mireya's question? Why or why not?

394–95
59–82
306–13

5. ***For Writing.*** Research a public high school near where you live — the school you attended or one near your college. Get permission from the school principal to **INTERVIEW** several teachers and students about their experiences with the curriculum, recreation facilities, lunch room, school library, and class sizes. Locate any recent newspaper accounts or school reports to supplement and verify the information you obtain from your interviews. Write a **REPORT** that **COMPARES** what you find out about the high school you researched with what Kozol reports about Fremont High. In what ways are the problems similar and in what ways are they different?

MIKE STOBBE

First U.S. Count Finds 1 in 200 Kids Are Vegetarian

Associated Press reporter Mike Stobbe writes essays on issues related to medicine and health. His work has appeared in the Los Angeles Times, *the* San Francisco Chronicle, *the* Charlotte Observer, *and the* Tampa Tribune, *among others. He also holds the membership chair at the Association of Health Care Journalists. The following report appeared in the online magazine* Salon *in 2009.*

SAM SILVERMAN IS CO-CAPTAIN of his high school football team — a safety accustomed to bruising collisions. But that's nothing compared with the abuse he gets for being a vegetarian.

"I get a lot of flak for it in the locker room," said the 16-year-old junior at Westborough High School in Massachusetts.

"All the time, my friends try to get me to eat meat and tell me how good it tastes and how much bigger I would be," said Silverman, who is 5-foot-10 and 170 pounds. "But for me, there's no real temptation."

Silverman may feel like a vegetable vendor at a butchers' convention, but about 367,000 other kids are in the same boat, according to a recent study that provides the government's first estimate of how many children avoid meat. That's about 1 in 200.

Other surveys suggest the rate could be four to six times that among 5
older teens who have more control over what they eat than young children do.

Vegetarian diets exclude meat, but the name is sometimes loosely worn. Some self-described vegetarians eat fish or poultry on occasion, while others — called vegans — cut out animal products of any kind, including eggs and dairy products.

Anecdotally, adolescent vegetarianism seems to be rising, thanks in part to YouTube animal slaughter videos that shock the developing sensibilities of many U.S. children. But there isn't enough long-term data to prove that, according to government researchers.

The new estimate of young vegetarians comes from a recent federal Centers for Disease Control and Prevention study of alternative medicine based on a survey of thousands of Americans in 2007. Information on children's diet habits was gleaned from about 9,000 parents and other adults speaking on the behalf of those under 18.

"I don't think we've done a good job of counting the number of vegetarian youth, but I think this is reasonable," Amy Lanou, a nutrition scientist at the University of North Carolina–Asheville, said of the government estimate. She works with the Physicians Committee for Responsible Medicine, a vegan advocacy group.

Vegetarians say it's animal welfare, not health, that most often 10
causes kids to stop eating meat.

"Compassion for animals is the major, major reason," said Richard Schwartz, president of Jewish Vegetarians of North America, an organization with a newsletter mailing list of about 800. "When kids find out the things they are eating are living animals — and if they have a pet. . . . "

Case in point is Nicole Nightingale, 14, of Safety Harbor, Florida. In 2007, Nightingale was on the Internet to read about chicken when she came across a video on YouTube that showed the birds being slaughtered. At the end, viewers were invited to go to the Web site peta.org — People for the Ethical Treatment of Animals [PETA].

A PETA sticker, shown actual size.

Nicole told her parents she was going vegan, prompting her mother to send an angry letter to PETA. But the vegan diet is working out, and now her mother is taking steps to become a vegetarian, too, said Nightingale, an eighth-grader.

She believes her experience was typical for a pre-adolescent vegetarian. "A lot more kids are using the Internet. They're curious about stuff and trying to become independent and they're trying to find out who they are," she said.

Vegetarians are most often female, from higher-income families 15
and living on the East or West coasts, according to previous studies. One good place to find teen vegetarians is Agnes Scott College, a mostly white, all-women's private school in suburban Atlanta with about 850 students. Roughly 5 to 10 percent of Agnes Scott students eat vegetarian, said Pete Miller, the college's director of food service.

Frequently, the most popular entree at the college dining hall is a fresh mozzarella sandwich with organic greens. And the comment board (called "the Beef Board," as in "what's your beef?") often contains plaudits for vegetarian dishes or requests for more. "They're very vocal," Miller said of his vegetarian diners.

Eating vegetarian can be very healthy — nutritionists often push kids to eat more fruits and vegetables, of course. For growing children, however, it's important to get sufficient amounts of protein, vitamins B12 and D, iron, calcium and other important nutrients that most people get from meat, eggs and dairy.

Also, vegetarian diets are not necessarily slimming. Some vegetarian kids cut out meat but fill up on doughnuts, french fries, soda or potato chips, experts said.

"Vegetarian doesn't mean low-calorie," said Dr. Christopher Bolling, who directs weight management research at Cincinnati Children's Hospital Medical Center. He said roughly 10 to 15 percent of the overweight kids who come to his medical center's weight loss program have tried a vegetarian diet at some point before starting the program.

Rayna Middlebrooks, 15, last year started a weight-loss program 20
offered by Children's Healthcare of Atlanta, a nonprofit hospital organization. She said she's been on a vegetarian diet for four years and now carries about 250 pounds on her 5-foot-3 inch frame.

Her mother confirmed that, and said that although Rayna does a great job of cooking vegetable-rich stir-fried meals for herself, the girl also loves pasta, soda and sweets, "I have to watch her with the candy," said Barbara Middlebrooks, of Decatur.

On the flip side is Silverman, the Boston-area football player. He's pleased with his health and has no problem sticking to his diet. Rather than try to negotiate the school cafeteria line, he brings his lunch to school. It's the same lunch every day — rye bread, some chicken-like tofu, cheese, a clementine, and an assortment of Nutrigrain, Cliff, granola and Power Bars.

He was raised vegetarian and said it's now so deeply ingrained that the idea of eating meat is nauseating. Recently, he ate something he belatedly realized might contain chicken. "I felt sick the rest of the day, until I threw up," he said.

Engaging with the Text

1. What information about vegetarians and vegetarian diets in Mike Stobbe's report did you find most surprising or interesting? Does this information change your thinking about vegetarian diets at all? If so, how?
2. 314–23 What terms does Stobbe **DEFINE** in his report? What do these defini-5–8 tions imply about the **AUDIENCE** he most wants to reach? Select two defined terms to support your response.
3. 261–67 How does Stobbe **BEGIN** his report? Why do you think he begins with this particular example? How does it prepare the reader for the rest of the essay?
4. 306–13 How does Stobbe use the strategy of **COMPARING AND CONTRASTING** in his report? How effective is this strategy for conveying the complexities of vegetarian diets as a lifestyle?
5. *For Writing.* Research a current health trend. It may have to do with diet, exercise, or some other activity for improving one's health. Interview several students about this trend and locate print or digital 59–82 sources that discuss it, then write a **REPORT** that informs your readers about this trend and whether or not it lives up to its promises. Include 410–13 **QUOTATIONS** from one or more of the people you interviewed about this trend.

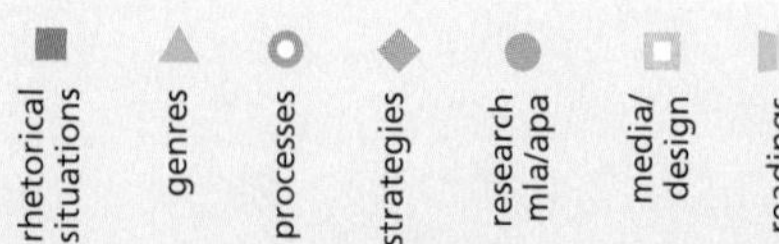

ALINA TUGEND

Multitasking Can Make You Lose . . . Um . . . Focus

Alina Tugend is a columnist for the New York Times. *Her work has also appeared in the* Los Angeles Times, *the* American Journalism Review, *and the* Saturday Evening Post, *as well as in anthologies and online magazines. This report on multitasking was published in the* New York Times *in 2008.*

AS YOU ARE READING THIS ARTICLE, are you listening to music or the radio? Yelling at your children? If you are looking at it online, are you e-mailing or instant-messaging at the same time? Checking stocks?

Since the 1990s, we've accepted multitasking without question. Virtually all of us spend part of most of our day either rapidly switching from one task to another or juggling two or more things at the same time.

While multitasking may seem to be saving time, psychologists, neuroscientists and others are finding that it can put us under a great deal of stress and actually make us less efficient.

Although doing many things at the same time — reading an article while listening to music, switching to check e-mail messages and talking on the phone — can be a way of making tasks more fun and energizing, "you have to keep in mind that you sacrifice focus when you do this," said Edward M. Hallowell, a psychiatrist and author of *CrazyBusy: Overstretched, Overbooked, and About to Snap!* (Ballantine, 2006). "Multitasking is shifting focus from one task to another in rapid succession. It gives the illusion that we're simultaneously tasking, but we're really not. It's like playing tennis with three balls."

5 Of course, it depends what you're doing. For some people, listening to music while working actually makes them more creative because they are using different cognitive functions.

But despite what many of us think, you cannot simultaneously e-mail and talk on the phone. I think we're all familiar with what

Dr. Hallowell calls "e-mail voice," when someone you're talking to on the phone suddenly sounds, well, disengaged.

"You cannot divide your attention like that," he said. "It's a big illusion. You can shift back and forth."

We all know that computers and their spawn, the smartphone and cellphone, have created a very different world from several decades ago, when a desk worker had a typewriter, a phone and an occasional colleague who dropped into the office.

Think even of the days before the cordless phone. Those old enough can remember when talking on the telephone, which was stationary, meant sitting down, putting your feet up and chatting — not doing laundry, cooking dinner, sweeping the floor and answering the door.

That is so far in the past. As we are required, or feel required, to do 10
more and more things in a shorter period of time, researchers are trying to figure out how the brain changes attention from one subject to another.

A pedestrian walking and texting.

Earl Miller, the Picower professor of neuroscience at the Massachusetts Institute of Technology, explained it this way: human brains have a very large prefrontal cortex, which is the part of the brain that contains the "executive control" process. This helps us switch and prioritize tasks.

In humans, he said, the prefrontal cortex is about one-third of the entire cortex, while in dogs and cats, it is 4 or 5 percent and in monkeys about 15 percent.

"With the growth of the prefrontal cortex, animals become more and more flexible in their behavior," Professor Miller said.

We can do a couple of things at the same time if they are routine, but once they demand more cognitive process, the brain has "a severe bottleneck," he said.

Professor Miller conducted studies where electrodes were attached 15
to the head to monitor participants performing different tasks.

He found that "when there's a bunch of visual stimulants out there in front of you, only one or two things tend to activate your neurons, indicating that we're really only focusing on one or two items at a time."

David E. Meyer, a professor of psychology at the University of Michigan, and his colleagues looked at young adults as they performed tasks that involved solving math problems or classifying geometric objects.

Their 2001 study, published in *The Journal of Experimental Psychology*, found that for all types of tasks, the participants lost time when they had to move back and forth from one undertaking to another, and that it took significantly longer to switch between the more complicated tasks.

Although the time it takes for our brains to switch tasks may be only a few seconds or less, it adds up. If we're talking about doing two jobs that can require real concentration, like text-messaging and driving, it can be fatal.

The RAC Foundation, a British nonprofit organization that focuses 20
on driving issues, asked 17 drivers, age 17 to 24, to use a driving simulator to see how texting affecting driving.

The reaction time was around 35 percent slower when writing a text message — slower than driving drunk or stoned.

All right, there are definitely times we should not try to multitask. But, we may think, it's nice to say that we should focus on one thing at a time, but the real world doesn't work that way. We are constantly interrupted.

A 2005 study, "No Task Left Behind? Examining the Nature of Fragmented Work," found that people were interrupted and moved from one project to another about every 11 minutes. And each time, it took about 25 minutes to circle back to that same project.

Interestingly, a study published last April, "The Cost of Interrupted Work: More Speed and Stress," found that "people actually worked faster in conditions where they were interrupted, but they produced less," said Gloria Mark, a professor of informatics at the University of California at Irvine and a co-author of both studies. And she also found that people were as likely to self-interrupt as to be interrupted by someone else.

25 "As observers, we'll watch, and then after every 12 minutes or so, for no apparent reasons, someone working on a document will turn and call someone or e-mail," she said. As I read that, I realized how often I was switching between writing this article and checking my e-mail.

Professor Mark said further research needed to be done to know why people work in these patterns, but our increasingly shorter attention spans probably have something to do with it.

Her study found that after only 20 minutes of interrupted performance, people reported significantly higher stress, frustration, workload, effort and pressure.

"I also argue that it's bad for innovation," she said. "Ten and a half minutes on one project is not enough time to think in-depth about anything."

Dr. Hallowell has termed this effort to multitask "attention deficit trait." Unlike attention deficit disorder, which he has studied for years and has a neurological basis, attention deficit trait "springs entirely from the environment," he wrote in a 2005 *Harvard Business Review* article, "Overloaded Circuits: Why Smart People Underperform."

30 "As our minds fill with noise — feckless synaptic events signifying nothing — the brain gradually loses its capacity to attend fully and gradually to anything," he wrote. Desperately trying to keep up with a multitude of jobs, we "feel a constant low level of panic and guilt."

But Dr. Hallowell says that despite our belief that we cannot control how much we're overloaded, we can.

"We need to recreate boundaries," he said. That means training yourself not to look at your BlackBerry every 20 seconds, or turning off your cellphone. It means trying to change your work culture so such devices are banned at meetings. Sleeping less to do more is a bad strategy, he says. We are efficient only when we sleep enough, eat right and exercise.

So the next time the phone rings and a good friend is on the line, try this trick: Sit on the couch. Focus on the conversation. Don't jump up, no matter how much you feel the need to clean the kitchen. It seems weird, but stick with it. You, too, can learn the art of single-tasking.

Engaging with the Text

1. According to Alina Tugend's research, what are the **EFFECTS** of multitasking? Tugend doesn't say much about the causes of this practice. Why do you think she doesn't treat causes? What do you think are the causes for multitasking? 278–82
2. How well does Tugend maintain a **TIGHT FOCUS** on her topic in this report? Given the claim she makes in her title, why might a tightly focused topic be important for helping readers understand the issue? 71
3. Tugend **DEFINES** several terms in her report. Locate one or more of the key terms she defines and discuss what these definitions contribute to this report. 314–23
4. What is Tugend's **STANCE** toward the practice of multitasking? Point out specific phrases that reveal her attitude. How appropriate is her stance, given her subject matter? 12–14
5. ***For Writing.*** Undertake your own study of multitasking. Spend time observing students, faculty, and staff in common spaces on your campus — the library, the student union, the dorms, and so on — to see how much multitasking occurs, if any. Speak with peers to find out their habits regarding multitasking. Write a **REPORT** on what you observe and what folks say about how beneficial or how detrimental multitasking can be. 59–82

DARA MAYERS

Our Bodies, Our Lives

Dara Mayers is a freelance writer whose work has been published in magazines such as U.S. News & World Report *and* Glamour, *and newspapers such as the* New York Times. *The following report appeared in 2004 in the* Ford Foundation Report, *a newsletter for that philanthropic organization.*

PUNE, INDIA — When Yogita Kasbe organizes meetings in the slum areas of this growing city in western India, she provides women with a forum to discuss the health issues that concern them. She also gives them a chance to learn about and participate in the development of microbicides, a new set of products that could enable millions of vulnerable women to protect themselves from H.I.V. Kasbe is a peer counselor who recruits women for the National AIDS Research Institute, which is conducting the clinical trials for microbicides. Working with the Global Campaign for Microbicides, based in Washington, D.C., NARI has developed a method of recruitment that is consistent with the ethical procedures at the heart of the campaign's work.

In the Janawadi slum, Kasbe's meetings sometimes take place in a small clearing under a streetlight in an alleyway. The conditions are cramped, but clean, and women sit on the sloping sidewalk. Because Kasbe is from the neighborhood, it is not difficult for her to gain access and trust in the community. "First, I'll find one woman I know, and tell her I want to conduct a group meeting," she says. "I won't initially talk about H.I.V. I'll talk about cleanliness and hygiene. Once I find one interested woman, I'll ask her to bring a few friends. The turnout, generally, is good, because people want to know how to improve their health."

When she introduces the topic of H.I.V./AIDS, she finds that although the women have heard of it, they have received only the most general information. Kasbe then explains what sexually transmitted diseases are, what the symptoms of AIDS are, and how to prevent transmission. Women who are interested in being tested for H.I.V. are

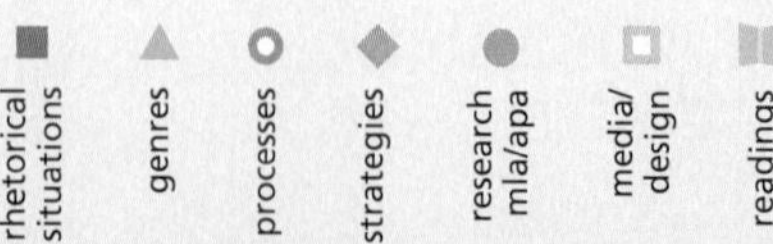

invited to the clinic. If they test negative, Kasbe will inform them of the benefits and risks of participating in phase-one clinical trials for microbicides. These trials help identify acute side effects and involve a small number of healthy volunteers. The women must weigh the benefits — possible protection from sexually transmitted diseases and free medical care during the trials — against the risk of allergic reaction. So far, reactions have been minimal.

There are 62 microbicide products in development around the world, designed as gels, lotions, creams, or suppositories that, when applied vaginally or rectally, will prevent the transmission of H.I.V. While microbicides may have applicability for gay men as well, they are being promoted specifically for women and will ultimately be available in both contraceptive and non-contraceptive forms. Because they are undetectable to men, microbicides have the added benefit of giving women the power to protect themselves without requiring their partner's knowledge or acquiescence. Married women are the fastest growing group of people being infected with H.I.V. in India, which soon will outpace South Africa as the country with the world's highest infection rate.

"The original conception of the AIDS challenge in the developing 5
world was that it was a supply-line problem," says Lori Heise, director of the Global Campaign for Microbicides. "There was no discussion of culture, of women's vulnerability. The fact is, many women in the developing world cannot ask their husbands to use condoms and cannot force them to be faithful. And even if they can elect to use condoms, they are forced to make a terrible choice. They can either not have children or potentially expose themselves to a fatal disease. If all I have to offer is condoms, I can't even begin the conversation."

Gender inequality in India puts women at great risk. Most women cannot choose who they will marry, says Jayshodhara Dasgupta, the coordinator of Sahayog, a resource center on gender and women's health and rights in Lucknow. In February she attended a workshop on women's vulnerability to H.I.V./AIDS that was offered as part of the annual meeting of the Indian Network of Nongovernmental Organizations on H.I.V./AIDS. According to Dasgupta, even suggesting the use of a condom would make the woman suspect in the eyes of her male partner: "It would imply that she is too informed to be chaste or a virgin. She simply cannot question her husband's sex life. The vast majority of Indian women are very, very far from being able to negotiate safe sex."

The first microbicides are expected to have an effectiveness rate of approximately 40 to 60 percent. But even with limited effectiveness, microbicides are more promising than anything offered to date to limit the spread of H.I.V. in the developing world, according to the Global Campaign and other advocacy groups. Mathematical models developed by the campaign estimate that a 60-percent-effective microbicide, offered in 73 poor countries, would prevent 2.5 million infections over three years and save $2.7 billion in public health-care costs — in addition to $1 billion saved on lost productivity and the cost of training replacement workers.

"Seeta," a mother of two who lives in Janawadi, is a 34-year-old participant in the study being carried out in Pune. She is excited about the potential for microbicides. "Abstinence will not work — our husbands would kick us out of our homes," she says. "And condoms are male controlled. Men decide whether to use them. With microbicides we can rely on ourselves, without depending on men. Current methods are not enough to protect us. The government should make these products available to us. They should promote them. And they should be cheap enough so that poor women can use them. I would advise other women to use the products, and I am telling other women to participate in the trials."

"Ratna," 26, a mother of two, says that she was glad to participate in the microbicide trials, because she wants to take part in the effort to stop the spread of H.I.V. "We will buy it because life is more important than money. It should come as fast as possible onto the market because AIDS is spreading fast." Before participating in the trials, Seeta and Ratna (not their real names) knew nothing about H.I.V.

Promoting community engagement in the process of developing the 10
technology that will give women more power over their personal health and safety is a hallmark of the Global Campaign. For example, in areas where people go through the trash, women could not dispose of the microbicide applicator. Trash pickers would find it and wonder what it

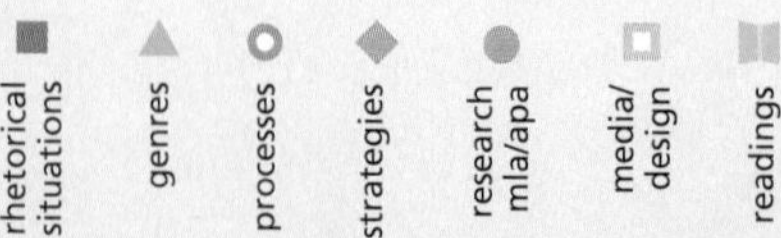

Seeta, one of several uninfected women who volunteered to participate in a study of microbicides.

was, potentially creating gossip and rumors about them. It is this kind of information that the Global Campaign feels is crucial in the development of microbicides. "These are things that you only find out by working with the communities directly," says Megan Gottemoeller, international programs coordinator for the Global Campaign. "Products need to be developed with the end user in mind, with the cooperation of the users themselves."

The Global Campaign is an umbrella organization with 25 partner organizations and more than 170 endorsing groups. Since 1998 it has promoted the development of microbicides internationally through grass-roots organizing, policy advocacy, lobbying and social science research. However, the campaign's goals go beyond microbicides.

"The origins of the Global Campaign are not in advancing a particular technology," says Gottemoeller. "They are in women's rights and the gender analysis of women's vulnerability to H.I.V./AIDS. Our ultimate goal is to help people have a range of prevention options that meet their particular needs. We've ended up focusing on microbicides because it is an area of research that is undervalued and underfunded. We saw that there was an opportunity to participate in a more meaningful way than civil society ever has in the scientific process and technology development."

Microbicides are at least five years away from being publicly available. The campaign does not anticipate investment from the pharmaceutical industry until at least one product has blazed the trail through the regulatory process, thereby providing a better idea of the costs of collecting the data necessary for the product to be licensed in the United States. "Virtually all funding for microbicide research is public or from private donors, coming from foundations or the government sector," says Gottemoeller. However, she adds that some small biotech and pharmaceutical companies in India and other developing countries are working with regulatory bodies to guide the process, rather than waiting it out.

Dr. S. M. Mehendale, deputy director of NARI, expresses a sense of urgency. "I believe microbicides would have a very significant impact," he says. "Women are getting infected by their husbands and giving birth to children with H.I.V. Microbicides would really help to break the chain of transmission from men to women, and fewer and fewer babies would be born with H.I.V. The health impact microbicides would have in India would be dramatic."

Advocating for something not yet widely available — and which 15
might prove to be ineffective — poses a difficult challenge for the Global Campaign, but most participants see the campaign for microbicides in the larger context of the struggle for gender equity. "I feel it is essentially a women's rights issue — having equal rights in all areas, including sexual health issues," says Bobby Ramakant, a campaign volunteer who also writes about health issues for the Health and Development Network, a nonprofit based in Thailand that helps disseminate health-related news through electronic discussions forums and newspapers.

"If you want to realize the larger public health goal of protection options for women, you have to address the issue of female empowerment in general," says Ramakant. "Even if 10 years down the line we don't have a microbicide, the campaign for them enables a conversation about the issues and helps to work on gender equality issues. A woman shouldn't have to rely on the mercy of a man to use a condom. If you put microbicides in that context it is definitely a rights issue."

Links to women's organizations, community-based groups, AIDS organizations, research institutions and government agencies have contributed to a remarkable movement for women's health and rights in poor countries, the reach of which extends beyond microbicides. "We have a very, very long way to go," says Dr. Radium Bhattacharya, president of both the Gujarat AIDS Awareness and Prevention Unit and the Indian Network of Nongovernmental Organizations on H.I.V./AIDS. "We have to bring some real structural changes to society. What we are doing now is part of that. We are really breaking the silence about women's health issues."

In a culture in which talking about sex is taboo, conversation about microbicides is in itself a revolutionary step. "Even the idea of a prevention option that women can control changes the minds of women," says Bhattacharya. "The campaign gives women the sense that they have sexual rights. It creates the idea in their minds. Women are starting to understand they have been exploited and are asking for things for themselves. Women are asking for microbicides as fast as they can come. Even just requesting microbicides is a good sign."

The campaign for microbicides has gained some powerful support in India.

"We recognize microbicides as a very important product that can 20
empower women to protect themselves against H.I.V. and other sexually transmitted infections," says Dr. Kamini Walia of the Indian Council of Medical Research. She also voices some common concerns: "The product should be safe, it should be easily accessible, and it should be low-priced."

Ramakant praises the Global Campaign for initiating dialogue to increase awareness about the potential of microbicides. "The Global Campaign has played a key role in bringing people together — researchers, clinicians, NGO communities and donors — in one forum," he says. "That is a big step. The challenge will be to capture the synergy and channel it to accelerate research and development of microbicides, to pressure donor agencies and government, and to integrate microbicides into family-welfare programs."

Heise calls the campaign a movement on behalf of today's 10- and 11-year-old girls and boys. "With sufficient investment and political will we should have a product available when these young people come of age," she says. "That is my hope, because we cannot afford to lose another entire generation."

Engaging with the Text

1. What is the general topic of this report? Done well, writing that reports 71 information is **TIGHTLY FOCUSED.** What is the specific focus of this report?
2. Since this piece was published in the *Ford Foundation Report*, who is 5–8 the intended **AUDIENCE?** How might this kind of report encourage philanthropic donors? What in this report would make it attractive to those who wish to support this kind of work?
3. 266–70 How does this report **END?** How would the ending appeal to readers of a *Ford Foundation Report?* What does it leave them thinking? How else might it end?
4. 528–32 What does the **IMAGE** contribute to the report? What does it say that words alone cannot?
5. ***For Writing.*** Identify a new medical product and do some research on it — what it does, whom it's for, and what effects it might have on the lives of those who use it (beyond improving their health). Write 59–82 up a **REPORT** on your findings, and consider including an image to help present your information.

Arguments 57

See also:

AMY GOLDWASSER

What's the Matter with Kids Today?

Amy Goldwasser is the editor of RED: Teenage Girls in America Write On What Fires Up Their Lives Today *(2007) and redthebook.com. Her editing and writing have appeared in many publications, including the* New Yorker, Seventeen, *and* Vogue. *She teaches editing at the Columbia Publishing Course and writing at the Lower Eastside Girls Club. The following argument was first published in the online magazine* Salon *in 2008.*

THE OTHER WEEK WAS ONLY THE LATEST TAKEDOWN of what has become a fashionable segment of the population to bash: the American teenager. A phone (land line!) survey of 1,200 17-year-olds, conducted by the research organization Common Core and released Feb. 26, found our young people to be living in "stunning ignorance" of history and literature.

This furthered the report that the National Endowment for the Arts came out with at the end of 2007, lamenting "the diminished role of voluntary reading in American life," particularly among 13-to-17-year-olds, and Doris Lessing's* condemnation, in her acceptance speech for the Nobel Prize in literature, of "a fragmenting culture" in which "young men and women . . . have read nothing, knowing only some specialty or other, for instance, computers."

Kids today — we're telling you! — don't read, don't write, don't care about anything farther in front of them than their iPods. The Internet, according to 88-year-old Lessing (whose specialty is sturdy typewriters, or perhaps pens), has "seduced a whole generation into its inanities."

**Doris Lessing*: British novelist and playwright; she was recognized by the United Kingdom in 1999 when she was appointed a Companion of Honour for "conspicuous national service." [Editor's note]

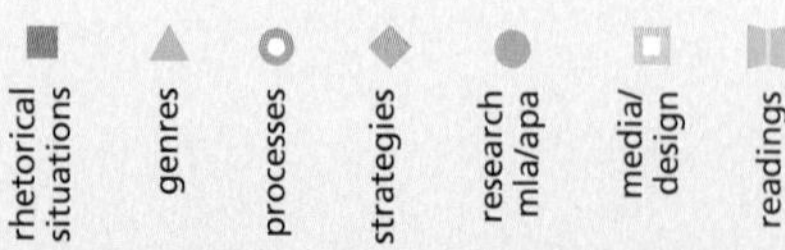

Or is it the older generation that the Internet has seduced — into the inanities of leveling charges based on fear, ignorance and old-media, multiple-choice testing? So much so that we can't see that the Internet is only a means of communication, and one that has created a generation, perhaps the first, of writers, activists, storytellers? When the world worked in hard copy, no parent or teacher ever begrudged teenagers who disappeared into their rooms to write letters to friends — or a movie review, or an editorial for the school paper on the first president they'll vote for. Even 15-year-old boys are sharing some part of their feelings with someone out there.

We're talking about 33 million Americans who are fluent in texting, 5
e-mailing, blogging, IM'ing and constantly amending their profiles on social network sites — which, on average, 30 of their friends will visit every day, hanging out and writing for 20 minutes or so each. They're connected, they're collaborative, they're used to writing about themselves. In fact, they choose to write about themselves, on their own time, rather than its being a forced labor when a paper's due in school. Regularly, often late at night, they're generating a body intimate written work. They appreciate the value of a good story and the power of a speech that moves: Ninety-seven percent of the teenagers in the Common Core survey connected "I have a dream" with its speaker — they can watch Dr. King deliver it on demand — and eight in 10 knew what *To Kill a Mockingbird* is about.

This is, of course, the kind of knowledge we should be encouraging. The Internet has turned teenagers into honest documentarians of their own lives — reporters embedded in their homes, their schools, their own heads.

But this is also why it's dangerous, why we can't seem to recognize that it's just a medium. We're afraid. Our kids know things we don't. They drove the presidential debates onto YouTube and very well may determine the outcome of this election. They're texting at the dinner table and responsible for pretty much every enduring consumer cultural phenomenon: iPod, iTunes, iPhone; Harry Potter, *High School Musical*; large hot drinks with gingerbread flavoring. They can sell ads on their social network pages, and they essentially made MySpace worth $580 million and *Juno* an Oscar winner.

Besides, we're tired of having to ask them every time we need to find Season 2 of *Heroes*, calculate a carbon footprint or upload photos to Facebook (now that we're allowed on).

Plus, they're blogging about us.

So we've made the Internet one more thing unknowable about the 10
American teenager, when, really, it's one of the few revelations. We conduct these surveys and overgeneralize — labeling like the mean girls, driven by the same jealousy and insecurity.

Common Core drew its multiple-choice questions for teens from a test administered by the federal government in 1986. Twenty-plus years ago, high school students didn't have the Internet to store their trivia. Now they know that the specific dates and what-was-that-prince's-name will always be there; they can free their brains to go a little deeper into the concepts instead of the copyrights, step back and consider what Scout and Atticus* were really fighting for. To criticize teenagers' author-to-book title matching on the spot, over the phone, is similar to cold-calling over-40s and claiming their long-division skills or date of *Jaws* recall is rusty. This is what we all rely on the Internet for.

That's not to say some of the survey findings aren't disturbing. It's crushing to hear that one in four teens could not identify Adolf Hitler's role in world history, for instance. But it's not because teenagers were online that they missed this. Had a parent introduced 20 minutes of researching the Holocaust to one month of their teen's Internet life, or a teacher assigned *The Diary of Anne Frank* (arguably a 13-year-old girl's blog) — if we worked with, rather than against, the way this generation voluntarily takes in information — we might not be able to pick up the phone and expose tragic pockets of ignorance.

---

*Scout and Atticus: characters in Harper Lee's Pulitzer Prize–winning novel *To Kill a Mockingbird*. [Editor's note]

The average teen chooses to spend an average of 16.7 hours a week reading and writing online. Yet the NEA report did not consider this to be "voluntary" reading and writing. Its findings also concluded that "literary reading declined significantly in a period of rising Internet use." The corollary is weak — this has a well been a period of rising franchises of frozen yogurt that doesn't taste like frozen yogurt, of global warming, of declining rates of pregnancy and illicit drug use among teenagers, and of girls sweeping the country's most prestigious high school science competition for the first time.

Teenagers today read and write for fun; it's part of their social lives. We need to start celebrating this unprecedented surge, incorporating it as an educational tool instead of meeting it with punishing pop quizzes and suspicion.

We need to start trusting our kids to communicate as they will 15
online — even when that comes with the risk that they'll spill the family secrets or campaign for a candidate who's not ours.

Once we stop regarding the Internet as a villain, stop presenting it as the enemy of history and literature and worldly knowledge, then our teenagers have the potential to become the next great voices of America. One of them, 70 years from now, might even get up there to accept the very award Lessing did — and thank the Internet for making him or her a writer and a thinker.

Engaging with the Text

1. Amy Goldwasser challenges the idea that "kids today" don't read or write. What **EVIDENCE** to the contrary does Goldwasser present to make her case? What is her **DEFINITION** of thinking, reading, and writing and how does it differ from those whose view she disputes?

287–93
314–23

2. What is Goldwasser's **STANCE** toward her topic? How effective is this stance for making her argument? Point to specific words and phrases that reveal her stance.

12–14

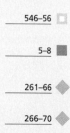

546–56
5–8

3. Goldwasser wrote her argument for a magazine on the **WEB**. How might it be different if she had written it for a print magazine? How would the **AUDIENCE** differ, and what different assumptions would she have had to make about that audience?

261–66
266–70

4. What role do Doris Lessing's comments in the **BEGINNING** of Goldwasser's essay play in her argument? How does this opening relate to her **ENDING** sentence? How else might she have begun or ended her essay?

83–110

5. ***For Writing.*** Write a companion piece to Goldwasser's essay titled "What's the Matter with Adults Today?" in which you explore how your parents or other adults might be considered illiterate about using electronic media. What technologies do these adults rely on? How are their communication practices different from yours? Write an essay **ARGUING A POSITION** on the value of the methods these adults use to communicate as compared with the electronic media you and your peers use.

STEPHEN L. CARTER

Just Be Nice

Stephen L. Carter is a professor at Yale Law School and has written extensively on such topics as affirmative action, the judicial confirmation process, and the place of religion in our legal and political cultures. The following argument was written for the Yale Alumni Magazine *in 1998, and was later included in* Civility: Manners, Morals, and the Etiquette of Democracy *(1998).*

WHEN I WAS A CHILD, attending grade school in Washington, D.C., we took classroom time to study manners. Not only the magic words "please" and "thank you" but more complicated etiquette questions, like how to answer the telephone ("Carter residence, Stephen speaking") and how to set the table (we were quizzed on whether knife blades point in or out). And somehow nobody — no children, no parents — objected to what nowadays would surely be viewed as indoctrination.

Today, instruction of this sort is so rare that when a school tries to teach manners to children, it makes news. So when the magazine *U.S. News & World Report* ran a story in 1996 about the decline of civility, it opened with what it must have considered the man-bites-dog vignette — an account of a classroom where young people were taught to be polite. Ironically, this newsworthy curriculum evidently teaches a good deal less about etiquette than we learned back at Margaret M. Amidon Elementary School in the sixties, but that is still a good deal more than children learn in most places. Deportment classes are long gone. Now and then the schools teach some norms of conduct, but almost always about sex, and never the most important ones: *Do not engage in harassment* and *Always use a condom* seem to be the outer limits of their moral capacity. The idea that sex, as a unique human activity, might require a unique morality, different from the general moral rules against physical harm to others and harm to the self, is not one that public schools are prepared to entertain.

Respect for rules of conduct has been lost in the deafening and essentially empty rights-talk of our age. Following a rule of good manners may mean doing something you do not want to do, and the weird rhetoric of our self-indulgent age resists the idea that we have such things as obligations to others. We suffer from what James Q. Wilson has described as the elevation of self-expression over self-control. So when a black student at a Connecticut high school was disciplined in 1996 for wearing pants that drooped (exposing his underwear), not only did he claim a right to wear what he liked, but some community leaders hinted at racism, on the theory that many young African American males dress this way. (The fact that the style is copied from prison garb, which lacks a belt, evidently makes no impression on these particular defenders of the race.)

When I was a child, had my school sought to discipline me, my parents would have assumed the school had good reason. And they probably would have punished me further at home. Unlike many of today's parents, they would not have begun by challenging the teacher or principal who thought I had done wrong. To the student of civility, the relevant difference between that era and the present is the collapse of trust, particularly trust in strangers and in institutions. My parents would have trusted the school's judgment — and thus trusted the school to punish me appropriately — but trust of that kind has largely dissolved. Trust (along with generosity) is at the heart of civility. But cynicism has replaced the healthier emotion of trust. Cynicism is the enemy of civility: it suggests a deep distrust of the motives of our fellow passengers, on trusting others even when there is risk. And so, because we no longer trust each other, we place our trust in the vague and conversation-stifling language of "rights" instead.

Consider again the boy with the droopy pants. To talk about wearing a particular set of clothes as a "right" is demeaning to the bloody struggles for such basic rights as the vote and an unsegregated education. But the illusion that all desires are rights continues its insidious spread. At about the same time, a fired waitress at a restaurant not far from Yale, where I teach, announced a "right" to pierce her face with 5

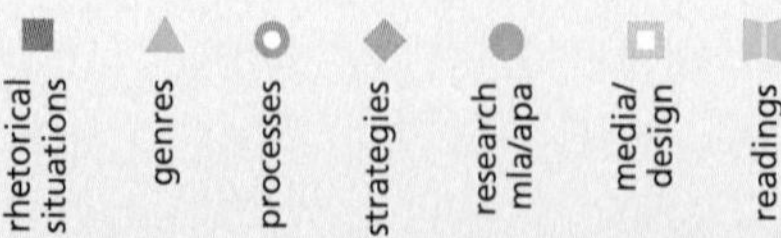

as many studs and rings as she wishes. And, not long ago, a television program featured an interview with a woman who insisted on the "right" to be as fat as she likes. Rights that are purchased at relatively low cost stand a fair chance of being abused, simply because there is no history behind them, and thus little pressure to use them responsibly — in short, because nobody knows why the right exists. But even a right that possesses a grimly instructive history — a right like freedom of speech — may fall subject to abuse when we forget where it came from.

This proposition helps explain *Cohen v. California*, a 1971 decision in which the Supreme Court overturned the conviction of a young man who wore on his jacket the benign legend F--- THE DRAFT. The case arose as the public language grew vulgar. The nineteenth and early twentieth centuries offered a tradition of public insults that were witty, pointed, occasionally cruel, but not obscene or particularly offensive. Politicians and other public figures competed to demonstrate their cleverness in repartee. (One of my favorites is Benjamin Disraeli's explanation of the difference between a misfortune and a calamity: "If Gladstone fell into the Thames, that would be a misfortune. And if anyone pulled him out, that would be a calamity.") Nowadays the tradition of barbed wit has given way to a witless barbarism, our lazier conversational habit of reaching for the first bit of profanity that comes to mind. The restraint and forethought that are necessary to be clever, even in insult, are what a sacrificed civility demands. When we are lazy about our words, we tell those at whom our vulgarity is directed that they are so far beneath us that they are not worth the effort of stopping to think how best to insult them; we prefer, animal-like, to make the first sound that comes to mind.

In *Cohen v. California*, the justices were unfortunately correct that what the dissenters called "Cohen's absurd and immature antic" was protected by the freedom of speech. But it is important to add that when the framers of the Constitution envisioned the rough-and-tumble world of public argument, they almost certainly imagined heated disagreements against a background of broadly shared values; certainly that was the model offered by John Locke, by then a kind of political folk hero. It is unlikely that the framers imagined a world in which I might feel (morally) free to say the first thing that came into my head. I do think

Cohen was rightly decided, but the danger deserves emphasis: when offensiveness becomes a constitutional right, it is a right without any tradition behind it, and consequently we have no norms to govern its use.

Consider once more the fired waitress. I do not deny that the piercing of one's body conveys, in many cultures, information of great significance. But in America, we have no tradition to serve as guide. No elder stands behind our young to say, "Folks have fought and died for your right to pierce your face, so do it right"; no community exists that can model for a young person the responsible use of the "right"; for the right, even if called self-expression, comes from no source other than desire. If we fail to distinguish desire from right, we will not understand that rights are sensible and wise only within particular contexts that give them meaning. The Constitution protects a variety of rights, but our moral norms provide the discipline in their exercise. Sometimes what the moral norm of civility demands is that we restrain our self-expression for the sake of our community. That is why Isaac Peebles in the nineteenth century thought it wrong for people to sing during a train ride; and why it is wrong to race our cars through the streets, stereos cranked high enough to be sure that everyone we pass has the opportunity to enjoy the music we happen to like; and why it was wrong for Cohen to wear his jacket, and why it is wrong for racists to burn crosses (another harmful act of self-expression that the courts have protected under the First Amendment). And it is why a waitress who encounters the dining public every day in her work must consider the interest of that public as she mulls the proper form of self-expression.

Consequently, our celebration of Howard Stern, Don Imus, and other heroes of "shock radio" might be evidence of a certain loss of moral focus. The proposition that all speech must be protected should not be confused with the very different proposition that all speech must be celebrated. When radio station WABC in New York dismissed a popular talk show host, Bob Grant, who refused to stop making racist remarks on the air, some of his colleagues complained that he was being cen-

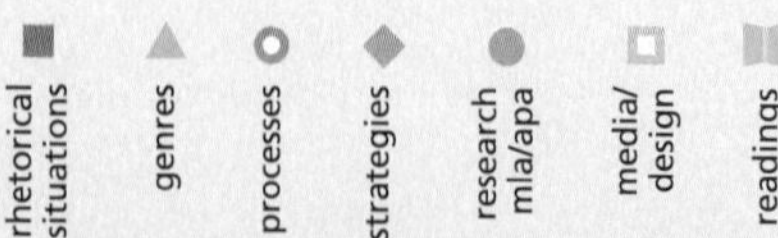

sored. Lost in the brouhaha was the simple fact that Grant's comments and conduct were reprehensible, and that his abuse of our precious freedoms was nothing to be celebrated.

10 The point is not that we should rule the offensive illegal, which is why the courts are correct to strike down efforts to regulate speech that some people do not like, and even most speech that hurts; the advantages of yielding to the government so much power over what we say have never been shown to outweigh the dangers. Yet we should recognize the terrible damage that free speech can do if people are unwilling to adhere to the basic precept of civility, that we must sometimes rein in our own impulses — including our impulses to speak hurtful words — for the sake of those who are making the democratic journey with us. The Proverb tells us, "Death and life are in the power of the tongue" (Proverbs 18:21). The implication is that the choice of how to use the tongue, for good or for evil, is ours.

Words are magic. We conjure with them. We send messages, we paint images. With words we report the news, profess undying love, and preserve our religious traditions. Words at their best are the tools of morality, of progress, of hope. But words at their worst can wound. And wounds fester. Consequently, the way we use words matters. This explains why many traditional rules of etiquette, from Erasmus's handbook in the sixteenth century to the explosion of guides to good manners during the Victorian era, were designed to govern how words — those marvelous, dangerous words — should be used. Even the controversial limits on sexual harassment and "hate speech" that have sprouted in our era, limits that often carry the force of law, are really just more rules of civility, more efforts, in a morally bereft age, to encourage us to discipline our desires.

How we treat one another is what civility is about.

My point is not to tell us how to speak. My point is to argue that how we speak is simply one point on a continuum of right and wrong ways to treat one another. And how we treat one another is what civility is about.

Engaging with the Text

273–75 286–87

1. What is Stephen Carter's **THESIS**? What good **REASONS** does he provide to back up his position? Do you accept these reasons? Why or why not?

289–90

2. How do the **ANECDOTES** about Carter's own experience in grade school and the boy with the droopy pants establish a context for his argument?

2–8

3. Carter wrote this piece for the *Yale Alumni Magazine*. What values do you think he assumes that his readers hold? How do you know? How does he appeal to this **AUDIENCE**? Refer to examples in his text.
4. For Carter, what is the role words play in civility, in how we ought to treat each other? Discuss the power of words as both "tools of morality" and weapons that can "wound." What are the implications of this power for your own speech and writing?

283–99 5–8 294–95

5. ***For Writing.*** Carter concludes by asserting that "how we treat one another is what civility is all about." What we wear, what we say, even how we move can affect and possibly offend others: wearing a t-shirt bearing a provocative slogan, talking loudly on a cell phone in a public space, putting feet up on the seat in a subway train. Identify other such actions that you or others find offensive. Choose one and write an essay **ARGUING A POSITION** on the issue of its propriety: does it violate norms of civility? How and why (or why not)? You should identify a clear **AUDIENCE** and keep their values in mind as you shape your essay. And remember: whatever position you take, you'll want to consider **OTHER POSITIONS**, including Carter's.

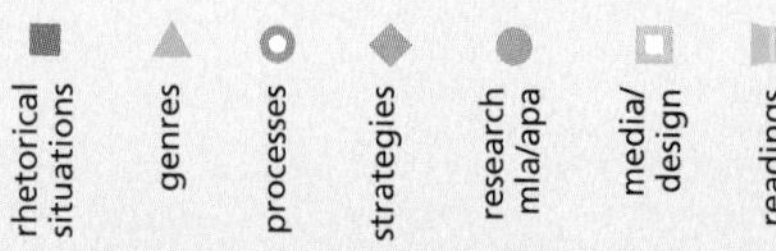

BARACK OBAMA

Election Night Remarks

On November 4, 2008, Barack Obama was elected President of the United States. That night he delivered the following speech to throngs of supporters in Grant Park, Chicago. His first public address as president-elect articulates his vision for moving the country forward, a vision significant for a country in severe economic crisis and at war. Like previous speeches, this one reveals Obama's skill as a rhetor—Quintilian's "good man speaking well." Obama is the author of several books, including his memoir Dreams from My Father: A Story of Race and Inheritance *(2004) and* The Audacity of Hope: Thoughts on Reclaiming the American Dream *(2006).* *For an analysis of this speech, see p. 610.*

IF THERE IS ANYONE OUT THERE who still doubts that America is a place where all things are possible; who still wonders if the dream of our founders is alive in our time; who still questions the power of our democracy, tonight is your answer.

It's the answer told by lines that stretched around schools and churches in numbers this nation has never seen; by people who waited three hours and four hours, many for the very first time in their lives, because they believed that this time must be different; that their voice could be that difference.

It's the answer spoken by young and old, rich and poor, Democrat and Republican, black, white, Latino, Asian, Native American, gay, straight, disabled and not disabled — Americans who sent a message to the world that we have never been a collection of Red States and Blue States: we are, and always will be, the United States of America.

It's the answer that led those who have been told for so long by so many to be cynical, and fearful, and doubtful of what we can achieve to put their hands on the arc of history and bend it once more toward the hope of a better day.

It's been a long time coming, but tonight, because of what we did 5
on this day, in this election, at this defining moment, change has come to America.

I just received a very gracious call from Senator McCain. He fought long and hard in his campaign, and he's fought even longer and harder for the country he loves. He has endured sacrifices for America that most of us cannot begin to imagine, and we are better off for the service rendered by this brave and selfless leader. I congratulate him and Governor Palin for all they have achieved, and I look forward to working with them to renew this nation's promise in the months ahead.

I want to thank my partner in this journey, a man who campaigned from his heart and spoke for the men and women he grew up with on the streets of Scranton and rode with on that train home to Delaware, the Vice President–elect of the United States, Joe Biden.

Barack Obama speaking in Grant Park, Chicago, on November 4, 2008.

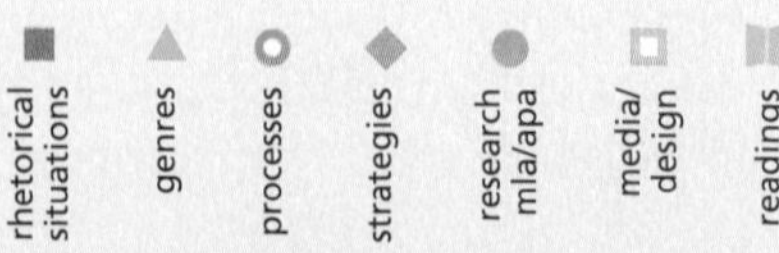

I would not be standing here tonight without the unyielding support of my best friend for the last sixteen years, the rock of our family and the love of my life, our nation's next First Lady, Michelle Obama. Sasha and Malia, I love you both so much, and you have earned the new puppy that's coming with us to the White House. And while she's no longer with us, I know my grandmother is watching, along with the family that made me who I am. I miss them tonight, and know that my debt to them is beyond measure.

To my campaign manager David Plouffe, my chief strategist David Axelrod, and the best campaign team ever assembled in the history of politics — you made this happen, and I am forever grateful for what you've sacrificed to get it done.

But above all, I will never forget who this victory truly belongs to — 10
it belongs to you.

I was never the likeliest candidate for this office. We didn't start with much money or many endorsements. Our campaign was not hatched in the halls of Washington — it began in the backyards of Des Moines and the living rooms of Concord and the front porches of Charleston.

It was built by working men and women who dug into what little savings they had to give five dollars and ten dollars and twenty dollars to this cause. It grew strength from the young people who rejected the myth of their generation's apathy; who left their homes and their families for jobs that offered little pay and less sleep; from the not-so-young people who braved the bitter cold and scorching heat to knock on the doors of perfect strangers; from the millions of Americans who volunteered, and organized, and proved that more than two centuries later, a government of the people, by the people and for the people has not perished from this Earth. This is your victory.

I know you didn't do this just to win an election and I know you didn't do it for me. You did it because you understand the enormity of the task that lies ahead. For even as we celebrate tonight, we know the challenges that tomorrow will bring are the greatest of our lifetime — two wars, a planet in peril, the worst financial crisis in a century. Even as we stand here tonight, we know there are brave Americans waking up in the deserts of Iraq and the mountains of Afghanistan to risk their lives for us. There are mothers and fathers who will lie awake after their children fall asleep and wonder how they'll make the mortgage, or pay their doctor's bills, or save enough for college. There is new energy to harness and new jobs to be created; new schools to build and threats to meet and alliances to repair.

The road ahead will be long. Our climb will be steep. We may not get there in one year or even one term, but America — I have never been more hopeful than I am tonight that we will get there. I promise you — we as a people will get there.

There will be setbacks and false starts. There are many who won't 15
agree with every decision or policy I make as President, and we know that government can't solve every problem. But I will always be honest with you about the challenges we face. I will listen to you, especially when we disagree. And above all, I will ask you join in the work of remaking this nation the only way it's been done in America for two-hundred-and-twenty-one years — block by block, brick by brick, calloused hand by calloused hand.

What began twenty-one months ago in the depths of winter must not end on this autumn night. This victory alone is not the change we seek — it is only the chance for us to make that change. And that cannot happen if we go back to the way things were. It cannot happen without you.

So let us summon a new spirit of patriotism; of service and responsibility where each of us resolves to pitch in and work harder and look after not only ourselves, but each other. Let us remember that if this financial crisis taught us anything, it's that we cannot have a thriving Wall Street while Main Street suffers — in this country, we rise or fall as one nation; as one people.

Let us resist the temptation to fall back on the same partisanship and pettiness and immaturity that has poisoned our politics for so long. Let us remember that it was a man from this state who first carried the banner of the Republican Party to the White House — a party founded on the values of self-reliance, individual liberty, and national unity. Those are values we all share, and while the Democratic Party has won a great victory tonight, we do so with a measure of humility and determination to heal the divides that have held back our progress. As Lincoln said to a nation far more divided than ours, "We are not enemies, but friends . . . though passion may have strained it must not break our bonds of affection." And to those Americans whose support I have yet to earn — I may not have won your vote, but I hear your voices, I need your help, and I will be your President too.

And to all those watching tonight from beyond our shores, from parliaments and palaces to those who are huddled around radios in the forgotten corners of our world — our stories are singular, but our destiny is shared, and a new dawn of American leadership is at hand. To those who would tear this world down — we will defeat you. To those who seek peace and security — we support you. And to all those who have wondered if America's beacon still burns as bright — tonight we proved once more that the true strength of our nation comes not from the might of our arms or the scale of our wealth, but from the enduring power of our ideals: democracy, liberty, opportunity, and unyielding hope.

For that is the true genius of America — that America can change. 20
Our union can be perfected. And what we have already achieved gives us hope for what we can and must achieve tomorrow.

This election had many firsts and many stories that will be told for generations. But one that's on my mind tonight is about a woman who cast her ballot in Atlanta. She's a lot like the millions of other s who stood in line to make their voice heard in this election except for one thing — Ann Nixon Cooper is 106 years old.

She was born just a generation past slavery; a time when there were no cars on the road or planes in the sky; when someone like her couldn't vote for two reasons — because she was a woman and because of the color of her skin.

And tonight, I think about all that she's seen throughout her century in America — the heartache and the hope; the struggle and the progress; the times we were told that we can't, and the people who pressed on with that American creed: Yes we can.

At a time when women's voices were silenced and their hopes dismissed, she lived to see them stand up and speak out and reach for the ballot. Yes we can.

When there was despair in the dust bowl and depression across the 25
land, she saw a nation conquer fear itself with a New Deal,* new jobs and a new sense of common purpose. Yes we can.

When the bombs fell on our harbor and tyranny threatened the world, she was there to witness a generation rise to greatness and a democracy was saved. Yes we can.

She was there for the buses in Montgomery, the hoses in Birmingham, a bridge in Selma, and a preacher from Atlanta who told a people that "We Shall Overcome."† Yes we can.

A man touched down on the moon, a wall came down in Berlin, a world was connected by our own science and imagination. And this year, in this election, she touched her finger to a screen, and cast her vote, because after 106 years in America, through the best of times and the darkest of hours, she knows how America can change. Yes we can.

America, we have come so far. We have seen so much. But there is so much more to do. So tonight, let us ask ourselves — if our children should live to see the next century; if my daughters should be so lucky to live as long as Ann Nixon Cooper, what change will they see? What progress will we have made?

This is our chance to answer that call. This is our moment. This is our time — to put our people back to work and open doors of opportunity for our kids; to restore prosperity and promote the cause of peace;

---

*_New Deal:_ economic initiatives and stimulus programs that President Franklin D. Roosevelt developed between 1933 and 1938 to help the United States recover from the Great Depression. [Editor's note]

†_Preacher:_ Martin Luther King Jr. (1929–1968). _Bridge:_ in March 1965, police and civil rights protestors met in a violent confrontation as protestors crossed a bridge in Selma, Alabama, on their way to the capital. _Hoses:_ in 1963, Birmingham, Alabama, high school students protesting segregation were sprayed with high-powered fire hoses. _Buses:_ in December 1955, Rosa Parks (1913–2005) refused to give up her seat to a white passenger, sparking the 385-day Montgomery, Alabama, bus boycott. [Editor's notes]

to reclaim the American Dream and reaffirm that fundamental truth — that out of many, we are one; that while we breathe, we hope, and where we are met with cynicism, and doubt, and those who tell us that we can't, we will respond with that timeless creed that sums up the spirit of a people:

Yes We Can. Thank you, God bless you, and may God bless the 30
United States of America.

Engaging with the Text

1. What is Barack Obama's central **ARGUMENT** in this victory speech? Where in his speech does this argument appear most clearly? 83–110
2. What is the central **PURPOSE** of Obama's speech? Identify specific phrases that reveal that purpose. 3–4
3. Who is the **AUDIENCE** for this speech, and how does Obama appeal to them? Cite specific passages in your response. Given his audience, why do you think Obama focuses on Ann Nixon Cooper? How does this example help his audience understand his argument? 5–8
4. In his **SPEECH,** Obama uses repetition as a rhetorical strategy, specifically, "It's the answer" at the beginning and "Yes we can" at the end. How does this repetition help him make his argument and achieve his purpose? 534–45
5. ***For Writing.*** Re-read Obama's speech, paying particular attention to his vision for moving America forward, and consider what changes you've seen in the country since Obama was elected — and in the course of your life. Do the changes you've seen support the vision for America that Obama articulates in this speech? Write an essay that **REFLECTS** on the historical changes you've seen and how they relate to Obama's vision. 534–45

MAGGIE CUTLER

Whodunit — The Media?

Maggie Cutler is one of several pen names used by Lynn Phillips, a journalist who has written widely on politics, the media, sex, and women. She also writes a biweekly satirical column called "The Secret Life of Maggie Cutler" for Nerve.com. The following essay appeared in a 2001 issue of the Nation, *a liberal magazine dedicated to "the discussion of political and social questions" in "a really critical spirit."*

WILL GIRLS IMITATE THE NEW, KICKASS HEROINES in the Japanese animé *Cardcaptors*? Will the impressionable 12-year-olds exposed to trailers for MGM's *Disturbing Behavior* forever after associate good teen behavior with lobotomies? Did Nine Inch Nails and the video game *DOOM* inspire the Trenchcoat Mafia's bloodbath at Columbine? Thousands of studies have been done to try to answer variants of the question: Does media violence lead to real-life violence, making children more antisocial and aggressive?

Like most complex issues, discussions about the impact of media violence on children suffer from that commonest of media problems: fudge. Almost any simple statement on the subject obscures the complexity of the facts, half-facts, and "results suggest" findings of the past forty years. The right-wing Parents Television Council, for example, announces that the per-hour rate in the United States of sexual and violent material and coarse language combined almost tripled from 1989 to 1999. But while PTC president Brent Bozell castigates the media for lowering standards of acceptable speech and behavior, he doesn't mention that in the final years of this avalanche of dreck the juvenile crime rate *dropped* more than 30 percent. Or, again, in August 1999 the Senate Judiciary Committee, headed by Orrin Hatch, reported confidently that "Television alone is responsible for 10 percent of youth violence." Given the overall juvenile crime count in 1997, the report implied, some 250 murders and 12,100 other violent crimes would not have been committed if it weren't for the likes of *Batman Beyond*.

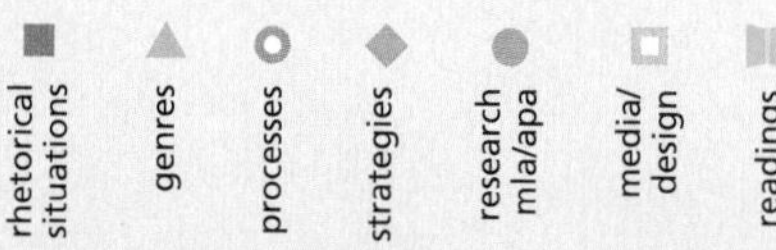

Doom 3, *a best-selling video game released in 2004.*

But this, of course, is deeply misleading. One of the reasons so many media violence studies have been done is that the phenomenon may be too complex to study conclusively. There's no way, after all, to lock two clones in a black box, feed them different TV, movie, and video-game diets, and open the box years later to determine that, yes, it was definitely those Bruce Lee epics that turned clone A into Jesse Ventura, while clone B's exposure to the movie *Babe* produced a Pee Wee Herman.

It has been hard, in other words, for media violence studies to shake the ambiguity of correlations. Several studies have shown that violent boys tend to watch more TV, choose more violent content, and get more enjoyment out of it. But the studies admittedly can't show exactly how or why that happens. Do temperamentally violent kids seek out shows that express feelings they already have, or are they in it for the adrenaline boost? Do the sort of parents who let kids pig out on gore tend to do more than their share of other hurtful things that encourage violent behavior? To what extent is violent media producing little Johnny's aggression — or inspiring it, making it appear glamorous, righteous, acceptably gratuitous, fun, or "normal" — and to what extent is it merely satisfying little Johnny's greater-than-average longings for the mayhem, vengeance, superhuman power, and sweet revenge that most people, at times, secretly crave?

5 According to James Garbarino, author of *Lost Boys: Why Our Sons Turn Violent and How We Can Save Them,* it makes no sense to talk about violent media as a direct cause of youth violence. Rather, he says, "it depends": Media violence is a risk factor that, working in concert with others, can exacerbate bad behavior.

Like Orrin Hatch's committee, Garbarino estimates the effect of violent media on juvenile violence at about 10 percent, but his ecology-of-violence formulation is far less tidy than the Hatch committee's pop-psych model. Garbarino himself reports in an e-mail that he would like to see media violence treated as a public health problem — dammed at its Hollywood source the way sewage treatment plants "reduce the problem of cholera." Nevertheless, his ecology model of how juvenile violence emerges from complex, interacting factors means that hyperaggressive, "asset poor" kids are likely to be harmed by graphic depictions of violence, while balanced, "asset rich" kids are likely to remain unscathed. A few studies have even found that a "cathartic effect" of media violence makes some kids *less* aggressive. This wide range of individual variance makes policy prescriptions a tricky matter.

The American Psychological Association's Commission on Violence and Youth (1994) mentions violent media as only one among many factors in juvenile violence. It stresses that inborn temperament, early parental abuse or neglect, poverty, cognitive impairment, plus a deficiency of corrective influence or role models in various combinations will put a child at greater risk for violence, both as perpetrator and as victim. The APA found that many damaged kids' lives can be salvaged with early intervention. By the age of 8, these at-risk kids can be identified. Once identified they can be taught skills that enable them to resolve conflicts peacefully. The APA adds that parental guidance along with reducing kids' exposure to graphic violence can help keep them out of the correctional system. But for the kids most at risk, reducing representational violence is obviously no cure. So this past fall, when Senators John McCain and Joseph Lieberman ordered the entertainment industry to stop advertising its nastier products to young children or else face (shudder) regulation, it was fair of media critics to castigate them for exploiting the media violence problem for its bipartisan glow rather than attempting to find the least coercive, most effective ways of keeping children safe and sane.

Perhaps the biggest problem in mitigating the effect of media violence on children is that it's hard to nail down just what "violent media" means to actual kids. As with adult pornography, we all think we know what it is until we have to define it. That's because kids not only process content differently depending on their temperament, background, and circumstances, they seem to process it differently at different ages, too.

A series of often-cited studies known as Winick and Winick (1979) charted distinct stages in media processing abilities. Fairly early, from about 6 until about 10, most — but not all — kids are learning to deal with media much as adults do: interactively rather than passively. In her 1985 book, *Watching* Dallas: *Soap Opera and the Melodramatic Imagination*, Ien Ang of the University of Western Sydney in Australia showed that different adult viewers rewrote the "messages" of shows to suit their own views. So a wise little girl whose parents discuss media with her might enjoy *Wrestlemania* as an amusing guide to crazy-guys-to-avoid, while an angry, abandoned, slow-witted child is more likely to enter its world of insult and injury with uncritical awe.

10 At first blush, measures like content labeling would seem to make more sense for the 2-to-6 set because young kids do get confused about reality, fantasy, information, and advertising. But again, what constitutes "violent" content isn't always obvious. The Winicks found that young children whose parents fought a lot responded with more distress to representations of people yelling and screaming — because it seemed real — than to blatant violence for which they had no frame of reference. Should there be a label for "loud and emotional"? And if so, should we slap it on *La Bohème?*

Because representational violence is so hard to define, the recently reported Stanford media effects studies, which focused on third and fourth graders, ducked the problem. The study team, headed by Thomas Robinson, simply worked with teachers, parents, and kids to help children lower their overall media use voluntarily. As a result of the six-month program, which involved classroom instruction, parental support, and peer pressure, kids used media about 30 percent less than usual. And, they found, verbal and physical aggression levels subsequently dropped 25 percent on average. These numbers are being taken especially seriously because they were established "in the field" rather than in the lab, so that the verbal and physical aggression measured was actual, not simulated by, say, asking a child to kick or insult a doll. As media violence studies predicted, the more aggressive kids were to begin with, the more their behavior improved when they consumed less of whatever it was they normally consumed.

Although the Stanford study — perhaps to stay popular with granters — is being promoted as a study on media violence, it is really a study of media overuse, self-awareness, and the rewards of self-discipline. Its clearest finding wasn't that media violence is always harmful but that too much mediated experience seems to impair children's ability to interact well with other people. Follow-up studies at

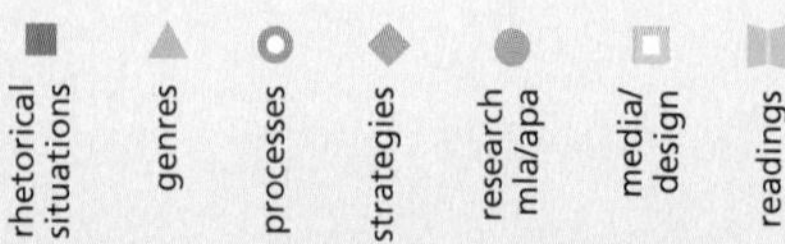

Stanford will show whether the remarkable benefits of its media reduction program last over a long period. If they do, such classes may be a helpful addition to school curriculums in conjunction, perhaps, with courses in conflict resolution. But in any case, its results demonstrate less the effects of specific content than what could be called "the rule of the real."

The rule of the real says that however strong media influences may be, real life is stronger. Real love, real money, real political events, and real-life, unmediated interpersonal experience all shape kids' lives, minds, and behavior more powerfully than any entertainment products. Even media seen or understood as real — news, documentaries, interviews — will have more impact than that which a kid knows is make-believe. As the Winicks found, kids understand early that cartoon violence is a joke, not a model. Even wrestling, once kids figure out that it's staged, gets processed differently from, say, a schoolyard beating.

Without belittling the importance of media research, it's time that the rule of the real governed policy as well. After all, boys whose dads do hard time tend to end up in jail, while boys who see *Fight Club* tend to end up in film clubs; it's more likely that the Santana High killer decided to shoot up his school after seeing the anniversary coverage of Columbine than because he watched *The Mummy*. Abused young women don't kill their battering husbands because they grew up watching *Charlie's Angels,* and teens who hear no criticism of the Gulf War tend to want another. Given limited energies and resources, if our politicians really wanted to reduce youth violence, they would push to reform prison policies, provide supervised after-school activities for teens, and get early, comprehensive help to high-risk children. As a community, we would do better to challenge the corporate conglomeration of news outlets than to legislate the jugs 'n' jugular quotient in *Tomb Raider*, its labeling, or ad placements — and this is true even though the stuff kids like is often quite nasty, and even though the better part of the scientific establishment now agrees that such excitements are less than benign. But setting priorities like these is hard because, while the real may rule children's lives as it rules our own, it's much more fun to imagine controlling their dreams.

Engaging with the Text

1. 284–86 What is Maggie Cutler's main **CLAIM**? Where does she state this 286–93 claim? What **REASONS** and **EVIDENCE** does she give to support her claim, and has she convinced you? If not, do you at least accept her argument as plausible?
2. 261–66 Cutler **BEGINS** with a series of questions. How do these questions prepare readers for her argument? What role do questions play in writing? Where else does she use questions, and to what effect?
3. "The rule of the real," Cutler writes, "says that however strong media influences may be, real life is stronger." How does the "rule of the real" relate to youth violence? In what ways does this rule complicate the notion that media violence in some way causes youth violence?
4. 13 How would you characterize Cutler's **TONE**? Point to examples in her text that reveal that tone. How does her tone affect the persuasiveness of her argument?
5. 97 *For Writing.* Take a **POSITION** for or against the commonplace assump- 384–99 tion that media violence causes actual violence. **RESEARCH** the issue and use the results of your research to support your argument. Make 294 sure to consider and **ACKNOWLEDGE** in your essay more than one position.

GRANT PENROD

Anti-Intellectualism: *Why We Hate the Smart Kids*

The following essay won second place in the Arizona State University Printer's Devil Contest, an annual competition open to all students enrolled in writing classes at Arizona State. Grant Penrod wrote the essay for a first-year composition course.

THE FOOTBALL TEAM FROM MOUNTAIN VIEW HIGH SCHOOL won the Arizona state championship last year. Again. Unbeknownst to the vast majority of the school's student body, so did the Science Bowl Team, the Speech and Debate Team, and the Academic Decathlon team. The football players enjoyed the attentions of an enthralled school, complete with banners, assemblies, and even video announcements in their honor, a virtual barrage of praise and downright deification. As for the three champion academic teams, they received a combined total of around ten minutes of recognition, tacked onto the beginning of a sports assembly. Nearly all of the graduating seniors will remember the name and escapades of their star quarterback; nearly none of them will ever even realize that their class produced Arizona's first national champion in Lincoln-Douglas Debate. After all, why should they? He and his teammates were "just the nerds."

This instance finds plentiful company in the experiences of everyday life; intellectuals constantly see their efforts trivialized in the rush to lavish compliments elsewhere. However, such occurrences present only a faint silhouette of true anti-intellectualism; trivialization seems insignificant when compared with the outright disdain for the educated harbored by much of society. That academia's proponents provoke the wrath of the populace is certain. As an illustration, a commentator under the screen name ArCaNe posted the following quote on TalkingCock.com, an online discussion board: "Man how I hate nerds . . . if I ever had a tommygun with me . . . I would most probably blow each one of their . . . heads off." Were this statement alone in its extremism, it could be written off a joke. Unfortunately, it represents just one statement along countless similar sites and postings, a veritable cornucopia of evidence attesting to society's distaste for intellectuals. The question, then, is not whether anti-intellectualism exists, but rather why it exists. Several factors seem to contribute to the trend, including social stereotypes, public examples, and monetary obsession. Any or all of these factors can contribute to anti-intellectualism, and the result is a crushing disregard for the lives and achievements of fellow human beings.

Perhaps the most obvious cause of anti-intellectualist tendencies, harmful social stereotypes begin to emerge as early as in high school. The idea of the "geek" or "nerd" of the class is a familiar one to most students, and it is not a pleasant one. One online venter, Dan6erous, describes the image well: "A+ this and . . . got a 1600 on my SAT and got all AP class[es] next year woohoo. That's all these people care about don't they have lives damn nerds." In this respect, the trend to dislike intellectuals stems at least in part from an inescapable perception that concern for grades and test scores excludes the coexistence of normal social activities. Sadly, this becomes somewhat of a self-fulfilling prophecy; "nerds" are excluded from social activity because of their label, and that label in turn intensifies through the resulting lack of social contact. The cycle seems unbreakable. Of course, not all "nerds" are socially excluded; most high school students could readily name a few intelligent people with at least a degree of popularity. The point, though, is that the *image* of intellectualism is disliked as anti-social, and the harms of even a fallacious perception to this effect spread to all of the intelligentsia.

This argument, however, merely accounts for the perpetuation of anti-intellectual feelings. Those feelings must also *originate* somewhere, possibly in the examples set by public figures. Certainly the image presented by modern celebrities suggests that intellectualism has no ties to success and social legitimacy. As an illustration, a Web site hosted by Angelfire.com features a compilation of the names of famous high

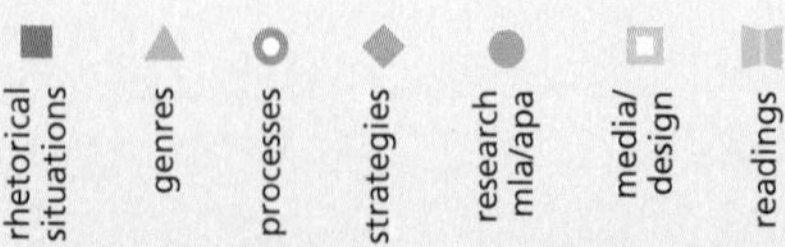

school dropouts ("Noted Dropouts"). With such well-known cultural icons as Christina Aguilera, Kid Rock, L. L. Cool J., and Sammy Sosa qualifying for such a list, any drive toward intelligence or education becomes laughable in the eyes of media-inundated young people ("Noted Dropouts"). Thus, intellectualism loses the respect that its rigor would otherwise tend to earn it. Uneducated success extends far beyond just singers and sports stars, too; even the current President of the United States* presents the image of the success of nonintellectualism. His reputation as a "C" student is widely touted, and his public speeches hardly exonerate his intellectual image. The fact that such a vital public figure can get away with saying things like "It's clearly a budget. It's got a lot of numbers in it," and "There needs to be a wholesale effort against racial profiling, which is illiterate children" reflects rather poorly on the regard in which most Americans hold intelligence (Lewis).

5 Sadly, the aforementioned examples of uneducated success are even further entrenched by the prodigious wealth of the celebrities involved. For example, Sammy Sosa earned an intimidating eighteen million dollars during the year 2002 ("Celebrity 100"). Indeed, as a writer for *The Carillon* put it, "In more than a few cases athletes' incomes surpass the gross national product of some third-world countries" (Brejak). In the eyes of an ever-watchful public, just the existence of such amazingly affluent yet strikingly uneducated individuals would seem to call into question the necessity and even legitimacy of intellectualism. Certainly, most of the people effected by these media images are teenagers, but these budding young anti-intellectuals carry the sentiments of education-bashing on into their adult lives as well. As an illustration, Robert T. Kiyosaki (no longer a teenager) claims in his book *If You Want to Be Rich and Happy, Don't Go to School?* that education is now merely an archaic institution that continues to cling to obsolete practices (Rev. of *If You Want to Be Rich*). The tendency to forgo enlightenment for "success" even leaks into the college community now: a recent article by

---

**President*: George W. Bush was president when this essay was written. [Editor's note]

Ethan Bronner states that "in the survey . . . 74.9 percent of freshmen chose being well off as an essential goal while only 40.8 percent" selected "developing a philosophy" as a similar goal (Bronner). Indeed, Americans seem enamored with wealth at the expense of intellectualism. Unfortunately for them, this supposed negative correlation between brains and buying power doesn't even exist; "People holding doctorate degrees earned more than twice the salary of high school graduates" in the year 2000 ("Census").

Regardless of the causes of anti-intellectualism, the effects are clear and devastating; society looks down on those individuals who help it to progress, ostracizing its best and brightest. Some may blame television or general societal degradation for the fall of the educated, but at heart the most disturbing issue involved is the destruction of promising personalities; ignoring intellectuals both in school and later on in life crushes its victims, as illustrated in the following lines:

> My loud and bitter screams aren't being heard
> No one is there to hear them or to care
> They do not come cuz I'm a nerd
> Dealing with this pain is a lot to bear. (Casey F.)

For the sake of the smart kids, we all need to "lay off" a little.

Works Cited

ArCaNe. "Re: A Gifted Student." *TalkingCock.com*. TalkingCock.com, 2 Sept. 2001. Web. 21 Apr. 2009. <http://www.talkingcock.com/html/article.php?sid=416>.

Brejak, Matt. "Money, Contracts and Switzerland." *The Carillon*. U. of Regina, 28 Oct. 1999. Web. 24 Apr. 2009.

Bronner, Ethan. "College Freshmen Aiming for High Marks in Income." *New York Times*. New York Times, 12 Jan. 1998. Web. 28 Apr. 2009.

"The Celebrity 100—Jocks." *Forbes.com*. Forbes.com Inc., 20 Jun. 2002. Web. 1. Oct. 2003.

"Census 2000: Education." *BDASUN*. Bermuda Sun, 18 Dec. 2002. Web. 21 Apr. 2009.

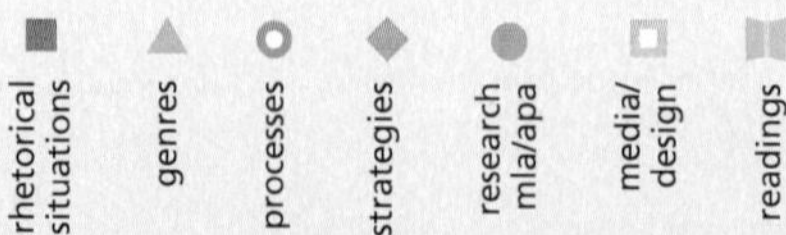

Dan6erous. Online posting. *Chilax.com*. Chilax.com, 31 Aug. 2003. Web. 1. Oct. 2003. <http://chilax.com/forum/index.php?showtopic=1331&st=60>.

F., Casey. "My loud and bitter screams aren't being heard." *TeenMag.com*. Hearst Communications, Inc., 9 Apr. 2002. Web. 1 Oct. 2003. <http://www.teenmag.com/allaboutyou/poetry/poetry_040902_8.html>.

Lewis, Jone Johnson, comp. "Bushisms Quotes." *WisdomQuotes.com*. N.p., 2009. Web. 28 Apr. 2009.

"Noted High School and Elementary School Dropouts." *Celebrity Research Lists*. Angelfire.com, 14 Apr. 2009. Web. 28 Apr. 2009. <http://www.angelfire.com/stars4/lists/dropouts.html>.

Rev. of *If You Want to Be Rich and Happy, Don't Go to School?* by Robert T. Kiyosaki. *EducationReformBooks.net*. World Prosperity, Ltd., n.d. Web. 28 Apr. 2009.

Engaging with the Text

1. Grant Penrod claims that the effects of anti-intellectualism are "clear and devastating," arguing that society "ostracizes its best and brightest." What **REASONS** and **EVIDENCE** does he provide to support his claim? Do you find his argument persuasive? Why or why not? 286–93
2. What does Penrod's **TITLE** tell us about his intended **AUDIENCE**? What values do you think he assumes they hold? How does he **APPEAL** to these readers? Do you think he is successful? 272–73 5–8 98
3. Penrod suggests that intellectuals are disliked in part because of the "perception that concern for grades and test scores excludes the coexistence of normal social activities" — and that this becomes a "self-fulfilling prophecy; 'nerds' are excluded from social activity because of their label, and that label in turn intensifies through the resulting lack of social contact." Do you agree? Why or why not?
4. To support his claim that anti-intellectualism is fueled in part by the media, Penrod names celebrities from sports, music, and politics who became successful without the benefit of an education. Do you agree

with Penrod that the success of these celebrities is partly responsible for anti-intellectualism? Why or why not? What **EVIDENCE** 287–93 could be offered to **REFUTE THIS ARGUMENT**? 295

5. ***For Writing.*** Penrod identifies "nerds" as one stereotypical high school group. "Jocks" are another familiar stereotype. How were students **CLASSIFIED** 300–305 into stereotyped groups at your high school? Were the classifications fair? Who did the classifying? What were the consequences for members of the group and for other students? Write an essay about one of these groups that **ARGUES A POSITION** 83–110 on what factors motivated the stereotyping. You'll need to support your argument with reasons and evidence, such as facts, statistics, and anecdotes.

GREGORY MANTSIOS

Class in America — 2003

Sociologist Gregory Mantsios is the director of the Murphy Institute for Worker Education and Labor Studies at Queens College of the City University of New York. He has written widely on socioeconomic class in America and is the editor of A New Labor Movement for the New Century *(1998), a collection of essays. The following argument appeared in* Race, Class, and Gender in the United States *(2004), a sociology textbook, and the notes are in the style of that publication. As you read, pay attention to how Mantsios identifies four myths about socioeconomic class in America and then structures his argument around them.*

PEOPLE IN THE UNITED STATES DON'T LIKE TO TALK ABOUT CLASS. Or so it would seem. We don't speak about class privileges, or class oppression, or the class nature of society. These terms are not part of our everyday vocabulary, and in most circles they are associated with the language of the rhetorical fringe. Unlike people in most other parts of the world, we shrink from using words that classify along economic lines or that point to class distinctions: phrases like "working class," "upper class," and "ruling class" are rarely uttered by Americans.

For the most part, avoidance of class-laden vocabulary crosses class boundaries. There are few among the poor who speak of themselves as lower class; instead, they refer to their race, ethnic group, or geographic location. Workers are more likely to identify with their employer, industry, or occupational group than with other workers, or with the working class.[1]

Neither are those at the other end of the economic spectrum likely to use the word "class." In her study of thirty-eight wealthy and socially prominent women, Susan Ostrander asked participants if they considered themselves members of the upper class. One participant responded, "I hate to use the word 'class.' We are responsible, fortunate people, old families, the people who have something."

Another said, "I hate [the term] upper class. It is so non-upper class to use it. I just call it 'all of us,' those who are wellborn."[2]

5 It is not that Americans, rich or poor, aren't keenly aware of class differences — those quoted above obviously are; it is that class is not in the domain of public discourse. Class is not discussed or debated in public because class identity has been stripped from popular culture. The institutions that shape mass culture and define the parameters of public debate have avoided class issues. In politics, in primary and secondary education, and in the mass media, formulating issues in terms of class is unacceptable, perhaps even un-American.

There are, however, two notable exceptions to this phenomenon. First, it is acceptable in the United States to talk about "the middle class." Interestingly enough, such references appear to be acceptable precisely because they mute class differences. References to the middle class by politicians, for example, are designed to encompass and attract the broadest possible constituency. Not only do references to the middle class gloss over differences, but these references also avoid any suggestion of conflict or exploitation.

This leads us to the second exception to the class-avoidance phenomenon. We are, on occasion, presented with glimpses of the upper class and the lower class (the language used is "the wealthy" and "the poor"). In the media, these presentations are designed to satisfy some real or imagined voyeuristic need of "the ordinary person." As curiosities, the ground-level view of street life and the inside look at the rich and the famous serve as unique models, one to avoid and one to aspire to. In either case, the two models are presented without causal relation to each other: one is not rich because the other is poor.

Similarly, when social commentators or liberal politicians draw attention to the plight of the poor, they do so in a manner that obscures the class structure and denies class exploitation. Wealth and poverty are viewed as one of several natural and inevitable states of being: differences are only differences. One may even say differences are the American way, a reflection of American social diversity.

We are left with one of two possibilities: either talking about class and recognizing class distinctions are not relevant to U.S. society, or we mistakenly hold a set of beliefs that obscure the reality of class differences and their impact on people's lives.

Let us look at four common, albeit contradictory, beliefs about the United States. 10

Myth 1: The United States is fundamentally a classless society. Class distinctions are largely irrelevant today, and whatever differences do exist in economic standing, they are — for the most part — insignificant. Rich or poor, we are all equal in the eyes of the law, and such basic needs as health care and education are provided to all regardless of economic standing.

Myth 2: We are, essentially, a middle-class nation. Despite some variations in economic status, most Americans have achieved relative affluence in what is widely recognized as a consumer society.

Myth 3: We are all getting richer. The American public as a whole is steadily moving up the economic ladder, and each generation propels itself to greater economic well-being. Despite some fluctuations, the U.S. position in the global economy has brought previously unknown prosperity to most, if not all, Americans.

Myth 4: Everyone has an equal chance to succeed. Success in the United States requires no more than hard work, sacrifice, and perseverance: "In America, anyone can become a millionaire; it's just a matter of being in the right place at the right time."

In trying to assess the legitimacy of these beliefs, we want to ask several important questions. Are there significant class differences among Americans? If these differences do exist, are they getting bigger or smaller, and do these differences have a significant impact on the way we live? Finally, does everyone in the United States really have an equal opportunity to succeed? 15

The Economic Spectrum

Let's begin by looking at difference. An examination of available data reveals that variations in economic well-being are, in fact, immense. Consider the following:

- The wealthiest 1 percent of the American population holds 38 percent of the total national wealth. That is, they own well over one-third of all the consumer durables (such as houses, cars, and stereos) and financial assets (such as stocks, bonds, property, and savings accounts). The richest 20 percent of Americans hold 83 percent of the total household wealth in the country.[3]
- Approximately 241,000 Americans, or approximately three quarters of 1 percent of the adult population, earn more than $1 million *annually*, with many of these individuals earning over $10 million and some earning over $100 million. It would take the average American, earning $34,000 per year, more than 65 *lifetimes* to earn $100 million.[4]

Affluence and prosperity are clearly alive and well in certain segments of the U.S. population. However, this abundance is in contrast to the poverty and despair that is also prevalent in the United States. At the other end of the spectrum:

- Approximately 12 percent of the American population — that is, nearly one of every eight people in this country — live below the official poverty line (calculated in 2001 at $9,214 for an individual and $17,960 for a family of four).[5] Among the poor are over 2.3 million homeless, including nearly 1 million homeless children.[6]
- Approximately one out of every five children in the United States under the age of six lives in poverty.[7]

The contrast between rich and poor is sharp, and with nearly one-third of the American population living at one extreme or the other, it is difficult to argue that we live in a classless society. Big-payoff reality shows, celebrity salaries, and multimillion-dollar lotteries notwithstanding, evidence suggests that the level of inequality in the United States is getting higher. Census data show the gap between the rich and the poor to be the widest since the government began collecting information in 1947[8] and that this gap is continuing to grow. While four out of five households in the United States saw their share of net worth fall between 1992 and 2000, households in the top fifth of the population saw their share increase from 59 percent to 63 percent.[9]

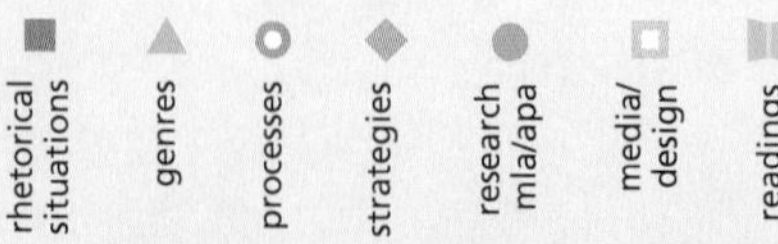

Nor is such a gap between rich and poor representative of the rest of the industrialized world. In fact, the United States has by far the most unequal distribution of household income.[10] The income gap between rich and poor in the United States (measured as the percentage of total income held by the wealthiest 20 percent of the population versus the poorest 20 percent) is approximately 11 to 1, one of the highest ratios in the industrialized world. The ratio in Japan and Germany, by contrast, is 4 to 1.[11]

Reality 1: There are enormous differences in the economic standing of 20
the American citizens. A sizable proportion of the U.S. population occupies opposite ends of the economic spectrum. In the middle range of the economic spectrum:

- Sixty percent of the American population holds less than 6 percent of the nation's wealth.[12]
- While the real income of the top 1 percent of U.S. families skyrocketed by 59 percent during the economic boom of the late 1990s, the income of the middle fifth of the population grew only slightly and its share of income (15 percent of the total compared to 48 percent of the total for the wealthiest fifth), actually declined during this same period.[13]
- Regressive changes in governmental tax policies and the weakening of labor unions over the last quarter century have led to a significant rise in the level of inequality between the rich and the middle class. Between 1979 and 2000, the gap in household income between the top fifth and middle fifth of the population rose by 31 percent.[14] During the economic boom of the 1990s, four out of five Americans saw their share of net worth decline, while the top fifth saw their share increase from 59 percent to 63 percent.[15] One prominent economist described economic growth in the United States as a "spectator sport for the majority of American families."[16] Economic decline, on the other hand, is much more "inclusive," with layoffs impacting hardest on middle- and lower-income families — those with fewer resources to fall back on.

The level of inequality is sometimes difficult to comprehend fully by looking at dollar figures and percentages. To help his students visualize the distribution of income, the well-known economist Paul Samuelson asked them to picture an income pyramid made of children's blocks, with each layer of blocks representing $1,000. If we were to construct Samuelson's pyramid today, the peak of the pyramid would be much higher than the Eiffel Tower, yet almost all of us would be within six feet of the ground.[17] In other words, the distribution of income is heavily skewed; a small minority of families take the lion's share of national income, and the remaining income is distributed among the vast majority of middle-income and low-income families. Keep in mind that Samuelson's pyramid represents the distribution of income, not wealth. The distribution of wealth is skewed even further.

Reality 2: The middle class in the United States holds a very small share of the nation's wealth and that share is declining steadily. The gap between rich and poor and between rich and the middle class is larger than it has ever been.

American Life-Styles

At last count, nearly 33 million Americans across the nation lived in unrelenting poverty.[18] Yet, as political scientist Michael Harrington once commented, "America has the best dressed poverty the world has ever known."[19] Clothing disguises much of the poverty in the United States, and this may explain, in part, its middle-class image. With increased mass marketing of "designer" clothing and with shifts in the nation's economy from blue-collar (and often better-paying) manufacturing jobs to white-collar and pink-collar jobs in the service sector, it is becoming increasingly difficult to distinguish class differences based on appearance.[20] The dress-down environment prevalent in the high-tech industry (what one author refers to as the "no-collars movement") has reduced superficial distinctions even further.[21]

Beneath the surface, there is another reality. Let's look at some "typical" and not-so-typical life-styles.

American Profile

Name	Harold S. Browning
Father	manufacturer, industrialist
Mother	prominent social figure in the community
Principal child-rearer	governess
Primary education	an exclusive private school on Manhattan's Upper East Side *Note:* a small, well-respected primary school where teachers and administrators have a reputation for nurturing student creativity and for providing the finest educational preparation *Ambition:* "to become President"
Supplemental tutoring	tutors in French and mathematics
Summer camp	sleep-away camp in northern Connecticut *Note:* camp provides instruction in creative arts, athletics, and sciences
Secondary education	a prestigious preparatory school in Westchester County *Note:* classmates included the sons of ambassadors, doctors, attorneys, television personalities, and well-known business leaders *After-school activities:* private riding lessons *Ambition:* "to take over my father's business" *High-school graduation gift:* BMW
Family activities	theater, recitals, museums, summer vacations in Europe, occasional winter trips to the Caribbean *Note:* as members of and donors to the local art museum, the Brownings and their children attend private receptions and exhibit openings at the invitation of the museum director

(*Continued on next page*)

Higher education	an Ivy League liberal-arts college in Massachusetts
	Major: economics and political science
	After-class activities: debating club, college newspaper, swim team
	Ambition: "to become a leader in business"
First full-time job (age 23)	assistant manager of operations, Browning Tool and Die, Inc. (family enterprise)
Subsequent employment	*3 years* — executive assistant to the president, Browning Tool and Die
	Responsibilities included: purchasing (materials and equipment), personnel, and distribution networks
	4 years — advertising manager, Lackheed Manufacturing (home appliances)
	3 years — director or marketing and sales, Comerex, Inc. (business machines)
Present employment (age 38)	executive vice president, SmithBond and Co. (digital instruments)
	Typical daily activities: review financial reports and computer printouts, dictate memoranda, lunch with clients, initiate conference calls, meet with assistants, plan business trips, meet with associates
	Transportation to and from work: chauffeured company limousine
	Annual salary: $315,000
	Ambition: "to become chief executive officer of the firm, or one like it, within the next five to ten years"
Present residence	eighteenth-floor condominium on Manhattan's Upper West Side, eleven rooms, including five spacious bedrooms and terrace overlooking river
	Interior: professionally decorated and accented with elegant furnishings, valuable antiques, and expensive artwork

(*Continued on next page*)

	Note: building management provides doorman and elevator attendant; family employs *au pair* for children and maid for other domestic chores
Second residence	farm in northwestern Connecticut, used for weekend retreats and for horse breeding (investment/hobby)
	Note: to maintain the farm and cater to the family when they are there, the Brownings employ a part-time maid, groundskeeper, and horse breeder

Harold Browning was born into a world of nurses, maids, and gov- 25
ernesses. His world today is one of airplanes and limousines, five-star restaurants, and luxurious living accommodations. The life and life-style of Harold Browning is in sharp contrast to that of Bob Farrell.

	American Profile
Name	Bob Farrell
Father	machinist
Mother	retail clerk
Principal child-rearer	mother and sitter
Primary education	a medium-size public school in Queens, New York, characterized by large class size, outmoded physical facilities, and an educational philosophy emphasizing basic skills and student discipline
	Ambition: "to become President"
Supplemental tutoring	none
Summer camp	YMCA day camp
	Note: emphasis on team sports, arts and crafts

(Continued on next page)

Secondary education	large regional high school in Queens
	Note: classmates included the sons and daughters of carpenters, postal clerks, teaches, nurses, shopkeepers, mechanics, bus drivers, police officers, salespersons
	After-school activities: basketball and handball in school park
	Ambition: "to make it through college"
	High-school graduation gift: $500 savings bond
Family activities	family gatherings around TV, bowling, an occasional trip to the movie theater, summer Sundays at the public beach
Higher education	a two-year community college with a technical orientation
	Major: electrical technology
	After-school activities: employed as a part-time bagger in local supermarket
	Ambition: "to become an electrical engineer"
First full-time job (age 19)	service-station attendant
	Note: continued to take college classes in the evening
Subsequent employment	mail clerk at large insurance firm; manager trainee, large retail chain
Present employment (age 38)	assistant sales manager, building supply firm
	Typical daily activities: demonstrate products, write up product orders, handle customer complaints, check inventory
	Transportation to and from work: city subway
	Annual salary: $39,261
	Ambition: "to open up my own business"
	Additional income: $6,100 in commissions from evening and weekend work as salesman in local men's clothing store
Present residence	the Farrells own their own home in a working-class neighborhood in Queens

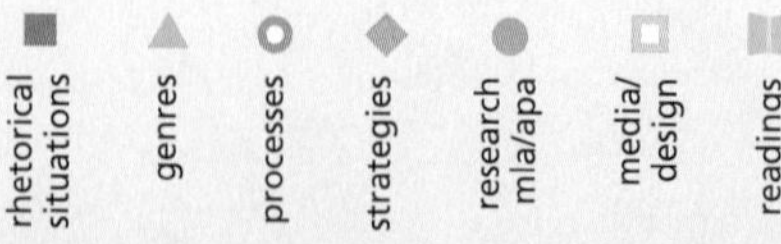

Bob Farrell and Harold Browning live very differently: the life-style of one is privileged; that of the other is not so privileged. The differences are class differences, and these differences have a profound impact on the way they live. They are differences between playing a game of handball in the park and taking riding lessons at a private stable; watching a movie on television and going to the theater; and taking the subway to work and being driven in a limousine. More important, the difference in class determines where they live, who their friends are, how well they are educated, what they do for a living, and what they come to expect from life.

Yet, as dissimilar as their life-styles are, Harold Browning and Bob Farrell have some things in common; they live in the same city, they work long hours, and they are highly motivated. More important, they are both white males.

Let's look at someone else who works long and hard and is highly motivated. This person, however, is black and female.

	American Profile
Name	Cheryl Mitchell
Father	janitor
Mother	waitress
Principal child-rearer	grandmother
Primary education	large public school in Ocean Hill-Brownsville, Brooklyn, New York
	Note: rote teaching of basic skills and emphasis on conveying the importance of good attendance, good manners, and good work habits; school patrolled by security guards
	Ambition: "to be a teacher"
Supplemental tutoring	none
Summer camp	none

(Continued on next page)

Secondary education	large public school in Ocean Hill-Brownsville *Note:* classmates included sons and daughters of hairdressers, groundskeepers, painters, dressmakers, dishwashers, domestics *After-school activities:* domestic chores, part-time employment as babysitter and housekeeper *Ambition:* "to be a social worker" *High-school graduation gift:* corsage
Family activities	church-sponsored socials
Higher education	one semester of local community college *Note:* dropped out of school for financial reasons
First full-time job (age 17)	counter clerk, local bakery
Subsequent employment	file clerk with temporary-service agency, supermarket checker
Present employment (age 38)	nurse's aide at a municipal hospital *Typical daily activities:* make up hospital beds, clean out bedpans, weigh patients and assist them to the bathroom, take temperature readings, pass out and collect food trays, feed patients who need help, bathe patients, and change dressings *Annual salary:* $15,820 *Ambition:* "to get out of the ghetto"
Present residence	three-room apartment in the South Bronx, needs painting, has poor ventilation, is in a high-crime area *Note:* Cheryl Mitchell lives with her four-year-old son and her elderly mother

When we look at the lives of Cheryl Mitchell, Bob Farrell, and Harold Browning, we see life-styles that are very different. We are not looking, however, at economic extremes. Cheryl Mitchell's income as a nurse's aide puts her above the government's official poverty line.[22] Below her on the income pyramid are 33 million poverty-stricken Americans. Far from being poor, Bob Farrell has an annual income as an assistant sales manager that puts him well above the median income level — that is, more than 50 percent of the U.S. population earns less money than Bob Farrell.[23] And while Harold Browning's income puts him in a high-income bracket, he stands only a fraction of the way up Samuelson's income pyramid. Well above him are the 241,000 individuals whose annual salary exceeds $1 million. Yet Harold Browning spends more money on his horses than Cheryl Mitchell earns in a year.

Reality 3: Even ignoring the extreme poles of the economic spectrum, 30
we find enormous class differences in the life-styles among the haves, the have-nots, and the have-littles.

Class affects more than life-style and material well-being. It has a significant impact on our physical and mental well-being as well.

Researchers have found an inverse relationship between social class and health. Lower-class standing is correlated to higher rates of infant mortality, eye and ear disease, arthritis, physical disability, diabetes, nutritional deficiency, respiratory disease, mental illness, and heart disease.[24] In all areas of health, poor people do not share the same life chances as those in the social class above them. Furthermore, lower-class standing is correlated with a lower quality of treatment for illness and disease. The results of poor health and poor treatment are borne out in the life expectancy rates within each class. Researchers have found that the higher your class standing, the higher your life expectancy. Conversely, they have also found that within each age group, the lower one's class standing, the higher the death rate; in some age groups, the figures are as much as two and three times as high.[25]

Reality 4: From cradle to grave, class standing has a significant impact on our chances for survival.

The lower one's class standing, the more difficult it is to secure appropriate housing, the more time is spent on the routine tasks of everyday life, the greater is the percentage of income that goes to pay for food and other basic necessities, and the greater is the likelihood of crime victimization.[26] Class can accurately predict chances for both survival and success.

Class and Educational Attainment

School performance (grades and test scores) and educational attainment 35
(level of schooling completed) also correlate strongly with economic class. Furthermore, despite some efforts to make testing fairer and schooling more accessible, current data suggest that the level of inequity is staying the same or getting worse.

In his study for the Carnegie Council on Children twenty-five years ago, Richard De Lone examined the test scores of over half a million students who took the College Board exams (SATs). His findings were consistent with earlier studies that showed a relationship between class and scores on standardized tests; his conclusion: "the higher the student's social status, the higher the probability that he or she will get higher grades."[27] Fifteen years after the release of the Carnegie report, College Board surveys reveal data that are no different: test scores still correlate strongly with family income.

Average Combined Scores by Income (440 to 1600 scale)[28]

Family Income	*Median Score*
More than $100,000	1130
$80,000 to $100,000	1082
$70,000 to $80,000	1058
$60,000 to $70,000	1043
$50,000 to $60,000	1030
$40,000 to $50,000	1011
$30,000 to $40,000	986
$20,000 to $30,000	954
$10,000 to $20,000	907
less than $10,000	871

These figures are based on the test results of 1,302,903 SAT takers in 1999.

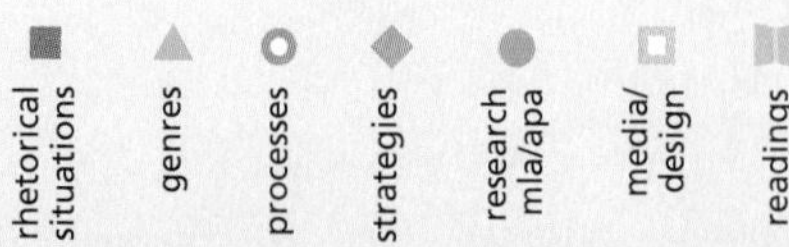

A little more than twenty years ago, researcher William Sewell showed a positive correlation between class and overall educational achievement. In comparing the top quartile (25 percent) of this sample to the bottom quartile, he found that students from upper-class families were twice as likely to obtain training beyond high school and four times as likely to attain a postgraduate degree. Sewell concluded: "Socioeconomic background . . . operates independently of academic ability at every stage in the process of educational attainment."[29]

Today, the pattern persists. There are, however, two significant changes. On the one hand, the odds of getting into college have improved for the bottom quartile of the population, although they still remain relatively low compared to the top. On the other hand, the chances of completing a college degree have deteriorated markedly for the bottom quartile. Researchers estimate the chances of completing a four-year college degree (by age 24) to be nineteen times as great for the top 25 percent of the population as it is for the bottom 25 percent.[30]

Reality 5: Class standing has a significant impact on chances for educational achievement.

Class standing, and consequently life chances, are largely deter- 40
mined at birth. Although examples of individuals who have gone from rags to riches abound in the mass media, statistics on class mobility show these leaps to be extremely rare. In fact, dramatic advances in class standing are relatively infrequent. One study showed that fewer than one in five men surpass the economic status of their fathers.[31] For those whose annual income is in six figures, economic success is due in large part to the wealth and privileges bestowed on them at birth. Over 66 percent of the consumer units with incomes of $100,000 or more have inherited assets. Of these units, over 86 percent reported that inheritances constituted a substantial portion of their total assets.[32]

Economist Harold Wachtel likens inheritance to a series of Monopoly games in which the winner of the first game refuses to relinquish his or her cash and commercial property for the second game. "After all," argues the winner, "I accumulated my wealth and income by my own wits." With such an arrangement, it is not difficult to predict the outcome of subsequent games.[33]

Reality 6: All Americans do not have an equal opportunity to succeed. Inheritance laws ensure a greater likelihood of success for the offspring of the wealthy.

Spheres of Power and Oppression

When we look at society and try to determine what it is that keeps most people down — what holds them back from realizing their potential as healthy, creative, productive individuals — we find institutional forces that are largely beyond individual control. Class domination is one of these forces. People do not choose to be poor or working class; instead, they are limited and confined by the opportunities afforded or denied them by a social and economic system. The class structure in the United States is a function of its economic system: capitalism, a system that is based on private rather than public ownership and control of commercial enterprises. Under capitalism, these enterprises are governed by the need to produce a profit for the owners, rather than to fulfill collective needs. Class divisions arise from the differences between those who own and control corporate enterprise and those who do not.

Racial and gender domination are other forces that hold people down. Although there are significant differences in the way capitalism, racism, and sexism affect our lives, there are also a multitude of parallels. And although class, race, and gender act independently of each other, they are at the same time very much interrelated.

On the one hand, issues of race and gender cut across class lines. 45
Women experience the effects of sexism whether they are well-paid professional or poorly paid clerks. As women, they face discrimination and male domination, as well as catcalls and stereotyping. Similarly, a wealthy black man faces racial oppression, is subjected to racial slurs, and is denied opportunities because of his color. Regardless of their class standing, women and members of minority races are constantly dealing with institutional forces that are holding them down precisely because of their gender, the color of their skin, or both.

On the other hand, the experiences of women and minorities are differentiated along class lines. Although they are in subordinate positions vis-à-vis white men, the particular issues that confront women and minorities may be quite different depending on their position in the class structure.

Power is incremental, and class privileges can accrue to individual women and to individual members of a racial minority. At the same time, class-oppressed men, whether they are white or black, have privileges afforded them as men in a sexist society. Similarly, class-oppressed whites, whether they are men or women, benefit from white privilege in a racist society. Spheres of power and oppression divide us deeply in our society, and the schisms between us are often difficult to bridge.

Whereas power is incremental, oppression is cumulative, and those who are poor, black, and female are often subject to all of the forces of class, race, and gender discrimination simultaneously. This cumulative situation is what is meant by the double and triple jeopardy of women and minorities.

Furthermore, oppression in one sphere is related to the likelihood of oppression in another. If you are black and female, for example, you are much more likely to be poor or working class than you would be as a white male. Census figures show that the incidence of poverty varies greatly by race and gender.

Chances of Being Poor in America[34]

White male / female	*White female head**	*Hispanic male / female*	*Hispanic female head**	*Black male / female*	*Black female head**
1 in 10	1 in 5	1 in 5	1 in 3	1 in 5	1 in 3

*Persons in families with female householder, no husband present.

In other words, being female and being nonwhite are attributes in our society that increase the chances of poverty and of lower-class standing. 50

Reality 7: Racism and sexism significantly compound the effects of class in society.

Notes

1. See Jay MacLead, *Ain't No Makin' It: Aspirations and Attainment in a Lower-Income Neighborhood* (Boulder, CO: Westview Press, 1995); Benjamin DeMott, *The Imperial Middle* (New York: Morrow, 1990); Ira Katznelson, *City Trenches: Urban Politics and Patterning of Class in the United States* (New York: Pantheon Books, 1981); Charles W. Tucker, "A Comparative Analysis of Subjective Social Class: 1945–1963," *Social Forces,* no. 46, June 1968, pp. 508–514; Robert Nisbet, "The Decline and Fall of Social Class," *Pacific Sociological Review,* vol. 2, Spring 1959, pp. 11–17; and Oscar Glantz, "Class Consciousness and Political Solidarity," *American Sociological Review,* vol. 23, August 1958, pp. 375–382.

2. Susan Ostander, "Upper-Class Women: Class Consciousness as Conduct and Meaning," in G. William Domhoff, *Power Structure Research* (Beverly Hills, CA: Sage Publications, 1980, pp. 78–79). Also see Stephen Birmingham, *America's Secret Aristocracy* (Boston: Little, Brown, 1987).

3. Lawrence Mishel, Jared Bernstein, and Heather Boushey, *The State of Working America: 2002–03* (Ithaca, NY: ILR Press, Cornell University Press, 2003, p. 277).

4. The number of individuals filing tax returns showing a gross adjusted income of $1 million or more in 2000 was 241,068 (Tax Stats at a Glance, Internal Revenue Service, U.S. Treasury Department, available at www.irs.ustreas.gov/taxstats/article/0,,id=102886,99.html).

5. Bernadette D. Proctor and Joseph Dalaker, "U.S. Census Bureau, Current Population Reports," *Poverty in the United States: 2001* (Washington, DC: U.S. Government Printing Office, 2002, pp. 1–5).

6. Martha Burt, "A New Look at Homelessness in America" (Washington, DC: The Urban Institute, February 2000).

7. Proctor and Dalaker, op. cit., p. 4.

8. Mishel et al., op. cit., p. 53.

9. Mishel et al., ibid., p. 280.

10. Based on a comparison of 19 industrialized states: Mishel et al., ibid., pp. 411–412.

11. See The Center on Budget and Policy Priorities, Economic Policy Institute, "Pulling Apart: State-by-State Analysis of Income Trends," Jan-

uary 2000, fact sheet; "Current Population Reports: Consumer Income" (Washington, DC: U.S. Department of Commerce, 1993); The World Bank, "World Development Report: 1992" (Washington, DC: International Bank for Reconstruction and Development, 1992); The World Bank, "World Development Report 1999/2000," pp. 238–239.

12. Derived from Mishel et al., op. cit., p. 281.

13. Mishel et al., ibid., p. 54.

14. Mishel et al., ibid., p. 70.

15. Mishel et al., ibid., p. 280.

16. Alan Blinder, quoted by Paul Krugman, in "Disparity and Despair," *U.S. News and World Report,* March 23, 1992, p. 54.

17. Paul Samuelson, *Economics,* 10th ed. (New York: McGraw-Hill, 1976, p. 84).

18. Joseph Dalaker, "U.S. Census Bureau, Current Population Reports, series P60–207," *Poverty in the United States: 1998* (Washington, DC: U.S. Government Printing Office, 1999, p. v).

19. Michael Harrington, *The Other America* (New York: Macmillan, 1962, pp. 12–13).

20. Stuart Ewen and Elizabeth Ewen, *Channels of Desire: Mass Images and the Shaping of American Consciousness* (New York: McGraw-Hill, 1982).

21. Andrew Ross, *No-Collar: The Humane Work Place and Its Hidden Costs* (New York: Basic Books, 2002).

22. Based on a poverty threshold for a family of three in 2003 of $15,260.

23. The median income in 2001 was $38,275 for men, $29,214 for women, and $42,228 for households. Carmen DeNavas-Walt and Robert Cleveland, "U.S. Census Bureau, Current Population Reports," *Money Income in the United States: 2001* (Washington, DC: U.S. Government Printing Office, 2002, p. 4).

24. E. Pamuk, D. Makuc, K. Heck, C. Reuben, and K. Lochner, *Socioeconomic Status and Health Chartbook, Health, United States, 1998* (Hyattsville, MD: National Center for Health Statistics, 1998, pp. 145–159); Vincente Navarro, "Class, Race, and Health Care in the United States," in Bersh Berberoglu, *Critical Perspectives in Sociology,* 2nd ed. (Dubuque, IA: Kendall/

Hunt, 1993, pp. 148–156); Melvin Krasner, *Poverty and Health in New York City* (New York: United Hospital Fund of New York, 1989). See also U.S. Dept. of Health and Human Services, *Health Status of Minorities and Low Income Groups*, 1985; and Dan Hughes, Kay Johnson, Sara Rosenbaum, Elizabeth Butler, and Janet Simons, *The Health of America's Children* (The Children's Defense Fund, 1988).

25. E. Pamuk et al., op. cit.; Kenneth Neubeck and Davita Glassberg, *Sociology; A Critical Approach* (New York: McGraw-Hill, 1996, pp. 436–438); Aaron Antonovsky, "Social Class, Life Expectancy, and Overall Mortality," in *The Impact of Social Class* (New York: Thomas Crowell, 1972; pp. 467–491). See also Harriet Duleep, "Measuring the Effect of Income on Adult Mortality Using Longitudinal Administrative Record Data," *Journal of Human Resources*, vol. 21, no. 2, Spring 1986.

26. E. Pamuk et al., op. cit., fig. 20; Dennis W. Roncek, "Dangerous Places: Crime and Residential Environment," *Social Forces*, vol. 60, no. 1, September 1981, pp. 74–96.

27. Richard De Lone, *Small Futures* (New York: Harcourt Brace Jovanovich, 1978, pp. 14–19).

28. Derived from The College Entrance Examination Board, "1999, A Profile of College Bound Seniors: SAT Test Takers"; available at www.collegeboard.org/sat/cbsenior/yr1999/NAT/natbk499.html#income.

29. William H. Sewell, "Inequality of Opportunity for Higher Education," *American Sociological Review*, vol. 36, no. 5, 1971, pp. 793–809.

30. The Mortenson Report on Public Policy Analysis of Opportunity for Postsecondary Education, "Postsecondary Education Opportunity" (Iowa City, IA: September 1993, no. 16).

31. De Lone, op. cit., pp. 14–19.

32. Howard Tuchman, *Economics of the Rich* (New York: Random House, 1973, p. 15).

33. Howard Wachtel, *Labor and the Economy* (Orlando, FL: Academic Press, 1984, pp. 161–162).

34. Derived from Proctor and Dalaker, op. cit., p. 3.

Engaging with the Text

1. Gregory Mantsios offers an either / or **CLAIM:** "Either talking about class and recognizing class distinctions are not relevant to U.S. society, or we mistakenly hold a set of beliefs that obscure the reality of class differences and their impact on people's lives." However, it's clear early on that his argument will focus on one possibility and not the other. What information does he provide that reveals his actual position? 284–86
2. Mantsios presents four beliefs about class and labels them "myths." How does his use of this synonym affect his **TONE?** How would you characterize his tone? Give examples from the text. 13
3. How does Mantsios argue against each of the four "myths" he identifies? What **REASONS** and **EVIDENCE** does he provide to support his position? What **OTHER VIEWPOINTS** does he consider? Does he convince you? (If not, why not?) 286–93 294–95
4. Mantsios uses **CHARTS** to **COMPARE** the disparate lifestyles of Bob Farrell, Harold Browning, and Cheryl Mitchell. How else might he have presented this information? How do the charts support his claim that class determines "where they live, who their friends are, how well they are educated, what they do for a living, and what they come to expect from life"? Use examples from the essay in your response. 529–32 306–13
5. ***For Writing.*** Explore the role of class at your school. For example, what can you learn about the social and economic status of students, faculty, and support staff by examining the cars in the parking lot (and where those lots are located)? Observe a campus social event: Who attends? What do they wear? What campus organization sponsors the event? What norms of behavior are expected at this event? Use the information you collect to **ARGUE A POSITION** on the way social class may affect campus life. 83–110

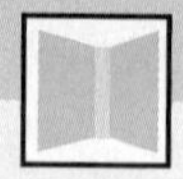

58 Evaluations

See also:

ALI HEINEKAMP
Juno: *Not Just Another Teen Movie* 125

DAVID POGUE

No Keyboard? And You Call This a BlackBerry?

David Pogue is the author of a number of how-to manuals and tech books, including PalmPilot: The Ultimate Guide *(1998), six editions of* MacWorld Mac Secrets *(with Joe Schorr), and several books in the "Dummies" series. In 1999, he launched Pogue Press, which publishes the Missing Manual series — "the book that should have been in the box" — and now boasts over 100 titles. He is also an Emmy Award–winning technology correspondent for CBS News and the personal-technology columnist for the* New York Times, *where the following evaluation appeared in 2008.*

Research in Motion (R.I.M.), the company that brought us the BlackBerry, has been on a roll lately. For a couple of years now, it's delivered a series of gorgeous, functional, supremely reliable smartphones that, to this day, outsell even the much-adored iPhone.

Here's a great example of the intelligence that drives R.I.M.: The phones all have simple, memorable, logical names instead of incomprehensible model numbers. There's the BlackBerry Pearl (with a translucent trackball). The BlackBerry Flip (with a folding design). The BlackBerry Bold (with a stunning design and faux-leather back).

Well, there's a new one, just out ($200 after rebate, with two-year Verizon contract), officially called the BlackBerry Storm.

But I've got a better name for it: the BlackBerry Dud.

The first sign of trouble was the concept: a touch-screen BlackBerry. 5
That's right — in its zeal to cash in on some of that iPhone touch-screen mania, R.I.M. has created a BlackBerry without a physical keyboard.

Hello? Isn't the thumb keyboard the defining feature of a BlackBerry? A BlackBerry without a keyboard is like an iPod without a scroll wheel. A Prius with terrible mileage. Cracker Jack without a prize inside.

R.I.M. hoped to soften the blow by endowing its touch screen with something extra: clickiness. The entire screen acts like a mouse button. Press hard enough, and it actually responds with a little plastic click.

As a result, the Storm offers two degrees of touchiness. You can tap the screen lightly, or you can press firmly to register the palpable click.

It's not a bad idea. In fact, it ought to make the on-screen keyboard feel more like actual keys. In principle, you could design a brilliant operating system where the two kinds of taps do two different things. Tap lightly to type a letter — click fully to get a pop-up menu of accented characters (é,è,ë and so on). Tap lightly to open something, click fully to open a shortcut menu of options. And so on.

10 Unfortunately, R.I.M.'s execution is inconsistent and confusing.

Where to begin? Maybe with e-mail, the most important function of a BlackBerry. On the Storm, a light touch highlights the key but doesn't type anything. It accomplishes nothing — a wasted software-design opportunity. Only by clicking fully do you produce a typed letter.

It's too much work, like using a manual typewriter. ("I couldn't send two e-mails on this thing," said one disappointed veteran.)

It's no help that the Storm shows you two different keyboards, depending on how you're holding it (it has a tilt sensor like the iPhone's).

When you hold it horizontally, you get the full, familiar Qwerty keyboard layout. But when you turn it upright, you get the less accurate SureType keyboard, where two letters appear on each "key," and the software tries to figure out which word you're typing.

15 For example, to type "get," you press the GH, ER and TY keys. Unfortunately, that's also "hey." You can see the problem. And trying to enter Web addresses or unusual last names is utterly hopeless.

Furthermore, despite having had more than a year to study the iPhone, R.I.M. has failed to exploit the virtues of an on-screen keyboard. A virual keyboard's keys can change, permitting you to switch languages or even alphabet systems within a single sentence. A virtual keyboard can offer canned blobs of text like ".com" and ".org" when it senses that you're entering a Web address, or offer an @ key when addressing e-mail.

But not on the Storm.

Incredibly, the Storm even muffs simple navigation tasks. When you open a menu, the commands are too close together; even if your

The BlackBerry Storm.

finger seems to be squarely on the proper item, your click often winds up activating something else in the list.

To scroll a list, you're supposed to flick your finger across the screen, just as on the iPhone. But even this simple act is head-bangingly frustrating; the phone takes far too long to figure out that you're swiping and not just tapping. It inevitably highlights some random list item when you began to swipe, and then there's a disorienting delay before the scrolling begins.

There's no momentum to the scrolling, either, as on the iPhone or 20
a Google phone; you can't flick faster to scroll farther. Scrolling through a long list of phone numbers or messages, therefore, is exhausting.

Nor is that the Storm's only delayed reaction. It can take two full seconds for the screen image to change when you turn it 90 degrees, three seconds for a program to appear, five seconds for a button-tap to register. (Remember: To convert seconds into BlackBerry time, multiply by seven.)

In short, trying to navigate this thing isn't just an exercise in frustration — it's a marathon of frustration.

I haven't found a soul who tried this machine who wasn't appalled, baffled or both.

And that's before they discovered that the Storm doesn't have Wi-Fi. It can't get onto the Internet using wireless hot spots, like the iPhone or other BlackBerrys. Verizon's high-speed (3G) cellular Internet network is now in 258 American cities, but that's still a far cry from everywhere.

But wait, there's less. Both of my review Storms had more bugs than 25
a summer picnic. Freezes, abrupt reboots, nonresponsive controls, cosmetic glitches.

My favorite: When I try to enter my Gmail address, the Storm's camera starts up unexpectedly, turning the screen into a viewfinder — even though the keyboard still fills half the screen. (R.I.M. executives steadfastly refused to acknowledge any bugs. I even sent them videos of the Storm's goofball glitches, but they offered only stony phone silence.)

It's all too bad, because behind that disastrous software and balky screen, there's a very nice phone.

It runs, after all, on Verizon's excellent cellphone network. If you're one of the few remaining rich people in this country, you can even use this phone overseas (roaming rates are as high as $5 a minute). The phone features are excellent; calls are loud and clear.

The Storm has voice dialing, copy-and-paste, programmable side buttons, removable battery and a standard headphone jack. You can open and even edit *Microsoft Word, Excel* and *Powerpoint* attachments. Even Mac fans can get in on the action, thanks to a free copy of the *Pocket Mac* software.

30 You also get expandable storage; an eight-gigabyte memory card comes in the box. The Web browser is the best yet on a BlackBerry: double-tap to zoom, drag a finger to scroll. The camera is dog slow, but it has a very good flash, a 2X zoom and a stabilizer; it takes decent, if pale, pictures and movies. (And goodness knows, it's easy to start up. Just enter a Gmail address . . .)

There's even GPS, with turn-by-turn directions as you drive ($10 a month extra). The Storm can show voice mail in a Inbox-like list, like the iPhone does ($3 a month extra). The screen (480 × 360 pixels) is bright and beautiful.

Honestly, though, you'll probably never get that far. When you look at your typing, slow and typo-ridden, and you repair the dents you've made banging your head against the wall, you'll be grateful that Verizon offers a 30-day return period.

How did this thing ever reach the market? Was everyone involved just too terrified to pull the emergency brake on this train?

Maybe R.I.M. is just overextended. After all, it has just introduced three major new phones — Flip, Bold, Storm — in two months, each with a different software edition. Quality-control problems are bound to result; the iPhone 3G went through something similar.

35 Web rumor has it that a bug-fix software update is in the works. Until then, maybe Storm isn't such a bad name for this phone. After all — it's dark, sodden and unpredictable.

Engaging with the Text

1. David Pogue's evaluation of the BlackBerry Storm is decidedly negative. Do you think it's a **BALANCED AND FAIR ASSESSMENT**? Point to passages in his review where he balances some of his negative assessment with positive. What does this balance contribute to his evaluation? 129
2. Who is the **AUDIENCE** for Pogue's evaluation? What does he assume about his audience's knowledge of the subject? Point to specific passages that reveal his assumptions. Considering his audience, what do you think of his **TONE**? Is it appropriate? Why or why not? 5–8 14

128–29

3. What **CRITERIA** does Pogue use to evaluate the BlackBerry Storm? What other criteria might he have used to assess this product?
4. The writer and philosopher Robert M. Pirsig observed that "Technology presumes there's just one right way to do things and there never is." How does his observation apply to the BlackBerry line in general and the Storm in particular?
5. ***For Writing.*** Select a recently released product that you (or someone you know) own to review. Develop a list of criteria relevant for that product and use it to write an **EVALUATION** of the product for potential consumers. Be sure to include well-supported reasons for your assessment.

125–32

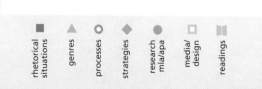

SETH SCHIESEL

Playing God, the Home Game

Seth Schiesel is a journalist who writes for the Arts and Culture section of the New York Times, *where the following review of the game* Spore *was published in September 2008. Schiesel regularly writes on the gaming industry, the impact and social relevance of video games, telecommunications, and international media conglomerates. Earlier in his career he wrote editorials for the* Boston Globe. *As you read, pay attention to the way Schiesel compares* Spore *to other games in order to support his evaluation.*

WHAT IS THE DIFFERENCE between a game and a toy? Does a game that feels more like a toy — even a scintillating, empowering toy — fall short on its own terms? Or is it enough just to be a great toy?

Those questions came to mind again and again as I spent more than 60 hours recently with *Spore*, the almost impossibly ambitious new brainchild of Will Wright. Best known for his popular evocations of urban sprawl *(SimCity)* and suburban Americana *(The Sims)*, Mr. Wright has spent the last eight years trying to figure out how to convey the vast sweep of evolution from a single cell to the exploration of the galaxy as an interactive entertainment experience. His answer, *Spore*, is being released in stores and online for PCs and Macs in Europe on Friday and in North America this weekend.

As an intelligent romp through the sometimes contradictory realms of science, mythology, religion and hope about the universe around us, *Spore* both provokes and amuses. And as an agent of creativity it is a landmark. Never before have everyday people been given such extensive tools to create their digital alter ego.

Beginning with all manner of outlandish creatures — want to make a seven-legged purple cephalopod that looks like it just crawled out of somewhere between the River Styx* and your brother-in-law's basement? — and proceeding through various buildings and vehicles, *Spore* gives users unprecedented freedom to bring their imaginations to some semblance of digital life. In that sense *Spore* is probably the coolest, most interesting toy I have ever experienced.

But it's not a great game, and that is something quite different. 5

The quintessential toys, like a ball or toy soldier, captivate with their versatility. Children can see in a toy what they wish, and are content. Adults, however, tend to lose interest in toys after a little while. Instead they can find deep intellectual and sometimes emotional engagement in the games that emerge around those simple toys, like soccer and chess. Those games are eternal not because I can make my rook look like a slavering alien or because David Beckham occasionally sprouts wings, but because their basic dynamics and rules are perfectly tuned to foster an almost infinitely interesting variety of tactics, strategies and results.

Spore does not have that magic, at least not at the world-beating level it so clearly could have. People who are more interested in playing *Spore* than in playing with *Spore* — that is, people who are more interested in a game than a toy — are likely to come away feeling a bit let down.

Yes, *Spore* is undeniably gorgeous; Mr. Wright and his development team at Maxis have accomplished a prodigious technical feat with the programming that allows members of *Spore's* interstellar menagerie variously to walk, stalk, flop and fly as they befriend and devour one another. For that matter, Mr. Wright and his publishers at Electronic Arts deserve all the credit they have received from some scientists merely for making a game about evolution (though it will be fascinating to see how the game fares among people who do not believe evolution is real). And yes, millions of people will surely spend countless hours, and dollars, on the fabulous computer toy that is *Spore*. And they should.

Yet like me, many players will end up crestfallen that the genius bestowed on *Spore's* creative facilities was clearly not matched by similar inspiration for deeply engaging gameplay. Beneath all the eye

---

**River Styx*: in Greek mythology, the river that divides the Earth from Hades (the Underworld). [Editor's note]

candy, most of the basic core play dynamics in *Spore* are unfortunately rather thin.

At some level that seems by design. As perhaps befits its subject matter, *Spore* is not one game but a collection of five discrete mini-games, each reflecting a different stage of biological and social evolution and a different archetypal game style. 10

Life begins in the cell stage, basically a simple prologue. Think of *Pac-Man* but more colorful. Drifting in the primordial soup, your cell eats pellets (plants or prey) and avoids ghosts (bigger organisms). After maybe 30 minutes (if you survive), you evolve onto land and into the creature stage.

That stage is where Mr. Wright's team seems to have spent the most effort, and for me it has been by far the most enjoyable and interesting part of the game. The entire *Spore* project might have been better handled if the cell and creature levels had been released together a couple years ago at a lower price (*Spore* now costs $49.95), allowing the more pedestrian later phases to receive a comparable level of time and attention as expansions.

Keep in mind that *Spore* includes no real-time multiplayer; that bizarre monster on the horizon is not being directly controlled by another player. Yet if you are connected to the Internet, that monster may have been made by another player in his own single-player universe and then used to populate your planet.

And so the creature stage rules *Spore*, because only there can you fully appreciate the range of expression possible using *Spore's* tool set. As you explore the planet and meet other players' progeny, the DNA you collect allows you to customize your creature with any of dozens of different body parts. Various mouths, hands, feet and wings convey different abilities, perhaps singing or dancing (for making allies of other species) or biting or clawing (for fighting).

But *Spore* goes a bit off the track as it reaches the tribal phase and beyond. Perhaps the biggest problem is that all that time you spent lovingly fine-tuning your otherworldly avatar in the creature phase basically doesn't matter anymore. After the creature phase the cosmetic appearance of your species is locked in, but the abilities it developed 15

The beginning of life, the cell stage, in the new video game Spore, *in which the microbes eat pellets and avoid bigger organisms.*

are largely meaningless. Instead, in the tribal stage, you get just a few choices of different weapons and clothing. In the civilization phase you devise airplanes, land vehicles and ships, and in the space phase you obviously make spacecraft. But as *Spore* goes along, those choices matter less and less in shaping how you can actually play the game.

Progressing out of the tribe and civilization stages requires either conquering or co-opting all the neighboring tribes or cities. These "conquer the world" stories are classic computer game styles, and *Spore* borrows heavily from the basic mechanics of some of the best strategy games ever made, like *Command & Conquer*, *StarCraft* and *Civilization*. (For example, send peasants to gather supplies while you deploy forces against your rivals.)

Once you leap to the space stage, *Spore's* strategic gameplay becomes a bit of a hash reminiscent of games like *Master of Orion* and

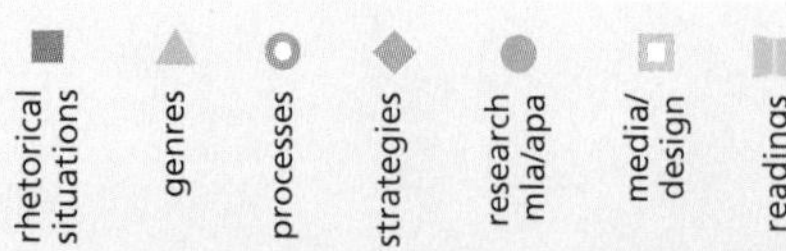

Then they evolve into the creature stage.

Galactic Civilizations, only with horrendous, almost carpal-tunnel-syndrome-inducing interface controls and insufficient tools for managing what is meant to be a galaxy-spanning empire. The exploration and planet-shaping functions of this phase are enjoyable, but they are largely obscured by a gratuitous amount of low-level tasks like warding off pirate invasions and manually moving trade goods from one system to another, over and over. In none of its later stages does the depth of *Spore's* play come close to matching the best-of-genre games available in each of the categories it derives from. (And then there are the inexplicable lapses in basic functionality, like the absence of an auto-save feature. The first time the program crashes, probably in the space phase, and you realize that hours of effort have been lost, you'll be mad. The second time, you may quit forever.)

In fairness, one could also note a similar lack of depth in the basic play systems of *The Sims*, which has proven enduringly popular. But there are some intersecting design reasons why that works better in *The Sims* than in *Spore*.

Most important, *The Sims* is profoundly noncompetitive and open ended. *The Sims* is structured so you can help your family putter around the house forever. There are other families in the neighborhood to interact with, but they aren't trying to eat your children or burn your house down.

Spore, like real life, is largely about the survival of the fittest. In each 20
stage your species either becomes dominant and evolves, or it becomes extinct (meaning you try over and over again until you "win"). In *The Sims* making a family dysfunctional is half the fun. In *Spore* a dysfunctional species basically loses the game. The competitive nature is one reason why, despite its cutesy looks, *Spore* is aimed both at adults and children. And that competitive aspects is why a relative dearth of rich and interesting play mechanics hurts *Spore* more than *The Sims*.

The real frustration with *Spore* is that the team behind it was capable of such high achievement in the areas it focused on, while other parts languished. As reflected in its prodigious creation tools, it succeeds on so many of the most important levels for media these days. Like Facebook, YouTube and the Internet itself, *Spore* is about giving people both the tools to express themselves and a group to share with. The fun of trading creatures with friends and family and exploring new worlds in *Spore* will probably never get old.

Now if Mr. Wright and the Maxis team just take another few passes through *Spore's* later stages and release a big revision patch next year, they may finally end up with a game to match the stellar toy they have already unleashed.

Engaging with the Text

1. According to Seth Schiesel, what distinguishes a toy from a game? What are the characteristics of each? Why is this **CLASSIFICATION** necessary in his review? 300–305
2. How does Schiesel demonstrate that he is **KNOWLEDGEABLE** about video games and gaming? Point to specific passages that reveal his familiarity with this subject. 129
3. Bill Gates claims that personal computers have become "the most empowering tool" ever created, that they're tools of communication, of creativity, and that "they can be shaped by their user." Of course, without software, none of these attributes of the personal computer can be realized. How does Gates's claim apply to the game *Spore* as Schiesel describes it?
4. What do the **IMAGES** from *Spore* contribute to this evaluation? How would this evaluation read without them? What other images might this piece have included? 528–32
5. ***For Writing.*** Select a recent video game made for the computer or TV — or, if you prefer, another type of game, like a board game or a role-playing game. Establish a list of criteria that are necessary for a good game. Write an **EVALUATION** of the game for potential users based on those criteria, aiming at either new gamers or advanced players, and be sure to offer a description of the game that provides as much information as your audience will need. Include images from the game in your review, if possible. 125–32

MICHIKO KAKUTANI

The End of Life As She Knew It

Michiko Kakutani is a book critic at the New York Times. *In 1998, she was awarded the Pulitzer Prize for Criticism. The following review of Joan Didion's memoir,* The Year of Magical Thinking *(2005), appeared in the* Times *in 2005. For a selection from Didion's book, see p. 929.*

IN JOAN DIDION'S WORK, there has always been a fascination with what she once called "the unspeakable peril of the everyday" — the coyotes by the interstate, the snakes in the playpen, the fires and Santa Ana winds of California. In the past, that peril often seemed metaphorical, a product of a theatrical imagination and a sensibility attuned to the emotional and existential fault lines running beneath society's glossy veneer: it was personal but it was also abstract.

There is nothing remotely abstract about what has happened to Ms. Didion in the last two years.

On Christmas Day 2003, her daughter Quintana, who had come down with flulike symptoms, went to the emergency room at Beth Israel North Hospital in New York City. Suffering from pneumonia and septic shock, she was suddenly in the hospital's intensive-care unit, hooked up to a respirator and being given a potent intravenous drug cocktail.

Five days later, Ms. Didion's husband of 40 years, John Gregory Dunne, sat down to dinner in their Manhattan apartment, then abruptly slumped over and fell to the floor. He was pronounced dead — of a massive heart attack — later that evening.

"The Broken Man," what Quintana as a young girl used to call "fear 5
and death and the unknown," had come for her father, even as it had come to wait for her in the I.C.U.

"Life changes fast," Ms. Didion would write a day or two later. "Life changes in the instant. You sit down to dinner and life as you know it ends."

Like those who lost loved ones in the terrorist attacks of 9/11, like those who have lost friends and family members to car accidents, airplane crashes, and other random acts of history, Ms. Didion instantly saw ordinary life morph into a nightmare. She saw a shared existence with shared rituals and shared routines shatter into a million irretrievable pieces.

In her devastating new book, *The Year of Magical Thinking,* Ms. Didion writes about the year she spent trying to come to terms with what happened that terrible December, a year she says that "cut loose any fixed idea I had ever had about death, about illness, about probability and luck, about good fortune and bad, about marriage and children and memory, about grief, about the ways in which people do and do not deal with the fact that life ends, about the shallowness of sanity, about life itself."

Throughout their careers, Ms. Didion and Mr. Dunne wrote about themselves, about their marriage, their nervous breakdowns, the screenplays they worked on together, and the glittering worlds they inhabited in New York and Los Angeles. Writing for both of them was a way to find out what they thought; the construction of a narrative was a means of imposing a pattern on the chaos of life.

And so, almost a year after the twin calamities of December 2003, 10
Ms. Didion began writing this volume. It is an utterly shattering book that gives the reader an indelible portrait of loss and grief and sorrow, all chronicled in minute detail with the author's unwavering reportorial eye. It is also a book that provides a haunting portrait of a four-decade-long marriage, an extraordinarily close relationship between two writers, who both worked at home and who kept each other company almost 24 hours a day, editing each other's work, completing and counterpointing each other's thoughts.

"I could not count the times during the average day when something would come up that I needed to tell him," Ms. Didion writes. "This impulse did not end with his death. What ended was the possibility of response."

Like so many of her fictional heroines, Ms. Didion says she always prized control as a means of lending life at least the illusion of order, and in an effort to cope with what happened to her husband and daughter, she turned to the Internet and to books. "Read, learn, work it up, go to the literature," she writes. "Information is control." She queried doctors, researched the subjects of grief and death, read everything from Emily Post on funeral etiquette to Philippe Ariès's *Western Attitudes toward Death.*

When Quintana suffered a relapse in March 2004 — she collapsed at the Los Angeles airport and underwent emergency neurosurgery at the U.C.L.A. Medical Center for a massive hematoma in her brain — Ms. Didion began researching the doctors' findings. She skimmed the appendices to a book called *Clinical Neuroanatomy* and studied *Intensive Care: A Doctor's Journal* in an effort to learn what questions to ask Quintana's doctors.

During those weeks at U.C.L.A., Ms. Didion says she realized that many of her friends in New York and California "shared a habit of mind usually credited to the very successful": "They believed absolutely in their own management skills. They believed absolutely in the power of the telephone numbers they had at their fingertips, the right doctor, the major donor, the person who could facilitate a favor at State or Justice." For many years, she shared those beliefs, and yet at the same time she says she always understood that "some events in life would remain beyond my ability to control or manage them" and that "some events would just happen. This was one of those events."

Nor could she control her own thoughts. Try as she might to sup- 15
press them, memories of her life with Mr. Dunne — of trips they had taken with Quintana to Hawaii, of homes they had lived in Los Angeles and Manhattan, of walks and meals shared — continually bobbed to the surface of her mind, creating a memory "vortex" that pulled her back in time only to remind her of all that she had lost. She began trying to avoid places she might associate with her husband or daughter.

The magical thinking of denial became Ms. Didion's companion. She found herself "thinking as small children think, as if my thoughts or wishes had the power to reverse the narrative, change the outcome." She authorized an autopsy of her husband, reasoning that an autopsy could show what had gone wrong, and if it were something simple —

a change in medication, say, or the resetting of a pacemaker — "they might still be able to fix it."

She similarly refused to give away his shoes, reasoning that it would be impossible for him to "come back" without anything to wear on his feet. When she heard that Julia Child had died, she thought: "this was finally working out: John and Julia Child could have dinner together."

In an effort to get her mind around what happened, Ms. Didion ran the events of December 30 through her mind again and again, just as she ran several decades of family life through her mind, looking for a way to de-link the chain of causation. What if they hadn't moved to New York so many years ago? What if Quintana had gone to a different hospital? What if they still lived in Brentwood Park in their two-story Colonial house with the center-hall plan?

Even when Quintana seems to be making a recovery, Ms. Didion finds it difficult to work: she has a panic attack in Boston, trying to cover the Democratic convention, and puts off finishing an article, thinking that without John, she has no one to read it. She feels "fragile, unstable," worried that when her sandal catches on the sidewalk, she will fall and there will be no one to take her to the emergency room. She takes to wearing sneakers about town and begins leaving a light on in the apartment throughout the night.

In this book, the elliptical constructions and sometimes mannered 20
prose of the author's recent fiction give way to stunning candor and piercing details that distinguished her groundbreaking early books of essays, *Slouching Towards Bethlehem* and *The White Album*. At once exquisitely controlled and heartbreakingly sad, *The Year of Magical Thinking* tells us in completely unvarnished terms what it is to love someone and lose him, what it is to have a child fall sick and be unable to help her.

It is a book that tells us how people try to make sense of the senseless and how they somehow go on.

The tragic coda to Ms. Didion's story is not recounted in these pages: the death — from an abdominal infection — of Quintana in August, a year and eight months after she first fell ill and a year and eight months after the death of her father.

Engaging with the Text

1. 261–66 Michiko Kakutani waits until the eighth paragraph of her book review to mention the title of the book she's reviewing, Joan Didion's *The Year of Magical Thinking*. How does she **BEGIN** her text, and how does this beginning appeal to readers? What would be the effect had she opened by referring to the book?
2. 408–19 Kakutani peppers her review with **QUOTATIONS** from Didion's memoir. What function do these quotations serve? What role, in general, do quotations play in evaluations?
3. Kakutani does not explicitly state her opinion of Didion's book, but how do we know what she thinks? Identify passages that reveal her evaluation.
4. 3–4 One **PURPOSE** of a book review is to help potential readers decide whether or not a book is worth reading. Does this review achieve that purpose? Why or why not? What other purpose might it serve? What other goals might Kakutani have had in writing it?
5. 125–32 128–29 ***For Writing.*** Write a review **EVALUATING** a book you've read — a novel, a how-to book, a textbook, whatever. Be sure to develop **CRITERIA** to determine the book's strengths and weaknesses and to cite specific examples from the book to support your evaluation.

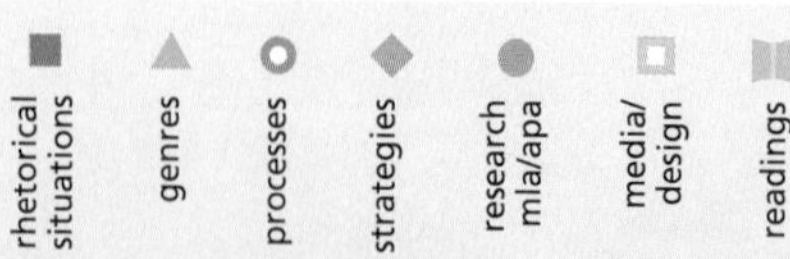

A. O. SCOTT

007 Is Back, and He's Brooding

A. O. Scott is a film critic for the New York Times *and a frequent contributor to* Slate. *A graduate of Harvard, Scott served as a book reviewer for* Newsday *and worked on the editorial staffs of the* New York Review of Books *and* Lingua Franca *before joining the* Times. *The following film review appeared in the* Times *in 2008.*

A REVIEWER MAY COME TO A NEW JAMES BOND MOVIE — *Quantum of Solace*, directed by Marc Forster and opening Friday, is the 22nd official installment of the series in 46 years — with a nifty theory or an elaborate sociocultural hermeneutic agenda, but the most important thing to have on hand is a checklist. It's all well and good to reflect upon the ways 007, the Harry Potter of British intelligence, has evolved over time through changes in casting, geopolitics, sexual mores and styles of dress.

But the first order of business must always be to run through the basic specs of this classic entertainment machine's latest model and see how it measures up.

So before we proceed to any consideration of the deeper meanings of *Quantum of Solace* (or for that matter the plain meaning of its enigmatic title), we need to assess the action, the villain, the gadgets, the babes and the other standard features.

The opening song, performed by Jack White and Alicia Keys (an intriguing duo on paper if nowhere else), is an abysmal cacophony of incompatible musical idioms, and the title sequence over which those idioms do squalling battle is similarly disharmonious: conceptually clever and visually grating. The first chase, picking up exactly where the 2006 *Casino Royale* left off, is speedy and thrilling, but the other action set-pieces are a decidedly mixed bag, with a few crisp footraces, some semi-coherent punch-outs and a dreadful boat pileup that brings back painful memories of the invisible car Pierce Brosnan tooled around in a few movies ago.

Picturesque locales? Bolivia, Haiti, Austria and Italy are featured or 5
impersonated, to perfectly nice touristic effect. Gizmos? A bit disappointing, to tell the truth. Technological advances in the real world may not quite have outpaced those in the Bond universe, but so many movies these days show off their global video surveillance set-ups and advanced smart-phone applications that it's hard for this one to distinguish itself.

What about the villain? One of the best in a while, I'd say, thanks to a lizardy turn from the great French actor Mathieu Amalric, who plays Dominic Greene, a ruthless economic predator disguised as an ecological do-gooder. The supporting cast is studded with equally excellent performers, including Jeffrey Wright and Giancarlo Giannini, both reprising their roles in *Casino Royale*.

And the women? There are two, as usual — not counting Judi Dench, returning as the brisk and impatient M — one (Gemma Arterton) a doomed casual plaything, the other a more serious dramatic foil and potential romantic interest. That one, called Camille, is played by Olga Kurylenko, whose specialty seems to be appearing in action pictures as the pouty, sexy sidekick of a brooding, vengeful hero. Not only Daniel Craig's Bond, but also Mark Wahlberg's Max Payne and Timothy Olyphant's Hitman.

James Bond is a much livelier character than either of those mopey video-game ciphers, but he shares with them the astonishing ability to resist, indeed to ignore, Ms. Kurylenko's physical charms.

This is not out of any professional scruple. The plot of *Quantum of Solace* is largely propelled by Bond's angry flouting of the discipline imposed by his job, and anyway when did James Bond ever let work get in the way of sex? No, what gets in the way is emotion. 007's grief and rage, the source of his connection to Camille, are forces more powerful than either duty or libido.

Mr. Brosnan was the first actor to allow a glimmer of complicated 10
emotion to peek through Bond's cool, rakish facade, and since Mr. Craig took over the franchise two years ago the character has shown a temperament at once rougher and more soulful than in previous incarnations. The violence in his first outing, *Casino Royale*, was notably intense,

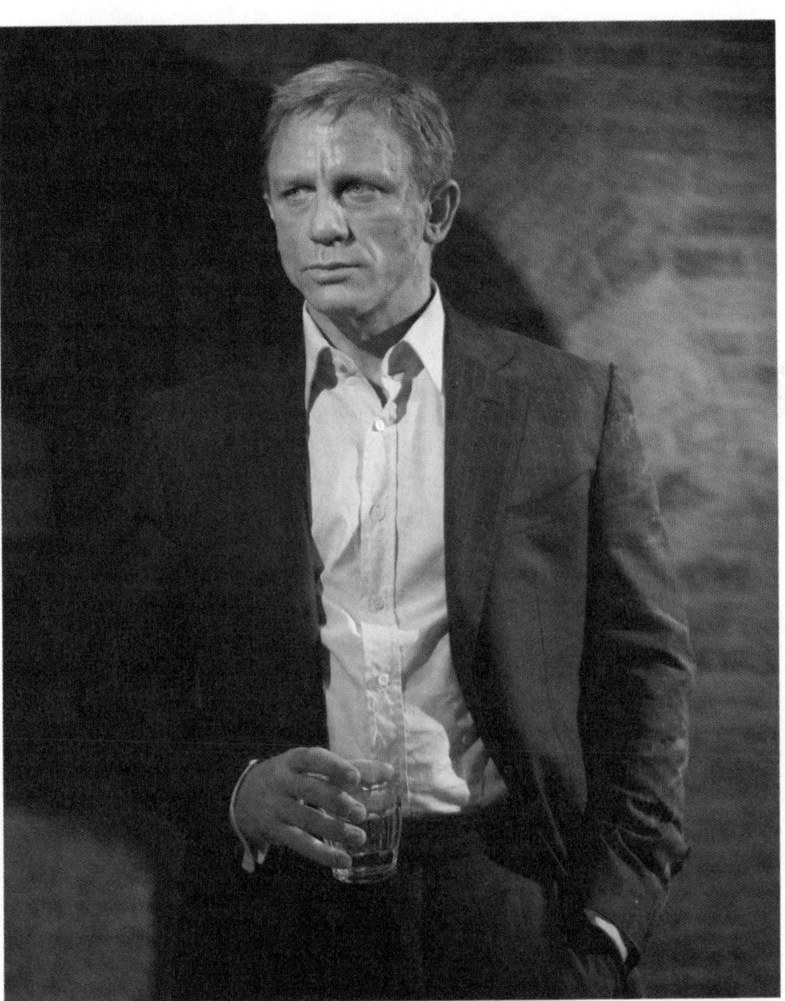

Daniel Craig in Quantum of Solace.

and while *Quantum of Solace* is not quite as brutal, the mood is if anything even more grim and downcast.

The death in *Casino* of Bond's lover Vesper Lynd (Eva Green), along with the possibility that she had betrayed him before dying, provides an obvious psychological explanation for his somber demeanor in *Quantum*. But while the exploration of Bond's psychology makes him, arguably at least, a deeper, subtler character — and there is certainly impressive depth and subtlety in Mr. Craig's wounded, whispery menace — it also makes him harder to distinguish from every other grieving, seething avenger at the multiplex.

Which is to say just about every one. And here, I suppose, the deeper questions bubble up. Is revenge the only possible motive for large-scale movie heroism these days? Does every hero, whether Batman or Jason Bourne, need to be so sad?

I know grief has always been part of the Dark Knight's baggage, but the same can hardly be said of James Bond, Her Majesty's suave, cynical cold war paladin. His wit was part of his — of our — arsenal, and he countered the totalitarian humorlessness of his foes with a wink and a *bon mot*.*

Are these weapons now off limits for the good guys? Or can moviegoers justify their vicarious enjoyment of on-screen mayhem — and luxury hotels, high-end cocktails and fast cars — only if there are some pseudoserious bad feelings attached? The Sean Connery James Bond movies of the 1960s were smooth, cosmopolitan comedies, which in the Roger Moore era sometimes ascended to the level of farce. With Mr. Craig, James Bond reveals himself to be — sigh — a tragic figure.

Quantum of Solace, a phrase never uttered in the course of this film 15
(though it has something to do with Greene's diabolical scheme, itself never fully explained), means something like a measure of comfort. Perhaps that describes what Bond is looking for, or maybe it is what this kind of entertainment tries to provide a fretful audience. If so, I prefer mine with a dash of mischief.

**Bon mot*: good word (French); a witty or clever phrase. [Editor's note]

Engaging with the Text

1. What **CRITERIA** does A. O. Scott list as necessary for assessing *Quantum of Solace* or for that matter any James Bond movie? In your opinion, are these the most relevant criteria for the movie he reviews? Why or why not? How does he use the list of criteria to structure his evaluation? 128–29
2. This review was written for a general **AUDIENCE** of *New York Times* readers. What are some of the reasons they might have for reading this review? What reasons would a more specialized audience — of producers, actors, or film directors, for example — have for reading this review? How might this evaluation be different if it had been written for a more specialized audience? 5–8
3. How does Scott's **DEFINITION** of the phrase "Quantum of Solace" support his overall assessment of the film? 314–23
4. What does the **IMAGE** from the film contribute to this review? How well does it reflect Scott's description of Daniel Craig in the role of James Bond? If you have seen the film, would you suggest any other scenes that might reflect Scott's assessment of it more effectively than this one does? 528–32
5. **For Writing.** Choose a film or book series (e.g., *Star Wars, Batman, Harry Potter*, or *Twilight*), and decide what the "standard features" are for the series. Using these as your **CRITERIA**, write a review in which you evaluate the latest work in relation to the rest, as Scott does. Cite specific **DETAILS** from the work to support your evaluation. 125–32 324–27

SARAH WILDMAN

Caught in the Ayatollah's Web

Sarah Wildman is a journalist who writes on culture and politics. Formerly a staff member at the New Republic *and the* Washington *correspondent for the* Advocate, *she is now a senior correspondent for the* American Prospect. *Her work has appeared in the* New York Times, *the* Guardian, Elle, Oprah, *and* Glamour, *and many other publications. The following review of Marina Nemat's* Prisoner of Tehran *(2007) and Zarah Ghahramani's* My Life as a Traitor *(2008) appeared in the* Times *in 2008. To read a selection from* Prisoner of Tehran, *see p. 571.*

HOW MANY MEN AND WOMEN HAVE BEEN BRUTALIZED in Evin, Tehran's notorious political prison? Built by the shah, the prison became a ghoulish instrument of the ayatollah after the Iranian revolution in 1979. Although Evin remains the repressive arm of the state, we rarely hear about its victims. (One notable exception is the Iranian-born Canadian photojournalist Zahra Kazemi, who made headlines after she died under interrogation there in 2003.)

Two women, Marina Nemat and Zarah Ghahramani, both safely ensconced in the West, have now come forward with memoirs of their imprisonment at Evin. Their testimonies, recounting experiences separated by more than 20 years, illuminate Iran's human rights abuses and speak to the moral dismemberment of a society based in fear and repression.

Nemat's and Ghahramani's accounts of arrest, torture and imprisonment are depressingly familiar. We have read these descriptions of beatings, humiliation and terror before, from Chile to Burma to Abu Ghraib. In each case, there is a weird sameness: the blindfolding, removal of human contact, debasing. Yet each victim has her own story to tell.

Marina Nemat grew up in 1970s Tehran in a middle-class Catholic family. But after the shah was toppled and the Islamists slowly consol-

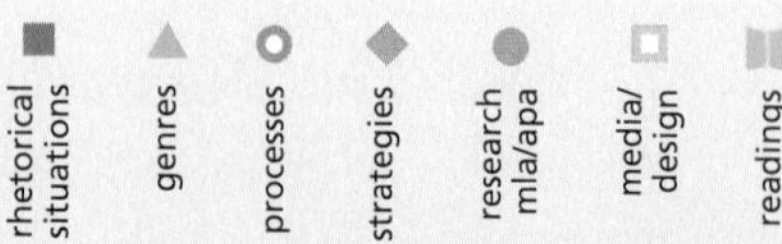

idated power, "the world in which I had grown up and the rules by which I had lived and which I had believed to be set in stone were falling apart," Nemat recalls. "I was a stranger in my own life." Here we hear echoes of other Iranian memoirs — namely *Persepolis*, Marjane Satrapi's graphic novel. Perfume and makeup disappear, girls and boys no longer hold hands, and Islam classes supplant school curriculum. The teachers in Nemat's high school are replaced by members of Khomeini's Revolutionary Guards. When Nemat raises her hand and asks to learn calculus rather than revolutionary theory, she starts an impromptu schoolwide walkout that begins her inevitable journey to Evin.

5 "I felt as if the country were slowly being submerged in water," she writes. In prison, she meets a cadre of young women, each accused of a vaguely formulated antigovernment activity.

Prisoner of Tehran is a gripping personal history, but not a high literary event. Nemat's prose is often treacly and hackneyed. Still, her testimony makes the book vital. She is best when relating painful stories of young people destroyed by Iran in the early 1980s. One fellow inmate, Sarah, descended into madness after her brother was executed and wrote the story of her life endlessly on her arms, legs and torso, refusing to wash lest her memories be forgotten. Nemat herself remained silent on her imprisonment for 20 years and concealed even the most bizarre twist in her story: She was briefly married to a prison interrogator, who helped commute her death sentence in exchange for her hand in marriage.

By contrast, Zarah Ghahramani wrote *My Life as a Traitor* soon after fleeing Iran for Australia. Born in 1981, she never knew a prerevolutionary Iran and held naïve hope that recent reforms would grant at least a modicum of personal freedom. In 2001, when she was 20, Ghahramani was tortured and imprisoned at Evin for her role in a protest at Tehran University. Wrapped in "a cloak of snobbishness," she writes, "I hadn't believed that my life could be invaded by people I considered beneath me."

The details here are sharp, evocative — and angry. Her hands turn a "weird blue" after being tied behind her for hours; her scalp bleeds and itches when her hair is aggressively shorn as punishment. She longs for small pleasures, like pink shoes. In the midst of a beating, she worries that a cut on her chin will become infected. "I will become deformed and ugly," she writes. "I will no longer be a pretty Persian girl. . . . How powerful my vanity is!"

Ghahramani's descriptions of torture are described unsparingly. She staves off insanity by talking to the man in an adjacent cell, her "madman," who keeps her alive partly by insistently speaking to her. Ghahramani, who had been studying translation and Spanish before her arrest, cites a poem by Federico García Lorca: "Oh, death awaits me / before I get to Córdoba!"

Ghahramani thinks of herself "as a Persian rather than as an Iranian." 10
Her book, written with the journalist Robert Hillman, is a defense of Persian and Kurdish identity (she has both), Farsi and her anger at those who have subverted Persia. "I want my children to read Sadi and Hafiz and Khayyam and Rumi," she writes. "Then I want them to read the Code of the Council of Guardians." Why, she asks, have the mullahs "squandered such a beautiful language on this nonsense?"

In *Prisoner of Tehran*, Nemat asks her godmother why the family never asked any questions about her incarceration. "We're afraid to ask because we're afraid of knowing," the woman answers.

Resistance to that fear animates these two important and chillingly universal memoirs.

Engaging with the Text

12–14
1. What **STANCE** does Sarah Wildman take toward the two books she reviews — *Prisoner of Tehran* and *My Life as a Traitor*? How does her stance relate to the political history each book recounts? Point to specific phrases in her review that reveal her stance and its relation to this history.

129
2. To what degree does Wildman's review offer a **BALANCED AND FAIR ASSESSMENT** of each book? Where are this balance and fairness most evident in her evaluation?

3. How does Wildman **COMPARE AND CONTRAST** the two books she reviews? What characteristics do they share? How do they differ? How does her comparison relate to the **CRITERIA** she uses to evaluate the two books?
4. How does Wildman **BEGIN** her evaluation of these two books? How appropriate is this beginning for this review? How does it prepare readers for the subject matter at the heart of the two memoirs?
5. ***For Writing.*** Choose two memoirs, novels, movies, or graphic narratives that deal with the same or similar subject, and develop a list of criteria to evaluate both works. Write an **EVALUATION** that compares the two works — and be sure to include specific examples and **QUOTATIONS** from each to support your assessment.

306–13
130
261–66
125–32
410–13

59 Literary Analyses

See also:

STEPHANIE HUFF
Metaphor and Society in Shelley's "Sonnet"
144

PHILIP NEL

Fantasy, Mystery, and Ambiguity

Philip Nel is an English professor at Kansas State University and the author of several books: J. K. Rowling's Harry Potter Novels: A Reader's Guide *(2001),* The Avant-Garde and American Postmodernity: Small Incisive Shocks *(2002), and* Dr. Seuss: American Icon *(2004). He is also co-editor with Julia Mackenborg of* Tales for Little Rebels: A Collection of Radical Children's Literature *(2008). The following piece is from his book about the Harry Potter novels, written after the publication of the fourth installment in the series.*

ONE ASPECT OF HARRY POTTER'S APPEAL is that of the apparently ordinary child who turns out to be special — which, surely, is a secret wish of many children. As J. K. Rowling has said, "I was aware when I was writing that this was a very common fantasy for children: 'These boring people cannot be my parents. They just can't be. I'm so much more special than that' " ("Pure Magic"). Like Taran in Lloyd Alexander's chronicles of Prydain (1964–1968), Will Stanton in Susan Cooper's *Dark Is Rising* series (1965–1977), and Lyra Silvertongue in Philip Pullman's *His Dark Materials* trilogy (1995–2000), Harry is special. And, like the children in all these books, he's on a mission. Though Rowling claims that fantasy is her least favorite genre (she prefers the realism of Roddy Doyle), her books owe a lot to the traditions of fantasy. Harry, a classic fantasy hero, is the oppressed child who fights back, proving himself and quashing his enemies. Featuring more than 100 characters, the *Harry Potter* series is an epic fantasy. Though we have only the first four novels by which to judge it, the series has every indication of leading toward a *Last Battle* — to borrow the title of the final Narnia novel — in which the forces of good vanquish the forces of evil.

While they attain the magical skills they will need in the confrontation toward which the narrative pushes them, a fantasy novel's young characters embark on a journey of self-discovery. As does Bilbo Baggins in J. R. R. Tolkien's *The Hobbit* (1937) and Ged in Ursula K. Le Guin's *A Wizard of Earthsea* (1968), Harry Potter gains a deeper understanding of himself as he moves toward the anticipated final battle. Initially worried that his Muggle upbringing will place him at a disadvantage among Hogwarts students, Harry discovers that he does have talents: he's great at flying and a natural Seeker on his house's Quidditch team. Just as we all must come to terms with who we are, Harry also wonders if some of his abilities make him a bad person. A Parselmouth, Harry can talk to snakes, a rare ability he shares with dark wizards like Voldemort and Salazar Slytherin. Possessing the capacity to speak Parseltongue worries Harry, because the Sorting Hat had offered to place him in Slytherin, only sending him to Gryffindor when he kept chanting "Not Slytherin, not Slytherin" (*Philosopher's Stone* 90–91). When he expresses this anxiety, Dumbledore advises, "It is our choices, Harry, that show us what we truly are, far more than our abilities" (*Chamber of Secrets* 245). Dumbledore's moral applies equally well to Ron and Hermione, who also come into their own during the course of the series. At first an overbearing school swot, Hermione grows more comfortable with herself, develops a strong sense of commitment to her friends, and — though she remains the smartest student in her year — learns to resist the impulse to display her intelligence at every available opportunity. Ron has thus far developed less than Hermione or Harry, but he is gradually emerging from the shadow of his older brothers, playing a key role in solving the mysteries of the first three novels and sharing some of Harry's limelight in *Goblet of Fire*.

As in many fantasy novels and fairy tales, the central character is on a quest; however, the narrative of Harry's quest unfolds more like a classic mystery. In the first novel, Harry seeks to protect the Philosopher's Stone; in the second, to stop the basilisk from attacking students; in the third, to elude and to be revenged upon Sirius Black, whom he believes was an accomplice in his parents' murder; and in the fourth, to win the Triwizard Tournament cup. In its effort to highlight Harry's quests, the previous sentence oversimplifies all four novels. Ron and Hermione often join in Harry's quests, and the implicit and explicit nature of each quest changes as Rowling's mystery unfolds. In *Harry Pot-*

ter and the Philosopher's Stone, the three characters first wonder what is hidden on the righthand side of the third-floor corridor; upon learning what it is, they puzzle over who wants it, suspect Snape, and finally decide to protect it themselves. Concurrent with this mystery quest, they also want to know: Who is Nicolas Flamel? Who or what has been attacking the unicorns? Why did Snape seem to be sabotaging Harry's broom at the Quidditch match? At the opening banquet, why did Harry's scar hurt when Snape appeared to be looking at him? Of course, two overriding questions in all of the novels are: How did Harry survive the Avada Kevadra curse that killed both of his parents? And why did Voldemort want to kill Harry in the first place? Harry asks Dumbledore both questions in *Philosopher's Stone*. The Hogwarts headmaster provides a partial answer to the first question when he says that Harry's mother died to save him, and that Voldemort cannot understand a love that powerful. In words that may echo the author's sentiments toward her own late mother, Dumbledore tells Harry, "to have been loved so deeply, even though the person who loved us is gone, will give us some protection for ever" (216). However, Dumbledore does not tell us why Voldemort wanted the Potters dead; that mystery persists.

If the first novel appears to have many mystery plots going at once, it is remarkably simple when compared with the subsequent three. Each of the next three books grows more complex as its mysteries grow more intricate and clever. The final hundred or so pages of *Harry Potter and the Prisoner of Azkaban* — themselves as gripping and elaborate a conclusion to a mystery as one could hope for — prove only to foreshadow the complexity of *Harry Potter and the Goblet of Fire*. In the *Prisoner of Azkaban*'s concluding pages, we witness the arc of Rowling's narrative expanding — an expansion that continues in its sequel. Though the first two novels provide a sense of narrative closure, the next two offer only an emotional resolution, coupled with an uneasy feeling that the dangerous world beyond Hogwarts will continue to bear down upon the young characters. After realizing that their perceptions of several major characters were incorrect, Harry and Hermione listen in disbelief as Dumbledore tells them, "I have no power to make other men see the truth, or to overrule the Minister for Magic" (*Prisoner of Azkaban* 287).

Then, in what can only be a reference to the endings of the previous two novels, Harry realizes that he "had grown used to the idea that Dumbledore could solve anything. He had expected Dumbledore to pull some amazing solution out of the air. But no . . . their last hope was gone" (288). We readers had grown used to the idea that Dumbledore could set things right, too. *Harry Potter and the Goblet of Fire* complicates matters further, revealing corruption in government ministries, the possibilities for global misunderstanding, and the alliance in disarray while Voldemort returns to power.

Underscoring their complexity, the novels view official systems of 5
power skeptically, placing greater faith in unofficial alliances. While not all bureaucrats are corrupt, many officials appear bumbling, misguided, or acting in their own self-interest instead of for the public good. Though Arthur Weasley is kind-hearted and works hard in the Misuse of Muggle Artefacts Office, Ludo Bagman pays more attention to gambling than running the Department of Games and Sports, Cornelius Fudge tends to fudge things (as his name suggests) as Minister for Magic, and Barty Crouch (the Minister for International Magical Co-operation) is more concerned with appearing correct than with being honest or just. Tellingly, when Crouch was head of the Department of Magical Law Enforcement, he sent the innocent Sirius Black to Azkaban without a trial. Unlike the criminal justice system and other official channels of power, the alliance that Dumbledore begins to reassemble in the penultimate chapter of *Harry Potter and the Goblet of Fire* holds more promise. Rowling evinces trust in the greater efficacy of *ad hoc* groups throughout the novels. When school officials either ignore them (*Philosopher's Stone*) or fail to solve the problem (*Chamber of Secrets*), Harry, Ron, and Hermione form their own alliance and solve the problem themselves. Rowling seems more comfortable when power courses through unofficial networks — as if its activist spirit is more democratic than power entrenched in official channels. No stranger to political activism herself, Rowling implies that activists are more worthy of our trust than public officials are.

As the series develops, it grows increasingly interested in questions of power: who has it, who has the right to exercise it over another, who has the moral authority to wield it, and how it should be exercised. Perhaps the most striking example occurs during the nineteenth chapter of *Prisoner of Azkaban*, when Harry intervenes to stop Black and Lupin from killing Pettigrew, the man directly responsible for Voldemort killing Harry's parents. This moment of moral decision-making gives both readers and characters pause: Sirius asks Harry if he's sure, and when Harry explains why he is, he displays a quiet heroism. Harry saves Pettigrew because he does not think his father would want his best friends to become killers (275). Wonderfully, Harry both regrets his noble decision and receives high praise for it. When Pettigrew escapes, Harry accuses himself of helping Voldemort, albeit inadvertently. "I stopped Sirius and Professor Lupin killing Pettigrew! That makes it my fault, if Voldemort comes back!" Dumbledore quietly disagrees: "Hasn't your experience with the Time-Turner taught you anything, Harry? The consequences of our actions are always so complicated, so diverse, that predicting the future is a very difficult business indeed." In addition, Dumbledore notes that in saving Pettigrew, Harry has given Voldemort a deputy who is in Harry's debt. Dumbledore then adds gently, "I knew your father very well, both at Hogwarts and later [. . .]. He would have saved Pettigrew too, I am sure of it" (311). If Voldemort is interested in power for its own sake, Harry wishes to use his power only when it is *right* to do so. He could have had Pettigrew killed, avenging his parents' deaths, but sensing that vengeance is the wrong motive, he saves Pettigrew's life. In her *New Yorker* essay, Joan Acocella develops a fascinating analysis of power in Rowling's books, arguing that "Each of the novels approaches the problem from a different angle": the first novel is heroic; the second is "secular, topical, political"; the third is psychological; the fourth is more ambitious in its politics, introducing new topics (such as sex) but not yet answering the question of whether power is "reconcilable with goodness" (77–78).

Acocella's analysis reminds us that one of the most compelling aspects of these novels may be their ambiguity. During each novel, we wonder whether characters have done or are doing the right thing; at the end, many questions remain unanswered. During *Harry Potter and the Goblet of Fire*, we wonder if Ludo Bagman is aligned with the dark wizards or merely unscrupulous? At the end of the novel, we know him to be unscrupulous but not bad, though we do not know which side he will end up assisting. A character like Bagman could go either way. In *Prisoner of Azkaban*, after Harry overhears the "facts" (which turn out to be false) that Sirius Black betrayed his parents, we see Harry's dark side. He wants revenge on Black: but will he risk his own life trying to catch him? Harry decides not to, but the incident does call attention to some potential weaknesses that Voldemort could exploit. In future novels, will Harry be able to keep his temper under control? Will his strong resolve be an asset, a hindrance, or a bit of both? Perhaps the fact that these books raise as many questions as they answer accounts — at least in part — for their enormous appeal.

Works Cited

Acocella, Joan. "Under the Spell." *New Yorker* 31 July 2000: 74–78. Print.

Le Guin, Ursula. *A Wizard of Earthsea*. 1968. New York: Bantam, 1975. Print.

"Pure Magic." *CBS Sunday Morning*. Writ. Mark Phillips. CBS. 26 Sept. 1999. Television.

Rowling, J. K. *Harry Potter and the Chamber of Secrets*. London: Bloomsbury, 1998. Print.

---. *Harry Potter and the Goblet of Fire*. London: Bloomsbury, 2000. Print.

---. *Harry Potter and the Philosopher's Stone*. London: Bloomsbury, 1997. Print.

---. *Harry Potter and the Prisoner of Azkaban*. London: Bloomsbury, 1999. Print.

Tolkien, J. R. R. *The Hobbit*. 1937. Rev. ed. New York: Ballantine Books, 1982. Print.

Engaging with the Text

272–73

1. The **TITLE** of this analysis is "Fantasy, Mystery, and Ambiguity." How does this title reflect the organization of the analysis? How effective do you find this organization? Try your hand at writing a different title, one that might provoke readers to read on.

2. Philip Nel frequently poses questions without answering them. How do they help **GUIDE** readers? Why do you think he doesn't offer answers to these questions? 272–77
3. Nel incorporates **QUOTATIONS** from the Harry Potter novels throughout his analysis. What role(s) do these quotations serve? Point to examples from the text in your response. 410–13
4. Nel claims that the Harry Potter novels are "interested in questions of power: who has it, who has the right to exercise it over another, who has the moral authority to wield it, and how it should be exercised." Discuss how Nel treats these questions in his **ANALYSIS** of the novels. 38–58 How significant are these questions for understanding the Harry Potter series? What do these questions reveal about Nel's **STANCE** toward the Potter novels? 12–14
5. ***For Writing.*** Power — who has it, who lacks it, what they do with it, how it affects them — is a common thread in many literary works. Choose a text you know — a novel, short story, or drama — and **ANALYZE** its treatment of the concept of power. 38–58

PETER N. GOGGIN

"Enjoy Illusions, Lad, and Let the Rocks Be Rocks": Le Guin's A Wizard of Earthsea

Peter N. Goggin is an English professor at Arizona State University, where he teaches courses in rhetoric and theories of literacy. The author of Professing Literacy in Composition Studies *(2007) and of numerous scholarly essays, he is founder and co-director of the Western States Rhetoric and Literacy Conference. His current research is on rhetorics of environmental sustainability. Goggin wrote the following analysis of Ursula K. Le Guin's* A Wizard of Earthsea *in 2007 and revised it for inclusion in this book.*

> My opinion is that in the world of knowledge the idea of good appears last of all, and is seen only with an effort; and when seen, is also inferred to be the universal author of all things beautiful and right, parent of light and of the lord of light in this visible world, and the immediate source of reason and truth in the intellectual; and that this is the power upon which he who would act rationally, either in public or private life must have his eye fixed.
>
> — PLATO, THE REPUBLIC, BOOK 7

PLATO'S ALLEGORY OF THE CAVE in *The Republic* addresses the perennial question about the nature of reality. It also evokes the notion that knowledge is power, along with the myriad rhetorical and ethical complications that accompany such a notion. Ursula Le Guin's fantasy novel *A Wizard of Earthsea* (1968) is strongly reminiscent of Plato's cave allegory as its protagonist, the young wizard Sparrowhawk / Ged (referred to simply as Ged for the remainder of this essay), embarks on a quest for knowledge and enlightenment about himself, the various denizens and inhabitants of the world of Earthsea, and the very nature of reality itself. Ged's quest is temporal as, like Plato's prisoner brought out of the cave and then returned to the darkness and shadows, he acquires knowledge and accumulates experiences that constantly challenge him to reconsider the reality of his world and his place in it. What Le Guin's novel offers is not only a wonderful story about wizards, education, good and evil — sort of a cross between Tolkien's *Lord of the Rings* trilogy and Rowling's *Harry Potter* series — but also a powerful saga about a search for harmony between self-actualization and social welfare; between human society and the natural world. It presents a model of reason, ambition, and appetite in balance as an alternative to dominant contemporary social models of dualistic thinking.

This essay explores the young wizard Ged's quest for knowledge and wholeness-of-being in the world of Le Guin's *A Wizard of Earthsea* as a tale of enlightenment in a realm where environment, social politics, awareness, and activism intersect. In its capacity as a work of adolescent literature, the book serves as a point of access into the often complex and contradictory aspects of coming to understand one's world and one's places in it.

In his allegory of the cave, Plato offers a hypothesis for a process of enlightenment, suggesting that without this, the bulk of humanity resides in unenlightened illusion and shadow, unaware of the truth of form. In the allegory, men (humanity) are chained up from childhood so that all they have ever seen in their field of vision are shadows cast on a screen in front of them. The source of the shadows comes from performers who operate puppets from behind the prisoners. Behind the puppeteers is a source of light (fire) that casts the shadow of the objects the prisoners see on the screen in front of them. Because they have no way to see anything but those shadows and the echoed voices of the puppeteers, the prisoners take the shadows to be real, and discuss among themselves the importance, meaning, and value of those shadows as if they were forms in and of themselves and not projected illusions. Plato contends that if one of the prisoners were dragged from the cave into the sunlight, he would at first struggle with the new reality, and perhaps resist it. Having existed all his life in the relative ignorance of the cave, the prisoner would be confused and frightened when faced with the light of truth. He would not be able to see sunlight as reality, and might even attempt to run away from it back into the security of ignorance. But he would eventually come to recognize and accept the reality of true form, begin to see the world and his place in it, and see his previous perception of existence as one based on illusion. Plato speculates that once enlightened, the prisoner would resist being dragged back into the cave. Once returned, he would never be able to accept the world of ignorance that was once so known and secure, and would always desire to return to the world of enlightenment.

Like Plato's reluctant prisoner, Ged's story is one of struggle with his emerging knowledge and enlightenment, and the choices he is faced with that not only allow him to move toward self-realization, but also have the potential to profoundly impact the world of Earthsea, its environment, and its people. His movement to maturity, marked by the names "Duny" to "Sparrowhawk" and eventually his true name, "Ged," is also marked by increasing self-awareness of the complexity of his own identity and the world he lives in, and by the increasing knowledge and enlightened nature of others he comes into contact with. Like Plato's prisoner, Ged does not find his own way to enlightenment, but is guided there by a series of mentors who bring him out of the cave of ignorance and into the light of knowledge. The process begins with his aunt, the village witch, who first identifies Ged's (then Duny's) potential for "the making of power" and teaches him his first simple spells:

> This was Duny's first step on the way he was to follow all his life, the way of magery, the way that led him at last to hunt a shadow over land and sea to the lightless coasts of death's kingdom. But in those first broad steps along the way, it seemed a broad, bright road. (Le Guin, *Wizard* 15)

While under the tutelage of his next guide, the mage Ogion, Ged gains access to the books that give him his first frightening experience with the shadow that he resists and fights for much of the remainder of the story. For Ged at this moment, the shadow appears to be only darkness and evil but is actually the very source of enlightenment, harmony, and self-realization that he ultimately comes to accept. Ogion's scolding of Ged's irresponsible act of using his new knowledge and power for self-gratification establishes themes of restraint and balance that are central to the story:

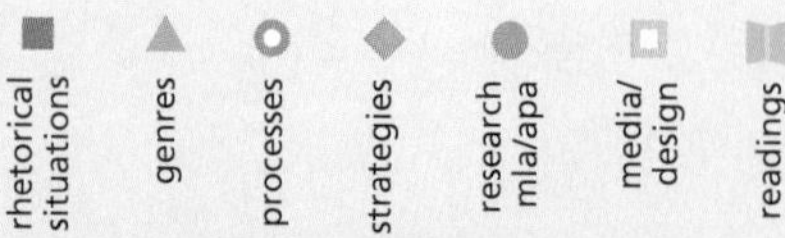

> Have you never thought how danger must surround power as a shadow does light? This sorcery is not a game we play for pleasure or praise. Think of this: that every word, every act of our Art is said and is either for good, or for evil. Before you speak or do you must know the price that is to pay. (Le Guin, *Wizard* 23)

Here Le Guin's story transcends the sheer fantasy of typical sword and sorcery tales. Good and evil are not absolutes but are made by choice. Like Plato's charioteer in another of his dialogues, the *Phaedrus*, the wisdom (reason) of the mage is necessary to keep altruistic and visceral desires, represented by the two winged horses, in balance. Ogion is telling Ged that his words and acts are rhetorical, constructed by choice and intent. The power to persuade and influence others, and to alter the natural world is an art, and in the hands of an ethical or unethical person can be wielded to various and differing purposes. In the allegory of the cave, Plato contends that those who have learned to see and understand the light of true knowledge have a responsibility to use that knowledge for the good of society. Plato refers to these as "just men" with the implication that unjust men may use knowledge and the ability to speak it to manipulate and distort. It is this latter element of his own awakening sense of self-identity that Ged must face in his encounters with the gebbeth/shadow. Like the charioteer, he must learn to control and balance darkness and light, good and evil, not as dualistic entities, but integrated parts of a whole. He must experience critical self-awareness and a sense of being-in-the-world to achieve enlightenment and connection with his environment. Thus, Ged must release the "evil" in order to recognize it for what it is and literally embrace it to become a true master of his Art.

5 As he progresses on to the Knoll of Roke and the school for wizards, Ged encounters, even more directly, lessons on the power of knowledge in the lectures of the Master Changer and the need to use such power with wisdom:

> You must not change one thing, one pebble, one grain of sand until you know what good and evil will follow on that act. The world is in balance, in Equilibrium. A wizard's power of Changing and of Summoning can shake the balance of the world. It is dangerous,

> that power. It is most perilous. It must follow knowledge and serve need. To light a candle is to cast a shadow. (Le Guin, *Wizard* 44)

The Master Changer's words serve not only as a traditional dire warning as a plot mechanism for the story, but also introduce Ged to concepts that Plato valued so highly. Doug Brown points out that Plato's ideal of self-realization for the individual consists of three elements: reason, ambition, and appetite. Self-realization is achieved when all three of these elements are in balance (40). However, as Ged has to discover, self-realization alone is not sufficient. Plato emphasized wisdom above all else, and it is wisdom that Ged ultimately must acquire in his quest to come to terms with the power of his increasing, and potentially destructive, knowledge. The Master Changer further emphasizes this point in his lecture:

> He looked down at the pebble again. "A rock is a good thing, too, you know," he said, speaking less gravely. "If the Isles of Earthsea were all made of diamond, we'd lead a hard life here. Enjoy illusions, lad, and let the rocks be rocks." (Le Guin, *Wizard* 44)

Ged's lesson on the consequences of using his knowledge (or not) to alter the natural world, i.e., letting the rocks be rocks, is his first lesson in living in harmony with and in the world. For Plato, a hallmark of wisdom is restraint, understanding when to act or not act on one's desire for self-gratification, whether that gratification is physical, intellectual, or spiritual.

For the sake of the story, of course, Ged chooses to ignore the warnings and uses his power to call forth the destructive force that becomes embodied in the Gebbeth. It is a lesson in choosing a path of insatiability over one of sustainability. Ged's final mentor, his best friend, Vetch, is strongly connected to family, culture, and environment. He models balance in living and maintaining a sustainable lifestyle. Vetch is the only one who can accompany Ged in the final stages of his quest, and Ged draws strength from his friend's ability to remain grounded and stable in his values, sense of responsibility, and restraint in using his power. Like Plato's prisoner who ultimately sloughs off the remnants of the illusionary reality of the cave, and accepts the light of knowledge and the truth of Form, Ged finally reckons with the shadow he has both resisted and run from, and finally accepts and embraces it. "Look, it is done. It is over," says Ged. "The wound is healed. . . . I am whole, I am free" (Le Guin, *Wizard* 180). This notion of wholeness, combined with Le Guin's narrated statement at the moment of Ged's healing, "light and darkness met, and joined, and were one" (Le Guin, *Wizard* 179), is echoed in the allegory of the cave in the following observation:

> Whereas, our argument shows that the power and capacity of learning exists in the soul already; and that just as the eye was unable to turn from darkness to light without the whole body, so too the instrument of knowledge can only by the movement of the whole soul be turned from the world of becoming into that of being, and learn by degrees to endure the sight of being, and of the brightest and best of being, or in other words, of the good. (Plato, bk. 7)

Plato's view that the individual's innate capacity for learning must be nurtured and guided, and that once true knowledge is achieved, must be used for just purposes is a theme that also drives Le Guin's protagonist. Ged's wholeness of being allows him to transcend a dualistic sense of himself as individual and the world as other. This is a tenet that can broaden the appeal of Le Guin's novel for an adolescent audience, who, like Ged, are finding their way in the world and are dependent on already established social norms of what constitutes learning and knowledge.[1] As such, *A Wizard of Earthsea* offers an important parable on critical self-awareness that can contribute to an understanding of "coming into that of being, and learn[ing] by degrees to endure the sight of being" (Plato, bk. 7).

Note

1. That *A Wizard of Earthsea* has a broad appeal was apparent when it was selected as one of two Le Guin novels, the other being *The Tombs of Atuan* (New York: Bantam Books, 1989), to be made into a movie, *Legend of Earthsea*, for the Sci-Fi channel. For Le Guin's response to the adaptation of her novels, see "A Whitewashed Earthsea."

Works Cited

Brown, Doug. *Insatiable Is Not Sustainable.* Westport, CT: Praeger, 2002. Print.

Legend of Earthsea. Prod. Robert Halmi. Dir. Rob Lieberman. Writ. Gavin Scott. The Sci-Fi Channel, 13 and 14 Dec. 2004. Television.

Le Guin, Ursula K. "A Whitewashed Earthsea: How the Sci-Fi Channel Wrecked My Books." *Slate.com.* Washington Post–Newsweek Interactive, 16 Dec. 2004. Web. 20 Feb. 2005.

---. *A Wizard of Earthsea.* 1968. New York: Bantam Books, 1975. Print.

Plato. *Plato's Phaedrus.* 1952. Trans. R. Hackforth. New York: Cambridge UP, 1993. Print.

---. *The Republic.* Trans. Benjamin Jowett. *Constitution Society.* Constitution Society, n.d. Web. 10 Feb. 2007.

Engaging with the Text

306–13

1. Throughout his essay, Peter N. Goggin **COMPARES** Plato's concepts of reality and human nature to those expressed in LeGuin's *A Wizard of Earthsea.* Why does Goggin turn to an ancient rhetorician to discuss a twentieth-century novel? What does this comparison with Plato help you understand about Le Guin's novel?

146
287–93

2. What is the **ARGUABLE THESIS** of Goggin's analysis of *A Wizard of Earthsea*? What **EVIDENCE** does he offer in support of this thesis? How effective is this evidence?

272–73

3. Goggin uses a quotation from the novel as part of his **TITLE.** How does this title prepare readers for the main argument of this analysis? Is this title effective? Why or why not?

5–8

4. Who do you think is the intended **AUDIENCE** for this essay? Point to passages in the text that provide clues to its audience.

143–52
410–13

5. ***For Writing.*** Many literary analyses involve comparisons between two or more works. Choose two poems, stories, or novels that share similar patterns or themes and write an **ANALYSIS** comparing the two works on the basis of those patterns or themes. Be sure to include **QUOTATIONS** from the works to support your analysis.

PATRICIA HAMPL

The Invention of Autobiography: Augustine's Confessions

Patricia Hampl is a professor of English at the University of Minnesota. A widely published poet and essayist, she has also written three memoirs: A Romantic Education *(1981), an exploration of her Czech heritage;* Virgin Time: In Search of the Contemplative Life *(1992), an account of her journey to understand Catholicism, the religion of her youth; and* The Florist's Daughter *(2008). The following analysis comes from* I Could Tell You Stories: Sojourns in the Land of Memory *(1999), a collection of essays that explores the genre of memoir.*

THE FIRST NINE BOOKS of the *Confessions* feel familiar to us. They are what we think of as autobiography. Augustine* casts before us incident and vignette, sketch and portrait, stringing these bright gemstones on the story line of his life as he writes his way from his birth in 354 in Thagaste (now Souk Ahras in the hills of eastern Algeria) to the bittersweet period following his baptism when his mother dies at the Roman port of Ostia as she and Augustine and their circle wait to sail home to Africa.

In these nine chapters of his life, Augustine muses about his babyhood, and even beyond that to his time in the womb, searching what a psychologized modern would call "the unconscious" for hints and clues to his nature. He is clearly troubled by the mystery of existence: "I do not know where I came from," he says with surprisingly agnostic wonder.

Augustine begins his great portrait of his devout Berber Christian mother in Book I as he reminds the Lord how he nursed at her breast, taking in, he knows, much more than milk. Monica's personality storms

**Aurelias Augustinus* (354–430): bishop of Hippo and one of the four "Latin Fathers" of the Roman Catholic Church. His *Confessions* (c. 400), often regarded as "the first autobiography," recounts his conversion to Christianity. After his death he was canonized a saint. [Editor's note]

and rainbows over the entire book. She is her son's biggest fan and greatest nag. She is also "my mother, my incomparable mother!" Her concern about her son verges on obsession. "Like all mothers, though far more than most," Augustine the bishop writes, still confounded after all these years by her passionate attachment, "she loved to have me with her." She follows him to the dock when he is about to leave Africa for Rome, weeping and wailing, begging him either to stay or to take her with him. Finally desperate to be rid of her, he lies about the time of his departure and makes his escape.

A good try, but Monica, of course, gets her way, on earth and in heaven. She follows Augustine to Rome and then to Milan when he secures a plum teaching position there. She prays him into the Church with more than pious wishes: she has a mother's spooky clairvoyance, and assures him she *knows* he will find his way to baptism. Her prophecy climaxes in Book IX during their mutual mystical experience in Ostia.

5 In marked contrast to his rhapsodic writing about Monica, Augustine mentions his father with telling coolness. Patricius was a small-time farmer who remained a pagan until receiving baptism on his deathbed. He was neither a success in life nor a questing soul. He died when Augustine was eighteen and he cast only a faint shadow on his son's consciousness. Augustine was his mother's son, and knew it.

No incident is too small for Augustine in the *Confessions* — provided it has metaphoric value. He is a gifted writer, after all, a pro, and he knows very well that his description of his boyhood theft of pears from a garden — a purely willful act because he didn't even want to eat the pears — rings a change on the first theft in another Garden.

He reports his first prayer — "not to be beaten at school." And reminds God that in response to this first intercession "You did not hear my prayer. . . . " Augustine recalls the harshness of his school days and the cruelty of his teachers with the scorekeeping precision of a true memoirist, immune to the irritating wisdom of forgiving and forgetting. The slap of his boyhood humiliations and the still-tender skin of the adult bishop who recounts them ring down the centuries. "We loved to play," he explains heatedly, appealing to God as if to a referee in a ghostly game of yore, "and we were punished by adults who nonetheless did the same themselves. But whereas the frivolous pursuits of grown-up people are called 'business,' children are punished. . . . Moreover, was the master who flogged me any better himself? If he had been worsted by a fellow-scholar in some pedantic dispute, would he not have been racked by even more bitter jealousy than I was when my opponent in a game of ball got the better of me?" Still arguing his case after all these years.

We see him grow into a young intellectual, sharpening his knives of argument, engaged in his first philosophical battles. The Manichees,* a gnostic sect whose dualism greatly appeals to him at first, later become a grave disappointment. He hopscotches from Manicheism to a fashionable skepticism, then into a mystical Neoplatonism† that leads him finally to the threshold of the Church. He enumerates his hesitations about Catholicism, and presents the process, both intellectual and spiritual, that leads him finally to the Baptistry in Milan. We feel the circumspection of his mind: After listening carefully to the great bishop Ambrose he says coolly, "I realized that the Catholic faith . . . was in fact intellectually respectable." This is not the response of a credulous seeker, but the balanced judgment of an educated, upwardly mobile provincial intent on climbing in Roman society, a classical Latin scholar still slightly uneasy with the folk elements in biblical texts. The urgency of his search for truth never leaves his story. It is the ground beat of the tale.

But we would not read the *Confessions* down the centuries if they were the testimony of an intellectual's struggles, no matter how passionately told. It is passion itself that makes Augustine alive to us. He insists that we understand this about him: Well after his intellectual questions had been answered, he continues to resist conversion because, to him, baptism means chastity. In fact, the most famous line in the *Confessions* is the prayer of his hot adolescence: "Grant me chastity and self-control, but please not yet."

**Manichees*: early Christian sect that adhered to a dualistic philosophy, i.e., a worldview that all phenomena are composed of opposites, such as good and evil. [Editor's note]

†Neoplatonism: philosophy, modified from the teachings of Plato, that espouses belief in a single source, the One, from which all else emanates, and with which the soul can reunite in trance or ecstasy. [Editor's note]

Augustine was not the promiscuous lover of popular imagination 10
— or of his own description. From the age of nineteen he lived in complete and apparently happy fidelity with his girlfriend, a woman of lower rank with whom marriage was not a possibility. We never learn her name. She and Augustine have a child together, a son named Adeodatus (Gift of God) who, like Monica and several youthful friends, compose his intimate circle.

When Augustine does abandon this lover of his youth, it is to make a prudent marriage, a logical career move which Monica promoted. The break is shattering. His girlfriend, he says, "was ripped from my side. . . . So deeply was she engrafted into my heart that it was left torn and wounded and trailing blood." While he waited two years for the girl to whom he was engaged to reach marriageable age, he says, with the crudeness of a broken heart, that he "got myself another woman." But even this indulgence does not help: "The wound inflicted on me by the earlier separation did not heal. . . . After the fever and the immediate acute pain had dulled, it putrefied, and the pain became a cold despair."

Is it possible to read the *Confessions* today with the same urgency that Augustine brought to writing them? This is not simply a modern's self-admiring question about a late fourth-century book's "relevance" to our own secular age. It is a question Augustine would have appreciated, believing as he did in sorting things out for oneself. He refused, for example, to accept the glossy reputation of Faustus, the Manichee sage who proved, when frankly questioned, to be a charming phony. The blunt question of Augustine's appeal to the modern reader must be posed.

The answer lies in Augustine's literary self. With all the theological and cultural differences and all the history that divide us from Augustine's first readers, our recognition of the originality and power of the *Confessions* resides fundamentally in the same place—in his voice. Not because his is a magically "modern" voice from antiquity, somehow chumming up to the reader. In any case, the book isn't written to us.

It is addressed expressly to God. *Magnus es, Domine,* it begins: Great are you, Lord. Augustine claims in the first breath of the *Confessions* that his intention is the innate one — "we humans," he says simply, " . . . long

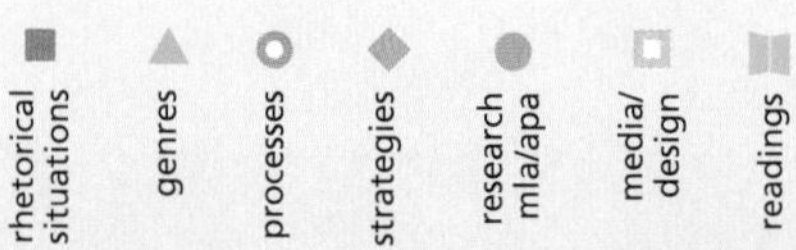

to praise you." But the real voice of the book is one of inquiry. He wants to *know*. At times it is heartbreaking, even comic, to see Augustine struggle with the mystery of existence. "Was there nothing before . . . except the life I lived in my mother's womb?" he asks in Book I. "But then, my God, my sweetness, what came before that? Was I somewhere else? Was I even someone? I have nobody to tell me. . . . Are you laughing at me for asking you these questions?" Augustine is willing to look foolish, even before God, if it will get him below the surface of things. This willingness to risk being a fool for the truth, which is all that literary courage is, keeps Augustine young for the ages.

The habitual way of approaching the *Confessions* is to see Augustine as a penitent, a man gazing with horror at his sinful past from the triumphant refuge of his conversion. Maybe the *Confessions* would have been such a book if Augustine had written them in 387, the year of his baptism and the death of Monica. It was certainly the great high-low year of his existence, the pivot of his life. But it is fully ten years after his baptism (a harrowing adult initiation experience, a true cult act signaling a changed life, not to be confused with the mild christening ceremonies of our own times) when Augustine turns to write the great searching book of his life.

The adjective is significant: What, after all, is a converted Christian properly searching for? Isn't the definition, the whole meaning of religious conversion, precisely that the great answer has been found, that one has moved from uncertainty to conviction? In its ardent, insistent questioning, the *Confessions* is not an ode. Like the Psalms of David, Augustine's great rhapsodic-furious model, it is a call to attention. But then, perhaps to call out to God, to demand a response, *is* to praise, though not in the pietistic way we routinely mistake as religious. The core of praise, for Augustine, lies in the fact that he, like all human beings, is so thoroughly God's creature that his *confessio,* his life quest for God, can never be finished. He was created to be that creature who beats its fists against the breast of the divine. "For Thou hast made us for Thyself," Augustine says on the first page of the *Confessions,* "and our hearts are restless till they rest in Thee."

Augustine's longing to know is not merely intellectual. He must know as one knows through love — by being known. *Deus, noverim te, noverim me,* he prays. God, let me know You and know myself. Probably no one since Job has inquired of his God as desperately and commandingly. Like Job, Augustine sees prayer as a form of thinking, a way of seeking truth, not a pious form of wishing. But Job is a character in a great primeval tale. Augustine, in the fine paradox of autobiography, is a character in a story *and* the narrator of that character. He bears in his voice the blood-beat of time. He belongs not to myth, but to history. As we do.

Engaging with the Text

1. 143–52 A **LITERARY ANALYSIS** makes an argument about a text — how it works and/or what it means. What is Patricia Hampl's argument about
273–75 Augustine's *Confessions?* Restate her **THESIS** in your own words.
2. 147 Hampl challenges conventional **INTERPRETATIONS** of Augustine's *Confessions* that see him "as a penitent, a man gazing with horror at his sinful past from the triumphant refuge of his conversion." What
287–93 **EVIDENCE** does she provide to support her analysis?
3. 300–305 Hampl **CLASSIFIES** Augustine's *Confessions* as an autobiography. Could
153–60 it be called a **MEMOIR?** What key features of an autobiography does she cite to support her classification, and could they be cited as features of a memoir? Why is the classification important?
4. Hampl explores why this ancient text continues to be appealing and relevant to contemporary readers, writing, "The answer lies in Augustine's literary self . . . in his voice." What does she means by this claim? How does she illustrate Augustine's "literary self"? What does she mean by "voice"?
5. ***For Writing.*** Identify a text that has been read by generations of readers (one of Plato's dialogues, perhaps, or Shakespeare's sonnets, or a *Canterbury Tale*) or that is often read in high school (*To Kill a Mockingbird, Julius Caesar,* "Stopping by Woods on a Snowy Evening"). Why do
38–58 you think this text is still read today? Write an **ANALYSIS** of the text that offers an explanation for its enduring popularity — or, conversely, that argues why it should no longer be read.

LESLIE MARMON SILKO

Language and Literature from a Pueblo Indian Perspective

Poet and fiction writer Leslie Marmon Silko grew up on the Laguna Pueblo Reservation in New Mexico. She is author of a collection of poetry, several novels, and a collection of essays, Yellow Woman and a Beauty of the Spirit: Essays on Native American Life Today *(1996), which addresses the cultural and social contexts that shape her poetry and fiction. The following essay began as a speech and first appeared in print in* English Literature: Opening Up the Canon *(1979), edited by Leslie A. Fiedler and Houston A. Baker. As you read, notice how Silko organizes her analysis and incorporates sample narratives to demonstrate the weblike, nonlinear pattern of Pueblo narratives.*

WHERE I COME FROM, the words most highly valued are those spoken from the heart, unpremeditated and unrehearsed. Among the Pueblo people, a written speech or statement is highly suspect because the true feelings of the speaker remain hidden as she reads words that are detached from the occasion and the audience. I have intentionally not written a formal paper because I want you to *hear* and to experience English in a structure that follows patterns from the oral tradition. For those of you accustomed to being taken from point A to point B to point C, this presentation may be somewhat difficult to follow. Pueblo expression resembles something like a spider's web — with many little threads radiating from the center, crisscrossing each other. As with the web, the structure emerges as it is made and you must simply listen and trust, as the Pueblo people do, that meaning will be made.

My task is a formidable one: I ask you to set aside a number of basic approaches that you have been using, and probably will continue to use, and instead, to approach language from the Pueblo perspective, one that embraces the whole of creation and the whole of history and time.

What changes would Pueblo writers make to English as a language for literature? I have some examples of stories in English that I will use to address this question. At the same time, I would like to explain the importance of storytelling and how it relates to a Pueblo theory of language.

So I will begin, appropriately enough, with the Pueblo Creation story, an all-inclusive story of how life began. In this story, Tséitsínako, Thought Woman, by thinking of her sisters, and together with her sisters, thought of everything that is. In this way, the world was created. Everything in this world was a part of the original creation; the people at home understood that far away there were other human beings, also a part of this world. The Creation story even includes a prophecy, which describes the origin of European and African peoples and also refers to Asians.

5 This story, I think, suggests something about why the Pueblo people are more concerned with story and communication and less concerned with a particular language. There are at least six, possibly seven, distinct languages among the twenty pueblos of the southwestern United States, for example, Zuñi and Hopi. And from mesa to mesa there are subtle differences in language. But the particular language spoken isn't as important as what a speaker is trying to say, and this emphasis on the story itself stems, I believe, from a view of narrative particular to the Pueblo and other Native American peoples — that is, that language is story.

I will try to clarify this statement. At Laguna Pueblo, for example, many individual words have their own stories. So when one is telling a story, and one is using words to tell the story, each word that one is speaking has a story of its own, too. Often the speakers or tellers will go into these word-stories, creating an elaborate structure of stories-within-stories. This structure, which becomes very apparent in the actual telling of a story, informs contemporary Pueblo writing and storytelling as well as the traditional narratives. This perspective on narrative — of story within story, the idea that one story is only the beginning of many stories, and the sense that stories never truly end — represents an important contribution of Native American cultures to the English language.

Many people think of storytelling as something that is done at bedtime, that it is something done for small children. But when I use the term *storytelling,* I'm talking about something much bigger than that. I'm talking about something that comes out of an experience and an understanding of that original view of creation — that we are all part of a whole; we do not differentiate or fragment stories and experiences. In the beginning, Tséitsínako, Thought Woman, thought of all things, and all of these things are held together as one holds many things together in a single thought.

So in the telling (and you will hear a few of the dimensions of this telling) first of all, as mentioned earlier, the storytelling always includes the audience, the listeners. In fact, a great deal of the story is believed to be inside the listener; the storyteller's role is to draw the story out of the listeners. The storytelling continues from generation to generation.

Basically, the origin story constructs our identity — within this story, we know who we are. We are the Lagunas. This is where we come from. We came this way. We came by this place. And so from the time we are very young, we hear these stories, so that when we go out into the world, when one asks who we are, or where we are from, we immediately know: we are the people who came from the north. We are the people of these stories.

In the Creation story, Antelope says that he will help knock a hole 10
in the earth so that the people can come up, out into the next world. Antelope tries and tries; he uses his hooves, but is unable to break through. It is then that Badger says, "Let me help you." And Badger very patiently uses his claws and digs a way through, bringing the people into the world. When the Badger clan people think of themselves, or when the Antelope people think of themselves, it is as people who are of *this* story, and this is *our* place, and we fit into the very beginning when the people first came, before we began our journey south.

Within the clans there are stories that identify the clan. One moves, then, from the idea of one's identity as a tribal person into clan identity, then to one's identity as a member of an extended family. And it is the notion of "extended family" that has produced a kind of story that some distinguish from other Pueblo stories, though Pueblo people do not. Anthropologists and ethnologists have, for a long time, differentiated the types of stories the Pueblos tell. They tended to elevate the old, sacred, and traditional stories and to brush aside family stories, the family's account of itself. But in Pueblo culture, these family stories are given equal recognition. There is no definite, present pattern for the way one will hear the stories of one's own family, but it is a very critical part of one's childhood, and the storytelling continues throughout one's life. One will hear stories of importance to the family — sometimes wonderful stories — stories about the time a maternal uncle got the biggest deer that was ever seen and brought it back from the mountains. And so an individual's identity will extend from the identity constructed around the family — "I am from the family of my uncle who brought in this wonderful deer and it was a wonderful hunt."

Family accounts include negative stories, too; perhaps an uncle did something unacceptable. It is very important that one keep track of all these stories — both positive and not so positive — about one's own family and other families. Because even when there is no way around it — old Uncle Pete *did* do a terrible thing — by knowing the stories that originate in other families, one is able to deal with terrible sorts of things that might happen within one's own family. If a member of the family does something that cannot be excused, one always knows stories about similar inexcusable things done by a member of another family. But this knowledge is not communicated for malicious reasons. It is very important to understand this. Keeping track of all the stories within the community gives us all a certain distance, a useful perspective, that brings incidents down to a level we can deal with. If others have done it before, it cannot be so terrible. If others have endured, so can we.

The stories are always bringing us together, keeping this whole together, keeping this family together, keeping this clan together. "Don't go away, don't isolate yourself, but come here, because we have all had these kinds of experiences." And so there is this constant pulling together to resist the tendency to run or hide or separate oneself during a traumatic emotional experience. This separation not only endangers the group but the individual as well — one does not recover by oneself.

Because storytelling lies at the heart of Pueblo culture, it is absurd to attempt to fix the stories in time. "When did they tell the stories?"

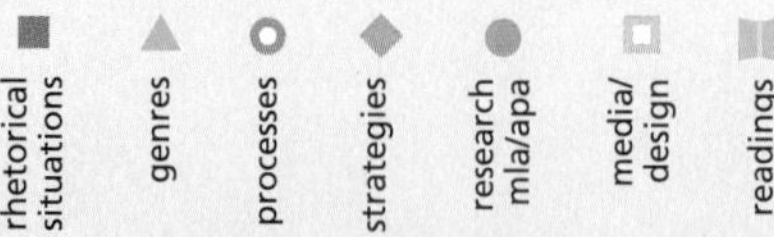

or "What time of day does the storytelling take place?" — these questions are nonsensical from a Pueblo perspective, because our storytelling goes on constantly: as some old grandmother puts on the shoes of a child and tells her the story of a little girl who didn't wear her shoes, for instance, or someone comes into the house for coffee to talk with a teenage boy who has just been in a lot of trouble, to reassure him that someone else's son has been in that kind of trouble, too. Storytelling is an ongoing process, working on many different levels.

Here's one story that is often told at a time of individual crisis (and 15
I want to remind you that we make no distinctions between types of story — historical, sacred, plain gossip — because these distinctions are not useful when discussing the Pueblo *experience* of language). There was a young man who, when he came back from the war in Vietnam, had saved up his army pay and bought a beautiful red Volkswagen. He was very proud of it. One night he drove up to a place called the King's Bar right across the reservation line. The bar is notorious for many reasons, particularly for the deep *arroyo** located behind it. The young man ran in to pick up a cold six-pack, but he forgot to put on his emergency brake. And his little red Volkswagen rolled back into the *arroyo* and was all smashed up. He felt very bad about it, but within a few days everybody had come to him with stories about other people who had lost cars and family members to that *arroyo,* for instance, George Day's station wagon, with his mother-in-law and kids inside. So everybody was saying, "Well, at least your mother-in-law and kids weren't in the car when it rolled in," and one can't argue with that kind of story. The story of the young man and his smashed-up Volkswagen was now joined with all the other stories of cars that fell into that *arroyo*.

Now I want to tell you a very beautiful little story. It is a very old story that is sometimes told to people who suffer great family or personal loss. This story was told by my Aunt Susie. She is one of the first generation of people at Laguna who began experimenting with English — who began working to make English speak for us — that is, to speak from the heart. (I come from a family intent on getting the stories told.)

**Arroyo*: ravine (Spanish). [Editor's note]

As you read the story, I think you will hear that. And here and there, I think, you will also hear the influence of the Indian school* at Carlisle, Pennsylvania, where my Aunt Susie was sent (like being sent to prison) for six years.

This scene is set partly in Acoma, partly in Laguna. Waithea was a little girl living in Acoma and one day she said, "Mother, I would like to have some *yashtoah* to eat." *Yashtoah* is the hardened crust of corn mush that curls up. *Yashtoah* literally means "curled up." She said, "I would like to have some *yashtoah*," and her mother said, "My dear little girl, I can't make you any *yashtoah* because we haven't any wood, but if you will go down off the mesa, down below, and pick up some pieces of wood and bring them home, I will make you some *yashtoah*." So Waithea was glad and ran down the precipitous cliff of Acoma mesa. Down below, just as her mother had told her, there were pieces of wood, some curled, some crooked in shape, that she was to pick up and take home. She found just such wood as these.

She brought them home in a little wicker basket. First she called to her mother as she got home, "*Nayah, deeni!* Mother, upstairs!" The Pueblo people always called "upstairs" because long ago their homes were two, three stories, and they entered from the top. She said, "*Deeni! UPSTAIRS!*" and her mother came. The little girl said, "I have brought the wood you wanted me to bring." And she opened her little wicker basket to lay out the pieces of wood but here they were snakes. They were snakes instead of crooked sticks of wood. And her mother said, "Oh my dear child, you have brought snakes instead!" She said, "Go take them back and put them back just where you got them." And the little girl ran down the mesa again, down below to the flats. And she put those snakes back just where she got them. They were snakes instead and she was very hurt about this and so she said, "I'm not going home. I'm going to *Kawaik*, the beautiful lake place, *Kawaik*, and drown myself in the lake, *byn'yah'nah* [the "west lake"]. I will go there and drown myself."

**Indian school*: the Carlisle Indian Industrial School, federally supported boarding school attended by more than 15,000 Native American children from 1879 to 1918. [Editor's note]

So she started off, and as she passed the Enchanted Mesa near Acoma she met an old man, very aged, and he saw her running, and he said, "My dear child, where are you going?" "I'm going to *Kawaik* and jump into the lake there." "Why?" "Well, because," she said, "my mother didn't want to make any *yashtoah* for me." The old man said, "Oh, no! You must not go my child. Come with me and I will take you home," He tried to catch her, but she was very light and skipped along. And every time he would try to grab her she would skip faster away from him.

The old man was coming home with some wood strapped to his back and tied with yucca. He just let the strap go and let the wood drop. He went as fast as he could up the cliff to the little girl's home. When he got to the place where she lived, he called to her mother. *"Deeni!"* "Come on up!" And he said, "I can't. I just came to bring you a message. Your little daughter is running away. She is going to *Kawaik* to drown herself in the lake there." "Oh my dear little girl!" the mother said. So she busied herself with making the *yashtoah* her little girl liked so much. Corn mush curled at the top. (She must have found enough wood to boil the corn meal and make the *yashtoah*.)

While the mush was cooking off, she got the little girl's clothing, her *manta* dress* and buckskin moccasins and all her other garments, and put them in a bundle — probably a yucca bag. And she started down as fast a she could on the east side of Acoma. (There used to be a trail there, you know. It's gone now, but it was accessible in those days.) She saw her daughter way at a distance and she kept calling: "Stsamaku! My daughter! Come back! I've got your *yashtoah* for you." But the little girl would not turn. She kept on ahead and she cried: "My mother, my mother, she didn't want me to have any *yashtoah*. So now I'm going to *Kawaik* and drown myself." Her mother heard her cry and said, "My little daughter, come back here!" "No," and she kept a distance away from her. And they came nearer and nearer to the lake. And she could see her daughter now, very plain. "Come back, my daughter! I have your *yashtoah*." But no, she kept on, and finally she reached the lake and she stood on the edge.

**Manta*: square, blanketlike cloth used as a cloak. [Editor's note]

She had tied a little feather in her hair, which is traditional (in death they tie this feather on the head). She carried a feather, the little girl did, and she tied it in her hair with a piece of string, right on top of her head she put the feather. Just as her mother was about to reach her, she jumped into the lake. The little feather was whirling around and around in the depths below. Of course the mother was very sad. She went, grieved, back to Acoma and climbed her mesa home. She stood on the edge of the mesa and scattered her daughter's clothing, the little moccasins, the *yashtoah*. She scattered them to the east, to the west, to the north, to the south. And the pieces of clothing and the moccasins and *yashtoah,* all turned into butterflies. And today they say that Acoma has more beautiful butterflies: red ones, white ones, blue ones, yellow ones. They came from this little girl's clothing.

Now this is a story anthropologists would consider very old. The version I have given you is just as Aunt Susie tells it. You can occasionally hear some English she picked up at Carlisle — words like "precipitous." You will also notice that there is a great deal of repetition, and a little reminder about *yashtoah,* and how it is made. There is a remark about the cliff trail at Acoma — that it was once there, but is there no longer. This story may be told at a time of sadness or loss, but within this story many other elements are brought together. Things are not separated out and categorized; all things are brought together. So that the reminder about the *yashtoah* is valuable information that is repeated — a recipe, if you will. The information about the old trail at Acoma reveals that stories are, in a sense, maps, since even to this day there is little information or material about trails that is passed around with writing. In the structure of this story the repetitions are, of course, designed to help you remember. It is repeated again and again, and then it moves on.

The next story I would like to tell is by Simon Ortiz, from Acoma Pueblo. He is a wonderful poet who also works in narrative. One of the things I find very interesting in this short story is that if you listen very closely, you begin to hear what I was talking about in terms of a story never beginning at the beginning, and certainly never ending. As the Hopis sometimes say, "Well, it has gone this far for a while." There is always that implication of a continuing. The other thing I want you to listen for is the many stories within one story. Listen to the kinds of stories contained within the main story — stories that give one a family identity and an individual identity, for example. This story is called "Home Country":

> "Well, it's been a while. I think in 1947 was when I left. My husband had been killed in Okinawa* some years before. And so I had no more husband. And I had to make a living. O I guess I could have looked for another man but I didn't want to. It looked like the war had made some of them into a bad way anyway. I saw some of them come home like that. They either got drunk or just stayed around a while or couldn't seem to be satisfied anymore with what was there. I guess now that I think about it, that happened to me although I wasn't in the war not in the Army or even much off the reservation just that several years at the Indian School. Well there was that feeling things were changing not only the men the boys, but things were changing.
>
> "One day the home nurse the nurse that came from the Indian health service was at my mother's home my mother was getting near the end real sick and she said that she had been meaning to ask me a question. I said what is the question. And the home nurse said well your mother is getting real sick and after she is no longer around for you to take care of, what will you be doing you and her are the only ones here. And I said I don't know. But I was thinking about it what she said made me think about it. And then the next time she came she said to me Eloise the government is hiring Indians now in the Indian schools to take care of the boys and girls I heard one of the supervisors saying that Indians are hard workers but you have to supervise them a lot and I thought of you well because you've been taking care of your mother real good and you follow all my instructions. She said I thought of you because you're a good Indian girl and you would be the kind of person for that job. I didn't say anything I had not ever really thought about a job but I kept thinking about it.
>
> "Well my mother she died and we buried her up at the old place the cemetery there it's real nice on the east side of the hill

**Okinawa*: southernmost Japanese island, site of fierce fighting between Japanese and American forces in World War II. [Editor's note] where the sun shines warm and the wind doesn't blow too much sand around right there. Well I was sad we were all sad for a while but you know how things are. One of my aunties came over and she advised me and warned me about being too sorry about it and all that she wished me that I would not worry too much about it because old folks they go along pretty soon life is that way and then she said that maybe I ought to take in one of my aunties kids or two because there was a lot of them kids and I was all by myself now. But I was so young and I thought that I might do that you know take care of someone but I had been thinking too of what the home nurse said to me about working. Hardly anybody at our home was working at something like that no woman anyway. And I would have to move away.

"Well I did just that. I remember that day very well. I told my aunties and they were all crying and we all went up to the old highway where the bus to town passes by every day. I was wearing an old kind of bluish sweater that was kind of big that one of my cousins who was older had got from a white person a tourist one summer in trade for something she had made a real pretty basket. She gave me that and I used to have a picture of me with it on it's kind of real ugly. Yeah that was the day I left wearing a baggy sweater and carrying a suitcase that someone gave me too I think or maybe it was the home nurse there wasn't much in it anyway either. I was scared and everybody seemed to be sad I was so young and skinny then. My aunties said one of them who was real fat you make sure you eat now make your own tortillas drink the milk and stuff like candies is no good she learned that from the nurse. Make sure you got your letter my auntie said. I had it folded into my purse. Yes I have one too a brown one that my husband when he was still alive one time on furlough he brought it on my birthday it was a nice purse and still looked new because I never used it.

"The letter said that I had a job at Keams Canyon the boarding school there but I would have to go to the Agency first for some papers to be filled and that's where I was going first. The Agency. And then they would send me out to Keams Canyon. I didn't even know where it was except that someone of our relatives said that it was near Hopi. My uncles teased me about watching out for the Hopi men and boys don't let them get too close they said well you

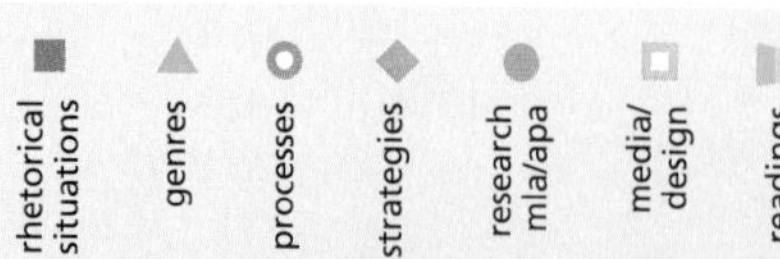

> know how they are and they were pretty strict too about those things and then they were joking and then they were not too and so I said aw they won't get near to me I'm too ugly and I promised I would be careful anyway.
>
> "So we all gathered for a while at my last auntie's house and then the old man my grandfather brought his wagon and horses to the door and we all got in and sat there for a while until my auntie told her father okay father let's go and shook his elbow because the poor old man was old by then and kind of going to sleep all the time you had to talk to him real loud. I had about ten dollars I think that was a lot of money more than it is now you know and when we got to the highway where the Indian road which is just a dirt road goes off the pave road my grandfather reached into his blue jeans and pulled out a silver dollar and put it into my hand. I was so shocked. We were all so shocked. We all looked around at each other we didn't know where the old man had gotten it because we were real poor two of my uncles had to borrow on their accounts at the trading store for the money I had in my purse but there it was a silver dollar so big and shrinking in my grandfather's hand and then in my hand.
>
> "Well I was so shocked and everybody was so shocked that we all started crying right there at the junction of that Indian road and the pave highway I wanted to be a little girl again running after the old man when he hurried with his long legs to the cornfields or went for water down to the river. He was old then and his eye was turned gray and he didn't do much anymore except drive the wagon and chop a little bit of wood but I just held him and I just held him so tightly.
>
> "Later on I don't know what happened to the silver dollar it had a date of 1907 on it but I kept it for a long time because I guess I wanted to have it to remember when I left my home country. What I did in between then and now is another story but that's the time I moved away,"

is what she said.[1]

There are a great many parallels between Pueblo experiences and 25
those of African and Caribbean peoples — one is that we have all had the conqueror's language imposed on us. But our experience with English has been somewhat different in that the Bureau of Indian Affairs

schools were not interested in teaching us the canon of Western classics. For instance, we never heard of Shakespeare. We were given Dick and Jane,* and I can remember reading that the robins were heading south for the winter. It took me a long time to figure out what was going on. I worried for quite a while about our robins in Laguna because they didn't leave in the winter, until I finally realized that all the big textbook companies are up in Boston and *their* robins do go south in the winter. But in a way, this dreadful formal education freed us by encouraging us to maintain our narratives. Whatever literature we were exposed to at school (which was damn little), at home the storytelling, the special regard for telling and bringing together through the telling, was going on constantly.

And as the old people say, "If you can remember the stories, you will be all right. Just remember the stories." When I returned to Laguna Pueblo after attending college, I wondered how the storytelling was continuing (anthropologists say that Laguna Pueblo is one of the more acculturated pueblos), so I visited an English class at Laguna Acoma High School. I knew the students had cassette tape recorders in their lockers and stereos at home, and that they listened to Kiss and Led Zeppelin and were all informed about popular culture in general. I had with me an anthology of short stories by Native American writers, *The Man to Send Rain Clouds*. One story in the book is about the killing of a state policeman in New Mexico by three Acoma Pueblo men in the early 1950s.[2] I asked the students how many had heard this story and steeled myself for the possibility that the anthropologists were right, that the old traditions were indeed dying out and the students would be ignorant of the story. But instead, all but one or two raised their hands — they had heard the story, just as I had heard it when I was young, some in English, some in Laguna.

One of the other advantages that we Pueblos have enjoyed is that we have always been able to stay with the land. Our stories cannot be separated from their geographical locations, from actual physical places

Dick and Jane: characters in an early-reading series common in American schools from the 1930s through the 1960s. [Editor's note]

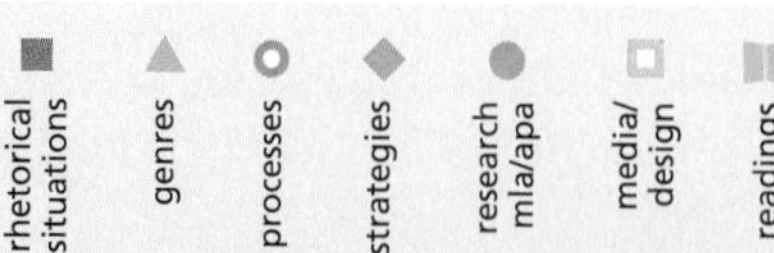

on the land. We were not relocated like so many Native American groups who were torn away from their ancestral land. And our stories are so much a part of these places that it is almost impossible for future generations to lose them — there is a story connected with every place, every object in the landscape.

Dennis Brutus has talked about the "yet unborn" as well as "those from the past," and how we are still *all* in *this* place, and language — the storytelling — is our way of passing through or being with them, or being together again. When Aunt Susie told her stories, she would tell a younger child to go open the door so that our esteemed predecessors might bring in their gifts to us. "They are out there," Aunt Susie would say. "Let them come in. They're here, they're here with us *within* the stories."

A few years ago, when Aunt Susie was 106, I paid her a visit, and while I was there she said, "Well, I'll be leaving here soon. I think I'll be leaving here next week, and I will be going over to the Cliff House." She said, "It's going to be real good to get back over there." I was listening, and I was thinking that she must be talking about our house at Paguate Village, just north of Laguna. And she went on, "Well, my mother's sister (and she gave her Indian name) will be there. She has been living there. She will be there and we will be over there, and I will get a chance to write down these stories I've been telling you." Now you must understand, of course, that Aunt Susie's mother's sister, a great storyteller herself, has long since passed over into the land of the dead. But then I realized, too, that Aunt Susie wasn't talking about death the way most of us do. She was talking about "going over" as a journey, a journey that perhaps we can only begin to understand through an appreciation for the boundless capacity of language that, through storytelling, brings us together, despite great distances between cultures, despite great distances in time.

Notes

1. Simon J. Ortiz, *Howabah Indians* (Tucson: Blue Moon Press, 1978).
2. See Simon J. Ortiz, "The Killing of a State Cop," in *The Man to Send Rain Clouds*, ed. Kenneth Rosen (New York: Viking Press, 1974), 101–108.

Engaging with the Text

1. Leslie Marmon Silko notes that for Pueblo and other Native American
peoples "language is story." What does she mean by this claim? How
146 does she **SUPPORT** this point?

2. 314–23 How does Silko **DEFINE** "storytelling," and how is this definition central to her analysis?

3. Silko claims that one of the advantages that Pueblos have enjoyed is
that "we have always been able to stay with the land. Our stories cannot be separated from their geographical locations, from actual physical places on the land." According to Silko, why is this connection
365–66 between the stories and their **LARGER CONTEXT** significant in Pueblo
culture?

4. Silko announces that readers "accustomed to being taken from point
223–24 A to point B to point C" may find her text difficult to follow. **OUTLINE**
the text to see how it is organized. What cues does Silko provide to
272–77 **GUIDE READERS**?

5. *For Writing.* The structure of a literary work is often an excellent subject for analysis, as the way a poem, song, story, novel, or drama is
structured strongly influences how we read it and how we interpret
143–52 it. Choose a literary text you like, and **ANALYZE ITS STRUCTURE**. How
does that structure affect the meaning of the text? Alternatively, select
one of the stories Silko includes in her essay and analyze its structure. Discuss how it exemplifies the organization of "a spider's web
— with many little threads radiating from the center, crisscrossing
each other."

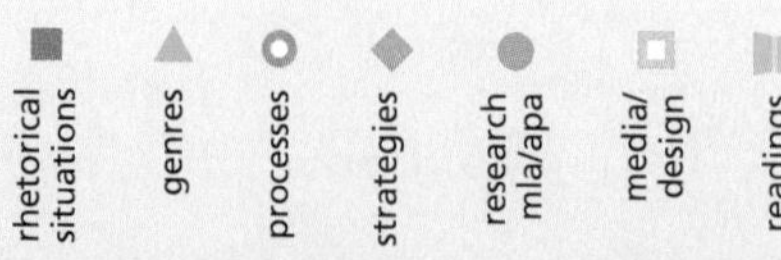

WILLOW D. CRYSTAL

"One of us . . . ": *Concepts of the Private and the Public in "A Rose for Emily"*

The following essay was written by Willow D. Crystal, a student at Harvard, as a model paper for The Norton Introduction to Literature. *As you read it, notice how Crystal draws on scholarly research to support her claims about the tensions between private and public constructs in Faulkner's "A Rose for Emily." See p. 787 if you want to read the story.*

THROUGHOUT "A ROSE FOR EMILY," William Faulkner introduces a tension between what is private, or belongs to the individual, and what is public, or the possession of the group. "When Miss Emily Grierson died," the tale begins, "our whole town went to her funeral: the men through a sort of respectful affection for a fallen monument, the women mostly out of curiosity to see the inside of her house . . . " (787). The men of the small town of Jefferson, Mississippi, are motivated to attend Miss Emily's funeral for public reasons; the women, to see "the inside of her house," that private realm which has remained inaccessible for "at least ten years" (787).

This opposition of the private with the public has intrigued critics of Faulkner's tale since the story was first published. Distinctions between the private and the public are central to Lawrence R. Rodgers's argument in his essay " 'We all said, "she will kill herself" ': The Narrator/Detective in William Faulkner's 'A Rose for Emily.' " The very concept of the detective genre demands that "there must be concealed facts that . . . must become clear in the end" (119), private actions which become public knowledge. In her feminist tribute, "A Rose for 'A Rose for Emily,' " Judith Fetterley uses the private-public dichotomy to demonstrate the "grotesque reality" (34) of the patriarchal social system in Faulkner's story. According to Fetterley, Miss Emily's "private life becomes a public document that the town folk feel free to interpret at will" (36). Thus, while critics such as Rodgers and Fetterley offer convincing — if divergent — interpretations of "A Rose for Emily," it is necessary first to understand in Faulkner's eerie and enigmatic story the relationship between the public and the private, and the consequences of this relationship within the story and for the reader.

The most explicit illustration of the opposition between the public and the private occurs in the social and economic interactions between the town of Jefferson, represented by the narrator's "our" and "we," and the reclusive Miss Emily. "Alive," the narrator explains, "Miss Emily had been a tradition, a duty, and a care; a sort of hereditary obligation upon the town, dating from that day in 1894 when Colonel Sartoris, the mayor, . . . remitted her taxes, the dispensation dating from the death of her father on into perpetuity" (787–88). Ironically (and this is one of the prime examples of the complexity of the relationship of private and public in the story), the price of privacy for Miss Emily becomes the loss of that very privacy. Despite — or perhaps because of — her refusal to buy into the community, the citizens of Jefferson determine that it is their "duty," their "hereditary obligation," to oversee her activities. When, for example, Miss Emily's house begins to emit an unpleasant smell, the town officials decide to solve the problem by dusting her property with lime. When she refuses to provide a reason why she wants to buy poison, the druggist scrawls "For rats" (793) across the package, literally and protectively overwriting her silence.

Arguably, the townspeople's actions serve to protect Miss Emily's privacy — by preserving her perceived gentility — as much as they effectively destroy it with their intrusive zeal. But in this very act of protection they reaffirm the town's proprietary relation to the public "monument" that is Miss Emily and, consequently, reinforce her inability to make decisions for herself.

While the communal narrator and Miss Emily appear to be polar 5
opposites — one standing for the public while the other fiercely defends her privacy — the two are united when an outsider such as Homer Barron appears in their midst. If Miss Emily serves as a representation — an icon, an inactive figure in a "tableau," an "idol" — of traditional antebellum southern values, then Homer represents all that is new and different. A "day laborer" (792) from the North, Homer comes to Jefferson

to pave the sidewalks, a task which itself suggests the modernization of the town.

The secret and destructive union between these two representational figures implies a complex relationship between the private and the public. When Miss Emily kills Homer and confines his remains to a room in her attic, where, according to Rodgers, "she has been allowed to carry on her illicit love affair in post-mortem privacy" (119), this grotesque act ironically suggests that she has capitulated to the code of gentility that Jefferson imagines her to embody. This code demands the end of a romantic affair which some residents deemed "a disgrace to the town and a bad example to the young people" (793), thus placing tradition and the good of the community above Miss Emily's own wishes. Through its insistence on Miss Emily's symbolic relation to a bygone era, the town — via the narrator — becomes "an unknowing driving force behind Emily's crime" (Rodgers 120). Her private act is both the result of and a support for public norms and expectations.

At the same time, however, the act of murder also marks Miss Emily's corruption of that very code. By killing Homer in private, Miss Emily deliberately flouts public norms, and by eluding explicit detection until after her own death, she asserts the primacy of the private. The murder of the outsider in their midst thus leads Miss Emily to achieve paradoxically both a more complete privacy — a marriage of sorts without a husband — and a role in the preservation of the community.

Yet the elaborate relationship between Jefferson and Miss Emily is not the only way in which Homer's murder may be understood as a casualty of the tension between the public and the private. When Miss Emily kills Homer, Rodgers contends, "from the town's point of view, it was the best thing. . . . Homer represents the kind of unwelcomed resident and ineligible mate the town wants to repel if it is to preserve its traditional arrangements" (125). The people of Jefferson and Miss Emily join in a struggle to "repel" the outside and to ensure a private, inner order and tradition. This complicity creates intriguing parallels between the illicit, fatal union of Homer and Miss Emily and the reunion of the North and the South following the Civil War. In this reformulation of the private and the public, Miss Emily becomes, as Fetterley notes, a "metaphor and mirror for the town of Jefferson" (43). Miss Emily's honor is the townspeople's honor, her preservation their preservation.

Finally, the parallels between Miss Emily's secretive habits and the narrator's circuitous presentation of the story lead to a third dimension of the negotiations between the private and the public in "A Rose for Emily," a dimension in which Faulkner as author and the collective "we" as narrator confront their public consumers, the readers. Told by the anonymous narrator as if retrospectively, "A Rose for Emily" skips forward and back in time, omitting details and deferring revelations to such a degree that many critics have gone to extreme lengths to establish reliable chronologies for the tale. The much-debated "we" remains anonymous and unreachable throughout the tale — maintaining a virtually unbreachable privacy — even as it invites the public (the reader) to participate in the narrator's acts of detection and revelation. Rodgers observes:

> The dramatic distance on display here provides an ironic layer to the narrative. As the observers of the conflict between the teller-of-tale's desire to solve the curious mysteries that surround Emily's life — indeed, his complicity in shaping them — and his undetective-like detachment from her crimes, readers occupy the tantalizing position of having insight into unraveling the mystery which the narrator lacks. (120–21)

The reader is thus a member of the communal "we" — party to the narrator's investigation and Jefferson's voyeuristic obsession with Miss Emily — but also apart, removed to a plane from which "insight" into and observation of the narrator's own actions and motives become possible. The reader, just like Miss Emily, Homer, and the town of Jefferson itself, becomes a crucial element in the tension between the public and the private.

10 Thus, public and private are, in the end, far from exclusive categories. And for all of its literal as well as figurative insistence on opposition and either/or structures, Faulkner's "A Rose for Emily" enacts the provocative idea of being "[o]ne of us" (796), of being both an individual

and a member of a community, both a private entity and a participant in the public sphere.

Works Cited

Faulkner, William. "A Rose for Emily." *The Norton Field Guide to Writing, with Readings*. 2nd ed. Ed. Richard Bullock and Maureen Daly Goggin. New York: Norton, 2010. 787–96. Print.

Fetterley, Judith. "A Rose for 'A Rose for Emily.' " *The Resisting Reader: A Feminist Approach to American Fiction*. Bloomington: Indiana UP, 1978. 34–45. Print.

Moore, Gene M. "Of Time and Its Mathematical Progression: Problems of Chronology in Faulkner's 'A Rose for Emily.' " *Studies in Short Fiction* 29.2 (1992): 195–204. Print.

Rodgers, Lawrence R. " 'We all said, "she will kill herself" ': The Narrator/Detective in William Faulkner's 'A Rose for Emily.' " *Clues: A Journal of Detection* 16.1 (1995): 117–29. Print.

Engaging with the Text

1. What is Willow Crystal's **THESIS**? Restate it in your own words. Read "A Rose for Emily" (on pp. 787–96) yourself. Do you agree with Crystal's analysis? Why or why not? 273–75
2. Crystal focuses on three examples of the tensions between concepts of public and private. What do these examples contribute to her **ANALYSIS**? 38–58
3. How would you characterize Crystal's **STANCE** toward Faulkner's story? Identify specific language in her essay that reveals that stance. 12–14
4. How does Crystal **SYNTHESIZE OTHER SCHOLARSHIP** on Faulkner's story in her analysis? How does she use this synthesis to support her own analysis? 406–7
5. ***For Writing.*** **ANALYZE** a literary work that intrigues you. You may base a literary analysis on your own reading and thinking about a text. 38–58

377–403

404–19

However, your analysis may be enriched by knowing what others have written about the text as well. **RESEARCH** scholarship on the literary piece to see what other scholars may have said about it. Write an essay that both presents your own analysis and also responds to what others say about the same work. You can agree with what they say, disagree, or both; the important thing is to think about what others say, and to **QUOTE**, **PARAPHRASE**, or **SUMMARIZE** their views in your text.

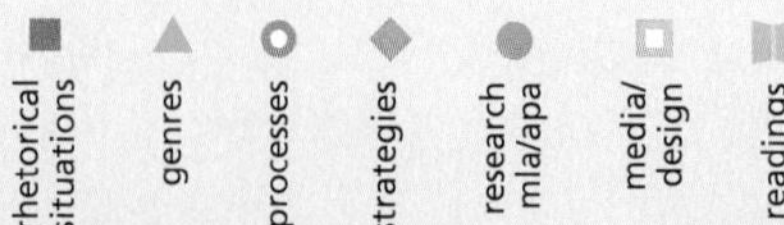

WILLIAM FAULKNER

A Rose for Emily

William Faulkner (1897–1962) is the author of twenty novels, including The Sound and the Fury *(1929),* As I Lay Dying *(1930), and* Absalom! Absalom! *(1936), as well as many short stories and six books of poetry. He received the Nobel Prize for Literature in 1949 and Pulitzer Prizes in 1954 and 1962. The story "A Rose for Emily" was first published in 1931.*

WHEN MISS EMILY GRIERSON DIED, our whole town went to her funeral: the men through a sort of respectful affection for a fallen monument, the women mostly out of curiosity to see the inside of her house, which no one save an old man-servant — a combined gardener and cook — had seen in at least ten years.

It was a big, squarish frame house that had once been white, decorated with cupolas and spires and scrolled balconies in the heavily lightsome style of the seventies,* set on what had once been our most select street. But garages and cotton gins had encroached and obliterated even the august names of that neighborhood; only Miss Emily's house was left, lifting its stubborn and coquettish decay above the cotton wagons and the gasoline pumps — an eyesore among eyesores. And now Miss Emily had gone to join the representatives of those august names where they lay in the cedar-bemused cemetery among the ranked and anonymous graves of Union and Confederate soldiers who fell at the battle of Jefferson.

Alive, Miss Emily had been a tradition, a duty, and a care; a sort of hereditary obligation upon the town, dating from that day in 1894 when Colonel Sartoris, the mayor — he who fathered the edict that no Negro woman should appear on the streets without an apron — remitted her taxes, the dispensation dating from the death of her father on into per-

---

**Seventies*: the 1870s, the decade after the Civil War (1861–65). [Editor's note] petuity. Not that Miss Emily would have accepted charity. Colonel Sartoris invented an involved tale to the effect that Miss Emily's father had loaned money to the town, which the town, as a matter of business, preferred this way of repaying. Only a man of Colonel Sartoris' generation and thought could have invented it, and only a woman could have believed it.

When the next generation, with its more modern ideas, became mayors and aldermen, this arrangement created some little dissatisfaction. On the first of the year they mailed her a tax notice. February came, and there was no reply. They wrote her a formal letter, asking her to call at the sheriff's office at her convenience. A week later the mayor wrote her himself, offering to call or to send his car for her, and received in reply a note on paper of an archaic shape, in a thin, flowing calligraphy in faded ink, to the effect that she no longer went out at all. The tax notice was also enclosed, without comment.

5 They called a special meeting of the Board of Aldermen. A deputation waited upon her, knocked at the door through which no visitor had passed since she ceased giving china-painting lessons eight or ten years earlier. They were admitted by the old Negro into a dim hall from which a stairway mounted into still more shadow. It smelled of dust and disuse — a close, dank smell. The Negro led them into the parlor. It was furnished in heavy, leather-covered furniture. When the Negro opened the blinds of one window, a faint dust rose sluggishly about their thighs, spinning with slow motes in the single sun-ray. On a tarnished gilt easel before the fireplace stood a crayon portrait of Miss Emily's father.

They rose when she entered — a small, fat woman in black, with a thin gold chain descending to her waist and vanishing into her belt, leaning on an ebony cane with a tarnished gold head. Her skeleton was small and spare; perhaps that was why what would have been merely plumpness in another was obesity in her. She looked bloated, like a body long submerged in motionless water, and of that pallid hue. Her eyes, lost in the fatty ridges of her face, looked like two small pieces of coal pressed into a lump of dough as they moved from one face to another while the visitors stated their errand.

She did not ask them to sit. She just stood in the door and listened quietly until the spokesman came to a stumbling halt. Then they could hear the invisible watch ticking at the end of the gold chain.

Her voice was dry and cold. "I have no taxes in Jefferson. Colonel Sartoris explained it to me. Perhaps one of you can gain access to the city records and satisfy yourselves."

"But we have. We are the city authorities, Miss Emily. Didn't you get a notice from the sheriff, signed by him?"

"I received a paper, yes," Miss Emily said. "Perhaps he considers 10
himself the sheriff. . . . I have no taxes in Jefferson."

"But there is nothing on the books to show that, you see. We must go by the — "

"See Colonel Sartoris. I have no taxes in Jefferson."

"But, Miss Emily — "

"See Colonel Sartoris." (Colonel Sartoris had been dead almost ten years.) "I have no taxes in Jefferson. Tobe!" The Negro appeared. "Show these gentlemen out."

II

So she vanquished them, horse and foot, just as she had vanquished 15
their fathers thirty years before about the smell. That was two years after her father's death and a short time after her sweetheart — the one we believed would marry her — had deserted her. After her father's death she went out very little; after her sweetheart went away, people hardly saw her at all. A few of the ladies had the temerity to call, but were not received, and the only sign of life about the place was the Negro man — a young man then — going in and out with a market basket.

"Just as if a man — any man — could keep a kitchen properly," the ladies said; so they were not surprised when the smell developed. It was another link between the gross, teeming world and the high and mighty Griersons.

A neighbor, a woman, complained to the mayor, Judge Stevens, eighty years old.

"But what will you have me do about it, madam?" he said.

“Why, send her word to stop it,” the woman said. “Isn't there a law?”

20 “I'm sure that won't be necessary,” Judge Stevens said. “It's probably just a snake or a rat that nigger of hers killed in the yard. I'll speak to him about it.”

The next day he received two more complaints, one from a man who came in diffident deprecation. “We really must do something about it, Judge. I'd be the last one in the world to bother Miss Emily, but we've got to do something.” That night the Board of Aldermen met — three gray-beards and one younger man, a member of the rising generation.

“It's simple enough,” he said. “Send her word to have her place cleaned up. Give her a certain time to do it in, and if she don't . . . ”

“Dammit, sir,” Judge Stevens said, “will you accuse a lady to her face of smelling bad?”

So the next night, after midnight, four men crossed Miss Emily's lawn and slunk about the house like burglars, sniffing along the base of the brickwork and at the cellar openings while one of them performed a regular sowing motion with his hand out of a sack slung from his shoulder. They broke open the cellar door and sprinkled lime there, and in all the outbuildings. As they recrossed the lawn, a window that had been dark was lighted and Miss Emily sat in it, the light behind her, and her upright torso motionless as that of an idol. They crept quietly across the lawn and into the shadow of the locusts that lined the street. After a week or two the smell went away.

25 That was when people had begun to feel really sorry for her. People in our town, remembering how old lady Wyatt, her great-aunt, had gone completely crazy at last, believed that the Griersons held themselves a little too high for what they really were. None of the young men were quite good enough for Miss Emily and such. We had long thought of them as a tableau; Miss Emily a slender figure in white in the background, her father a spraddled silhouette in the foreground, his back to her and clutching a horsewhip, the two of them framed by the back-flung front door. So when she got to be thirty and was still single, we were not pleased exactly, but vindicated; even with insanity in the family she wouldn't have turned down all of her chances if they had really materialized.

When her father died, it got about that the house was all that was left to her; and in a way, people were glad. At last they could pity Miss Emily. Being left alone, and a pauper, she had become humanized. Now she too would know the old thrill and the old despair of a penny more or less.

The day after his death all the ladies prepared to call at the house and offer condolence and aid, as is our custom. Miss Emily met them at the door, dressed as usual and with no trace of grief on her face. She told them that her father was not dead. She did that for three days, with the ministers calling on her, and the doctors, trying to persuade her to let them dispose of the body. Just as they were about to resort to law and force, she broke down, and they buried her father quickly.

We did not say she was crazy then. We believed she had to do that. We remembered all the young men her father had driven away, and we knew that with nothing left, she would have to cling to that which had robbed her, as people will.

III

She was sick for a long time. When we saw her again, her hair was cut short, making her look like a girl, with a vague resemblance to those angels in colored church windows — sort of tragic and serene.

The town had just let the contracts for paving the sidewalks, and 30
in the summer after her father's death they began to work. The construction company came with niggers and mules and machinery, and a foreman named Homer Barron, a Yankee — a big, dark, ready man, with a big voice and eyes lighter than his face. The little boys would follow in groups to hear him cuss the niggers, and the niggers singing in time to the rise and fall of picks. Pretty soon he knew everybody in town. Whenever you heard a lot of laughing anywhere about the square, Homer Barron would be in the center of the group. Presently we began to see him and Miss Emily on Sunday afternoons driving in the yellow-wheeled buggy and the matched team of bays from the livery stable.

At first we were glad that Miss Emily would have an interest, because the ladies all said, "Of course a Grierson would not think seriously of a Northerner, a day laborer." But there were still others, older people, who said that even grief could not cause a real lady to forget *noblesse oblige* — without calling it *noblesse oblige*.* They just said, "Poor Emily. Her kinsfolk should come to her." She had some kin in Alabama; but years ago her father had fallen out with them over the estate of old lady Wyatt, the crazy woman, and there was no communication between the two families. They had not even been represented at the funeral.

And as soon as the old people said, "Poor Emily," the whispering began. "Do you suppose it's really so?" they said to one another. "Of course it is. What else could . . . " This behind their hands; rustling of craned silk and satin behind jalousies† closed upon the sun of Sunday afternoon as the thin, swift clop-clop-clop of the matched team passed: "Poor Emily."

She carried her head high enough — even when we believed that she was fallen. It was as if she demanded more than ever the recognition of her dignity as the last Grierson; as if it had wanted that touch of earthiness to reaffirm her imperviousness. Like when she bought the rat poison, the arsenic. That was over a year after they had begun to say "Poor Emily," and while the two female cousins were visiting her.

"I want some poison," she said to the druggist. She was over thirty then, still a slight woman, though thinner than usual, with cold, haughty black eyes in a face the flesh of which was strained across the temples and about the eyesockets as you imagine a lighthouse-keeper's face ought to look. "I want some poison," she said.

"Yes, Miss Emily. What kind? For rats and such? I'd recom — " 35

"I want the best you have. I don't care what kind."

The druggist named several. "They'll kill anything up to an elephant. But what you want is — "

"Arsenic," Miss Emily said. "Is that a good one?"

"Is . . . arsenic? Yes ma'am. But what you want — "

**Noblesse oblige*: the traditional obligation of the nobility to treat the lower classes with respect and generosity (French). [Editor's note]

†*Jalousies*: slatted window blinds. [Editor's note]

"I want arsenic." 40

The druggist looked down at her. She looked back at him, erect, her face like a strained flag. "Why, of course," the druggist said. "If that's what you want. But the law requires you to tell what you are going to use it for."

Miss Emily just stared at him, her head tilted back in order to look him eye for eye, until he looked away and went and got the arsenic and wrapped it up. The Negro delivery boy brought her the package; the druggist didn't come back. When she opened the package at home there was written on the box, under the skull and bones: "For rats."

IV

So the next day we all said, "She will kill herself"; and we said it would be the best thing. When she had first begun to be seen with Homer Barron, we had said, "She will marry him." Then we said, "She will persuade him yet," because Homer himself had remarked — he liked men, and it was known that he drank with the younger men in the Elk's Club — that he was not a marrying man. Later we said, "Poor Emily," behind the jalousies as they passed on Sunday afternoon in the glittering buggy, Miss Emily with her head high and Homer Barron with his hat cocked and a cigar in his teeth, reins and whip in a yellow glove.

Then some of the ladies began to say that it was a disgrace to the town and a bad example to the young people. The men did not want to interfere, but at last the ladies forced the Baptist minister — Miss Emily's people were Episcopal — to call upon her. He would never divulge what happened during that interview, but he refused to go back again. The next Sunday they again drove about the streets, and the following day the minister's wife wrote to Miss Emily's relations in Alabama.

So she had blood-kin under her roof again and we sat back to watch 45
developments. At first nothing happened. Then we were sure that they were to be married. We learned that Miss Emily had been to the jeweler's and ordered a man's toilet set in silver, with the letters H. B. on each piece. Two days later we learned that she had bought a complete outfit of men's clothing, including a nightshirt, and we said, "They are

married." We were really glad. We were glad because the two female cousins were even more Grierson than Miss Emily had ever been.

So we were not surprised when Homer Barron — the streets had been finished some time since — was gone. We were a little disappointed that there was not a public blowing-off, but we believed that he had gone on to prepare for Miss Emily's coming, or to give her a chance to get rid of the cousins. (By that time it was a cabal, and we were all Miss Emily's allies to help circumvent the cousins.) Sure enough, after another week they departed. And, as we had expected all along, within three days Homer Barron was back in town. A neighbor saw the Negro man admit him at the kitchen door at dusk one evening.

And that was the last we saw of Homer Barron. And of Miss Emily for some time. The Negro man went in and out with the market basket, but the front door remained closed. Now and then we would see her at a window for a moment, as the men did that night when they sprinkled the lime, but for almost six months she did not appear on the streets. Then we knew that this was to be expected too; as if that quality of her father which had thwarted her woman's life so many times had been too virulent and too furious to die.

When we next saw Miss Emily, she had grown fat and her hair was turning gray. During the next few years it grew grayer and grayer until it attained an even pepper-and-salt iron-gray, when it ceased turning. Up to the day of her death at seventy-four it was still that vigorous iron-gray, like the hair of an active man.

From that time on her front door remained closed, save for a period of six or seven years, when she was about forty, during which she gave lessons in china-painting. She fitted up a studio in one of the downstairs rooms, where the daughters and grand-daughters of Colonel Sartoris' contemporaries were sent to her with the same regularity and in the same spirit that they were sent on Sundays with a twenty-five cent piece for the collection plate. Meanwhile her taxes had been remitted.

Then the newer generation became the backbone and the spirit of 50
the town, and the painting pupils grew up and fell away and did not send their children to her with boxes of color and tedious brushes and pictures cut from the ladies' magazines. The front door closed upon the

last one and remained closed for good. When the town got free postal delivery Miss Emily alone refused to let them fasten the metal numbers above her door and attach a mailbox to it. She would not listen to them.

Daily, monthly, yearly we watched the Negro grow grayer and more stooped, going in and out with the market basket. Each December we sent her a tax notice, which would be returned by the post office a week later, unclaimed. Now and then we would see her in one of the downstairs windows — she had evidently shut up the top floor of the house — like the carven torso of an idol in a niche, looking or not looking at us, we could never tell which. Thus she passed from generation to generation — dear, inescapable, impervious, tranquil, and perverse.

And so she died. Fell ill in the house filled with dust and shadows, with only a doddering Negro man to wait on her. We did not even know she was sick; we had long since given up trying to get any information from the Negro. He talked to no one, probably not even to her, for his voice had grown harsh and rusty, as if from disuse.

She died in one of the downstairs rooms, in a heavy walnut bed with a curtain, her gray head propped on a pillow yellow and moldy with age and lack of sunlight.

V

The Negro met the first of the ladies at the front door and let them in, with their hushed, sibilant voices and their quick, curious glances, and then he disappeared. He walked right through the house and out the back and was not seen again.

The two female cousins came at once. They held the funeral on the 55
second day, with the town coming to look at Miss Emily beneath a mass of bought flowers, with the crayon face of her father musing profoundly above the bier and the ladies sibilant and macabre; and the very old men — some in their brushed Confederate uniforms — on the porch and the lawn, talking of Miss Emily as if she had been a contemporary of theirs, believing that they had danced with her and courted her perhaps, confusing time with its mathematical progression, as the old do, to whom all the past is not a diminishing road, but, instead, a huge

meadow which no winter ever quite touches, divided from them now by the narrow bottleneck of the most recent decade of years.

Already we knew that there was one room in that region above stairs which no one had seen in forty years, and which would have to be forced. They waited until Miss Emily was decently in the ground before they opened it.

The violence of breaking down the door seemed to fill this room with pervading dust. A thin, acrid pall as of the tomb seemed to lie everywhere upon this room decked and furnished as for a bridal: upon the valance curtains of faded rose color, upon the rose-shaded lights, upon the dressing table, upon the delicate array of crystal and the man's toilet things backed with tarnished silver, silver so tarnished that the monogram was obscured. Among them lay a collar and tie, as if they had just been removed, which, lifted, left upon the surface a pale crescent in the dust. Upon a chair hung the suit, carefully folded; beneath it the two mute shoes and the discarded socks.

The man himself lay in the bed.

For a long while we just stood there, looking down at the profound and fleshless grin. The body had apparently once lain in the attitude of an embrace, but now the long sleep that outlasts love, that conquers even the grimace of love, had cuckolded him. What was left of him, rotted beneath what was left of the nightshirt, had become inextricable from the bed in which he lay; and upon him and upon the pillow beside him lay that even coating of the patient and biding dust.

Then we noticed that in the second pillow was the indentation of 60
a head. One of us lifted something from it, and leaning forward, that faint and invisible dust dry and acrid in the nostrils, we saw a long strand of iron-gray hair.

RITA DOVE

The First Book

Rita Dove is a professor of English at the University of Virginia and a former Poet Laureate of the United States. She is the author of nine books of poetry, including Thomas and Beulah *(1986) and* American Smooth *(2004), as well as a book of short stories, a novel, a book of essays, and a play. She has received several awards for her writing, including the Pulitzer Prize in Poetry and the National Humanities Medal. Her poem "The First Book" appears in* On the Bus with Rosa Parks *(1999).*

Open it.

Go ahead, it won't bite.
Well . . . maybe a little.

More a nip, like. A tingle.
It's pleasurable, really.

You see, it keeps on opening.
You may fall in.

Sure, it's hard to get started;
remember learning to use

knife and fork? Dig in:
You'll never reach bottom.

It's not like it's the end of the world —
just the world as you think

you know it.

JIMMY SANTIAGO BACA
Count-time

Poet and prose writer Jimmy Santiago Baca is the author of several volumes of poetry, including Black Mesa Poems *(1995) and* Immigrants in Our Own Land *(1979), from which this poem is taken. He has also written a memoir, a screenplay, a short-story collection, and an essay collection, and has received several awards for his writing, including an American Book Award and a Pushcart Prize. In addition, Baca is founder of Cedar Tree, Inc., a nonprofit organization that conducts writing workshops in prisons, schools for at-risk youth, and elsewhere. For a glimpse into this poet's life,* *see p. 838.*

Everybody to sleep the guard symbolizes
on his late night tour of the tombs.
When he leaves, after counting still bodies
wrapped in white sheets, when he goes,

the bodies slowly move, in solitary ritual,
counting lost days, mounting memories,
numbering like sand grains
the winds drag over high mountains
to their lonely deaths; like elephants
they go bury themselves
under dreamlike waterfalls,
in the silence.

LANGSTON HUGHES

Theme for English B

Langston Hughes (1902–1967) was a central player in the Harlem Renaissance in the 1920s and 1930s. He penned some sixty books, including novels, short-story collections, nonfiction and autobiographical works, and several volumes of poetry. Among the best-known volumes of poetry is Montage of a Dream Deferred *(1951), in which the following poem was first published. One of the dominant voices of the time speaking out on race issues, Hughes earned critical acclaim for his realistic portrayal of African American characters, such as the speaker in the following poem.*

The instructor said,

Go home and write
a page tonight.
And let that page come out of you —
Then, it will be true.

I wonder if it's that simple?
I am twenty-two, colored, born in Winston-Salem.
I went to school there, then Durham,* then here
to this college† on the hill above Harlem.
I am the only colored student in my class.
The steps from the hill lead down into Harlem,
through a park, then I cross St. Nicholas,
Eighth Avenue, Seventh, and I come to the Y,
the Harlem Branch Y, where I take the elevator
up to my room, sit down, and write this page:

**Winston-Salem, Durham*: cities in North Carolina.
†*This college*: City College of the City University of New York (CCNY).

It's not easy to know what is true for you or me
at twenty-two, my age. But I guess I'm what
I feel and see and hear, Harlem, I hear you:
hear you, hear me — we two — you, me, talk on this page.
(I hear New York, too.) Me — who?
Well, I like to eat, sleep, drink, and be in love.
I like to work, read, learn, and understand life.
I like a pipe for a Christmas present,
or records — Bessie, bop,* or Bach.
I guess being colored doesn't make me *not* like
the same things other folks like who are other races.
So will my page be colored that I write?
Being me, it will not be white.
But it will be
a part of you, instructor.
You are white —
yet a part of me, as I am a part of you.
That's American.
Sometimes perhaps you don't want to be a part of me.
Nor do I often want to be a part of you.
But we are, that's true!
I guess you learn from me —
although you're older — and white —
and somewhat more free.

This is my page for English B.

**Bop*: a type of fast-paced jazz music that became popular in the 1940s. *Bessie*: American blues singer Bessie Smith (1898–1937).

Memoirs 60

See also:

RICK BRAGG
All Over But the Shoutin' 153

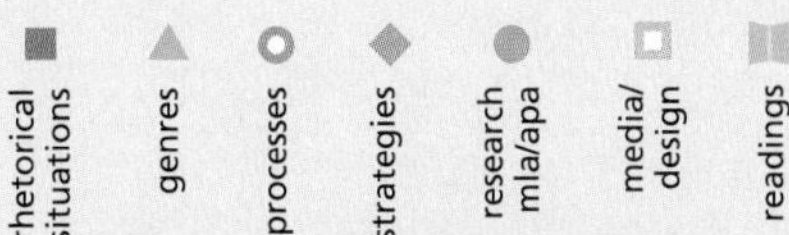

DAVID SEDARIS

Us and Them

Humorist David Sedaris is the author of several collections of personal essays, including Naked *(1997),* Me Talk Pretty One Day *(2000), and* When You Are Engulfed in Flames *(2008). He is a frequent commentator on National Public Radio and a playwright whose works include* Santa-Land Diaries & Seasons Greetings: 2 Plays *(1998), as well as works coauthored with his sister, Amy Sedaris. In 2001,* Time *magazine named Sedaris "Humorist of the Year." The following essay comes from Sedaris's book-length memoir* Dress Your Family in Corduroy and Denim *(2004).*

WHEN MY FAMILY FIRST MOVED to North Carolina, we lived in a rented house three blocks from the school where I would begin the third grade. My mother made friends with one of the neighbors, but one seemed enough for her. Within a year we would move again and, as she explained, there wasn't much point in getting too close to people we would have to say good-bye to. Our next house was less than a mile away, and the short journey would hardly merit tears or even good-byes, for that matter. It was more of a "see you later" situation, but still I adopted my mother's attitude, as it allowed me to pretend that not making friends was a conscious choice. I could if I wanted to. It just wasn't the right time.

Back in New York State, we had lived in the country, with no sidewalks or streetlights; you could leave the house and still be alone. But here, when you looked out the window, you saw other houses, and people inside those houses. I hoped that in walking around after dark I might witness a murder, but for the most part our neighbors just sat in their living rooms, watching TV. The only place that seemed truly different was owned by a man named Mr. Tomkey, who did not believe in television. This was told to us by our mother's friend, who dropped by one afternoon with a basketful of okra. The woman did not editorialize — rather, she just presented her information, leaving her listener to make of it what she might. Had my mother said, "That's the craziest

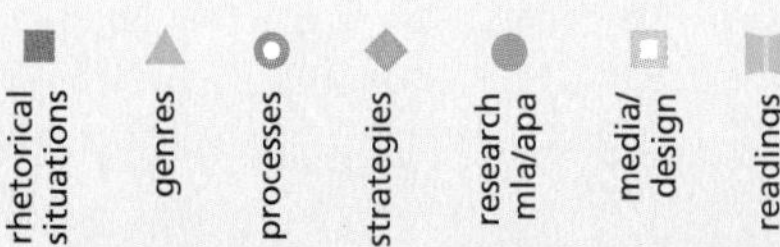

thing I've ever heard in my life," I assume that the friend would have agreed, and had she said, "Three cheers for Mr. Tomkey," the friend likely would have agreed as well. It was a kind of test, as was the okra.

To say that you did not believe in television was different from saying that you did not care for it. Belief implied that television had a master plan and that you were against it. It also suggested that you thought too much. When my mother reported that Mr. Tomkey did not believe in television, my father said, "Well, good for him. I don't know that I believe in it, either."

"That's exactly how I feel," my mother said, and then my parents watched the news, and whatever came on after the news.

Word spread that Mr. Tomkey did not own a television, and you began 5
hearing that while this was all very well and good, it was unfair of him to inflict his beliefs upon others, specifically his innocent wife and children. It was speculated that just as the blind man develops a keener sense of hearing, the family must somehow compensate for their loss. "Maybe they read," my mother's friend said. "Maybe they listen to the radio, but you can bet your boots they're doing *something*."

I wanted to know what this something was, and so I began peering through the Tomkeys' windows. During the day I'd stand across the street from their house, acting as though I were waiting for someone, and at night, when the view was better and I had less chance of being discovered, I would creep into their yard and hide in the bushes beside their fence.

Because they had no TV, the Tomkeys were forced to talk during dinner. They had no idea how puny their lives were, and so they were not ashamed that a camera would have found them uninteresting. They did not know what attractive was or what dinner was supposed to look like or even what time people were supposed to eat. Sometimes they wouldn't sit down until eight o'clock, long after everyone else had finished doing the dishes. During the meal, Mr. Tomkey would occasionally pound the table and point at his children with a fork, but the moment he finished, everyone would start laughing. I got the idea that he was imitating someone else, and wondered if he spied on us while we were eating.

When fall arrived and school began, I saw the Tomkey children marching up the hill with paper sacks in their hands. The son was one grade lower than me, and the daughter was one grade higher. We never spoke, but I'd pass them in the halls from time to time and attempt to view the world through their eyes. What must it be like to be so ignorant and alone? Could a normal person even imagine it? Staring at an Elmer Fudd lunch box, I tried to divorce myself from everything I already knew: Elmer's inability to pronounce the letter *r*, his constant pursuit of an intelligent and considerably more famous rabbit. I tried to think of him as just a drawing, but it was impossible to separate him from his celebrity.

One day in class a boy named William began to write the wrong answer on the blackboard, and our teacher flailed her arms, saying, "Warning, Will. Danger, danger." Her voice was synthetic and void of emotion, and we laughed, knowing that she was imitating the robot in a weekly show about a family who lived in outer space. The Tomkeys, though, would have thought she was having a heart attack. It occurred to me that they needed a guide, someone who could accompany them through the course of an average day and point out all the things they were unable to understand. I could have done it on weekends, but friendship would have taken away their mystery and interfered with the good feeling I got from pitying them. So I kept my distance.

In early October the Tomkeys bought a boat, and everyone seemed 10
greatly relieved, especially my mother's friend, who noted that the motor was definitely secondhand. It was reported that Mr. Tomkey's father-in-law owned a house on the lake and had invited the family to use it whenever they liked. This explained why they were gone all weekend, but it did not make their absences any easier to bear. I felt as if my favorite show had been canceled.

Halloween fell on a Saturday that year, and by the time my mother took us to the store, all the good costumes were gone. My sisters dressed as witches and I went as a hobo. I'd looked forward to going in disguise to the Tomkey's door, but they were off at the lake, and their house was dark. Before leaving, they had left a coffee can full of gumdrops on the

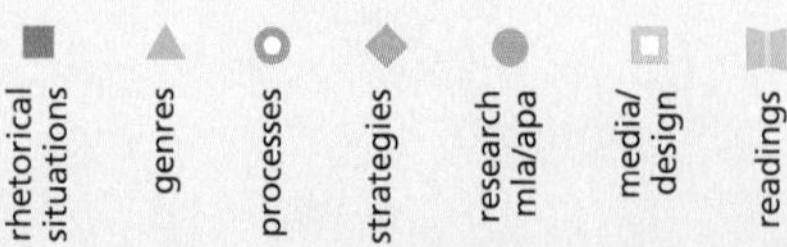

front porch, alongside a sign reading DON'T BE GREEDY. In terms of Halloween candy, individual gumdrops were just about as low as you could get. This was evidenced by the large number of them floating in an adjacent dog bowl. It was disgusting to think that this was what a gumdrop might look like in your stomach, and it was insulting to be told not to take too much of something you didn't really want in the first place. "Who do these Tomkeys think they are?" my sister Lisa said.

The night after Halloween, we were sitting around watching TV when the doorbell rang. Visitors were infrequent at our house, so while my father stayed behind, my mother, sisters, and I ran downstairs in a group, opening the door to discover the entire Tomkey family on our front stoop. The parents looked as they always had, but the son and daughter were dressed in costumes — she as a ballerina and he as some kind of a rodent with terry-cloth ears and a tail made from what looked to be an extension cord. It seemed they had spent the previous evening isolated at the lake and had missed the opportunity to observe Halloween. "So, well, I guess we're trick-or-treating *now,* if that's okay," Mr. Tomkey said.

I attributed their behavior to the fact that they didn't have a TV, but television didn't teach you everything. Asking for candy on Halloween was called trick-or-treating, but asking for candy on November first was called begging, and it made people uncomfortable. This was one of the things you were supposed to learn simply by being alive, and it angered me that the Tomkeys did not understand it.

"Why of course it's not too late," my mother said. "Kids, why don't you . . . run and get . . . the candy."

"But the candy is gone," my sister Gretchen said. "You gave it away 15
last night."

"Not *that* candy," my mother said. "The other candy. Why don't you run and go get it?"

"You mean *our* candy?" Lisa said. "The candy that we *earned*?"

This was exactly what our mother was talking about, but she didn't want to say this in front of the Tomkeys. In order to spare their feelings, she wanted them to believe that we always kept a bucket of candy lying around the house, just waiting for someone to knock on the door and ask for it. "Go on, now," she said. "Hurry up."

My room was situated right off the foyer, and if the Tomkeys had looked in that direction, they could have seen my bed and the brown paper bag marked MY CANDY. KEEP OUT. I didn't want them to know how much I had, and so I went into my room and shut the door behind me. Then I closed the curtains and emptied my bag onto the bed, searching for whatever was the crummiest. All my life chocolate has made me ill. I don't know if I'm allergic or what, but even the smallest amount leaves me with a blinding headache. Eventually, I learned to stay away from it, but as a child I refused to be left out. The brownies were eaten, and when the pounding began I would blame the grape juice or my mother's cigarette smoke or the tightness of my glasses — anything but the chocolate. My candy bars were poison but they were brand-name, and so I put them in pile no. 1, which definitely would not go to the Tomkeys.

Out in the hallway I could hear my mother straining for something 20
to talk about. "A boat!" she said. "That sounds marvelous. Can you just drive it right into the water?"

"Actually, we have a trailer," Mr. Tomkey said. "So what we do is back it into the lake."

"Oh, a trailer. What kind is it?"

"Well, it's a *boat* trailer," Mr. Tomkey said.

"Right, but is it wooden, or you know . . . I guess what I'm asking is what *style* trailer do you have?"

Behind my mother's words were two messages. The first and most 25
obvious was "Yes, I am talking about boat trailers, but also I am dying." The second, meant only for my sisters and me, was "If you do not immediately step forward with that candy, you will never again experience freedom, happiness, or the possibility of my warm embrace."

I knew that it was just a matter of time before she came into my room and started collecting the candy herself, grabbing indiscriminately, with no regard to my rating system. Had I been thinking straight, I would have hidden the most valuable items in my dresser drawer, but instead, panicked by the thought of her hand on my doorknob, I tore off the wrappers and began cramming the candy bars into my mouth, desperately, like someone in a contest. Most were miniature, which made them easier to accommodate, but still there was only so much room, and it was hard to chew and fit more in at the same time. The headache began immediately, and I chalked it up to tension.

My mother told the Tomkeys she needed to check on something, and then she opened the door and stuck her head inside my room. "What the *hell* are you doing?" she whispered, but my mouth was too full to answer. "I'll just be a moment," she called, and as she closed the door behind her and moved toward my bed, I began breaking the wax lips and candy necklaces pulled from pile no. 2. These were the second-best things I had received, and while it hurt to destroy them, it would have hurt even more to give them away. I had just started to mutilate a miniature box of Red Hots when my mother pried them from my hands, accidentally finishing the job for me. BB-size pellets clattered onto the floor, and as I followed them with my eyes, she snatched up a roll of Necco wafers.

"Not those," I pleaded, but rather than words, my mouth expelled chocolate, chewed chocolate, which fell onto the sleeve of her sweater. "Not those. Not those."

She shook her arm, and the mound of chocolate dropped like a horrible turd upon my bedspread. "You should look at yourself," she said. "I mean, *really* look at yourself."

Along with the Necco wafers she took several Tootsie pops and half 30
a dozen caramels wrapped in cellophane. I heard her apologize to the Tomkeys for her absence, and then I heard my candy hitting the bottom of their bags.

"What do you say?" Mrs. Tomkey asked.

And the children answered, "Thank you."

While I was in trouble for not bringing my candy sooner, my sisters were in more trouble for not bringing theirs at all. We spent the early part of the evening in our rooms, then one by one we eased our way back upstairs, and joined our parents in front of the TV. I was the last to arrive, and took a seat on the floor beside the sofa. The show was a Western, and even if my head had not been throbbing, I doubt I would have had the wherewithal to follow it. A posse of outlaws crested a rocky hilltop, squinting at a flurry of dust advancing from the horizon, and I thought again of the Tomkeys and of how alone and out of place they had looked in their dopey costumes. "What was up with that kid's tail?" I asked.

"Shhhh," my family said.

For months I had protected and watched over these people, but now, 35
with one stupid act, they had turned my pity into something hard and ugly. The shift wasn't gradual, but immediate, and it provoked an uncomfortable feeling of loss. We hadn't been friends, the Tomkeys and I, but still I had given them the gift of my curiosity. Wondering about the Tomkey family had made me feel generous, but now I would have to shift gears and find pleasure in hating them. The only alternative was to do as my mother had instructed and take a good look at myself. This was an old trick, designed to turn one's hatred inward, and while I was determined not to fall for it, it was hard to shake the mental picture snapped by her suggestion: here is a boy sitting on a bed, his mouth smeared with chocolate. He's a human being, but also he's a pig, surrounded by trash and gorging himself so that others may be denied. Were this the only image in the world, you'd be forced to give it your full attention, but fortunately there were others. This stagecoach, for instance, coming round the bend with a cargo of gold. This shiny new Mustang convertible. This teenage girl, her hair a beautiful mane, sipping Pepsi through a straw, one picture after another, on and on until the news, and whatever came on after the news.

Engaging with the Text

272–73

1. David Sedaris **TITLES** his essay "Us and Them." Whom does this title refer to? With whom are we meant to sympathize — "us" or "them"? How do you know?

157

2. Successful memoirs tell **A GOOD STORY.** Do you think "Us and Them" meets that requirement? Why or why not? Refer to the text in your response.

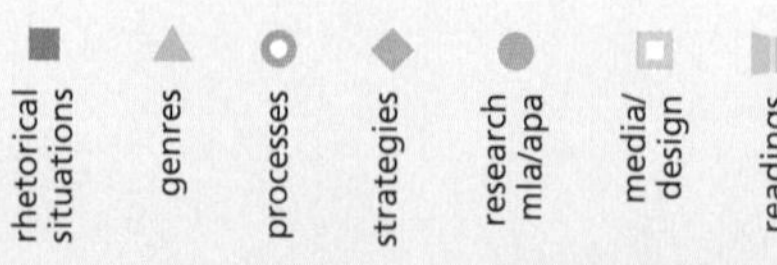

3. Sedaris describes two handwritten signs from Halloween night. The first is attached to a "coffee can full of gumdrops" telling trick or treaters "DON'T BE GREEDY." The second graces young Sedaris's bag of candy: "MY CANDY. KEEP OUT." What significance do these two signs have in the story? What do they tell us about Sedaris?
4. How would you characterize Sedaris's **STANCE**? What specific passages indicate his attitude about the events he recalls? 12–14
5. *For Writing.* Recall a time when a person or event taught you something about yourself, something that perhaps you could not fully understand until now. Write a **MEMOIR** that describes the person or narrates the event. Include **VIVID DETAIL** and be sure to make clear what **SIGNIFICANCE** the person or event had in your life. 153–60 157 157–58

ALBERTO ÁLVARO RÍOS

The March of the Altar Boy Army

Alberto Álvaro Ríos is an English professor at Arizona State University, where he teaches creative writing. A highly acclaimed writer, Ríos is author of eight books of poetry and three collections of short stories. The following selection is from his memoir Capirotada: A Nogales Memoir *(1999), which recounts his experience growing up Catholic in the Mexican-American border town of Nogales, Arizona. His title —* Capirotada *— is the name of a common Mexican bread pudding made with apples, raisins, and cinnamon that is traditionally eaten during Lent.*

WHEN I WAS GROWING UP IN NOGALES we lived right behind the Catholic church, on Rodriguez Street, on a small hill. A curious thing about my mother, having come from England, is that she was Catholic, which was something of a rarity then in that Protestant country. But she didn't move behind the church on purpose. Rather than religious conviction, no matter how fervent, it turned out to be on account of the Saint of Affordable Housing that we ended up living there.

The Catholic church in Nogales in the Fifties used to do an odd thing, which they have kept up to this day. They would send old Irish priests there to retire, even though the town was maybe 90 percent Spanish-speaking—which as kids we thought was great because, when we had to go to confession, we waited and we went straight for one of the Irish priests, so that we could give our confessions in Spanish, which of course they didn't understand.

We had this confession thing pegged, we thought, but they thought they had this thing pegged, too. They had something like a stop-watch method: How long did you talk? That's how bad you were.

But we got that figured out, so we went into the confessional and talked fast. You could go in there and say the worst thing, forgive me Father, *¡maté a alguien!*, forgive me Father, I killed someone, but say it fast and like it was nothing and you were out of there sometimes with only a Hail—not even a whole Hail Mary. You were out of

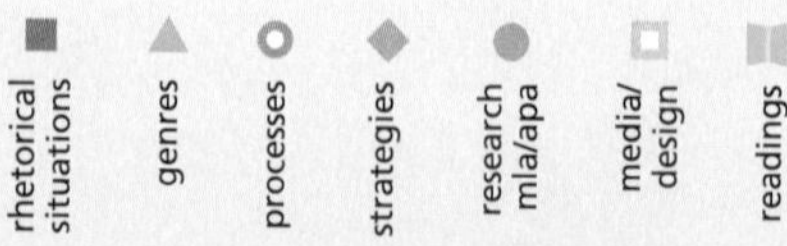

there. We had this routine down pat, and it was a nice, good, happy relationship.

. . .

The priests in this town finally did just fine. They did their jobs as priests, but as men they were in true exile, in true retirement. This part about the Irish priests was not finally very funny. They had no one to talk to, even after they learned Spanish enough to know what was what. Learning a language is only learning words, which are not themselves the experiences they represent. And even when they later took in more about this place and its people, what they learned was secondhand information. 5

So, whether as a kid I liked it or not, it made some sense that my mother started inviting them over. They could talk to my mother. They shared some sense of exile, and some commonness of culture, and to talk was a happy thing. A happy thing—except for me. And especially the first time she invited them over.

. . .

My brother and I sat by the window, which was our place. We essentially lived in a building with four small, two-room apartments, which is there to this day. To make things fit, everything was combined. Though there were some partial dividing walls, there wasn't really anything like a dining room and a living room or anything else. Things just went where they fit best. A chair was just a chair—never a dining room chair or a bedroom chair. It was also a stool and a toy and a desk.

As I looked out the window on this Saturday afternoon and early dusk, I watched as two of the priests came out of the church still dressed in their cassocks. They looked like they were wearing dresses, but nobody said so. It's that confessions had gone long that day, and the priests hadn't had time to change.

I watched them walk toward our building, and started to say something to my mother, but she shushed me. When I was sure it was our building they were aiming for, I started to say "I think something is wrong with Doña Cuquita, she's sick, it's something." Doña Cuquita was our downstairs neighbor. She was old, and not doing too well. And I knew why priests came to people's houses.

But my mother said to stop it, that there was nothing wrong with 10
Doña Cuquita. I heard them coming up the steps, and thought it was our neighbors next door, then, but my mother said no. And then they knocked. On our door.

I looked around at all of us. Nobody looked like they were about to die.

. . .

She welcomed them in, and that was that. Who would know that letting them in was to change my life.

One particular priest came over regularly, and a running routine developed between us. The first time he came over, my mother said, be nice, shake hands with Father So-and-So. Of course, So-and-So was not his name, but that was another thing.

I've asked my mother, and she's told me, but I can't get it quite right. She says something like Father McCaughy, but just try pronouncing that. Add to it my mother's English spin, and I can't even begin to spell it. She says something like "Father McCargy." All my life she added things to words like someone walking into the kitchen might put some more salt in the soup. I grew up thinking my grandmother was called "Nan-nan," when really what my mother was saying was "Nana."

On the other hand, and just to keep things interesting, she also left 15
sounds out. I was a junior in high school reading a book in class, which is what the teacher had us do when he was exasperated beyond all measure, which was most of the time, and which meant I got a lot of reading done. Well, I was reading a book and suddenly I burst out laughing.

Everybody looked at me, but I couldn't explain. It was mine. I had read a word, which had an apostrophe in it, but at the beginning, signifying that something was left out. The word was " 'ell," and meant "hell." My mother must have said "bloody 'ell" every day of my life, and the whole time I thought it was simply some perverse comment on the letter "L," which was my only reference for that sound. After all those years, however, I could see now that it wasn't the letter "L" at all. Not at all.

All of this means that calling the priest Father So-and-So is the best I can do. Those who spoke only Spanish had a different name for him

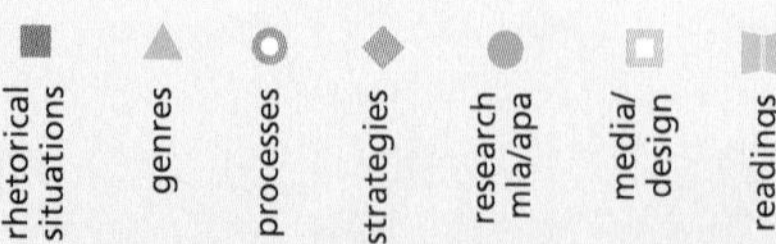

altogether, but stemming from the same trouble with pronunciation. He was Padre Fulano, "Fulano" being the equivalent of "So-and-So." It comes across as something like, that priest over there, you know who I mean. Father Whatever-that-name-is. There was no disrespect in this, and no doubt the priests had just as much trouble remembering our names. The lucky thing for us was, when you met the priest, all you had to say was "Father." That worked out all right for us. The priests, I think, stuck with "my child" for everybody.

Well, be nice, shake hands with Father So-and-So, my mother said.

I was a nice kid. I went right up and put my hand out. He put his hand up, too, but went right past mine and headed straight for my cheek, pinching it hard and lifting me in the process—he had strong fingers—and saying, what a handsome young man you are, while my feet dangled in the air.

The next week arrives, and he comes to dinner again, my mother 20
says be nice, shake hands with Father So-and-So, and so, okay, I put my hand up again. But this time, I bury my face in the side of my arm so there's no way he can get it. He puts his hand up too, just like the last time, and just like the last time it goes right past mine again, but this time, instead of going for the cheek, he goes for the hair, giving it a good, strong, memorable mussing.

This went on and on, and we developed this relationship where, whenever he came over, I'd start circling the room in one direction and he'd move around in the other. I would later see this in wrestling matches on television, which my mother loved to watch, and as the wrestlers would circle each other with menacing intent, I'd think, hey, I invented this.

But one day he came over, and instead of circling around, he just stood there, and put his hands on his hips. He was quiet for a minute, and I just watched. He looked at me, carefully, up and down, and said, "So, then. I think it's time." And he said it in an Irish accent, which made it sound different, and even scarier.

Well, I was still quite young, a little kid, and a priest standing there looking ominously at you and saying "it's time" was pretty scary. It doesn't matter what kind of accent he has.

"What a fine, young altar boy you'd make."

Oh no. Busted. Life as I knew it, I was sure, had come to an end. 25 Altar boy. I knew what altar boys did. I mean, they probably changed their underwear, and took baths. I didn't really know. But they looked shiny up there on the altar. I didn't want any of that—who would—but I didn't know what to do.

I just politely, because I was a nice kid, tried to summon up this "no thank you, Father," but before I could even come close to getting it out my mother jumped right in and said, "of course, of course, he'd love to, Father, anything you say."

And so I was drafted into the Altar Boy Army. If you've been an altar boy, you know that being up on the altar, well that's about five seconds of what you do. The rest of it is, clean the church, and that's what we did, clean the church. It's like you buy five hundred brooms, bring in a bunch of altar boys, and say, that looks like a match. We cleaned, and we cleaned. And we cleaned again.

I really was too young. I learned a lot, though, maybe more than my share. I didn't learn probably what altar boys should be learning in the way they should be learning it, but in the big picture I think I was all right. Something I particularly remember is carrying a very large votive candle one day, the mega-mortal sin size. It was a big, and red, and heavy candle, too much for a little kid. I was walking in, and I tripped in the doorway. The candle fell onto the ground and it broke. But I didn't look down. I looked up.

Because the noise that came out of that candle in that church, that large, cavernous church, was huge—this was my first experience with an echo chamber. And that noise—kapow, wow, wow, wow, ow—it wouldn't stop. That noise is still in the church. It waits for me, every time I come back.

I remember thinking, well, that's kind of neat. And the next thing 30 I did—I knew the priest wasn't there—was the most courageous act I could have concocted at that moment, the most illegal thing I could do. I looked around, to make sure the coast was clear, and I went, "HEY!"

Hey, ey, ey ey. That noise went around and around. You're not supposed to yell in a church, I think, I don't know. It's what I thought at

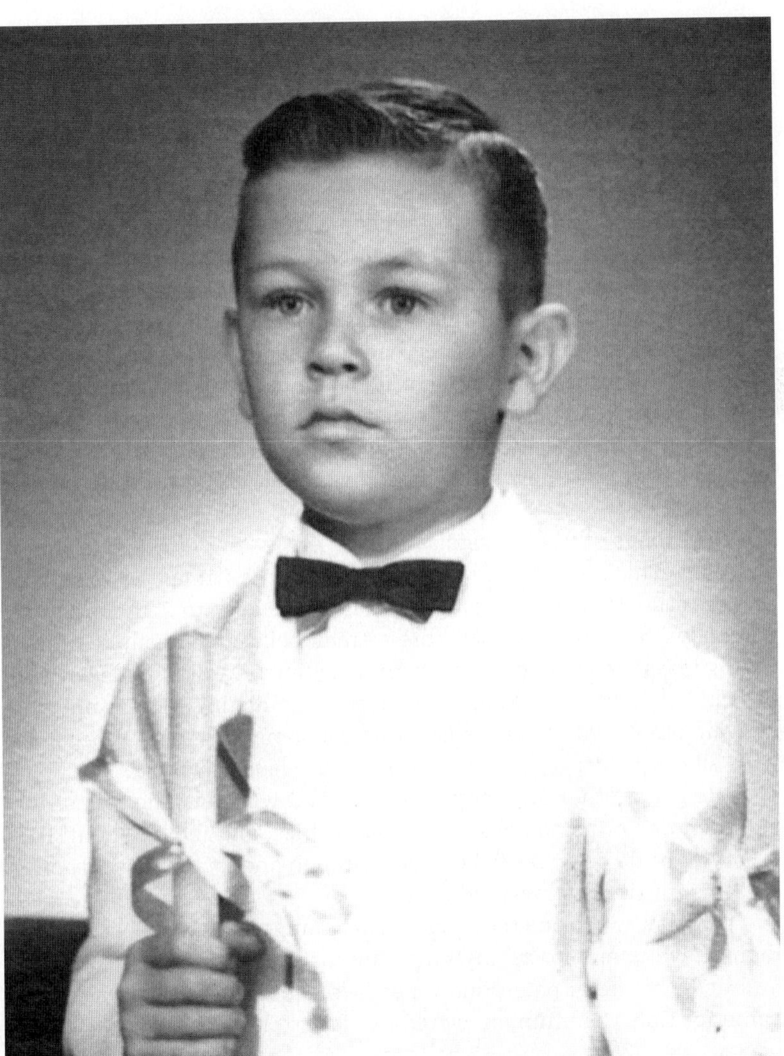

Me in my first communion photograph. If you grew up in Nogales, sooner or later, for one event or another, you had your photograph taken at Tessar's in Nogales, Sonora. That way, you always looked good at least once in your life.

the time. You can't yell, but I yelled. And the noise going around, I thought well that was all right, and I felt pretty good.

I think back now and that was right. It was some way of feeling bigger. It was a big sound that came out of me. It felt good. I remember going back to my friend Sergio, another altar boy who was always telling me things to do in church, and I told him what I had done.

Oh that's nothing, he said, that's nothing. Come over here. And he took me over to the rack of little *manda* candles, which are promise candles. When you make a promise, you light a *manda* candle, at least in the Mexican churches. But the candles all burn at different rates, and that's what was important. They had big candle snuffers lying next to them, and he picked one up and said, listen to this: "do do do be, do do do be," which was a little musical scale sound he made by tapping the glass rims of the candles with the snuffer, from low to high and back down, jazzlike. He knew just which ones to hit, and got a little rhythm going, too.

Hey, that's all right, I said.

Wait. That's not all. He looked at me with a smile. We went back into the sacristy, into the storage area. If you've been to Catholic church, you know that altar boys have these small bells, and a couple of times during mass the altar boy rings them. Ting ting ting. But a little boy with bells in his hands, who's supposed to go ting ting ting—That's not what he wants to do with those bells. So we got some more sets of bells, and with all of them together we went KA-CHING CHING CHING.

We got another altar boy to join us and we spent the rest of that summer, one of us on bells, Sergio on candles, and me on Shout! HEY, ching, do be do be do be do be. It was a rough and loud but sturdy offering, this music, this invented prayer.

My job was the one they gave to the youngest altar boy because you didn't have to memorize anything. You just followed the priest around and held the metal paten under people's chins so the host,* as people came for Holy Communion, would not fall to the ground.

---

*Host: Eucharist bread, a small thin wafer that represents Christ's body during Holy Communion. *Paten*: a small disk made from a precious metal, typically silver or gold, that is used in a Catholic mass to hold the host. [Editor's note]

The only other thing you need to know is, like with my first experience with an echo chamber, this was my first experience with a carpet. We didn't have any money, and so didn't have any carpets in our house, which wasn't a house anyway. It was an apartment behind the church.

My friend Sergio taught me a real interesting thing about carpets. He said, you know, if you rub your foot a little bit hard along a carpet, you can produce . . . well, I will simply say that I was about to move from music to physics.

. . .

To keep Christ from falling, I held the metal plate under chins, while on the thick red carpet of the altar I dragged my feet and waited for the precise moment: Plate to chin I delivered without expression the Holy Electric Shock!—the kind that produces a really large swallowing, and makes people think. I thought of it as justice.

But on other Sundays the first in my eyes was different, my mission somehow changed. I would hold the metal plate a little too hard against those certain, same, nervous chins, and I, I would look with authority down the tops of white dresses.

Well, I did it once, anyway. And afterward, I went running back to Sergio to tell him what I had done.

"I did it," I said, "I did it, I looked down Mrs. So-and-So's dress"—there was no relation to the priest—"I looked down Mrs. So-and-So's dress." I said it with great bravado, and I did it, but the truth is I wasn't so sure why.

. . . It was Sergio who had told me how I had the best job in church.

"You get to look down all the dresses," he had said. But he hadn't told me how come. I pretended it was great and said stuff and acted tough, but the truth was it would be a couple of years before I even heard the phrase "birds and bees."

That's why they gave this job to the youngest altar boy, and I really was too young, if only at first. Father So-and-So had done this, truthfully, as a favor to my mother, not because I was trained or ready or had any particular aptitude for the job. It was all right, I think. I didn't think so then, but it was all right, and got better. And I did start to understand about things, enough to know better than to do everything Sergio told me to. Mostly.

Engaging with the Text

1. Alberto Álvaro Ríos describes the Irish priests who served the predominantly Spanish parish of Nogales as men who "were in true exile. . . . They had no one to talk to, even after they learned Spanish enough to know what was what." He then compares them to his British-born mother, who he also saw as living in exile. What does Ríos suggest here about the relationship among culture, language, and identity? Why can someone who learns the language of a different culture still remain in exile with "no one to talk to"?

2. Why do you think Ríos titles his essay "The March of the Altar Boy 272–73 Army"? How effective is this **TITLE** for preparing the reader for this piece? What about for enticing readers to read further?

3. 157 One of the features of a memoir is that it tells **A GOOD STORY**. Is Ríos's essay a good story? Why or why not? What elements are necessary for a good story, and which does Ríos incorporate into his piece?

4. 12–14 What is Ríos's **STANCE** toward being an altar boy? Identify specific passages that reveal his attitude and tone. In what ways is his stance appropriate for both the genre and his subject matter?

5. *For Writing.* In his memoir, Ríos recalls very specific, albeit questionable, lessons he learned from his fellow altar boys. Recall a time you learned a lesson from a friend, or by acting on something your friend 153–60 told you. Write a **MEMOIR** about the lesson. **DESCRIBE** your friend, the 324–32 setting, and any other people involved, and be sure to indicate the 157–58 **SIGNIFICANCE** of this lesson for yourself.

LILLIAN SMITH

When I Was a Child

Social critic and civil rights activist Lillian Smith (1897–1966) addressed issues of race, sexuality, and gender equality in her fiction and nonfiction writing and worked tirelessly against segregation and social inequality during the first half of the twentieth century. Indeed, she is mentioned in Martin Luther King Jr.'s "Letter from Birmingham Jail" as one of the few whites then sympathetic to the African American cause. Perhaps best known for her novel Strange Fruit *(1944), Smith was also author of a several other books. The following selection is from her book* Killers of the Dream *(1961), a work that mixes personal memoir and social commentary to examine racial segregation in the South.*

I WAS BORN AND REARED in a small Deep South town whose population was about equally Negro and white. There were nine of us who grew up freely in a rambling house of many rooms, surrounded by big lawn, back yard, gardens, fields, and barn. It was the kind of home that gathers memories like dust, a place filled with laughter and play and pain and hurt and ghosts and games. We were given such advantages of schooling, music, and art as were available in the South, and our world was not limited to the South, for travel to far places seemed a simple, natural thing to us, and usually there was one of the family in a remote part of the earth.

We knew we were a respected and important family of this small town but beyond this knowledge we gave little thought to status. Our father made money in lumber and naval stores for the excitement of making and losing it—not for what money can buy nor the security which it sometimes gives. I do not remember at any time wanting "to be rich" nor do I remember that thrift and saving were ideals which our parents considered important enough to urge upon us. Always in the family there was an acceptance of risk, a mild delight even in burning bridges, an expectant "what will happen now!" We were not irresponsible; living according to the pleasure principle was by no means our way of life. On the contrary we were trained to think that each of us should do something that would be of genuine usefulness to the world, and the family thought it right to make sacrifices if necessary, to give each child adequate preparation for this life's work. We were also trained to think learning important, and books, but "bad" books our mother burned. We valued music and art and craftsmanship but it was people and their welfare and religion that were the foci around which our lives seemed naturally to move. Above all else, the important thing was what we "planned to do with our lives." That each of us must do something was as inevitable as breathing for we owed a "debt to society which must be paid." This was a family commandment.

While many of our neighbors spent their energies in counting limbs on the family tree and grafting some on now and then to give symmetry to it, or in reliving the old bitter days of Reconstruction* licking scars to cure their vague malaise, or in fighting each battle and turn of battle of that Civil War which has haunted the southern conscience so long, my father was pushing his nine children straight into the future. "You have your heritage," he used to say, "some of it good, some not so good; and as far as I know you had the usual number of grandmothers and grandfathers. Yes, there were slaves, far too many of them in the family, but that was your grandfather's mistake, not yours. The past has been lived. It is gone. The future is yours. What are you going to do with it?" Always he asked this question of his children and sometimes one knew it was but an echo of the old question he had spent his life trying to answer for himself. For always the future held my father's dreams; always there, not in the past, did he expect to find what he had spent his life searching for.

We lived the same segregated life as did other southerners but our parents talked in excessively Christian and democratic terms. We were

---

*_Reconstruction_: the political policies that addressed social and political issues of the post–Civil War era (1865–1877), including the abolition of slavery and the restoration of Southern states to the Union in agreement with the Constitution. Although the collapse of the Republican state governments in the South was final by 1877, the animosity and debates over reconstruction lasted into the twentieth century. [Editor's note]

told ten thousand times that status and money are unimportant (though we were well supplied with both); we were told that "all men are brothers," that we are a part of a democracy and must act like democrats. We were told that the teachings of Jesus are real and important and could be practiced if we tried. We were told also that to be "radical" is bad, silly too; and that one must always conform to the "best behavior" of one's community and make it better if one can. We were taught that we were superior not to people but to hate and resentment, and that no member of the Smith family could stoop so low as to have an enemy. No matter what injury was done us, we must not injure ourselves further by retaliating. That was a family commandment too.

5 We had family prayers once each day. All of us as children read the Bible in its entirety each year. We memorized hundreds of Bible verses and repeated them at breakfast, and said "sentence prayers" around the family table. God was not someone we met on Sunday but a permanent member of our household. It never occurred to me until I was fourteen or fifteen years old that He did not see every act and thought and chalk up the daily score on eternity's tablets.

. . .

Against this backdrop the drama of the South was played out one day in my life:

A little white girl was found in the colored section of our town, living with a Negro family in a broken-down shack. This family had moved in only a few weeks before and little was known of them. One of the ladies in my mother's club, while driving over to her washerwoman's, saw the child swinging on a gate. The shack, as she said, was hardly more than a pigsty and this white child was living with ignorant and dirty and sick-looking colored folks."They must have kidnapped her," she told her friends. Genuinely shocked, the clubwomen busied themselves in an attempt to do something, for the child was very white indeed. The strange Negroes were subjected to a grueling questioning and finally grew frightened and evasive and refused to talk at all. This only increased the suspicion of the white group, and the next day the clubwomen, escorted by the town marshal, took the child from her adopted family despite their tears.

She was brought to our home. I do not know why my mother consented to this plan. Perhaps because she loved children and always showed tenderness and concern for them. It was easy for one more to fit into our ample household and Janie was soon at home there. She roomed with me, sat next to me at the table; I found Bible verses for her to say at breakfast; she wore my clothes, played with my dolls and followed me around from morning to night. She was dazed by her new comforts and by the interesting activities of this big lively family; and I was as happily dazed, for her adoration was a new thing to me; and as time passed a quick, childish, and deeply felt bond grew up between us.

But a day came when a telephone message was received from a colored orphanage. There was a meeting at our home, whispers, shocked exclamations. All afternoon the ladies went in and out of our house talking to Mother in tones too low for children to hear. And as they passed us at play, most of them looked quickly at Janie and quickly looked away again, though a few stopped and stared at her as if they could not tear their eyes from her face. When my father came home in the evening Mother closed her door against our young ears and talked a long time with him. I heard him laugh, heard Mother say, "But Papa, this is no laughing matter!" And then they were back in the living room with us and my mother was pale and my father was saying, "Well, work it out, honey, as best you can. After all, now that you know, it is pretty simple."

10 In a little while my mother called my sister and me into her bedroom and told us that in the morning Janie would return to Colored Town. She said Janie was to have the dresses the ladies had given her and a few of my own, and the toys we had shared with her. She asked me if I would like to give Janie one of my dolls. She seemed hurried, though Janie was not to leave until next day. She said, "Why not select it now?" And in dreamlike stiffness I brought in my dolls and chose one for Janie. And then I found it possible to say, "Why? Why is she leaving? She likes us, she hardly knows them. She told me she had been with them only a month."

"Because," Mother said gently, "Janie is a little colored girl."

"But she can't be. She's white!"

"We were mistaken. She is colored."

"But she looks—"

"She is colored. Please don't argue!"

"What does it mean?" I whispered.

"It means," Mother said slowly, "that she has to live in Colored Town with colored people."

"But why? She lived here three weeks and she doesn't belong to them, she told me she didn't."

"She is a little colored girl."

"But you said yourself that she has nice manners. You said that," I persisted.

"Yes, she is a nice child. But a colored child cannot live in our home."

"Why?"

"You know, dear! You have always know that white and colored people do not live together."

"Can she come over to play?"

"No."

"I don't understand."

"I don't either," my young sister quavered.

"You're too young to understand. And don't ask me again, ever again, about this!" Mother's voice was sharp but her face was sad and there was no certainty left there. She hurried out and busied herself in the kitchen and I wandered through that room where I had been born, touching the old familiar things in it, looking at them, trying to find the answer to a question that moaned in my mind like a hurt thing. . . .

And then I went out to Janie, who was waiting, knowing things were happening that concerned her but waiting until they were spoken aloud.

I do not know quite how the words were said but I told her that she was to return in the morning to the little place where she had lived because she was colored and colored children could not live with white children.

"Are you white?" she said.

"I'm white," I replied, "and my sister is white. And you're colored. And white and colored can't live together because my mother says so."

"Why?" Janie whispered.

"Because they can't," I said. But I knew, though I said it firmly, that something was wrong. I knew my father and mother whom I passionately admired had done that which did not fit in with their teachings. I knew they had betrayed something which they held dear. And I was shamed by their failure and frightened, for I felt that they were no longer as powerful as I had thought. There was something Out There that was stronger than they and I could not bear to believe it. I could not confess that my father, who had always solved the family dilemmas easily and with laughter, could not solve this. I knew that my mother who was so good to children did not believe in her heart that she was being good to this child. There was not a word in my mind that said it but my body knew and my glands, and I was filled with anxiety.

But I felt compelled to believe they were right. It was the only way 35
my world could be held together. And, like a slow poison, it began to seep through me: *I was white. She was colored. We must not be together. It was bad to be together. Though you ate with your nurse when you were little, it was bad to eat with any colored person after that. It was bad just as other things were bad that your mother had told you. It was bad that she was to sleep in the room with me that night. It was bad. . . .*

I was suddenly full of guilt. For three weeks I had done things that white children are not supposed to do. And now I knew these things had been wrong.

I went to the piano and began to play, as I had always done when I was in trouble. I tried to play Paderewski's *Minuet** and as I stumbled through it, the little girl came over and sat on the bench with me. Feeling lonely, lost in these deep currents that were sweeping through our house that night, she crept closer and put her arms around me and I shrank away as if my body had been uncovered. I had not said a word, I did not say one, but she knew, and tears slowly rolled down her little white face.

**Ignacy Jan Paderewski* (1860–1941): a Polish composer, pianist, politician and diplomat. Popular in the 1920s and 1930s, his *Minuet* is one of many pieces he composed for the piano. [Editor's note]

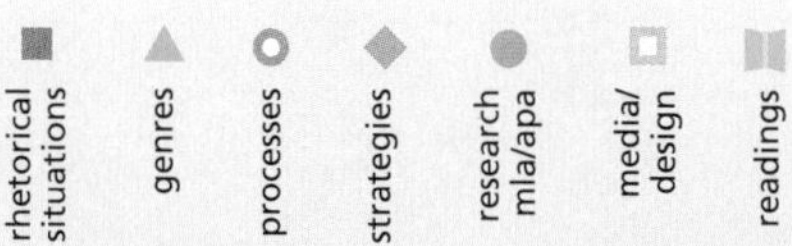

Engaging with the Text

1. The event at the center of Lillian Smith's narrative took place in the early part of the twentieth century, several decades before the civil rights movement challenged segregation on legal grounds. How relevant is Smith's memoir today? How might her memoir inform current discussions about segregation in the United States?
2. How does Smith **BEGIN** her memoir? What is the importance of this beginning to her memoir's **SIGNIFICANCE**?

261–66
157–58

3. Authors of well-written memoirs often use **DIALOGUE** strategically. Where does Smith incorporate dialogue in her piece? Why do you think she chose to use dialogue at these points and not others?

333–37

4. What is the conflict Smith experiences between her parents' teachings and beliefs and their actions at the end of the story? Why do you think she chose to write about this particular event in her memoir? How does that relate to her **PURPOSE** in this piece? What outcome do you think she was seeking?

3–4

5. ***For Writing.*** Smith relates an early experience of the harsh realities of racism, one among many that led her to become a civil rights activist. Recall an event from your past that taught you something about some kind of injustice—whether social, political, religious, or cultural. Write a **MEMOIR** that **NARRATES** that event and makes clear its significance both for you personally and for the larger society and / or culture.

153–60
343–51

VALERIE STEIKER

Our Mother's Face

Valerie Steiker is the culture editor at Vogue *and a writer whose essays have appeared in the* New Yorker *and other publications. She is also co-editor with Chris Knutsen of the essay collection* Brooklyn Was Mine *(2008). The following piece is from Steiker's memoir,* The Leopard Hat: A Daughter's Story *(2002), which tells of the lasting influence Steiker's mother had on her life, from her charmed childhood in New York City to the time she spent, in her twenties, at Harvard and in Paris.*

AT THE BEGINNING OF MARCH, my mother's doctor let us know there was truly nothing more he could do for her in the hospital, and my father decided we should bring her home, where she would be more at ease, surrounded by the family and things and memories that she loved. She was happy to come home — we could hear it in her voice as she directed us to pack up her belongings — as if she had worried without telling us that she would never see it again.

The last week of her life I spent at home. It was spring break. My sister and I sat by her bed, talking softly, watching television. We played the sound track to *A Room with a View** over and over, all of us soothed by its ethereal quality. "That's nice," my mother said at one point from her bed. We took turns bringing her things: lunches she couldn't or wouldn't eat, highball glasses filled with 7-Up or ginger ale. She drank constantly. The disease parched her and nothing was enough to quench her thirst.

Although there was a nurse, it was we who administered her pills, careful to take note of the time and to follow the doctor's instructions. At one point, she was in so much pain she threatened to kill herself if we didn't give her another dose of medication. Frantic, we called the doctor so he could tell her we weren't doing anything wrong, and she got on the phone and accused us of all being in a conspiracy to hurt her. My mother, once so full of warmth and love and vitality, had become

*A *Room with a View*: film (1985) of E. M. Forster's novel. [Editor's note]

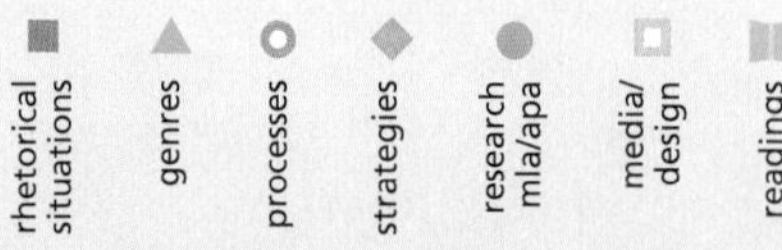

suspicious, paranoid. The morphine was taking her usual anxieties and feeding them until they grew to monstrous proportions. One afternoon she insisted I escort her to the library. Painted hunter green and filled with books and musical instruments, it was the best-loved room in the house. She explained to me, her voice strict with instruction, that she wanted us to make sure there were no samurai there. Without questioning her, I held her, felt her body's efforts under the peach satin robe as we walked slowly down the hallway, through the bright red foyer where she had so often entertained, and into the library. I turned on the light, and said softly, "See, Mommy? There isn't anyone here." In her quasi-dream state, she seemed satisfied, and we returned to her room. I helped her to her bed, wondering at the speed with which we had all had to surrender our grip on normalcy. . . .

A few days later, Bella came from Belgium. Bella, one of my mother's beloved *tantes,** whom she had been close to ever since she was a child. I went to pick her up at the airport with my uncle, my father's older brother, and on the way back we got caught in traffic on the Fifty-ninth Street Bridge. It seemed inconceivable to me that my mother could die without me, while I was trapped in something so mundane as a traffic jam. When we finally got home, Bella wept over my mother's weakened body, her stark skull, her unblinking, watery eyes. Later she cried to me that she hadn't seen a human being look so ravaged since Auschwitz.† None of us knew what to do with ourselves, with the pain — hers and ours — that was everywhere, pervading every available space in the house. With the exception of her bedroom, which was filled with the plastic accoutrements of illness and no longer recognizable as her usual headquarters, the apartment looked as it always had. Only everything was very still. On the tables my mother had arranged so lovingly, the silver-framed photographs of past adventures and delicate porcelain bouquets and figurines sat silently waiting. The couch pillows puffed just so, the tall chairs standing at attention around the dining room

**Tantes*: aunts (French). [Editor's note]

†*Auschwitz*: town in Poland that was the site of a Nazi concentration camp in World War II. [Editor's note]

table: all was in abeyance. The spirit that had animated each room, every seductive curve of furniture, every woven flowery vine, was withdrawing, its life force waning. She was being taken from us, and nothing, not even our boundless love, could stop the process; no amount of knowledge or money existed that could keep her from going away.

On the morning of the day she died, I looked in the bathroom mirror and 5
cried for myself, for the almost unrecognizable girl before me. I didn't get dressed, staying in the same nightshirt I had slept in, which was covered in dark burgundy stripes, and which later I would put away at the back of a shelf, never to be worn again. Whenever I wasn't in my mother's room that day, I spent time cleaning mine. My belongings had gotten out of hand, so I cleaned furiously, folding the clothes that were strewn everywhere and angrily putting books and papers in order on my desk. When the time came — for what, I didn't dare to imagine — I wanted to be ready. A few hours later I got my period. I stared at the clouds of tissue, like pale pink roses, floating in the bowl and took the blood as a benison, a tribute to the children I would have in her memory.

Bella and my father and my sister and I spent that afternoon and evening in my mother's room, holding her hands and stroking her forehead, my sister and I begging her to promise she would watch over us always. In the middle of the night, not knowing what else to do with ourselves, we sat down to play boraco, the family card game, perhaps trying to evoke the Renoir-like afternoons we had spent in Belgian tea gardens together. Just as the cards were laid out, as if she were annoyed by our choosing to play at such a time, the steady rasp of my mother's breathing became jagged, uneven. We flew from the card table and gathered around her bed. It was a sound like something being torn. Ourselves choking, we stroked her face and arms until the last catch in her throat. The life had not flowed out of her; it had been seized.

My father and sister and I drew away from the bed and held one another tightly, a crying circle of three. On the table in her room, there was a nineteenth-century brass lamp: an angel holding up a torch of light. When I looked up from our embrace, the light from next to her bed had cast a silhouette of the angel against the white closet doors,

The author and her mother.

and I remember thinking to myself that it made perfect sense, that her spirit must have been borne away by angels.

It was about three o'clock in the morning by the time we got into bed. My father slept on the pullout couch in his den — it was too upsetting for him to go into their bedroom without her. Stephanie and I decided to sleep together in my room. As we faced each other in bed, too tired and brokenhearted even to say good night to each other, I watched in amazement as my sister's features became my mother's. I was staring at the face of my mother in my bed, she was right next to me, looking at me lovingly, her eyes melting into mine. Yes, I knew that the undertaker had just come and taken her body away, carrying it on a gurney through the marble lobby where she had so often clipped in her high heels. But this was real. The next morning when I told Stephanie what I had seen as we fell asleep, she looked at me as if I were crazy and then started half laughing, half crying. She had had the exact same experience. She, too, had seen our mother's face, in mine.

Engaging with the Text

3–4 1. One **PURPOSE** for writing a memoir is to explore our past, to think about people, places, and events that are important to us. What other purpose does Valerie Steiker's memoir serve, both for herself as the writer and us as the readers?

324–27 2. What **DETAILS** does Steiker present — of what the apartment looked like, what they ate, what they said, what happened — and what do these reveal about Steiker, and about her feelings for her mother? How does this detailed focus on the mundane create a sense of the profound?

277 345–46 3. How does Steiker use **TRANSITIONS** and **TIME MARKERS** to guide readers through the days preceding and following her mother's death? Aside from guiding readers, what is their effect?

9–11 4. Steiker chose to explore her mother's death through a memoir. What other **GENRES** might she have used? How would her story be different if she had used another genre, such as a **REFLECTION** or a **REPORT**? In what situations would another genre be more appropriate, and why? 180–87 59–82

5. ***For Writing.*** Steiker's memoir focuses on the death of her mother as it unfolded in the space of her family's apartment. Identify a place that you hold important in your life and recall an event that occurred there that has some significance for you. Write a **MEMOIR** about the event, using detail to help readers to see, hear, and otherwise sense the event and the key people involved. Include **DIALOGUE** if appropriate, and be sure to indicate the **SIGNIFICANCE** of the event in your life. 153–60 333–37 157–58

HENRY LOUIS GATES JR.

A Giant Step

The director of the W. E. B. Du Bois Institute for African and African American Research at Harvard University, Henry Louis Gates Jr. is a scholar of African American literature and literary criticism. He is the author of The Signifying Monkey: A Theory of Afro-American Literary Criticism *(1988) and one of the general editors of* The Norton Anthology of African American Literature *(1997, second edition 2004). The following essay first appeared in the* New York Times Magazine *in 1990 and was later incorporated in Gates's 1994 autobiography* Colored People: A Memoir.

"WHAT'S THIS?" the hospital janitor said to me as he stumbled over my right shoe.

"My shoes," I said. 5

"That's not a shoe, brother," he replied, holding it to the light. "That's a brick."

It *did* look like a brick, sort of.

"Well, we can throw these in the trash now," he said.

"I guess so."

We had been together since 1975, those shoes and I. They were orthopedic shoes built around molds of my feet, and they had a $2\frac{1}{4}$-inch lift. I had mixed feelings about them. On the one hand, they had given me a more or less even gait for the first time in 10 years. On the other hand, they had marked me as a "handicapped person," complete with cane and special license plates. I went through a pair a year, but it was always the same shoe, black, wide, weighing about four pounds.

It all started 26 years ago in Piedmont, West Virginia, a backwoods town of 2,000 people. While playing a game of touch football at a Methodist summer camp, I incurred a hairline fracture. Thing is, I didn't know it yet. I was 14 and had finally lost the chubbiness of my youth. I was just learning tennis and beginning to date, and who knew where that might lead?

Not too far. A few weeks later, I was returning to school from lunch when, out of the blue, the ball-and-socket joint of my hip sheared apart. It was instant agony, and from that time on nothing in my life would be quite the same.

I propped myself against the brick wall of the schoolhouse, where the school delinquent found me. He was black as slate, twice my size, mean as the day was long and beat up kids just because he could. But the look on my face told him something was seriously wrong, and — bless him — he stayed by my side for the two hours it took to get me into a taxi.

"It's a torn ligament in your knee," the surgeon said. (One of the signs of what I had — a "slipped epithysis" — is intense knee pain, I later learned.) So he scheduled me for a walking cast.

I was wheeled into surgery and placed on the operating table. As the doctor wrapped my leg with wet plaster strips, he asked about my schoolwork.

"Boy," he said, "I understand you want to be a doctor."

I said, "Yessir." Where I came from, you always said "sir" to white people, unless you were trying to make a statement.

Had I taken a lot of science courses?

"Yessir. I enjoy science."

"Are you good at it?"

"Yessir, I believe so."

"Tell me, who was the father of sterilization?"

"Oh, that's easy, Joseph Lister."

Then he asked who discovered penicillin.

Alexander Fleming.

And what about DNA?

Watson and Crick.

The interview went on like this, and I thought my answers might get me a pat on the head. Actually, they just confirmed the diagnosis he'd come to.

He stood me on my feet and insisted that I walked. When I tried, the joint ripped apart and I fell on the floor. It hurt like nothing I'd ever known.

The doctor shook his head. "Pauline," he said to my mother, his voice kindly but amused, "there's not a thing wrong with that child. The problem's psychosomatic. Your son's an overachiever."

Back then, the term didn't mean what it usually means today. In Appalachia, in 1964, "overachiever" designated a sort of pathology: the overstraining of your natural capacity. A colored kid who thought he could be a doctor — just for instance — was headed for a breakdown.

What made the pain abate was my mother's reaction. I'd never, ever heard her talk back to a white person before. And doctors, well, their words were scripture.

Not this time. Pauline Gates stared at him for a moment. "Get his 30
clothes, pack his bags — we're going to the University Medical Center," which was 60 miles away.

Not great news: the one thing I knew was that they only moved you to the University Medical Center when you were going to die. I had three operations that year. I gave my tennis racket to the delinquent, which he probably used to club little kids with. So I wasn't going to make it to Wimbledon. But at least I wasn't going to die, though sometimes I wanted to. Following the last operation, which fitted me for a metal ball, I was confined to bed, flat on my back, immobilized by a complex system of weights and pulleys. It was six weeks of bondage — and bedpans. I spent my time reading James Baldwin, learning to play chess and quarreling daily with my mother, who had rented a small room — which we could ill afford — in a motel just down the hill from the hospital.

I think we both came to realize that our quarreling was a sort of ritual. We'd argue about everything — what time of day it was — but the arguments kept me from thinking about that traction system.

I limped through the next decade — through Yale and Cambridge . . . as far away from Piedmont as I could get. But I couldn't escape the pain, which increased as the joint calcified and began to fuse over the next 15 years. My leg grew shorter, as the muscles atrophied and the ball of the ball-and-socket joint migrated into my pelvis. Aspirin, then Motrin, heating pads and massages, became my traveling companions.

Most frustrating was passing store windows full of fine shoes. I used to dream about walking into one of those stores and buying a pair of shoes. "Give me two pairs, one black, one cordovan," I'd say. "Wrap 'em up." No six-week wait as with the orthotics in which I was confined. These would be real shoes. Not bricks.

In the meantime, hip-joint technology progressed dramatically. But no surgeon wanted to operate on me until I was significantly older, or until the pain was so great that surgery was unavoidable. After all, a new hip would last only for 15 years, and I'd already lost too much bone. It wasn't a procedure they were sure they'd be able to repeat.

This year, my 40th, the doctors decided the time had come.

I increased my life insurance and made the plunge.

The nights before my operations are the longest nights of my life — but never long enough. Jerking awake, grabbing for my watch, I experience a delicious sense of relief as I discover that only a minute or two have passed. You never want 6 A.M. to come.

And then the door swings open. "Good morning, Mr. Gates," the nurse says. "It's time."

The last thing I remember, just vaguely, was wondering where amnesiac minutes go in one's consciousness, wondering if I experienced the pain and sounds, then forgot them, or if these were somehow blocked out, dividing the self on the operating table from the conscious self in the recovery room. I didn't like that idea very much. I was about to protest when I blinked.

"It's over, Mr. Gates," says a voice. But how could it be over? I had merely *blinked*. "You talked to us several times," the surgeon had told me, and that was the scariest part of all.

Twenty-four hours later, they get me out of bed and help me into a "walker." As they stand me on my feet, my wife bursts into tears. "Your foot is touching the ground!" I am afraid to look, but it is true: the surgeon has lengthened my leg with that gleaming titanium and chrome-cobalt alloy ball-and-socket-joint.

"You'll need new shoes," the surgeon says. "Get a pair of Dock-Sides; they have a secure grip. You'll need a 3/4-inch lift in the heel, which can be as discreet as you want."

I can't help thinking about those window displays of shoes, those elegant shoes that, suddenly, I will be able to wear. Dock-Sides and sneakers, boots and loafers, sandals and brogues. I feel, at last, a furtive sympathy for Imelda Marcos, the queen of soles.

The next day, I walk over to the trash can, and take a long look at 45
the brick. I don't want to seem ungracious or unappreciative. We have walked long miles together. I feel disloyal, as if I am abandoning an old friend. I take a second look.

Maybe I'll have them bronzed.

Engaging with the Text

261–66

1. Henry Louis Gates Jr. **BEGINS** his memoir about something that happened to him when he was fourteen by telling us about what happened to him twenty-six years later. This opening sets up a frame for his memoir. What does this frame contribute to your understanding of the earlier event in Gates's life?

5–8

2. Who was Gates's original **AUDIENCE** for this piece? How did he shape this memoir for that audience? Point to examples in your response. How might the text be different had he written it for an audience of doctors? For an audience of lawyers?

314–23

3. Gates explains that the white doctor used the word "overachiever" to mean something very different from what it means today. How does he **DEFINE** "overachiever"? What is the significance of this definition? What details does he provide to flesh out his definition?

333–37

4. Much of this memoir is told through **DIALOGUE.** Imagine that Gates had simply told what happened, summarizing what was said rather than letting the reader "hear" the key conversations. You might try rewriting the text without dialogue to see the difference. What can you conclude about when and why you might want to use dialogue in your own writing?

153–60

5. ***For Writing.*** Think of an event from your past that you remember as significant, or perhaps just interesting. Write about this event in a way that tells readers something about yourself. Try to structure your **MEMOIR** as Gates does, juxtaposing the event from your past with one from the present.

Profiles 61

See also:

LAURA M. HOLSON
Rural Idaho Town Seeks to Turn Film's Cult Status into Prosperity 161

ROB BAKER

Jimmy Santiago Baca: Poetry as Lifesaver

Rob Baker is a freelance creative writer who teaches English and creative writing at Barrington High School in Illinois. The following profile appeared in a 2008 issue of the Council Chronicle, *a monthly magazine published by the National Council of Teachers of English (NCTE). As you read, notice how Baker focuses his profile on the significance of poetry for Baca, using details from Baca's life to support his point.* *To read one of Jimmy Santiago Baca's poems, see p. 798.*

Chicano poet Jimmy Santiago Baca was born with rattlesnake poison in his blood. In January, 1952, just before his mother gave birth, she was bitten by a rattler. The healer who tended to her wound and then brought Baca into the world said that because of the venom Baca would be able to see in the dark and that he would change many times throughout his life, just as a snake sloughs its skin. And change many times he did.

As related in his award-winning autobiography, *A Place to Stand,* Baca's parents abandoned him when he was seven; he lived briefly with his grandparents and then in a series of detention centers from which he constantly ran away. He attended junior high, but dropped out after less than a year because he could not keep up academically nor mesh with the "normal" kids who had families. As a teenager, he lived a haphazard existence on the streets of Albuquerque, fighting, drinking, and doing drugs. He worked piecemeal jobs — loading food on planes, operating a vending machine route, a handyman business. Then, during stints in California and Arizona, he became a very successful drug dealer.

That he would morph into a renowned poet is perhaps the least likely change anyone would have predicted for Baca who, as a young adult, could barely read or write, who "hated books, hated reading," who had "never owned a book and had no desire to own one." And this change probably wouldn't have happened if Baca hadn't been sentenced, at age 21, to five to ten years in prison.

To read of Baca's prison years is to marvel at the human capacity for survival and renewal. In a place more reminiscent of Dante's *Inferno* than of an institution for rehabilitation, where blood was shed more often than light, and where the inmates' chronic lassitude, fear, and anger led to depression, murder, rape, and paranoia, Baca — remarkably — endured, and exited not only sane and alive, but as a poet.

Chance encounters catalyzed Baca's transformation. A couple years 5 into his incarceration, Baca received a letter from a man as part of a church program to write to prisoners without families. As a result of their continued correspondence, Baca painstakingly taught himself to read and write, activities that helped bring purpose into his monotonous days. The man then put Baca in touch with a poet friend. Poetry changed Baca's life forever.

"I believe something in my brain or something in my nervous system was impacted by poetry, by the way the lines and the words were arranged," said Baca. "I was such an emotional animal and I had never read any poetry. When I read it, it just tolled so many bells in my head, it was like, 'Wow! I can actually communicate like this. There are actually people who talk like this and write like this.' I was just absorbed into it, into the vortex of this ecstasy."

Baca published poems while still in prison. His first collection, *Immigrants in Our Own Land* (Louisiana State University Press, 1979), came out just after his release.

Baca's writing explores his fractured family and personal life, his prison experiences, and his ethnicity. In addition to his autobiography, he has penned ten poetry collections, a book of short stories, and a screenplay, the 1993 film *Blood In, Blood Out*.

"Language gave me a way to keep the chaos of prison at bay and prevented it from devouring me," he wrote in his prologue to *A Place to Stand*. "It was a resource that allowed me to confront and understand my past . . . and it opened a way toward the future that was based not on fear or bitterness or apathy but on compassionate involvement."

In another life change, Baca ultimately morphed into a teacher. He 10 began by working with gang members who regularly congregated near his home, though his initial contact with them seemed more likely to result in violence than poetry. One night, when the youths hanging out on his street were particularly raucous, Baca went outside in his pajamas, baseball bat in hand. He told them that they had awakened his baby and that they had to leave.

"They said, 'We ain't got no other place to go,'" Baca recounted. "So I said, 'All right, meet me at St. Anne's church tomorrow and I'll ask the priest if we can use the barracks there.' And you know what? They all met me there and I had my first workshop ever, and I realized with a sort of vague ignorance that I was really gifted at working with kids."

Baca now does many workshops a year and receives frequent visits from public school educators who come to observe his techniques. He says he's "very much into Latin American poets," but he also uses more frequently taught poets such as William Carlos Williams, Denise Levertov, Lawrence Ferlinghetti, and Walt Whitman.*

> Language gave me a way to keep the chaos of prison at bay and prevented it from devouring me. It was a resource that allowed me to confront and understand my past.

Baca encourages students to tell the stories no one else has: the stories of their own lives. He also encourages students to use poetry to discuss issues they might not normally talk about. "Most of the time there are subtle protocols you have to abide by. You're sitting at a table with friends, there are certain things you don't talk about. With these kids, ninety percent of their lived experience is stuff you don't talk about."

Baca believes poetry is able to reach the people he works with — people often considered by society to be "the worst of the worst" — because "there's nothing that is required for you to speak poetically from your heart."

To Baca, his mission as a teacher — and the role of poetry in 15
general — is nothing less than to save lives.

"My job is simply to keep the light inside [my students] burning. That's it. My job is to make sure they do not fall into despair. And I guess

---

**William Carlos Williams* (1883–1963), *Denise Levertov* (1923–1997), *Lawrence Ferlinghetti* (b. 1919), *and Walt Whitman* (1819–1892): American poets who composed in free verse. With the exception of Whitman, all wrote during the twentieth century. [Editor's note]

that's the answer to why I work with unwed mothers, I go to prisons, I work with homeless and gang kids, because their light's starting to go off, to dim, and I have to come in there and fire it up, and I do that with poetry, and I do that with commitment, and I do that with compassion."

Engaging with the Text

1. Rob Baker begins his profile of the poet Jimmy Santiago Baca with an **ANECDOTE**. How does this anecdote foreshadow the changes Baca experiences during his life? What role does language play in those changes?

265–66

2. What **ENGAGING DETAILS** does Baker provide in his profile to create an impression of Baca as someone who sees "his mission as a teacher — and the role of poetry in general — [as] nothing less than to save lives"?

166

3. This piece was published in a magazine for English teachers. How does Baker shape his profile of Baca to appeal to that **AUDIENCE**? How might his profile be different if he had written it for an audience of high school students? Prison inmates?

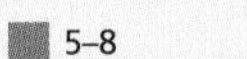
5–8

4. How much **BACKGROUND** on Baca does Baker provide in this profile? Why is this background important? How does it help the reader better understand who Baca is today?

165–66

5. ***For Writing.*** Identify someone with an interesting career, job, or hobby that has played a significant role in his or her life. Interview that person and write a **PROFILE** that demonstrates how that hobby or job has changed him or her. Use **DIALOGUE** and engaging details to help reveal your subject's character.

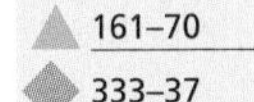
161–70
333–37

SAMUEL G. FREEDMAN

Camp Leads a Drumbeat for a Marching Band's Style

Samuel G. Freedman is a professor of journalism at Columbia University. An award-winning author and journalist who has written widely on education, ethics, and religion, he has been a reporter and contributor for several news organizations and is currently a columnist for the New York Times. *Freedman has published six nonfiction books, including* Small Victories: The Real World of a Teacher, Her Students and Their High School *(1990);* Jew vs. Jew: The Struggle for the Soul of American Jewry *(2000); and* Letters to a Young Journalist *(2006). The following profile of a marching band camp appeared in the* Times *in 2008.*

AS HIS EXTENDED FAMILY GATHERED AROUND THE TABLE for dinner last Christmas, Ben Brock received one final present. It was a scrapbook, each page adorned with photos of him as a child and handwritten notes from his relatives. Then, on the last sheet, the names of his mother, sister, uncles and aunts appeared, with a dollar figure next to each.

Those numbers reflected the money they had pledged to send Ben, 16, almost as far from his home in Seattle as it was possible to go within the continental United States. At the end of that journey lay the dream he had nurtured since watching the movie "Drum Line" in sixth grade: to become part of the Marching 100, the renowned band at Florida A&M University.

So on a gauzy gray morning seven months later Ben and his snare drum strode onto the dewy grass of the band's practice field on the Tallahassee campus. He had been awakened at 5 a.m. and the day's last rehearsal would not end until 10 p.m. His feet screamed. His shoulders ached. Gnats swarmed around his face, daring him to break rhythm and lose composure.

"Snap, precision, lock in with the tempo," called out an instructor, very much in the manner of a Marine drill sergeant. "Now step it up, get some volume."

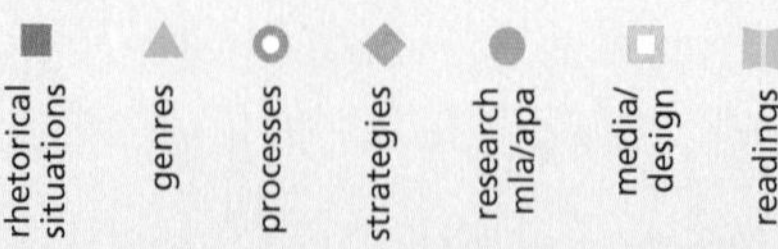

But this, all this, is what Ben Brock had sought, he and 450 other 5
high school students, drawn from throughout the United States and as far as Germany. They had enrolled in the summer band camp operated by the Marching 100. For the campers, these eight days offered a kind of initiation; for the band, they offered the chance to recruit future members and to spread its ecstatic performance style literally around the world.

In the nation's historically black colleges, marching bands have long provided far more than "The Star-Spangled Banner" for football crowds, and none, arguably, has grown more famous than Florida A&M's.

The group's traditional and official name, the Marching 100, is a rare bit of false modesty: the group now numbers upward of 350 musicians, drum majors and flag-carriers. The unit has built a national, even global, following with appearances at the Super Bowl, both of President Bill Clinton's inaugural parades, the Grammy Awards and the bicentennial of the French republic.

The only reason Florida A&M was not explicitly identified as the inspiration for "Drum Line" is that the script called for the Marching 100

Tallie Brinson warmed up on his trombone at summer band camp run by the Marching 100.

to finish second in a battle of the bands, and, as the group's director, Professor Julian E. White, put it the other day, "We don't lose."

The Marching 100 has created a revolution in band style, radically infusing the traditional catalog of songs and formations with the sounds and dances of black popular culture. "It slides, slithers, swivels, rotates, shakes, rocks and rolls," the band's founding director, Professor William P. Foster, wrote in his memoirs. "It leaps to the sky, does triple twists, and drops to earth without a flaw, without missing either a beat or a step."

It also attracts plenty of acolytes. When Dr. White began the 10
summer camp 18 years ago, he expected to attract mainly African-American students from the Southeast. Not only has the enrollment soared to 450 from an initial 90, the geographical and racial range has expanded. (Tuition is $475, with many students receiving scholarships.)

Three busloads of campers came this summer from Michigan alone. Dozens of Hispanic and white teenagers have flocked to the program, including the archetypal slacker this summer who wore a T-shirt explaining, "I'm Probably Late."

"They come here, they ignore the gnats, they ignore the heat, because of the uniqueness of what we do and the pride we feel, the dedication," Dr. White said. "And when they leave here, their parents say they sleep for a week."

Ralph Jean-Paul remembers those sensations well. Now the band president and a tuba instructor for the summer program, he started out eight years ago as a camper.

"I felt I had come to an empire," Mr. Jean-Paul recalled. "To see this magnitude of musicians, all working in one place, 30 tubas alone. That first day, I told myself, 'This is where I want to be.'"

Technology has enhanced and challenged the summer camp. On 15
the one hand, teenagers anywhere in the world can find clips of the Marching 100 on YouTube or visit its MySpace page.

"I saw people doing a dance routine with their drums that I thought was completely impossible," Mr. Rock said of his online exploration. "I said to myself, 'I've got to learn how to do that.'"

On the other hand, the rise of hip-hop and the computerized music programs like GarageBand has depleted the pool of young instrumentalists. In addition, many public schools have reduced or eliminated music classes to provide double periods of math and reading, which are tested annually under the education law No Child Left Behind.*

The camp makes no concession to any of it. Within the program's single week, every student is expected to learn a pregame and half-time show, and to perform with a symphonic, chamber or jazz ensemble. Veterans know to bring along insect repellant and ice packs.

"They're serious down here," said L'Dante Brown, a 14-year-old drummer from the Virgin Islands. "When they tell you to stand still and be quiet, you can hear the mosquitoes flying."

And when they tell Mr. Brown and the rest to move and make noise, 20
and all the French horns and piccolos and saxophones and trombones sashay into action, the syncopated sound echoes across the hilly campus.

"I know I'm not the best player," said Dana Dixon, 16, a clarinetist from Cedar Rapids, Iowa. "But I've learned notes. I've learned steps. I'm happy and I'm sore. I thought waking up at 5 o'clock would be terrible, but it's nothing. It's, like, let's wake up and do it."

Engaging with the Text

1. Samuel G. Freedman **BEGINS** his profile not with the marching band summer camp but with an anecdote about one of its recent participants, Ben Brock. Why do you think he chose to start his piece this way? How effective is this beginning? How does it prepare readers for the rest of the profile? 261–66

No Child Left Behind (NCLB): a national education reform policy signed into law by former president George W. Bush in January 2002. Developed to improve primary and secondary education by creating accountability measures for schools, it requires that states perform basic skills assessments of all students in certain grades. [Editor's note]

2. 166 What kinds of **ENGAGING DETAILS** does Freedman include in his profile? 330–31 What **DOMINANT IMPRESSION** of this marching band camp do these details create? Point to specific phrases to support your response.
3. 165 Well-written profiles focus on an **INTERESTING SUBJECT**. Does Freedman's profile accomplish this goal? If so, how does Freedman sustain interest in this subject throughout his profile? If not, how might Freedman revise this piece to bring his subject to life?
4. As the headnote preceding this profile indicates, Freedman has written widely on education in the United States. Considering his inter- 3–4 est in education, what might be the **PURPOSE** of his profile? From what 166 **ANGLE** does Freedman approach his subject in order to achieve that purpose?
5. ***For Writing.*** Identify a student group on your campus you'd like to learn more about. (You can probably find a list of student organiza- 394–95 tions on your school's website.) **INTERVIEW** one or more of the group's 396 leaders and members to find out how the group functions, its role on campus, and its range of activities. Attend gatherings of this group to **OBSERVE** it in action and collect details for your profile. Based on your interviews, first-hand observations, and any relevant print sources (such as the school newspaper or magazine accounts of your subject), 161–70 write a **PROFILE** of the group.

NICHOLAS HOWE

Writing Home:
High Street

Nicholas Howe (1953–2006) was a professor of English at the University of California, Berkeley, where his primary work was on the literature and culture of Anglo-Saxon England. His books include The Old English Catalogue Poems *(1985),* Migration and Mythmaking in Anglo-Saxon England *(2002), and the Norton Critical Edition of* Beowulf *(2001). The following profile is of a street in Columbus, Ohio, home of the Ohio State University, where Howe taught before moving to Berkeley. It comes from* Across an Inland Sea: Writing in Place from Buffalo to Berlin *(2003). Before reading Howe's profile, think of a street near your school that you could write about, and read with an eye for the way Howe helps readers to envision a street they've likely never before seen.*

HIGH STREET RUNS THROUGH Columbus, Ohio, as a spine. Its character shifts along its length to reflect the surrounding area: the old downtown with government and commercial offices; the rehabbed gallery district; an amorphous university community; quiet residential neighborhoods with wood-frame houses from the early twentieth century. But it remains always the main street of the city, the north-south line that separates cross-streets into east and west, that serves as the origin point for giving directions. High Street is the main axis for Columbus's grid pattern so that, if you can find it, you are never really lost in the central city. Its name comes from those New Englanders who settled this part of the country after the Revolutionary War, and the occasional anglophile will slip in the definite article as if speaking of an English town: The High Street. But that usage seems almost comic because it is not a street of half-timbered houses, pub signs, and hanging flower baskets.

Over the years the foursquare, though rarely distinguished, brick buildings that line the street have suffered more from botched attempts at modernization than outright neglect. Their slapped-on false facades, out-of-date neon signs, unused upper floors all testify in one way or

High Street, Columbus, Ohio.

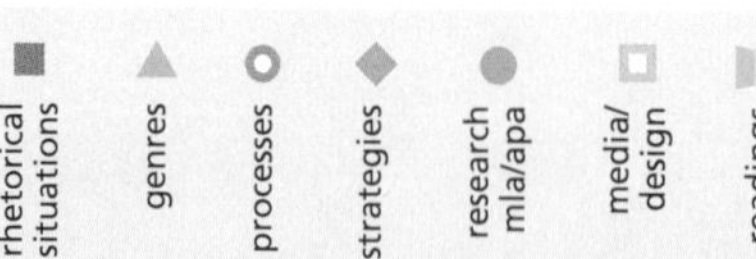

another to their owners' doomed efforts to stem the drift of businesses to the suburbs in the 1950s and 1960s where life was newer and parking easier. Along some stretches, the street has been cut into jaggedly: original buildings were torn down and replaced with one-story strips or supermarkets set far back so shoppers can park in front. This exploitative use of space makes what once had been a symmetrical main street with a trim curbline appear ragged and disconnected. Only in the last several years have zoning regulations been changed to limit setbacks; new buildings must now abut the sidewalk and have their parking lots in the rear, as was the custom in the early 1900s. This return to older practice has become a selling point. A recent for-sale sign on an empty lot along High Street featured a drawing of a typical, early-1900s storefront with signs for imagined businesses that read "Upscale Restaurant" and "Delicious Bakery." A fashionable coffeeshop has just been built on that site with no setback. Even as the building was being finished, it was hard to remember that it was replacing a drive-through beer store that had in turn been a gas station.

The traffic along High Street is steady, sometimes heavy, and always punctuated by buses running north and south. That it has the most regular service in the city, with a bus every seven to ten minutes, is another sign that it is a main drag. In a city that belongs to the car culture of the American heartland, High Street is one of the few places where you will see people walking. Except for several gentrified blocks in the Short North section, with chic restaurants and galleries, much of High Street can still evoke, for those willing to see it, the sense of a small city from early in the twentieth century. But it takes patience to find that city amid the parking lots, the chain drugstores, the fast-food franchises that fill the air with their aromas, the constant flow of traffic that passes along the street without looking at what lines each side.

The few square miles of the world that I know best fall along High Street between Clintonville, the neighborhood of World War I–era houses where I live, and the Ohio State University, where I teach. The distance is about two miles or perhaps forty minutes by foot but I almost never make it in less than an hour because I stop to look in store windows or explore the ways people use the street and its adjacent network of alleys. For ten years or so I have wandered in this neighborhood, buying necessities like food and hardware, spending too much money on used books and cameras, always trying to ease some of the restlessness that comes with a steady life set in one place. Making an alley do the work of the exotic unknown may seem silly, perhaps even pathetic, but it is better for the imagination than reading exploraporn or watching action movies. It gets one out of the house, and that is the first benefit of travel.

5 Clintonville along High Street is a neighborhood that needs to be walked, not because it is scenic, but because it must be peeled back layer by layer. That way you can see how it has shifted from generation to generation, how it shifts as you walk it day by day. These changes rarely force themselves on you; they can easily be ignored. But paying so little attention to where you live leaves you increasingly unable to appreciate anywhere else, no matter how dramatic. Looked at carefully, though, these two miles of High Street record a changing America. Different moments from the past have left their traces along the street, and they can be read like geological striations or the *pentimento* of an artist's canvas. The painted signs on brick buildings — for long-gone places like Burkart's Economy Stores and a lunchroom called Clinton Villa, or still thriving ones like Schreiner's Hardware and Pace-Hi Beer and Wine Shop — are now so faded as to be barely readable. When they were fresh and garish in their deep colors, these signs must have seemed as arresting as the neon fast-food signs of today. The few that survive along High Street have paled into the brick walls of buildings and no longer catch the eye.

Some of the old back-lit signs that preceded neon remain in place, though the names on them change as tenants come and go. Clintonville Hardware becomes Midwest Photo Exchange, but the sign remains in place. Along this stretch, other buildings have been turned from their original uses as auto showrooms and furniture stores to more improvised purposes, and sheds off of alleys hide old cars soon to be vintage. Nothing here is abandoned in a derelict or wasteful way, nothing here gives cause for fear or even much regret. It's just that people seem to have forgotten to use the upper floors of buildings or the sheds behind them. As life goes on elsewhere, these spaces have lost their purpose.

Wandering around these alleys, down these nooks and crannies, has given density to my life; it has taught me about the uncelebrated persistence of what was built and occupied more than a generation or two ago. I have not lived here long enough to see ghosts turning these corners, nor do I have family ties that run back several generations, as I do in Buffalo. Yet walking these blocks and looking through alleyways behind buildings toward High Street has given me a sense of how the lives passed in a place leave their scars on it. It matters to these wanderings that this is not a "quaint" or "charming" stretch, one gentrified to sterile tastefulness. Instead, it is visibly a mixed-up area with convenience stores, insurance agencies, transmission shops, and a few local bars set beside deeply expert dealers from whom you can purchase a used Ferrari or Mercedes-Benz, an antique Stickley* chair, or a new Leica camera. No one planned the neighborhood to be this way, no one has yet driven out the service stores to make room for more boutiques. In an impromptu way, it simply happened, and in happening found its comfortably jumbled character.

Engaging with the Text

1. According to Nicholas Howe, how has High Street changed over the years? What **BACKGROUND** and **CONTEXT** does Howe supply to help his readers understand the changes? How can the character of High Street be described today? 165
2. A good profile generally focuses on an unusual subject, or on something very ordinary shown in an interesting way. How does Howe make a fairly ordinary street in Columbus, Ohio, an **INTERESTING SUBJECT**? 165
3. According to Howe, what has **CAUSED** the various changes on High Street? Why do you think he addresses these causes in his profile of High Street? What do they contribute to the overall profile?  278–82

**Gustav Stickley* (1858–1942): American furniture maker and spokesman for the Arts and Crafts movement. [Editor's note]

4. Howe tells us that "Clintonville along High Street is a neighborhood that needs to be walked, not because it is scenic, but because it must be peeled back layer by layer." What does he mean by the phrase "layer by layer"? In his **DESCRIPTION** of High Street, how does he peel the layers back for the reader?
5. ***For Writing.*** Select an interesting street, building, or other structure in your neighborhood. Spend some time **OBSERVING** it, do some **RESEARCH** on its history, and write a **PROFILE** that explores how it came to be the way it is today.

324–32
396
375–403
161–70

JOAN DIDION

Georgia O'Keeffe

Joan Didion is a novelist and journalist, the author of five screenplays and several best-selling essay collections, including A Book of Common Prayer *(1977) and* The White Album *(1979). A selection from her memoir* The Year of Magical Thinking *(2005) appears on p. 929. The following profile of artist Georgia O'Keeffe, published when O'Keeffe was 92, comes from* The White Album.

"WHERE I WAS BORN and where and how I have lived is unimportant," Georgia O'Keeffe told us in the book of paintings and words published in her ninetieth year on earth. She seemed to be advising us to forget the beautiful face in the Stieglitz photographs. She appeared to be dismissing the rather condescending romance that had attached to her by then, the romance of extreme good looks and advanced age and deliberate isolation. "It is what I have done with where I have been that should be of interest." I recall an August afternoon in Chicago in 1973 when I took my daughter, then seven, to see what Georgia O'Keeffe had done with where she had been. One of the vast O'Keeffe "Sky above Clouds" canvases floated over the back stairs in the Chicago Art Institute that day, dominating what seemed to be several stories of empty light, and my daughter looked at it once, ran to the landing, and kept on looking. "Who drew it," she whispered after a while. I told her. "I need to talk to her," she said finally.

My daughter was making, that day in Chicago, an entirely unconscious but quite basic assumption about people and the work they do. She was assuming that the glory she saw in the work reflected a glory in its maker, that the painting was the painter as the poem is the poet, that every choice one made alone — every word chosen or rejected, every brush stroke laid or not laid down — betrayed one's character. *Style is character.* It seemed to me that afternoon that I had rarely seen so instinctive an application of this familiar principle, and I recall being

Georgia O'Keeffe, 1930.

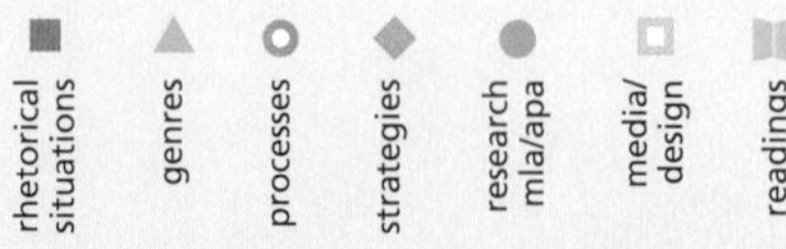

pleased not only that my daughter responded to style as character but that it was Georgia O'Keeffe's particular style to which she responded: this was a hard woman who had imposed her 192 square feet of clouds on Chicago.

"Hardness" has not been in our century a quality much admired in women, nor in the past twenty years has it even been in official favor for men. When hardness surfaces in the very old we tend to transform it into "crustiness" or eccentricity, some tonic pepperiness to be indulged at a distance. On the evidence of her work and what she has said about it, Georgia O'Keeffe is neither "crusty" nor eccentric. She is simply hard, a straight shooter, a woman clean of received wisdom and open to what she sees. This is a woman who could early on dismiss most of her contemporaries as "dreamy," and would later single out one she liked as "a very poor painter." (And then add, apparently by way of softening the judgment: "I guess he wasn't a painter at all. He had no courage and I believe that to create one's own world in any of the arts takes courage.") This is a woman who in 1939 could advise her admirers that they were missing her point, that their appreciation of her famous flowers was merely sentimental. "When I paint a red hill," she observed coolly in the catalogue for an exhibition that year, "you say it is too bad that I don't always paint flowers. A flower touches almost everyone's heart. A red hill doesn't touch everyone's heart." This is a woman who could describe the genesis of one of her most well-known paintings — the "Cow's Skull: Red, White, and Blue" owned by the Metropolitan — as an act of quite deliberate and derisive orneriness. "I thought of the city men I had been seeing in the East," she wrote. "They talked so often of writing the Great American Novel — the Great American Play — the Great American Poetry. . . . So as I was painting my cow's head on blue I thought to myself, 'I'll make it an American painting. They will not think it great with the red stripes down the sides — Red, White and Blue — but they will notice it.' "

The city men. The men. They. The words crop up again and again as this astonishingly aggressive woman tells us what was on her mind when she was making her astonishingly aggressive paintings. It was

Georgia O'Keeffe, Red Canna.

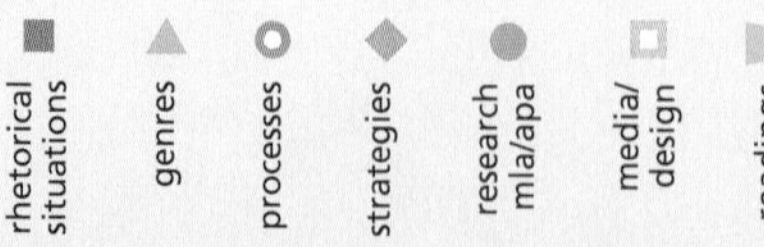

those city men who stood accused of sentimentalizing her flowers: "I made you take time to look at what I saw and when you took time to really notice my flower you hung all your associations with flowers on my flower and you write about my flower as if I think and see what you think and see — and I don't." *And I don't.* Imagine those words spoken, and the sound you hear is *don't tread on me.* "The men" believed it impossible to paint New York, so Georgia O'Keeffe painted New York. "The men" didn't think much of her bright color, so she made it brighter. The men yearned toward Europe so she went to Texas, and then New Mexico. The men talked about Cézanne, "long involved remarks about the 'plastic quality' of his form and color," and took one another's long involved remarks, in the view of this angelic rattlesnake in their midst, altogether too seriously. "I can paint one of those dismal-colored paintings like the men," the woman who regarded herself always as an outsider remembers thinking one day in 1922, and she did: a painting of a shed "all low-toned and dreary with the tree beside the door." She called this act of rancor "The Shanty" and hung it in her next show. "The men seemed to approve of it," she reported fifty-four years later, her contempt undimmed. "They seemed to think that maybe I was beginning to paint. That was my only low-toned dismal-colored painting."

5 Some women fight and others do not. Like so many successful guerrillas in the war between the sexes, Georgia O'Keeffe seems to have been equipped early with an immutable sense of who she was and a fairly clear understanding that she would be required to prove it. On the surface her upbringing was conventional. She was a child on the Wisconsin prairie who played with china dolls and painted watercolors with cloudy skies because sunlight was too hard to paint and, with her brother and sisters, listened every night to her mother read stories of the Wild West, of Texas, of Kit Carson and Billy the Kid. She told adults that she wanted to be an artist and was embarrassed when they asked what kind of artist she wanted to be: she had no idea "what kind." She had no idea what artists did. She had never seen a picture that interested her, other than a pen-and-ink Maid of Athens in one of her mother's books, some Mother Goose illustrations printed on cloth, a tablet cover that showed a little girl with pink roses, and the painting of Arabs on horseback that

hung in her grandmother's parlor. At thirteen, in a Dominican convent, she was mortified when the sister corrected her drawing. At Chatham Episcopal Institute in Virginia she painted lilacs and sneaked time alone to walk out to where she could see the line of the Blue Ridge Mountains on the horizon. At the Art Institute in Chicago she was shocked by the presence of live models and wanted to abandon anatomy lessons. At the Art Students League in New York one of her fellow students advised her that, since he would be a great painter and she would end up teaching painting in a girls' school, any work of hers was less important than modeling for him. Another painted over her work to show her how the Impressionists did trees. She had not before heard how the Impressionists did trees and she did not much care.

At twenty-four she left all those opinions behind and went for the first time to live in Texas, where there were no trees to paint and no one to tell her how not to paint them. In Texas there was only the horizon she craved. In Texas she had her sister Claudia with her for a while, and in the late afternoons they would walk away from town and toward the horizon and watch the evening star come out. "That evening star fascinated me," she wrote. "It was in some way very exciting to me. My sister had a gun, and as we walked she would throw bottles into the air and shoot as many as she could before they hit the ground. I had nothing but to walk into nowhere and the wide sunset space with the star. Ten watercolors were made from that star." In a way one's interest is compelled as much by the sister Claudia with the gun as by the painter Georgia with the star, but only the painter left us this shining record. Ten watercolors were made from that star.

Engaging with the Text

161–70
1. "Style is character," Joan Didion observes. How does her **PROFILE** of Georgia O'Keeffe support this observation?

409–13
2. Didion includes a number of **QUOTATIONS** in her profile of Georgia O'Keeffe. Why do you think Didion chose so often to quote O'Keeffe

directly, rather than **SUMMARIZING** or **PARAPHRASING** her words? You might try paraphrasing one of the quotations to see the difference. 413–17

3. Didion **CONTRASTS** O'Keeffe with "the men." What does she mean by "the men"? What beliefs and personalities does she ascribe to them? How does describing them illuminate aspects of O'Keeffe's character? 306–13

4. When this profile was first published, in *The White Album* (1979), it did not include any **ILLUSTRATIONS**; we added the two reproduced here. Obviously, this reproduction of *Red Canna* helps readers see one of O'Keeffe's "famous flowers," but what might be the downside of including it here? 528–32

5. ***For Writing.*** Identify someone you know who is an artist, professional or amateur (e.g., a musician, a painter, a quilter, or an actor). **INTERVIEW** that person about the specific art he or she practices. Write a **PROFILE** of the person. 394–95 161–70

SEAN SMITH

Johnny Depp:
Unlikely Superstar

Sean Smith is a senior writer for Newsweek, *where he covers entertainment and the film industry. He was previously the West Coast editor for* Premiere *magazine. The following profile of actor Johnny Depp was prompted by the release of the film* Pirates of the Caribbean: Dead Man's Chest *(2006) and appeared in the June 26 issue of* Newsweek *that year. Notice that although much of the profile is based on Smith's interview with Depp, Smith also incorporates quotes and other information from other sources.*

FATHERHOOD HAS A WAY of changing people, even iconoclasts. "When I became a dad for the first time, it was like a veil being lifted," Johnny Depp says, as he leans forward, rolling loose tobacco into dark brown paper and using his knee as a table. "I've always loved the process of acting, but I didn't find the occupational hazards particularly rewarding." Occupational hazards like being stalked by paparazzi, mauled by strangers, packaged to sell bubble gum and other side effects of fame. "I can't use the word 'fame' with myself, but yeah," he says. "I just . . . there was a long period of confusion and dissatisfaction, because I didn't understand any of it. There was no purpose to it." He leans back, lights the cigarette, exhales. "I was never horribly self-obsessed or wrapped up in my own weirdness, but when my daughter was born, suddenly there was clarity. I wasn't angry anymore. It was the first purely selfless moment that I had ever experienced. And it was liberating. In that moment, it's like you become something else. The real you is revealed."

The Real Johnny Depp. How long have we searched for him? No one in Hollywood, it's fair to say, has worked harder at *not* being a movie star than Depp has, and yet he has evolved into one of the most adored actors of his generation not in spite of that persistence but because of it. *Pirates of the Caribbean: The Curse of the Black Pearl* may have grossed $653 million worldwide, made Depp a $20 million man and earned him an Oscar nomination, but he still seems an unlikely addition to the A-list. Top-tier stars,

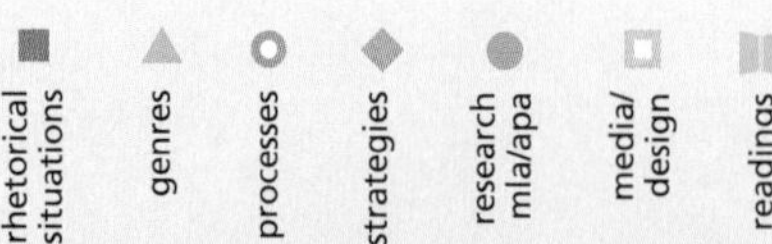

Johnny Depp as Captain Jack Sparrow in Pirates of the Caribbean: Dead Man's Chest *(2006).*

even those who are great actors, stay on top by being true to their personas. We pay $10 to see Will Smith or Julia Roberts precisely because they don't surprise us. It's not that they're playing themselves. It's just that the force of their personalities swamps everything else. They're more than actors. They're brands. Depp, 43, is almost pathologically unpredictable. He can be bizarre, hilarious, unsettling — even annoying. But he is never the same. He's the anti-Tom Cruise. "Nothing against Tom, but Johnny may be a bigger star now," says director John Waters, who cast Depp in 1990's *Cry-Baby*. "Nobody is sick of Johnny Depp."

Pirates of the Caribbean: Dead Man's Chest, which opens on July 7, will likely be the highest-grossing movie of the summer. And judging from *Newsweek*'s first look in the editing room, it also promises to be a welcome blast of sunshine in a season when Cruise has crashed and burned, and

The Da Vinci Code has proved to be a joyless blockbuster. In this second leg of the *Pirates* trilogy — the third installment will be released next summer — lovebirds Will (Orlando Bloom) and Elizabeth (Keira Knightley) are arrested on their wedding day for aiding the escape of Depp's louche Narcissus, Captain Jack Sparrow. To win freedom for his bride and himself, Will must find Captain Jack, get him to hand over his mysterious compass and give it to the wormy Lord Beckett, who plans to use it to rid the world of pirates forever. Jack, meanwhile, has more immediate problems. He owes his soul to undersea Captain Davey Jones, is in danger of being destroyed by a giant sea creature called a *kraken* and has landed on an island of cannibals who have made him their god. Which would be great if the natives didn't make a habit of eating their gods.

Returning director Gore Verbinski, producer Jerry Bruckheimer and team have cranked up the action this time around. One huge set piece includes an elaborate three-way sword fight on a massive water wheel that has snapped off its frame and is rolling at top speed through the jungle. ("It's those moments when you realize how absurd your job is," Depp says. "It's great fun, but it was a bastard to shoot.") Luckily, they've also given Depp plenty of playtime, too. Even more than in the first film, Depp's exaggerated expressions and unexpected line deliveries turn "cute" moments into hilarious ones. At one point, Elizabeth tells Jack, "You're a good man." Depp replies, sloppily, under his breath, "All evidence to the contrary."

Sitting in a bungalow at the Chateau Marmont in Los Angeles, Depp 5
flashes a bit of Captain Jack every time he opens his mouth. Those gold pirate teeth are bonded onto his own. With the shoot for the third *Pirates* resuming in August, Depp figured it was just easier to keep them. "They don't come off until the ride stops," he says, and smiles. "It's a horrible process. I didn't want to go through yanking them off and putting them back on. And it leaves some residue of the character behind." Time slows down when you're with Johnny Depp. He seems like a man who has never rushed to, or from, anywhere in his life. He is chronically late for interviews — sometimes four or five hours, sometimes days — but this time around just a gentlemanly 50 minutes. And once he's with you, he never seems in a hurry to leave. His voice is a soft, low mumble. His body is in almost constant motion—rolling those cigarettes, rubbing an elbow, reach-

ing for a glass — but the rhythm is tranquil and fluid, like a cat licking its paw. He's a calm, almost hypnotic presence. "He's always been true to who he is," says director Tim Burton, who has made five films with Depp, including last year's *Charlie and the Chocolate Factory*. "He's never been ruled by money, or by what people think he should or shouldn't do. Maybe it's just in America, but it seems that if you're passionate about something, it freaks people out. You're considered bizarre or eccentric. To me, it just means you know who you are."

Depp arrived in Hollywood in the early '80s. Despite a physical beauty that had studio executives slobbering to make him into a Romantic Leading Man and hordes of teenage girls (and a few boys) dreaming of touching his hair *just once*, Depp escaped from the Hollywood star machine around 1990, and managed to elude capture for almost two decades. He hid out in strange, sometimes beautiful films, playing unforgettable characters — Edward Scissorhands, Ed Wood, Hunter S. Thompson, Gilbert Grape — in movies that rarely made a dent at the box office. Of the 20 films Depp starred in before 2003, only one, Burton's *Sleepy Hollow*, squeaked past the $100 million mark. Depp got a reputation for being outré and unbankable. "Oh, yeah," he says, then rolls off the list of crimes: "'That guy can't open a film. He does all those weird art movies. He works with directors whose names we can't pronounce.'" He smiles. "But there are worse things they could say."

When news hit years ago that Depp was going to make the first *Pirates*, the buzz around town was that he must be broke, and that after years of taking the artistic high road, he had finally sold out. Depp says he never worried about that. "Never, not once, and I don't know why, because one would think that I would have," he says. "I suppose it's because I feel like I have a voice. The idea of commercial success never bothered me necessarily. What bothered me was *striving* for that, and lying to get that. If I was going to do something, it had to be on my terms — not because I'm some hideous control freak — but because I don't want to live a lie. You really don't want to look back on your life and go, 'I was a complete fraud.'"

The battle to remain authentic has been long and bloody, and it made Depp an angry young man for most of his twenties. Born in Kentucky, the youngest of four kids, and raised in Florida by parents who fought and finally divorced when he was fifteen, Depp dreamed of playing guitar in a band. By sixteen he had dropped out of school and was doing just that, his group opening for acts like Iggy Pop. "It was wonderful," he says. "I couldn't have been happier." But after the band arrived in Los Angeles, Depp found himself broke. A musician he was briefly married to at the time introduced Depp to Nicolas Cage, who suggested that he give acting a try. On little more than a whim, he did, and ended up with a supporting role in *A Nightmare on Elm Street* and a small part in *Platoon*. Still struggling financially, he signed for *21 Jump Street*, a slick TV series about young cops going undercover in high schools. It made Depp a teen idol, and made him miserable just as fast. "Everything flips," he says. "Suddenly, you go into restaurants and people are pointing at you and whispering. You feel spooked by it because that freedom of anonymity is gone. You never get used to that. You'd leave the hotel to go to dinner and there'd be tons of cameras and flashbulbs. 'Smile, Johnny! Smile!'" He looks annoyed by it, even now. "I thought, 'Jesus, I just want to go home.' But there was no home."

Depp was locked into a multiyear contract with the Fox network. "They turned me into this product, and I didn't have a say in it," he says. "You have no voice, you know? I felt like I was a captive." So he lashed out, becoming a disruptive force on the *Jump Street* set in the hope that the network would fire him. "I was the only one who confronted him on what an a--hole he was being," says costar Holly Robinson Peete. "I totally understood his position, but I was over the moon to be a part of this show, and it's hard to come to work every day with someone who is p---ing all over it. So I went into his dressing room and told him how I felt, and right after that he trashed his Winnebago." Peete doesn't have any hard feelings toward Depp, and chalks it up to youth and inexperience. "He's got a really great heart, but he was frustrated," she says. "He just hated the idea of being on a lunch box or some teenage girl's wall."

Finally freed from *Jump Street*, Depp played a succession of iconic lon- 10
ers and dreamers for visionary, unconventional directors, such as Waters, Burton, Jim Jarmusch and Terry Gilliam. But the anger, which Depp calls his "hillbilly rage," never quite dissipated. He was famously arrested for trashing a New York City hotel room in 1994, and while Depp says the incident was blown out of proportion — "I wasn't the Wild Man of Borneo" — he still believed that his fame and success lacked a point, meaning. "I had these sort of self-destructive periods," he says. "We all go

through times where we poison ourselves a bit. Looking back on it now, it was simply a waste of time, all the self-medicating and boozing."

Depp was rescued, in part, by Marlon Brando. The two worked together on 1995's *Don Juan DeMarco*, and hit it off at the first rehearsal. "Within minutes, Johnny was in Marlon's lap with, I think, a bottle of gin," says director Jeremy Leven. "And I think he stayed there the whole time." It's easy to imagine the bond between the two men, both actors with unconventional visions, talent to burn and a disdain for art compromised by commerce. "Marlon was a pioneer," Depp says, quietly. "So I wouldn't even put myself in the same thought bubble with him, but he understood a lot of things about me, and was incredibly generous and helpful and caring. Very rarely did we talk about movies or acting, so it wasn't that. He saw me going through stuff that he had been through — my weird hillbilly rage — so yeah, the connection was strong and deep."

But it wasn't until Depp met and fell in love with French actress-singer Vanessa Paradis that everything seemed to fall into place for the actor. After a series of highly public, long-term romances — Sherilyn Fenn, Jennifer Grey, Winona Ryder, Kate Moss — his relationship with Paradis seemed to anchor him. The couple's daughter, Lily-Rose, was born in 1999; their son, Jack, in 2002. Being a father released him from the pressure of finding meaning and identity exclusively in his work. "I think it softened him on one level, and then invigorated him on an artistic one," says Burton. "It's an interesting juxtaposition." Depp himself puts it more directly: "Now I know where home is."

It was Depp's desire to make a movie for his kids that led him to *Pirates*. In a visit to the Disney lot about five years ago, he mentioned to studio chairman Dick Cook that he'd been watching a lot of Disney movies with his daughter, loved them and was hoping to voice a character in a Pixar movie. Cook mentioned that the studio was developing a movie based on the theme-park ride *Pirates of the Caribbean*. "And he got very excited," Cook recalls. "He said, 'Like a real pirate movie? With swords?' And I said, 'Yeah — with swords.' And he said, 'I'm in.' "

As is now well known to *Pirates* fans, studio executives were nonplussed when they began to see the footage of Depp in character. Whereas Captain Jack Sparrow was initially conceived as a young Burt Lancaster, Depp had re-imagined him as a debauched, vain, slightly fey rock star, inspired by Rolling Stones icon Keith Richards and cartoon skunk Pepe Le Pew. "The studio was, like, 'Is he gay? Is he drunk? We don't know *what* he's doing!' " says producer Bruckheimer. "It took a little while to calm everybody down." For his part, Verbinski, the director, loved it. "You know, there's a lot of conspiring that goes on between actors and directors that I think is very healthy," he says. "You should be a little concerned as a director if you're *not* making the studio nervous."

Depp's off-kilter performance, of course, was the very thing that cat- 15
apulted *Pirates* into a cultural phenomenon. "First of all, Johnny is a pirate in real life," says John Waters. "It's the closest part he's ever played to his real self, but the fact that he played it kind of nelly was a big risk." Pause. "If only real gay pirates were that much fun." After decades of being daring and unexpected in daring and unexpected little films, Depp was now staying true to himself in a big summer blockbuster. He didn't have to be an outsider on the outside. He could be an outsider on the inside. "You feel like you have infiltrated the enemy camp, like you got in there somehow and chiseled your name in the castle wall," he says. The huge success of the film "made perfect sense to me on the one hand, and at the same time, it made no sense at all, which I kind of enjoyed." He takes another drag, exhales. "Yeah, it just felt right. Even now, with the dolls and the cereal boxes and snacks and fruit juices, it all just feels fun to me, in a Warholian way. It's absurd. It doesn't get more absurd." Depp's not ready to let go of Captain Jack just yet. "He's a blast to play," he says. "I'll be in a deep, dark depression saying goodbye to him." He laughs. "I'll keep the costume and just prance around the house, entertain the kids." Or the rest of the world. "Maybe '*Pirates* 4, 5 and 6,' " he says. "If they had a good script, why not? I mean, at a certain point, the madness must stop, but for the moment, I can't say that he's done."

These days, Depp and his family divide their time between homes in Los Angeles and France, when they're not on some movie set or other. He says the media perception of him as an expat and wanna-be Frenchman has been overstated. "But, yeah, I love it there," he says. "I've always loved it there. The phones don't ring as much. Movies are never brought up in conversation. I'll take the kids and we'll go out to the trampoline and the swing set, and we'll stop by the garden and see how our tomatoes are

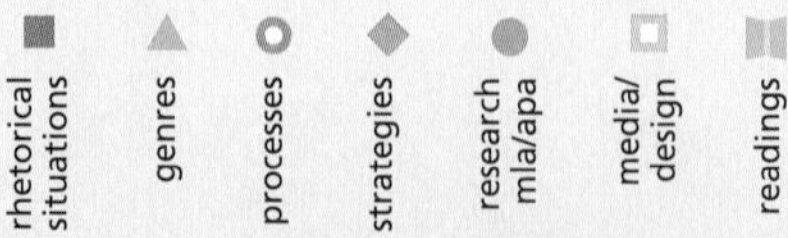

doing. You know, old-fart stuff. Good stuff." At last, Depp has learned to quit fighting fate / fame / whatever. "I think everything happened the way it was meant to happen, but I don't know why," he says. "I remember every bump in the road, and I still don't know how I got here. But who am I to ask why? The fact is, this is where I am. So I enjoy it, salute it and keep moving forward." He smiles, a flash of gold. "None of it makes any sense to me, but then, why should it?"

Engaging with the Text

1. Good profiles see their subjects from an **INTERESTING ANGLE.** What do you think is Sean Smith's angle on Johnny Depp? Identify places in the text that make that angle clear. 166
2. Smith **BEGINS** his profile of Johnny Depp with an observation: "Fatherhood has a way of changing people, even iconoclasts." Why was having children a turning point in Depp's life? How does this opening set the stage for the rest of the profile? How effective is this opening? 261–66
3. What is Smith's **STANCE** toward Depp, his subject? Point to specific places in the text that reveal this stance. 12–14
4. In what ways has Johnny Depp been made into a commodity over the years? How did Depp move from being angry about being commodified—"hat[ing] the idea of being on a lunch box or some teenage girl's wall"—to embracing it, noting that "the dolls and cereal boxes and snacks and fruit juices, it all feels fun to me, in a Warholian way"? How do you feel about this attitude?
5. ***For Writing.*** Identify a person who is near the top of his or her career (a teacher, a police officer, a business person, an artist—in short, any profession). You might consider finding someone who is in a career you would like to pursue. Interview that person to find out how he or she came to be in the chosen career, how that career has played itself out, and what he or she plans to do next. Write a **PROFILE** that incorporates **ANECDOTES** and **DIALOGUE** from your subject to help readers understand how that person arrived where he or she is now. 161–70 343–51 333–37

62 Proposals

See also:

MICHAEL GRANOF
Course Requirement: Extortion 171

JENNIFER CHURCH
Biodiversity Loss and Its Effect on Medicine 178

DENNIS BARON

Don't Make English Official — Ban It Instead

Dennis Baron is a professor of English and linguistics at the University of Illinois at Urbana-Champaign. His essays on the history of English usage, language legislation, and technology and literacy have been widely published in newspapers and magazines. His books include Grammar and Good Taste: Reforming the American Language *(1983) and* The English-Only Question: An Official Language for Americans? *(1992). He also serves as a consultant to policy makers, lawyers, and journalists on questions concerning language. The following proposal originally appeared in the* Washington Post *in 1996.*

CONGRESS IS CONSIDERING, and may soon pass, legislation making English the official language of the United States. Supporters of the measure say that English forms the glue that keeps America together. They deplore the dollars wasted translating English into other languages. And they fear a horde of illegal aliens adamantly refusing to acquire the most powerful language on earth.

On the other hand, opponents of official English remind us that without legislation we have managed to get over ninety-seven percent of the residents of this country to speak the national language. No country with an official language law even comes close. Opponents also point out that today's non-English-speaking immigrants are picking up English faster than earlier generations of immigrants did, so instead of official English, they favor "English Plus," encouraging everyone to speak both English and another language.

I would like to offer a modest proposal to resolve the language impasse in Congress. Don't make English official, ban it instead.

That may sound too radical, but proposals to ban English first surfaced in the heady days after the American Revolution. Anti-British sentiment was so strong in the new United States that a few superpatriots wanted to get rid of English altogether. They suggested replacing English with Hebrew, thought by many in the eighteenth century to be the world's first language, the one spoken in the garden of Eden. French was also considered, because it was thought at the time, and especially by the French, to be the language of pure reason. And of course there was Greek, the language of Athens, the world's first democracy. It's not clear how serious any of these proposals were, though Roger Sherman* of Connecticut supposedly remarked that it would be better to keep English for ourselves and make the British speak Greek.

Even if the British are now our allies, there may be some benefit to 5
banning English today. A common language can often be the cause of strife and misunderstanding. Look at Ireland and Northern Ireland, the two Koreas, or the Union and the Confederacy. Banning English would prevent that kind of divisiveness in America today.

Also, if we banned English, we wouldn't have to worry about whose English to make official: the English of England or America? of Chicago or New York? of Ross Perot or William F. Buckley?†

We might as well ban English, too, because no one seems to read it much lately, few can spell it, and fewer still can parse it. Even English teachers have come to rely on computer spell checkers.

Another reason to ban English: it's hardly even English anymore. English started its decline in 1066, with the unfortunate incident at Hastings.‡ Since then it has become a polyglot conglomeration of French, Latin, Italian, Scandinavian, Arabic, Sanskrit, Celtic, Yiddish and Chinese, with an occasional smiley face thrown in.

More important, we should ban English because it has become a world language. Remember what happened to all the other world languages: Latin, Greek, Indo-European? One day they're on everybody's tongue; the next day they're dead. Banning English now would save us that inevitable disappointment.

---

*_Roger Sherman_ (1721–1793): American revolutionary leader and signer of the Declaration of Independence and the U.S. Constitution. [Editor's note]

†_William F. Buckley Jr._ (1925–2008): conservative political commentator. _Ross Perot_: American industrialist and independent presidential candidate. [Editor's note]

‡_Hastings_: port on south coast of England, site of Saxon army's defeat by the invading Norman forces led by William of Normandy (c. 1028–1087). [Editor's note]

10 Although we shouldn't ban English without designating a replacement for it, there is no obvious candidate. The French blew their chance when they sold Louisiana. It doesn't look like the Russians are going to take over this country anytime soon — they're having enough trouble taking over Russia. German, the largest minority language in the U.S. until recently, lost much of its prestige after two world wars. Chinese is too hard to write, especially if you're not Chinese. There's always Esperanto, a language made up a hundred years ago that is supposed to bring about world unity. We're still waiting for that. And if you took Spanish in high school you can see that it's not easy to get large numbers of people to speak another language fluently.

In the end, though, it doesn't matter what replacement language we pick, just so long as we ban English instead of making it official. Prohibiting English will do for the language what Prohibition did for liquor. Those who already use it will continue to do so, and those who don't will want to try out what has been forbidden. This negative psychology works with children. It works with speed limits. It even worked in the Garden of Eden.

Engaging with the Text

1. Dennis Baron **BEGINS** his essay by presenting two views on whether or not English should be the official language of the United States. What is the central problem that both sides are trying to address? Is this an effective beginning? Why or why not? How else might he have begun? 261–66
2. Baron signals that his proposal is meant to be read as satire when he writes "I would like to offer a modest proposal to resolve the language impasse in Congress. Don't make English official, ban it instead." Here Baron alludes to Jonathan Swift's "A Modest Proposal," an essay that is a *tour de force* of satire. If we aren't meant to take his proposal at face value — and we aren't — what is the **PURPOSE** of Baron's proposal? What, in other words, is the real argument he is making? 3–4

286–87

3. Baron offers six **REASONS** for accepting his "solution." What are those reasons? What is the central point that holds these different reasons together?

9–11

4. If Baron's purpose is not actually to propose banning English in America, why do you think he chose to use the proposal genre to put forth his argument? What other **GENRES** might he have used?

171–79
283–99

5. ***For Writing.*** Identify a current hotly debated issue in the country, your state, your town, or your school. **PROPOSE** an outlandish solution for the problem and provide a plausible, if ironic, **ARGUMENT** for your solution. Be sure to anticipate — and respond to — possible objections to your proposed solution.

PETER SINGER

The Singer Solution to World Poverty

Australian philosopher Peter Singer is a professor of bioethics in the University Center for Human Values at Princeton University and a professor in the Center for Applied Philosophy and Public Ethics at the University of Melbourne in Australia. The author of eighteen books, among them Animal Liberation *(revised edition 2001),* One World: Ethics and Globalization *(2002), and* The Life You Can Save: Acting Now to End World Poverty *(2009), he is considered one of the founders of the modern animal rights movement. The following proposal was first published in 1999 in the* New York Times Magazine.

IN THE BRAZILIAN FILM *Central Station*, Dora is a retired schoolteacher who makes ends meet by sitting at the station writing letters for illiterate people. Suddenly she has an opportunity to pocket $1,000. All she has to do is persuade a homeless nine-year-old boy to follow her to an address she has been given. (She is told he will be adopted by wealthy foreigners.) She delivers the boy, gets the money, spends some of it on a television set, and settles down to enjoy her new acquisition. Her neighbor spoils the fun, however, by telling her that the boy was too old to be adopted — he will be killed and his organs sold for transplantation. Perhaps Dora knew this all along, but after her neighbor's plain speaking, she spends a troubled night. In the morning Dora resolves to take the boy back.

Suppose Dora had told her neighbor that it is a tough world, other people have nice new TVs too, and if selling the kid is the only way she can get one, well, he was only a street kid. She would then have become, in the eyes of the audience, a monster. She redeems herself only by being prepared to bear considerable risks to save the boy.

At the end of the movie, in cinemas in the affluent nations of the world, people who would have been quick to condemn Dora if she had not rescued the boy go home to places far more comfortable than her apartment. In fact, the average family in the United States spends almost one-third of its income on things that are no more necessary to them than Dora's new TV was to her. Going out to nice restaurants, buying new clothes because the old ones are no longer stylish, vacationing at beach resorts — so much of our income is spent on things not essential to the preservation of our lives and health. Donated to one of a number of charitable agencies, that money could mean the difference between life and death for children in need.

All of which raises a question: in the end, what is the ethical distinction between a Brazilian who sells a homeless child to organ peddlers and an American who already has a TV and upgrades to a better one — knowing that the money could be donated to an organization that would use it to save the lives of kids in need?

Of course, there are several differences between the two situations 5
that could support different moral judgments about them. For one thing, to be able to consign a child to death when he is standing right in front of you takes a chilling kind of heartlessness; it is much easier to ignore an appeal for money to help children you will never meet. Yet for a utilitarian philosopher like myself — that is, one who judges whether acts are right or wrong by their consequences — if the upshot of the American's failure to donate the money is that one more kid dies on the streets of a Brazilian city, then it is, in some sense, just as bad as selling the kid to the organ peddlers. But one doesn't need to embrace my utilitarian ethic to see that, at the very least, there is a troubling incongruity in being so quick to condemn Dora for taking the child to the organ peddlers while, at the same time, not regarding the American consumer's behavior as raising a serious moral issue.

In his 1996 book *Living High and Letting Die*, the New York University philosopher Peter Unger presented an ingenious series of imaginary examples designed to probe our intuitions about whether it is wrong to live well without giving substantial amounts of money to help people who are hungry, malnourished, or dying from easily treatable illnesses like diarrhea. Here's my paraphrase of one of these examples:

Bob is close to retirement. He has invested most of his savings in a very rare and valuable old car, a Bugatti, which he has not been able to insure. The Bugatti is his pride and joy. In addition to the pleasure he gets from driving and caring for his car, Bob knows that its rising market value means that he will always be able to sell it and live comfortably after retirement. One day when Bob is out for a drive, he parks the Bugatti near the end of a railway siding and goes for a walk up the track. As he does so, he sees that a runaway train, with no one aboard, is running down the railway track. Looking farther down the track, he sees the small figure of a child very likely to be killed by the runaway train. He can't stop the train and the child is too far away to warn of the danger, but he can throw a switch that will divert the train down the siding where his Bugatti is parked. Then nobody will be killed — but the train will destroy his Bugatti. Thinking of his joy in owning the car and the financial security it represents, Bob decides not to throw the switch. The child is killed. For many years to come, Bob enjoys owning his Bugatti and the financial security it represents.

Bob's conduct, most of us will immediately respond, was gravely wrong. Unger agrees. But then he reminds us that we, too, have opportunities to save the lives of children. We can give to organizations like Unicef or Oxfam America. How much would we have to give one of these organizations to have a high probability of saving the life of a child threatened by easily preventable diseases? (I do not believe that children are more worth saving than adults, but since no one can argue that children have brought their poverty on themselves, focusing on them simplifies the issues.) Unger called up some experts and used the information they provided to offer some plausible estimates that include the cost of raising money, administrative expenses, and the cost of delivering aid where it is most needed. By his calculation, $200 in donations would help a sickly two-year-old transform into a healthy six-year-old — offering safe passage through childhood's most dangerous years. To show how practical philosophical argument can be, Unger even tells his readers that they can easily donate funds by using their credit card and calling one of these toll-free numbers: (800) 367-5437 for Unicef; (800) 693-2687 for Oxfam America.

Now you, too, have the information you need to save a child's life. How should you judge yourself if you don't do it? Think again about Bob and his Bugatti. Unlike Dora, Bob did not have to look into the eyes of the child he was sacrificing for his own material comfort. The child was a complete stranger to him and too far away to relate to in an intimate, personal way. Unlike Dora, too, he did not mislead the child or initiate the chain of events imperiling him. In all these respects, Bob's situation resembles that of people able but unwilling to donate to overseas aid and differs from Dora's situation.

10 If you still think that it was very wrong of Bob not to throw the switch that would have diverted the train and saved the child's life, then it is hard to see how you could deny that it is also very wrong not to send money to one of the organizations listed above. Unless, that is, there is some morally important difference between the two situations that I have overlooked.

Is it the practical uncertainties about whether aid will really reach the people who need it? Nobody who knows the world of overseas aid can doubt that such uncertainties exist. But Unger's figure of $200 to save a child's life was reached after he had made conservative assumptions about the proportion of the money donated that will actually reach its target.

One genuine difference between Bob and those who can afford to donate to overseas aid organizations but don't is that only Bob can save the child on the tracks, whereas there are hundreds of millions of people who can give $200 to overseas aid organizations. The problem is that most of them aren't doing it. Does this mean that it is all right for you not to do it?

Suppose that there were more owners of priceless vintage cars — Carol, Dave, Emma, Fred and so on, down to Ziggy — all in exactly the same situation as Bob, with their own siding and their own switch, all sacrificing the child in order to preserve their own cherished car. Would that make it all right for Bob to do the same? To answer this question affirmatively is to endorse follow-the-crowd ethics — the kind of ethics that led many Germans to look away when the Nazi atrocities were being committed. We do not excuse them because others were behaving no better.

We seem to lack a sound basis for drawing a clear moral line between Bob's situation and that of any reader of this article with $200 to spare who does not donate it to an overseas aid agency. These readers seem to be acting at least as badly as Bob was acting when he chose to let the runaway train hurtle toward the unsuspecting child. In the light of this conclusion, I trust that many readers will reach for the phone and donate that $200. Perhaps you should do it before reading further.

Now that you have distinguished yourself morally from people who 15
put their vintage cars ahead of a child's life, how about treating yourself and your partner to dinner at your favorite restaurant? But wait. The money you will spend at the restaurant could also help save the lives of children overseas! True, you weren't planning to blow $200 tonight, but if you were to give up dining out just for one month, you would easily save that amount. And what is one month's dining out, compared to a child's life? There's the rub. Since there are a lot of desperately needy children in the world, there will always be another child whose life you could save for another $200. Are you therefore obliged to keep giving until you have nothing left? At what point can you stop?

Hypothetical examples can easily become farcical. Consider Bob. How far past losing the Bugatti should he go? Imagine that Bob had got his foot stuck in the track of the siding, and if he diverted the train, then before it rammed the car it would also amputate his big toe. Should he still throw the switch? What if it would amputate his foot? His entire leg?

As absurd as the Bugatti scenario gets when pushed to extremes, the point it raises is a serious one: only when the sacrifices become very significant indeed would most people be prepared to say that Bob does nothing wrong when he decides not to throw the switch. Of course, most people could be wrong; we can't decide moral issues by taking opinion polls. But consider for yourself the level of sacrifice that you would demand of Bob, and then think about how much money you would have to give away in order to make a sacrifice that is roughly equal to that. It's almost certainly much, much more than $200. For most middle-class Americans, it could easily be more like $200,000.

Isn't it counterproductive to ask people to do so much? Don't we run the risk that many will shrug their shoulders and say that morality, so conceived, is fine for saints but not for them? I accept that we are unlikely to see, in the near or even medium-term future, a world in which it is normal for wealthy Americans to give the bulk of their wealth to strangers. When it comes to praising or blaming people for what they do, we tend to use a standard that is relative to some conception of normal behavior. Comfortably off Americans who give, say, 10 percent of their income to overseas aid organizations are so far ahead of most of their equally comfortable fellow citizens that I wouldn't go out of my way to chastise them for not doing more. Nevertheless, they should be doing much more, and they are in no position to criticize Bob for failing to make the much greater sacrifice of his Bugatti.

At this point various objections may crop up. Someone may say: "If every citizen living in the affluent nations contributed his or her share I wouldn't have to make such a drastic sacrifice, because long before such levels were reached, the resources would have been there to save the lives of all those children dying from lack of food or medical care. So why should I give more than my fair share?" Another, related objection is that the government ought to increase its overseas aid allocations, since that would spread the burden more equitably across all taxpayers.

Yet the question of how much we ought to give is a matter to be 20
decided in the real world — and that, sadly, is a world in which we know that most people do not, and in the immediate future will not, give substantial amounts to overseas aid agencies. We know, too, that at least in the next year, the United States government is not going to meet even the very modest United Nations–recommended target of 0.7 percent of gross national product; at a moment it lags far below that, at 0.09 percent, not even half of Japan's 0.22 percent or a tenth of Denmark's 0.97 percent. Thus, we know that the money we can give beyond that theoretical "fair share" is still going to save lives that would otherwise be lost. While the idea that no one need do more than his or her fair share is a powerful one, should it prevail if we know that others are not doing their fair share and that children will die preventable deaths unless we do more than our fair share? That would be taking fairness too far.

Thus, this ground for limiting how much we ought to give also fails. In the world as it is now, I can see no escape from the conclusion that each one of us with wealth surplus to his or her essential needs should be giving most of it to help people suffering from poverty so dire as to be life-threatening. That's right: I'm saying that you shouldn't buy that new car, take that cruise, redecorate the house, or get that pricey new suit. After all, a $1,000 suit could save five children's lives.

So how does my philosophy break down in dollars and cents? An American household with an income of $50,000 spends around $30,000 annually on necessities, according to the Conference Board, a nonprofit economic research organization. Therefore, for a household bringing in $50,000 a year, donations to help the world's poor should be as close as possible to $20,000. The $30,000 required for necessities holds for higher incomes as well. So a household making $100,000 could cut a yearly check for $70,000. Again, the formula is simple: Whatever money you're spending on luxuries, not necessities, should be given away.

Now, evolutionary psychologists tell us that human nature just isn't sufficiently altruistic to make it plausible that many people will sacrifice so much for strangers. On the facts of human nature, they might be right, but they would be wrong to draw a moral conclusion from those facts. If it is the case that we ought to do things that, predictably, most of us won't do, then let's face that fact head-on. Then, if we value the life of a child more than going to fancy restaurants, the next time we dine out we will know that we could have done something better with our money. If that makes living a morally decent life extremely arduous, well, then that is the way things are. If we don't do it, then we should at least know that we are failing to live a morally decent life — not because it is good to wallow in guilt but because knowing where we should be going is the first step toward heading in that direction.

When Bob first grasped the dilemma that faced him as he stood by that railway switch, he must have thought how extraordinarily unlucky he was to be placed in a situation in which he must choose between the life of an innocent child and the sacrifice of most of his savings. But he was not unlucky at all. We are all in that situation.

Engaging with the Text

1. 3–4 What is the **PURPOSE** of Peter Singer's proposal? What is he actually 171–79 **PROPOSING**? What action does he want us to take? Point to passages where his purpose is made explicit.
2. Singer begins his essay with reference to the Brazilian film *Central Station* 290–91 and follows it with a hypothetical **SCENARIO**. What role do the film and the scenario play in his proposal? What do they contribute to the persuasiveness of his argument? Do you find them effective? Why or why not?
3. Singer argues that "whatever money you're spending on luxuries, not necessities, should be given away." To what degree do you agree with this claim? How much faith in this claim does Singer himself appear to have?
4. 175 What **QUESTIONS** does Singer anticipate? How does he address potential naysayers?
5. ***For Writing.*** Think of a large societal problem (for example, poverty, pollution, or unemployment) and how the actions of individuals might help alleviate it (volunteering at a food bank, recycling soda cans, restructuring a company to create more positions). Describe the problem 171–79 and write a **PROPOSAL** for how you and other individuals can help to solve it.

H. STERLING BURNETT

A Modest Proposal to Improve Forest Management: State Forest Block Grants

Specializing in issues related to environmental policy and gun policy, H. Sterling Burnett has held positions in several public policy organizations. He is a Senior Fellow for the National Center for Policy Analysis (NCPA), a conservative nonprofit think tank. Burnett regularly discusses energy and environmental policy as a guest on national radio and television, and his writing has appeared in USA Today, *and the* Washington Times, *among other publications. This proposal appeared on the NCPA website in 1998.*

THE UNITED STATES FOREST SERVICE (USFS) IS A LIGHTNING ROD for both fiscal conservatives and liberal environmentalists, two groups not often on the same side of issues. Fiscal conservatives decry its money-losing programs. Environmentalists claim that its programs cause environmental harm. Both sets of criticisms are correct. But because neither group trusts the other's motives, when either group proposes reforms that would streamline the USFS's operating procedures, alter its goals, or shift its budget priorities the other group stymies the effort. And year after year passes with no changes made to the failed policies.

Logging is the most criticized of the USFS's money-losing efforts — but it is not the biggest money loser. That distinction goes to recreation. Hikers, birders and campers pay even less of their own way than loggers. Researchers at the Political Economy Research Center in Bozeman, Montana, found that while the timber program in 1988 made more than $5 million in Forest Service Region 1, the recreation program lost almost $15 million. Neither program has made money since then. In 1992, the Region 1 timber program lost $18,967,660 and recreation lost $23,415,573 (25 percent more than logging and five times more than the grazing program).

In contrast, state and county forests typically make money. For instance, from 1988–1992 while state forests in Montana made $13.3 million, Montana's 10 national forests lost $42 million. State forests yielded an average of $2.16 for every dollar spent; federal forests lost between $.09 and $.73 for every dollar spent.

Most of these losses were due to the much higher management costs for national forests. The average wages were comparable — $15.30 per hour for state forests versus $15.63 for national forests, but it took 11.6 hours of administration and management per 1000 board feet harvested on federal land versus 4.5 hours on state land.

The figures are similar for county forests in Minnesota. From 1990– 5
1993 the Superior National Forest lost $15.83 for every thousand board feet of timber logged, while St. Louis County forest lands in the same region made $8.44 on every thousand board feet of timber harvested.

The environment benefits from state management as well. Independent teams of experts in both Montana and Minnesota concluded that state foresters did a better job of protecting watersheds and waterways from the impacts of various activities than did federal forest managers.

- In Montana 99 percent of the watersheds in state forests were protected from all impacts from logging, compared to 92 percent of watersheds on federal forests.
- In Minnesota county lands had a 90 percent compliance rate with best management practices for protecting water quality, compared to 87 percent for national forests.
- Federal forests had an 87 percent compliance rate.

State forests also have better annual growth rates than federal forests. In the Southwest-central region of Montana the state forests averaged 67 percent of their productive potential, while the Gallatin National Forest, where more trees are dying than growing, actually had a negative growth rate.

In theory, the better water quality and superior timber growth should give state forests greater biodiversity than federal forests.

With these facts in mind Congress could implement a demonstration project, allowing any state that has demonstrated both superior economic and environmental performance with its forests to take over the management of the national forests within its boundaries. Congress could give fixed but declining block grants to the participating states to help them manage the forests during the transition period.

10 Each state that undertook such control would have to be allowed to run the program a sufficient number of years to counteract years of federal mismanagement and demonstrate improved environmental quality. At the end of the time period, any state that showed both improved economic and environmental performance on federal forests would be granted those forests outright and federal payments would end. Federal forests that did not improve could revert to federal management and new management experiments could be tried.

State and county foresters in underperforming states faced with the prospect of additional revenues would have the incentive to improve the performance on their forests in an effort to win authority to manage federal lands. And USFS managers, faced with a loss of revenues and authority would have the incentive to improve performance in an effort to maintain control of what federal forests remain.

Several states have shown that the public can have the best of both worlds, forests that make a profit and that promote environmental quality. Armed with this knowledge, a courageous Congress could allow states to manage the federal forests within their borders. Wildlife and the U.S. taxpayer would owe these farsighted legislators a debt of gratitude.

Engaging with the Text

1. H. Sterling Burnett **BEGINS** his proposal with an observation that fiscal conservatives and liberal environmentalists mistrust one another, and thus, "when either group proposes reforms . . . the other group stymies the effort." Why do you think Burnett begins by emphasizing this conflict? How does this approach help establish the context for his topic and prepare readers for the rest of his proposal?

261–66

2. What is Burnett's **CALL TO ACTION** in his proposal? How effective are his arguments for persuading his readers to agree with and act on this call?

175

3. In describing the problem at the heart of his proposal, H. Sterling 306–13 Burnett **COMPARES AND CONTRASTS** federal with state and local forest management. What method does he use to organize his comparison? How else might he have presented this information? What other 524–32 **DESIGN** elements — charts, tables, and so on — might he have used?
4. 5–8 Burnett wrote this proposal for an **AUDIENCE** of environmentalists and environmental policy makers who would likely be familiar with the topic and terms he uses to discuss it. How might this proposal need to be revised for an audience of first-year college students? Which terms would need to be defined? What else about the proposal might need to be explained for this new audience?
5. ***For Writing.*** Identify a service on your campus — dining, the bookstore, the recreation center, or computer services, for example — that you think could be improved. Research how the service is currently run, and interview a manager of the service to determine how it might be managed differently to provide better service to students. Write a 171–79 **PROPOSAL** that identifies problems with the current service and suggests methods of improving its management for the benefit of your campus community.

HEIDI POLLOCK

You Say You Want a Resolution?

The following proposal was first published in 2003 in h2so4, *a magazine "dedicated to provoking thought on politics and philosophy, art and love, without giving up the potential to delight, amuse, and entertain." Heidi Pollock is a frequent contributor.*

I HAVE FINALLY MASTERED THE ART of making New Year's resolutions, a skill honed by years of abject failure. Seven years ago I developed a fine-tuned Resolution Philosophy which has proven consistently successful in numerous clinical trials (and tribulations). In the interests of humanitarian aid, I am going to share my hard-won methodology with the world, in the hope that we may forever end the vicious cycle of making vain, fruitless, and doomed resolutions such as "I will lose ten pounds this year," "I will go to the gym three times a week," and "I will not park illegally ever again."

For starters, a New Year's resolution should not be about improving your life; it should be about enriching it in a potentially unpredictable way. The new year provides you with a chance to do new things. Therefore, a New Year's resolution should not be something that you've already thought about doing; it should not be on your existing agenda. "Quit smoking," for instance, doesn't count because the fact that you shouldn't be smoking is old news. A true resolution should be an addition to your life, should expand your horizons and help you grow as a person. It should be process-oriented and not require major psychological or physical changes. A solid resolution should not be too fixated on a specific goal; it should not be subject to a Pass/Fail grade; it should strive for a wide spectrum of achievement(s).

Here are the rules: You should always make three resolutions. This is partly to increase the odds of success, but mostly to direct the focus of enhancement outside the body. The tyranny of "diet" and "gym" resolutions is distinctly unhealty. Resolutions should also be made to benefit your intellectual, emotional, or artistic well-being. Make one resolution in the Health & Lifestyle category, another in the Education/Practice category and, most importantly, make one resolution in the Project/Task category. This last category is the wildcard designed to help your chances of actually fulfilling at least one of your three resolutions by year's end.

My approach to making New Year's resolutions may strike you as contrived to guarantee success, but I assure you, it isn't. Last year, for example, I couldn't even remember my Education resolution — so, obviously, that was a big failure. I also failed to succeed in the Health category: "Eat one vegetable everyday." I'm a bread/cheese/fruit girl, so this was a bona fide resolution for me, a real challenge. Even after I began to count pea soup, pickles, and red pasta sauce as vegetables, I still failed to live up to this laughably attainable goal. On the plus side, I now have a markedly improved tendency to order entrees that come with "julienned vegetables" instead of "mashed potatoes." I may have failed to meet my goal, but I certainly acquired slightly better dining habits.

Luckily, thanks to my three-resolution rule, I was able to celebrate 5
partial success this year thanks to my Project achievement: "File taxes." Admittedly, this included nine years of back taxes and was therefore a far cry from the simple task you might think. It is also important to note that I resolved to "file" taxes without mentioning the need to "pay" them, thereby increasing the resolution's likelihood of success, if not the IRS's happiness with my substandard citizenship.

Lesson the First: One person's habitual practice is another's daunting resolution. You might find that the laws of this country are motivation enough for filing your taxes, but it certainly wasn't working for me. Never underestimate the value of any resolution, no matter how obvious, unnecessary, trivial, or slight. My friend Susanne, for example, set her Practice resolution one year as "Stop buying new black and grey clothing." Three years ago, her wardrobe contained exactly three things that weren't primarily black or grey; today, the majority of her clothes are of many colors. It's worth noting that the subclauses of her resolution allowed her to replace existing black or grey items as well as permitting her to acquire black or grey items in a "new" clothing category (e.g., the purchase of a new black cardigan was allowed because, although she owned a black turtleneck sweater, a black "heavy" sweater, and a black v-neck "light" sweater, she did not, technically, possess a black cardigan sweater).

Lesson #2: Developing a new habit is more important than attaining an absolute goal. So what if Susanne fudged with the clothing "categories"; her resolution trained her to evaluate her purchasing habits. As for myself, I used to be in the habit of reading constantly, and while I don't have proof, I believe I've slacked off in this regard over the years. This year my Education/Practice resolution is: "Read 2–3 books per month." The goal seems too easily obtainable, even by my lax standards, but the resolution is designed to reinvigorate my reading habit, not to foster my acquisition of specific knowledge. I once resolved to "Take a multivitamin daily" — five years later, I still carry a small plastic vial filled with vitamins to support this acquired habit. (Should you take this habit on, I strongly recommend that you choose vitamins bearing a popular brand-name stamp if you are likely to be a traveler subject to security searches). Of course, under the rubric of my resolution program, "daily" resolutions are actively discouraged, but insofar as they lead to new habits, they can be acceptable.

Lesson #3: Include fail-safes. Although my reading goal is three books per month, if I pick up George Eliot's *Middlemarch* I'm not going to berate myself for squeezing in *The Tao of Pooh* just to make my minimum number. While habit development is decidedly the critical feature of a good resolution, your goal should be attainable. Case in point: I happen to have very lazy bedtime habits, so this year my Health resolution is "Wash face before going to sleep." My intent is to use cleanser and, in an ideal world, moisturizer, but if all I manage to do is splash some cold water near the vicinity of my head, then at least I'll still stand the chance of meeting my stated goal.

Lesson #4: Keep it simple. The "cold water provision" won't just help me achieve the habit formation and goal attainment of "washing my face"; it really represents a much larger and infinitely more important aspect of good resolution making: the theory of greater returns. I happen to know that if I'm standing at a sink, about to slosh some water on my face in an effort to maintain my resolve, I'm highly likely to cave in, locate some cleanser, and actually do some scrubbing. Furthermore, I also know that every time I clean my face I feel guilty about not doing the same for my teeth. Regressing even farther, brushing my teeth often leads to flossing them as well. But what I really know about myself is that there is absolutely no way I could ever, in a million years, possibly "wash my face, brush my teeth, and floss — every single night before going to sleep — for the whole year!" So, I've kept the resolution simple: I'm aiming for cleanser, hoping for floss, but ultimately counting on water to see me through.

Lesson #5: Plan ahead. What I mean by this is plan ahead for your next 10
New Year's Eve and make sure one of your resolutions is entertaining enough to discuss. Pick up a new skill — plumbing, knitting, bird watching, playing the ocarina. Develop a random expertise — opera, knowledge of where the rotating bars are, olive tasting, croquet, formal gardening. Memorize something — poems, star constellations, the common ingredients of shampoo. Vow to write a letter once a month — to a grandparent, a politician, a company that has brought you joy ("Dear Mars, Inc. Thank you for the M&M!"). Read something you normally wouldn't — *Scientific American, Architectural Digest*, Edward Gibbon, *Teen People*. Eat things, visit places, make stuff.

The point: Remember. It is almost impossible in life to master a skill, interest, or knowledge that is completely pointless. If you disagree, then try to prove me wrong! Seriously. I really have no interest in going to a New Year's party next year with a bunch of unimaginative, grumpy, starving, thin people.

Engaging with the Text

1. Heidi Pollock begins by stating her own philosophy about New Year's resolutions. A good New Year's resolution, she tells us, "should be an addition to your life, should expand your horizons and help you grow as a person. It should be process-oriented and not require major psychological or physical changes." What exactly is she **PROPOSING** — and what is the **PROBLEM** she aims to solve? 171–79 174
2. Pollock supports her proposal with **EXAMPLES** from her own life. How persuasive are these examples? 288
3. This piece originally appeared in *h2so4*, a magazine whose website says that it mixes the "serious and silly, arcane and mundane." Imagine it had been written instead for *Martha Stewart Living* or *Real Simple*, two magazines that offer how-tos and advice for the home. How might it be different? How would the **TITLE** be different, for example? How else might the writing be different? 272–73
4. The title is an allusion to a Beatles song; what does it tell readers about Pollock's **STANCE**? How does it help establish her **TONE**? 12–14 14
5. ***For Writing.*** Identify a practice you engage in (such as studying for tests, blogging, exercising regularly) that you feel you have mastered. Write a humorous **PROPOSAL** arguing that others should try your method. 171–79

MEGAN HOPKINS

Training the Next Teachers for America: *A Proposal for Reconceptualizing Teach for America*

Megan Hopkins was a doctoral student in the Graduate School of Education and Information Studies at the University of California, Los Angeles at the time she wrote this proposal. It appeared in a 2008 issue of Phi Delta Kappan, *a journal that addresses education policy and practice. As you read, notice how Hopkins uses evidence from several studies to support her proposal for improving the Teach for America program. Hopkins documents her sources according to* The Chicago Manual of Style, *as required for articles published in* Phi Delta Kappan.

SOON AFTER I BEGAN my first year as a Teach for America (TFA) corps member, I realized how underprepared I felt teaching first grade. Not only was I unsure how to manage and organize my classroom, but I also lacked the necessary content and pedagogical knowledge to teach my students effectively. Perhaps most important, I did not have deep understandings of or appreciation for the experiences of my students or their community. The five-week training institute I attended during the prior summer had not been enough to develop my educational "toolkit" or to prepare me to provide my students with the type of education that might begin to equalize their chances in the system.

Although I grew as an educator over time and am still committed to working in education, it was an uphill battle. And, like most other TFA corps members, I left teaching within the first three years. Since my involvement with Teach for America, the organization has made considerable efforts to refine its preparation model, yet the program continues to draw criticism for teacher underpreparation and low retention rates.

In light of my experience and this continuing criticism, I wish to recommend alterations in the preparation of corps members that would: (1) extend the TFA commitment to three years; (2) convert the first year of teaching to a residency training year, offering classroom training with expert veteran teachers while corps members also complete coursework toward certification; and (3) offer incentives for corps members to teach longer than three years. I recommend these changes with the goal of improving the effectiveness of corps members and motivating TFA teachers to remain in their assignments for longer than two or three years. These changes could help TFA fulfill its mission of creating leaders who will make lasting changes in the field of education, while also enhancing program quality during the time these potential leaders serve in our nation's most underresourced schools.

These recommendations could be supported, in part, by the Teaching Residency Act, introduced by Sen. Barack Obama (D-Ill.), and the Preparing Excellent Teachers Act, introduced in the House by Rep. Rahm Emanuel (D-Ill.). Both bills, introduced last summer, would enable prospective teachers to work under the wing of expert mentor teachers for an academic year while they complete their coursework for certification. The bills aim to expand the reach of highly successful models for urban teacher residencies — programs that provide substantial preparation for carefully selected novice teachers who commit to teaching for a minimum of three to four years in the districts that sponsor them. The passage of this legislation would create an opportunity for Teach for America to embrace promising new strategies for teacher preparation and induction.

Why Change TFA?

Recent research on corps members' effectiveness suggests the need for 5
a change in TFA's approach. The TFA model assumes that extensive formal teacher training is not essential for its recruits — most of them graduates of top colleges with strong leadership abilities and a desire to improve educational opportunities for the nation's children.

Yet the reality is that Teach for America teachers are initially less successful in supporting student learning than are traditionally prepared teachers who are fully certified when they enter the profession.[1] One study found that TFA recruits had more positive effects on students' math achievement as corps members finished their certification and training; however, they continued to have negative effects on elementary students' reading achievement throughout all the years of the study.[2]

A small study comparing the performance of the students of 41 beginning and experienced TFA teachers with that of the students of other teachers in their schools reported that the TFA-taught students performed as well as the others in reading and better than the others in math. But the teachers of the comparison group were even less likely to be trained or certified than the TFA teachers.[3] The slight increases in mathematics achievement that the more experienced TFA teachers contributed were not substantial.

While the research is limited to comparing student performance on standardized tests, and it is arguable whether these tests accurately measure student achievement, these studies show that TFA corps members are not, in fact, as successful as the organization assumes they will be. Particularly when they begin teaching, TFA teachers are less successful than their peers who receive more formal training.

In addition to criticism involving the preparation of its teachers, Teach for America is often criticized for its high turnover rates, as studies have found that 80 percent or more of corps members have left their teaching positions by the end of the third year, just when they are beginning to be more successful. This figure compares to about 30 percent to 40 percent of traditionally certified teachers in the same districts who leave by the end of the third year.[4] Districts — and their schools and students — bear the cost of this high level of attrition, and not surprisingly, some district officials have expressed concerns about this turnover rate. For example, Chicago administrators have indicated their desire for TFA corps members to stay longer, noting the longer tenures of other recruits and emphasizing their own responsibility to be "conscientious consumers" when making hiring decisions.[5] These observations suggest that TFA should consider incentives for corps members who are willing to remain longer in the classroom.

What Approaches Might Improve the Model?

In comparative international studies of teacher preparation, the U.S. has 10
been shown to undervalue preservice training. In particular, it is much less likely in the U.S. than in other developed nations that prospective

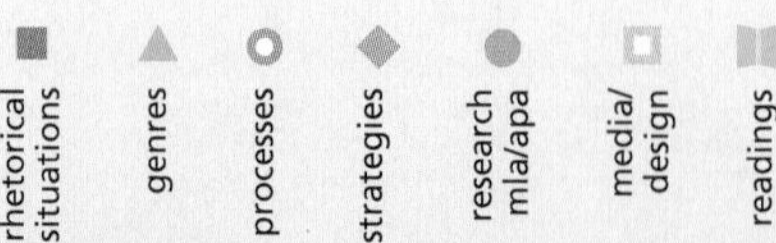

teachers will learn to teach under the wing of a master teacher while they are learning about curriculum, instruction, learning, and child development. Most European countries include a full year of closely supervised clinical practice in a school associated with the university as part of universal preservice preparation. Other countries, such as Japan, require extensive on-the-job training for teachers in their initial "apprenticeship," with coaching and 60 days per year of seminars and classroom visits providing guidance and support that prepare novice teachers to lead their own classrooms.[6] Master teachers supervise beginning teachers by observing, suggesting areas for improvement, and discussing effective instructional strategies.

Similarly, in an attempt to strengthen teacher preparation in the U.S. and to alter experienced teachers' roles in teacher training, some schools and universities across the country are collaborating to create professional development schools. These schools are designed to support the learning of new and experienced teachers and to restructure schools of education.[7] In partnership with universities, veteran teachers serve as mentors for new teachers and work with university faculty members to develop the preparation curriculum and make decisions about instructional practices. Not only do such schools promote collaboration and provide hands-on training for new teachers, but they also redefine the roles of experienced teachers by giving them an opportunity to take on leadership positions. Studies show that teachers trained in professional development schools feel better prepared, more often apply theory to practice, are more confident and enthusiastic about teaching, and are more highly rated than teachers prepared in other ways.[8]

More recently, shortages of high-quality teachers have led large urban school districts to initiate their own versions of the professional development school approach. For example, the Boston Public Schools and the Boston Plan for Excellence collaborated to create the Boston Teacher Residency; Chicago implemented the Academy for Urban School Leadership through a nonprofit agency chartered by the city schools; and Denver started the Boettcher Teachers Program in two of its schools, with the help of the Boettcher Foundation, the Public Education and

Business Coalition, and the University of Denver.[9] Together, these programs form the Coalition of Urban Teacher Residencies. Each program builds on a medical residency approach to train new teachers, very much like the professional development school model. The programs recruit recent college graduates and midlife career changers to complete a yearlong paid residency with an expert mentor teacher while they also take coursework toward certification and a master's degree in education. When they have completed a year-end portfolio evaluation and the required coursework, program graduates begin teaching independently within their residency districts the following year. They continue to receive mentoring while they begin to teach. Finally, program participants must commit to teach in the district for at least three or four years. This model of preparation brings committed, well-prepared individuals into high-need urban schools with the hope of keeping them there.

A Teach for America Residency

In view of TFA teachers' limited preparation and considering the promise of these innovative approaches, I recommend that Teach for America develop a residency training model with the following features:

1. *Extend the program's current two-year commitment to three years.* Corps members will serve as residents during their first year. Then they will go on to teach on their own for at least two subsequent years.
2. *Require all first-year corps members to complete a residency year in an expe-* 15
rienced teacher's classroom within their placement district and at (or near) their placement grade level. During this year, corps members will co-teach with a mentor teacher who is deemed highly effective at raising student achievement. The mentor teacher, in collaboration with a TFA program director or university instructor, will scaffold the corps member's training, so that the corps member first observes the mentor teacher and discusses instructional strategies and eventually leads the classroom while the mentor assesses and provides feedback on the corps member's performance. During this year of residency, not only will corps members acquire collaborative skills and instructional

expertise, but they will also gain an understanding of the community context in which they will teach, and they will complete coursework for certification.

3. *Cluster TFA "residents" at high-performing urban schools.* Each of the programs in the Coalition of Urban Teacher Residencies concentrates its participants at a small number of schools that have a large number of expert teachers and adept administrators. Like prospective teachers who train in professional development schools, residents under this model would collaborate within a school community that provides a positive culture and support.
4. *Offer courses through a university partner for first-year corps members to obtain certification and a master's degree.* During the residency year, corps members will also take courses through a local partner university so that they may complete their teacher certification requirements and have the opportunity to obtain a master's degree. While TFA currently partners with local universities in most of its placement sites, stronger relationships between TFA and these partners — and between coursework and clinical experiences — must be developed if residents are to integrate theory and practice and apply what they are learning.
5. *Provide incentives to teach longer than three years.* A range of incentives could be offered, including opportunities to take on leadership roles, as well as stipends and forgivable loans for accepting additional responsibilities. Teachers who serve for longer than three years could also serve as liaisons among members of the partnership and provide support and professional development to novice teachers. After gaining substantial teaching experience, these longer-term corps members could serve as mentors in one of the residency training schools and partner with university colleagues in offering support and coursework.

Challenges to Implementation

Since these strategies would require an overhaul of Teach for America's approach to teacher preparation, there are many issues to address before proceeding.

Funding. School districts currently provide full salaries to TFA corps 20
members. A different funding structure would need to be developed to support first-year corps members during their residency year, as many districts could not afford to support two teachers for a single classroom. Additional funds would also be needed to compensate mentor teachers and longer-term TFA teachers who took on leadership roles, although these roles already exist in a number of districts. Some possibilities follow:

- As the Chicago teacher residency does, TFA and the districts could adopt a graduated pay scale that would pay first-year corps members less than the normal first-year teacher salary, while longer-term corps members would receive a stipend in addition to their regular salary for fulfilling a mentor or leadership role. In addition, teachers who decided to remain at their placement sites for longer than their commitments could be granted forgivable student loans, with a specific percentage of the balance forgiven for each additional year teaching at the site. Federal funds are available to help underwrite such programs to keep teachers in high-need schools.
- Model first-year funding on the Boston Teacher Residency (BTR) model. This program offers a small stipend ($10,000) to first-year residents. In addition, residents must pay tuition of $10,000 for their university coursework, but BTR offers them a no-interest loan to cover this cost, which is reduced and ultimately eliminated if residents remain as teachers in the district for three years. Teach for America could use a similar approach.
- If Teach for America alters its approach to include a year of residency, it may be able to reduce its summer institute training or even replace it with training administered within the cities or school districts where corps members are placed, thereby greatly reducing the costs. Corps members may be better served by completing an intensive training in their placement district under the guidance of an expert mentor teacher from that district so that they can acquire knowledge about the specific context in which they will teach.

- Instead of devoting funding to recruitment and to expanding the corps at the current rapid rate, Teach for America could use this funding to implement the preparation model proposed. While this may hinder TFA from meeting its expansion goals, the model would produce a number of high-quality teachers who would be likely to remain for more than two or three years at their placement sites. This would reduce the demand for new teachers and provide greater benefit to districts, schools, and students.

Capacity. If Teach for America desires to initiate these changes, it will 25
need to consider its capacity to do so. One issue will be recruiting enough mentor teachers to match the number of first-year corps members. TFA currently recruits veteran teachers for its summer institute, and these people are certainly candidates for mentoring positions during the school year. Furthermore, because TFA has been placing teachers in some cities for over 10 years, there are some sites that have a reasonable number of alumni still in teaching, and they would be an excellent pool of mentors and could also provide connections to other experienced teachers.

In addition, the organization would need to form partnerships with local universities and with local school districts. Thus far, Teach for America has been successful at securing such partnerships within each placement city, but none has thus far been as involved as this new strategy would require. New models of coursework may need to be developed, and instructors may need to be hired. The Boston Teacher Residency has a curriculum coordinator who works to develop the coursework and to seek university faculty members to help design and to teach each of the required courses. The Chicago Residency works with National-Louis University and the University of Illinois at Chicago to design and offer coursework that is linked to the clinical experience.

Existing structures. Teach for America would have to make some decisions about the existing structures of the organization. For example, it would have to consider making changes to or eliminating the summer institute to supply funding for a new system. It would also have to consider the current support systems within each placement city. For example, the roles and responsibilities of program directors would change within this model, as they not only would work with corps members but also would collaborate with mentor teachers, school principals, and university faculty members.

Possible objections. If the Teach for America commitment is extended to three years, some applicants may be reluctant to apply, thus limiting the pool of highly qualified candidates. However, better training and support should encourage other recruits, and the incentives offered in the third year and beyond should overcome some resistance. Surveying and conducting focus groups with current corps members regarding the use of a residency model would help TFA determine which kinds of recruits would be interested in participating in a longer-term alternative track. Furthermore, some school districts will prefer the model, as it provides better-prepared entrants who have a better chance of staying in teaching longer. This improvement may encourage districts to contribute funds, just as a growing number are creating residency and intern programs of their own.

Next steps. Before implementing a programwide change, Teach for America would be wise to pilot the new strategy in one placement site and assess its effectiveness. Such a site should be chosen after assessing such resources as the availability of mentor teachers, the number of effective schools to serve as residency sites, and the potential for district and university support. New strategies should be implemented for no less than three years before evaluating results, as this would provide enough time for at least one cohort of corps members to complete their service under the new model.

Conclusion

While these proposals would require substantial redesign of the TFA 30
model, the results are likely to be worth the investment. Teach for America has the potential to effect large-scale change in the field of edu-

cation. It recruits highly qualified, motivated corps members who appreciate the importance of equal educational opportunities, and many go on to devote their lives to this mission. However, these bright individuals are not as effective in the classroom as they could be, and their students do not perform as well as students in classrooms where teachers have more formal training. Corps members who are given a full year to learn effective instructional practices and to fully prepare to work within the context of their placement site will be better prepared to enter their classrooms as skilled teachers. If TFA can prepare its recruits to be more successful in their classrooms from the beginning of their service, it may be able to achieve its vision more effectively, so that, as the TFA mission states, "One day, all children in this nation will have the opportunity to attain an excellent education."

Notes

1. Ildiko Laczko-Kerr and David C. Berliner, "The Effectiveness of 'Teach for America' and Other Under-Certified Teachers on Student Academic Achievement: A Case of Harmful Public Policy," *Education Policy Analysis Archives,* 6 September 2002, http://epaa.asu.edu/epaa/v10n37; Linda Darling-Hammond et al., "Does Teacher Preparation Matter? Evidence About Teacher Certification, Teach for America, and Teacher Effectiveness," www.schoolredesign.net/binaries/teachercert.pdf, 2005; and Thomas J. Kane, Jonah E. Rockoff, and Douglas O. Staiger, "What Does Certification Tell Us About Teacher Effectiveness? Evidence from New York City," Working Paper 12155, National Bureau of Economic Research, Cambridge, Mass., April 2006.

2. Donald Boyd et al., "How Changes in Entry Requirements Alter the Teacher Workforce and Affect Student Achievement," *Education Finance and Policy,* vol. 1, 2006, pp. 176–216.

3. Paul Decker, Daniel Mayer, and Steven Glazerman, *The Effects of Teach for America on Students: Findings from a National Evaluation* (Princeton, N.J.: Mathematica Policy Research, MPR Reference No: M-8792750, 2004).

4. Boyd et al., op. cit.; Darling-Hammond, op. cit.; and Kane, Rockoff, and Staiger, op. cit.

5. Bess Keller, “Chicago Wants TFA to Commit Longer,” *Education Week*, 22 September 2004, p. 14.

6. Harold W. Stevenson and James W. Stigler, *The Learning Gap* (New York: Simon & Schuster, 1992).

7. Linda Darling-Hammond, Marcella L. Bullmaster, and Velma L. Cobb, “Rethinking Teacher Leadership Through Professional Development Schools,” *Elementary School Journal*, vol. 96, 1995, pp. 87–106.

8. Renee L. Clift and Patricia Brady, “Research on Methods Courses and Field Experiences,” in Marilyn Cochran-Smith and Kenneth M. Zeichner, eds., *Studying Teacher Education: The Report of the AERA Panel on Research and Teacher Education* (Mahwah, N.J.: Erlbaum, 2005), pp. 309–424; Gloria A. Neubert and James B. Binko, “Professional Development Schools: The Proof Is in the Performance,” *Educational Leadership*, February 1998, pp. 44–46; and Suzanne Yerian and Pamela L. Grossman, “Preservice Teachers’ Perceptions of Their Middle-Level Teacher Education Experience: A Comparison of a Traditional and a PDS Model,” *Teacher Education Quarterly*, Fall 1997, pp. 85–101.

9. Information about the Boston Teacher Residency is available at www.bpe.org/btr; information about the Academy for Urban School Leadership, at www.ausl-chicago.org; and information about the Boettcher Teachers Program, at www.boettcherteachers.org.

Engaging with the Text

1. Megan Hopkins identifies specific problems with the Teach for America program, and proposes three changes to help solve those problems. What specific changes does she suggest? How does she build a 175 convincing **ARGUMENT** to persuade readers to accept the solutions she proposes?

2. 266–70 Hopkins **ENDS** her proposal with a powerful quotation from the Teach for America mission statement: “One day all children in this nation will have the opportunity to attain an excellent education.” How effective is this ending? In what ways would Hopkins’s proposed solutions contribute to this goal?

3. Who is the intended **AUDIENCE** for this proposal? How does the content of the proposal as well as its place of publication lead you to identify this particular audience? 5–8

4. How does Hopkins **ANTICIPATE QUESTIONS** about and potential objections to her proposal? Point to two specific passages in which she anticipates questions and objections. Can you think of any additional questions about or potential objections to her proposal that she has not addressed? 175

5. ***For Writing.*** Writing from the perspective of a teacher, Hopkins proposes ways to reconceptualize the Teach for America program to help it better realize its "potential to effect large-scale change in the field of education." Consider your own experience as a student in the educational system. What aspect of your education — class sizes, teaching methods, required courses, peer mentoring, and so on — might be improved? Write a **PROPOSAL** that identifies one or more problems with your education as you have experienced it and argues for your recommended solutions. 171–79

63 Reflections

See also:

JONATHAN SAFRAN FOER
My Life as a Dog 180

DAVE BARRY

Guys vs. Men

Dave Barry is a well-known humorist who is the author of thirty books and countless columns. Two of his books — Dave Barry Turns 40 *(1990) and* Dave Barry's Greatest Hits *(1988) — served as the basis for the TV sitcom* Dave's World*, which ran for four seasons from 1993 to 1997. In 1988, Barry was awarded a Pulitzer Prize for Commentary. Formerly a syndicated columnist, he has had writing published in over 500 newspapers in the United States and abroad. The following reflection is from his book* Dave Barry's Complete Guide to Guys *(1995).*

MEN ITSELF IS A SERIOUS WORD, not to mention *manhood* and *manly*. Such words make being male sound like a very important activity, as opposed to what it primarily consists of, namely, possessing a set of minor and frequently unreliable organs.

But men tend to attach great significance to Manhood. This results in certain characteristically masculine, by which I mean stupid, behavioral patterns that can produce unfortunate results such as violent crime, war, spitting, and ice hockey. These things have given males a bad name.* And the "Men's Movement," which is supposed to bring out the more positive aspects of Manliness, seems to be densely populated with loons and goobers.

So I'm saying that there's another way to look at males: not as aggressive macho dominators; not as sensitive, liberated, hugging drummers; but as *guys*.

And what, exactly, do I mean by "guys"? I don't know. I haven't thought that much about it. One of the major characteristics of guyhood is that we guys don't spend a lot of time pondering our deep innermost feelings. There is a serious question in my mind about whether guys

*Specifically, "asshole."

actually *have* deep innermost feelings, unless you count, for example, loyalty to the Detroit Tigers, or fear of bridal showers.

5 But although I can't define exactly what it means to be a guy, I can describe certain guy characteristics, such as:

Guys Like Neat Stuff

By "neat," I mean "mechanical and unnecessarily complex." I'll give you an example. Right now I'm typing these words on an *extremely* powerful computer. It's the latest in a line of maybe ten computers I've owned, each one more powerful than the last. My computer is chock full of RAM and ROM and bytes and megahertzes and various other items that enable a computer to kick data-processing butt. It is probably capable of supervising the entire U.S. air-defense apparatus while simultaneously processing the tax return of every resident of Ohio. I use it mainly to write a newspaper column. This is an activity wherein I sit and stare at the screen for maybe ten minutes, then, using only my forefingers, slowly type something like:

Henry Kissinger looks like a big wart.

I stare at this for another ten minutes, have an inspiration, then amplify the original thought as follows:

Henry Kissinger looks like a big fat wart.

10 Then I stare at that for another ten minutes, pondering whether I should try to work in the concept of "hairy."

This is absurdly simple work for my computer. It sits there, humming impatiently, bored to death, passing the time between keystrokes via brain-teaser activities such as developing a Unified Field Theory of the universe and translating the complete works of Shakespeare into rap.*

In other words, this computer is absurdly overqualified to work for me, and yet soon, I guarantee, I will buy an *even more powerful* one. I won't be able to stop myself. I'm a guy.

---

*To be or not? I got to *know*.
Might kill myself by the end of the *show*.

Probably the ultimate example of the fundamental guy drive to have neat stuff is the Space Shuttle. Granted, the guys in charge of this program *claim* it has a Higher Scientific Purpose, namely to see how humans function in space. But of course we have known for years how humans function in space: They float around and say things like; "Looks real good, Houston!"

No, the real reason for the existence of the Space Shuttle is that it is one humongous and spectacularly gizmo-intensive item of hardware. Guys can tinker with it practically forever, and occasionally even get it to work, and use it to place *other* complex mechanical items into orbit, where they almost immediately break, which provides a great excuse to send the Space Shuttle up *again*. It's Guy Heaven.

Other results of the guy need to have stuff are Star Wars, the recreational boating industry, monorails, nuclear weapons, and wristwatches that indicate the phase of the moon. I am not saying that women haven't been involved in the development or use of this stuff. I'm saying that, without guys, this stuff probably would not exist; just as, without women, virtually every piece of furniture in the world would still be in its original position. Guys do not have a basic need to rearrange furniture. Whereas a woman who could cheerfully use the same computer for fifty-three years will rearrange her furniture on almost a weekly basis, sometimes in the dead of night. She'll be sound asleep in bed, and suddenly, at 2 A.M., she'll be awakened by the urgent thought: *The blue-green sofa needs to go perpendicular to the wall instead of parallel, and it needs to go there RIGHT NOW*. So she'll get up and move it, which of course necessitates moving other furniture, and soon she has rearranged her entire living room, shifting great big heavy pieces that ordinarily would require several burly men to lift, because there are few forces in Nature more powerful than a woman who needs to rearrange furniture. Every so often a guy will wake up to discover that, because of his wife's overnight efforts, he now lives in an entirely different house.

(I realize that I'm making gender-based generalizations here, but my feeling is that if God did not want us to make gender-based generalizations, She would not have given us genders.)

Guys Like a Really Pointless Challenge

Not long ago I was sitting in my office at the *Miami Herald*'s Sunday magazine, *Tropic,* reading my fan mail,* when I heard several of my guy coworkers in the hallway talking about how fast they could run the forty-yard dash. These are guys in their thirties and forties who work in journalism, where the most demanding physical requirement is the ability to digest vending-machine food. In other words, these guys have absolutely no need to run the forty-yard dash.

But one of them, Mike Wilson, was writing a story about a star high-school football player who could run it in 4.38 seconds. Now if Mike had written a story about, say, a star high-school poet, none of my guy coworkers would have suddenly decided to find out how well they could write sonnets. But when Mike turned in his story, they became *deeply* concerned about how fast they could run the forty-yard dash. They were so concerned that the magazine editor, Tom Shroder, decided that they should get a stopwatch and go out to a nearby park and find out. Which they did, a bunch of guys taking off their shoes and running around barefoot in a public park on company time.

This is what I heard them talking about, out in the hall. I heard Tom, who was thirty-eight years old, saying that his time in the forty had been 5.75 seconds. And I thought to myself: This is ridiculous. These are middle-aged guys, supposedly adults, and they're out there *bragging* about their performance in this stupid juvenile footrace. Finally I couldn't stand it anymore.

"Hey!" I shouted. "I could beat 5.75 seconds." 20

So we went out to the park and measured off forty yards, and the guys told me that I had three chances to make my best time. On the first try my time was 5.78 seconds, just three-hundredths of a second slower than Tom's, even though, at forty-five, I was seven years older than he. So I just *knew* I'd beat him on the second attempt if I ran really, really hard, which I did for a solid ten yards, at which point my left hamstring muscle, which had not yet shifted into Spring Mode from Mail-Reading Mode, went, and I quote, "pop."

*Typical fan letter: "Who cuts your hair? Beavers?"

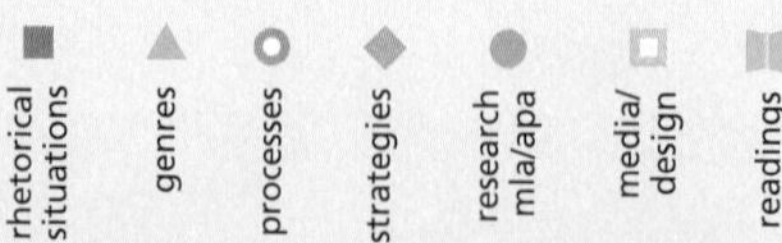

I had to be helped off the field. I was in considerable pain, and I was obviously not going to be able to walk right for weeks. The other guys were very sympathetic, especially Tom, who took the time to call me at home, where I was sitting with an ice pack on my leg and twenty-three Advil in my bloodstream, so he could express his concern.

"Just remember," he said, "*you didn't beat my time.*"

There are countless other examples of guys rising to meet pointless challenges. Virtually all sports fall into this category, as well as a large part of U.S. foreign policy. ("I'll bet you can't capture Manuel Noriega!"[*] "Oh YEAH??")

Guys Do Not Have a Rigid and Well-Defined Moral Code

25 This is not the same as saying that guys are bad. Guys *are* capable of doing bad things, but this generally happens when they try to be Men and start becoming manly and aggressive and stupid. When they're being just plain guys, they aren't so much actively *evil* as they are *lost*. Because guys have never really grasped the Basic Human Moral Code, which I believe was invented by women millions of years ago when all the guys were out engaging in some other activity, such as seeing who could burp the loudest. When they came back, there were certain rules that they were expected to follow unless they wanted to get into Big Trouble, and they have been trying to follow these rules ever since, with extremely irregular results. Because guys have never *internalized* these rules. Guys are similar to my small auxiliary backup dog, Zippy, a guy dog[†] who has been told numerous times that he is *not* supposed to (1) get into the kitchen garbage or (2) poop on the floor. He knows that these are the rules, but he has never really understood *why*, and sometimes he gets to thinking: Sure, I am *ordinarily* not supposed to get into the garbage, but obviously this rule is not meant to apply when there are certain extenuating[‡] circumstances, such as (1) somebody just threw

---

[*] *Manuel Noriega:* former military dictator in Panama; he was removed from power by the United States in 1989. [Editor's note]

[†] I also have a female dog, Earnest, who *never* breaks the rules.

[‡] I am taking some liberties here with Zippy's vocabulary. More likely, in his mind, he uses the term *mitigating*.

away some perfectly good seven-week-old Kung Pao Chicken, and (2) I am home alone.

And so when the humans come home, the kitchen floor has been transformed into GarbageFest USA, and Zippy, who usually comes rushing up, is off in a corner disguised in a wig and sunglasses, hoping to get into the Federal Bad Dog Relocation Program before the humans discover the scene of the crime.

When I yell at him, he frequently becomes so upset that he poops on the floor.

Morally, most guys are just like Zippy, only taller and usually less hairy. Guys are *aware* of the rules of moral behavior, but they have trouble keeping these rules in the forefronts of their minds at certain times, especially the present. This is especially true in the area of faithfulness to one's mate. I realize, of course, that there are countless examples of guys being faithful to their mates until they die, usually as a result of being eaten by their mates immediately following copulation. Guys outside of the spider community, however, do not have a terrific record of faithfulness.

I'm not saying guys are scum. I'm saying that many guys who consider themselves to be committed to their marriages will stray if they are confronted with overwhelming temptation, defined as "virtually any temptation."

Okay, so maybe I *am* saying guys are scum. But they're not *mean-* 30
spirited scum. And few of them — even when they are out of town on business trips, far from their wives, and have a clear-cut opportunity — will poop on the floor.

Engaging with the Text

1. Dave Barry claims that he isn't able to say what he means by the term "guys" because "one of the major characteristics of guyhood is that we guys don't spend a lot of time pondering our deep innermost feelings," and yet in this piece — indeed even this sentence — he identifies specific characteristics of "guys" that suggest he has indeed

pondered this state of maleness thoroughly. How do you account for this contradiction?

2. Despite his assertion that he can't define the term, Barry essentially provides an **EXTENDED DEFINITION** of the term "guy," detailing several characteristics. What are the characteristics of guys, according to Barry? Do you agree with these characteristics and his description of each? What other characteristics would you add, if any?

316–20

3. Barry includes several **EXAMPLES** of the behavior he identifies as characteristic of guys. Identity several passages that include such examples and discuss what these contribute to his reflection.

320

4. What is Barry's **STANCE** toward his topic of guys? Point to specific passages that reveal that stance. Is this stance appropriate for Barry's **PURPOSE**? Why or why not?

12–14

3–4

5. ***For Writing.*** Identify a specific group of people, animals, things, or places, and reflect on what distinguishing characteristics are shared by its members. Write a **REFLECTION** on the group that identifies those major characteristics. Study Barry's reflection to see what techniques he uses to elicit a smile or chuckle. Try your hand at one or more of these.

180–87

GEETA KOTHARI

If You Are What You Eat, Then What Am I?

Geeta Kothari's stories and essays have been published in numerous newspapers, journals and anthologies. She teaches writing at the University of Pittsburgh and is the editor of Did My Mama Like to Dance? and Other Stories About Mothers and Daughters *(1994). The following reflection first appeared in 1999 in the* Kenyon Review, *a literary journal published at Kenyon College. As you read, notice how Kothari incorporates vivid anecdotes to illustrate the competing cultural experiences that complicate her sense of identity.*

> To belong is to understand the tacit codes of the people you live with.
> —MICHAEL IGNATIEFF, *BLOOD AND BELONGING*

THE FIRST TIME MY MOTHER and I open a can of tuna, I am nine years old. We stand in the doorway of the kitchen, in semidarkness, the can tilted toward daylight. I want to eat what the kids at school eat: bologna, hot dogs, salami — foods my parents find repugnant because they contain pork and meat byproducts, crushed bone and hair glued together by chemicals and fat. Although she has never been able to tolerate the smell of fish, my mother buys the tuna, hoping to satisfy my longing for American food.

Indians, of course, do not eat such things.

The tuna smells fishy, which surprises me because I can't remember anyone's tuna sandwich actually smelling like fish. And the tuna in those sandwiches doesn't look like this, pink and shiny, like an internal organ. In fact, this looks similar to the bad foods my mother doesn't want me to eat. She is silent, holding her face away from the can while peering into it like a half-blind bird.

"What's wrong with it?" I ask.

She has no idea. My mother does not know that the tuna everyone 5
else's mothers made for them was tuna *salad*.

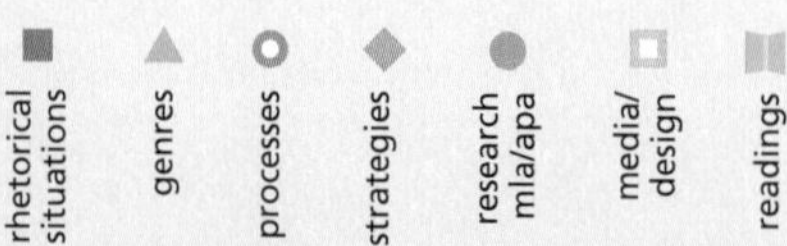

"Do you think it's botulism?"

I have never seen botulism, but I have read about it, just as I have read about but never eaten steak and kidney pie.

There is so much my parents don't know. They are not like other parents, and they disappoint me and my sister. They are supposed to help us negotiate the world outside, teach us the signs, the clues to proper behavior: what to eat and how to eat it.

We have expectations, and my parents fail to meet them, especially my mother, who works full-time. I don't understand what it means, to have a mother who works outside and inside the home; I notice only the ways in which she disappoints me. She doesn't show up for school plays. She doesn't make chocolate-frosted cupcakes for my class. At night, if I want her attention, I have to sit in the kitchen and talk to her while she cooks the evening meal, attentive to every third or fourth word I say.

We throw the tuna away. This time my mother is disappointed. I 10
go to school with tuna eaters. I see their sandwiches, yet cannot explain the discrepancy between them and the stinking, oily fish in my mother's hand. We do not understand so many things, my mother and I.

When we visit our relatives in India, food prepared outside the house is carefully monitored. In the hot, sticky monsoon months in New Delhi and Bombay, we cannot eat ice cream, salad, cold food, or any fruit that can't be peeled. Definitely no meat. People die from amoebic dysentery, unexplained fevers, strange boils on their bodies. We drink boiled water only, no ice. No sweets except for jalebi, thin fried twists of dough in dripping hot sugar syrup. If we're caught outside with nothing to drink, Fanta, Limca, Thums Up (after Coca-Cola is thrown out by Mrs. Gandhi) will do. Hot tea sweetened with sugar, served with thick creamy buffalo milk, is preferable. It should be boiled, to kill the germs on the cup.

My mother talks about "back home" as a safe place, a silk cocoon frozen in time where we are sheltered by family and friends. Back home, my sister and I do not argue about food with my parents. Home is where they know all the rules. We trust them to guide us safely through the maze of city streets for which they have no map, and we trust them to feed and take care of us, the way parents should.

Finally, though, one of us will get sick, hungry for the food we see our cousins and friends eating, too thirsty to ask for a straw, too polite to insist on properly boiled water.

At my uncle's diner in New Delhi, someone hands me a plate of aloo tikki, fried potato patties filled with mashed channa dal and served with a sweet and a sour chutney. The channa, mixed with hot chilies and spices, burns my tongue and throat. I reach for my Fanta, discard the paper straw, and gulp the sweet orange soda down, huge drafts that sting rather than soothe.

When I throw up later that day (or is it the next morning, when a 15
stomachache wakes me from deep sleep?), I cry over the frustration of being singled out, not from the pain my mother assumes I'm feeling as she holds my hair back from my face. The taste of orange lingers in my mouth, and I remember my lips touching the cold glass of the Fanta bottle.

At that moment, more than anything, I want to be like my cousins.

In New York, at the first Indian restaurant in our neighborhood, my father orders with confidence, and my sister and I play with the silverware until the steaming plates of lamb biryani arrive.

What is Indian food? my friends ask, their noses crinkling up.

Later, this restaurant is run out of business by the new Indo-Pak-Bangladeshi combinations up and down the street, which serve similar food. They use plastic cutlery and Styrofoam cups. They do not distinguish between North and South Indian cooking, or between Indian, Pakistani, and Bangladeshi cooking, and their customers do not care. The food is fast, cheap, and tasty. Dosa, a rice flour crepe stuffed with masala potato, appears on the same trays as chicken makhani.

Now my friends want to know, Do you eat curry at home? 20

One time my mother makes lamb vindaloo for guests. Like dosa, this is a South Indian dish, one that my Punjabi mother has to learn from a cookbook. For us, she cooks everyday food — yellow dal, rice, chapati, bhaji. Lentils, rice, bread, and vegetables. She has never referred to anything on our table as "curry" or "curried," but I know she has made chicken curry for guests. Vindaloo, she explains, is a curry too. I understand then that curry is a dish created for guests, outsiders, a food for people who eat in restaurants.

I look around my boyfriend's freezer one day and find meat: pork chops, ground beef, chicken pieces, Italian sausage. Ham in the refrigerator, next to the homemade bolognese sauce. Tupperware filled with chili made from ground beef and pork.

He smells different from me. Foreign. Strange.

I marry him anyway.

He has inherited blue eyes that turn gray in bad weather, light brown 25
hair, a sharp pointy nose, and excellent teeth. He learns to make chili with ground turkey and tofu, tomato sauce with red wine and portobello mushrooms, roast chicken with rosemary and slivers of garlic under the skin.

He eats steak when we are in separate cities, roast beef at his mother's house, hamburgers at work. Sometimes I smell them on his skin. I hope he doesn't notice me turning my face, a cheek instead of my lips, my nose wrinkled at the unfamiliar, musky smell.

I have inherited brown eyes, black hair, a long nose with a crooked bridge, and soft teeth with thin enamel. I am in my twenties, moving to a city far from my parents, before it occurs to me that jeera, the spice my sister avoids, must have an English name. I have to learn that haldi = turmeric, methi = fenugreek. What to make with fenugreek, I do not know. My grandmother used to make methi roti for our breakfast, cornbread with fresh fenugreek leaves served with a lump of homemade butter. No one makes it now that she's gone, though once in a while my mother will get a craving for it and produce a facsimile ("The cornmeal here is wrong") that only highlights what she's really missing: the smells and tastes of her mother's house.

I will never make my grandmother's methi roti or even my mother's unsatisfactory imitation of it. I attempt chapati; it takes six hours, three phone calls home, and leaves me with an aching back. I have to write translations down: jeera = cumin. My memory is unreliable. But I have always known garam = hot.

If I really want to make myself sick, I worry that my husband will one day leave me for a meat-eater, for someone familiar who doesn't sniff him suspiciously for signs of alimentary infidelity.

Indians eat lentils. I understand this as absolute, a decree from an 30
unidentifiable authority that watches and judges me.

So what does it mean that I cannot replicate my mother's dal? She and my father show me repeatedly, in their kitchen, in my kitchen. They coach me over the phone, buy me the best cookbooks, and finally write down their secrets. Things I'm supposed to know but don't. Recipes that should be, by now, engraved on my heart.

Living far from the comfort of people who require no explanation for what I do and who I am, I crave the foods we have shared. My mother convinces me that moong is the easiest dal to prepare, and yet it fails me every time: bland, watery, a sickly greenish yellow mush. These imperfect limitations remind me only of what I'm missing.

But I have never been fond of moong dal. At my mother's table it is the last thing I reach for. Now I worry that this antipathy toward dal signals something deeper, that somehow I am not my parents' daughter, not Indian, and because I cannot bear the touch and smell of raw meat, though I can eat it cooked (charred, dry, and overdone), I am not American either.

I worry about a lifetime purgatory in Indian restaurants where I will complain that all the food looks and tastes the same because they've used the same masala.

Engaging with the Text

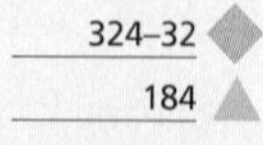
324–32 184

1. Geeta Kothari uses food as a way to explore the larger issue of cultural identity. How does she **DESCRIBE** Indian and American food? What **SPECIFIC DETAILS** does she include to help her readers understand the pulls of both American and Indian culture?

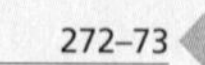
272–73

2. A good **TITLE** indicates what the piece is about and makes readers want to read it. How well does this title do those things? How does Kothari answer the question her title asks?

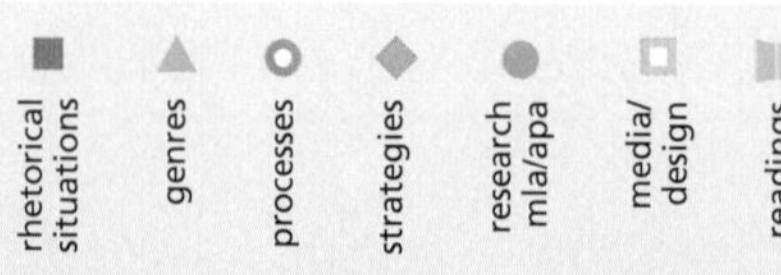

3. How does Kothari **BEGIN**? Is this an effective beginning? Why or why not? How does it signal to readers what Kothari will address in the rest of the piece? 261–66

4. For Kothari, cultural identity shapes, and is shaped by, the foods one eats and the ways one eats them. Her reflection reveals a struggle over two cultures — Indian and American — and she worries that she cannot locate herself fully in either. At the end of her text, she notes: "I worry that this antipathy toward dal signals something deeper, that somehow I am not my parents' daughter, not Indian, and because I cannot bear the touch and smell of raw meat . . . I am not American either." What does it mean to live on the border between two cultures in the ways Kothari describes?

5. ***For Writing.*** Think about the kinds of foods you grew up with and the ways they were similar or dissimilar to those of your peers. Write an essay **REFLECTING** on the role food has played in your own sense of your cultural heritage and identity. 180–87

ZORA NEALE HURSTON

How It Feels to Be Colored Me

A novelist, folklorist, and anthropologist, Zora Neale Hurston (1891–1960) was a major figure in the Harlem Renaissance of the early twentieth century. She is the author of short stories, novels, and books of nonfiction — including her autobiography, Dust Tracks on a Road *(1942) — but she is best known for the novel* Their Eyes Were Watching God *(1937). The following essay first appeared in 1928 in* The World Tomorrow, *a leftist Christian journal. It was reprinted nearly fifty years later in a volume of Hurston's writings titled* I Love Myself When I Am Laughing . . . and Then Again When I Am Looking Mean and Impressive *(1979). As you read, notice how Hurston examines her identity from several different social vantage points — race, region, and gender — to explore the complex question, Who am I?*

I **AM COLORED** but I offer nothing in the way of extenuating circumstances except the fact that I am the only Negro in the United States whose grandfather on the mother's side was *not* an Indian chief.

I remember the very day that I became colored. Up to my thirteenth year I lived in the little Negro town of Eatonville, Florida. It is exclusively a colored town. The only white people I knew passed through the town going to or coming from Orlando. The native whites rode dusty horses, the Northern tourists chugged down the sandy village road in automobiles. The town knew the Southerners and never stopped cane chewing when they passed. But the Northerners were something else again. They were peered at cautiously from behind curtains by the timid. The more venturesome would come out on the porch to watch them go past and got just as much pleasure out of the tourists as the tourists got out of the village.

The front porch might seem a daring place for the rest of the town, but it was a gallery seat for me. My favorite place was atop the gatepost. Proscenium box for a born first-nighter. Not only did I enjoy the

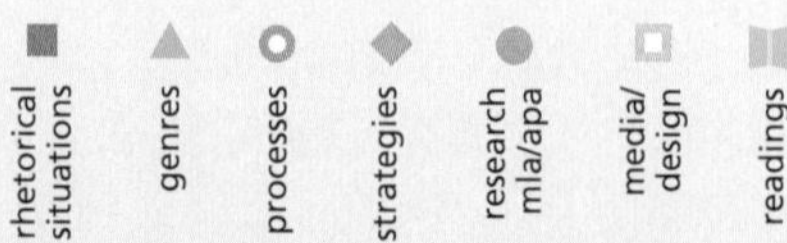

show, but I didn't mind the actors knowing that I liked it. I usually spoke to them in passing. I'd wave at them and when they returned my salute, I would say something like this: "Howdy-do-well-I-thank-you-where-you-goin'?" Usually automobile or the horse paused at this, and after a queer exchange of compliments, I would probably "go a piece of the way" with them, as we say in farthest Florida. If one of my family happened to come to the front in time to see me, of course negotiations would be rudely broken off. But even so, it is clear that I was the first "welcome-to-our state" Floridian, and I hope the Miami Chamber of Commerce will please take notice.

During this period, white people differed from colored to me only in that they rode through town and never lived there. They liked to hear me "speak pieces" and sing and wanted to see me dance the parse-me-la, and gave me generously of their small silver for doing these things, which seemed strange to me for I wanted to do them so much that I needed bribing to stop. Only they didn't know it. The colored people gave no dimes. They deplored any joyful tendencies in me, but I was their Zora nevertheless. I belonged to them, to the nearby hotels, to the county — everybody's Zora.

But changes came in the family when I was thirteen, and I was sent 5
to school in Jacksonville. I left Eatonville, the town of the oleanders, as Zora. When I disembarked from the river-boat at Jacksonville, she was no more. It seemed that I had suffered a sea change. I was not Zora of Orange County anymore, I was now a little colored girl. I found it out in certain ways. In my heart as well as in the mirror, I became a fast brown — warranted not to rub nor run.

But I am not tragically colored. There is no great sorrow dammed up in my soul, nor lurking behind my eyes. I do not mind at all. I do not belong to the sobbing school of Negrohood who hold that nature somehow has given them a lowdown dirty deal and whose feelings are all hurt about it. Even in the helter-skelter skirmish that is my life, I have seen that the world is to the strong regardless of a little pigmentation more or less. No, I do not weep at the world — I am too busy sharpening my oyster knife.

Someone is always at my elbow reminding me that I am the granddaughter of slaves. It fails to register depression with me. Slavery is sixty years in the past. The operation was successful and the patient is doing well, thank you. The terrible struggle that made me an American out of a potential slave said "On the line!" The Reconstruction said "Get set!"; and the generation before said "Go!" I am off to a flying start and I must not halt in the stretch to look behind and weep. Slavery is the price I paid for civilization, and the choice was not with me. It is a bully adventure and worth all that I have paid through my ancestors for it. No one on earth ever had a greater chance for glory. The world to be won and nothing to be lost. It is thrilling to think — to know that for any act of mine, I shall get twice as much praise or twice as much blame. It is quite exciting to hold the center of the national stage, with the spectators not knowing whether to laugh or to weep.

The position of my white neighbor is much more difficult. No brown specter pulls up a chair beside me when I sit down to eat. No dark ghost thrusts its leg against mine in bed. The game of keeping what one has is never so exciting as the game of getting.

I do not always feel colored. Even now I often achieve the unconscious Zora of Eatonville before the Hegira.* I feel most colored when I am thrown against a sharp white background.

For instance at Barnard.† "Beside the waters of the Hudson" I feel 10
my race. Among the thousand white persons, I am a dark rock surged upon, and overswept, but through it all, I remain myself. When covered by the waters, I am; and the ebb but reveals me again.

Sometimes it is the other way around. A white person is set down in our midst, but the contrast is just as sharp for me. For instance, when I sit in the drafty basement that is The New World Cabaret with a white

---

**Hegira:* Exodus or pilgrimage (Arabic); Hurston refers here to the migration of millions of African Americans from the South to the North in the early twentieth century. [Editor's note]

†*Barnard:* Barnard College in New York City, where Hurston received her B.A. in 1927. [Editor's note]

person, my color comes. We enter chatting about any little nothing that we have in common and are seated by the jazz waiters. In the abrupt way that jazz orchestras have, this one plunges into a number. It loses no time in circumlocutions, but gets right down to business. It constricts the thorax and splits the heart with its tempo and narcotic harmonies. This orchestra grows rambunctious, rears on its hind legs and attacks the tonal veil with primitive fury, rending it, clawing it until it breaks through to the jungle beyond. I follow those heathen — follow them exultingly. I dance wildly inside myself; I yell within, I whoop; I shake my assegai above my head, I hurl it true to the mark *yeeeeooww!* I am in the jungle and living in the jungle way. My face is painted red and yellow and my body is painted blue. My pulse is throbbing like a war drum. I want to slaughter something — give pain, give death to what, I do not know. But the piece ends. The men of the orchestra wipe their lips and rest their fingers. I creep back slowly to the veneer we call civilization with the last tone and find the white friend sitting motionless in his seat, smoking calmly.

"Good music they have here," he remarks, drumming the table with his fingertips.

Music. The great blobs of purple and red emotion have not touched him. He has only heard what I felt. He is far away and I see him but dimly across the ocean and the continent that have fallen between us. He is so pale with his whiteness then and I am *so* colored.

At certain times I have no race, I am *me*. When I set my hat at a certain angle and saunter down Seventh Avenue, Harlem City, feeling as snooty as the lions in front of the Forty-Second Street Library, for instance. So far as my feelings are concerned, Peggy Hopkins Joyce on the Boule Mich* with her gorgeous raiment, stately carriage, knees knocking together in a most aristocratic manner, has nothing on me. The cosmic Zora emerges. I belong to no race nor time. I am the eternal feminine with its string of beads.

**Boule Mich:* Boulevard St. Michel, a street on the left bank of Paris. *Peggy Hopkins Joyce* (1893–1957): American actress and celebrity. [Editor's note]

15 I have no separate feeling about being an American citizen and colored. I am merely a fragment of the Great Soul that surges within the boundaries. My country, right or wrong.

Sometimes, I feel discriminated against, but it does not make me angry. It merely astonishes me. How *can* any deny themselves the pleasure of my company? It's beyond me.

But in the main, I feel like a brown bag of miscellany propped against a wall. Against a wall in company with other bags, white, red and yellow. Pour out the contents, and there is discovered a jumble of small things priceless and worthless. A first-water diamond, an empty spool, bits of broken glass, lengths of string, a key to a door long since crumbled away, a rusty knife-blade, old shoes saved for a road that never was and never will be, a nail bent under the weight of things too heavy for any nail, a dried flower or two still a little fragrant. In your hand is the brown bag. On the ground before you is the jumble it held — so much like the jumble in the bags, could they be emptied, that all might be dumped in a single heap and the bags refilled without altering the content of any greatly. A bit of colored glass more or less would not matter. Perhaps that is how the Great Stuffer of Bags filled them in the first place — who knows?

Engaging with the Text

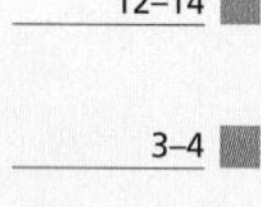
261–66 12–14 3–4

1. This essay **BEGINS** with an attention-grabbing statement. How does it signal Zora Neale Hurston's **STANCE**? Find other passages in the essay that reveal that stance.
2. What do you think Hurston's **PURPOSES** were in writing this essay — to explore her topic? entertain? provoke readers? argue a point? something else?
3. This essay is filled with references to color. Highlight all the words that refer to colors. Can you **IDENTIFY ANY PATTERNS**? What are some of the things colors are attributed to? Do they in any way relate to her title? What do you think Hurston is saying with all the color imagery?

361–63

4. Hurston **ENDS** with a **SIMILE** about bags: "brown . . . white, red and yellow . . . a jumble of small things priceless and worthless." How does this simile — and the last four paragraphs — relate to her central point about our differences and commonalities?

266–70
311–12

5. ***For Writing.*** Think about a time when you realized you were not the same as everyone around you. How did you become aware of your differences? How did you view any differences at the time, and how do you view them today? Write an essay that **REFLECTS** on the same subject Hurston does, how it feels to be you.

180–87

DIANE DEERHEART RAYMOND

Strawberry Moon

Diane Deerheart Raymond is an occupational therapy assistant. In addition, she is a teaching assistant and tutor at Bay Path College in Longmeadow, Massachusetts. The granddaughter of Chief Wise Owl of the Chaubunagungamaug Nipmuck tribe and the daughter of Loving One, the clan mother, Deerheart Raymond has volunteered in the public school system for many years educating children about Native history and culture. She has recently co-produced a documentary on her tribe's denial of recognition from the federal government. The following reflection was written in 2006 while Deerheart Raymond was a student at Bay Path College.

I ALWAYS KNEW I WAS INDIAN. It was a part of who I was growing up. Attending Pow Wows and moon celebrations on the reservation was commonplace. Religion was taught at home, not in a church. I am familiar with our Native language, for my mother used to scold us in Algonquin so that my white dad would not know what she was saying. We had certain Native customs and traditions we upheld. My favorite custom was burying the first ripe fruit from our garden (it was usually a tomato) back into Mother Earth. This allowed us to give thanks for the harvest we would receive that fall. After all, since my grandfather is the chief of the tribe and my mother its clan mother, it was inevitable that I would travel a Native path. One might think you cannot get much more Indian than with my particular lineage. What I have come to realize is that you actually can. I like to think of myself as continuously evolving into my Native skin and broadening my Native path.

I am very fair with green eyes. Both my siblings and I have inherited more of the physical traits of my full-blooded Swedish dad, and to be honest, we were always completely happy with them. It enabled us to mainstream comfortably into our all-white, suburban school. We were Indian at home and even sometimes at school, when the occasion fit. For instance, around Thanksgiving, elementary school-aged children study the colonists and the Indians. It might be at this time that one of

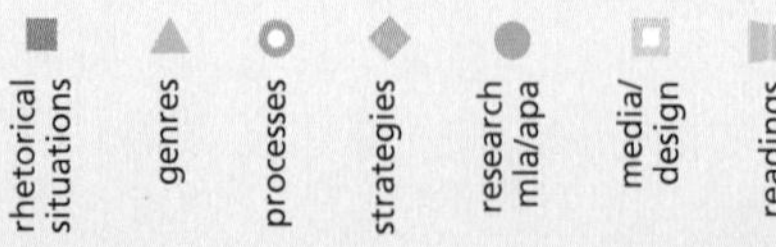

us might confess our Native heritage. This would cause a surge of interest and then a request to have my mom come in and talk with the class. It was always an interesting experience watching my classmates in awe of my mother and her stories. I never quite understood the fascination until I was much older. Thanksgiving always came and went and we resumed our average, white roles in our average, white schools.

Adolescence quickly enveloped me and I took a detour off of my Native path. I became quite uninterested in Pow Wows and Native ceremonies, for most of them were held on the weekends and I certainly had better things to do with my time. My white friends were going to parties and shopping and hanging out. I wanted to be with them and to be doing what they were doing. I stopped even mentioning I was Native, because it always promoted a lengthy discussion that I was not always willing to have. Being Native made me different from my other friends and as a teenager that's the last thing you want. However, this is where my knowing mother was ever so wise. She never forced my heritage down my throat. My Native culture was more like an omnipotent force in the background of my life, ever present and always receptive to how much I wished to utilize it. I always knew it was there, should I need it or want it. When the student is ready, a teacher will appear. I was not yet truly ready to encompass all the richness and lessons that my heritage had to offer.

Life carried on and I found myself married and with child at a fairly young age. I had decided to have a church wedding because my husband-to-be was Catholic. It's what all of my friends were doing. It's what I thought I should do. Through it all, my mother was wonderfully supportive. She never disapproved or made me feel guilty; she just embraced all that was me. Because I was so young and off of my true life path, my marriage began failing. It didn't happen all of a sudden; it was a gradual seven-year process. We were not only growing up with our baby, but also growing apart as well. We were becoming very different from each other. In the meantime, I had developed a new connection with my mother as well as a newfound respect for her. Having become a mother myself, I had a fuller understanding of her intuition and perspective. I now understood the depth of her unconditional love, for the awakenings within me with my own daughter's birth had confirmed this concept. I began to revel in this new light of motherhood and in my mom as my friend and confidante.

I would discuss my marital issues with my mom. I would explain 5
how angry I was at my husband that he didn't help me with the baby and the housework. How irresponsible he was when it came to finances, how all he wanted to do was party with his friends and how he couldn't keep a job. How our marriage counselor had said, "Never mind husband and wife, when did you two stop being friends?" I cried that all of our discussions ended as a screaming match. My loving mother would just smile empathetically at me and stroke my hair, letting me vent. Her validation of my complaints resulted in her naming my husband "Screeching Hawk" at our Harvestfest one year.

One day my mom asked me if I would go to the reservation and help with the Strawberry Moon festivities. She would periodically ask me to assist her in some Native activities and there were times I would take her up on it and others I wouldn't. She didn't ask me very often. However her request this time seemed a little different somehow. There was a sense of urgency about her, similar to the day when my daughter was born and she convinced me with her powerful grace that my daughter's middle name should be "Wunnegin." Wunnegin is a very positive word in our Native tongue, meaning "beautiful, welcomed one." Her utter conviction that this was meant to be this child's name ensured the incorporation of this Native name on my daughter's birth certificate.

Once again, this urgency I sensed within her convinced me to attend our Strawberry Moon. After all, my daughter had gone with her dad to the house of relatives that he had been staying with, so I had nothing better to do. We had recently separated for the fourth time. Impending divorce loomed. Besides that, it would really piss him off if I weren't home when he came to drop her off, so needless to say, that sealed the deal.

It was an overcast day and I was feeling melancholy at best. I picked up the strawberries at the market per Mom's request and met her at the reservation. She was standing at the entrance of the circle upon my arrival. She instructed me to place the strawberries in a basket, to enter

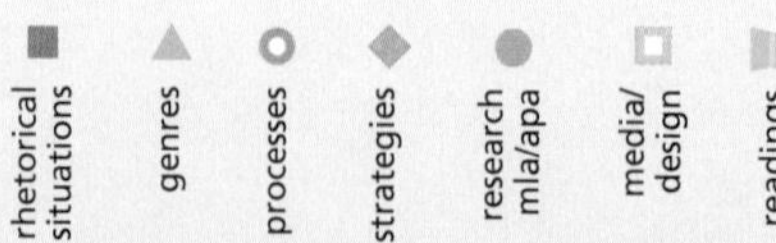

the circle last and then to proceed to offer everyone in the circle a strawberry, ending with her. I remembered the tradition. I had first handed out the strawberries to the members of the circle when I was five years old. Mom usually chooses a younger girl to pass the strawberries and I had guessed that she was having me do it today for nostalgic reasons.

I watched as each participant smudged and entered the circle. This purification ritual using the smoke created from burning sage or sweet grass allows you to cleanse yourself of negativity. I needed to get in the proper mindset before smudging because the Strawberry Moon was the moon of forgiveness. One was not supposed to enter the circle angry or resentful. I took some deep breaths. Could I forgive my soon-to-be ex-husband for all his hatefulness, condescension and selfishness? I was sure I could. We were making the right decision to split up. We were no longer happy in the relationship. This was the best decision for all of us. Perhaps if we stayed together, forgiveness would be much more difficult, but choosing to break allowed us to forgive much more readily. When not faced with the viciousness of each other on a daily basis, there was room for it.

I approached my relative standing at the entrance of the circle with 10
the burning sage. From head to toe, I washed myself clean with its smoke. I cleared my mind and allowed the smoke to encompass me wholly, to heal me. I could forgive. I entered the circle. The trees my grandfather had planted several years ago as a young buck had formed a gloriously imperfect circle for us in which to gather. The arbor that hosted the drum had become worn and tattered and the drummers were sure to get wet should it rain. The fire beckoned from the center of the circle, awaiting the dancers that would soon surround it.

Each member of the circle chose one strawberry from my basket. Each greeted me with a gentle smile or a warm embrace. The circle itself was medicinal. Everyone within it was magical. I ended with my mother's strawberry selection, which seemed to be the biggest and most vibrant one of all. My mom proceeded to the center of the circle and reminded us of the meaning behind this particular gathering. She talked about forgiveness and it being one of our greatest gifts, for while anger and resentment are all consuming, forgiveness is much more healing for the forgiver than for the one being forgiven. She went on to tell us about the quarreling siblings and our tribal legend of the Strawberry Moon. I listened as members of the circle talked about their own stories of forgiveness. I witnessed them consuming their strawberries and throwing the stem of the strawberry into the fire, allowing the smoke to carry their words to the Creator. I watched heartfelt handshakes in reconciliation. Foes became friends. The force within that circle radiated and I felt the earth vibrate.

I had to shield my eyes from the sun that began to reveal itself. It cast a lonely shadow of a hawk that was flying above us. It was a quiet, hovering, almost pensive hawk. It circled a few times and then finally floated away triumphantly, decisively. I felt my eyes being to burn and a lump chisel its way into my throat. My husband and I had chosen our separate paths and that decision had brought us relief and solace. I suddenly realized what had been buried for so long: I had actually forgiven him a long time ago. On some level I had always known we were much too young to be married. I had always known emotionally and spiritually we did not complement each other. I had always known we could not truly nurture one another and grow together. My anger, resentment, and my own continuous mistakes throughout my marriage had stemmed from this deep-rooted knowledge. For me to bury this, to not acknowledge it fully, was to conceal a part of myself. Denying my husband and, even more importantly, myself of my true essence doomed our relationship from the start. It caused me to egg him on, act out, behave childishly, blame him, and then feel guilty. My lack of responsibility and honesty had certainly been a major contribution to our failure as a couple. I had to take ownership for my wayward path. I needed to be accountable for my own mistakes. My eyes cleared and the lump in my throat melted away.

Forgiving him was much simpler than what it was I needed to do. My epiphany erupted — I had to forgive myself.

I shared my story with all my relations. I ate my strawberry. I placed the stem into the fire, thanking the Creator for enriching me with this clarity. My words were carried with the smoke, my spirit set forth toward healing. My mom came over and held me for a long time, grateful for my return to my Native path.

I left the reservation early that day, forgoing the potlatch and social 15 that followed the ceremony. This food and gift-giving exchange is the most enjoyable part of the day's events for most participants; however, I had already received the best possible gift. Following the circle, my graciously intuitive mother walked me directly to the car, knowing my direction. I was no longer interested in pissing off my future ex-husband and I arrived home in a timely fashion to receive our daughter. This sense of peace I now emulated was contagious. My ex eventually seemed to become more affable and agreeable. We became and continue to be co-parents, productively and separately. I now find my Native path broader with each new day. I find more and more ways to incorporate my culture's beliefs and values into my everyday life experiences. I find myself guiding my own daughter down her life's path and being present just enough so that she never wanders too far off her own Native path.

Nukkeeteetookum. (I have spoken.)

Engaging with the Text

1. At the beginning of her reflection, Diane Deerheart Raymond tells us, "I like to think of myself as continuously evolving into my Native skin and broadening my Native path." How does her essay support this **THESIS**?

273–75

2. One goal of a reflection is to explore a topic of significance to the writer in a way that will interest others. What is the **TOPIC** of Deerheart Raymond's reflection? Why do you think she chose this topic? Does she succeed in making her topic of interest to readers? Why or why not?

183–85

3. Deerheart Raymond wrote this reflection as a student in college, and her writing has a personal, introspective tone. To what extent is this appropriate for this **GENRE**? How might the tone be different if she had chosen a different genre — a **REPORT**, for example? What other genre might she have chosen, and how would this piece be different if she had written it in that genre?

9–11
59–82

266–70 4. Why do you think Deerheart Raymond chose to **END** her essay with the Algonquin phrase Nukkeeteetookum, meaning "I have spoken"? How does this ending phrase relate to her title, "Strawberry Moon"?

5. ***For Writing.*** Deerheart Raymond's essay grapples with what it means 306–13 to live on the border between two cultures. **COMPARE AND CONTRAST** Deerheart Raymond's identity struggle with those described by other authors writing on this topic — such as Geeta Kothari in "If You Are What You Eat, Then What Am I?" (pp. 910–15) and Tanya Barrientos in "Se Habla Español" (pp. 560–63). What challenges do these authors share as they navigate through different cultures? What are unique 180–87 to each? Write an essay that **REFLECTS** on the topic of cross-cultural identity and what it can mean to live on the borders between cultures.

JOAN DIDION

Grief

A novelist and journalist, Joan Didion is perhaps best known for her collections of essays, including Slouching Toward Bethlehem (1968), The White Album (1979), *and* Political Fictions (2001). *The following reflection on grief comes from Didion's National Book Award–winning memoir,* The Year of Magical Thinking (2005), *which chronicles her experiences of loss and grief following the death of her husband. (For a review of this book, see p. 732.) As you read, pay attention to how Didion structures her text, moving the reader through time from her early childhood to her adulthood and interweaving her reflections about how to make sense of life after the loss of a loved one.*

GRIEF TURNS OUT TO BE A PLACE none of us know until we reach it. We anticipate (we know) that someone close to us could die, but we do not look beyond the few days or weeks that immediately follow such an imagined death. We misconstrue the nature of even those few days or weeks. We might expect if the death is sudden to feel shock. We do not expect this shock to be obliterative, dislocating to both body and mind. We might expect that we will be prostrate, inconsolable, crazy with loss. We do not expect to be literally crazy, cool customers who believe that their husband is about to return and need his shoes. In the version of grief we imagine, the model will be "healing." A certain forward movement will prevail. The worst days will be the earliest days. We imagine that the moment to most severely test us will be the funeral, after which this hypothetical healing will take place. When we anticipate the funeral we wonder about failing to "get through it," rise to the occasion, exhibit the "strength" that invariably gets mentioned as the correct response to death. We anticipate needing to steel ourselves for the moment: will I be able to greet people, will I be able to leave the scene, will I be able even to get dressed that day? We have no way of knowing that this will not be the issue. We have no way of knowing that the funeral itself will be anodyne, a kind of narcotic regression in which we are wrapped in the care of others and the gravity and meaning of the occasion. Nor can we know ahead of the fact (and here lies the heart of the difference between grief as we imagine it and grief as it is) the unending absence that follows, the void, the very opposite of meaning, the relentless succession of moments during which we will confront the experience of meaninglessness itself.

As a child I thought a great deal about meaninglessness, which seemed at the time that most prominent negative feature on the horizon. After a few years of failing to find meaning in the more commonly recommended venues I learned that I could find it in geology, so I did. This in turn enabled me to find meaning in the Episcopal litany, most acutely in the words *as it was in the beginning, is now and ever shall be, world without end,* which I interpreted as a literal description of the constant changing of the earth, the unending erosion of the shores and mountains, the inexorable shifting of the geological structures that could throw up mountains and islands and could just as reliably take them away. I found earthquakes, even when I was in them, deeply satisfying, abruptly revealed evidence of the scheme in action. That the scheme could destroy the works of man might be a personal regret but remained, in the larger picture I had come to recognize, a matter of abiding indifference. No eye was on the sparrow. No one was watching me. *As it was in the beginning, is now and ever shall be, world without end.* On the day it was announced that the atomic bomb had been dropped on Hiroshima those were the words that came immediately to my ten-year-old mind. When I heard a few years later about mushroom clouds over the Nevada test site those were again the words that came to mind. I began waking before dawn, imagining that the fireballs from the Nevada test shots would light up the sky in Sacramento.

Later, after I married and had a child, I learned to find equal meaning in the repeated rituals of domestic life. Setting the table. Lighting the candles. Building the fire. Cooking. All those soufflés, all that crème caramel, all those daubes and albóndigas and gumbos. Clean sheets, stacks of clean towels, hurricane lamps for storms, enough water and food to see us through whatever geological event came our way. *These fragments I have shored against my ruins,** were the words that came to mind then. These fragments mattered to me. I believed in them. That I could find meaning in the intensely personal nature of my life as a wife and mother did not seem inconsistent with finding meaning in the vast indifference of geology and the test shots; the two systems existed for me on parallel tracks that occasionally converged, notably during earthquakes. In my unexamined mind there was always a point, John's and my death, at which the tracks would converge for a final time. On the Internet I recently found aerial photographs of the house on the Palos Verdes Peninsula in which we had lived when we were first married, the house to which we had brought Quintana home from St. John's Hospital in Santa Monica and put her in her bassinet by the wisteria in the box garden. The photographs, part of the California Coastal Records Project, the point of which was to document the entire California coastline, were hard to read conclusively, but the house as it had been when we lived in it appeared to be gone. The tower where the gate had been seemed intact but the rest of the structure looked unfamiliar. There seemed to be a swimming pool where the wisteria and box garden had been. The area itself was identified as "Portuguese Bend landslide." You could see the slumping of the hill where the slide had occurred. You could also see, at the base of the cliff on the point, the cave into which we used to swim when the tide was at exactly the right flow.

The swell of clear water.

That was one way my two systems could have converged. 5

We could have been swimming into the cave with the swell of clear water and the entire point could have slumped, slipped into the sea around us. The entire point slipping into the sea around us was the kind of conclusion I anticipated. I did not anticipate cardiac arrest at the dinner table.

**These fragments I have shored against my ruins*: a line from T. S. Eliot's poem *The Waste Land* (1922). [Editor's note]

Engaging with the Text

1. Joan Didion reflects on what she thought grief would be and how different it turned out to be when her husband died. What role does this contrast — between what she thought would happen and what she actually experienced — play in the way she **STRUCTURES** her thoughts? 184

2. How would you characterize Didion's **STANCE?** Does it seem appropriate for her topic? Why or why not? What does her tone convey about her stance toward her subject ? 13–14

3. How does Didion **DESCRIBE** her "rituals of domestic life"? What specific details does she supply? What **DOMINANT IMPRESSION** of her domestic life is created by these details? Why is that impression important to Didion? 324–32 330–31

4. What is the **PURPOSE** of Didion's reflection? Where is that purpose made most explicit? 3–4

5. ***For Writing.*** Grief is a powerful and sometimes surprising emotion. Think about a time when you experienced a strong emotion — such as grief, anger, or elation. Consider how this emotion affected you, and write an essay that **REFLECTS** on this emotion and your experience of it. 180–87

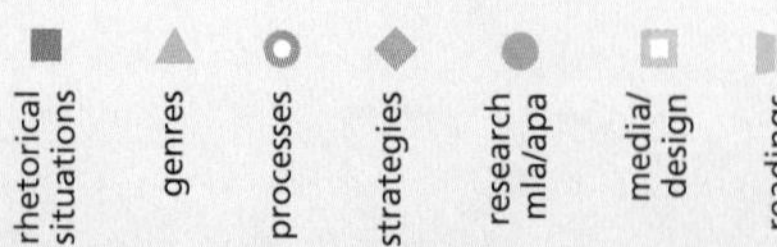

Multi-Genre Texts 64

See also:

ANNA QUINDLEN
Write for Your Life 201

RUTH BEHAR

The Anthropologist's Son

Ruth Behar was born in Cuba and moved to the United States as a young girl. She was the first Latina woman to receive a MacArthur Fellowship, and is now a professor of anthropology at the University of Michigan. Behar's work focuses on the role of the personal in ethnography, and she is the author of several books, including The Vulnerable Observer: Anthropology That Breaks Your Heart *(1996) and* An Island Called Home: Returning to Jewish Cuba *(2007), in which she explores her roots and those of other Jewish people in Cuba. The following argument appeared in the* Chronicle of Higher Education *in November 2008, shortly after Barack Obama was elected president.*

STANLEY ANN DUNHAM SOETORO earned a Ph.D. in anthropology with an 800-page dissertation about blacksmithing in Indonesia. She spent long stretches of time learning to love and rescue the cultures and communities of total strangers, at the cost of not always being around while her son was coming of age in Hawaii. Yet she had an indelible impact on him, teaching him to appreciate cultural diversity and have faith in people's ability to understand each other across borders and identities.

The fact that Barack Obama's mother was a cultural anthropologist has been noted with curiosity and amusement. A few commentators dismiss her anthropology credentials by describing her as part of a radical American fringe, while others represent her favorably, but as "unconventional," "free-spirited," or "bohemian." That reputation is based on her two brief (and interracial) marriages and her wanderings through Japanese villages in an era when the stay-at-home mom was the public model of the American mother. Many now find it difficult to comprehend her passion for her adopted culture and her desire to live for years among the subjects of her research and advocacy work, though what she did was nothing out of the ordinary within anthropology.

As a cultural anthropologist, I think Obama's family background is something to celebrate. But even more important, I think the time is ripe for cultural anthropology to become a fundamental part of American education and public culture. Anthropology needs to be taught alongside math, science, language arts, and history as early as elementary school and definitely throughout the high-school years. Its insights about the perils of ethnocentrism, racialization, and exoticized stereotypes need to become part of our everyday vocabulary.

Students shouldn't have to stumble upon cultural anthropology, as I did, in their last year of college. I remember being thrilled to discover an academic discipline that focused on the complications of developing empathy with people who hold different worldviews. And I was enthralled by the idea of fieldwork, which calls for immersion in the day-to-day existence of people who might initially seem strange and incomprehensible, so that by grappling with our differences through face-to-face interactions, we might move beyond dehumanizing portrayals of "the Other." For a Cuban-Jewish immigrant like me, who'd become all too familiar with the fraught experience of explaining who and what I was to others who wanted to box me into a single identity, the study of cultural difference was absolutely liberating.

I eventually learned that the discipline's origins were not as human- 5
istic as my ideals. Anthropology's fascination with cultural diversity arose in the early 20th century from Westerners' ruthless pursuit of colonial power and the arrogance of their presumed cultural superiority. The role of anthropologists was to elucidate the worldviews of "savages" in the third world before those cultures were swept away by modernity and capitalist development. Then in the 1950s and 60s, testimonies about the Holocaust revealed savagery in the heart of civilized Europe. Decolonization liberated Africa and Asia, and those who were once colonized began to ask, who was calling whom savage?

The discipline survived that crisis, and anthropologists became expert interpreters of cultures in transition. In the 1970s, anthropology was turned upside down by the civil-rights struggle, feminism, and the Native American and Chicano movements. Anthropologists again reinvented themselves by introducing the concept of "reflexivity," which posed key questions about who has the right to tell whose story. Since the 1980s and 90s, anthropology has undergone an even more-dramatic transformation. A wide range of Latino, African-American, Asian, and "halfie" anthropologists have seized the discipline that once viewed them as "Other" and put it to a new use in analyzing their own complex entanglements with home communities and countries.

Having overcome our shameful history after years of self-critique, anthropologists have transformed our discipline into the most optimistic of the social sciences, and the one that most forcefully speaks to the times in which we live, when so much is global but the heart longs for a place to call home. Nowadays our subject is the staggering variety of languages and cultures that crisscross the globe in an age of extreme displacement. We celebrate human creativity while keeping a close watch on the ways diversity is endangered by MacDonaldization of various kinds. We interrogate the idea of race and refute racist preconceptions, both explicit and subtle. We act as grass-roots ambassadors by seeking reciprocal understandings.

To borrow a term from Obama, there is a real audacity in the hopes anthropologists have for tolerance and peace through the twin practices of empathy and fieldwork. Obama's remarkable ability to build a coalition of support among mainstream white voters, minority groups — including African-Americans, Asians, Jews, and Latinos — and young people of all backgrounds demonstrates a deep understanding of his mother's discipline. . . . Perhaps he will seek counsel from cultural anthropologists; previous presidents have missed out on the insights we can offer regarding international issues and debates about identity, heritage, and memory.

. . .

May the anthropologist's son never be afraid of embracing all the different cultures he embodies — Anglo-American, African-American, Kenyan, Indonesian — for fear that some in the United States will think him "too foreign." Today we are all foreigners, and all natives. More than any president before him, Barack Obama has the potential to make Babel represent the possibility of dialogue rather than chaos. The legacy that Stanley Ann Dunham Soetoro left to her son is relevant to us all, now urgently so. The mending of our fractured nation and world depends on it.

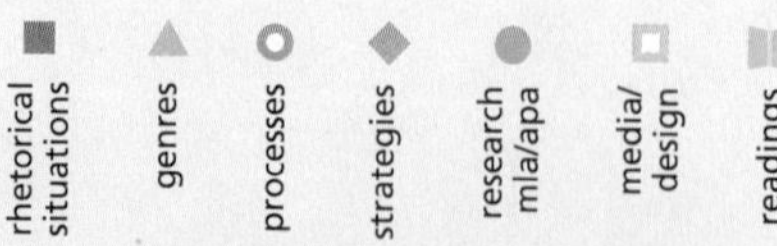

Engaging with the Text

1. Ruth Behar **MIXES SEVERAL GENRES** in order to develop her argument about the value of cultural anthropology in public life. What genre does she use to **BEGIN** her essay? What purpose does this beginning serve in relation to the rest of this piece? 201–8 262–66
2. What **REASONS** does Behar give to support her claim that "cultural anthropology [should] become a fundamental part of American education and public culture"? Do you find her reasons persuasive? Why or why not? 286–87
3. Why does Behar provide a history of anthropology? What does this background information suggest that Behar assumes about her **AUDIENCE**? 5–8
4. Behar writes that "Today we are all foreigners, and all natives." What does she mean by this observation? How does this statement relate to the historical background of anthropology she provides, especially "having overcome our shameful history after years of self-critique"? In what ways can anthropologists — indeed all of us — be understood to be both foreigners and natives?
5. ***For Writing.*** What other subjects or knowledge should be a fundamental part of education that is currently not taught? Write an **ARGUMENT** to persuade your readers that this knowledge of a concept, a practice, subject, etc., is crucial for all Americans — and be sure to consider what other genres might be useful to support your argument. For example, your argument might include an **EVALUATION** of a contemporary social practice, a **REPORT** on subjects currently being taught, or a **PROFILE** of the person who came up with your concept. 83–110 125–32 59–82 161–70

JAY PARINI

Of Value and Values: *Warren Buffett and the American Dream*

Jay Parini is a professor of English and creative writing at Middlebury College. Novelist, poet, critic, and biographer, Parini writes in diverse genres, and he is a frequent contributor to the Chronicle of Higher Education, *a publication aimed at educators in colleges and universities. The following article appeared in the* Chronicle Review *in December 2008 near the beginning of the most severe financial crisis the United States has seen since the Great Depression.*

WARREN BUFFETT, THE ORACLE OF OMAHA, is a modern business legend. In addition to being one of the richest men in America (even with recent losses, he is still worth tens of billions), he's an investment guru whose conversational asides can roil, or arouse, global markets. He is also something of a folk hero: the mild-mannered, relentless genius from nowhere who built a financial empire from nothing (more or less). His extraordinary life is the subject of a recent exhaustive and engaging biography, *The Snowball: Warren Buffett and the Business of Life* (Bantam Books), by Alice Schroeder, herself a financial analyst who understands investing and can explain it. In the latest downturn, Buffett has made headlines for making huge investments in General Electric and Goldman Sachs, just when everyone else was selling.

That he should attract such interest should surprise no one. As Calvin Coolidge once reminded us: "The business of America is business." Anyone who thinks otherwise is looking at some other country. For that reason, Americans have always had a certain fascination with successful figures in the world of finance and commerce, especially those who manage to pull themselves up by the bootstraps, emulating the saga that turned Horatio Alger into a best-selling author in the late 19th century. That was a period when the so-called robber barons — men like Cornelius Vanderbilt and J. P. Morgan — loomed large in the popular imagination. (Alger published more than a hundred "dime novels" that told the same story again and again, like *Ragged Dick; or, Street Life in New York With the Boot-Blacks,* published in 1868.

Yet Buffett — despite his vast wealth and power — hardly seems like a robber baron. He is far too modest for such a characterization, and his politics too generous. Howard Buffett, his father, was a right-wing politician in Nebraska, a member of the John Birch Society, and something of an embarrassment to his son, who opted for the Democrats in the 60s because of their commitment to civil rights. Warren Buffett is now an adviser on the economy to Barack Obama, who consistently invoked his name during the election, as if to assure nervous voters that he was, after all, a guy with solid connections in the world of capitalism.

The figure Buffett harks back to is Benjamin Franklin, the most congenial of our Founding Fathers. Franklin was the simple man of business, a genius in a leather apron. He gave a good name to capitalism, founding a library, a hospital, and a university. He organized a fire department and thought about public sanitation. He put his mind to a thousand tasks and generally improved whatever interested him, inventing bifocals and the Franklin stove when he wasn't experimenting with electricity or helping write the U.S. Constitution. In his *Autobiography* (which lay unfinished at the time of his death and was first published in English in 1793), he comes across as a boy from a Boston family of modest means who runs away from home at 17 and fetches up in Philadelphia with few assets, little money, and three loaves of bread (giving two of them away to a hungry young woman and her child). Already he thinks of himself as someone who will give away what he has to those in need.

5 Generations of entrepreneurs in the United States — Buffett among them — have regarded Franklin as their scrappy hero, someone to emulate. His model has been especially useful to this nation of immigrants. Except for American Indians, most of our ancestors came to these shores without a dime. That was true from the outset, beginning with the original waves of settlers from Northern Europe. Although some certainly came to the New World in search of religious freedom, the lure of financial success played a part in each wave of immigration, beginning with the settlements in Jamestown and Plymouth.

American entrepreneur Warren Buffett.

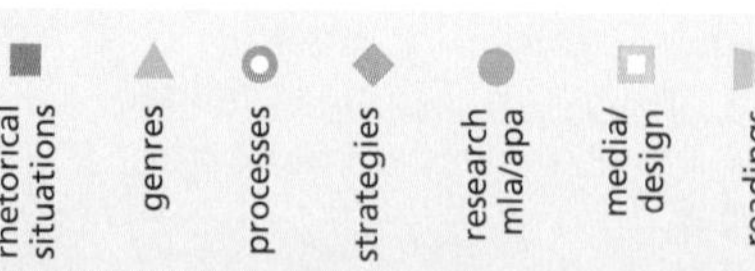

We see a ratcheting up of interest in the rags-to-riches narrative in the 19th and early 20th centuries, as millions more came from Southern and Eastern Europe to walk the streets of major American cities, eager to find a foothold in the economy. As one leafs through the numerous immigrant memoirs of this period, one sees that it was not only fantasies about getting rich that attracted so many to our shores. The image of the American character put forward by Franklin had considerable staying power. People honored someone self-made, to be sure, but they also believed in the dream of equality, the possibility of a rich communal life, where a man with three bread loaves might share two of them. There was a bright hopefulness in that character, a commonsensical quality, with that famous "can do" spirit.

One sees that spirit vividly in Mary Antin's *The Promised Land,* published in 1912, one of the finest immigrant memoirs. Her book serves as a template for the American immigrant experience, which begins far away in the Pale of Settlement, in Russia, where the boot of the law is heavy and uncomfortable. America is seen as the land of milk and honey; then comes the difficult ocean crossing in steerage, and the cold reception on the shores of Boston. But Antin writes a celebratory narrative as she moves to New York and the local community gradually surrounds her. In particular, she praises the democratic approach to education that makes her new life possible, allowing her to become a prominent writer: "The public school has done its best for us foreigners, and for the country, and turned us into good Americans."

That sounds a trifle naïve, as does Franklin at times. But it's easy to become cynical about the process of assimilation. I recall only too well my own father's stories: His parents were Italian immigrants, poor and uneducated. My father himself spoke only Italian until he enrolled in the first grade. He dropped out of school early — during the Depression — to help his family survive. My grandparents would have been surprised to know that I became a professor, relatively comfortable in the world, and far removed from the peasant life they had known in Italy. My point is simply that I, like so many Americans, understand the promise of our country and have a gut feeling that one should celebrate success, as in someone like Buffett, but also see his success as part of a larger American story that is more than simply a rags-to-riches myth. It's a more-inclusive story that speaks to the richness of community and the idea of equality.

Not surprisingly, there has always been a market for books about those who manage to make their way in the world by dint of ingenuity and hard work. *The Snowball* (forgive the odd title, which is taken from a Buffett quotation about a snowball needing only a downhill slope and enough snow to grow) falls into that category. It's the story of a quiet, unpretentious fellow with a head for numbers who managed to accumulate vast sums by choosing just the right companies, and then acquired large holdings in those companies for himself and those lucky enough to have him managing their investments. From what I can tell from various books about him (I've read three), he has remained a decent man, living modestly in the same house in Omaha that he bought decades ago. Apart from a large private jet, he seems immune to the trappings of wealth, although he counts Bill Gates and many other celebrities among his close friends. Famously, he plans to give most of his money away to the Bill & Melinda Gates Foundation. That charitable act will make him one of the great philanthropists of all time.

Schroeder is writing an authorized biography here, with her sub- 10
ject's close cooperation, and so she treads lightly on his private life. Nevertheless she tells us about his decidedly idiosyncratic ways, not least ignoring his wife and children during the early years of his marriage and keeping his mind on business. Later he attaches himself to a mistress, apparently with the consent of his wife. That goes against the American grain: Marriage, we've been told by various preachers and politicians, consists of one man and one woman, not one man and two women. Yet as a nation, we tend to forgive those, like Buffett, who succeed (and punish those who don't).

As noted, Schroeder understands the investment world, and her expertise makes *The Snowball* a particularly informative book for people who spend very little time thinking about the net worth of various companies. From an early age, Buffett was interested in making money, and he had a gut sense of how to do it: selling chewing gum, Cokes, and peanuts to neighbors, saving his money to invest while still in high school. As a college student, he idolized Benjamin Graham, an investment guru who pioneered the idea of "value investing." Graham's ideas were put forward in *Security Analysis* (1934), a textbook written with David L. Dodd, both of them professors at Columbia University. With an eye for the main chance, Buffett went to Columbia after his undergraduate studies at the Wharton School of the University of Pennsylvania to study with Dodd, then Graham.

He became fascinated with the notion that every company has an intrinsic value that may or may not be reflected in the price of its stock. One had to determine the value of a company through painstaking research, taking into account its assets, subtracting its liabilities. As Schroeder notes, the art of security analysis lay in the details: The intelligent investor had to play detective, "probing for what assets were really worth, excavating hidden assets and liabilities, considering what the company could earn — or not earn — and stripping apart the fine print to lay bare the rights of shareholders."

The story of Warren Buffett's rise to wealth is surprisingly gripping. He worked in New York for a while, as Graham's associate. Then he retreated to Omaha with his wife and young family, where he set about buying cheap and selling dear with a single-mindedness rarely seen in the annals of business. He often took inspired leaps of faith, as when in 1964 he decided to purchase vast quantities of American Express, whose stock had been recently battered by a scandal. Shrewdly, Buffett saw that news of the scandal was not widely known; the stock was cheap, but unfairly so. "Warren began to invest in American Express at a hyperactive sprint," Schroeder tells us. The gambit paid off handsomely, as the price of the stock kept rising, and Buffett kept investing.

One usually thinks that diversification is a key to intelligent investing, but here Buffett seems to have moved in a contrary direction, as he explained in one letter to his investors: "We diversify substantially less than most investment operations. We might invest up to 40 percent of our net worth in a single security under conditions coupling an extremely high probability that our facts and our reasoning are correct with a very low probability that anything could drastically change the underlying value of the investment."

Buffett liked partners, who served as sounding boards for his investment ideas. He made an early connection to Charles T. Munger, a lawyer-turned-investor, and eventually they became full partners in Berkshire Hathaway, a former textile mill that Buffett acquired and transformed into a holding company for his many investments. That partnership was solid by 1983, when the two men spelled out the nature of their investment philosophy: "We do not view the company as the ultimate owner of our business assets, but, instead, view the company as a conduit through which our shareholders own the assets." Such a philosophy deviates from the usual model these days, wherein corporate directors often view stockholders as a nuisance. Yet Buffett and Munger have always gone their own way. 15

Schroeder gives a good sense of Buffett's evolving fame as well as his riches. In the early 90s, he managed to redeem the reputation of Salomon Brothers by stepping in to run the company at a point when it seemed doomed to collapse, becoming something of a hero in the process. "The success of his unorthodox approach to scandal — embracing regulators and law enforcers instead of hunkering down — touched the yearning for nobility in many people's hearts: The dream that honesty is rewarded," as Schroeder tells it. "When Buffett walked into a room, the electricity was palpable."

One of the people attracted to Buffett was Bill Gates, Buffett's main competitor for the top spot on the *Forbes* list of American billionaires. The two met at a party arranged by Katharine Graham, owner of *The Washington Post*, who was among the inner circle of Buffett friends (and with whom he had had an affair). It was love at first sight, and the friendship evolved in interesting ways, with the two men helping each other with advice. That connection led, eventually, to Buffett's decision in 2006 to give away 85 percent of his Berkshire Hathaway stock, then worth more than $30-billion, with the bulk of the money going to the Gates Foundation.

One can hardly imagine such numbers. But Warren Buffett is all about numbers, big and small ones. His charm, I think, is the astonishing focus of his life. He has stood by basic principles, investing only in companies he can really understand, and sticking to his fundamental ideas through up and down times. His "value investing" looked extremely old-fashioned during the tech boom of the late 90s, but the value of value proved its staying power in the years of bust that followed. Buffett is perhaps the model capitalist, someone who takes community values into account as he accumulates great wealth, which he then gives away to good causes. In a period when greed and disregard for regulation have pushed the American economy into a downward spiral, he and his commonsensical approach to fiscal responsibility shine like a beacon on the hill.

Engaging with the Text

1. According to Jay Parini, what kind of man is Warren Buffett? What lesson are we meant to take away from Buffett's life?
2. In his essay, Parini shifts between two primary genres, an **EVALUATION** of Buffett's autobiography and a **PROFILE** of Buffett. Why do you suppose he chose to rely on these two genres? What would be lost if he relied on one genre to the exclusion of the other? 125–32 161–70
3. How have times changed economically since Buffett began accumulating his wealth? How do we make sense of Buffett's life and philosophy of wealth today?
4. Why do you think Parini chooses to **COMPARE** Buffett to Benjamin Franklin? What does this comparison convey about Buffett that might be hard to understand otherwise? 306–13
5. ***For Writing.*** Read a biography or autobiography of a person you admire, and consider what kind of lesson can be learned from that person's life. Write an essay that **PROFILES** that person, focusing on those qualities that provide a clear lesson. Draw from your research for support, and be sure to consider what other **GENRES** it might be helpful to incorporate. 161–70 201–8

PETER J. BOYER

Eviction:
The Day They Came for Addie Polk's House

Peter J. Boyer is an award-winning journalist whose work has appeared in several publications, including the New York Times, Vanity Fair, *and the* Los Angeles Times. *He is currently a staff writer at the* New Yorker, *where this piece was published in November 2008. The story of eviction which Boyer relates in the following profile of Addie Polk is one shared by many affected by the foreclosure crisis he describes.*

IN THE EARLY AFTERNOON ON OCTOBER 1ST, Donald Fatheree, a sheriff's deputy in Akron, Ohio, drove his black-and-gold cruiser into one of Akron's dying neighborhoods and came to a stop in front of a small white wood-frame house, with a neatly trimmed lawn and a beige Chevrolet parked in the driveway. He had been there many times before. Part of Fatheree's job is to execute writs of possession, legal orders turning people out of their foreclosed homes — a disagreeable task mitigated, if only slightly, by the long grind of the process. Akron is so beset by foreclosures (there were several hundred last month) that it often takes a year or more for a foreclosure to result in an eviction. Fatheree tried to use that time to accustom people gradually to the idea of losing their home. He believed that a successful eviction required a skilled salesman (himself), who could negotiate, unofficially, between banks and evictees, possibly avoiding a forcible removal. Fatheree would explain to the resident that remaining in the house was not an option—it had already been sold at auction — but if the resident took steps to move out Fatheree might be able to negotiate a little extra time from the banks. Most people followed Fatheree's advice and removed themselves before their final eviction date arrived. For the others, there was a standard procedure: they were escorted from the premises by a sheriff's deputy, and a moving van transported all their possessions to a local storage facility; if the belongings were not claimed within a month, they were sold.

Fatheree had already handled one forcible eviction that day, and the little white house was next on his list. The prospect made him a bit uneasy. In only the rarest cases — maybe one in a hundred — did eviction day arrive without his having had some contact with the resident of the home. The little white house was such a case. Fatheree had gone there countless times, delivering official notices and, sometimes, just stopping by on his own. His knocks on the door were never answered, but he believed that someone was inside; the notices he left, bright-yellow documents with "Sheriff" written on them, were always gone when he returned. A month before the eviction, he had, as required by Ohio law, posted the formal eviction notice by attaching it with duct tape to the front door. He'd returned to the house the day before, leaving one last note, along with his office and cell-phone numbers, in case the resident wished to talk. When, finally, he arrived for the eviction, Fatheree knew little more about the person inside than the information contained in the original foreclosure complaint: "Addie Polk, an unmarried woman."

You could never be sure what awaited on the other side of the door. As a precaution, Fatheree brought along another deputy, Jason Beam. Fatheree knocked on the front door, and, once again, no answer came. According to department policy, the evicting officers could not enter the premises unless they were accompanied by a representative from the bank. In this case, the defaulted loan had been made by Countrywide Home Loans,* and had been assumed by the Federal National Mortgage Association, or Fannie Mae, which had acquired the house at a sheriff's auction in June. The house, appraised at forty-two thousand dollars, had sold for twenty-eight thousand. No one from Countrywide had yet arrived, and the two deputies decided to wait. Another deputy, Dave Bailey, happened by, and stopped to say hello. It was a lovely day, and soon the three officers were chatting in the sunshine just a few paces from the front porch. After a time, they were joined by a curious neighbor, Robert Dillon, who owned the house next door.

**Countrywide Home Loans*: the largest independent mortgage lender in the United States. [Editor's note]

Dillon told the deputies that, yes, Addie Polk did live there. She and her husband, Robert, had moved into the neighborhood in 1970, the same year that Dillon and his wife bought their house. The community, largely black, had been solidly working class back then. Akron's three rubber giants — Goodyear, Goodrich, and Firestone — had provided more than enough opportunity for anyone who wanted work. But Akron's factories were challenged by innovations abroad. As jobs disappeared, the neighborhood began to fray. The street's brick roadbed now pushes up through the asphalt in big patches, and nearly every other house is empty or for sale. Robert Polk, who retired from the Goodrich plant, died in 1995, and Dillon, a taciturn Mississippi transplant, helps his widowed neighbor when he can, installing her air-conditioner and shovelling snow in winter.

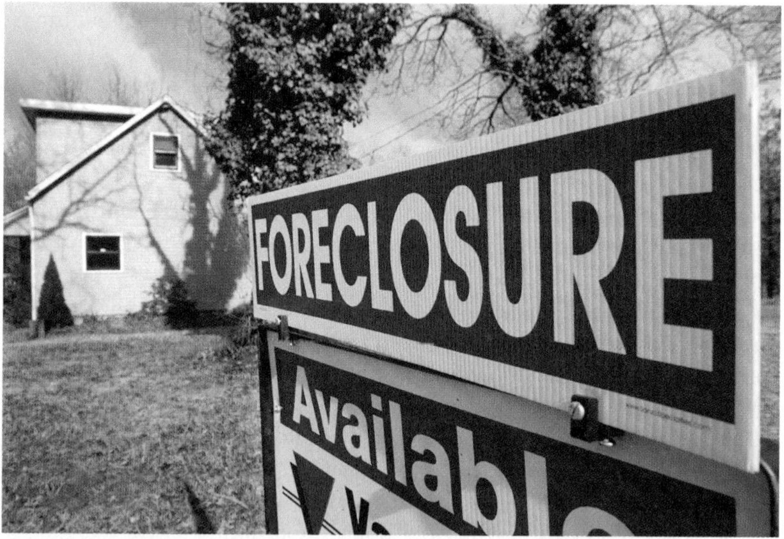

More than 2 million homes were in foreclosure or prolonged delinquency by the summer of 2008.

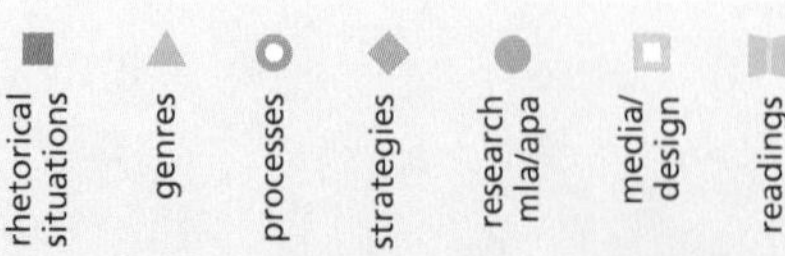

Dillon was surprised to hear that Addie Polk's home had been fore- 5
closed. She'd never let on about any financial difficulties. But, then, she was a very private person. She often didn't answer her door or her telephone (Dillon had failed to reach her by phone that morning), and she had no children and no other relatives in Akron. But even in her old age Miss Polk, as Dillon called her, remained determinedly independent. She drove herself to the grocery store and, every Sunday morning at nine o'clock, to services at Antioch Baptist Church, half a mile away.

Countrywide's representative never arrived. Fatheree was ready to leave, and have the eviction rescheduled, when the men heard a noise inside the house. Dillon, worried that Addie had fallen and needed help, said that he knew a way to get in, and Fatheree told him to try. Dillon fetched a ladder, climbed to a second-floor bathroom window, and worked it open. He stepped inside and called for Addie, but heard no reply. Fatheree's official eviction notice, the duct tape attached, lay on a bedroom dresser. Dillon found Addie in bed, reclined on her side, apparently asleep. A gun lay beside her, and he recalls wondering, Huh? Why is Miss Polk sleeping with a gun in her bed?

Two days later, Dennis Kucinich, the Democratic congressman from Cleveland, was in his Washington office browsing the Internet when he came across the story of Addie Polk from the Akron *Beacon-Journal*:

> At the age of 90, Addie Polk found herself in foreclosure this week, about to be forced from the home she's lived in for nearly 40 years.
>
> So, with a gun in her hand, the Akron widow apparently shot herself in the chest Wednesday afternoon as deputies were knocking on her door with eviction papers in hand.
>
> While a nation reels in financial crisis from years of mortgage abuse, Polk is recovering at Akron General Medical Center, awaiting word on where she will live when she's released.

For Kucinich, the story seemed providential. At the moment, his colleagues in the House were in the final stages of debate over the Bush Administration's bailout of the U.S. financial system, a plan that Kucinich angrily opposed. He saw the plan as an undeserved rescue of the very institutions that had caused the crisis, while guaranteeing no relief for people who were losing their homes to foreclosure. The Addie Polk story seemed to capture the disparity; Countrywide and Fannie Mae had been bailed out, but Addie Polk was left fearfully hiding from her fate.

Kucinich ran from his office, in the Rayburn House Office Building, to the Capitol, reaching the floor of the House as debate was winding down, and told Addie's story. "This bill does nothing for the Addie Polks of the world," Kucinich said. "This bill fails to address the fact that millions of homeowners are facing foreclosure, are facing the loss of their home. This bill will take care of Wall Street, and the market may go up for a few days, but democracy is going downhill."

10 Kucinich later told me that Addie Polk's predicament had struck a particular chord with him. "My story's a little bit different than some of the members of Congress," he said. "When I grew up in Cleveland, the oldest of seven, my parents never owned a home. They moved around a lot. We lived in twenty-one different places by the time I was seventeen, including a couple of cars. I've had the experience of being evicted. I understand what it's like to have people carrying your stuff out and putting it down on the curb. I did this as a child. Children are pretty resilient — they can overcome just about anything. But when someone's a little bit older, and you're the breadwinner, or, in Addie Polk's case, you're a widow, and you're ninety years old, where do you go?"

After his speech on the House floor, Kucinich returned to his office and instructed an aide to get in touch with Fannie Mae about Addie's case, "and see what the hell they are doing." That afternoon, a Fannie Mae spokesman, Brian Faith, announced that the institution would forgive Addie's debt and cancel further proceedings against her. "Just given the circumstances, we think it's appropriate," Faith said. "It certainly made our radar screen." Three weeks later, the same attorney for Countrywide who had filed the complaint arranged a transfer of deed, putting the house back in Addie Polk's name.

Even so, Kucinich said that he means to investigate the case through the Oversight and Government Reform subcommittee on domestic policy, which he chairs. The circumstances of Addie Polk's debt do seem curious. Summit County property records show that Addie and Robert Polk bought their home in 1970, for ten thousand dollars, and that when Robert died and Addie became the sole owner, in 1995, the house was fully paid for. Then, in 1997, Addie was offered a new mortgage on the place, which she accepted, for twenty-one thousand dollars. Four years later, after interest rates declined and real-estate values increased, an independent mortgage broker sold Addie a new loan, for $46,400, and peddled it to America's Wholesale Lender, a division of Countrywide. Then in 2004, after interest rates dropped further and housing prices increased even more, she took out yet another loan from Countrywide. That loan, in the amount of $45,620, was paired with a line of credit for $11,380. Addie was eighty-six. The mortgage was scheduled to be paid off on May 1, 2034.

"What I'm interested in determining is the extent to which lenders targeted elderly people as potential customers in order to go after a class of people that they knew, actuarially, it was impossible that they were going to be around to the conclusion of the mortgage," Kucinich says. "And they had a limited ability to repay. Lenders had to know this. And they did it anyhow, because it appears they were more interested in booking higher and higher sales."

Kucinich says that he wants to find out who at Countrywide wrote the loan for Addie, and how it got approved. "The forensics of this have to be thoroughly explored," he said. "As we get into it, I think it's going to demonstrate the degree of depravity in this mortgage business."

15 Lolita Adair became a real-estate agent in 1963, and a broker in 1979, at a time when Akron had few black brokers, none of them women. When the current foreclosure crisis hit, the city-council president, Marco Sommerville, asked Adair to head a task force on predatory lending. Now, when constituents come to him with mortgage problems, he directs them to Adair. "She knows the answer to questions before you finish asking them," Sommerville says.

I met Adair, a stately woman in her sixties, in her office, in downtown Akron, a few days after the Addie Polk incident, and she agreed to show me around. As we made our way through town in her white Cadillac, past the housing project where LeBron James* once lived, through neighborhoods where "For Sale" signs competed for space with "Obama" signs, Adair told me stories about the predatory lending that had occurred. "Mortgage brokers started cropping up like dandelions on your front lawn after a spring rain," she said. Solicitations for easy loans, using one's house as collateral, came in the mail, in telephone calls, and sometimes from door-to-door hucksters. "You put a slick and a con man together," she said, "and you have predatory lenders." People who accepted loans on terms that seemed too good to be true later found themselves confronted with hidden costs or huge balloon payments, or sudden, upward adjustments in the rates they thought they had agreed to. When they couldn't make their payments, many of them, embarrassed or confused, ignored the legal notices that began to arrive, and soon found themselves ruined and dislodged.

"Some of the stories are so tragic," Adair said. She spoke of how the business had turned upside down in the forty-five years since she entered it. Back then, the tragedy belonged to those who couldn't get loans because they lived in black neighborhoods and were redlined by banks out of the possibility of getting a loan. Adair says that is part of the reason that she became a broker; she served several terms on the local fair-housing board.

By 1970, when the Polks bought their house, the federal government had begun making it easier for the less well off to buy homes. But, Adair says, reform was too often reflexive, rather than measured, and that brought a new set of problems. By the nineteen-nineties, the government had all but mandated that more loans be made to people once considered too risky. Some lenders were eager to venture into the untapped marketplace, and property values (and profits) soared. Angelo Mozilo, Countrywide's chief executive, told the *Wall Street Journal* in 1996 that he personally reviewed two hundred low-income minority loan

---

***LeBron James*: highly regarded National Basketball Association player for the Cleveland Cavaliers. [Editor's note]

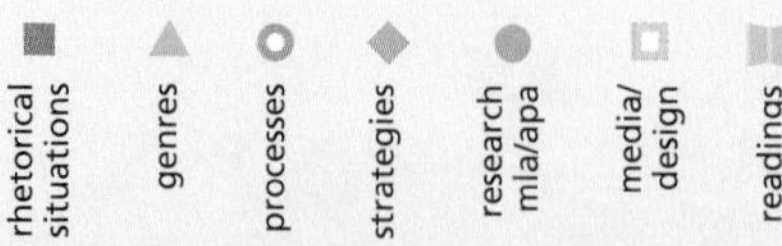

applications that had concerned his underwriters, and approved about seventy per cent of them, in order to send a message to his organization. Approving such loans, Mozilo conceded, meant that "lenders have had to stretch the rules a bit."

People who once found it too difficult to get loans, because of where 20
they lived, and who they were, now found it almost too easy. "What happened was, once the lenders got into the community and found that where interest rates for normal borrowers were somewhere around five per cent to six per cent — you could start with a credit-impaired borrower at nine per cent," Adair said. "As a result, it was, like, 'There's money there! We can make money.' "

A key player in these changes was Fannie Mae, created during the Depression to loosen money in the home-mortgage market. Fannie Mae does not make loans directly; rather, it buys loans made by primary lenders, thus freeing capital for other loans. Fannie Mae's requirements for loan-worthiness set the standard for the industry; loan applications that did not meet Fannie's standards were, by definition, subprime candidates. In 1999, in response to government pressure to expand low-to-moderate-income homeownership, Fannie Mae began to lower its credit-approval standards.

What is striking about Addie Polk's loan is that it wasn't "predatory," in the common usage of that term. Her 2004 Countrywide mortgage was a conventional prime loan, with a fixed thirty-year mortgage. In Adair's view, that makes Addie no less a victim. "Just because Addie Polk's loan is not an adjustable-rate mortgage," she said, "the fact that this was someone who had her home paid off and was encouraged to mortgage her home, time after time, without sound lending practices, makes it a predatory loan."

When Fannie Mae (or its younger cousin, Freddie Mac*) bought a loan, it pooled it with other loans and sold it to investors as a security — like a share of stock. These mortgage-backed securities came to be prized

---

***Freddie Mac*: the Federal Home Loan Mortgage Corporation, created in 1970 by the U.S. federal government to expand the secondary market for home mortgages. [Editor's note]

by investors, because they were seen as being a safe investment, backed, as they were, by American real estate. As home prices spiralled upward and demand for the securities increased, here and abroad, so did marketplace pressure to create more mortgages. Primary lending institutions were happy to oblige; it's easier to make a risky loan if it's going to be bought by Fannie Mae, bundled with other loans, and turned into a security. Whether it got bundled and sold again or stayed on Fannie's books, Addie Polk's mortgage almost certainly found its way into someone's investment portfolio.

That investment, though, was still seen as relatively safe, partly because of Fannie Mae's peculiar nature as a quasi-governmental enterprise. When an investor bought a security that was backed by loans like Addie Polk's, Fannie Mae guaranteed payment even if the borrower defaulted. Fannie was able to do this by exploiting its ability, as a government-sponsored enterprise, to borrow money at lower rates than its competitors. "Because it had the word 'federal' in it, and because it was a government entity, it could borrow at near Treasury rates," Jim Leach, the former Republican congressman who attended last week's G-20 conference* on behalf of President-elect Obama, said.

In Addie Polk's case, Fannie bought the loan for which she prom- 25
ised to pay Countrywide 6.375 percent interest on forty-five thousand dollars, and may have then packaged that loan with others into a security that paid investors a lower amount — say, 6.125 percent. Fannie's quarter-point profit amounted to an insurance pool against defaults. This worked, until Fannie Mae became swamped by defaults; in the event, the government stepped in for a rescue. Countrywide had passed the risk on to Fannie, which, in essence, passed the risk up to the government — a circumstance that critics have called "privatizing profit but socializing risk."

---

*G-20: a group of finance ministers and central bank governors from twenty economies that meet annually to discuss global economic and financial issues. The November 2008 conference, attended by heads of government, addressed the global financial crisis. [Editor's note]

When home values dropped and credit markets tightened, making refinancing difficult, strapped borrowers had no recourse but default, and eventual foreclosure. Last week, Fannie and Freddie announced a plan meant to address that inequity for some borrowers, promising to sponsor loan modifications for homeowners who are at least three months late on payments. By the end of June, there were 2.4 million homes in foreclosure or prolonged delinquency, accounting for 4.5 percent of all mortgages in the country — the highest level ever recorded. The primary lenders servicing those loans — like Countrywide — would earn new fees for the loan adjustments.

Adair turned onto La Croix Avenue and came to a step across from Addie's house. When we got out of the car, we were met by Robert Dillon, who had been told by Adair to expect us. We talked about Addie, and when the subject of her loan came up Dillon looked at Addie's house and shook his head. The roof was patched, the fascia was rotting, and the porch sagged underfoot. He remarked, "When they said forty-five thousand dollars, I said, 'Where'd the money go? I don't see it.' " (Marco Sommerville, the council president, had wondered the same thing. "It's the obvious question," he'd told me, and suggested that an investigation might be warranted. "There are some people who feel there's a snake in the cockpit somewhere.")

Adair, however, was annoyed by the question, and thought the answer was self-evident, considering the string of loans that Addie took out beginning in 1997. "Everybody asks what happened to the money!" she said. "But twenty-some thousand of it went to pay off that first mortgage, when she had that forty-six-thousand-dollar mortgage. Then she was back with a forty-five-thousand-odd mortgage a year and a half later. That's when they gave her the eleven-thousand-dollar line of credit. The lady, just on pure, simple mathematics — if her husband's been dead since 1995, that's thirteen years for her to be living on her own, and she probably did not work — "

"No, no, she didn't," Dillon said.

" — and her only income would have been from his retirement." 30

"I don't know. Four hundred a month? Plus Social Security."

"She probably didn't have a thousand dollars a month that she was living on."

Adair said that she didn't know Addie Polk, but she had known lots of people like her, and could imagine the circumstances that led to her catastrophe. "Here was an elderly lady whose home was paid off, who was getting telephone calls, or people knocking on the doors," she said. "You'd be surprised in some of our neighborhoods how many people have told me that they actually came knocking on their door. They tell you you might have some medical bills, or you can consolidate all of your loans into one payment. You can repair your house, or you might want to take a vacation. I mean, they go through all of this, and they do it in a way of asking you, 'Do you have some credit cards you could pay off? Do you have some medical bills?' And, of course, if you're elderly, and you say yes, you have medical bills or what have you, 'Oh, well, we can put them all into one payment, and this will not hurt you, because it's the equity you have in your home.' What they don't tell you is, those doctors' bills are not charging you any interest; now we're gonna start charging you some interest."

Most of the money that Addie received was automatically used to pay off the previous loan; in the process, the home that she'd once owned outright was stripped of its equity. She kept up with her payments on the last mortgage — $284.61 — for a time, then missed a few; by last year, she had stopped making payments altogether. When Countrywide called to inquire about late payments, she would listen for a few minutes and then hang up the phone.

35 Dillon said that the week after Addie shot herself he and his wife visited her in the hospital. The gun she had used, a .38-calibre handgun, had inflicted a serious wound in her shoulder, and no journalists have been allowed to speak with her. Dillon said that Addie seemed remorseful about the incident, and told him, "It was a crazy thing to do."

She brightened, Dillon said, when he told her that she was getting her home back. "She said, 'I am?' I said, 'Yeah, you're gonna get it back.' She was real happy to hear that." But Dillon didn't know how or if she would return home.

Engaging with the Text

1. According to Peter J. Boyer, what **CAUSED** the 2008 housing crisis? What role did the government play in this crisis? What does the phrase "privatizing profit but socializing risk" mean and how does it relate to Boyer's explanation? 278–82
2. Boyer organizes his essay around a **PROFILE** of Addie Polk, describing her story in great detail. Is this approach effective? Why or why not? What other **GENRES** does he mix into his essay? 161–70 19
3. What **DOMINANT IMPRESSION** of Addie Polk's Akron neighborhood does Boyer create through his vivid description of it? Point to specific details from the essay in your response. 330–31
4. Why do you think Boyer incorporates the lengthy quotation from the Akron *Beacon-Journal*? How does it help Boyer **TRANSITION** between his focus on Addie Polk and a focus on Dennis Kucinich? What other function does the quotation serve? 204
5. ***For Writing.*** Identify a social issue you feel strongly about. **RESEARCH** the issue, locating a person in your school, community, or family who gives a face to that issue. Write a **PROPOSAL** to detail the problem and offer a solution to it. Include a profile of that person who embodies the issue to strengthen your proposal. 373–407 171–79

HAL NIEDZVIECKI

Facebook in a Crowd

Novelist, columnist, and cultural critic, Canadian author Hal Niedzviecki has written several works of fiction and nonfiction. His books include Hello, I'm Special: How Individuality Became the New Conformity *(2004) and* The Big Book of Pop Culture: A How-to Guide for Young Artists *(2007). Cofounder of the magazine* Broken Pencil, *a guide to underground arts and zine culture, Niedzviecki has published essays in* Adbusters, Utne Reader, *and the* National Post, *among others. The following piece appeared in the* New York Times Magazine *in 2008. As you read, notice how Niedzviecki embeds an implicit argument about online social networks in his humorous reflection.*

ONE DAY THIS PAST SUMMER, I logged on to Facebook and realized that I was very close to having 700 online "friends." Not bad, I thought to myself, absurdly proud of how many cyberpals, connections, acquaintances and even strangers I'd managed to sign up.

But the number made me uneasy as well. I had just fallen out with a friend I'd spent a lot of time with. I'd disconnected with a few other ones for the usual reasons — jobs in other cities, family life limiting social time. I was as much to blame as they were. I had a 2-year-old kid of my own at home. Add to that my workaholic irritability, my love of being left alone and my lack of an office environment or mysterious association with the Masons from which to derive an instant network of cronies. I had fewer friends to hang out with than I'd ever had before.

So I decided to have a Facebook party. I used Facebook to create an "event" and invite my digital chums. Some of them, of course, didn't live in Toronto, but I figured, it's summer and people travel. You never know who might be in town. If they lived in Buffalo or Vancouver, they could just click "not attending," and that would be that. Facebook gives people the option of RSVP'ing in three categories — "attending," "maybe attending" and "not attending."

After a week the responses stopped coming in and were ready to be tabulated. Fifteen people said they were attending, and 60 said maybe.

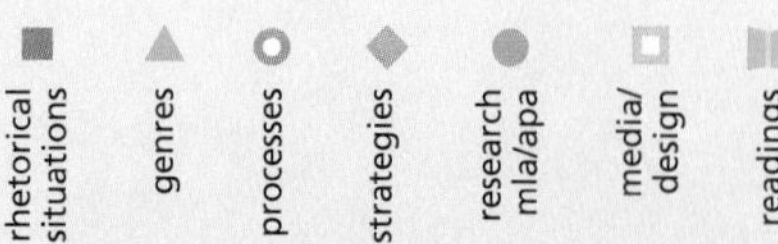

A few hundred said not, and the rest just ignored the invitation altogether. I figured that about 20 people would show up. That sounded pretty good to me. Twenty potential new friends.

On the evening in question I took a shower. I shaved. I splashed on 5
my tingly man perfume. I put on new pants and a favorite shirt. Brimming with optimism, I headed over to the neighborhood watering hole and waited.

And waited.

And waited.

Eventually, one person showed up.

I chatted with my new potential friend, Paula, doing my best to pretend I wasn't dismayed and embarrassed. But I was too self-conscious to be genuine. I kept apologizing for the lack of attendance. I looked over my shoulder every time the door opened and someone new came in. Paula was nice about it, assuring me that people probably just felt shy about the idea of making a new friend. She said she herself had almost decided not to come.

"And now you have me all to yourself," I said, trying to sound benef- 10
icent and unworried. We smiled at each other awkwardly.

We made small talk. I found out about her job, her boyfriend, her soccer team. Paula became my Facebook friend after noticing I was connected to a friend of hers. She thought it would be interesting to drop by and meet me.

Eventually we ran out of things to say. Anyway, she had to work in the morning. I picked up the tab on her Tom Collins and watched as she strode out into the night, not entirely sure if our friendship would grow.

After she left, I renewed my vigil, waiting for someone to show. It was getting on 11 o'clock and all my rationalizations — for example, that people needed time to get home from work, eat dinner, relax a bit — were wearing out.

I would learn, when I asked some people who didn't show up the next day, that "definitely attending" on Facebook means "maybe" and "maybe attending" means "likely not." So I probably shouldn't have taken it personally. But the combination of alcohol and solitude turned my thoughts to self-pity. Was I really that big of a loser? Or was it that no one wants to get together in real life anymore? It wasn't Facebook's fault; all those digital pals were better than nothing. For chipping away at past friendships and blocking honest new efforts, you really have to blame the entire modern world. People want to hang out with you, I assured myself. They just don't have the time.

By now it was nearing midnight. My head was clouded by drink, 15
and it was finally starting to sink in: no one else was coming. I'd have to think up some other way to revitalize my social life. I ordered one more drink.

The beer arrived, a British import: Young's Double Chocolate Stout. I raised my glass in a solitary toast and promised myself I'd spend less time online. Then I took a gulp: the beer was delicious but bittersweet. Seven hundred friends, and I was drinking alone.

Engaging with the Text

1. Hal Niedzviecki's essay offers a subtle critique about the alienating effects of the Internet. Where in this essay is that critique made evident? How does it relate to the **TITLE** of his piece? 272–73
2. How does Niedzviecki use **NARRATION** in his essay? What does this humorous story help us understand about his position on technology? 343–51
3. Who is the **AUDIENCE** for Niedzviecki's essay? How can you tell? Point to specific places in the text that make clear his intended audience. 5–8
4. What does Niedzviecki's essay suggest about the nature of "friendships" on social networking sites such as Facebook? If you belong to a social networking site, how does his experience of the relationships that blossom there compare with yours?
5. *For Writing.* **RESEARCH** the trends in online social networks, and **INTERVIEW** (either online or in person) others who use an online social network to see what they believe about the nature of friendships online. Write a **REPORT** on your findings that incorporates some of your own experience with one or more of these sites. 373–407 394–95 59–82

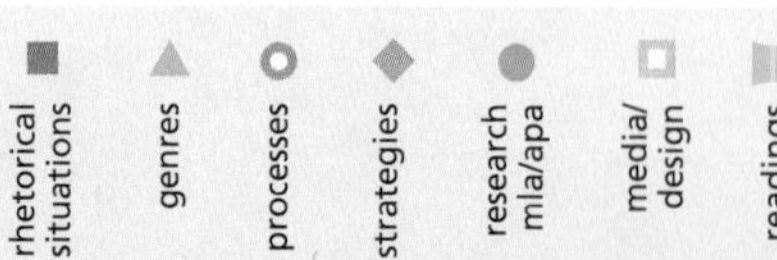

NICHOLAS G. CARR

Is Google Making Us Stupid?

Nicholas G. Carr has written widely on technology, business, and culture. His books include Does IT Matter? Information Technology and the Corrosion of Competitive Advantage *(2004), and* The Big Switch: Rewiring the World, From Edison to Google *(2008). In addition to his blog* Rough Type, *in which he makes observations about the latest technologies and related issues, he regularly contributes to several periodicals. The following piece has been widely debated since its appearance as a cover article of the* Atlantic *in 2008. As you read, notice how Carr mixes in genres such as report and reflection to support his argument about the effects of the Internet on literacy, cognition, and culture.*

"DAVE, STOP. STOP, WILL YOU? Stop, Dave. Will you stop, Dave?" So the supercomputer HAL pleads with the implacable astronaut Dave Bowman in a famous and weirdly poignant scene toward the end of Stanley Kubrick's *2001: A Space Odyssey*. Bowman, having nearly been sent to a deep-space death by the malfunctioning machine, is calmly, coldly disconnecting the memory circuits that control its artificial "brain." "Dave, my mind is going," HAL says, forlornly. "I can feel it. I can feel it."

I can feel it, too. Over the past few years I've had an uncomfortable sense that someone, or something, has been tinkering with my brain, remapping the neural circuitry, reprogramming the memory. My mind isn't going — so far as I can tell — but it's changing. I'm not thinking the way I used to think. I can feel it most strongly when I'm reading. Immersing myself in a book or a lengthy article used to be easy. My mind would get caught up in the narrative or the turns of the argument, and I'd spend hours strolling through long stretches of prose. That's rarely the case anymore. Now my concentration often starts to drift after two or three pages. I get fidgety, lose the thread, begin looking for something else to do. I feel as if I'm always dragging my wayward brain back to the text. The deep reading that used to come naturally has become a struggle.

I think I know what's going on. For more than a decade now, I've been spending a lot of time online, searching and surfing and sometimes adding to the great databases of the Internet. The Web has been a godsend to me as a writer. Research that once required days in the stacks or periodical rooms of libraries can now be done in minutes. A few Google searches, some quick clicks on hyperlinks, and I've got the telltale fact or pithy quote I was after. Even when I'm not working, I'm as likely as not to be foraging in the Web's info-thickets reading and writing e-mails, scanning headlines and blog posts, watching videos and listening to podcasts, or just tripping from link to link to link. (Unlike footnotes, to which they're sometimes likened, hyperlinks don't merely point to related works; they propel you toward them.)

For me, as for others, the Net is becoming a universal medium, the conduit for most of the information that flows through my eyes and ears and into my mind. The advantages of having immediate access to such an incredibly rich store of information are many, and they've been widely described and duly applauded. "The perfect recall of silicon memory," *Wired*'s Clive Thompson has written, "can be an enormous boon to thinking." But that boon comes at price. As the media theorist Marshall McLuhan pointed out in the 1960s, media are not just passive channels of information. They supply the stuff of thought, but they also shape the process of thought. And what the Net seems to be doing is chipping away my capacity for concentration and contemplation. My mind now expects to take in information the way the Net distributes it: in a swiftly moving stream of particles. Once I was a scuba diver in the sea of words. Now I zip along the surface like a guy on a Jet Ski.

I'm not the only one. When I mention my troubles with reading to 5
friends and acquaintances — literary types, most of them — many say they're having similar experiences. The more they use the Web, the more they have to fight to stay focused on long pieces of writing. Some of the bloggers I follow have also begun mentioning the phenomenon. Scott Karp, who writes a blog about online media, recently confessed that he has stopped reading books altogether. "I was a lit major in college, and used to be [a] voracious book reader," he wrote. "What happened?" He speculates on the answer: "What if I do all my reading on the web not so much because the way I read has changed, i.e. I'm just seeking convenience, but because the way I THINK has changed?"

Bruce Friedman, who blogs regularly about the use of computers in medicine, also has described how the Internet has altered his mental habits. "I now have almost totally lost the ability to read and absorb a longish article on the web or in print," he wrote earlier this year. A pathologist who has long been on the faculty of the University of Michigan Medical School, Friedman elaborated on his comment in a telephone conversation with me. His thinking, he said, has taken on a "staccato" quality, reflecting the way he quickly scans short passages of text from many sources online. "I can't read *War and Peace* anymore," he admitted. "I've lost the ability to do that. Even a blog post of more than three or four paragraphs is too much to absorb. I skim it."

Anecdotes alone don't prove much. And we still await the long-term neurological and psychological experiments that will provide a definitive picture of how Internet use affects cognition. But a recently published study of online research habits, conducted by scholars from University College London, suggests that we may well be in the midst of a sea change in the way we read and think. As part of the five-year research program, the scholars examined computer logs documenting the behavior of visitors to two popular research sites, one operated by the British Library and one by a U.K. educational consortium, that provide access to journal articles, e-books, and other sources of written information. They found that people using the sites exhibited "a form of skimming activity," hopping from one source to another and rarely returning to any source they'd already visited. They typically read no more than one or two pages of an article or book before they would "bounce" out to another site. Sometimes they'd save a long article, but there's no evidence that they ever went back and actually read it. The authors of the study report:

> It is clear that users are not reading online in the traditional sense; indeed there are signs that new forms of "reading" are emerging as users "power browse" horizontally through titles, contents pages and abstracts going for quick wins. It almost seems that they go online to avoid reading in the traditional sense.

Thanks to the ubiquity of text on the Internet, not to mention the popularity of text-messages on cell phones, we may well be reading more today than we did in the 1970s or 1980s, when television was our medium of choice. But it's a different kind of reading, and behind it lies a different kind of thinking — perhaps even a new sense of the self. "We are not only *what* we read," says Maryanne Wolf, a developmental psychologist at Tufts University and the author of *Proust and the Squid: The Story and Science of the Reading Brain*. "We are *how* we read." Wolf worries that the style of reading promoted by the Net, a style that puts "efficiency" and "immediacy" above all else, may be weakening our capacity for the kind of deep reading that emerged when an earlier technology, the printing press, made long and complex works of prose commonplace. When we read online, she says, we tend to become "mere decoders of information." Our ability to interpret text, to make the rich mental connections that form when we read deeply and without distraction, remains largely disengaged.

Reading, explains Wolf, is not an instinctive skill for human beings. It's not etched into our genes the way speech is. We have to teach our minds how to translate the symbolic characters we see into the language we understand. And the media or other technologies we use in learning and practicing the craft of reading play an important part in shaping the neural circuits inside our brains. Experiments demonstrate that readers of ideograms, such as the Chinese, develop a mental circuitry for reading that is very different from the circuitry found in those of us whose written language employs an alphabet. The variations extend across many regions of the brain, including those that govern such essential cognitive functions as memory and the interpretation of visual and auditory stimuli. We can expect as well that the circuits woven by our use of the Net will be different from those woven by our reading of books and other printed works.

Sometime in 1882, Friedrich Nietzsche* bought a typewriter — a Malling- 10
Hansen Writing Ball, to be precise. His vision was failing, and keeping

---

***Friedrich Nietzsche* (1844–1900): nineteenth-century German philosopher whose work has been influential in several disciplines, including philosophy, literary studies, rhetoric, and linguistics. [Editor's note] his eyes focused on a page had become exhausting and painful, often bringing on crushing headaches. He had been forced to curtail his writing, and he feared that he would soon have to given it up. The typewriter rescued him, at least for a time. Once he had mastered touch-typing, he was able to write with his eyes closed, using only the tips of his fingers. Words could once again flow from his mind to the page.

But the machine had a subtler effect on his work. One of Nietzsche's friends, a composer, noticed a change in the style of his writing. His already terse prose had become even tighter, more telegraphic. "Perhaps you will through this instrument even take to a new idiom," the friend wrote in a letter, noting that, in his own work, his "'thoughts' in music and language often depend on the quality of pen and paper."

"You are right," Nietzsche replied, "our writing equipment takes part in the forming of our thoughts." Under the sway of the machine, writes the German media scholar Friedrich A. Kittler, Nietzsche's prose "changed from arguments to aphorisms, from thoughts to puns, from rhetoric to telegram style."

The human brain is almost infinitely malleable. People used to think that our mental meshwork, the dense connections formed among the 100 billion or so neurons inside our skulls, was largely fixed by the time we reached adulthood. But brain researchers have discovered that that's not the case. James Olds, a professor of neuroscience who directs the Krasnow Institute for Advanced Study at George Mason University, says that even the adult mind "is very plastic." Nerve cells routinely break old connections and form new ones. "The brain," according to Olds, "has the ability to reprogram itself on the fly, altering the way it functions."

As we use what the sociologist Daniel Bell has called our "intellectual technologies" — the tools that extend our mental rather than our physical capacities — we inevitably begin to take on the qualities of those technologies. The mechanical clock, which came into common use in the 14th century, provides a compelling example. In *Technics and Civilization*, the historian and cultural critic Lewis Mumford described how the clock "disassociated time from human events and helped create the belief in an independent world of mathematically measurable sequences." The "abstract framework of divided time" became "the point of reference for both action and thought."

15 The clock's methodical ticking helped bring into being the scientific mind and the scientific man. But it also took something away. As the late MIT computer scientist Joseph Weizenbaum observed in his 1976 book, *Computer Power and Human Reason: From Judgment to Calculation,* the conception of the world that emerged from the widespread use of time-keeping instruments "remains an impoverished version of the older one, for it rests on a rejection of those direct experiences that formed the basis for, and indeed constituted, the old reality." In deciding when to eat, to work, to sleep, to rise, we stopped listening to our senses and started obeying the clock.

The process of adapting to new intellectual technologies is reflected in the changing metaphors we use to explain ourselves to ourselves. When the mechanical clock arrived, people began thinking of their brains as operating "like clockwise." Today, in the age of software, we have come to think of them as operating "like computers." But the changes, neuroscience tells us, go much deeper then metaphor. Thanks to our brain's plasticity, the adaptation occurs also at a biological level.

The Internet promises to have particularly far-reaching effects on cognition. In a paper published in 1936, the British mathematician Alan Turing proved that a digital computer, which at a time existed only as a theoretical machine, could be programmed to perform the function of any other information-processing device. And that's what we're seeing today. The Internet, an immeasurably powerful computing system, is subsuming most of our other intellectual technologies. It's becoming our map and our clock, our printing press and our typewriter, our calculator and our telephone, and our radio and TV.

When the Net absorbs a medium, that medium is re-created in the Net's image. It inject the medium's content with hyperlinks, blinking ads, and other digital gewgaws, and it surrounds the content with the content of all the other media it has absorbed. A new e-mail message, for instance, may announce its arrival as we're glancing over the latest headlines at a newspaper's site. The result is to scatter our attention and diffuse our concentration.

The Net's influence doesn't end at the edges of a computer screen, either. As people's minds become attuned to the crazy quilt of Internet media, traditional media have to adapt to the audience's new expectations. Television programs add text crawls and pop-up ads, and magazines and newspapers shorten their articles, introduce capsule summaries, and crowd their pages with easy-to-browse info-snippets. When, in March of this year, the *New York Times* decided to devote the second and third pages of every edition to article abstracts, its design director, Tom Bodkin, explained that the "shortcuts" would give harried readers a quick "taste" of the day's news, sparing them the "less efficient" method of actually turning the pages and reading the articles. Old media have little choice but to play by the new-media rules.

Never has a communications system played so many roles in our 20
lives — or exerted such broad influence over our thoughts — as the Internet does today. Yet, for all that's been written about the Net, there's been little consideration of how, exactly, it's reprogramming us. The Net's intellectual ethic remains obscure.

About the same time that Nietzsche started using his typewriter, an earnest young man named Frederick Winslow Taylor carried a stopwatch into the Midvale Steel plant in Philadelphia and began a historic series of experiments aimed at improving the efficiency of the plant's machinists. With the approval of Midvale's owners, he recruited a group of factory hands, set them to work on various metalworking machines, and recorded and timed their every movement as well as the operations of the machines. By breaking down every job into a sequence of small, discrete steps and then testing different ways of performing each one, Taylor created a set of precise instructions — an "algorithm," we might say today — for how each worker should work. Midvale's employees grumbled about the strict new regime, claiming that it turned them into little more than automatons, but the factory's productivity soared.

More than a hundred years after the invention of the steam engine, the Industrial Revolution had at last found its philosophy and its philosopher. Taylor's tight industrial choreography — his "system," as he liked to call it — was embraced by manufacturers throughout the country and, in time, around the world. Seeking maximum speed, maximum efficiency, and maximum output, factory owners used time-and-motion studies to organize their work and configure the jobs of their workers. The goal, as Taylor defined it in his celebrated 1911 treatise, *The Principles of Scientific Management,* was to identify and adopt, for every job, the "one best method" of work and thereby to effect "the gradual substitution of science for rule of thumb throughout the mechanic arts." Once his system was applied to all acts of manual labor, Taylor assured his followers, it would bring about a restructuring not only of industry but of society, creating a utopia of perfect efficiency. "In the past the man has been first," he declared; "in the future the system must be first."

Taylor's system is still very much with us; it remains the ethic of industrial manufacturing. And now, thanks to the growing power that computer engineers and software coders wield over our intellectual lives, Taylor's ethic is beginning to govern the realm of the mind as well. The Internet is a machine designed for the efficient and automated collection, transmission, and manipulation of information, and its legions of programmers are intent on finding the "one best method" — the perfect algorithm — to carry out every mental movement of what we've come to describe as "knowledge work."

Google's headquarters, in Mountain View, California — the Googleplex — is the Internet's high church, and the religion practiced inside its walls is Taylorism. Google, says its chief executive, Eric Schmidt, is "a company that's founded around the science of measurement," and it is striving to "systematize everything" it does. Drawing on the terabytes of behavioral data it collects through its search engine and other sites, it carries out thousands of experiments a day, according to the *Harvard Business Review,* and it uses the results to refine the algorithms that increasingly control how people find information and extract meaning from it. What Taylor did for the work of the hand, Google is doing for the work of the mind.

The company has declared that its mission is "to organize the 25
world's information and make it universally accessible and useful." It

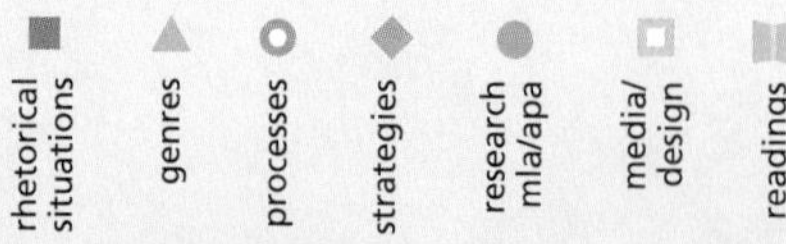

seeks to develop "the perfect search engine," which it defines as something that "understands exactly what you mean and gives you back exactly what you want." In Google's view, information is a kind of commodity, a utilitarian resource that can be mined and processed with industrial efficiency. The more pieces of information we can "access" and the faster we can extract their gist, the more productive we become as thinkers.

Where does it end? Sergey Brin and Larry Page, the gifted young men who founded Google while pursuing doctoral degrees in computer science at Stanford, speak frequently of their desire to turn their search engine into an artificial intelligence, a HAL-like machine that might be connected directly to our brains. "The ultimate search engine is something as smart as people — or smarter," Page said in a speech a few years back. "For us, working on search is a way to work on artificial intelligence." In a 2004 interview with *Newsweek*, Brin said, "Certainly if you had all the world's information directly attached to your brain, or an artificial brain that was smarter than your brain, you'd be better off." Last year, Page told a convention of scientists that Google is "really trying to build artificial intelligence and to do it on a large scale."

Such an ambition is a natural one, even an admirable one, for a pair of math whizzes with vast quantities of cash at their disposal and a small army of computer scientists in their employ. A fundamentally scientific enterprise, Google is motivated by a desire to use technology, in Eric Schmidt's words, "to solve problems that have never been solved before," and artificial intelligence is the hardest problem out there. Why wouldn't Brin and Page want to be the ones to crack it?

Still, their easy assumption that we'd all "be better off" if our brains were supplemented, or even replaced, by an artificial intelligence is unsettling. It suggest a belief that intelligence is the output of a mechanical process, a series of discrete steps that can be isolated, measured, and optimized. In Google's world, the world we enter when we go online, there's little place for the fuzziness of contemplation. Ambiguity is not an opening for insight but a bug to be fixed. The human brain is just an outdated computer that needs a faster processor and a bigger hard drive.

The idea that our minds should operate as high-speed data-processing machines is not only built into the workings of the Internet, it is the network's reigning business model as well. The faster we surf across the Web — the more links we click and pages we view — the more opportunities Google and other companies gain to collect information about us and to feed us advertisements. Most of the proprietors of the commercial Internet have a financial stake in collecting the crumbs of data we leave behind as we flit from link to link — the more crumbs, the better. The last thing these companies want is to encourage leisurely reading or slow, concentrated thought. It's in their economic interest to drive us to distraction.

Maybe I'm just a worrywart. Just as there's a tendency to glorify tech- 30
nological progress, there's a countertendency to expect the worst of every new tool or machine. In Plato's *Phaedrus,* Socrates bemoaned the development of writing. He feared that, as people came to rely on the written word as a substitute for the knowledge they used to carry inside their heads, they would, in the words of one of the dialogue's characters, "cease to exercise their memory and become forgetful." And because they would be able to "receive a quantity of information without proper instruction," they would "be thought very knowledgeable when they are for the most part quite ignorant." They would be "filled with the conceit of wisdom instead of real wisdom." Socrates wasn't wrong — the new technology did often have the effects he feared — but he was shortsighted. He couldn't foresee the many ways that writing and reading would serve to spread information, spur fresh ideas, and expand human knowledge (if not wisdom).

The arrival of Gutenberg's printing press,* in the 15th century, set off another round of teeth gnashing. The Italian humanist Hieronimo Squarciafico worried that the easy availability of books would lead to

**Johannes Gutenberg* (1398–1468): a German goldsmith and printer credited with the invention of the printing press and the first mechanically printed Bible. [Editor's note]

intellectual laziness, making men "less studious" and weakening their minds. Others argued that cheaply printed books and broadsheets would undermine religious authority, demean the work of scholars and scribes, and spread sedition and debauchery. As New York University professor Clay Shirky notes, "Most of the arguments made against the printing press were correct, even prescient." But, again, the doomsayers were unable to imagine the myriad blessings that the printed word would deliver.

So, yes, you should be skeptical of my skepticism. Perhaps those who dismiss critics of the Internet as Luddites or nostalgists will be proved correct, and from our hyperactive, data-stoked minds will spring a golden age of intellectual discovery and universal wisdom. Then again, the Net isn't the alphabet, and although it may replace the printing press, it produces something altogether different. The kind of deep reading that a sequence of printed pages promotes is valuable not just for the knowledge we acquire from the author's words but for the intellectual vibrations those words set off within our own minds. In the quiet spaces opened up by the sustained, undistracted reading of a book, or by any other act of contemplation, for that matter, we make our own associations, draw our own inferences and analogies, foster our own ideas. Deep reading, as Maryanne Wolf argues, is indistinguishable from deep thinking.

If we lose those quiet spaces, or fill them up with "content," we will sacrifice something important not only in our selves but in our culture. In a recent essay, the playwright Richard Foreman eloquently described what's at stake:

> I come from a tradition of Western culture, in which the ideal (my ideal) was the complex, dense and "cathedral-like" structure of the highly educated and articulate personality — a man or woman who carried inside themselves a personally constructed and unique version of the entire heritage of the West. [But now] I see within us all (myself included) the replacement of complex inner density with a new kind of self — evolving under the pressure of information overload and the technology of the "instantly available."

As we are drained of our "inner repertory of dense cultural inheritance," Foreman concluded, we risk turning into "'pancake people' — spread wide and thin as we connect with that vast network of information accessed by the mere touch of a button."

I'm haunted by that scene in *2001*. What makes it so poignant, and so weird, is the computer's emotional response to the disassembly of its mind: its despair as one circuit after another goes dark, its childlike pleading with the astronaut — "I can feel it. I can feel it. I'm afraid" — and its final reversion to what can only be called a state of innocence. HAL's outpouring of feeling contrasts with the emotionlessness that characterizes the human figures in the film, who go about their business with an almost robotic efficiency. Their thoughts and actions feel scripted, as if they're following the steps of an algorithm. In the world of *2001*, people have become so machinelike that the most human character turns out to be a machine. That's the essence of Kubrick's dark prophecy: as we come to rely on computers to mediate our understanding of the world, it is our own intelligence that flattens into artificial intelligence.

Engaging with the Text

1. Sergey Brin has noted, "Some say Google is God. Others say Google is Satan. But if they think Google is too powerful, remember that with search engines, unlike other companies, all it takes is a single click to go to another search engine." How does Nicholas G. Carr's essay support or challenge this assertion? Why do you think this topic elicits such strong responses?
2. According to Carr, what has been the effect of the Internet on the way we read, think, and live? What **EVIDENCE** does he offer to support his claims? How does his discussion of the changes wrought by other technologies help him make his argument? 287–93
3. Where in his argument does Carr **INCORPORATE OTHER VIEWPOINTS**? Is this an effective strategy for his piece? Why or why not? 294–95

4. Why does Carr **BEGIN** and **END** by referring to HAL from the film *2001: A Space Odyssey*? How do the quotes he chooses from the film help him appeal to his **AUDIENCE**?

5. ***For Writing.*** What is your view of how technology is affecting the way we think, read, write, and live? Write an **ARGUMENT** in which you support or challenge Carr's conclusion that "as we come to rely on computers to mediate our understanding of the world, it is our own intelligence that flattens into artificial intelligence." Consider mixing in a **REFLECTION** on your own use of computers to help make your argument.

261–71
5–8
83–110
180–87

Acknowledgments

IMAGE ACKNOWLEDGMENTS

45: Courtesy ResiCal, Inc.; **46:** Courtesy Unilever; **48:** © McNEIL-PPC, Inc. 2007. LISTERINE® is a registered trademark of Johnson & Johnson. Used with permission; **69:** Bettman / Corbis; **72:** Steve Morris / Air Team Images; **90:** (both) Bettmann / Corbis; **164:** Brian Nicholson / The New York Times / Redux; **292:** © Reagan Louie; **304:** Naum Kazhdan / Redux; **310:** (top) From Stiglitz, Joseph. *Economics*. New York: Norton, (bottom) www.ivillage.com; **328:** Courtesy Glaxo Smith Kline; **341:** From Beranbaum, Rose Levy. *The Bread Bible*. New York: Norton; **386, 389, 390:** Courtesy of University of Wyoming Library; **450:** (wolf) Jim Krueger, (beagle) DlILL / Corbis, text courtesy of *The Bark*; **455:** Courtesy of Forum on Religion and Ecology, Yale University and J. Baird Callicott; **457:** Reprinted with permission of EBSCO Publishing, 2008; **469:** Bettmann / Corbis; **496:** Ethics & Behavior. 18(1). 59–92 © Taylor & Francis Group, LLC; **497:** Lisa Takeuchi Cullen, "Freshen Up Your Drink": Copyright TIME INC. Reprinted by permission. TIME is a registered trademark of Time Inc. All rights reserved, (David Stern) Amanda Friedman / Icon International, (Justin Timberlake) Tobias Schwartz / Reuters; **501:** Reprinted from the Federal Reserve Bank of San Francisco Economic Letter 2001-29. The opinions expressed in this article do not necessarily reflect the views of the management of the Federal Reserve Bank of San Francisco, or of the Board of Governors of the Federal Reserve System. Glenn D. Rudebusch; **502:** Reprinted with permission of EBSCO Publishing, 2008; **529:** (top) Peter Turnley / Corbis, (second image) from Stiglitz and Walsh. *Principles of Microeconomics*. 3rd ed. New York: Norton, (third image) From Ginsberg, Lowi, Weir. *We the People*. 5th ed. New York: Norton, (fourth image) From Stiglitz, Joseph. *Economics*. New York: Norton, (fifth image) From Maier, Smith, Keyssar, Kevles. Inventing America. New York: Norton, (sixth image) From Ginsberg, Lowi, Weir. *We the People*. 5th ed. New York: Norton; **531:** (top two) Photo: Don Nowak, (bottom two) AP Photo; **552:** (clockwise from top left) Courtesy of the author, AP Photo, Courtesy of Dr. R. Standleer, Warner Brothers / Photofest; **553:** Courtesy Illinois State University; **554:** (top) Courtesy Illinois State University, (bottom) Clare Robertson, www.loobylu.com; **555:** Courtesy Julia Gilkinson; **578:** Time / Life Pictures / Getty Images; **583:** Cover of FUN HOME: A Family Tragicomic by Alison Bechdel. Jacket art © 2006 by Alison Bechdel. Reprinted by permission of Houghton Mifflin Harcourt Publishing Company. All rights reserved; **605:** Courtesy *Men's Health* magazine; **615:** Chris Barrett@Hedrich Blessing; **617, 619:** Flad Architects; **624:** Courtesy Children, Inc.; **650:** Courtesy of PETA; **654:** Daniel Acker / Bloomberg News / Landov; **661:** Anita Khemka / Contact Press Images; **678:** John Gress / Corbis; **685:** Getty Images; **721:** Denis / REA / Redux; **728–29:** Electronic Arts, Inc.; **739:** Karen Ballard / Columbia Pictures; **815:** Courtesy of Alberto Rios; **829:** Courtesy Pantheon Books and Valerie Steiker; **843:** Mike Ewen / Tallahassee Democrat; **848:** By Nicholas Howe; **854:** Granger Collection; **856:** © 2006 The Georgia O'Keeffe Museum / Artists Rights Society

(ARS), New York. Collection of the University of Arizona Museum of Art, Tucson, Gift of Oliver James; **861:** © Walt Disney / Courtesy Everett Collection; **940:** Bonnie Schiffman / Corbis; **948:** Mel Evans / AP.

TEXT ACKNOWLEDGMENTS

Marjorie Agosín: "Always Living in Spanish," *The Literary Life*, p. 25. Reprinted by permission of the author.

Jimmy Santiago Baca: "Count-time" by Jimmy Santiago Baca, from *Immigrants In Our Own Land*, copyright © 1979 by Jimmy Santiago Baca. Reprinted by permission of New Directions Publishing Corp.

E.J. Bader: "Homeless on Campus" Reprinted by permission from *The Progressive*.

Rob Baker: "Jimmy Santiago Baca: Poetry as Lifesaver," *The Council Chronicle*, Sept. 2008, pp. 23–24. Copyright 2008 by the National Council of Teachers of English. Reprinted with permission.

Dennis Baron: "Don't Make English Official—Ban It Instead." Reprinted by permission of the author.

Tanya Barrientos: "Se Habla Español," from the August 2004 issue of *Latina*. Reprinted by permission of *Latina* magazine.

Dave Barry: "Introduction: Guys vs. Men" and "Guys vs. Men (Table)" from *Dave Barry's Complete Guide to Guys* by Dave Barry, copyright © 1995 by Dave Barry. Used by permission of Random House, Inc. For on-line information about other Random House, Inc. books and authors, see the Internet web site at http://www.randomhouse.com.

Alison Bechdel: Excerpt from "The Canary-Colored Caravan of Death" from *Fun Home: A Family Tragicomic* by Alison Bechdel. Copyright © 2006 by Alison Bechdel. Reprinted by permission of Houghton Mifflin Harcourt Publishing Company. All rights reserved.

Ginia Bellafante: "In the '24' World, Family Is the Main Casualty" from *The New York Times*, 5/20/2007, © 2007 The New York Times. All rights reserved. Used by permission and protected by the Copyright Laws of the United States. The printing, copying, redistribution, or retransmission of the Material without express written permission is prohibited. www.nytimes.com.

Michael Benton, Mark Dolan, and Rebecca Zinch: "Teen Film$: An Annotated Bibliography," from *Journal of Popular Film and Television*, Volume 25, pp. 83–88, Summer 1997. Reprinted by permission of the Helen Dwight Reid Educational Foundation. Published by Heldref Publications, 1319 Eighteenth St., NW, Washington, DC 20036-1802. © 1997.

Dylan Borchers: "Against the Odds: Harry S. Truman and the Election of 1948." Reprinted by permission of the author.

Peter J. Boyer: "Eviction: The Day They Came for Addie Polk's House." Originally published in *The New Yorker*, Nov. 24, 2008. Peter J. Boyer is a staff writer at *The New Yorker*. Reprinted by permission of the author.

Rick Bragg: "All Over But the Shoutin'," from *All Over But the Shoutin'* by Rick Bragg, copyright © 1997 by Rick Bragg. Used by permission of Pantheon Books, a division of Random House, Inc.

H. Sterling Burnett: "A Modest Proposal to Improve Forest Management: State Forest Block Grants," Opinion Editorial, National Center for Policy Analysis, Sept. 15, 2008. H. Sterling Burnett is a senior fellow with the National Center for Policy Analysis. Reprinted with permission.

Nicholas Carr: "Is Google Making Us Stupid?" This article originally appeared in the July/August 2008 issue of *The Atlantic*. Copyright 2008 by Nicholas Carr. Reprinted with permission.

Sean B. Carroll: From *Endless Forms Most Beautiful: The New Science of Evo Devo and the Making of the Animal Kingdom* by Sean B. Carroll. Copyright © 2005 by Sean B. Carroll. Used by permission of W.W. Norton & Company. This selection may not be reproduced, stored in a retrieval system, or transmitted in any form or by any means without the prior written permission of the publisher.

Stephen L. Carter: "Just Be Nice," *Civility: Manners, Morals, and the Etiquette of Democracy*, pp. 66–71. © 1998 by Stephen L. Carter. Reprinted by permission of Basic Books, a member of Perseus Books Group.

Jennifer Church: "Proposal for Biodiversity." Reprinted by permission of the author.

Maggie Cutler: "Whodunit—the Media?" by Maggie Cutler. Reprinted by permission from the March 26, 2001 issue of *The Nation*. For subscription information, call 1-800-3333-8536. Portions of each week's Nation magazine can be accessed at http://www.thenation.com.

Jeffrey DeRoven: "The Greatest Generation: The Great Depression and the American South" from *Etude & Techne*. Reprinted by permission of the author.

Joan Didion: "Georgia O'Keeffe" by Joan Didion. Copyright © 1979 by Joan Didion. Originally published in *The White Album*. Reprinted by permission of the author.

Joan Didion: From *The Year of Magical Thinking* by Joan Didion, copyright © 2005 by Joan Didion. Used by permission of Alfred A. Knopf, a division of Random House, Inc.

Rita Dove: "The First Book" from *On the Bus with Rosa Parks* by Rita Dove. Copyright © 1999 by Rita Dove. Used by permission of W. W. Norton & Company, Inc.

A. Roger Ekirch: From *At Day's Close: Night in Times Past* by A. Roger Ekirch. Copyright © 2005 by A. Roger Ekirch. Used by permission of W.W. Norton & Company. This selection may not be reproduced, stored in a retrieval system, or transmitted in any form or by any means without the prior written permission of the publisher.

James Fallows: "Throwing Like a Girl," *The Atlantic Monthly*, August 1996. Copyright 1996 The Atlantic Monthly Group, as first published in *The Atlantic Monthly*. Distributed by Tribune Media Services.

William Faulkner: "A Rose for Emily," from *Collected Stories of William Faulkner* (New York: Random House, 1950). Reprinted by permission.

Jonathan Safran Foer: "My Life as a Dog," *The New York Times*, November 27, 2006. © 2006, The New York Times. Reprinted by permission.

Samuel Freedman: "Camp Leads a Drumbeat for a Marching Band's Style" from *The New York Times*, 7/23/2008. © 2008 The New York Times. All rights reserved. Used by permission and protected by the Copyright Laws of the United States. The printing, copying, redistribution, or retransmission of the Material without express written permission is prohibited.

Henry Louis Gates, Jr.: "A Giant Step" by Henry Louis Gates, Jr. Copyright © 1990 by Henry Louis Gates, Jr. Originally published in *The New York Times Magazine*. Reprinted by permission of the author.

Diana George: "Changing the Face of Poverty: Nonprofits and the Problem of Representation" by Diana George from *Popular Literacy: Studies in Cultural Practices and Poetics*, edited by John Trimbur, © 2001. Reprinted by permission of the University of Pittsburgh Press.

Peter N. Goggin: "'Enjoy Illusions, Lad, and Let the Rocks Be Rocks': Le Guin's *A Wizard of Earthsea* as a Parable for a Rhetoric of Sustainability and Environmental Literacy." Reprinted by permission of the author.

Amy Goldwasser: "What's the Matter with Kids Today?" This article first appeared in Salon.com, at http://www.Salon.com. An online version remains in the Salon archives. Reprinted with permission.

Michael Granof: "Course Requirement: Extortion," *The New York Times*, August 12, 2007. © 2007, The New York Times. Reprinted by permission.

Patricia Hampl: "The Invention of Autobiography" from *I Could Tell You Stories: Sojourns in the Land of Memory* by Patricia Hampl. Copyright © 1999 by Patricia Hampl. Used by permission of W. W. Norton & Company, Inc.

Ali Heinekamp: "*Juno*: Not Just Another Teen Movie." Copyright © 2008 by Ali Heinekamp. Reprinted by permission of the author.

Gregory Hoadley: "Classic Nuance: Simon Hall at Indiana University by Flad Architects," ArchNewsNow.com, July 18, 2008. Reprinted with permission.

Laura Holson: "Rural Idaho Town Seeks to Turn Film's Status into Prosperity" from *The New York Times*, 7/10/2006, © 2006 The New York Times. All rights reserved. Used by permission and protected by the Copyright Laws of the United States. The printing, copying, redistribution, or retransmission of the Material without express written permission is prohibited. www.nytimes.com.

Megan Hopkins: "Training the Next Teachers for America: A Proposal for Reconceptualizing Teach for America," *Phi Delta Kappan*, June 2008, pp. 721–725. Reprinted by permission of the author.

Nicholas Howe: "Writing Home: High Street," Howe, Nicholas; *Across an Inland Sea*. © 2003 Princeton University Press. Reprinted by permission of Princeton University Press.

Stephanie Huff: "Metaphors and the Counterfeit Nature of Our Society." Reprinted by permission of the author.

Langston Hughes: "Theme for English B" from *The Collected Poems of Langston Hughes* by Langston Hughes, edited by Arnold Rampersad with David Roessel, Associate Editor, copyright © 1994 by the Estate of Langston Hughes. Used by permission of Alfred A. Knopf, a division of Random House, Inc.

Zora Neale Hurston: "How It Feels to Be Colored Me," from *I Love Myself When I'm Laughing*. Used with permission of the Estate of Zora Neale Hurston.

Michiko Kakutani: "The End of Life as She Knew It" from *The New York Times*, 10/4/2005. © 2005 The New York Times. All rights reserved. Used by permission and protected by the Copyright Laws of the United States. The printing, copying, redistribution, or retransmission of the Material without express written permission is prohibited.

Geeta Kothari: "If You Are What You Eat, Then What Am I?" Reprinted by permission of the author.

Jonathan Kozol: From *The Shame of the Nation* by Jonathan Kozol, copyright © 2005 by Jonathan Kozol. Used by permission of Crown Publishers, a division of Random House, Inc.

Doug Lantry: "Stay Sweet As You Are." Reprinted by permission of the author.

Lawrence Lessig: "Some Like It Hot"—Wired Magazine article, from *Free Culture* by Lawrence Lessig, copyright © 2004 by Lawrence Lessig. Used by permission of The Penguin Press, a division of Penguin Group (USA) Inc. For on-line information about other Penguin Group (USA) books and authors, see the Internet website at: http://www.penguin.com.

Joanna MacKay: "Organ Sales Will Save Lives." Reprinted by permission of the author.

Gregory Mantsios: "Class in America—2003," from *Race, Class, and Gender in the United States*, ed. Paula Rothenberg. Reprinted by permission of the author.

Dara Mayers: "Our Bodies, Our Lives" from the Ford Foundation report, Summer 2004. Reprinted with permission from the Ford Foundation. © Ford Foundation.

Sarah McGlone: "Effect of Biofeedback Training on Muscle Tension and Skin Temperature." Reprinted by permission of the author.

Philip Nel: "Fantasy, Mystery, and Ambiguity," from *J.K. Rowling's Harry Potter Novels: A Reader's Guide* by Philip Nel. © 2001. Reprinted by permission of the Continuum International Publishing Group.

Marina Nemat: Reprinted with the permission of the Free Press, a Division of Simon & Schuster, Inc., from *Prisoner of Tehran: One Woman's Story of Survival Inside of An Iranian Prison* by Marina Nemat. Copyright © 2007 by Marina Nemat. All rights reserved.

Shannon Nichols: " 'Proficiency'." Reprinted by permission of the author.

Hal Niedzviecki: "Facebook in a Crowd," *The New York Times, T Magazine*, 10/26/2008. © 2008 The New York Times. All rights reserved. Used by permission and protected by the Copyright Laws of the

United States. The printing, copying, redistribution, or retransmission of the Material without express written permission is prohibited.

Denise Noe: "Parallel Worlds: The Surprising Similarities (and Differences) of Country-and-Western and Rap," reprinted by permission of the author.

Jessica Ann Olson: "Annotated Bibliography on Global Warming." Copyright © 2008 by Jessica Ann Olson. Reprinted by permission of the author.

Jay Parini: "Of Value and Values: Warren Buffett and the American Dream," *The Chronicle Review*, Vol. 15, Issue 15, Dec. 5, 2008, p. B14. Reprinted by permission of Jay Parini.

Grant Penrod: "Anti-Intellectualism: Why We Hate the Smart Kids." Reprinted by permission of the author.

David Pogue: "No Keyboard? And You Call This a BlackBerry?" from *The New York Times*, 11/26/2008. © 2008 The New York Times. All rights reserved. Used by permission and protected by the Copyright Laws of the United States. The printing, copying, redistribution, or retransmission of the Material without express written permission is prohibited.

Heidi Pollock: "You Say You Want a Resolution?" Reprinted by permission of *H2so4*.

Anna Quindlen: "Write for Your Life." Reprinted by permission of International Creative Management, Inc. Copyright © 2007 by Anna Quindlen. First appeared in *Newsweek*, January 22, 2007.

Diane Deerheart Raymond: "Strawberry Moon." Reprinted by permission of the author.

Alberto Alvaro Rios: "The March of the Altar Boy Army," *Capirotada: A Nogales Memoir* by Alberto Alvaro Rios, pp. 22-31. © 1999. Reprinted by permission of University of New Mexico Press.

William Safire: "A Spirit Reborn," *The New York Times*, September 9, 2002. © 2002, The New York Times. Reprinted by permission.

Seth Schiesel: "Playing God, The Home Game" from *The New York Times*, 9/5/2008. © 2008 The New York Times. All rights reserved. Used by permission and protected by the Copyright Laws of the United States. The printing, copying, redistribution, or retransmission of the Material without express written permission is prohibited.

A.O. Scott: "007 Is Back, And He's Brooding" from *The New York Times*, 5/9/2008. © 2008 The New York Times. All rights reserved. Used by permission and protected by the Copyright Laws of the United States. The printing, copying, redistribution, or retransmission of the Material without express written permission is prohibited.

David Sedaris: "Us and Them," from *Dress Your Family in Corduroy and Denim* by David Sedaris. Copyright © 2004 by David Sedaris. By permission of Little, Brown & Company.

Katharine Q. Seelye: "Lurid Numbers on Glossy Pages! (Magazines Exploit What Sells)," *The New York Times*, 2/10/2006. © 2006 The New York Times. All rights reserved. Used by permission and protected by the Copyright Laws of the United States. The printing, copying, redistribution, or retransmission of the Material without express written permission is prohibited.

Leslie Marmon Silko: "Language and Literature from a Pueblo Indian Perspective," *Yellow Woman and A Beauty of the Spirit*. Copyright © 1981by Leslie Marmon Silko, reprinted by permission of The Wylie Agency LLC.

Peter Singer: "The Singer Solution to World Poverty," © by Peter Singer. Reprinted by permission of the author.

Lillian Smith: "When I Was a Child" from *Killers of the Dream* by Lillian Smith. Copyright 1949, © 1961 by Lillian Smith. Used by permission of W. W. Norton & Company, Inc.

Sean Smith: "A Pirate's Life," from *Newsweek*, June 26, 2006. © 2006 Newsweek, Inc. All rights reserved. Used by permission and protected by the Copyright Laws of the United States. The printing, copying, redistribution, or retransmission of the Material without express written permission is prohibited.

Valerie Steiker: "The Girl Who Cried Wolf" from *The Leopard Hat: A Daughter's Story* by Valerie Steiker, copyright © 2002 by Valerie Steiker. Used by permission of Pantheon Books, a division of Random House, Inc.

Susan Stellin: "The Inevitability of Bumps" from *The New York Times*, 6/12/2007, © 2007 The New York Times. All rights reserved. Used by permission and protected by the Copyright Laws of the United States. The printing, copying, redistribution, or retransmission of the Material without express written permission is prohibited. www.nytimes.com.

Martha Stewart: Reprinted from *Favorite Comfort Food: Classic Favorites and Great New Recipes* by Martha Stewart. Copyright © 1999 Martha Stewart Living Omnimedia, Inc. Published by Clarkson Potter Publishers, a division of Random House, Inc.

Mike Stobbe: "First US Count Finds 1 in 200 Kids Are Vegetarian," The Associated Press, January 11, 2009. Used with permission of The Associated Press. Copyright © 2009.

Carolyn Stonehill: "Modern Dating, Prehistoric Style." Reprinted by permission of the author.

Amy Tan: "Mother Tongue." Copyright © 1990 by Amy Tan. First appeared in *The Threepenny Review*. Reprinted by permission of the author and the Sandra Dijkstra Literary Agency.

Gary Taubes: "What If It's All Been a Big Fat Lie?," *The New York Times*, July 7, 2002. © 2002, The New York Times. Reprinted by permission.

Alina Tugend: "Multitasking Can Make You Lose . . . Um . . . Focus," *The New York Times*, 10/25/2008. © 2008 The New York Times. All rights reserved. Used by permission and protected by the Copyright Laws of the United States. The printing, copying, redistribution, or retransmission of the Material without express written permission is prohibited.

Jerry Weinberger: "Pious Princes and Red-Hot Lovers: The Politics of Shakespeare's Romeo and Juliet," *The Journal of Politics* (2003), 65, p. 350. Copyright © 2003, Southern Political Science Association. Reprinted with the permission of Cambridge University Press.

Sarah Wildman: "Caught in the Ayatollah's Web," *The New York Times*, 1/6/2008. © 2008 The New York Times. All rights reserved. Used by permission and protected by the Copyright Laws of the United States. The printing, copying, redistribution, or retransmission of the Material without express written permission is prohibited.

James Wood: "Victory Speech" by James Wood. Copyright © 2008 Condé Nast Publications. All rights reserved. Originally published in *The New Yorker*. Reprinted by permission.

Emily Yantis: "Informal Reflections on Honor." Copyright © 2008 by Emily Yantis. Reprinted by permission of the author.

Every effort has been made to gain permission for images and selections used in this book. Unless otherwise noted, all images not cited in this section have been provided by the editors and author of this publication. Rights holders of any images or selections not properly credited should contact Permissions Department, W.W. Norton & Company, Inc., 500 Fifth Avenue, New York, NY 10110, in order for a correction to be made in the next reprinting of our work.

Glossary/Index

A

abstract, 111–15 A GENRE of writing that summarizes a book, an article, or a paper, usually in 100–200 words. Authors in some academic fields must provide, at the top of a report submitted for publication, an abstract of its content. The abstract may then appear in a journal of abstracts, such as *Psychological Abstracts*. An *informative abstract* summarizes a complete report; a briefer *descriptive abstract* works more as a teaser; a standalone *proposal abstract* (also called a TOPIC PROPOSAL) requests permission to conduct research, write on a topic, or present a report at a scholarly conference. Key Features: SUMMARY of basic information • objective description • brevity

***ad hominem* argument, 296–97** A logical FALLACY that attacks someone's character rather than address the issues.

Note: This glossary/index defines key terms and concepts and directs you to pages in the book where you can find specific information on these and other topics. Please note the words set in SMALL CAPITAL LETTERS are themselves defined in the glossary/index.

analysis A GENRE of writing that methodically examines a topic or text by breaking it into its parts and noting how they work in relation to one another.

anecdotes Brief NARRATIVES used to illustrate a point.

annotated bibliography, 116–24 A GENRE of writing that gives an overview of published research and scholarship on a topic. Each entry includes complete publication information and a SUMMARY or an ABSTRACT for each source. A *descriptive annotation* summarizes the content of a source without commenting on its value; an *evaluative annotation* gives an opinion about the source along with a description of it. Key Features: statement of the scope • complete bibliographic information • relevant commentary • consistent presentation

APA style, 477–519 A system of documenting sources in the social sciences. APA stands for the American Psychological Association. *See also* DOCUMENTATION.

appendix A section at the end of a written work for supplementary material that would be distracting in the main part of the text.

B

C

its consequences will be. Sometimes cause and effect serves as the ORGANIZING principle for a whole text.

chronological order, 343–44 A way of ORGANIZING text that proceeds from the beginning of an event to the end. Reverse chronological order proceeds in the other direction, from the end to the beginning.

citation In a text, the act of giving information from a source. A citation and its corresponding parenthetical DOCUMENTATION or footnote or endnote provide minimal information about the source, and complete bibliographic information appears in a list of WORKS CITED or REFERENCES at the end of the text.

claim A statement that asserts a belief or position. In an ARGUMENT, a claim needs to be stated in a thesis or clearly implied, and requires support with REASONS and other kinds of EVIDENCE.

classify and divide, 300–305 A STRATEGY that either groups (classifies) numerous individual items by their similarities (for example, classifying cereal, bread, butter, chicken, cheese, ice cream, eggs, and oil as carbohydrates, proteins, and fats) or breaks (divides) one large category into small categories (for example, dividing food into carbohydrates, proteins, and fats). Sometimes classification and/or division serves as the ORGANIZING principle for a whole text. *See also* classifying; dividing.

clustering, 221–22 A PROCESS for GENERATING IDEAS AND TEXT, in which a writer visually connects thoughts by jotting them down and drawing lines between related items.

coherence The quality that allows an AUDIENCE to follow a text's meaning and to *see* the connections among ideas, sentences, and paragraphs. Elements that can help to achieve coherence include the title, a clearly stated or implied THESIS, topic sentences, an easy-to-follow organization with clear TRANSITIONS, and parallelism among comparable ideas.

collaboration, 215–18 The PROCESS of working with others.

D

definition, 314–23 A STRATEGY that gets at the meaning of something. Three main kinds of definitions are the *formal definition*, which may identify the category that something belongs to and tell what distinguishes it from other things in that category: for example, defining a worm as an invertebrate (a category) with a long, rounded body and no appendages (distinguishing features): the *extended definition*, which, as its name suggests is longer: for example, a paragraph explaining why the antagonist of a story is wormlike; and the *stipulative definition*, which gives a writer's own, particular use of a term: for example, using the term *worm* to refer to a kind of gummy candy. Sometimes definition serves as the ORGANIZING principle for a whole text.

description, 324–32 A STRATEGY that tells how something looks, sounds, smells, feels, or tastes. Effective description creates a clear DOMINANT IMPRESSION built from specific details. Description can be *objective*, *subjective*, or both. Sometimes description serves as the ORGANIZING principles for a whole text.

design, 15–17, 521–56 The way a text is arranged and presented visually. Elements of design include typeface, color, illustration, layout, and white space. One component of a RHETORICAL SITUATION, design plays an important part in reaching a text's AUDIENCE and achieving its PURPOSE.

dialogue, 333–37 A STRATEGY for adding people's own words to a text.

discovery drafting, 225 A PROCESS of DRAFTING something quickly, mostly for the purpose of discovering what one wants to say.

documentation, 425–27 Publication information about the sources cited in a text. The documentation usually appears in an abbreviated form in parentheses at the point of CITATION or in an endnote or a footnote. Complete documentation usually appears as a list of WORKS CITED or REFERENCES at the end of the text. Documentation styles vary by discipline. For example, Modern Language Association (MLA) style requires an author's complete first name if it appears in a source, whereas American Psychological Association (APA) style requires only the initial of an author's first name.

dominant impression, 330–31 The overall effect created through specific details when a writer DESCRIBES something.

drafting, 226–28 The PROCESS of putting words on paper or screen. Writers often write several drafts, REVISING each until they achieve their goal or reach a deadline. At that point, they submit a finished final draft.

E

editing The PROCESS of fine-tuning a text—examining each word, phrase, sentence, and paragraph—to be sure that the text is correct and precise and says exactly what the writer intends. *See also* PROOFREADING and REVISING.

either-or argument, 297 A logical FALLACY that oversimplifies to suggest that only two possible POSITIONS exist on a complex issue. The fallacy is also known as a false dilemma.

F

G

genre, 9–11, 19–208 A kind of text marked by and expected to have certain key features and to follow certain conventions of style and presentation. In the literary world, readers recognize such genres as the short story and novel (which are expected to have plots) and the poem (which may not have a plot but has other characteristics, such as rhythm); in academic and workplace settings, readers and writers focus on other genres, which also meet expectations in content, style, and appearance. Genres covered in the *Norton Field Guide* include ABSTRACTS, ANNOTATED BIBLIOGRAPHIES, APPLICATION LETTERS, ARGUMENTS, EVALUATIONS, LAB REPORTS, LITERACY NARRATIVES, LITERARY ANALYSES, PROFILES, PROPOSALS, REFLECTIONS, RÉSUMÉS, REPORTS, and TEXTUAL ANALYSES.

H

hasty generalization, 298 A FALLACY that reaches a conclusion based on insufficient or inappropriately qualified EVIDENCE.

home page, 549 The introductory page of a website. *See also* websites.

I

informal writing Writing not intended to be evaluated, sometimes not even to be read by others. Informal writing is produced primarily to explore ideas or to communicate casually with friends and acquaintances. *See also* FORMAL WRITING.

inquiry, writing as, 211–14 A PROCESS for investigating a topic by posing questions, searching for multiple answers, and keeping an open mind.

interpretation, 213 The act of making sense of something or explaining what one thinks it means. Interpretation is the goal of writing a LITERARY ANALYSIS or TEXTUAL ANALYSIS.

J

K

keyword A term that a researcher inputs when searching databases and the World Wide Web for information.

L

lab report, 133–42 A GENRE of writing that covers the process of conducting an experiment in a controlled setting. Key Features: explicit title • ABSTRACT • PURPOSE • methods • results and discussion • REFERENCES • APPENDIX • appropriate format

layout, 525 The way text is arranged on a page or screen—for example, in paragraphs, in lists, on charts, with headings, and so on.

letter writing, 224 A process of GENERATING IDEAS AND TEXT by going through the motions of writing to someone to explain a topic.

link In a Web page, a URL, a word, or an image that, when clicked, opens a different page.

listing, 220–21 A PROCESS for GENERATING IDEAS AND TEXT by making lists while thinking about a topic, finding relationships among the notes, and arranging the notes as an outline (*see* OUTLINING).

literacy narrative, 21–37 A GENRE of writing that tells about a writer's experience learning to read or write. Key Features: well-told story • vivid detail • indication of the narrative's significance

literacy portfolio, 257 An organized collection of materials showing examples of one writer's progress as a reader and/or writer.

literary analysis, 143–52 A GENRE of writing that argues for a particular INTERPRETATION of a literary text—most often fiction, poetry, or drama. *See also* ANALYSIS and TEXTUAL ANALYSIS. Key Features: arguable THESIS • careful attention to the language of the text • attention to patterns or themes • clear interpretation • MLA style

literature Literary works—including fiction, poetry, drama, and some nonfiction; also, the body of written work produced in given field.

looping, 220 A PROCESS for GENERATING IDEAS AND TEXTin which a writer writes about a topic quickly for several minutes and summarizes the most important or interesting idea in a sentence, which becomes the beginning of another round of writing and summarizing . . . and so on until finding an angle for a paper.

M

medium (pl. media), 15–16, 521–56 A means for communicating—for example, in print, with speech, or online. Texts consisting of words are said to use *verbal media*, whereas photographs, films, and sculptures are examples of *visual media* (though some verbal texts include visual images, and some visual texts include words).

N

narration, 21, 343–51 A STRATEGY for presenting information as a story, for telling "what happened." It is a pattern most often associated with fiction, but it shows up in all kinds of writing. When used in an essay, a REPORT, or another academic GENRE, a narrative must support a point—not merely tell an interesting story for its own sake. It must also present events in some kind of sequence and include only pertinent detail. Sometimes narrative serves as the ORGANIZING principle for a whole text. *See also* LITERACY NARRATIVE.

O

plagiarism Using another person's words, syntax, or ideas without giving appropriate credit and DOCUMENTATION. Plagiarism is a serious breach of ethics.

point of view A position from which something is considered.

portfolio, 247–58 A collection of writing selected by a writer to show his or her work, something including a statement assessing the work and explaining what it demonstrates.

position A statement that asserts a belief or CLAIM. In an ARGUMENT, a position needs to be stated in a THESIS or clearly implied, and requires support with REASONS and other kinds of EVIDENCE.

***post hoc, ergo propter hoc*, 297** Latin for "after this, therefore because of this"; also called FAULTY CAUSALITY. A FALLACY of assuming that the first of two events causes the second.

primary source, 384–85 A source such as a literary work, historical document, art, or performance that a researcher examines firsthand. Primary sources also include experiments and FIELD RESEARCH. In writing about the Revolutionary War, a researcher would likely consider the Declaration of Independence a primary source and a textbook's description of the writing of the document a SECONDARY SOURCE.

process, 209–58 In writing a series of actions that may include GENERATING IDEAS AND TEXT, DRAFTING, REVISING, EDITING, and PROOFREADING a text. *See also* EXPLAINING A PROCESS *and specific processes.*

profile, 161–70 A GENRE that presents an engaging portrait of a person, place, or event based on firsthand FIELD RESEARCH. Key Features: interesting subject • necessary background • interesting angle • firsthand account • engaging details

proofreading, 245–46 The final PROCESS of writing, when a writer checks for correct spelling and punctuation as well as for page order, missing copy, and consistent use of typefaces and FONTS. *See also* EDITING, REVISING, and REWRITING.

proposal, 171–79 A GENRE that argues for a solution to a problem or suggests some action. *See also* TOPIC PROPOSAL. Key Features: well-defined problem • recommended solution • answers to anticipated questions • call to action • appropriate TONE

purpose, 3–4 A writer's goal: to explore; to express oneself; to entertain; to demonstrate learning; to report; to persuade; and so on. Purpose is one element of the RHETORICAL SITUATION.

ject. Key Features: topic intriguing to the writer • some kind of structure • specific details • speculative TONE

reporting, 59–81 A GENRE of writing that presents information as objectively as possible to inform readers on a subject. *See also* LAB REPORT. Key Features: tightly focused topic • accurate, well-researched information • various writing strategies • clear DEFINITIONS • appropriate DESIGN

response, 235–36 A PROCESS of writing in which a reader responds to a writer's work by giving his or her thoughts about the writer's title, beginning, clarity of THESIS, support and DOCUMENTATION, ORGANIZING, STANCE, treatment of AUDIENCE, achievement of PURPOSE, handling of the GENRE, ending, and other matters.

résumé, 188–95 A GENRE that summarizes someone's academic and employment history, generally written to submit to potential employers, DESIGN and word choice depend on whether a résumé is submitted as a print document or in an electronic or scannable form. Key Features: organization that suits goals and experience • succinctness • design that highlights key information (for print) or that uses only one typeface (for scannable).

revision, 236–39 The PROCESS of making substantive changes, including additions and cuts, to a draft so that it contains all the necessary information in an appropriate organization. During revision, a writer generally moves from whole-text issues to details with the goals of sharpening the focus and strengthening the argument.

rewriting, 239–41 A PROCESS of composing a new draft from another perspective—from a different POINT OF VIEW, AUDIENCE, STANCE, GENRE, MEDIUM, sequence, and so on.

rhetorical situation, 1–17 The context within which writing or other communication takes place, including PURPOSE, AUDIENCE, GENRE, STANCE, and MEDIA/DESIGN.

S

secondary source, 384–85 An ANALYSIS of INTERPRETATION or a PRIMARY SOURCE. In writing about the Revolutionary War, a researcher would likely consider the Declaration of Independence a primary source and a textbook's description of writing of the document a secondary source.

signal phrase A phrase used to attribute quoted, paraphrased, or summarized material to a source, as in "she said" or "he claimed."

simile, 311 A figure of speech that compares two items using *like* or *as*: "Still we live meanly, like ants" (Henry David Thoreau, *Walden*), "The Wind begun to knead the Grass — / As Women do a Dough — " (Emily Dickinson).

slippery slope, 298 A FALLACY that asserts, without EVIDENCE, that one event will lead to a series of other events that will culminate in a cataclysm.

T

tone, 13 A writer's or speaker's attitude toward his or her readers and subject. A writer's tone reflects his or her STANCE and may be formal or informal, optimistic or pessimistic, playful, ironic, and so on.

topic proposal, 178–79 A statement of intent to examine a topic; also called a proposal ABSTRACT. Some instructors require a topic proposal in order to assess the feasibility of the writing project that a student has in mind. Key Features: concise discussion of the subject • clear statement of the intended focus • rationale for choosing the subject • mention of resources

transitions, 277 Words or PHRASES used to make clear the connection between ideas and text.

U

V

vantage point, 329–30 The physical position from which a writer DESCRIBES something.

W

works-cited list (MLA), 439 At the end of a researched text prepared MLA style, the list, with full bibliographic information, for all the sources cited in the text.

Y

Z

A Directory to MLA Style

MLA IN-TEXT DOCUMENTATION

MLA LIST OF WORKS CITED

BOOKS

PERIODICALS

ELECTRONIC SOURCES

THER KINDS OF SOURCES

A Directory to APA Style

APA IN-TEXT DOCUMENTATION

APA REFERENCE LIST

OOKS

PERIODICALS

ELECTRONIC SOURCES

OTHER KINDS OF SOURCES

A Menu of Readings